The Routledge Handbook of Translation Studies and Linguistics

The Routledge Handbook of Translation Studies and Linguistics explores the interrelationships between Translation Studies and Linguistics in six sections of state-of-the-art chapters, written by leading specialists from around the world. The first part, on the nature of language, translation and interpreting, begins by addressing the relationships between translation studies and linguistics as major topics of study in themselves before focusing, in individual chapters, on the relationships between translation on the one hand and semantics, semiotics and the sound system of language on the other. Part II is concerned with the nature of meaning and the ways in which meaning can be shared or semi-shared in text pairs that are related to each other as first-written texts and their translations, while Part III focuses on relationships between translation and interpreting and the written and spoken word. In Part IV, the users of language, and language in use in situations involving more than one language are covered, and in Part V technological tools that can assist language users are brought onto the scene. Finally, Part VI presents chapters on the links between areas of applied linguistics and translation and interpreting. With an introduction by the editor and an extensive bibliography, this handbook is an indispensable resource for advanced students of Translation Studies, interpreting studies and applied linguistics.

Kirsten Malmkjær is Professor of Translation Studies at the University of Leicester, UK, where she founded the Research Centre for Translation and Interpreting Studies and the MA in Translation Studies. She is the editor of the *Routledge Linguistics Encyclopedia* (third edition, 2010) and, with Kevin Windle, of the *Oxford Handbook of Translation Studies* (2011). She is the author of *Linguistics and the Language of Translation* (2005) and, with Murray Knowles, of *Language and Control in Children's Literature* (Routledge, 1996).

Routledge Handbooks in Translation and Interpreting Studies

Routledge Handbooks in Translation and Interpreting Studies provide comprehensive overviews of the key topics in translation and interpreting studies. All entries for the handbooks are specially commissioned and written by leading scholars in the field. Clear, accessible and carefully edited, *Routledge Handbooks in Translation and Interpreting Studies* are the ideal resource for both advanced undergraduates and postgraduate students.

For a full list of titles in this series, please visit https://www.routledge.com/Routledge-Handbooks-in-Translation-and-Interpreting-Studies/book-series/RHTI.

The Routledge Handbook of Translation Studies and Linguistics

Edited by Kirsten Malmkjær

LONDON AND NEW YORK

First published 2018
by Routledge
2 Park Square, Milton Park, Abingdon, Oxon OX14 4RN

and by Routledge
711 Third Avenue, New York, NY 10017

Routledge is an imprint of the Taylor & Francis Group, an informa business

British Library Cataloguing-in-Publication Data
A catalogue record for this book is available from the British Library

Library of Congress Cataloging in Publication Data
A catalog record has been requested for this book

ISBN: 978-1-138-91126-0 (hbk)
ISBN: 978-1-315-69284-5 (ebk)

Typeset in Times New Roman
by Sunrise Setting Ltd, Brixham, UK

Contents

Contents

Illustrations

Figures

Tables

Acknowledgements

I would like to acknowledge the invaluable work that my former colleague, Adelina Ivanova Hild, devoted to this volume in its early stages. I hope that she will approve of the way I took the project forward.

I am immensely grateful to all the contributors for their good natures and intellects and to the team at Routledge, particularly Louisa Semlyen and Laura Sandford, for their patience and help.

Every effort has been made to contact copyright-holders. Please advise the publisher of any errors or omissions, and these will be corrected in subsequent editions.

Contributors

Barbara Ahrens graduated in 1995 in conference interpreting (A: German, B: Spanish, C: English) at Heidelberg University, Germany. Since then, she has been working as a freelance conference interpreter, and she is a member of AIIC (the International Association of Conference Interpreters). In 2003, she obtained her PhD in Translation Studies from the University of Mainz, Faculty of Applied Linguistics and Cultural Studies in Germersheim with a doctoral thesis on prosody in simultaneous interpreting. From 2003 to 2006, she held a Junior Professorship in Translation Studies at Germersheim. In 2006, she was appointed Full Professor of Interpreting (Spanish) at Cologne University of Applied Sciences (now TH Köln) where she teaches interpreting Spanish-German and interpreting studies. From 2007 to 2015, she has been head of the MA programme in conference interpreting. Her research focuses on prosody and speaking skills in interpreting as well as on note-taking and cognitive aspects of speech processing in interpreting.

Alfredo Ardila is a full-time Professor at the Department of Communication Sciences and Disorders, Florida International University, Miami, Florida, USA. His current research focuses on bilingualism, and the brain organisation of language in normal and abnormal conditions.

Nune Ayvazyan holds a BA in English Studies from the Universitat Rovira i Virgili (Spain), an MA in Translation Studies from the Universitat Pompeu Fabra (Spain), and a PhD in Translation and Intercultural Studies. She teaches English and translation at BA and Masters levels at the Universitat Rovira i Virgili. Her research interests are in teaching foreign languages through translation, Soviet translation theories and multilingualism in minority communities.

Mona Baker is Professor of Translation Studies and Director of the Centre for Translation and Intercultural Studies at the University of Manchester, UK. She holds a BA in English and Comparative Literature from the American University in Cairo, an MA in Special Applications of Linguistics from the University of Birmingham and a DSc from the University of Manchester Institute of Technology (UMIST). In 1995, she founded St Jerome Publishing and the international journal *The Translator*. She is Vice President of the International Association of Translation and Intercultural Studies.

Rocío Baños is Senior Lecturer in Translation at the Centre for Translation Studies (CenTraS) at University College London, UK, where she teaches Audiovisual Translation and Translation Technology. Her research focuses mainly on audiovisual translation, with particular emphasis on the language of dubbing.

Stefan Baumgarten is a Lecturer in German and Translation Studies at Bangor University. His research interests centre on (critical) translation theories and the role of translation as an ideological practice, specifically in its impact on political and philosophical discourse and underground literature. His work also concentrates on questions of globalised political discourse as expressed in the rise of activist, post-anarchist and pro-democratic movements that challenge the current political domination and hegemonic orthodoxy of neoliberal regimes.

Silvia Bernardini is full Professor of English at the Department of Interpreting and Translation of the University of Bologna, Italy, where she teaches English linguistics and translation from English into Italian. Her main research interests are in the areas of corpus linguistics and Translation Studies, both descriptive and applied.

Łucja Biel is an Associate Professor at the Institute of Applied Linguistics, University of Warsaw, Poland. She was a Visiting Lecturer on the MA in Legal Translation at City University London, UK, from 2009 to 2014. She is deputy editor of the *Journal of Specialised Translation* and Secretary General of the European Society for Translation Studies. Her research interests focus on legal translation, translator training and corpus-based genre analysis. She has published over 40 papers in this area, for example in *The Translator*, *Meta*, *Jostrans*, *LANS*, *Fachsprache* and a book *Lost in the Eurofog: The Textual Fit of Translated Law* (2014).

Jean Boase-Beier is Professor Emerita of Literature and Translation at the University of East Anglia, UK, and author of many academic works on translation, poetry and stylistics, such as *Stylistic Approaches to Translation* (Routledge, 2006) and *A Critical Introduction to Translation Studies* (2011). She is a translator of poetry from and into German; collections include translations from the work of Ernst Meister, Rose Ausländer and Volker von Törne. She is also the editor of four series of translated poetry books for Arc Publications. Her current research is mainly concerned with the translation of Holocaust poetry; two recent publications in this area are *Translating the Poetry of the Holocaust* (2015) and the co-edited volume *Translating Holocaust Lives* (2017).

Sabine Braun is Professor of Translation Studies and Director of the Centre for Translation Studies at the University of Surrey, UK. Her research focuses on new modalities and socio-technological practices of translation and interpreting. She has a long-standing interest in video-mediated interpreting, and she has adopted discourse analytic, pragmatic and socio-logical approaches combining qualitative and quantitative methods to investigate and inform the integration of videoconferencing technologies into professional practice. She has led several international projects in this field, and has worked with the European Council Working Party on e-Justice and several justice-sector institutions to advise on, develop guidelines for, and provide training in videoconferencing and interpreting. Further interests include audio description as an emerging modality of intersemiotic translation and the use of multimodal technologies in interpreter education. She recently led an international consortium which developed the first 3D virtual environment to simulate interpreting practice.

Michael Carl is a Professor at Renmin University of China, Beijing and Professor with Special Responsibilities for Human and Machine Translation and Director of the Center for Research and Innovation in Translation and Translation Technology (CRITT) at the Copenhagen Business School, Denmark. His current research interest is related to the investigation of human translation processes and interactive machine translation. Prior to his position in Denmark he has been working on machine translation, terminology tools and the implementation of natural language processing software. Dr Carl has organised numerous workshops, scientific meetings and panels on machine translation and translation process-related topics.

Ying Cui received her PhD from the Department of Chinese, Translation and Linguistics, City University of Hong Kong. Her major research interests include translation practice and theories as well as linguistics. She teaches at the School of Translation Studies, Shandong University, Weihai (China).

Helle V. Dam is Professor of Interpreting and Translation Studies and Director of the Conference Interpreting Study Program at Aarhus University, Denmark. She currently serves as a member of the Executive Board of the European Society for Translation Studies (EST) and of the Advisory Board of the journal *Interpreting*. Her publications cover a wide variety of aspects (linguistic, cognitive, sociological) of both interpreting and translation and include a number of contributions to authoritative handbooks and encyclopedias in the field of translation and interpreting studies (e.g. John Benjamin's *Handbook of Translation Studies* and *Routledge Encyclopedia of Interpreting Studies*). Among several collective volumes, she is the co-editor of *Getting Started in Interpreting Research* (2001), *Knowledge Systems and Translation* (2005) and *The Translation Profession: Centers and peripheries* (2016). She is the editor of *Translation Studies: Moving Boundaries* based on the theme of the 8th EST Congress, which was organised under her chairmanship.

Jorge Díaz-Cintas is Professor in Translation at the Centre for Translation Studies (CenTraS), University College London, UK. Author of numerous articles and books on audiovisual translation, he is the recipient of the Jan Ivarsson Award (2014) and the Xènia Martínez Award (2015) for invaluable services to the field of audiovisual translation.

James Dickins is Professor of Arabic at the University of Leeds, UK. He has a BA in Arabic and Turkish from the University of Cambridge (1980) and a PhD in Arabic Linguistics from Heriot-Watt University (1990). He taught English in Sudan from 1980 to 1982, and has taught Arabic and Arabic-English translation at the University of Cambridge, Heriot-Watt University, and the universities of St Andrews, Durham, Salford and Leeds. His publications include *Standard Arabic: An Advanced Course* (1998, with Janet Watson), *Extended Axiomatic Linguistics* (1999), *Thinking Arabic Translation* (2002; second edition 2016, with Sandor Hervey and Ian Higgins) and *Sudanese Arabic: Phonematics and Syllable Structure* (2007).

Grażyna Drzazga completed her PhD in the Cognitive Science of Language at McMaster University in Canada and has MA degrees in Applied Linguistics (Translation) from Maria Curie-Skłodowska University in Lublin (Poland) and York University in Toronto (Canada). Currently she is an Adjunct Lecturer at the University of Florida English Language Institute, USA. Her research interests include language and gender, linguistic borrowings, political correctness and empirical studies of translation as a process.

Federico M. Federici holds a Laurea in Foreign Languages (Rome La Sapienza University, Italy), and a PhD in Translation (University of Leeds, UK). He is a Reader in Translation Studies at the Centre for Translation Studies, University College London, UK. He founded and directed the European Master's in Translation (EMT) MA in Translation Studies at

Durham University, UK (2008–2014), where he also founded and directed the Centre for Intercultural Mediation. He served as a member of the Board of the EMT Network (2011–2014). Together with journal articles, he authored *Translation as Stylistic Evolution* (2009), edited *Mediating Emergencies and Conflicts* (2016), *Translating Dialects and Languages of Minorities* (2011), *Translating Regionalized Voices in Audiovisuals* (2009), and co-edited with Dario Tessicini *Translators, Interpreters and Cultural Mediators* (2014). His research focuses on translators and interpreters as intercultural mediators and on reception of translated texts. He is involved in projects focusing on translators working in crises.

Aline Ferreira is a Lecturer of Portuguese at the University of Toronto in Canada. She is also a Postdoctoral Research Fellow in the Language and Literacy Research Laboratory at Wilfrid Laurier University in Waterloo, Canada.

Henrik Gottlieb studied English and Applied Linguistics at the University of Copenhagen, Denmark, where he wrote a prize thesis and later a PhD dissertation on Translation Studies, with a focus on polysemiotic translation, especially subtitling. He worked as a subtitler with public broadcaster Danmarks Radio 1980–1995, became Associate Professor at the University of Copenhagen in 2000 and was the chief editor of *Perspectives – Studies in Translatology* 2006–2011. He has published widely on screen translation since 1989 and has lectured extensively in Europe and abroad. Apart from Translation Studies proper, his present research interests are lexicography, language politics and contact linguistics, with special emphasis on the impact of English on other languages – via translations and other channels of influence.

James Luke Hadley is Ussher Assistant Professor in Literary Translation at Trinity College Dublin, Ireland. He is the author of several articles addressing translation in historically under-researched contexts. His current project employs digital humanities methodologies to systematise the study of the concatenation effect in indirect translations. His aim is to demonstrate that the generation of context-neutral, testable and falsifiable hypotheses in Translation Studies is not only possible, but desirable for the continued development of the discipline.

Ida Kiltgård is an Associate Professor in English and Translation Studies at Roskilde University in Denmark. She teaches various subjects in the English Studies programme as well as general Academic English Writing. She has published widely on literary translation with a particular interest in the Danish translations of James Joyce's *Ulysses*, for example "Taking the Pun by the Horns: The Translation of Wordplay in James Joyce's Ulysses" (*Target* 17(1) 2005) and *Fictions of Hybridity: Translating Style in James Joyce's Ulysses* (2007). She has also worked on the internationalisation of Higher Education (Bent Preisler, Ida Klitgård and Anne Fabricius, eds., *Language and Learning in the International University: From English Uniformity to Diversity and Hybridity*, 2011) and recently with translation in other learning contexts (TOLC) focusing on the kind of covert translation which takes place when Danish university students write assignments in English as a foreign language based on reading sources in English (Isabelle Génin and Ida Klitgård, eds., *Translating the Voices of Theory/La traduction des voix de la théorie*, 2015). Finally, Klitgård has contributed to a successful textbook for students of translation: Anne Schjoldager, Henrik Gottlieb and Ida Klitgård, *Understanding Translation* (2008, 2010).

Benoît Krémer is a professional translator and conference interpreter and a Senior Lecturer at the Faculty of Translating and Interpreting, University of Geneva, Switzerland, where he has been teaching translation and interpretation at BA and MA level for the last 25 years. He was President of the International Association of Conference Interpreters (AIIC) from 2006 to 2012.

Kirsten Malmkjær studied English and Philosophy at Birmingham University, UK, from 1978 to 1981, and completed her PhD, "Translation in Context", there in 1984. She lectured at Birmingham for four years before moving to the University of Cambridge, Research Centre for English and Applied Linguistics, whose MPhil she directed until 1999 when she was appointed Professor of Translation Studies at Middlesex University, North London. In September, 2010, she was appointed Professor of Translation Studies at the University of Leicester, where she established the Research Centre for Translation and Interpreting Studies and its MA. She has published widely in the field of Translation Studies, including the *Oxford Handbook of Translation Studies* (co-edited with Kevin Windle, 2011), *Linguistics and the Language of Translation* (2005), and numerous book and journal articles in her areas of interest, which include translation and philosophy, translation and language learning, the theory of translation, and translation and creativity.

Siobhán McElduff is an Associate Professor at the University of British Columbia. She is the author of *Roman Theories of Translation* (2013), and co-editor of a collection of papers on ancient Mediterranean translation (*Complicating the History of Western Translation*, 2012). She is currently working on the translation of gesture from Greece to Rome, and on a separate project on the working classes and classics in the 18th and 19th centuries. She is a practising translator and has published a volume of Cicero's speeches (*In Defense of the Republic*) for Penguin Classics.

Claudia Mejía Quijano linguist and semiologist, has been a Lecturer at the University of Geneva and a researcher at the University of Lausanne, Switzerland. She is now Professor of Translation at the University of Antioquia (Colombia). She has applied Saussurian semiology to various practical fields (psychoanalytical clinic of psychic traumas, discourse analysis in clinical research, analysis of text data, translation and language teaching) and has developed the project of a diachronic semiology.

Anthony Pym teaches at The University of Melbourne, Australia. He is Distinguished Professor of Translation and Intercultural Studies at the Universitat Rovira i Virgili in Tarragona, Spain, and Extraordinary Professor at Stellenbosch University in South Africa. He works on sociological approaches to translation and intercultural studies. With Kirsten Malmkjær and Mar Gutiérrez he led the European research project *Translation and Language Learning* (2013). He is the author of *Exploring Translation Theories* (second edition, Routledge 2014) and *Translation Solutions for Many Languages* (2016).

Mariachiara Russo is a conference interpreter and full Professor of Spanish at the Department of Interpreting and Translation of the University of Bologna, Italy, where she teaches Interpreting Theory and Simultaneous and Consecutive Interpreting from Spanish into Italian. Her main research interests are in the areas of aptitude testing for interpreting, corpus-based interpreting studies and remote interpreting.

Moritz Schaeffer received his PhD from the University of Leicester and has since worked as a Research Associate at the Center of Research and Innovation in Translation and Translation Technology (CRITT), Copenhagen Business School, Denmark, and at the Institute for

Language, Cognition and Computation, University of Edinburgh, UK. He is currently a Research Associate at the TRACO-Lab of the Johannes Gutenberg University Mainz, Germany.

Christina Schäffner is Professor Emerita at Aston University, Birmingham, UK. Until her retirement in September 2015, she was the Head of Translation Studies at Aston University, teaching courses in Translation Studies and in Interpreting, and supervising Master dissertations and PhD students. Her main research interests are political discourse in translation, news translation, metaphor in translation and translation didactics, and she has published widely on these topics.

Melani Schröter is Associate Professor in German Linguistics at the University of Reading, UK. Her research focuses on Critical Discourse Analysis, in particular public and political discourse, partly from a comparative, cross-linguistic perspective. She published a monograph, *Silence and Concealment in Political Discourse*, in 2013 and worked on comparative analyses on keywords in European Migration Discourses as well as on the use of German Nazi vocabulary in other languages. She is also interested in discourses of resistance and has published on German punk song lyrics.

John W. Schwieter is an Associate Professor of Spanish and Linguistics and a Faculty of Arts Teaching Scholar at Wilfrid Laurier University in Waterloo, Canada. He is also a Visiting Professor of Applied Linguistics in the Centre for Applied Research and Outreach in Language Education at the University of Greenwich in London, UK.

Gregory M. Shreve is Professor Emeritus of Translation Studies at Kent State University, USA, and Adjunct Professor of Translation, Interpreting and Foreign Languages at New York University, where he has taught since 2011. The founding Director of the Institute for Applied Linguistics and past Chair of the Department of Modern and Classical Languages Studies at Kent State, Professor Shreve was instrumental in establishing one of the first comprehensive Translation Studies programmes in the United States. Shreve's research interests include text linguistics and translation, cognitive translation studies, translation expertise, empirical approaches to translation studies and translation informatics. He is the co-author/co-editor of several books including (with Albrecht Neubert) *Translation as Text*, (with Joseph Danks, 1992) *Cognitive Processes in Translation and Interpreting* (1997) and (with Erik Angelone, 2010) *Translation and Cognition*.

Mark Shuttleworth has been involved in Translation Studies research and teaching since 1993, first at the University of Leeds, UK, then at Imperial College London, where for many years he was course leader of the MSc in Scientific, Technical and Medical Translation with Translation Technology, and now at University College London. His publications include the *Dictionary of Translation Studies* (1997), several articles and a monograph on metaphor in translation, and works on translation technology, translator training and medical translation. More recently, he has been developing an interest in translation and the Web, in particular as it is manifested in Wikipedia. He studied at the Universities of Oxford and Birmingham, and has a PhD from the University of London. He is a fluent speaker of Russian, German, Polish and French and has some knowledge of several other languages.

Magda Stroińska has a PhD in Linguistics from Edinburgh University, UK, and an MA in German and Applied Linguistics (Translation) from Warsaw University, Poland. She is a

Professor of German and Linguistics at McMaster University in Hamilton ON, Canada. Her major areas of research include sociolinguistics and cross-cultural pragmatics, in particular cultural stereotyping, theory of translation, language and politics, propaganda, the issues of identity in exile, ageing and bilingualism. Her most recent interest and research focus on language and psychological trauma.

Sven Tarp is Professor and Head of the Centre for Lexicography at Aarhus University, Denmark. He is also Extraordinary Professor at the Department of Afrikaans and Dutch at Stellenbosch University (South Africa), Extraordinary Board Member of the International Centre for Lexicography at the University of Valladolid (Spain), Founding Member of the Sino-Danish Sindberg Centre of Lexicography, Translation and Business Communication at Guangdong University of Finance (China) and Distinguished Visitor of the City of Santiago (Cuba). He holds a PhD in specialised lexicography (1993) and a Doctor's Degree in learners' lexicography (2006). He is the editor or co-editor of several specialised dictionaries and has published many contributions in journals and well-known series. He is the author of *Lexicography in the Borderland Between Knowledge and Non-knowledge* (2008), co-author of *Theory and Practice of Specialised Online Dictionaries* (with Pedro A. Fuertes-Olivera, 2014) and co-editor of *Manual of Specialised Lexicography* (with Henning Bergenholtz, 1995). He is one of the founders of the Function Theory of Lexicography.

Stefanos Vlachopoulos is Professor of German Language in the Department of Business Administration at the Technological Educational Institute of Epirus in Greece. His main areas of expertise are domain-specific communication, legal translation, legal interpreting, lexicography, creativity and translating as well as curriculum development.

Yanli Zhao is a Senior Lecturer at the School of Translation Studies, Shandong University, Weihai (China). Her research interests include literature, cultural studies and discourse analysis.

Introduction

Kirsten Malmkjær and the contributors

This handbook highlights, explicitly and unapologetically, in each of its chapters, relationships that obtain between Translation Studies and Linguistics; and each chapter generally assumes that this relationship is mutually beneficial. In this respect, the volume echoes stances adopted by many members of both the Translation Studies community and of the Linguistics community before the 1980s. In that decade, a sense arose in parts of the Translation Studies community that Linguistics was a malevolent bedfellow for their young discipline to snuggle down with. The worry has generally been that the "stronger", older discipline of Linguistics would hijack Translation Studies and obscure its special nature; but this volume illustrates that since the discipline of Translation Studies has overcome its youthful reticence, the benefits of mutual interaction between the disciplines have become recognized, just as, indeed, the benefits of mutual interaction between the study of translation and the study of languages were in the days before Translation Studies acquired its name (see Chapter 1).

Each of the contributors or pairs of contributors to this handbook has been able to illustrate this mutual relevance of the disciplines in ample measure and they were, of course, approached with their ability to do this in mind. If there remains, nonetheless, a bias in favour of the Translation Studies community, this is a reflection of the greater likelihood of finding scholars within Translation Studies with an understanding of and interest in Linguistics than of finding scholars within Linguistics with an understanding of and interest in Translation Studies. Perhaps this handbook will encourage more evenly balanced cooperation between our fields than has been achieved to date.

One of the joys of working in Translation Studies is the international nature of the scholarly community engaged with it, as illustrated in this handbook. The contributors originate from a large number of different nations, and many live and work outside their countries of origin. They are members of a field of scholarship that is generally collegiate and mutually supportive, in which friendships and collaborations outnumber competitions. This may reflect the fact that just as language is a shared human trait, so are translating and interpreting. There is no nation where these activities are not valued, and we would like to believe that benevolent reasons for their perceived value – e.g. enabling friendly and knowledge-sharing intercultural communion – outnumber reasons relating to international distrust and enmity. It is important for the continuing progress of translation and interpreting studies to keep abreast of developments in the study of languages, including in Linguistics, and it is important for the study of languages and for Linguistics to draw upon insights from translation and interpreting studies. We hope that this handbook will encourage continuing and enhanced interaction between Linguistics and translation and interpreting studies so that each will continue to benefit from interaction with the other, as the chapters in this volume amply demonstrate that they have since their naissance as disciplines.

The handbook has six major sections: I. The nature of language, translation and interpreting; II. Meaning making; III. Texts in speech and writing; IV. Individuals and their interactions; V. Translation, interpreting, media and machines; and VI. Applications. A different division would of course have been possible, but the one selected was chosen because it seemed to us to prioritise neither discipline at the expense of the other, while reflecting the diversity of areas in which interaction between the two takes place. An exception to this rule is the title of section V, which, in the interest of brevity, neglects to mention Linguistics while mentioning both translation and interpreting; but the content of the individual chapters is not similarly negligent of Linguistics.

The four chapters in Part I on the nature of language, translation and interpreting cover the main, traditional areas of Linguistics: "general" theory, semantics, semiotics and the sound system in relation to the discipline of Translation Studies. Chapter 1, "Theories of linguistics and of translation and interpreting", charts the history of the relationship between the study of languages on the one hand and of translation and interpreting on the other hand, in the 20th and 21st centuries. Linguists have studied languages in contact with each other in situations involving translation or interpreting in order to identify the similarities and differences between the languages, while some Translation Studies scholars have drawn upon linguistic theories in order to develop theories of translation. Some scholars fall equally comfortably into both the linguistic and the Translation Studies disciplines; however, a number have striven to keep their discipline firmly independent of Linguistics and to develop theories and research methodologies of their own. Given that it would not be possible in this chapter to deal in detail with every version of linguistic theory, the chapter emphasises theories and concepts from Linguistics that have especially resonated within Translation Studies, such as systemic functional grammar, the theory of linguistic relativity, the search for universals and the notion of language as social semiotics. More "formal", transformational accounts of language have not been included, despite Nida's (1964) early, brief infatuation, because although they have much to contribute to our understanding of human language, they have tended to avoid considerations of multilingual minds and have had little appeal within the community of translation and interpreting studies.

Chapter 2, "Semantics and translation", is concerned with meaning, which is a central concept in both Translation Studies and in Linguistics. The chapter deals with accounts of the nature of meaning, and with the comfort translators may draw from Austin's (1962) and Searle's (1969) accounts of speech acts. It is, however, within analytical philosophy of language that the concept of translation or, more accurately, interpreting, between languages is central, and this is also where we find a decisive argument against malevolent relativism. Quine's (1960) thesis of the indeterminacy of translation raises this spectre unintentionally, but Davidson's (1973; 1974) response lays it permanently to rest. In the current climate where factuality is being seriously questioned as a concept, this is an immensely important contribution to the life of nations. More pragmatic, application-oriented discussions of aspects of meaning are presented in Chapters 6 and 7.

In Chapter 3, "Semiotics and translation", Henrik Gottlieb deals with the communication of meaning through systems of signs, including not only the linguistic sign system, but also translation between linguistic signs and signs belonging to other systems. He presents a taxonomy that covers both intrasemiotic and intersemiotic types of translation, and he emphasises that most texts employ more than one type of sign, as for example audiovisual texts do (sounds and images); and that the non-linguistic signs may belong to a "text" that is translated from linguistic signs, as in the case of the "translation" of a novel into film. Here, the written text is translated into speech on the one hand but also into pictures of physical phenomena like landscapes and buildings, which, in the novel, will have been described using linguistic signs. Nor need there be any linguistic signs present in a translation between signs. For example, numerical relations can be presented as, translated into graphics, as is commonly done during PowerPoint-style presentations.

The final chapter of Part I, Chapter 4 "Phonetics, phonology, and interpreting" by Barbara Ahrens, introduces the linguistic sub-disciplines that focus on communication through spoken language, namely phonetics and phonology. Phonetics is concerned with the sounds of speech and with the ways in which they are produced by the human vocal organs and perceived by the auditory mechanisms. Phonology considers sounds as parts of language systems. The chapter explains the role of speech sounds in interpreting, focusing on pauses, speech rate and segmentation, intonation and fundamental frequency, and accentuation and stress. These elements affect the comprehensibility of the interpretation because they contain clues to how the message is to be understood, but they may be difficult to produce naturally and fluently in interpreting, especially in simultaneous interpreting, where the interpreter must listen to and produce speech at the same time. Often, an interpreter is compelled to wait for information that s/he needs before s/he can begin to interpret, and this can cause pausing followed by a sudden rush in delivery once the information has been made available, as the interpreter rushes to keep up with the development of meaning in the speaker's output. As a consequence, the interpretation may sound forced and unnatural to the listener, and this may impair their comprehension.

The chapters in Part I having covered large-scale, general aspects of language: its nature, meaning, signification and sound in relation to translation and interpreting, Part II, on meaning making, enters into details about the second and third areas especially, that is, meaning and signification. We are accustomed to thinking of translation and interpreting as dealing with the verbal: with texts in writing or in speech, although as Henrik Gottlieb clearly shows in Chapter 3, "Semiotics and translation", numerous other channels of communication are used by humans. In Chapter 5, "Non-verbal communication and interpreting" by Benoît Krémer and Claudia Mejía Quijano, non-verbal elements that are present in contexts of spoken communication are discussed. As also made clear in Chapter 4, these include prosody, intonation and aspects of the situation in which the interpretation takes place. An interpreter needs to perceive, comprehend and decode these non-verbal elements in order to understand the speaker fully, but speech is ephemeral and fast, and given the need to pass the speech on to another audience, interpreters often have to make quick decisions about what can be missed out and what must be conveyed. Furthermore, in situations that involve distance or remote interpreting, the myriad contextual elements that are available in face-to-face interpreting are missing, so that an interpreter may be forced to assume aspects of the information that they are required to convey. This is clearly challenging for interpreters, while for scholars of both Linguistics and Interpreting it is intriguing and promising of important insights about the effect of context on communication. Remote interpreting is also discussed in Chapter 24 in Part V of this volume.

In Chapter 6, "Relevance Theory, interpreting and translation" by Magda Stroińska and Grażyna Drzazga, we return to issues of meaning, but also to the issue just discussed, of how an interpreter can best decide what can be missed out and what must be included in order to convey within the time available a text that is optimally representative of the original. The chapter focuses on cases in which this is especially problematic, namely cases in which the interpreter works without previous knowledge of the texts to be translated. The authors argue that Relevance Theory offers insights into two aspects of messages that need to be understood in communication: explicatures, which are inferences about information required to make complete sense of utterances (elaborations on meaning); and implicatures, which are inferences that add extra propositions to the speaker's utterance (implied meaning). While implicatures may seem more problematic to resolve in real-life situations than explicatures, explicatures often pose significant difficulty in interpretation, as illustrated in this chapter with examples from courtroom interpretation.

Implicature features again, along with the notion of presupposition, in Chapter 7, "Implicature and presupposition in translation and interpreting" by Ying Cui and Yanli Zhao. The chapter discusses two major types of presupposition, the semantic and the pragmatic. Semantic presuppositions arise on the basis of logical relations. They tend not to be affected in translation or interpretation, because linguistic items which give rise to semantic presuppositions are very similar in different languages. In contrast, pragmatic presuppositions, which are concerned with speakers and the communicative situation, are subject, in translation, to the vagaries of situations, many and varied across languages and cultures. From the perspective of translation and interpretation, presuppositions can be regarded as translators' and interpreters' assumptions about the target context and about the needs and expectations of the target readers or audience. The authors propose that presuppositions in relation to a translation or an interpretation can be analysed on the basis of three features: audience needs analysis, communication principles and textualisation principles, the last of which relate to text organisation.

In the final chapter of Part II of the volume, Chapter 8, "Rhetoric, oratory, interpreting and translation", Siobhán McElduff and James Luke Hadley discuss the intersections between rhetoric, oratory and a range of translation practices and theories. The chapter begins by examining the culturally loaded Classical language traditionally used to describe diverse oratorical and rhetorical traditions, before moving to an historical examination of rhetoric from Greece and Rome through modern China and Japan. Situating rhetoric and its concerns historically, the first half of the chapter examines the important role of translation in Greek and Roman rhetorical education, before discussing the problematic position Greek language and culture had for Rome and the Roman elite. The chapter also investigates a number of East Asian rhetorical traditions, and the effect that the importation of European rhetorical paradigms had on these traditions, before discussing the later rejection of Greek or Latin terms as appropriate translations for Asian forms of rhetoric and their discussion. The chapter concludes by examining the need for and interest in historically and culturally grounded studies of rhetoric and translation that focus on regional and contextual differences, and that do not assume a starting point in Classical Greece, along with suggestions for further investigation.

The rhetorical tradition formed the foundation for the types of textual analysis that are the foci of Part III of the volume entitled "Texts in speech and writing". In Chapter 9, "Discourse Analysis, interpreting and translation", Stefan Baumgarten and Melani Schröter draw a distinction between Discourse Analysis and Critical Discourse Analysis, and discuss their relevance and applicability to Translation Studies. Discourse Analysis analyses language as a social practice by accounting for discursive, situational and (inter)textual dimensions of communicative exchanges, while Critical Discourse Analysis highlights the ideological dimensions of language with reference to the way in which discourse shapes and is shaped by manipulative and discriminatory practices that readers and listeners may not be aware of. Both approaches tend to concentrate on ideologies embedded within patterns of communication within one culture; but in this chapter, a case is made for contrastive, intercultural and Crosscultural Discourse Analysis. The authors argue that a method of enquiry which they label Contrastive Cultural Discourse Analysis could counteract the bias that they perceive within Discourse and Critical Discourse Analysis in favour of intracultural analyses, as well as their Eurocentrism and overreliance on dominant languages, especially English. The crosscultural dimension of Contrastive Cultural Discourse Analysis would focus on translation and interpreting as instances of crosscultural communication based on linguistic mediations through cultural recontextualisations and examine the ways in which translation and interpreting are embedded in crosscultural networks of social and economic power, influence and authority against the backdrop of globalisation.

One of the purposes of the analysis of discourse is the identification of types, or genres, of text, and in Chapter 10, "Genre analysis and translation", Łucja Biel discusses the applications of genre analysis in translation research and training. A genre is a text or discourse type which is recognised by its characteristic formal, stylistic features and by the functions of texts belonging to the genre. Genre analysis identifies these distinctive features, known as generic conventions, and the social, communicative, cultural, cognitive and ideological factors behind the use of genres. The main methods used in genre analysis in the past were qualitative but more recently quantitative, corpus-based methods have been used, especially to study lexico-grammatical patterns. The chapter discusses three major models of genre analysis: the English for Specific Purposes (ESP) model, the Sydney School that emerged from systemic functional linguistics, and the New Rhetoric model. The ESP approach and the Sydney School are oriented towards preparing learning resources for non-native speakers of English whereas the New Rhetoric model has a special interest in North American native writing and focuses on social purposes. Translation-oriented genre analysis has focused on identifying differences in generic structures, conventions and expectations across languages and cultures. Genres develop in recurring situations which prompt responses in the form of "inaugurals, eulogies, courtroom speeches and the like" (Miller 1984, 152), which become conventionalised through repetition and precedent. But the rhetorical situation, which is "a complex of persons, events, objects and relations" (Bitzer 1968) may vary across cultures, and so may the concomitant generic conventions. For example, a PhD examination in most European countries is a public event, whereas in the UK it takes place behind closed doors with only the candidate and the examiners, and possibly the supervisor and a chairperson present. In China, an intermediate situation is common, where the candidate presents their research to a panel along with a smaller audience, usually consisting of the candidate's fellow students and any interested members of staff. Naturally enough, the rhetorical structures used by a PhD candidate when presenting their research will differ in these situations. But even across cultures which share the open examination convention, the forms of address that candidates use to address and greet their audience are likely to be culture specific. Since an understanding of genre is important for our ability to react appropriately to a text, the internalisation of genre knowledge is important for professional translators' ability to perform effectively, and genre analysis is an important component in the training of translators in both source text interpretation and target text production.

Retaining a focus on text organisation, in Chapter 11, "Text linguistics, translation, and interpreting", Gregory M. Shreve considers translation and interpreting as non-random activities that function through groupings of words in sequences of sentences. These groupings are assembled deliberately for communicative purposes and become texts as a consequence of this selection process. Texts are "interaction structures", whose formal and semantic properties are structured to suit the communicative purposes of situated social interactions, and they have specific language characteristics that can allow, for instance, for classification into text types. Any actions taken by the translator or interpreter in the process of creating a new vehicle for situated communication in the target culture must account for these characteristics or properties and for the cultural differences in them. Much of text linguistics developed in parallel with Translation Studies. Both had early and continuing relationships to systemic functional linguistics and were concerned with the nature of textuality. Their core concepts are coherence, cohesion, intentionality, situationality, acceptability, informativity and intertextuality. Text linguistics is a means to examine the transformations that a text undergoes when it is translated, beyond the scope of the rendition of individual words and sentences. Texts have structural and semantic features that reflect relationships between sentences, and the chapter asks to what extent translation preserves, alters or destroys those relationships. When dealing with translation, text linguistics places our focus squarely on the nature of texts – textuality – and how the textuality of a source text is related to the textuality of its target.

In Chapter 12, "Narrative analysis and translation", Mona Baker offers an overview of socio-narrative theory and some of its applications in translation and interpreting studies, beginning with an account of the theory's basic assumptions. She explores some of the main differences between the concept of narrative, as defined and applied in this approach, and the concept of discourse, as understood and applied in Critical Discourse Analysis, and explains the theoretical and research implications of these differences. This is followed by an explanation and detailed exemplification of two sets of conceptual tools elaborated in socio-narrative theory. The first is a fluid typology of different types of narrative that has been revisited and adapted in a number of studies. The second is an interdependent set of dimensions that define narrativity and are deployed in any attempt to make sense of experience by embedding it within a narrative world. The typology proposed in Baker (2006) consists of four categories: personal, public, conceptual and meta-narratives. The chapter draws on existing studies to exemplify the meaning of each category and demonstrate the dynamic interplay between them. The set of dimensions discussed and exemplified are temporality (covering both time and space), relationality, selective appropriation, causal emplotment, particularity, genericness, normativeness/canonicity and breach, and narrative accrual. The typology and the set of dimensions are both exemplified with reference to a diverse set of materials, including poetry, theatre translation, political advocacy programmes of translation, author branding and subtitling. The chapter ends by acknowledging the difficulty of applying this version of narrative theory in the context of existing research traditions in Translation Studies, and proposes a number of avenues and genres that lend themselves readily to narrative analysis and that may be explored in future research.

Whereas the previous chapter eschews the concept of narratology, which is focused mainly on literature, Chapter 13, "Stylistics and translation", by Jean Boase-Beier, answers the questions that it raises largely with reference to works of literature, poetry in particular. The questions are the following: How do style and translation interact? What is a stylistic approach to translation and what is a translational approach to stylistics? The chapter begins by considering the location of stylistics with respect to both Linguistics and to the study of literature, tracing its origins in early work of the Prague and Moscow Linguistic Circles, and setting its development alongside that of the discipline of Translation Studies. Both disciplines are concerned with similar linguistic issues: the relation of meaning to form; the choices the originator of a text makes; and how these choices are reconstructed by the reader. For stylistics, we can gain interesting insights into the minute detail of a text, and the relations between its form and its meaning, by confronting the text with its translations. For Translation Studies, conversely, we can consider what a stylistic approach involves and what questions it raises: questions about the role of style in the production of the translation and in its reception. We must also ask in what sense stylistics can affect the practice of translation; one way of doing this is to consider how a stylistically aware translation might differ from one that takes less account of the nuances of style. Future research might take this practical question further, paying more attention to the way a reader processes the stylistic detail of a translated text, and exploring the differences between (a) reading on the assumption that a translated text does not differ in any interesting way from its source text and (b) a reading experience that takes full account of the fact that the translation has changed the text stylistically, and incorporated elements of the style of the translator.

Chapters 9 to 13, having dealt with theories of text writ large, and with the structuring of texts into specific types or genres, the two remaining chapters in Part III address details of texts that often present translators with particularly inviting opportunities for creativity in the form of tropes and wordplay. Chapter 14, "Tropes and translation", by James Dickins, identifies and defines a set of key tropes and presents a number of notions which are essential for trope analysis. The chapter provides a preliminary analysis of non-lexicalised tropes, including metaphor, simile, metonymy and synecdoche, followed by an analysis which is necessary if lexicalised tropes are to be accounted for. In a lexicalised trope, the figurative sense depends on the semantic conventions of the language. For example, in "That argument's rubbish", "rubbish" acquires a secondary lexicalised metaphorical sense "Worthless or absurd ideas, talk, or writing; nonsense" in addition to its basic lexicalised sense of refuse, which, however, limits the sense of the metaphor. By contrast, in "The past is a foreign country", "foreign country" is a non-lexicalised metaphor; there are no basic semantic conventions of English which limit and specify the sense of "foreign country" used non-literally. The chapter discusses Goatly's categories of core, periphery, approximation and transfer in relation to tropes, concluding that these represent a continuum rather than categorical differences, and that the differences between metaphor, metonymy and synecdoche are also matters of degree rather than of category. It offers a revised analysis of non-lexicalised tropes, taking into account the continuum arguments, and considers metaphorical force, mainly using Goatly's dead, sleeping, tired and active scale, before discussing Lakoff and Johnson's influential conceptual metaphor theory. Turning more specifically to translation issues, the chapter surveys works on the translation of tropes, and provides a chronologically oriented overview of approaches to the translation of metaphor, which is typically thought of as the most challenging trope to translate.

In Chapter 15, "Wordplay and translation", Ida Klitgård discusses the nature of wordplay, especially the pun, in relation to translation. The pun manipulates sounds and senses that produce meanings that are taken for granted within cultures, in such a way that unexpected combinations ensue, which typically make us laugh. Translating puns may be difficult if cultural references differ between the two languages. The chapter provides a thorough account of wordplay from a lexico-grammatical point of view where the pun is defined as a bisociation formed through an acoustic knot. The secondary, unexpected meaning of the pun takes us by surprise as it challenges lexical priming in terms of the principles of collocations and colligations. Following the exposition of definitions, the chapter discusses methods and current debates on the translation of puns. The article concludes with examples from the

Danish translations of James Joyce's novel *Ulysses* (1922), which is a playful fabric of interconnected multilingual imagery, motifs and extensive wordplay.

Part IV of the volume "Individuals and their interactions" moves from a focus on texts to a focus on the users of language. It is divided into four chapters. In Chapter 16, "Bilingualism, translation, and interpreting", John W. Schwieter and Aline Ferreira discuss the role of individual bilingualism in translation and interpreting research. The chapter begins by presenting definitions of translation, interpreting and the complex notion of bilingualism followed by a brief historical account of important research in this area. Next, several core issues are discussed, including language proficiency and translation direction, lexical-conceptual representation and mediation, a dynamic view of bilingual and trilingual memory, and working memory and lexical retrieval. Investigations of these topics have moved translation and interpreting studies forward significantly, and many of these investigations have been informed by theoretical models in bilingualism, which are also presented. The chapter reviews interdisciplinary methodologies that demonstrate how techniques from cognitive science have situated themselves effectively within translation and interpreting studies. Finally, the chapter discusses how technologies affect translation and interpreting research and practice and suggests how future work in bilingualism can continue to inform translation and interpreting studies.

Chapter 17, "Language disorders, interpreting, and translation" by Alfredo Ardila, addresses situations in which all is not well with an individual's language, and the consequences for the person's ability to translate and interpret. The chapter presents a clinical description of the language disorders associated with brain pathology and introduces a distinction between the fundamental or major aphasic syndromes, known as Wernicke's and Broca's aphasia, that impair phonology, lexicon, semantics and grammar, on the one hand; and other aphasic syndromes that affect the ability to produce language, or the executive control of the language, on the other. The chapter examines the organisation of language in the bilingual brain, emphasising crucial variables, such as the age of acquisition of the second language, that significantly affect the patterns of organisation of language in the brain. The final section approaches the question of aphasia in bilinguals. It distinguishes between different patterns of clinical manifestation and recovery, and considers disturbances in the translation ability observed in bilinguals.

In Chapter 18, "Language processing in translation", Moritz Schaeffer considers the investigation of linguistic processing during translation in unimpaired individuals. He focuses on the methodological issues that have arisen and play a role in the quest for a model of the translation process. The advantages and disadvantages of each method are considered and compared. Key findings from both Bilingualism Studies and Translation Process Research are explained and highlighted. Findings from experimental studies, eye movement corpus studies, product-based translation corpus studies and brain imaging studies are discussed. The relationship between research methods in Translation Process Research and those employed in Psychology and Bilingualism Studies are examined in detail and future avenues of research are identified.

The final contribution to Part IV of the volume moves from the individual into the wider context of society, with Federico M. Federici's chapter, Chapter 19, on "Sociolinguistics, translation, and interpreting". The chapter considers translating and interpreting as sociolinguistic activities, and starts by presenting an account of interaction between early translation and interpreting scholarship and concepts from sociolinguistics. Sociolinguistics focuses on how social and linguistic factors influence communication and organise meaning, and these issues are of crucial importance for any language and culture mediator. Concepts such as register, which covers the choice of appropriate language given a particular con-stellation of discourse participants and the relationships between them, topic and message function, are central in translating and interpreting and the chapter reflects on the influence of sociolinguistic concepts on approaches to translation and interpreting research and practice. The chapter reviews debates focused on topics that demonstrate the interrelationship between the two disciplines, and new perspectives on translation and interpreting emerging in sociolinguistic scholarship. As translators and interpreters operate in ever more technologi-cally complemented contexts, in which social interactions occur in mixed modes and on a number of physical and virtual platforms, the chapter suggests that a competent grasp of sociolinguistic concepts is likely to remain an intrinsic part of the skillsets of translators and interpreters.

This focus on technology moves us towards Part V of the volume, which considers the relationship between humans and machines in the context of translating and interpreting. In Chapter 20, "Language and translation in film", Rocío Baños and Jorge Díaz-Cintas discuss the professional practices that are usually considered part of audiovisual translation (AVT), including accessibility to the media for audiences with sensory disabilities. After a brief historical overview, the chapter outlines the main characteristics of AVT, in particular the semiotic nature of the source text and the technical issues that constrain the translation sol-utions that can be adopted in subtitling and dubbing. Special attention is paid to the pre-fabricated nature of the dialogue found in audiovisual texts and to the transition that takes place from the oral to the written mode in the case of subtitling. Interdisciplinarity is a dis-tinctive trademark of AVT and the chapter discusses the main research methods traditionally used to investigate this area, emphasising the Descriptive Translation Studies paradigm and the use of corpora to identify the features and patterns of translated films. The chapter explores the efforts made by AVT scholars to test the validity of their theories experimentally, to explore the cognitive effort involved in the translational process and to measure human behaviour by means of instruments such as eye trackers, in order to acquire a better under-standing of their target audience. The final section of the chapter focuses on the automation of subtitling through the application of statistical machine translation technology, the potential of AVT for foreign language teaching and learning and the proliferation of amateur practices like fansubbing and fandubbing on the net.

In Chapter 21, "Language, interpreting, and translation in the news media" Christina Schäffner explores the effect of globalisation on the translation of news-related material. Globalisation has resulted in rapid developments in the professional practices involved in multilingual communication and in a growth of non-professional translation. Journalists often resort to a type of translation when information initially provided in another language becomes a source for their own text production. In Translation Studies, the unique role translation plays in the production and dissemination of international news has been addressed systematically since the mid-2000s, and the chapter comments on this tradition of research, which explores linguistic and textual aspects of news texts in different languages and cultures, the translation strategies used and their effects, the practices in specific media settings and the agents involved and their understanding of translation. The chapter discusses the conceptual challenges news translation poses to Translation Studies, especially in relation to the concept of transediting, the activity of editing the text one is translating, a practice often engaged in by journalists.

Moving away from specific text genres, Chapter 22, "Corpus linguistics, translation and interpreting" by Silvia Bernardini and Mariachiara Russo, explores the effect of corpus lin-guistics, an approach to the study of language that developed in the late 20th century, on research methodology in translation and interpreting studies. The development of corpus linguistics enabled researchers to move away from analytical methods that relied mainly on introspection and on decontextualised, artificial examples. Access was made available to vast quantities of examples of texts in use, which could be collected according to explicitly defined criteria, stored electronically and searched using dedicated software known as corpus query tools. The chapter reviews the origins and basic assumptions of corpus linguistics, drawing attention in particular to the interest in phraseological and lexical perspectives on language that it brought about. Surveying the main analytical methods, insights and practical applications of corpora in the fields of translation and interpreting studies, the chapter focuses on widely used corpus designs. It identifies three issues of special relevance to corpus-based studies of translation, here intended in the narrower sense, i.e. written translation, namely typical features of translated language, translation shifts and translator style. Concerning the specificities of corpus-based interpreting studies, it draws attention especially to the triangulation of methods from corpus linguistics and other disciplines such as sociolinguistics and ethnography of communication. The chapter identifies challenges, debates and future directions in both research areas, and concludes with an outline of uses of corpus research and of corpora in the translation and interpreting professions, including corpus use for machine and computer-aided translation, translator–learner corpora and corpora for the training of translators and interpreters.

The World Wide Web can in many ways be considered the biggest corpus of all, and in Chapter 23, "Language and translation on the Web", Mark Shuttleworth shows how translation may be implemented, supported, promoted, facilitated, discussed and made available over the Web. The chapter locates its topic within web studies and provides an overview of linguistic issues relating to the Web, with particular reference to translation. Topics such as the characteristics of web-based discourse and how different languages are represented on the Web are covered, along with a range of different translation practices, such as crowdsourced translation, translation in Wikipedia, web localisation and fansubbing. The chapter also discusses the online medium itself and the kinds of material that are typically being translated online. It reports on how the Web is used as a site for translation activities, focusing on machine translation and post-editing, web-based software and online translation resources such as translation memories and terminology. In addition, the chapter examines the social context in which translation takes place on the Web, as represented by blogs, translation portals and translators' websites.

Concluding Part V of the handbook, Chapter 24, "Translation, interpreting and new technologies" by Michael Carl and Sabine Braun, sets out how new developments in information and communication technologies (ICT), have sparked a technological revolution in the translation and interpreting profession. They identify three strands of development. First, machine translation (MT), automatic speech recognition (ASR) and speech-to-speech translation (SST) systems are increasing in speed, diversity, accuracy and availability. Second, as more documents are translated than ever before, the translation profession is diversifying and adapting to changing market needs, including by using a plethora of tools to assist the process of translating and the production of translations. This has led to the expansion and diversification of computer-assisted translation (CAT) and human-assisted machine translation (HAMT). Third, the demand for interpreting services has grown rapidly along with requirements for the timeliness and sustainability of their delivery. This, combined with an increase in the required language combinations and local shortages of qualified interpreters, has encouraged the development of ICT-supported solutions including teleconference interpreting (TCI) and remote interpreting (RI) via telephone and videoconference.

The chapter explains the key terms and concepts associated with each of these areas and provides an overview of their historical development and an outline of the main current trends, issues, debates and future directions in relation to translation and interpreting technologies, referring to current and emerging practice and to insights from research. The chapter concludes with a brief discussion of the practical implications that the developments outlined are likely to have for translation and interpreting.

The chapter on technologies leads us naturally towards the concluding part of the volume, which focuses on applications of research in Linguistics and translation and interpreting to teaching, lexicography and the use of languages for specific purposes. The section opens with Chapter 25, "Linguistics, translation and interpreting in foreign-language teaching contexts", by Anthony Pym and Nune Ayvazyan. The chapter outlines the history of the use of translation and interpreting in language teaching from the Renaissance through to the present day. Before the late 19th century, translation was a regular part of the teaching of foreign languages, alongside spoken and picture-based activities. This practice was challenged by Romantic learning theories that sought to imitate the "natural" learning process of the young child, and subsequently, and more significantly, by language teachers who had migrated to the United States and wanted to replicate their own experience of immersion. A method like Berlitz's, dating from the end of the 19th century, still shuns translation. However, translation has maintained a key role in language teaching and learning in Eastern Europe and in Asia, and is increasingly advocated by new generations of teachers and scholars elsewhere, including in Western Europe, where research in the 21st century has shown no empirical evidence that judicious use of communicative translation has a negative effect on language learning. The chapter suggests that the lack of research into the use of translation in language teaching and learning in the late 20th century can be attributed to the limited attention that translation scholars paid to language education at that time, when Translation Studies was developing as an independent discipline.

Chapter 26, "Translation, Interpreting and Lexicography", by Helle V. Dam and Sven Tarp, explores another important area of interaction between translation and interpreting studies and another discipline. Although translation, interpreting and lexicography are three separate areas of human activity, each with its own theories, models and methods and, hence, its own disciplinary underpinnings, all three disciplines share a marked interdisciplinary dimension: their practice fields are typically "about something else". Translators may, for example, be called upon to translate medical texts, and interpreters may be assigned to work on medical speeches. Similarly, practical lexicography may produce medical dictionaries. In this perspective, the three disciplines frequently come into contact with each other. This chapter discusses and explores some of the basic aspects of this interrelationship, focusing on the (potential) contribution of lexicography to translation and interpreting. In the mutual relation between translation, interpreting and lexicography, translation and interpreting represent the main activity in which translators and interpreters are engaged, whereas the consultation of dictionaries is a secondary activity which is only relevant to them when experiencing information needs during the translation or interpreting process. As such, lexicography is above all viewed as an auxiliary discipline. The relationship between (written) translation and lexicography is strong and well established, whereas the link between interpreting and lexicography is much weaker. The chapter shows that there is no reason that this should continue to be the case, especially because the current introduction of disruptive technologies into lexicography is creating new possibilities of satisfying both old and new user needs.

The handbook's closing chapter, Chapter 27 on "Language for Specific Purposes and translation", by Stefanos Vlachopoulos, begins by outlining the historical background and major trends in the interaction between domain-specific language use, or Language for Specific Purposes (LSP) and translation. The chapter also discusses practical issues and illustrates how translators of specialised discourse perform by way of examples of translated legal texts, the cultural extremes of domain-specific discourse.

References

Austin, J. L. 1962. *How to Do Things with Words*. Oxford: Oxford University Press.

Baker, M. 2006. *Translation and Conflict: A Narrative Account*. London: Routledge.

Bitzer, L. F. 1968. The rhetorical situation. *Philosophy and Rhetoric* 1, pp. 1–14.

Davidson, D. 1973. Radical interpretation. *Dialectica* 27, pp. 313–328.

Davidson, D. 1974. On the very idea of a conceptual scheme. *Proceedings and Addresses of the American Philosophical Association* 47, pp. 5–20.

Miller, C. R. 1984. Genre as social action. *Quarterly Journal of Speech* 70, pp. 151–167.

Nida, E. A. 1964. *Toward a Science of Translating: With Special Reference to Principles and Procedures Involved in Bible Translating*. Leiden: E. J. Brill.

Quine, W. V. O. 1960. *Word and Object*. Cambridge, MA: The MIT Press.

Searle, J. R. 1969. *Speech Acts: An Essay in the Philosophy of Language*. Cambridge: Cambridge University Press.

Part I

The nature of language, translation and interpreting

1

Theories of linguistics and of translation and interpreting

Kirsten Malmkjær

Introduction and definitions

Linguistics is the academic discipline that focuses on languages, and since translation can be seen, in Catford's (1965, 1) words as "an operation performed on languages", many scholars interested in translation and interpreting have looked to linguistics for theoretical input (Nida 1964; Vinay and Darbelnet 1958/1995; Neubert 1973, 1985; Halverson 2007, 2010, 2013, 2014). Equally, though, linguists have sought enlightenment about language and languages through the study of languages in contact with each other in situations involving translation or interpreting (Sapir 1921; Jakobson 1959). Some scholars, especially those with a geographical background in Europe (e.g. Jakobson) and/or a disciplinary leaning towards field linguistics and/or anthropology (e.g. Sapir) fall equally comfortably into both the linguistic and the Translation Studies discipline.

Catford's definition has been criticised by Snell-Hornby (1995 [1988], 3) for expressing too narrow a view of what translation is and for deriving translation rules from "isolated and even absurdly simplistic sentences" (1995 [1988], 20). For their part, interpreting studies scholars like Seleskovitch (1975, 1978) and Seleskovitch and Lederer (1984, 1989) have warned that linguistics is too focused on words and expressions to be able to account for interpreting. Instead, they prefer the so-called theory of sense developed by Seleskovitch, according to which an interpreter abstracts sense from words in the source language in order to express a similar sense in the target language. Of course, a linguist might argue that the role of language in this process remains significant, and given the heightened concentration in the late 20th and early 21st centuries on the cognitive processes involved in translating and interpreting (see Chapter 18 in this volume), such criticisms seem less pertinent than they were when originally posed.

It is possible that at least some negative views of linguistics as a foundation for the development of translation and interpreting studies were based on a desire to forge independent disciplines and a concern that the complex processes of translating and interpreting would be overlooked in the effort to relate languages to each other, often with little regard for empirical data and even less attention paid to context. To a limited extent, these fears have been realised in the work by Gutt (1991), for example. Gutt draws heavily on Sperber and Wilson's (1986) relevance theoretic account of linguistic interaction (see Chapter 6 in this volume), so he pays considerable attention to context; nevertheless, he also claims that, given relevance theory, there is no need for a separate theory of translation Gutt (1990, 135, italics original):

> *the phenomenon commonly referred to as "translation" can be accounted for naturally within the relevance theory of communication developed by Sperber and Wilson: there is no need for a distinct general theory of translation.*

Of course, there are also translation scholars who have viewed linguistics positively. In addition to Catford, who bases his theory on the linguistic theory of Halliday (1961), these include Vinay and Darbelnet (1958), who believe with Trager and Smith (1951, 81) that linguistics is "the most exact of human sciences" (Vinay and Darbelnet 1958/1995, 7) and who draw heavily on Saussure's theory of signs (see in particular Vinay and Darbelnet 1958/1995, 12–15); Nida (1964, 9), who refers to Chomsky (1957; 1962 [published as 1964]); and Halverson (2007, 2010, 2013, 2014), who draws on the cognitive linguistic theory developed by Langacker (1983, 1987, 1991a, 1991b, 1999, 2008).

Historical perspectives

It is likely that people have been studying language for as long as there has been speech, and documented speculation about language, especially about its origins, dates back at least as far as the seventh century BCE (Mufwene 2013, 16). Each of the great traditions (Arab, Chinese, Greco-Roman, Indian, Near Eastern, Semitic, Western, and so on) has its own history (Law 1990, 784 and ff), but linguistics as such can still be considered a relatively young discipline. According to Fox (2006, 317) the discipline became established in the nineteenth century as what Burridge (2013, 141) describes as "a new science, distinct from literary studies and philosophical enquiry"; and what is generally thought of as the first major publication in modern linguistics, Ferdinand de Saussure's *Cours de linguistique générale* was published in 1916 (references here are to the Fontana/Collins edition introduced by Jonathan Culler and first published in 1974). Part four of this course concerns geographical linguistics, and in it, Saussure considers the diversity of languages to which he refers as "The most striking thing about the study of languages" and "the first observation made in linguistics" (1916/1974, 191); and, he adds, "Having noticed that two idioms differ, one instinctively looks for similarities" (1916/1974, 192). Saussure, however, does not dwell on the concept or practice of translation, an omission that sets him at odds with his contemporary, Edward Sapir, for whom comparison between languages is undertaken as field-work by way of informant-aided translation of words and expressions. This is not a mere matter of methodological difference between the founders of two scholarly traditions; followers of Sapir's comparative methodology consider, in the words of Roman Jakobson, that comparison through translation is the only legitimate method of linguistic inquiry. As Jakobson puts it (1959, 234): "No linguistic specimen may be interpreted by the science of language without a translation of its signs into other signs of the same system or into signs of another system". This approach to linguistic data collection is illustrated especially clearly by Edward Sapir (1921).

For example, Sapir (1921, 92–93) identifies thirteen concepts expressed in the sentence, "the farmer kills the duckling".

I. Concrete concepts:

1. First subject of discourse: *farmer*
2. Second subject of discourse: *duckling*
3. Activity: *kill*

These concrete subjects can be analysed into:

A. Radical concepts

1. Verb *(to) farm* (concept 1)
2. Noun: *duck* (concept 2)
3. Verb: *kill* (concept 3)

and

B. Derivational concepts

1. Agentive: expressed by the suffix *-er* (concept 4)
2. Diminutive: expressed by the suffix *-ling* (concept 5)

II. Relational concepts: including two instances of Definiteness of Reference expressed by "the" (concepts 6 and 7); Declarative modality expressed by the position of the subject and verb (concept 8); two instances of Personal Relations realised by the subjectivity of "farmer" and the objectivity of "duckling" (concepts 9 and 10); two instances of singular number expressed by the lack of plural suffix on "farmer" and on "duckling" (concepts 11 and 12) and one instance of time expressed by lack of any past tense indication on the verb and by the suffixed "-s" (concept 13).

In other languages, Sapir (1921, 94–98) points out, some or all of these concepts may be ordered differently, and some may not be expressed, while concepts that the English sentence does not express are expressed in other languages. In the German "equivalent sentence", as Sapir (1921, 95) refers to the sentence, *"Der Bauer tötet das Entelein"*, for example, the expression of definiteness:

> is unavoidably coupled with three other concepts – number (both *der* and *das* are explicitly singular), case (*der* is subjective; *das* is subjective or objective, by elimination therefore objective), and gender, a new concept of the relational order that is not in this case explicitly involved in English (*der* is masculine, *das* is neuter).

In Yana, an extinct language that was spoken in north-central California:

> Literally translated, the equivalent sentence would read something like "kill-s-he farmer [although the Yana did not farm] he to duckling," in which "he" and "to" are rather awkward English renderings of a general third person pronoun ... and an objective particle which indicates that the following noun is connected with the verb otherwise than as a subject. The suffixed element in "kill-s" corresponds to the English suffix with the important exceptions that it makes no reference to the number of the subject and that the statement is known to be true, that it is vouched for by the speaker.
>
> (Sapir 1921, 96)

17

Sapir (1921, 96–98) also compares the sentence with its Chinese and Kwakiutl translations (Kwakiutl was spoken in what is now British Columbia), noting numerous differences, but concluding, nevertheless, that (1921, 126):

> No language wholly fails to distinguish noun and verb, though in particular cases the nature of the distinction may be an elusive one. It is different with the other parts of speech. Not one of them is imperatively required for the life of language.

This is important, because this finding in linguistics (that all languages examined employ noun-like and verb-like elements), arrived at through a research method that is empirical, immensely thorough and profoundly translational, coincides with the findings of logico-philosophical analysis of language that subject and predicate are fundamental elements of expression. Both disciplines provide a basis in similarity against which the prolific differences between languages can be measured.

Core issues and topics

Can there be translation?

It is widely, although not universally, agreed that the common core of languages referred to in the previous section suffices to ensure that some degree of translation between languages can always be achieved. This does not mean that there are not profound differences between languages which can have significant effects on how speakers of these languages understand their surroundings, on the societies that they live in and on the processes of translation between the languages; but it does mean that the concept of linguistic relativity, popularised by Benjamin Lee Whorf (e.g. Whorf *circa* 1936), but also supported to an extent by Sapir himself (e.g. Sapir 1929/Mandelbaum 1949, 69), has been rethought, as Gumperz and Levinson's (1996a) book title suggests. For Translation Studies, it means that its *metier* is not spurious, as it would be if languages differed so radically that no translation could be conceived of (though how that would be established is a moot point). This possibility is considered by Whorf (1936/Carroll 1956) on the basis of information he learnt from a speaker of the Hopi Indian language whom he met in New York. According to this informant, the Hopi language contains:

> no words, grammatical forms, constructions or expressions that refer directly to what we call "time," or to past, present, or future, or to enduring or lasting, or to motion as kinematic rather than dynamic ... or that even refer to space in such a way as to exclude that element of extension or existence that we call "time". ... In this Hopi view, time disappears and space is altered ... At the same time, new concepts and abstractions flow into the picture, taking up the task of describing the universe without reference to such time or space – abstractions for which our language lacks adequate terms.
>
> (Whorf 1936/Carroll 1956, 57–58)

In Hopi, rather than time and space being, as Kant (1781, A26/B42 and A33/B49–50) has it, the forms of human experience, there are two "cosmic forms" (1936/Carroll 1956, 59), Manifested and Manifesting. The Manifested "comprises all that is or has been accessible to the senses"; the Manifesting comprises:

all that we call future, BUT NOT MERELY THIS; it includes ... all that we call mental – everything that appears or exists in the mind, or, as the Hopi would prefer to say, in the HEART, not only the heart of man, but the heart of animals, plants, and things.

(Whorf 1936/Carroll 1956, 59; small caps in the original)

Differences of this type between distant languages led Whorf to suggest "a new principle of relativity" (1940/Carroll 1956, 214) according to which "all observers are not led by the same physical evidence to the same picture of the universe, unless their linguistic backgrounds are similar, or can in some way be calibrated"; and since by calibration Whorf appears to mean setting a sentence of language *a* together with a sentence in language *b* in such a way that the word classes and their associated concepts in the two sentences match up fairly well, "translated" serves as at least a close synonym; and, according to Whorf, it is doubtful whether this is possible between even simple sentences of for example Hopi and English (1940/Carroll 1956, 216): "The Hopi do not say, 'I stayed five days,' but 'I left on the fifth day'". In the same article (*ibid.*), Whorf also makes the assertions about snow which are probably the best-known aspect of his work (even though most people could probably not name the originator of the remarks, and tend to be more precise about the number of words for snow that Eskimos are said to have than Whorf is); in its context, his discourse on snow runs as follows:

Hopi has one noun that covers every thing or being that flies, with the exception of birds, which class is denoted by another noun ... The Hopi actually call insect, airplane and aviator all by the same word ... This class seems to us too large and inclusive, but so would our class "snow" to an Eskimo ... an Eskimo ... would say that falling snow, slushy snow, and so on, are sensuously and operationally different ... he uses different words for them and for other kinds of snow.

In Gumperz and Levinson's (1996b, 1) summary, then, "The essential idea of linguistic relativity is 'that culture, *through* language, affects the way we think, especially perhaps our classification of the experienced world'". As they remark (1996b, 13 fn. 10), "controversies about language difference" have played a considerable part in discussions about equality between peoples. For example, "the Spanish champions of the Indians like Las Casas were keen to show that the Indian languages had a systematic grammar, while their detractors tried to establish that they lacked abstractions fundamental for intellectual and spiritual development". It is, then, a debate that has ramifications well beyond academic circles, and it is explored in the articles collected in Gumperz and Levinson (1996a). The debate about translatability within philosophy is addressed in Chapter 2 in this volume on semantics and translation.

The antidote to the relativism espoused by Whorf is of course latent in Sapir's insistence (see above) that "No language wholly fails to distinguish noun and verb, though in particular cases the nature of the distinction may be an elusive one" (1921, 126). This notion hints at universalism, and for a time, Translation Studies became preoccupied with this notion, which clearly echoes Chomsky's notion of universals of language, even though Translation Studies scholars searching for universals of translation have been reticent with respect to that relationship. In any case Chomsky himself insists that nothing follows concerning translating from the possible existence of linguistic universals (Chomsky 1965, 30):

The existence of deep-seated formal universals ... implies that all languages are cut to the same pattern, but does not imply that there is any point by point correspondence between particular languages. It does not, for example, imply that there must be some reasonable procedure for translating between languages.

Nevertheless, the existence of such universals would, as mentioned above, imply that translation would at least not be impossible in principle. A second major issue in Translation Studies has centred exactly around this question of whether there are, or are not, translation universals, but that debate has not generally addressed any relationship that there might be between translation universals and linguistic universals.

Are there universals of translation?

One of the major debates in modern Translation Studies has centred on the relationship between norms and universals in Translation Studies. As Malmkjær (2004/2007, 13) explains:

> Norms have played a central role in descriptive translation studies, because (Toury 1995, 61, emphasis in the original) **"it is norms that determine the (type and extent of) equivalence manifested by actual translations"**. Equivalence is the name given to the relationship, of whatever type and extent, between a translation and its source text, and the existence of such a relationship is axiomatic in the theory.
>
> (Toury 1980a, 45)

There is theoretical tension between Toury's concept of norms and the notion of the universal, since it is only on the assumption that behaviour may vary that "there is a point in assuming the existence of norms" (Toury 1995, 55), and the concept of the universal suggests invariance. So if translational behaviour is in principle highly variable, norms may have an important role in attempts at explaining regularities in translational behaviour; but if translational behaviour is constrained by universals, there is less need to resort to the norm concept in explaining regularities.

Toury (1977/1980b, 60) suggests that some features of translated text are, if not exactly universal, then at least very common. For example:

> there is an almost general tendency – irrespective of the translator's identity, language, genre, period, and the like – to explicate in the translation information that is only implicit in the original text.

Explicitation is one of the phenomena referred to by Baker (1993), who defines translation universals as "features which typically occur in translated text rather than original utterances and which are not the result of interference from specific linguistic systems" (Baker 1993, 243). Here, Baker adopts the somewhat counterintuitive practice shared by some scholars in linguistics of including among universals phenomena that are only present *typically* (that is, not actually universally). Among linguists following this practice is Greenberg (1966), on whose list of forty-five universals developed on the basis of study of thirty languages we find both absolute universals such as "All languages have pronominal categories involving at least three persons and two numbers" (Universal 42); and universal tendencies, like "In languages with prepositions, the genitive almost always follows the governing noun, while in languages with postpositions it almost always precedes ... " (Universal 2). In this tradition a universal is defined as a property "which must at least be true of the majority of the human languages" (Song, 2001, 8). Their regular presence is explained in terms of ease of language comprehension and production (Hawkins 1994), historical development (Bybee *et al.* 1990) or a combination of these explanations (Greenberg 1957; Hall 1988), whereas in the Chomskyan tradition universals are absolute and explained in terms of Universal Grammar, the initial state of the language acquisition device. The universals in Chomskyan theory include principles that constrain the forms of languages and parameters that define the binary variations which languages display (Chomsky 1981; Radford 2004). Given that principles and parameters are innate, they differ absolutely from norms. Norms are matters of socio-linguistics; universals of psycholinguistics.

As for translation universals, Baker's original definition of translation universals as features that *typically* occur in translated texts suggests a social explanation of their existence (if they exist) whereas the notion that they are not the result of features of the languages involved at least hints at a cognitive source and explanation of translation universals. This conundrum is solved by way of a differentiation later in the article between universals and norms. Translation universals, she contends (Baker, 1993, 246):

> can be seen as a product of constraints which are inherent in the translation process itself and this accounts for the fact that they are universal (or at least we assume they are, pending further research). They do not vary across cultures. Other features have been observed to occur consistently in certain types of translation within a particular socio-cultural and historical context. These are the product of norms of translation which represent another type of constraint on translational behaviour.

Baker lists as possible translation universals, explicitation, disambiguation, simplification, conventionalisation, avoidance of repetition, exaggeration of features of the target language, referred to as "normalisation" in Baker (1997, 183) and manifestations of the so-called "third code" (1993, 243–245). The third code is a notion Baker borrows from Frawley (1984/2000; quotation from the 2000 reprint). It arises, according to Frawley, as a result of the confrontation of the source text and the target text to be. Translation, he explains:

> is the bilateral accommodation of a matrix and target code … The translation itself … is essentially a third code which arises out of the bilateral consideration of the matrix and target codes: it is, in a sense, a subcode of each of the codes involved: That is, since the translation truly has a dual lineage, it emerges as a code in its own right, setting its own standards and structural presuppositions and entailments, though they are necessarily derivative of the matrix information and target parameters.
>
> (Frawley 1984/2000, 258)

Toury (1979/1980c, 72), too, had earlier referred to something of this kind, which he considers a manifestation of "interlanguage forms in translation", as a "translation universal".

It was Baker's intention to identify the linguistic characteristics of this third code, and these were indeed found to include some of the features she listed as translation universals. For example, normalisation had already been established as a characteristic of translated texts by Toury (1977/1980b), who examined the occurrence of binominals in texts respectively first written in and translated into Hebrew, and by Vanderauwera (1985), who examined unusual language use in Dutch fiction translated into English. It was subsequently confirmed in Kenny (1998), but contradicted by Xiao and Dai (2013/2014). Explicitation was identified by Blum-Kulka (1986) and subsequently confirmed by Øverås (1998) and Xiao and Dai (2013/2014), although a study of translation between English and Korean contradicts it (Cheong 2006).

Simplification was identified by Laviosa-Braithwaite (1997) and supported by Xiao and Dai (2013/2014). Exaggeration of phenomena specific to the target text language and not shared by the source language has been noted by Gellerstam (1986) and Lykke Jakobsen (1986). On the other hand, Eskola (2004) and Tirkkonen-Condit (2004) both find underrepresentation in translated text of features of the target language that are not shared by the source language; not surprising, one might think, given that there will obviously be nothing in the source language that will trigger the construction in the target language, and Malmkjær (2011) suggests that this feature is probably a translation universal.

According to Kruger (2002, 99), Baker had lost faith in the notion of the translation universal by 2001 "and opted instead to call these features of translated texts simply 'translational patterns and regularities'", and by 2004 something of an impasse had been reached with respect to the notion (see the papers collected in Mauranen and Kujamäki 2004). With regard to the phenomena originally thought of as potential candidates for the position of translation universals, therefore, we are left with the notion of norms as the best general explanation. Some, no doubt, arise as a result of teaching or of translators' desire to produce texts that are clear, unambiguous, easy to read, conventional, non-repetitive and respectful of target language features, which may become exaggerated as a result of the translators' efforts at being "natural" in the target language.

However, Malmkjær (2011) suggests that in addition to the underrepresentation in translated text of features of the target language that are not shared by the source language, identified by Tirkkonen-Condit (2004), two further universals of translation may be identified. One might be called "the first translational response". This can be assumed to be universal insofar as something has to be the first response that a translator has to a text to be translated. Comparing it with the response that a translator eventually chooses, she suggests (2011, 92):

> Might tell us a great deal about the bilingual language store (how items in the two languages are connected) and about translation competence (How much editing is it necessary to perform after the first response? Do some translators' first responses require less editing than those of others?), and about how translational cognitive activity differs from unilingual cognitive activity and from bilingual cognitive activity that is not translational.

Further, she proposes that segmentation might be a third translation universal (*ibid.*): "first responses to longer stretches of text will occur in segmented form", and this kind of segmentation has no counterpart in unilingual activity (Malmkjær 2011, 93):

> It involves simultaneous suppression and activation of the right features of the linguistic systems at the right time in the right proportions to each other before the translator or interpreter can get started on the conscious part of the translation process.

Investigating these might provide interesting insights into inter-linguistic relationships and into the relationships between items and concepts in the translating bilingual's mind (*ibid.*).

Main research methods

The main research method in linguistically oriented Translation Studies is comparison between source and target texts, a tradition which, according to Gellerstam (1996, 54), dates back to the third century AD. The comparison can be undertaken by way of what Lindquist (1989, 23) refers to as parallel reading, that is, reading "the SL text in parallel with the TL text, noting anything that is remarkable, and then to list deficiencies (or felicities) of all kinds". The fact that this quotation places the possibility that felicities might be highlighted by the comparative method in parentheses illustrates the propensity of followers of this method to pay particular attention to deficiencies in translated texts, and there has been considerable scepticism among scholars about the value of translated text as a source of information about language (see e.g. Lauridsen 1996, 65). However, as Gellerstam (1996, 53) points out – with reference to Sweden, but the point holds true for very many languages of limited diffusion – translations form a major part of the language people encounter in their daily lives, and should therefore be studied. Baker (1993) was similarly inspired by the habitual distrust and deprecation of translated texts to seek to develop a methodology that would show what the actual characteristics of translated texts are (see below).

The comparative method can be augmented by electronic means if the collections of texts to be examined are stored and therefore searchable electronically, and it can proceed from the source text to the target text or from the target text to the source text. The latter method was famously advocated by Toury (1980a) as an antidote to the tendency, before then, to:

> consider translation from the point of view of its being a reconstruction – in general a maximal (or at least optimal) reconstruction – of ST (i.e., the formalization of ST's systemic relationships), or even of SL, in TL, in such a way and to such an extent that TT and ST are interchangeable according to some preconceived definition of this interchangeability.
>
> (1980, 35)

Such theories postulate that translations have to meet certain conditions, but postulate, in addition, that these conditions cannot be met. For example, Ingarden (1931/1973, 266) maintains that:

> no genuine, really valuable lyric poem can be translated into a foreign language, precisely because the phonetic stratum is then replaced by a completely different verbal material, which cannot ever perform all those functions which were performed effortlessly in the original.

As Toury points out, such an approach cannot account for existing texts which are considered to be translations and which function as translations in their cultures. He therefore advocates an approach that begins from the target text and moves from it to the source text to discover which relationships in fact obtain between the two, and these relationships will then be taken to be relationships of translational equivalence (Toury 1980a, 39). Given that more than one possible relationship of equivalence typically exists between texts and text segments, the notion of the translation norm is invoked to explain why one such relationship rather than any other has been selected.

Toury's norm concept is broad, and can arguably be used to explain a great deal of what happens to the language of translated texts. However, Boase-Beier (2004; 2006) and Malmkjær (2003, 2004/2007) have both sought to develop an approach that is more detailed and explicitly "stylistically-aware", as Boase-Beier (2006, 111) puts it. In Boase-Beier's case, the approach is informed by cognitive stylistics (e.g. Stockwell 2002); Malmkjær's approach is a development of the more surface-oriented type of stylistic analysis described by, for example, Leech (1969) and Leech and Short (1981) (see Chapter 13 in this volume).

Instead of comparing texts and their translations, Baker (1993, 245) suggested the creation of "a corpus of texts translated into, say, English [or any other language] from a variety of languages" which could be compared with a corpus of texts originally written in English (or any other language). Were a number of corpus pairs to become available, it might be conceivable that certain differences between corpus pair parts were shared across the pairs, and these might then qualify as "universal features of translation" (*ibid.*) (though see the previous section). Baker and colleagues at the University of Manchester Institute of Technology (UMIST) created a corpus of English original texts and one of texts of the same types, namely newspaper articles and narrative prose, which, by 1998, amounted to two million words (Laviosa 1998, 557) and which was machine searchable. See Chapter 22 on corpus linguistics, translation and interpreting in this volume for an account of research undertaken using this and similar corpora. Machine readable corpora of interpreted text were also constructed, as were mixed corpora containing both interpreted and translated texts (Shlesinger 2009; Shlesinger and Ordan, 2012).

Current debates and future directions

In addition to the foci for future research suggested by Malmkjær (2011) and mentioned in the section on core issues and topics above, House (2013, 46) makes an impassioned "plea for a new linguistic-cognitive orientation" in Translation Studies, to balance the "predominance of cultural, social, ideological and personal concerns" that she perceives in Translation Studies and which, she considers, is in danger of ignoring "the essence of translation" (*op. cit.*: 47) to the detriment of any enhanced understanding of translated text. She points out that research methodologies involving key logging and eye tracking directly measure behaviour, and that related claims about translators' mental activity are hypotheses (*op. cit.*: 51). She advocates a return to her own model of linguistic-textual analysis of source texts and translations (House 1997), combined with Paradis' (2004) neurolinguistic theory of bilingualism, because without a descriptively and explanatorily adequate model of the bilingual mind, which Paradis provides, hypotheses about the translating activities of such a mind cannot be tested, however precise the textual analysis of its products may be.

House's model of translation and its assessment is based in part on Hallidayan systemic functional linguistics (see House 2015, 21). In similar vein, according to Kim and Matthiessen (2015, 335), "ways to move forward in translation studies" include the application of Hallidayan systemic functional linguistics as set out in Halliday (1978) to texts and their translations. They review studies of thematic progression in texts and their translations, and suggest that the systemic functional approach to linguistic and textual analysis can supply the rigorous framework that descriptive Translation Studies has hitherto lacked (Kim and Matthiessen 2015, 346). This is interesting given that it was basically the same framework, at a slightly earlier stage in its development, that appealed to Catford (1965) (see the first section in this chapter). There has been considerable interest in this framework and in the idea of applying it in Translation Studies in China, in particular, where Halliday studied (Peng 2015), and where interest in Translation Studies burgeoned around the turn of the century. This is to the advantage of the linguistically oriented aspects of the discipline, because it has meant a broadening of the language pairs that come under scrutiny within it and therefore of the phenomenon of translation itself, as called for by House (2013; see above). For example, Wang (2016) examines the impact of grammatical differences between Chinese and English on interpreting between the two languages and Choi (2013) analyses the discourse of original and translated speeches made by Lee Myung-bak, president of South Korea 2008–2013.

Translation Studies scholars can be expected to continue to test claims concerning languages and language pairs in translation. For example, Munday (2015) examines the use of reporting verbs, and hypothesises that the intensity of engagement and attitude that source text reporting verbs can convey tends to be downgraded in translations, while Steiner (2015) calls for further studies of cohesion in texts and their translations. Given that there is hardly a limit to the linguistic and textual features that are open to examination by Translation Studies scholars along with the upsurge in interest in this area, we can look forward to a steady stream of scholarship in the years to come.

Implications for practice

Malmkjær (forthcoming) suggests that studying translations and their source texts can enhance cross-linguistic awareness not only among language learners and trainee translators, but more generally. Language awareness, she suggests:

> involves the ability to think about language as a structured phenomenon that humans use to get along in the world of sentient beings, processes and things and by means of which a number of human purposes can be pursued more or less successfully, depending, at least partly, on how finely tuned interactants' language awareness is.

Language awareness, in her conception, includes awareness of the existence of different languages and dialects; of idiolect; of the close relationship between language and context; of the reality-building and reality-reflecting nature of language, and of the power of language to persuade. She suggests that each of these awarenesses can be enhanced through exercises involving translations. Since, as Thompson (1984, 132; italics in the original) reminds us, individuals have different abilities "*to make a meaning stick*" and since "relations of domination are sustained by a *mobilisation of meaning*", raising awareness of how meaning can be mobilised is of immense importance for the general good of all members of society. Because languages differ, a source text and its translation almost always realise different variants of the "same" narration, and studying these differences can highlight the importance of language choice within one language as well as the fact that some things cannot be expressed in exactly the same way, or at all, in all languages. By the use of "back-translations", which are translations of a translation back into the language of the source text for the translation, this method works for people who have different language pairs (as long as one language is shared among them) or with monolinguals as well as with language learners.

Further reading

Catford, J. C. 1965. *A Linguistic Theory of Translation: An Essay in Applied Linguistics*. Oxford: Oxford University Press.
A classic of linguistically oriented writings on translation.

House, J. 2015. *Translation as Communication Across Languages and Cultures*. London: Routledge.
Repositions Translation Studies within modern applied linguistics.

Malmkjær, K. 2005. *Linguistics and the Language of Translation*. Edinburgh: Edinburgh University Press. Intended for students of translation, languages and linguistics who would like to enhance their understanding of the relationships between these disciplines.

Vinay, J.-P. and Darbelnet, J. 1958. *Stylistique comparée du français et de l'anglais*. Paris: Les éditions Didier. English translation and edition by J. Sager and M.-J. Hamel. 1995. *Comparative Stylistics of French and English: A Methodology for Translation*. Amsterdam: John Benjamins Publishing Company.

A thorough account of relationships between French and English and of how these affect translation between the two languages.

Related topics

Implicature and presupposition in translation and interpreting; Relevance Theory, interpreting, and translation; Semantics and translation; Semiotics and translation, Discourse analysis, interpreting and translation; Linguistics, translation and interpreting in FL teaching contexts; Phonetics, phonology and interpreting.

References

Baker, M. 1993. "Corpus Linguistics and Translation Studies: Implications and Applications". In *Text and Technology: In Honour of John Sinclair*, edited by M. Baker, G. Francis and E. Tognini-Bonelli, 233–250. Amsterdam and Philadelphia: John Benjamins.

Baker, M. 1997. "Corpus-based Translation Studies: The Challenges that Lie Ahead". In *Terminology, LSP and Translation: Studies in Language Engineering in Honour of Juan C, Sager*, edited by H. Somers, 175–186. Amsterdam: John Benjamins.

Blum-Kulka, S. 1986. "Shifts of cohesion and coherence in translation". In *Interlingual and Intercultural Communication*, edited by J. House and S. Blum-Kulka, 17–35. Tübingen: Gunter Narr Verlag.

Boase-Beier, J. 2004. Knowing and not knowing: style, intention and the translation of a Holocaust poem. *Language and Literature* 13(1), pp. 25–35.

Boase-Beier, J. 2006. *Stylistic Approaches to Translation*. Manchester: St Jerome.

Burridge, K. 2013. "Nineteenth-century study of sound change from Rask to Saussure". In *The Oxford Handbook of the History of Linguistics*, edited by K. Allan, 141–165. Oxford: Oxford University Press.

Bybee, J. L., Pagliua, W. and Perkins, R. D. 1990. "On the Asymmetries in the Affixation of Grammatical Material". In *Studies in Typology and Diachrony*, edited by W. Croft, S. Kemmer and K. Denning, 43–58. Amsterdam: John Benjamins.

Catford, J. C. 1965. *A Linguistic Theory of Translation: An Essay in Applied Linguistics*. Oxford: Oxford University Press.

Cheong, H.-J. 2006. Target text contraction in English-into-Korean translations: a contradiction of presumed translation universals? *Meta* 51(2), pp. 343–367.

Choi, J. 2013. Discourse analysis on the originals and translations of speeches by the president of Korea, Lee Myung-bak. *The Journal of Translation Studies* 14(3), pp. 7–39.

Chomsky, N. 1957. *Syntactic Structures*. The Hague: Mouton.

Chomsky, N. 1964. "The Logical Basis of Linguistic Theory". In *Proceedings of the Ninth International Congress of Linguistics*, edited by H. Lunt, 914–978. The Hague: Mouton.

Chomsky, N. 1965. *Aspects of the Theory of Syntax*. Cambridge, MA: The MIT Press.

Chomsky, N. 1981. *Lectures on Government and Binding*. Dordrecht: Foris.

Eskola, S. 2004. "Untypical Frequencies in Translated Language: A Corpus-based Study on a Literary Corpus of Translated and Non-translated Finnish". In *Translation Universals – Do They Exist?*, edited by A. Mauranen and P. Kujamäki, 83–100. Amsterdam: John Benjamins.

Fox, A. 2006. "Historical and Comparative Linguistics in the 19th Century". In *Encyclopedia of Language and Linguistics*. 2nd ed., Vl. 5, edited by K. Brown, 317–326. Oxford: Elsevier.

Frawley, W. 1984. "Prolegomenon to a Theory of Translation". In *Translation: Literary, Linguistic, and Philosophical Perspectives*, edited by W. Frawley. London: Associated University Press. Reprinted (2000) in *The Translation Studies Reader*, edited by L. Venuti, 250–263. London: Routledge.

Gellerstam, M. 1986. "Translationese in Swedish Novels Translated from English". In *Translation Studies in Scandinavia*, edited by L. Wollin and H. Lindquist, 88–95. Lund, Sweden: CWK Gleerup.

Gellerstam, M. 1996. "Translations as a Source for Cross-linguistic Studies". In *Languages in Contrast: Papers from a Symposium on Text-based Cross-linguistic Studies, Lund 4–5 March 1994*, edited by K. Aijmer and B. Altenberg, 53–62. Lund: Lund University Press.

Greenberg, J. H. 1957. "Order of Affixing: A Study in General Linguistics". In *Essays in Linguistics* edited by J. H. Greenberg. Chicago: University of Chicago Press.

Greenberg, J. H. 1966. Some universals of grammar with particular reference to the order of meaningful elements. In *Universals of Language*, edited by J. H. Greenberg, 73–113. Cambridge, MA: MIT Press.

Gumperz, J. J. and Levinson, S. C., eds. 1996a. *Rethinking Linguistic Relativity*. Cambridge: Cambridge University Press.

Gumperz, J. J. and Levinson, S. C. 1996b. "Introduction: Linguistic Relativity Re-examined". In *Rethinking Linguistic Relativity*, edited by J. J. Gumperz and S. C. Levinson, 1–18. Cambridge: Cambridge University Press.

Gutt, E.-A. 1990. A theoretical account of translation – without a translation theory. *Target* 2(2), pp. 135–164.

Gutt, E.-A. 1991. *Translation and Relevance: Cognition and Context*, Oxford: Basil Blackwell. 2nd ed. (2000) Manchester: St Jerome.

Hall, C. J. 1988. "Integrating Diachronic and Processing Principles in Explaining the Suffixing Preference". In *Explaining Linguistic Universals*, edited by J. A. Hawkins, 321–349. Oxford: Blackwell.

Halliday, M. A. K. 1961. Categories of the theory of grammar. *Word* 17, pp. 241–292.

Halliday, M. A. K. 1978. *Language as Social Semiotic: The Social Interpretation of Language and Meaning*. London: Edward Arnold.

Halverson, S. L. 2007. A cognitive linguistic approach to translation shifts. *Belgian Journal of Linguistics* 21, pp. 105–121.

Halverson, S. L. 2010. "Towards a Cognitive Theory of Translation". In *Translationswissenschaft– Stand und Perspektiven. Innsbrucker Ringvorlesungen zur Translationswissenschaft VI*, edited by L. Zybatow, 15–33. Frankfurt: Peter Lang.

Halverson, S. L. 2013. "Implications of Cognitive Linguistics for Translation Studies". In *Cognitive Linguistics and Translation: Advances in Some Theoretical Models and Applications*, edited by A. Rojo, 33–73. Berlin: Mouton de Gruyter.

Halverson, S. 2014. "Reorienting Translation Studies: Cognitive Approaches and the Centrality of the Translator". In *Translation: A Multidisciplinary Approach*, edited by J. House, 116–139. Houndsmill: Palgrave Macmillan.

Hawkins, J. A. 1994. *A Performance Theory of Order and Constituency*. Cambridge: Cambridge University Press.

House, J. 1997. *Translation Quality Assessment: A Model Revisited*. Tübingen: Gunter Narr.

House, J. 2013. Towards a new linguistic-cognitive orientation in translation studies. *Target* 25(1), pp. 46–60.

House, J. 2015. *Translation Quality Assessment: Past and Present*. London: Routledge.

Ingarden, R. 1931/1973. *The Literary Work of Art: An Investigation on the Borderlines of Ontology, Logic, and Thepry of Literature. With an Appendix on the Function of Language in the Theatre*. Translated, with an Introduction, by G. G. Grabowicz from the 3rd ed. of *Das literarische Kunstwerk*, copyright 1965 by Max Niemeyer Verlag, Tübingen (1st ed. 1931). Evanston: Northwestern University Press.

Jakobson, R. 1959. "On linguistic aspects of translation". In *On Translation*, edited by R A. Brower, 232–239. Cambridge, MA: Harvard University Press.

Kant, E. 1781. *Kritik der reinen Vernunft*. 2nd ed. 1787 translated by Norman Kemp Smith 1929 as *Critique of Pure Reason*. London: The Macmillan Press.

Kenny, D. 1998. Creatures of habit? What translators usually do with words. *Meta* XLIII(4), pp. 515–523.

Kim, M. and Matthiessen, C. M. I. M. 2015. Ways to move forward in translation studies: a textual perspective. *Target* 27(3), pp. 325–334.

Kruger, A. 2002. Corpus-based translation research: its development and implications for general, literary and Bible translation. *Acta Theologica Supplementum* 2, pp. 70–106.

Langacker, R. W. 1983. *Foundations of Cognitive Grammar.* Bloomington: Indiana University Linguistics Club.

Langacker, R. W. 1987. *Foundations of Cognitive Grammar, Vol. I, Theoretical Prerequisites.* Stanford, CA: Stanford University Press.

Langacker, R. W. 1991a. *Concept, Image, and Symbol: The Cognitive Basis of Grammar.* Berlin: Mouton de Gruyter.

Langacker, R. W. 1991b. *Foundations of Cognitive Grammar, Vol. II, Descriptive Application.* Stanford, CA: Stanford University Press.

Langacker, R. W. 1999. *Grammar and Conceptualization.* Berlin: Mouton de Gruyter.

Langacker, R. W. 2008. *Cognitive Grammar: A Basic Introduction.* New York: Oxford University Press.

Lauridsen, K. 1996. "Text Corpora and Contrastive Linguistics: Which Type of Corpus for Which Type of Analysis?". In *Languages in Contrast: Papers from a Symposium on Text-based Cross-linguistic Studies, Lund 4–5 March 1994*, edited by K. Aijmer and B. Altenberg, 63–71. Lund: Lund University Press.

Laviosa, S. 1998. Core patterns of lexical use in a comparable corpus of English narrative prose. *Meta* 43(4), pp. 557–570.

Laviosa-Braithwaite, S. 1997. "Investigating Simplification in an English Comparable Corpus of Newspaper Articles". In *Transferre Necesse Est*, edited by K. Klaudy and J. Kohn, 530–540. Budapest: Scholastica.

Law, V. 1990. "Language and its Students: The History of Linguistics". In *An Encyclopaedia of Language*, edited by N. E. Collinge, 784–842. London: Routledge.

Leech, G. 1969. *A Linguistic Guide to English Poetry.* London: Longman.

Leech, G. and Short, M. 1981. *Style in Fiction: A Linguistic Introduction to English Fictional Prose.* London: Longman.

Lindquist, H. 1989 *English Adverbials in Translation: A Corpus Study of Swedish Renderings.* Lund: Lund University Press.

Lykke Jakobsen, A. 1986 "Lexical Selection and Creation in Translation". In *Proceedings from the Third Nordic Conference for English Studies, Hesselby, Sept 25–27, 1986*, Vol. I, edited by I. Lindblad and M. Ljung, 101–112. Stockholm, Sweden: Almqvist and Wiksell International.

Malmkjær, K. 2003. What happened to God and the angels: an exercise in translational stylistics. *Target* 15(1), pp. 37–58.

Malmkjær, K. 2004/2007. Norms and nature in translation studies. *SYNAPS* 16, pp. 13–19. Reprinted in Anderman, G. and Rogers, M. (eds). 2007. *Incorporating Corpora: Corpora and the Translator*, Clevedon: Multilingual Matters, pp. 49–59.

Malmkjær, K. 2011. "Translation Universals". In *The Oxford Handbook of Translation Studies*, edited by K. Malmkjær and K. Windle, 83–93. Oxford: Oxford University Press.

Malmkjær, K. forthcoming. "Language Awareness and Translation". In *The Routledge Handbook of Language Awareness*, edited by P. Garrett and J. M. Cots. London: Routledge.

Mauranen, A. and Kujamäki, P., eds. 2004. *Translation Universals: Do they Exist?* Amsterdam: John Benjamins Publishing Company.

Mufwene, S. S. 2013. "The Origins and the Evolution of Language". In *The Oxford Handbook of the History of Linguistics*, edited by K. Allan, 13–52. Oxford: Oxford University Press.

Munday, J. 2015. Engagement and graduation resources as markers of translator/interpreter positioning. *Target* 27(3), pp. 406–421.

Neubert, A. 1973. Theorie und Praxis für die Übersetzungswissenschaft. *Linguistische Arbeitsberichte* 7, pp. 120–144.

Neubert, A. 1985. *Text and Translation.* Leipzig: VEB Verlag Enzyklopädie.

Nida, E. A. 1964. *Toward a Science of Translating: With Special Reference to Principles and Procedures Involved in Bible Translating*. Leiden: E. J. Brill.

Øverås, L. 1998. In search of the third code: an investigation of norms in literary translation. *Meta* XLIII (4), pp. 571–588.

Paradis, M. 2004. *A Neurolinguistic Theory of Bilingualism*. Amsterdam: John Benjamins.

Peng, X. 2015. "Halliday in China: Legacies and Advances from Lou, Wang and Beyond". In *The Bloomsbury Comnpanion to M. A. K. Halliday*, edited by J. Webster. London: Bloomsbury.

Radford, A. 2004. *Minimalist Syntax: Exploring the Structure of English*. Cambridge: Cambridge University Press.

Sapir, E. 1921. *Language: An Introduction to the Study of Speech*. New York: Harcourt, Brace.

Sapir, E. 1929. The status of linguistics as a science. *Language* 5, pp. 207–214. Reprinted in Mandelbaum, D. (ed). 1949. *Selected Writings of Edward Sapir in Language, Culture and Personality*. Berkeley: University of California Press, pp. 45–60.

Saussure, Ferdinand de. 1916. *Cours de linguistique générale*. 1974. *Course in General Linguistics*. London: Fontana/Collins.

Seleskovitch, D. 1975. *Langage, langues et mémoire*, Paris: Minard lettres modernes.

Seleskovitch, D. 1978. *Interpreting for International Conferences: Problems of Language and Communication*. Washington, DC: Pen and Booth, translated by S. Dailey & E. N. Mcmillan. First published in French as *L'interprète dans les conférences internationales –problèmes de langage et de communication*, 1968.

Seleskovitch, D. and Lederer, M. 1984. *Interpréter pour traduire*. Paris: Didier erudition.

Seleskovitch, D. and Lederer, M. 1989. *Pédagogie raisonnée de l'interprétation*, 1989. 2nd augmented ed. 2002. Translation by J. Harmer, 1995. *A Systematic Approach to Teaching Interpretation*. Washington, DC: RID.

Shlesinger, M. 2009. "Towards a Definition of Interpretese: An Intermodal, Corpus-based Study". In *Efforts and Models in Interpreting and Translation Research: A Tribute to Daniel Gile*, edited by G. Hansen, A. Chesterman and H. Gerzymisch-Arbogast, 237–253. Amsterdam/Philadelphia: John Benjamins.

Shlesinger, M. and Ordan, N. 2012. More spoken or more translated? Exploring a known unknown of simultaneous interpreting, *Target* 24(1), pp. 43–60.

Snell-Hornby, M. 1995 [1988]. *Translation Studies: An Integrated Approach*. Amsterdam and Philadelphia: John Benjamins.

Song, J. J. 2001. *Linguistic Typology: Morphology and Syntax*. Harlow: Pearson Educational.

Sperber, D. and Wilson, D. 1986. *Relevance: Communication and Cognition*. Oxford: Basil Blackwell.

Steiner, E. 2015. Contrastive studies of cohesion and their impact on our knowledge of translation (English-German). *Target* 27(3), pp. 351–369.

Stockwell, P. 2002. *Cognitive Poetics: An Introduction*. London: Routledge.

Thompson, J. B. 1984. *Studies in the Theory of Ideology*. Cambridge: Polity Press.

Tirkkonen-Condit, S. 2004. "Unique Items: Over- or Under-Represented in Translated Language?" In *Translation Universals: Do They Exist?* edited by A. Mauranen and P. Kujamäki, Pekka, 177–184. Amsterdam and Philadelphia: John Benjamins.

Toury, G. 1980a. "Translated Literature: System, Norm, Performance: Toward a TT-Oriented Approach to Literary Translation". In *In Search of a Theory of Translation*, Tel Aviv: The Porter Institute for Poetics and Semiotics, Tel Aviv University, pp. 35–50. Reprinted in: *Poetics Today* 1981 2(4), pp. 9–27.

Toury, G. 1977/1980b. The nature and role of norms in literary translation. Reprinted from Toury, G. 1977 *Translational Norms and Literary Translation into Hebrew, 1930–1945*. Tel Aviv: The Porter Institute for Poetics and Semiotics, Tel Aviv University, in G. Toury, *In Search of a Theory of Translation*, Tel Aviv: The Porter Institute for Poetics and Semiotics, Tel Aviv University, pp. 51–62.

Toury, G. 1979/1980c. "Interlanguage and its Manifestations in Translation." Reprinted from *Meta* 1979: 24(2) pp. 223–231, in *In Search of a Theory of Translation*, Tel Aviv: The Porter Institute for Poetics and Semiotics, Tel Aviv University, pp. 71–78.

Toury, G. 1995. *Descriptive Translation Studies and Beyond*. Amsterdam and Philadelphia: John Benjamins.

Trager, G. L. and Smith, H. L. 1951. *Outline of English Structure*. Norman, OK: Battenburg Press.

Vanderauwera, R. 1985. *Dutch Novels Translated into English: The Transformation of a "Minority" Literature*. Amsterdam: Rodopi.

Vinay, J.-P. and Darbelnet, J. 1958. *Stylistique comparée du français et de l'anglais*. Paris: Les éditions Didier. English translation and edition by J. Sager and M.-J. Hamel. 1995. *Comparative Stylistics of French and English: A Methodology for Translation*. Amsterdam: John Benjamins.

Wang, M. 2016. The impact of grammatical differences on simultaneous interpreting: English into Chinese. *International Journal of Social, Behavioural, Educational, Economic, Business and Industrial Engineering* 10(10), pp. 3234–3248.

Whorf, B. L. *circa* 1936. "An American Indian Model of the University". Found among Whorf's papers and published in Carroll, J. B. (ed.) 1956. *Language, Thought and Reality: Selected Writings of Benjamin Lee Whorf*, 57–64. Cambridge, MA: The MIT Press.

Whorf, B. L. 1940. "Science and Linguistics". Reprinted in Carroll, J. B. (ed.), 1956. *Language, Thought and Reality: Selected Writings of Benjamin Lee Whorf*. Cambridge, MA: The MIT Press, pp. 207–219, 1956 from *Technology Review* 42(6), pp. 229–231, 247–248.

Xiao, R. and Dai, G. 2013/2014. Lexical and grammatical properties of translational Chinese: translation universal hypotheses revaluated from the Chinese perspective. *Corpus Linguistics and Linguistic Theory* 10(1), pp. 11–55.

2

Semantics and translation

Kirsten Malmkjær

Introduction and definitions

Semantics is the study of meaning and to the extent that translation concerns the conveyance of a message in one language that "means the same" as a message previously conveyed in another language, meaning is a central concept in translation theory. Furthermore, as we shall see, translation is a central concept in theories of meaning. But meaning is not an easy concept to define or to theorise and at least one philosopher has been driven to wonder "Why is the theory of meaning so *hard*?" (Putnam 1970/1975, 139). Scholars in Translation Studies may feel that this is not their problem: they do not need to explain what meaning is; they only need to be able to discuss the relationships between texts that interest them. But almost any discussion of such relationships takes for granted some sort of *tertium comparationis*, something that the two texts do or do not have in common, and this is often referred to as their meaning (not forgetting that other concepts, such a text function, serve as the *tertium comparationis* in some theories of translation; see Nord 1997).

Much confusion can be engendered by listing scholars' varied ways of categorising kinds of meaning. However, at least one broad distinction must be drawn between what I shall call *basic* meaning and *connotational* meaning. Basic meaning includes Lyons' (1977, 50) descriptive, social and expressive meaning, Halliday's (1970, 143) ideational/experiential, interpersonal and textual meaning, and what is known variously as referential, cognitive, propositional, designative, literal, representational (Bühler 1934), thin (Strawson 1950/1972) and denotative meaning. It is the kind of meaning about which some agreement can be reached through discussion, because it has an air of objectivity about it. Connotational meaning, in contrast, has to do with the associations a person has with parts of their language(s). This is less open to discussion and it is not the topic of this chapter. In order to become clearer about the focus here, let us look at ways in which the terms "mean"", "means", "meant" and "meaning" are used in English. Lyons (1977, 1–2) and Palmer (1981, 3) between them offer the following examples:

1. I did not mean to hurt you.
2. He means well, but he's rather clumsy.

3. Life without love has no meaning.
4. Fame and riches mean nothing to the true scholar.
5. Dark clouds mean rain.
6. A red light means "stop".
7. Calligraphy means "beautiful handwriting".
8. What do you mean by the word "concept".
9. It was John I meant not Harry.
10. He never says what he means.
11. She rarely means what she says.

In (1) and (2), what is at issue is what a person intends as the outcome of their actions. But an intended outcome, or purpose, of an action cannot be identified with its meaning. Many utterances might have similar outcomes; it is possible to hurt someone in several ways, both by saying and doing, and we do not want an account of meaning that makes all hurtful linguistic (and non-linguistic) actions synonymous. In (3), we are dealing with the purpose of life, and in (4) with the importance someone attaches to something. Here, again, we are not dealing with linguistic meaning, but with aspects of the psychology of persons, or with the emotions. It is in (5) that we begin to approximate towards the meaning of meaning we are interested in, because in (5) there is at least a proper relationship of what we might call signification between clouds and rain (see Chapter 3 on semiotics and translation in this volume). To an experienced observer, the presence of dark clouds will signify the likelihood of rain in the near future. But the clouds are natural signs, and the signifying relationship between them and the rain is a relationship of what Grice (1957) has referred to as natural meaning, as opposed to non-natural meaning. It is non-natural meaning which interests us as semanticists.

A major difference between natural and non-natural meaning is that we cannot ascribe to the clouds the intention to warn or tell us that it will rain, whereas we can assume that someone uttering the words "It is going to rain" intends to warn or tell us that it is going to rain. Another way of demonstrating the difference is to point out that it would not make sense to say of the clouds that they mean "rain". In contrast, it makes perfect sense to say of the example in (6) that the red light means "stop". In the case of non-natural meaning, there exists a convention according to which we accept that certain signs have certain meanings which could typically also have been conveyed by means of a linguistic expression. The red light stands in for the word "stop"; the clouds do not stand in for the word "rain".

However, neither example (6) nor example (7) fully covers the phenomenon that interests us as semanticists, as we can see by contemplating the nature and functions of definitions in dictionaries. The definition of "calligraphy" in (7) can only help a person who already knows what "beautiful handwriting" means. If you do not have a point of entry into a dictionary then the dictionary cannot help you. To find the meaning of, say, the German word "gelb", you would, if you did not know enough German to use a monolingual dictionary, go to a dictionary which links German to your mother tongue. If you were English, for example, you would not go to a German/Danish dictionary, because that would just tell you that "gelb" means "gul" which would not help you.

In examples (8) and (9), we begin to get close to the sense of "meaning" that we are interested in. What is at issue here is what entity in the world someone is referring to with a given expression. The concept in (8) and the person in (9) are non-linguistic entities which are *referents* for the expressions; they are what the expressions denote. In addition to the relationships which expressions form with other expressions in a language, expressions also relate to the non-linguistic world, and it is not possible to provide a coherent, non-circular theory of meaning without taking this relationship into account.

In examples (10) and (11) a contrast is set up between what Searle (1979, 93) refers to as "speaker's utterance meaning" and "word or sentence meaning". We shall return to this distinction, but notice that for it to be possible to be aware that someone has said one thing (conveyed by the sentence meaning) and apparently meant another (the speaker's utterance meaning), one must have a reasonable idea about what the sentence meaning was.

An excursion into the history of attempts to define meaning will take us some way towards understanding the difficulties involved in giving an account of meaning. Such an account has to provide answers to two main questions, which Davidson (1973/1984, 125) formulates within the following scenario (my addition of numbers in square brackets):

> Kurt utters the words 'Es regnet' and under the right conditions we know that he has said that it is raining. Having identified his utterance as intentional and linguistic, we are able to go on to interpret his words: we can say what his words, on that occasion, meant. [1] What could we know that would enable us to do this? [2] How could we come to know it? The first of these questions is not the same as the question what we *do* know that enables us to interpret the words of others. For there may easily be something we could know and don't, knowledge of which would suffice for interpretation, while on the other hand it is not altogether obvious that there is anything we actually know which plays an essential role in interpretation. The second question, how we could come to have knowledge that would serve to yield interpretations, does not, of course, concern the actual history of language acquisition. It is thus a doubly hypothetical question: given a theory that would make interpretation possible, what evidence plausibly available to a potential interpreter would support the theory to a reasonable degree?

In the following section, we shall explore some attempts at providing answers to these two questions.

Historical perspectives

First attempt: The ideational theory of meaning

A common-sense view of meaning is that ideas in the mind are the meanings of expressions. Grayling (1982, 186) calls this the ideational theory of meaning. In Britain, Locke is the most famous proponent of this theory in its purest form. Locke (1689/1964, Book Three, Chapter II) writes:

> *Words are sensible signs, necessary for communication.* Man, though he have great variety of thought, and such from which others as well as himself might receive profit and delight; yet they are all within his own breast, invisible and hidden from others, nor can of themselves be made to appear. The comfort and advantage of society not being to be had without communication of thoughts, it was necessary that man should find some external signs, whereof those invisible ideas, which his thoughts are made up of, might be known to others. For this purpose nothing was so fit, either for plenty or quickness, as those articulate sounds, which with so much ease and variety he found himself able to make. Thus we may conceive how *words*, which were by nature so well adapted to that purpose, came to be made use of by men as the signs of their ideas; not by any natural

connexion that there is between particular sounds and certain ideas, for then there would be but one language amongst all men; but by a voluntary imposition, whereby such a word is made arbitrarily the mark of such an idea. The use, then, of words, is to be sensible marks of ideas; and the ideas they stand for are their proper and immediate signification.

As Grayling (1982, 186) points out, there are a number of problems with this theory, among them the assumption that thought precedes speech both logically and historically: our ancestors found themselves enjoying a rich thought-life which they decided that they would share with each other, so they began to experiment with verbal sounds. But this is an unlikely scenario; it is far more likely that the richness of human language grew in tandem with the richness of human thought; indeed, it is hard to see how anything but rudimentary thought could be possible without language.

Another question that faces the ideational theory of meaning concerns how the language would have developed. Imagine that your ancestor wanted to make a link between his or her idea of a cave and the word "cave". How could s/he check, the next time s/he wanted to mention the cave, that s/he had remembered the right word for it? This is the crux of Wittgenstein's (1958) anti-private-language argument. If you were trying to use such a language, then:

> there would be no difference between your being under the correct impression that you were following a rule and your being under the incorrect impression that you were following a rule, or, at least, there would be no detectable difference even for you. So there would be no effective rules in this so-called 'language'. Anything you said would do.
>
> (Pears 1971, 159)

But the severest difficulty is that even if you should happen to get it right for yourself, you could not know whether other language users were using the language in the same way as you. I can refer to my idea with the word "cave", but I cannot know that the word conjures up the same kind of idea in your mind. Nor is it clear how an idea-language could be taught, because ideas, private as they are, cannot serve as teaching links. I cannot present a learner with my idea of a cave and say: "Look, this is what I mean by 'cave'".

So the ideational theory of meaning cannot answer both questions raised by Davidson: ideas are not evidence that could be plausibly available to someone trying to understand what another person means.

Second attempt: Augustine's theory of reference

Augustine writes in *Confessions*, I.8 (between 397 and 400 CE) (see Wittgenstein 1958, paragraph 1, note 1):

> When they (my elders) named some object ... I saw this and I grasped that the thing was called by the sound they uttered ... Thus, as I heard words repeatedly used in their proper place in various sentences, I gradually learned to understand what objects they signified.

This theory considers aspects of the world to provide evidence of meaning. Many of these are, at least, visible; if I say "cave", pointing to my cave, then you might get the idea that I mean by "cave", cave. However, as Wittgenstein (1958, §28 and *passim*) points out, ostension is not that simple: if I point to my cave and say "cave", my interlocutor might take me to mean "cave"; however, they might just as well take me to be referring to the darkenss in the cave, or to its shape, or to the number 1, as there is just one cave, and so on. As Wittgenstein puts it "ostensive definition can be variously interpreted in *every* case". Furthermore, even if I refer with "cave" to my cave, my cave is not the meaning of "cave". As Strawson (1950/1972, 40) has pointed out, this would have the absurd consequence that if I take my pencil out of my pocket I am taking the meaning of the term "pencil" out of my pocket. And even if we were to extend the theory so that "pencil" came to refer to all the pencils there are, have been and will be, this would not help because it would commit us to the absurd idea that every person uttering the term would be referring to this infinite number of pencils, something that is both conceptually and logically impossible.

Furthermore, several words or phrases can refer to the same thing without meaning the same, as in the case of "the morning star" and "the evening star". If the meaning of expressions were just the referent, then these expressions should mean the same; but it is possible for one and the same person to believe at one and the same time "the morning star is in the sky" and "it is not the case that the evening star is in the sky". A closely related mystery for the theory is the possibility that a true identity statement can convey new information. For example, the utterance "The morning star is the evening star" may be news to someone. Clearly, if the planet Venus, the object, were the sole component of the meaning of each expression, then anyone who understood the meaning of them both would already have known that both referred to Venus, and, consequently, that they referred to the same.

Finally, even though some expressions do not refer, we would not want to say that they are meaningless. Consider, "The present king of France is bald". This whole utterance, and even the part of it that does not refer, has meaning, so its meaning obviously cannot be its referent.

These problems were addressed by the German philosopher and logician, Gottlob Frege.

Third attempt: Frege's theory of sense and reference

Frege (1892/1977, 57) suggests that in addition to "that to which the sign refers, which may be called the reference of the sign" there is also "the *sense* of the sign, wherein the mode of presentation is contained". Then "The reference of 'evening star' would be the same as that of 'morning star,' but not the sense".

A name or definite description "*expresses* its sense, *stands for* or *designates* its reference" (1892/1977, 61). The sense, or mode of presentation, is made publicly available by the expression; it is shared by everyone who knows the language and it must not be confused with a subjective idea, or with connotations (1892/1977, 59) or with the specific form of the expression because Frege also believes that different expressions, whether in the same or different languages, can convey the same sense (1892/1977, 58). This is a conundrum for stylistics, where there tends to be an assumption that the way in which something is expressed matters to meaning, but it seems tempting for translation scholars until, that is, they read that Frege (1918–1919) wants to say that, e.g. "steed" has the same sense as "cart horse", at which point the Translation Studies scholar will probably join forces with the stylistician and reject sense as helpful, at least to his or her practical endeavours. It could be maintained, however, in this connection, that translators and, in particular interpreters, for whom thinking on their feet and time constraints loom large, might on occasion find themselves forced, through lack of terminology or mental agility, to forgo precision of differentiation of the type between "steed" and "cart horse" and opt for the neutral term, "horse". Arguably, this is a strategy that succeeds in conveying a sense of the original.

To every expression, according to Frege, there corresponds a sense, whereas there are plenty of expressions which do not refer. So "in grasping a sense, one is not certainly assured of a reference" (1892/1977, 58). In the case of "the present king of France", we grasp its sense even though it has no reference. The meaning, in this case, is exhausted by the sense, and the sense rescues the expression from the meaninglessness to which the primitive reference theory would condemn it. In the case of whole sentences, their sense is the thought they express. But, as Frege (1892/1977, 63) points out, we are often not satisfied simply to know the thought that a sentence or utterance expresses; we generally want to know, also, whether the sentence expresses a truth, and:

> We are therefore driven into accepting the *truth value* of a sentence as constituting its reference. By the truth value of a sentence I understand the circumstance that it is true or false. There are no further truth values. For brevity I call the one the True and the other the False.

The True and the False are objects, just like Venus is an object, and a sentence is a proper name for one of these objects just like "Venus" or "the morning star" are names for the object Venus. Given that the reference of a sentence is its truth value, all true sentences have the same reference and so do all false sentences. This may seem peculiar, but it allows us to understand how sense and reference together contribute to the meaning of a sentence (1892/1977, 65):

> We can never be concerned only with the reference of a sentence; but again the mere thought alone yields no knowledge, but only the thought together with its reference, i.e. its truth value. Judgements can be regarded as advances from a thought to a truth value.

However, the theory allows for some sentences not to have truth values, namely those whose parts fail to refer, and this disturbed logicians like Russell (1905), according to whom any sentence containing a definite description asserts existence. To assert the existence of the non-existent is to say something false; ergo, sentences containing reference-lacking definite descriptions are false.

Faced with these and related difficulties, attempts were made to build on Frege's theory in such a way that its weaknesses would be eradicated and its strengths retained. For example, according to the verification theory of meaning, a consistent and satisfactory theory of meaning can be provided for a set of sentences that are, in Ayer's terms "factually significant" (Ayer 1936/1971, 48):

> a sentence is factually significant to any given person, if, and only if, he knows how to verify the proposition which it purports to express – that is, if he knows what observations would lead him, under certain conditions, to accept the proposition as being true, or reject it as being false.

However, this so-called verification principle proved too restrictive. The general laws of science are not verifiable, because they are universally quantified. The statements of history fare no better, for how can present observation verify statements about the past? Nor is it clear how the verification principle itself should be verified, and if it cannot be verified, then it is not factually significant. For a time, it was thought that the verification principle might be saved by Schlick's verification theory of meaning (1936), according to which the meaning of a proposition is its method of verification:

> Stating the meaning of a sentence amounts to stating the rules according to which the sentence is to be used, and this is the same as stating the way in which it can be verified (or falsified).
>
> (Schlick 1936; see Grayling 1982, 205)

This theory considers meaning to be a method, rather than something that sentences "have" or do not have, which might be an advantage; and if it were true, then so would Ayer's principle be. Schlick believed that there were certain "protocol sentences" which consisted in incorrigible reports of observation and which required no other kind of verification. These constituted "the unshakable points of contact between knowledge and reality", and all other factually significant sentences were derivable from these. Objections to this proposal include Quine's (1960) that it is not possible to verify or falsify individual sentences in isolation, because our theory of nature is holistic, so that all observation is theory laden, a notion that will be discussed below along with "Quine's pessimism" (with thanks to Putnam 1970/1975, 146–149) regarding a theory of translation. But first, let us consider a theory of language which has captured the imagination of at least some Translation Studies scholars, namely that pioneered by J. L. Austin.

Fourth attempt: Speech-act theory (this section draws on Malmkjær 1995/2002/2010/2013)

Speech-act theory was developed by Austin in the 1930s and published in 1962 on the basis of a series of lectures that Austin gave at Harvard University in 1955. The theory arises in reaction to what Austin (1962, 3) calls the descriptive fallacy, the view that a declarative sentence is always used to describe some state of affairs truly or falsely. Austin points out that there are many declarative sentences which do not describe, report or state anything, and of which it makes no sense to ask whether they are true or false. The utterance of such sentences is, or is part of, an action that would not normally be described as simply saying something. Austin (1962, 5) gives a number of examples: "I do", as uttered as part of a marriage ceremony; "I name this ship the Queen Elizabeth", as uttered by the appropriate person while smashing a bottle against the stem of the ship in question; "I give and bequeath my watch to my brother", as written in a will; or "I bet you sixpence it will rain tomorrow". To utter such sentences in the appropriate circumstances is not to describe what you are doing: it *is* doing it, or part of doing it, and Austin calls such utterances performatives or performative utterances, distinguishing them from constatives or constative utterances, which are used to state a fact or describe a state of affairs. Only constatives can be true or false; performatives are happy or unhappy.

The criterion for a happy performative is that the circumstances in which it is uttered should be appropriate: certain felicity conditions must obtain. If a performative is unhappy, or infelicitous, something has gone wrong in the connection between the utterance and the circumstances in which it is uttered.

There are four main types of condition for the happy functioning of a performative (Austin 1962, 14–15):

1. It must be a commonly accepted convention that the uttering of particular words by particular people in particular circumstances will produce a particular effect.
2. All participants in this conventional procedure must carry out the procedure correctly and completely.
3. If the convention is that the participants in the procedure must have certain thoughts, feelings and intentions, then the participants must in fact have those thoughts, feelings and intentions.
4. If the convention is that any participant in the procedure binds her/himself to behave subsequently in a certain way, then s/he must in fact behave subsequently in that way.

If any of these criteria is unfulfilled, the performative will be unhappy in one of two ways. If we sin against either (1) or (2), the conventional act is *not* achieved: a person who is already married may go through another marriage ceremony, but this second marriage will be null and void because its circumstances were faulty (1). Or, a couple may go through all of the marriage ceremony except signing the register; the marriage will then be null and void because the ceremony was not carried out completely (2). Cases in which the act is *not* achieved are called misfires.

If we sin against (3) and (4), the conventional act *is* achieved, but the procedure will have been abused. A person may say "I congratulate you" without having the appropriate feelings of joy for the addressee; or s/he may say "I promise to be there" without having any intention of being there. In such cases, the act will be insincere (3). Or, a person may say "I welcome you" and then proceed to treat the addressee as an unwelcome intruder, in which case s/he will have breached the commitment inherent in the greeting subsequently to behave in a certain manner (4).

So the connection between performatives and constatives is that for a performance to be happy, certain constatives must be true (1962, 45): for "I congratulate you" to be happy, "I feel pleased for you" must be true.

However, Austin points out that the distinction between the truth/falsity dimension and the happiness/unhappiness dimension is not as clear as it first seemed to be. First, it seems that not only performatives can be unhappy: "All John's children are bald" uttered when John has no children is just as unhappy as "I give and bequeath my watch to my brother" written in the will of a person who has no watch. In each case, certain things are presupposed by the utterance: that John has children, and that the will writer owns a watch. These presuppositions fail for lack of reference. Similarly, "The cat is on the mat" uttered by somebody who does not believe that the cat is on the mat is just as much abused as "I promise to be there" uttered by someone who has no intention of being there. Both are unhappy because their implications are unfulfilled: the utterance of "The cat is on the mat" implies that the speaker believes that the cat is on the mat just as "I promise to be there" implies that the speaker intends to be there. So constatives can be as unhappy as performatives, and the unhappinesses arise for the same types of reason in the case of both types of utterance. Furthermore, performatives seem to be able to be untrue just as constatives. "I advise you to do it" could be considered false in the sense of conflicting with the facts if my belief about what is best for you is mistaken. Similarly, "I declare you guilty" conflicts with the facts if you are innocent. So, in general (Austin 1962, 52):

> In order to explain what can go wrong with statements we cannot just concentrate on the proposition involved ... as has been done traditionally. We must consider the total

situation in which the utterance is issued – the total speech-act – if we are to see the parallel between statements and performative utterances, and how each can go wrong. So the total speech-act in the total speech-situation is emerging from logic piecemeal as important in special cases: and thus we are assimilating the supposed constative utterance to the performative.

Furthermore, although some performatives are marked as such by containing a verb that stands for the action being performed, as when in saying "I promise", I am promising, many performatives do not contain these so-called speech-act verbs or performative verbs, and are not even declarative sentences; in many cases, uttering words such as "dog", "bull" or "fire" constitutes an action of warning just as much as uttering "I warn you that there is a dog/bull/ fire", and we would want to say that these utterances, too, are performatives. A distinction is therefore drawn between explicit performatives and implicit or primary performatives. Any primary performative is expandable into a sentence with a verb in the first person singular indicative active or the second or third person indicative passive, which names the action carried out by the performative. Austin calls these verbs performative verbs or speech-act verbs, and since "state" is one of them, any constative is an implicit performative which can be made explicit by being prefaced by "I hereby state that".

So *any* utterance is part of or all of doing of some action, and the only distinction that remains is between performative and non-performative *verbs*. Performative verbs name actions that are performed, wholly or partly, by saying something ("state", "promise"); non-performative verbs name types of action which are independent of speech ("walk", "sleep"). Austin estimates that there are up to 9,999 performative verbs and he tries to place them into a number of broad classes according to their illocutionary forces. The illocutionary force of an utterance is distinguished from its locution and from its perlocutionary effect as follows:

Directing language at an audience involves performing three simultaneous acts: a locutionary act, an illocutionary act and a perlocutionary act. To perform a locutionary act is to say something in what Austin (1962, 94) calls "the full normal sense". It includes:

- The phonic act: uttering noises, phones.
- The phatic act: uttering noises that are part of a certain language, phemes.
- The rhetic act: using these noises with a certain sense and reference, rhemes.

But each locutionary act carries with it an illocutionary act, such as stating, promising, warning, betting, and so on. If a hearer, through her/his knowledge of the conventions of the language, grasps this act, there is uptake on her/his part of the illocutionary force of the utterance. The effect the illocutionary act has on the hearer is called the perlocutionary act, for example persuading, deterring, surprising, misleading or convincing. Perlocutionary acts are performed *by* saying something rather than *in* saying it, and the speaker has less control over them than over the illocutionary act: you cannot be sure that a warning will deter a person or that a plea will persuade them, and so on.

Austin (1962, Lecture 12) suggests that it is possible to distinguish a number of broad classes or families of speech acts, classified according to their illocutionary force:

Verdictives, e.g. giving a verdict, estimate, reckoning, appraisal or finding.
Excersitives, e.g. exercising powers, rights or influence, exemplified by voting, ordering, urging, advising, warning, etc.

Commissives, e.g. typified by promising or otherwise undertaking.

Behabitives, which have to do with social behaviour and attitudes, for example apologizing, congratulating, commending, condoling, cursing and challenging.

Expositives, which show how our utterances fit into the course of an argument or conversation, e.g. "I reply"; "I argue"; "I concede"; "I illustrate"; "I assume"; "I postulate".

In Searle's development of the theory to perform speech acts comes to be seen as engaging in rule-governed behaviour. For example, the rules for the use of any illocutionary force indicator for promising are that (Searle 1969, 63):

1. Any illocutionary force indicating device, P, for promising is to be uttered only in the context of an utterance ... which predicates some future act, A, of the speaker, S.
2. P is to be uttered only if the hearer, H, would prefer S's doing A to her/his not doing A.
3. P is to be uttered only if it is not obvious to both S and H that S will do A in the normal course of events.
4. P is to be uttered only if S intends to do A.
5. The utterance of P counts as an undertaking of an obligation to do A.

According to Searle (1979) knowing the rules for performing speech acts helps interlocutors to determine when an utterance having a particular mood, say interrogative (e.g. "Is that your coat on the floor?"), functions as a question, and when it does not; or when an utterance in the imperative (e.g. "take a chair") functions as an order, and when not; or when an utterance in the declarative (e.g. "it is cold in here") functions as a statement and when it does not. In such cases, Searle suggests, a speaker means what s/he says but means something else as well, so that the utterance meaning includes the sentence meaning but extends beyond it; such speech acts have two illocutionary forces, one direct and one indirect. For a hearer to grasp both these forces at once, s/he must: know the rules for performing speech acts; share some background information with the speaker; exercise her/his powers of rationality and inference; and know certain general principles of cooperative conversation (see Chapter 7 on implicature and presupposition in translation and interpreting in this volume).

Implications for practice of the notion of the speech act

There are two major advantages to be drawn from the notion of the speech act from the point of view of translation theory and practice. First, it can remind translators that it is permissible or even necessary not to render the exact "meaning" of whatever a speaker says in cases where that is not the main or only issue. To give a trite example, when a French host wishes his or her Danish guests "bon appetite", it is not appropriate for their interpreter to render this into Danish as "god appetit", because the equivalent invitation to begin to eat in Danish is "værsgo" (which is a contraction of an expression in the imperative that would translate as "be so good" ("vær så god"), inviting the guests to be so good as to begin to eat). Second, Searle's account suggests that it is possible to draw up guidelines for types of linguistic event for which classes of Austinian speech acts may be appropriate or inappropriate, depending on circumstances. For example, it may be inappropriate in some cultures to employ any exemplar from the verdictive class of speech acts in circumstances where the speaker is considered to be of a lower rank than the person whose possession or action is being referred to.

The notion of the speech act has been used to define a speech (Reisigl 2008, 243; quoted by Vuorikoski 2012, 154) as "a structured verbal chain of coherent speech acts uttered on a special occasion for a specific purpose by a single person and addressed to a more or less specific audience". Vuorikoski (2012, 161) herself focuses on the speech act "request", which accounts for 14% of the 2,070 sentences contained in her corpus of speeches delivered in English and interpreted into Finnish, German and Swedish during plenary sessions of the European Parliament (EP). She suggests "that language philosophy may provide some aid for interpreters for understanding the EP political rhetoric" (2012, 156), although her own research is based on Sadock's (1990) understanding of speech acts.

This kind of potential notwithstanding, speech-act theory fails to find an answer to the questions posed by Davidson (1973/1984, 125) for the theory of meaning. As Austin (1962, 149) puts it (italics in the original):

> We may well suspect that the theory of 'meaning' as equivalent to 'sense and reference' will certainly require some weeding-out and reformulating in terms of the distinction between locutionary and illocutionary acts (*if these notions are sound*: they are only adumbrated here). I admit that not enough has been done here: I have taken the old 'sense and reference' on the strength of current views.

It is worth bearing this insight in mind: pragmatic theories generally take for granted that the semantics is given.

Current debates and their implications

Quine's pessimism regarding a theory of translation is part of his more general pessimism about whether there can be a theory of meaning at all; it is formulated and partly motivated by Quine's (1960, 26) strictly empiricist theory of how we learn:

> Surface irritations generate, through language, one's knowledge of the world. One is taught so to associate words with words and other stimulations that there emerges something recognizable as talk of things, and not to be distinguished from truth about the world.

To illustrate the effect of this, imagine "*radical* translation, i.e. translation of the language of a hitherto untouched people" (Quine 1960, 28, italics in the original). In this scenario (1960, 29), "A rabbit scurries by, the native says 'Gavagai', and the linguist notes down the sentence 'Rabbit' (or 'Lo, a rabbit') as tentative translation, subject to testing in further cases". But, Quine points out (1960, 31 and 51–52):

> It is important to think of what prompts the native's assent to 'Gavagai?' as stimulations and not rabbits ... it is stimulations that must be made to match, not animals. [And] consider 'gavagai'. Who knows but that the objects to which this term applies are not rabbits after all, but mere stages, or brief temporal segments, of rabbits. In either event, the stimulus situations that prompt assent to 'Gavagai' would be the same as for 'Rabbit'. Or perhaps the objects to which 'gavagai' applies are all and sundry undetached parts of rabbits; again the stimulus meaning would register no difference. When from the sameness of stimulus meanings of 'Gavagai' and 'Rabbit' the linguist leaps to the conclusion that a gavagai is a whole enduring rabbit, he is just taking for granted that the native is enough like us to have a brief general term for rabbits and no brief general term for rabbit stages or parts.

As Hookway (1988, 134) points out, returning to the Wittgensteinian point about the inscrutability of ostension, it is not clear whether "Gavagai" means "There's a rabbit" or,

"An undetached part of a rabbit is over there", or "Rabbithood is instantiated over there", or "A stage in the history of a rabbit is over there", or "That spot is one mile to the left of an area of space one mile to the right of a rabbit". Given the presence of the rabbit, each would be a possible meaning, depending on what the speaker's "ontological commitment" was: to middle-sized objects like rabbits, or to rabbit parts, or to stages in the history of rabbits, or to areas of space. The only reliable evidence there is for what someone means are the circumstances attendant on their utterance, but these circumstances are subject to different ways of understanding the world, and we have no access to these different ways of understanding the world except for the speakers' utterances. This conundrum is known as the circle of belief and meaning (see e.g. Lepore and Ludwig 2013), and unless we can break into it, the prospects for a theory of meaning are poor.

The problem, as we have seen, with the theories we have examined lies with the notion of reference or denotation, with the idea that there must be something that words "stand for", in virtue of which (perhaps in conjunction with something like Frege's sense (1892)) they have meaning. This notion, as Davidson (1967, 307) puts it, does not seem to "oil the wheels of a theory of meaning". Given this, he suggests, it might be helpful to place a different predicate between one sentence and another sentence that is supposed to be the meaning of the first. He suggests that the predicate "is true" would be a good candidate, because truth is (1973/1984, 134) "a single property which attaches, or fails to attach, to utterances, while each utterance has its own interpretation" and because holding true is an attitude that it is reasonable to assume that most speakers have to their own utterances most of the time.

According to Tarski (1956), the truth predicate functions in such a way that for any sentence S here is a statement of the form, "S is true iff p", where p is the translation of S into the language of the theory. An example of such a so-called T-sentence would be "'Es regnet' is true-in-German when spoken by x at time t if and only if it is raining near x at t" (Davidson 1973/1984, 135). A theory of truth assumes that speakers are able to agree, for any utterance, U, that "U" is true if and only if C where C is a description of the circumstances in which "U" is held true. And to have language, it is necessary to have a theory of truth: you have to believe that speakers utter what they believe to be true most of the time; if they did not, their language would not work and could not be taught/learnt. Therefore (Davidson 1973/1984, 137):

> The methodological advice to interpret in a way that optimizes agreement should not be conceived as resting on a charitable assumption about human intelligence that might turn out to be false. If we cannot find a way to interpret the utterances and other behaviour of a creature as revealing a set of beliefs largely consistent and true by our own standards, we have no reason to count that creature as rational, as having beliefs or as saying anything.

It has been mooted by e.g. Lakoff and Johnson (1980, 181) that truth may be culture specific and hence variable across cultures:

> People with very different conceptual systems than our own may understand the world in a very different way than we do. Thus they may have a very different body of truths than we have and even different criteria for truth and reality.

But as Davidson (1974/1984, 183–189) points out, this position relies on a separation between the world "out there", and the human conceptual systems that "organize" it:

> Philosophers ... are prone to talk of conceptual schemes ... ways of organizing experience ... points of view from which individuals, cultures ... survey the passing

scene. There may be no translating from one scheme to another, in which case the beliefs, hopes, and bits of knowledge that characterize one person have no true counterparts for the subscriber to another scheme . . . Even those thinkers who are certain there is only one conceptual scheme are in the sway of the scheme concept; even monotheists have religion . . . Conceptual relativism is a heady and exotic doctrine, or would be if we could make good sense of it. The trouble is, as so often in philosophy, it is hard to improve intelligibility while retaining the excitement. . . . The notion of fitting the totality of experience, like the notion of fitting the facts, or of being true to the facts, adds nothing intelligible to the simple concept of being true. Nothing . . . no *thing*, makes sentences and theories true: not experience, not surface irritations, not the world, can make a sentence true. *That* experience takes a certain course . . . [makes] sentences and theories true.

So relativism does not threaten translation/interpreting viciously. The account places translation centrally in any act of communication by language and hence centrally in providing an account of it. Translation clearly merits serious investigation and serious consideration by anyone with an interest in the language sciences.

Further reading

Grayling, A. C. 1982. *An Introduction to Philosophical Logic*. Sussex: The Harvester Press.
An excellent introduction to a number of issues in semantics that are only touched on in this chapter.

Hookway, C. 1988. *Quine: Language, Experience and Reality*. Cambridge: Polity Press and Stanford: Stanford University Press.
Introduces and explains the work of Willard van Orman Quine, one of the most important American philosophers of the 20th century. It focuses particularly on Quine's theory of translational indeterminacy and compares it with Davidson's counterargument.

Searle, J. R., ed. 1971. *The Philosophy of Language*. Oxford: Oxford University Press.
The first three contributions to this volume, by Austin, Strawson and Searle, provide a comprehensive introduction to the theory of speech as action, which was fundamental in the development of pragmatics.

Related topics

Semiotics and translation. Implicature and presupposition in translation and interpreting.

References

Austin, J. L. 1962. *How to Do Things with Words*. Oxford: Oxford University Press.
Ayer, A. J. 1936/1971. *Language, Truth and Logic*. Harmondsworth: Pelican Books. First published by Victor Gollancz in 1936.
Bühler, K. 1934. *Sprachtheorie*. Jena: Fischer.
Davidson, D. 1967. Truth and meaning. *Synthese* 17(3), pp. 304–323.
Davidson, D. 1973/1984. "Radical Interpretation". Reprinted from *Dialectica* 27, pp. 313–328, in *Inquiries into Truth and Interpretation*, 125–139. Oxford: Clarendon Press.
Davidson, D. 1974/1984. "On the Very Idea of a Conceptual Scheme". Reprinted from *Proceedings and Addresses of the American Philosophical Association*. Vol. 47, in *Inquiries into Truth and Interpretation*, 183–189. Oxford: Clarendon Press.
Frege, G. 1892/1977. "On Sense and Reference". Reprinted from *Zeitschrift für Philosophie und philosophische Kritik*. Vol. 100, 25–50, in 1977 *Translations from the Philosophical Writings of Gottlob Frege*, edited by P. Geach and M. Black, 56–78. Oxford: Basil Blackwell.

Frege, G. 1918–19. "Der Gedanke: Eine logische Untersuchung" ("The Thought: A Logical Inquiry"). In *Beiträge zur Philosophie des Deutschen Idealismus* pp. 58–77. Reprinted 1956 in *Mind*, New Series, 65(259), pp. 289–311.

Grayling, A. C. 1982. *An Introduction to Philosophical Logic*. Sussex: The Harvester Press.

Grice, H. P. 1957. "Meaning". *Philosophical Review* 66, pp. 377–388. Reprinted in *Philosophical Logic*, 1967, edited by P. F. Strawson, 39–48. Oxford: Oxford University Press.

Halliday, M. A. K. 1970. Functional diversity in language. *Foundations of Language* 6, pp. 322–361.

Lakoff, G. and Johnson, M. 1980. *Metaphors We Live By*. Chicago: University of Chicago Press.

Lepore, E. and Ludwig, K. 2013. "Introduction". In *A Companion to Donald Davidson*, edited by E. Lepore and K. Ludwig, 1–13. Oxford: Blackwell.

Locke, J. 1689/1964. *An Essay Concerning Human Understanding*. Glasgow: William Collins Sons & Co Ltd.

Lyons, J. 1977. *Semantics*, Vol. 1. Cambridge: Cambridge University Press.

Malmkjær, K. 1995/2002/2010/2013. "Speech Act Theory". In *The Linguistics Encyclopedia*, 3rd ed., edited by K. Malmkjær, 497–505. 1st ed. 1995.

Nord, C. 1997. *Translating as a Purposeful Activity: Functionalist Approaches Explained*. Manchester: St Jerome.

Palmer, F. R. 1981. *Semantics*, 2nd ed. Cambridge: Cambridge University Press.

Pears, D. 1971. *Wittgenstein*. London: Fontana/Collins.

Putnam, H. 1970/1975. "Is Semantics Possible?" Reprinted from *Languages, Belief and Metaphysics*, edited by H. Kiefer and M. Munitz, New York: State University of New York Press in Putnam, H. 1975. *Mind, Language and Reality: Philosophical Papers*, Vol. 2: 139–152. Cambridge: Cambridge University Press.

Quine, W. V. O. 1960. *Word and Object*. Cambridge, MA: The MIT Press.

Reisigl, M. 2008. "Rhetoric of Political Speeches". In *Handbook of Communication in the Public Sphere*, edited by R. Wodak and V. Koller, 243–270. Berlin: Mouton de Gruyter.

Russell, B. 1905. On denoting. *Mind* 14(56), pp. 479–493.

Sadock, J. M. 1990. "Comments on Vanderveken and on Cohen and Levesque". In *Intentions in Communication*, edited by P. R. Cohen, J. Morgan and M. E. Pollack, 257–270. Cambridge, MA: The MIT Press.

Schlick, M. 1936. Meaning and verification. *Philosophical Review* 45(4), pp. 339–369.

Searle, J. R. 1969. *Speech Acts: An Essay in the Philosophy of Language*. Cambridge: Cambridge University Press.

Searle, J. R. 1979. "Metaphor". In *Metaphor and Thought*, edited by A. Ortony, 92–123. Cambridge: Cambridge University Press.

Strawson, P. F. 1950/1972. "On referring". *Mind* 1950, pp. 320–344. Reprinted in *New Readings in Philosophical Analysis*, edited by H. Feigl, W. Sellars, and K. Lehrer. 1972, 35–50. New York: Appleton-Century-Crofts.

Tarski, A. 1956. "The Concept of Truth in Formalized Languages". In *Logic, Semantics, Metamathematics* edited by A. Tarski. Oxford: Oxford University Press.

Vuorikoski, A.-R. 2012. "Fine-tuning SI Quality Criteria: Could Speech Act Theory be of any Use?" Available from: https://www.academia.edu/3352593/Fine-tuning_SI_Quality_Criteria_Could_Speech_Act_Theory_be_of_any_Use.

Wittgenstein, L. 1958. *Philosophical Investigations*, 2nd ed. Translated by G. E. M. Anscombe. Oxford: Basil Blackwell.

3

Semiotics and translation

Henrik Gottlieb

Translation: More than just words

In the novel *Il nome della rosa*, written by the semiotician Umberto Eco in 1980 (English translation by William Weaver, *The Name of the Rose* published in 1983), the protagonist, Brother William of Baskerville, tells his young novice: "I have never doubted the truth of signs, Adso; they are the only things man has with which to orient himself in the world. What I did not understand was the relation among signs" (Eco 1983, 527). ["*Non ho mai dubitato della verità dei segni, Adso, sono la sola cosa di cui l'uomo dispone per orientarsi nel mondo. Ciò che io non ho capito è stata la relazione tra i segni*" (Eco 1980, 321).]

In this chapter (based on Gottlieb 2003, 2005, 2008) I will focus on one key aspect of that "relation among signs" – namely the semiotic nature of translation. Traditional conceptions of translation have only included *intrasemiotic* translation (translation within a given sign system), and almost exclusively its subcategory *interlingual* translation, i.e. the transfer of verbal messages from one speech community to another. However, any kind of translation – even interlingual types – is a multi-faceted phenomenon, and the word "translation" covers at least two dimensions in which the given message is expressed: (1) time, i.e. the temporal progression of the translational *process*; and (2) space, including the semiotic composition of the translational *product*.

The central role of interlingual translation, the phenomenon that most people will associate with the term *translation*, has been succinctly described by Vassallo (2015, 171): "This post-Babelian phenomenon is a constant and inevitable aspect of our lives, anchored as they are in the interpretation and communication of linguistic and non-linguistic signs which surround us".

Indeed, surrounded by an ever-increasing communicational output – from written online information to live multi-media presentations – we experience a growing need for translation. Mass-media products as well as acts of communication with more limited audiences are being translated – by professionals, by fan communities, by machines and by ourselves – in unprecedented numbers. Little wonder that recent decades have witnessed a growing scholarly interest in all the ramifications of translation.

New media require new methods of translation, and audiovisual media, in particular, represent challenges to the translator not known before the invention of sound film in 1927. Nevertheless, whether we work as literary or drama translators, interpret at conferences, localise computer software or subtitle TV series, what we translate is words – speech acts, to be exact (see Chapter 2, in this volume).

As stated above, a primary aim of this chapter is to expand the notion of translation in order to accommodate not only the nonverbal channels present in much modern communication, but also the types of communication not involving language in a traditional sense. Getting to grips with the nature of translation and the multitude of new texts representing – or *re-presenting* – existing texts also implies dealing with the myriad types of "multi-channel" texts so typical of contemporary society. While most of what was written on translation in the first decades after the breakthrough of Translation Studies in the 1970s dealt with written (interlingual) translation, since around 2000, audiovisual and nonverbal aspects of translation have enjoyed growing scholarly attention. Among the first titles dealing with "paraverbal" translation are Poyatos (1997) and Gambier and Gottlieb (2001). More recent titles on semiotic aspects of translation include Kourdis and Kukkonen (2015), and others that are listed in Gottlieb (2013). Finally, the issue of multimodality has been dealt with in Baldry and Thibault (2006) and in Kress (2010).

Taking as my point of departure the complex (*polysemiotic*) textual nature of communication, in which several semiotic channels are used simultaneously, in this chapter I intend to provide conceptual tools for dealing systematically with any type of translation encountered in today's communicative landscape, by establishing a semiotically based taxonomy of translation. This semiotic mapping of the landscape of translation is based on an analysis of which channels constitute originals and translations, and – as we will see – not all translated texts use the same communicative channels as their originals.

The semantics of semiotics

The link between translation and semiotics has been forcefully expressed by Bassnett: "The first step towards an examination of the processes of translation must be to accept that although translation has a central core of linguistic activity, it belongs most properly to semiotics" (Bassnett 2014, 24).

The word "semiotics" shares the root "*sema*" (Greek for "sign") with the term "semantics", which is the scholarly discipline concerned with meaning, and semiotics can be defined as the discipline that deals with the communication of meaning through systems of signs. One such sign system is vocal language (e.g. Afrikaans) based on speech, another is signing (or sign language, e.g. British Sign Language) based on gestures – the type of non-vocal language used by the Deaf. As stated above, translation within one sign system is intrasemiotic, while translation between sign systems is intersemiotic. By "sign system", I mean a disparate rule-based organisation of meaningful signs unlike any other such entity. This implies that I consider all so-called natural languages, e.g. Finnish, Xhosa and Japanese, representatives of one common system: that of vocal languages.

However, some semioticians consider individual languages disparate semiotic systems: "From the perspective of semiotics, translation is studied as a purely semiotic act that involves the transition from one semiotic system (source language) to another (target language)" (Kourdis 2015, 303). Even translation scholars like Gideon Toury tend to see languages as different systems (Toury 1986). I believe this is an unfortunate view, as all vocal languages use the same oral (and often written) semiotic channels. Only communication between a (deaf) sign language user and a (hearing) user of a vocal language – no matter which – represents two semiotic systems, and for that reason deserves to be labelled "intersemiotic translation".

The terms "semiotics" and "semiotic" have been used widely, and in widely different ways and contexts, even within Translation Studies.

Some scholars maintain that of the two traditional approaches within semiotics, the "structural" school initiated by Ferdinand de Saussure and the "interpretive" school based on Charles Peirce's work, the latter is better suited to describing translational phenomena (Stecconi 2010, 314). The reason for this is that while the structuralists operate with a simple signifier–signified match, interpretive semiotics enters a human agent in this equation, thus yielding a triangular relationship between sign, object and interpretant – the latter concept referring to the effect on the interpreter (ibid.).

The process of translation involves a chain of disparate and consecutive acts, ranging from the conceiver(s) of the original text, via the text itself to the receiver(s) of the translated version. Even the translational product is a complex notion. As a synthesis of signs, the translated text encompasses much more than the rephrasing of the original message – a multifarious entity in its own right. Interpretation is key, and as phrased by Torop, "no translation is fundamentally a unique text but one of many possibilities to render the original text" (Torop 2008, 255).

As mentioned above, the starting point of 20th-century Translation Studies was to deal with texts that were seen as verbal only, whether written or spoken. Although all human experience is polysensorial, i.e. based on the combined input from all our five senses, for centuries we have communicated through, and translated, monosemiotic texts. These texts operate through one semiotic channel only, typically the written word, but they are not merely abstract verbalisations of a message just waiting for someone to read them, hear them or translate them.

As Zabalbeascoa, having studied film translation, aptly puts it, "no text can be made entirely of verbal signs because such signs always need some sort of physical support" (Zabalbeascoa 1997, 338). This physical support – represented by typographical conventions regarding layout and typefaces, etc. – gains semantic momentum in genuinely polysemiotic texts. The most prominent polysemiotic text type is the audiovisual text, defined by Chaume as "a semiotic construct comprising several signifying codes that operate simultaneously in the production of meaning" (Chaume 2004, 16). Polysemiotic texts are not always found in the media; a classical example of a polysemiotic text is the "artefact plus wall-panel explanation" text found in museums (Neather 2012), often expanded by means of a leaflet or audio description.

Stecconi states that "semiotics can be described as the discipline that studies how people make sense of their experience of the world and how cultures develop and give currency to this understanding" and that "semiotics is ultimately a theory of how we produce, interpret and negotiate meaning through signs" (Stecconi 2010, 314). As especially the former aspect, that of the production of signs, needs to be developed in order to understand the scope and impact of translation(s), this aspect will be the focus of this chapter.

In the following section we will look at the parameters that constitute texts (in a wide sense of that word) as well as those that shape the profile of the products of translations. Of special interest here are the possible differences in semiotic composition between source and target texts, and the effect of nonverbal factors on the verbal rephrasing of polysemiotic texts, e.g. films and TV productions.

Translation in the web of semiotics: Distinctions and definitions

As semiotics is intertwined with semantics – signs, by definition, make sense – any channel of expression in any act of communication carries meaning. For this reason, even exclusively nonverbal communication deserves the label "text", thus accommodating phenomena such as music and graphics, as well as sign language (for the Deaf) and tactile messages in Braille (for the blind). In a Translation Studies context, the two latter categories represent strictly convention-based communication. This means that there is a (more or less) fixed relationship between the way a message is expressed in the two types of texts, ranging from an absolute 1:1 relationship – as found between Morse code and the Latin alphabet – to the degrees of freedom open to the translator of an advertising slogan from English into Spanish, for instance. Returning to sign language and Braille, these types of communication may very well be considered along with verbal-only (monosemiotic) and multi-channel (polysemiotic) texts. As opposed to what is true of music and graphics, relatively simple algorithms exist that would transform messages in Braille or in one of the world's many sign languages into a vocal language – either written or spoken. As a case in point, the intersemiotic process of translating from the tactile to the visual mode – e.g. when a text in Braille is translated into "the same" text using alphanumeric characters – is certainly simpler and more rule-governed than the process of translating a printed text from one verbal language into another. Both communicative acts, however, deserve the label "conventional translation", as opposed to, say, the less constrained communicative act performed by a radio reporter commentating on a baseball match for his listeners, i.e. the act of describing physical action through words (in any language). Such an act will be labelled "adaptational translation".

Table 3.1 Intersemiotic types of translation

Target text compared with original		Target text semiotics		
		Diasemiotic (different channel(s) than in the original)	*Ultrasemiotic (more channels than in the original)*	*Infrasemiotic (fewer channels than in the original)*
Adaptational translation	**Nonverbal**	1. Music based on photo	2. Animation film based on music	3. Sketch of bee dance in encyclopedia
	Deverbalised	4. Manual illustrated for illiterates	5. Screen adaptation of novel	6. Painting based on drama
	Verbalised	7. Ball game on radio	8. Ball game on TV	9. Audio-described film on DVD
Conventional translation	**Nonverbal**	10. Written music	11. Statistical pie charts	12. Notation of ballet
	Deverbalised	13. Pictograms	14. Acted stage directions	15. International traffic sign
	Verbalised	16. Morse code decryption	17. Interpreted sign language user	18. Charts mediated to the blind

Table 3.2 Intrasemiotic types of translation

Target text compared with original		Target text semiotics — Isosemiotic (same channel(s) as original)					
		Synchronic translation	**Diachronic translation**	**Dialectal translation**	**Diaphasic translation**	**Transliteration**	**Diamesic**
Adaptational translation	**Nonverbal**	19. New musical arrangement of standard tune					
	Verbal Interlingual	20. Remake of foreign film					
	Verbal Intralingual	21. Contemporary adaptation of "classic" film					
Conventional translation	**Nonverbal**	22. Transposition of music; interpreting between two sign languages					
	Verbal — Interlingual	27. Chinese poem into English		23. Manually translated for foreign customers	24. Hamlet into modern Danish	25. US hip-hop lyrics into standard Dutch	26. Novel translated for children
		28. Subtitled foreign film					
Intralingual		29. Abridged version of manual	30. Dante into modern Italian	31. Verlan into standard French	32. Legal text made popular	33. Arabic text rendered in Latin letters	34. Subtitles for the Deaf

Since not all languages are verbal, we may define language as *any communicative system working through the combination of sensory signs.* This implies that, in turn, text may be defined as *any combination of sensory signs carrying communicative intention.*

Based on this communicative definition of text, an equally broad definition of translation may be ventured, namely: *any process, or product hereof, in which a text is replaced by another text reflecting, or inspired by, the original entity.* As pointed out by Stecconi (2009, 263), "it is logically impossible to label as translation a text that is not perceived as speaking on behalf of another – i.e. that does not mediate between source and target environments".

Tables 3.1 and 3.2 illustrate the colossal range of translational phenomena encompassed by this multidimensional definition. Below, the various dimensions and the resulting semiotic categorisation of translational phenomena will be discussed in detail.

Types of translation

All translations – and, indeed, all texts – have an intended audience, whether well defined or not. For this reason, the typological classification presented in Tables 3.1 and 3.2 is functional by nature, based on audience perception, i.e. on how each type of translation is cognitively processed by the intended audience.

The taxonomy represented in Tables 3.1 and 3.2 is based on four translational dimensions:

I   semiotic identity or non-identity between source and target texts, distinguishing intra-semiotic types of translation from intersemiotic types
II   possible changes in semiotic composition of the translation, which may be (a) isosemiotic (using the same channel(s) of expression as the source text), (b) diasemiotic (using different channels), (c) ultrasemiotic (using more channels) or (d) infrasemiotic (using fewer channels than the original text)
III   varying degrees of freedom for the translator, distinguishing adaptational (free) from conventional (bound) types of translation
IV   the presence or absence of verbal material in source and/or target texts, creating a distinction between translations that (a) remain verbal, (b) introduce nonverbal elements, (c) introduce verbal elements or (d) remain nonverbal.

In Tables 3.1 and 3.2, an example is given for each translation type of the taxonomy. Each of the 34 types will be discussed, and the examples will be explained.

Before discussing the vast array of translational types, the four central distinctions listed above will have to be defined:

I   Intersemiotic vs. intrasemiotic translation

(a)   In intersemiotic translation, the channel(s) of communication used in the translated text will differ from the channel(s) used in the original text. In other words, the source and target texts are semiotically non-equivalent, yet – as phrased by Dusi (2015, 184) – the target text is "intersubjectively recognized as being linked" to a given source text. This link between source and target text embodies similarity rather than sameness or equivalence – the latter concept not even universally acknowledged by scholars studying monosemiotic translation.

(b) In intrasemiotic translation, the sign systems used in source and target texts are identical; a case of semiotic equivalence. Whereas intersemiotic translation is a notion directly borrowed from Jakobson (1959), the term "intrasemiotic translation" – also used by Toury (1986) – encompasses Jakobson's interlingual and intralingual types of translation. Within intrasemiotic translation, I distinguish between six different sub-categories of verbal conventional translation, whether interlingual (involving two languages) or intralingual (involving only one):

(i) synchronic translation (with original and translation as contemporaries),
(ii) diachronic translation (between texts belonging to different ages),
(iii) dialectal translation (between different geographical, social or generational language variants),
(iv) diaphasic translation (making expert texts accessible to the public, adult fiction suited for children, etc.),
(v) transliteration (which involves a change in alphabet), and
(vi) diamesic translation (involving a change in language mode; i.e. from speech to writing or vice versa).

II Isosemiotic vs. diasemiotic, ultrasemiotic and infrasemiotic translation

(a) The prototypical translation, sometimes termed "translation proper", is isosemiotic: it uses the same communicative channel(s) as the original. In addition, it is also isomesic, i.e. it retains the language mode (oral or written) of the original. All sorts of printed translations are isomesic. Isomesic translation encompasses both monosemiotic texts (e.g. oral discourse being interpreted for foreign-language speakers) and polysemiotic texts (e.g. film dubbing, in which spoken source-language lines are replaced by lines spoken in the target language).

(b) Diasemiotic translation uses different channels than the original text, while the number of channels (one or more) is the same. While the transfer from written into played music is an example of diasemiotic translation of a monosemiotic text, turning a silent movie into a radio play would constitute a polysemiotic example of diasemiotic translation: from verbal and nonverbal images to verbal and nonverbal sounds.

(c) In ultrasemiotic translation, the translated texts display more semiotic channels than the original – as when a novel is semiotically unfolded into a film.

(d) Lastly, the term infrasemiotic translation implies that the semiotic "bandwidth" (range of activated semiotic channels) of the translation is narrower than that of the original. We see this when, for instance, a mime artist performs a piece of drama originally including spoken lines; audio-described stage plays for the blind, for instance, fall into this category as well.

III Conventional vs. adaptational translation

As opposed to *en bloc* labelling of intersemiotic translation as adaptation – as does Eco (2004, 158–159) – I believe it necessary to distinguish between adaptational and conventional intersemiotic translation. The defining feature here is the degrees of freedom available to the translator. In other words, processes that follow conventional procedures, e.g. for transforming written music (i.e. notes) into performed music, are termed "conventional translations", while processes in which the translator is not bound by existing "conversion tables" are named "adaptational translations". An oft-mentioned example of the latter type is screen adaptation (type 5 in Table 3.1).

(a) Conventional translation – with both intrasemiotic and intersemiotic types represented – uses some degree of formulaic conversion of the source text *en route* to the target text. With target texts created through anything from strict conversion algorithms (as in Morse encryption, for instance) to methods relying on norms and conventions (as when dictionaries and other sources of reference are used as tools in interlingual, written translation), the direct link between source and target texts is obvious, and criteria for evaluation are easily established – although not always totally agreed upon.

(b) Adaptational translation, on the other hand, is found whenever the existence and reception of one text triggers the production of another based on the first. The resulting text will relate to the original in a way which is more detached and less predictable than in conventional translation. Following from this is the inability to reconstruct the original from the translated version, something which – to a certain extent – is possible with conventional translation.

The terms "conventional" and "adaptational" have been employed partly in order to pinpoint the difference between the two conceptual counterparts, partly to make room for a wider interpretation of the notion of translation than seen whenever "translation proper" and "adaptation" are juxtaposed. However, these two counterparts are not poles at each end of a line; rather, they constitute two halves of a cline ranging from zero degrees of freedom (as in intralingual transliteration – type 33 in Table 3.2) to almost total freedom, as when music is translated into moving pictures (type 2 in Table 3.1).

IV Verbal vs. nonverbal translation

(a) Verbal translations are translations that retain their verbal channel. These include all inter- and intralingual translations, ranging from an American remake of a Japanese movie to the transliteration of Arabic words into Latin lettering, as found in written Maltese. Verbal translations are by definition intrasemiotic.

(b) Translations that introduce nonverbal elements include genres as disparate as poetry turned into songs and non-smoking pictograms in bars and restaurants. These are examples of deverbalised translation.

(c) Some translations introduce verbal elements, as when a sign language user is interpreted into a vocal language, or a text in Morse code is decrypted. These types are examples of verbalised translation.

(d) Finally, translations that remain nonverbal include linguistic entities (such as interpreting between two sign languages) as well as non-linguistic ones, e.g. a two-dimensional drawing of a sculpture. Here we talk about nonverbal translation. As is true of deverbalising and verbalising translation, nonverbal translation is by definition intersemiotic.

Different roles of translation: Substitutes vs. supplements

The taxonomy represented by Tables 3.1 and 3.2 is based on the four main distinctions listed as points I–IV above. Through this systematic categorisation, all existing and potential types of translation should be represented – categorised according to their semiotic qualities.

Based on the broad definition of "text" provided earlier in this chapter, the taxonomy categorises the various types of translation from the end user's perspective, and in doing so, encompasses three kinds of cognitive decoding activity:

1. Translations acting as text substitutes for audiences who, due to (a) sensory, or (b) linguistic impairment are expected to be unable to decode the original, as well as (c) people who for practical reasons cannot make use of it. An example of the first case is signed news on television, which – to a deaf audience – replaces radio news for hearing audiences. In the second case, when DVD audiences lack the command of the foreign language heard on screen and select a domestic-language soundtrack, the resulting viewing experience emulates that of watching a domestic production. The third type of audience is made up of people who, for example, want to enjoy a book while driving a car or doing household chores, by listening to an audiobook.
2. Translations as text enhancers, e.g. when a PowerPoint presentation shows numerical relations turned into graphics, thus boosting the impact of the original figures, which on their own terms may not be cognitively fully comprehensible to the audience.
3. Translations that are cognitively supplementary, as when audiences have simultaneous access to, and (partly) understand, the original text. This phenomenon is mainly found in the audiovisual media, as multilingual audiences read subtitles while listening to the original dialogue. In this mode of reception, widespread in subtitling countries, the polyglot viewer processes dialogue and subtitles as "diamesic twins", while oscillating between using subtitles as an aid to understanding the original dialogue, and using the original dialogue to evaluate, and often criticise, the subtitles. This doubling of verbal channels is also found when a DVD is played with both subtitles and soundtrack in the target language.

Whereas reception modes 1 and 2 are intended by the translational agents (the translator, the publisher/broadcaster, etc.), mode 3 is an unintended spin-off from mode 1b, disturbing traditional views of translation as text substitutes, or at least (intersemiotic) text enhancers. The game of "spot-the-error" enabled by reception mode 3 has long been a national pastime in Scandinavia, the result being that in working from English, subtitlers – in constant fear of being accused of not giving the "precise" translation of what is said – sometimes prefer unnatural-sounding constructions (Gottlieb 2014). Hopefully, when optional subtitles find their way from DVD to digital TV reception mode 3 in viewers watching foreign productions will vanish, leaving subtitlers with the degrees of freedom enjoyed by translators producing substitutional translations (Gottlieb 2015, 40–41).

The translational range explained through examples

In the following sections, each type of translation found in the comprehensive taxonomy presented in Tables 3.1 and 3.2 will be treated successively.

Intersemiotic translation

Intersemiotic translation, in which the semiotic channels used in the translated product differ from those of the original, encompasses the following types:

Adaptational types

Nonverbal translation: Nonverbal → nonverbal text

1. In this diasemiotic type, the human agent operates between two different, monosemiotic types of expression (= texts), e.g. when converting a visual expression to a musical one.
2. A striking example of this ultrasemiotic type, in which the semantic texture becomes more complex in translation, is the animated Disney cartoon *Fantasia* (1940), which presents the musical works of Bach, Tchaikovsky, Stravinsky and others while at the same time reflecting the musical score in moving images.
3. A case of the opposite movement, that of semiotic simplification, is found when, for instance, a person draws a sketch of the way bees communicate to give directions to an attractive flowerbed. While the original text produced by the bee is spatial and includes sound signals, the drawing – meant for an encyclopedia, for example – is two-dimensional and mute.

Deverbalised translation: Verbal → not (only) verbal text

4. When making a written manual useful to illiterates by replacing the written signs with nonverbal illustrations, the translator will produce a text of similar semiotic complexity as that of the original, i.e. a monosemiotic text.
5. One of the few non-interlingual examples often discussed in Translation Studies belongs in this ultrasemiotic category: screen adaptation – in which a monosemiotic work (typically, a novel) is semiotically "dissected" and recreated using the underlying (poly)semiotic structure of the dramatic work.
6. When, for instance, a play is turned into mime, vocal language is lost, and movements matter more than when they are counterbalanced by words. With this type of translation, there are fewer channels to carry the semantic load that was shared by a larger number of channels in the original. A documented example of this infrasemiotic type is Max Ernst's painting *Oedipus Rex*, a conversion of the Greek drama by the same name (Stathi 2015, 324).

Verbalised translation: Nonverbal → verbal text

7. Verbalised texts in this diasemiotic category include phenomena that are relayed to an audience bereft of the ability to comprehend the original text, i.e. a radio-transmitted baseball match, in which the natural sound effects are kept in the background, while the visual action on the field is substituted by verbal narration.
8. Representing the same ballgame on TV constitutes a different type of translation. Here, the verbal layer added by the commentator supplements what the viewer already sees on the TV screen. In this way, apart from the missing ambience of the stadium, TV viewers get "more" information than the spectators at the stadium.
9. Perhaps the best-known example of infrasemiotic translation is novelisation – screen adaptation reversed, so to speak, as relevant nonverbal filmic elements are verbalised and – together with the spoken lines – published in book format. A further example of the complexities of polysemiotic translation is audio description on TV. In this procedure, the translator transfers the content of two channels – nonverbal image (pictorial content) and verbal image (existing captions and displays; sometimes even interlingual subtitles) – into one: a verbal depiction, presented (optionally) as an integral part of the film soundtrack, whether original or dubbed. Audio description is thus a modern-day

version of the classic tradition of *ekphrasis*, in which "a verbal text describes a work of visual art" (Eco 2004, 110). The reason for considering this type (which might be considered additive) infrasemiotic is that although some of the visual information of a film is represented through audio description, the fact remains that the entire film is now communicated to the intended audience through two channels only: the verbal oral and the nonverbal oral channels. The verbal visual and nonverbal visual channels remain inaccessible to the Blind, who are the very *raison d'être* of audio description – a type of translation that has gained much scholarly attention (see, for instance, Benecke 2004; Kruger and Orero 2010; and Szarkowska 2011).

Conventional types

Nonverbal translation: Nonverbal → nonverbal text

10. A classic example of this diasemiotic type is written music, in which each note in a sequence denotes pitch as well as duration. As with other types of conventional translation, there is some leeway of interpretation – not only when working from written to performed music, but also when trying to translate (notate) live music to paper.

11. Instead of merely switching between channels of representation – as in the previous example – we are concerned here with adding new semiotic layers to the original text, *in casu* statistical information. Dealing with numbers, which – although part of the alphanumerical reality of written communication – can hardly be termed verbal, illustrating numerical relations by means of bar or pie charts while keeping the actual figures as part of the graphic whole is an example of this ultrasemiotic type of translation.

12. In contrast to the previous two types, we are talking here about translations that use fewer semiotic channels than those present in the original – a case in point being ballet notation, in which choreography, i.e. complex three-dimensional movements in real time, is represented on paper.

Deverbalised translation: Verbal → not (only) verbal text

13. Pictograms, road signs and nonverbal logos are examples of conventional translation of verbal messages. Interestingly, certain speech communities use these nonverbal messages much more than others. As regards traffic signs, for instance, the Anglo-American tradition is heavily verbal, with messages like "No entry" (Figure 3.1) commonly seen on roads, while elsewhere, the international nonverbal sign (Figure 3.3) is favoured.

14. Translating stage directions into theatrical performance is a key example of ultrasemiotic translation, in which an all-verbal message is "fleshed out" into spoken lines plus body language and movements on stage.

15. An example of infrasemiotic deverbalisation is found when the Anglophone "combined" no entry sign (Figure 3.2) is replaced by the international (nonverbal) traffic sign with the same message (Figure 3.3) – a reversal of the process exemplified in type 13.

Verbalised translation: Nonverbal → verbal text

16. The encryption and decryption of Morse code is a perfect example of diasemiotic translation, with the unique feature that a 1:1 relationship is found between original and translation, meaning that translating the same message back and forth will not in any way alter the semantic content. Morse code is an extreme exponent of conventional translation, with no "artistic license" granted to the translator.

Figure 3.1   Monosemiotic verbal visual text

Figure 3.2   Polysemiotic verbal and nonverbal visual text

Figure 3.3   Monosemiotic nonverbal visual text

17. When perceived by target-language audiences other than those intended, certain semiotic channels may yield little or no information. As a case in point, hearing conference participants (who do not understand sign language) for whom a sign language user is being interpreted into a vocal language will experience two semiotic layers in the message addressed to them: the almost entirely incomprehensible (soundless) sign language and the spoken language. So although this is a case of "more channels" perceived by the user – providing that s/he is not blind or visually impaired – the original text (signing) remains almost void of information. Here, the hearing target user possesses the sensory capabilities for comprehension, but lacks the skills for encryption of the sign language code.

18. A typical source text for this infrasemiotic type of translation, a "conventional" parallel to type 9, is graphics (3-D pie charts including numbers), the target text of type 11. When communicating the content of such charts to blind audiences, the information from two semiotic channels is condensed into one: oral communication.

Intrasemiotic translation

In intrasemiotic translation we are dealing with what can be termed "reformulation of a given expression within the same semiotic system" (Eco 2004, 131).

Adaptational types

Certain intrasemiotic adaptational translations, e.g. a stage play turned into a film (with both texts using the same semiotic channels) may strictly speaking be a result of two intersemiotic processes: that of turning the "live" play into a written screenplay, followed by the process of unfolding that monosemiotic text and creating the final movie. Still, by comparing the resulting text with the original, the total process may fairly be labelled intrasemiotic translation.

Nonverbal translation: Nonverbal → nonverbal text

19. A well-known exponent of this type is re-interpretation in the form of a new musical arrangement of an existing work, for instance a jazz standard. The result is a different textual expression within the semiotic confines of performed music. (In contradistinction to this, transposing a piece of music is conventional and thus a type 22 translation.)

Interlingual translation: L1 text → L2 text

20. In the interlingual subcategory falls the remaking of films. A remake transplants the entire film, setting and all, into the target culture. The resulting film may appear to be an original work, but as it is based on an existing storyline etc., it is indeed a translation (Evans 2014).

Intralingual translation: L1 text → new L1 text

21. Remaining within the realm of film, an intralingual example of adaptational translation is the remake of a domestic film classic. With the exception of screen adaptations of plays by authors like Shakespeare, such new versions of old films either alter outdated elements of the script, or base themselves on an entirely new dialogue list.

Conventional types

Nonverbal translation: Nonverbal → nonverbal text

22. Nonverbal translation includes a wide range of translational acts. When transposing (written) music from one key to another, the "transposer" stays within the semiotic boundaries of written music. Likewise, when, for instance, American Sign Language users are interpreted for deaf audiences in Britain who use British Sign Language, this is done through a bilingual sign interpreter – strictly within the confines of the semiotic system "signing", in this taxonomy categorised as "nonverbal".

Interlingual translation: L1 text → L2 text

Synchronic translation

23. To most non-experts, of the 34 types offered in this taxonomy, only this and types 24 and 27 qualify as translation. In traditional terms, interlingual, conventional and isomesic translation *is* translation. And, to be fair, cell 23 in the matrix of translation is packed with a number of translational sub-types and genres. Apart from printed translations, community interpreting and dubbing are also examples of this dominant type of translation. What is common to all these interlingual sub-types is that they retain the semiotic composition of the original while recreating the semantic content in another (vocal) language.

Diachronic translation

24. When studying translation, a striking paradox lies in the fact that translations often come closer to a meaningful representation of the original than the original itself. This is not only true of carefully edited translations of sloppy originals, but especially relevant when the time dimension is involved. Old texts in any language are more difficult to read than new translations in the same language.

Dialectal translation

25. More often than not, dialectal elements in a foreign text are standardised as part of "normal" (type 23 or 24) interlingual translation. However, some texts are written entirely in dialect, a fairly recent example being the 1993 novel *Trainspotting*, written (by Irvine Welsh) in what is best described as a near-phonetic spelling of modern Scots' junkie lingo. The Norwegian version was a clear-cut example of interlingual dialectal translation; the localised version reading (almost) like a standard Norwegian novel.

Diaphasic translation

26. One much-cited example of this interlingual type is the foreign versions of Hans Christian Andersen's fairy tales. These were – and still are – typically retold for children, rather than translated in extenso, with both children and adults in mind, as the author originally intended (Pedersen 2004).

Transliteration

27. This type of interlingual translation is found whenever verbal messages in one writing system are translated to verbal messages in another language and another writing system.

This means that a very high proportion of the world's language combinations yield this type of translation, for example whenever translating between Chinese and Western languages. Even in the European Union, now with three writing systems (Latin, Greek and Cyrillic), interlingual transliteration is a common occurrence.

Diamesic translation

28. It has been pointed out that "[f]ilm adaptations are visible remains of an invisible process" (Stathi 2015, 336). This is true of most types of translation, but subtitling, with the original still audible and visible onscreen, is a different story. Subtitling is an additive type of translation, in which intersemiotic feedback and redundancy play a major role (Gottlieb 2013). Although "crossing over" from the oral to the written mode, and thus deserving the term "diagonal translation" (Gottlieb 1994), subtitling is considered intrasemiotic in this taxonomy. It could be argued that as part of the diamesic shift (from speech to writing) subtitling – as well as its semiotic twin, opera surtitling (Dewolf 2001) – would qualify as intersemiotic (cf. Chuang 2006). However, as what is verbal in the source text remains verbal, this movement from spoken lines to written text is considered intralingual, while the transfer from language 1 to language 2 – whenever foreign-language productions are subtitled – is what places "normal" subtitling firmly in the interlingual category. Another argument in favour of considering subtitling inter-semiotic, namely that the written subtitles are an added semiotic channel only found in the translated film, must be refuted as well. The reason for this is that as (original-language) film and television make use of written signs – in the form of captions and displays – the semiotic *composition* as such is not changed through subtitling, although the semiotic *balance* is undeniably shifted from largely aural to predominantly visual-language reception. However, with time – and depending on national educational systems, etc. – the communicative power of the written subtitles may decrease as audiences pick up not only intonational cues, but also substantial semantic and stylistic elements in the original dialogue.

Intralingual translation: L1 text → new L1 text

Synchronic translation

29. Synchronic translation includes cases where a target text is presented as an alternative to the source text, while aimed at the same audience and written in the same language and register. Target texts may range from abridged print versions of manuals to expanded online versions of magazine articles.

Diachronic translation

30. As mentioned above (see type 24), intralingual "updating" of texts is not always well received in literary circles; although the Dano-Norwegian playwright Holberg may be difficult to understand for modern Scandinavians, modernised versions of his plays are rarely offered. However, few protest if non-literary texts, e.g. technical instructions, are brought up to date. The dialogue in dubbed film classics, especially in animated Disney-style pictures, is also often exposed to diachronic translation – normally an intralingual procedure, as the original dialogue need not be consulted.

Dialectal translation

31. It is not always considered politically correct to translate sociolectal features or utterances by dialect speakers into standard language. However, it often happens in subtitling countries whenever immigrants or people speaking with a "heavy" local accent are interviewed on TV. Equally relevant is the reverse phenomenon, where messages in standard language are translated into the local dialect, often for political rather than communicative reasons.

Diaphasic translation

32. This type of translation is commonly seen in situations where public authorities wish to communicate more effectively with clients or voters by making syntactically complex and expert-sounding texts easier to read for the non-expert. The focal point here is adapting the message to a different – yet still domestic – audience.

Transliteration

33. In communicating speech sounds in Arabic to Western readers, for instance, it may be necessary to transliterate the Arabic letters into Latin letters; an indisputable case of transliteration. A borderline case is found when, for example, aged German texts written in *Fraktur* (Gothic letters) are reset in a modern font in order for young Germans to be able to read them.

Diamesic translation

34. The simplest example of this intralingual type is transcription (taking speech down in writing), as when the spoken slogan in a TV commercial is reinforced by simultaneously presenting it in writing. The same diamesic duplication is found when hearing audiences watch domestic-language TV programmes with subtitles intended for non-hearing viewers. Although aimed at deaf people, domestic productions with optional (teletext or digital) subtitles are enjoyed by many elderly people and others with a hearing deficiency (Neves 2005; Matamala and Orero 2010; Romero-Fresco 2015). Most of these subtitles are simply diamesic – albeit sometimes condensed – versions of the lines spoken onscreen; hence this categorisation as "intralingual". Still, seen in isolation, the instances where sound effects are rendered in the subtitles – as for instance "Doorbell rings" or "Waves washing ashore" – would qualify for membership of the intersemiotic type 18: infrasemiotic verbalisation. A reverse example of intralingual diamesic translation is the production of audiobooks, which – as pointed out earlier – are listened to not only by visually impaired or dyslexic audiences, but also by normally sighted persons.

On categorisation and beyond

Having established a supposedly all-embracing taxonomy of translation, in which no translational act or artefact should be deprived of categorisation, I must hasten to state that with semiotically complex entities such as various online texts and other electronic media products, categorisation is not always a matter of course. Different foci may lead to different categorisations, or – more accurately phrased – as several text types are semiotic composites or mosaics, any categorisation of such hybrid entities will have to consider the "odd" parts of the text.

As a case in point, some video games are marketed with translated captions (i.e. written onscreen messages) while the spoken dialogue is the original (English) lines (see also O'Hagan and Mangiron 2013; Bernal-Merino 2015). Similarly, localised web pages often "forget" to translate certain textual elements, ranging from drop-down menus to videoclips.

Some translated audiovisual productions may also be categorised differently, depending on which elements are considered. An interesting example is found when foreign films with captions and displays in Latin letters are voiced-over – an interlingual isosemiotic translation procedure favoured especially in Slavonic speech communities (Franco, Matamala and Orero 2010) – into languages using Cyrillic script. Not only will such written signs be read aloud by the narrator, thus representing interlingual diamesic translation; even "untranslatable" names will have to be read aloud, since they are encoded in an alphabet unknown to the common viewer – a case of transliteration. This means that different elements of, for instance, an American movie voiced-over for Russian audiences may be referred to three different translational categories: type 23 (interlingual synchronic translation of dialogue) and types 28 and 27 combined (interlingual diamesic translation of original English captions via transliteration) – a logical outcome of the intricate relations between the original polysemiotic mosaic and its translated version.

Acknowledging such hybrid entities as part of the fascination in the multidimensional world of translation, it is my hope that the taxonomy discussed above will prove exhaustive and accommodate all types of present and future translational phenomena – no matter in which medium they will take place.

Further reading

BITRA, Bibliography of Translation and Interpreting. University of Alicante: https://aplicacionesua.cpd. ua.es/tra_int/usu/buscar.asp?idioma=en (DOI: 10.14198/bitra)
This online bibliography, accessible in several languages, contains over 69,000 entries (by August 2017). It includes not only nearly all publications on translation, but also a large number of unpublished university dissertations and theses.

Kourdis, E. and Kukkonen, P., eds. 2015. *Semiotics of Translation, Translation in Semiotics*. Special issue of *Punctum: International Journal of Semiotics* 1(2). Available from: http://punctum.gr/wp-content/uploads/2016/03/Punctum12-final.pdf.
A collection of scholarly articles including titles on the semiotics and the role of language in translating films, advertisements and visual art.

O'Hagan, M., ed. 2006. *Anime, Manga and Video Games*. Special issue of *Perspectives: Studies in Translatology* 14(4).
The first collection published on the translation of these polysemiotic genres.

Petrilli, S. 2014. *Sign Studies and Semioethics: Communication, Translation and Values*. Berlin: Mouton de Gruyter.
An impressive and thorough discussion of translation in the wider context of theoretical semiotics by an author who has published widely in this field.

Remael, A., Orero, P and Carroll, M., eds. 2012. *Audiovisual Translation and Media Accessibility at the Crossroads. Media for All 3*. Amsterdam: Rodopi.
A splendid and diverse collection of papers on various aspects and methods of audiovisual translation.

Related topics

Semantics and translation; Non-verbal communication and interpreting.

References

Baldry, A. and Thibault, P. J. 2006. *Multimodal Transcription and Text Analysis: A Multimedia Toolkit and Coursebook*. London: Equinox.

Bassnett, S. 2014. *Translation Studies*. 4th ed. [1st ed. 1980]. London: Routledge.

Benecke, B. 2004. Audio-description. *Meta* 49(1), pp. 78–80.

Bernal-Merino, M. Á. 2015. *Translation and Localisation in Video Games: Making Entertainment Software Global*. London: Routledge.

Chaume, F. 2004. Film studies and translation studies: two disciplines at stake in audiovisual translation. *Meta* 49(1), pp. 12–24.

Chuang, Y.-T. 2006. Studying subtitle translation from a multi-modal approach. *Babel* 52(4), pp. 372–383.

Dewolf, L. 2001. "Surtitling Operas. With examples of Translations from German into French and Dutch". In *(Multi) Media Translation: Concepts, Practices, and Research*, edited by Y. Gambier and H. Gottlieb, 179–188. Amsterdam: John Benjamins.

Dusi, N. 2015. Intersemiotic translation: theories, problems, analyses. *Semiotica* 206, pp. 181–205.

Eco, U. 1980. *Il nome della rosa*. Milan: Bompiani. Available from: https://profssamonicaguido.files.wordpress.com/2013/11/rosa.pdf.

Eco, U. 1983. *The Name of the Rose*. William Weaver (trans.). New York: Harcourt Brace Jovanovich.

Eco, U. 2004. *Mouse or Rat? Translation as Negotiation*. London: Phoenix. [Original edition 2003.]

Evans, J. 2014. Film remakes, the black sheep of translation. *Translation Studies* 7(3), pp. 300–314.

Franco, E., Matamala, A. and Orero, P. 2010. *Voice-Over Translation. An Overview*. Bern: Peter Lang.

Gambier, Y. and Gottlieb, H., eds. 2001. *(Multi) Media Translation: Concepts, Practices, and Research*. Amsterdam: John Benjamins.

Gottlieb, H. 1994. Subtitling: diagonal translation. *Perspectives: Studies in Translatology* 2(1), pp. 101–121.

Gottlieb, H. 2003. Parameters of translation. *Perspectives: Studies in Translatology* 11(3), pp. 167–187.

Gottlieb, H. 2005. "Multidimensional Translation: Semantics turned Semiotics". In *Proceedings of the Marie Curie Euroconferences MuTra: Challenges of Multidimensional Translation – Saarbrücken 2–6 May 2005*, edited by S. Nauert and H. Gerzymisch-Arbogast, 33–61. Available from: www.translationconcepts.org/pdf/MuTra_2005_Proceedings.pdf#page=37.

Gottlieb, H. 2008 [2010]. "Multidimensional Translation". In *Understanding Translation*, edited by A. Schjoldager with H. Gottlieb and I. Klitgård, 39–65. Copenhagen: Academica.

Gottlieb, H. 2013. "Subtitles: Readable Dialogue?" In *Eye Tracking in Audiovisual Translation*, edited by E. Perego, 37–79. Roma: Aracne Editrice.

Gottlieb, H. 2014. "Foreign Voices, Local Lines: In Defense of Visibility and Domestication in Subtitling". In *Subtitling and Intercultural Communication*, edited by B. Garzelli and M. Baldo, 27–54. Interlinguistica 1. Studi contrastivi tra Lingue e Culture. Pisa: Edizioni ETS.

Gottlieb, H. 2015. "Different Viewers, Different Needs: Personal Subtitles for Danish TV?" In *The Reception of Subtitles for the Deaf and Hard of Hearing in Europe*, edited by P. Romero Fresco, 17–44. Bern: Peter Lang.

Jakobson, R. 1959 [2000]. "On Linguistic Aspects of Translation". In *On Translation*, edited by R. A. Brower, 232–239. Cambridge, MA: Harvard University Press. Reprinted in L. Venuti, ed. 2000. *The Translation Studies Reader*, 113–118. London: Routledge. (Second edition 2004.)

Kourdis, E. 2015. "Semiotics of Translation: An Interdisciplinary Approach to Translation". In *International Handbook of Semiotics*, edited by P. P. Trifonas, 303–320. Dordrecht: Springer.

Kress, G. 2010. *Multimodality: A Social Semiotic Approach to Contemporary Communication*. London: Routledge.

Kruger, J.-L. and Orero, P., eds. 2010. Audio Description, Audio Narration: A New Era in AVT. Special issue of *Perspectives: Studies in Translatology* 18(3).

Matamala, A. and Orero, P., eds. 2010. *Listening to Subtitles: Subtitles for the Deaf and Hard of Hearing*. Bern: Peter Lang.

Neather, R. 2012. Intertextuality, translation, and the semiotics of museum presentation: the case of bilingual texts in Chinese museums. *Semiotica* 192, pp. 197–218.

Neves, J. 2005. *Audiovisual Translation: Subtitling for the Deaf and Hard-of-Hearing*. PhD dissertation, School of Arts, Roehampton University. Available from: http://rrp.roehampton.ac.uk/cgi/artstheses/1.

O'Hagan, M. and Mangiron, C. 2013. *Game Localization: Translating for the Global Digital Entertainment Industry*. Amsterdam: John Benjamins.

Pedersen, V. H. 2004. *Ugly Ducklings? Studies in the English Translations of Hans Christian Andersen's Tales and Stories*. Odense: University Press of Southern Denmark.

Poyatos, F., ed. 1997. *Nonverbal Communication and Translation*. Amsterdam: John Benjamins.

Romero-Fresco, P., ed. 2015. *The Reception of Subtitles for the Deaf and Hard of Hearing in Europe*. Bern: Peter Lang.

Stathi, I. 2015. "Inter-semiotic Translation and Transfer Theory in Cinematic/Audiovisual Adaptations of Greek Drama". In *International Handbook of Semiotics*, edited by P. P. Trifonas 321–338. Dordrecht: Springer.

Stecconi, U. 2009. "Semiotics". In *Routledge Encyclopedia of Translation Studies*, 2nd ed., edited by M. Baker and G. Saldanha. London: Routledge.

Stecconi, U. 2010. "Semiotics and Translation". In *Handbook of Translation Studies*, Vol. 1, edited by Y. Gambier and L. van Doorslaer, 314–319. Philadelphia: John Benjamins.

Szarkowska, A. 2011. Text-to-speech audio description: towards wider availability of AD. *Journal of Specialised Translation* 15, pp. 142–162. Available from: www.jostrans.org/issue15/art_szarkowska.pdf.

Torop, P. 2008. Translation and semiotics. *Sign Systems Studies* 2, pp. 253–258. Available from: www.ceeol.com.

Toury, G. 1986/2010. "Translation, a Cultural-Semiotic Perspective". In *Encyclopedic Dictionary of Semiotics*, edited by T. A. Sebeok (3rd revised and updated ed. 2010, edited by Marcel Danesi). Berlin: Mouton de Gruyter.

Vassallo, C. 2015. What's so proper about translation? Or interlingual translation and interpretive semiotics. *Semiotica* 206, pp. 161–179.

Zabalbeascoa, P. 1997. "Dubbing and the Nonverbal Dimension of Translation". In *Nonverbal Communication and Translation*, edited by F. Poyatos, 327–342. Amsterdam: John Benjamins.

Phonetics, phonology and interpreting

Barbara Ahrens

Introduction and definitions

> 'I don't mind what she said, but I don't like the way she said it' is a complaint we all heard some time or other, and probably have uttered ourselves. What does it mean?
>
> (Bolinger 1986, 3)

As the quotation above suggests, in oral communication, the message is encoded in elements that go beyond mere words (Henderson 1980; Key 1980): the way something is said contains important information for the listener (Lehtonen 1982, 37). As early as at the beginning of the 20th century, Behaghel (1900) underlined the role non-verbal and extralinguistic factors play in oral communication, but it took another 60 years before linguistic research started to focus on spoken language and its special features (Enkvist 1982, 17; Schönherr 1997).

The linguistic subdisciplines focusing on spoken language and oral communication are phonetics and phonology. Phonetics, on the one hand, deals with the actual sounds of spoken human speech. Different sounds and the physiological-articulatory processes underlying their production as well as their acoustic properties and auditory perception are described and researched within the discipline of phonetics (Catford 2001; Pétursson and Neppert 1996). Phonology, on the other hand, focuses on the function of sounds in a language system, i.e. the organisation of sounds as functional (distinctive) units in a language (Clark, Yallop and Fletcher 2007; Katamba 1989). The function of sounds can be distinctive on all levels: syllables, words, phrases, sentences or even longer utterances. Especially on the phrase, sentence and utterance levels, sound and its variation are important for conveying different linguistic meanings. In this respect, phonetic and phonological phenomena are expressed by prosody, which is inherent to oral speech processes, be it monolingual or bilingual as in interpreting (see the following section).

Both subdisciplines – phonetics and phonology – are complex areas of study because of their interdisciplinary nature, involving anatomy, physics or neurology, for example, and because phonetic and phonological categories are highly interdependent.

Initially, research into these phenomena of spoken language was very limited due to technical challenges, such as recording, quantity of data, time-consuming transcription and analyses. Another factor influencing this kind of research is the lack of a homogeneous terminology, e.g. for describing prosodic features in spoken language (Heuft 1999, 14; Schönherr 1997, 3). Terminological heterogenity is reflected by the synonymous use of terms such as "prosody", "intonation" or "suprasegmental features". American structuralism opts for the term "suprasegmental features" for describing "[. . .] features whose arrangement in contrastive patterns in the time dimension is not restricted to single segments defined by their phonetic quality [. . .]" (Lehiste 1970, 2–3). In European linguistics, the dominant term is "prosodic" because it is not associated with a specific linguistic school (Crystal 1969, 6).

Prosody can be defined as a phenomenon of spoken language which comprises all suprasegmental features that depend on tonal, dynamic and durational parameters (Ahrens 2004). Tonal features include intonation (pitch contour) and pitch range. Their acoustic parameter is fundamental frequency (F_0), which is perceived as pitch. Dynamic features depend on changes of the acoustic parameter of intensity, which is perceived as loudness. Rhythm, for example, is a dynamic element. Time is the conditioning factor of durational features like pauses or speech rate. There is a fourth category of prosodic features: they depend on the interplay of tonal, dynamic and/or durational parameters and can therefore be described as "hybrid phenomena". A typical hybrid phenomenon is accent (accentuation, stress).

Prosody is a complex non-verbal phenomenon that has several characteristics and functions. The most important characteristics are *structure* and *prominence* (Ahrens 2004, 2005): the acoustic continuum produced by the speaker is structured prosodically and elements the speaker considers to be important are emphasised by prosody too. As a consequence, prosodic elements guide and support the listener's process of comprehension (Cutler 1983, 91). In addition to these main functions, prosodic features also serve an indexical purpose: the listener can usually tell from prosody if the speaker is a man or a woman (Lehiste 1970, 58).

Furthermore, prosody has a complementary-compensatory function: it can complement what is being said by providing additional information or it can even compensate for what is not being said. Finally, prosodic features can substitute for each other: in whispering for example, there is no pitch, so accents are conditioned by variations of intensity and duration.

The relation between cognition and speaking becomes evident in interruptions or hesitations in the acoustic signal of speech flow. Thus, prosodic features, such as pauses, are indicators of cognitive processes underlying speech planning and production: "Time to pause seems to be a condition for the kind of central processes (thinking) which underlie new organisation in speech to take place" (Goldman-Eisler 1958, 67).

The durational aspect of pauses is emphasised by many authors who describe pauses as an interruption of the acoustic signal over a certain period of time (e.g. Cruttenden 1997, 30; Crystal 1969, 166; Goldman-Eisler 1961, 18), although pauses can also be perceived when there is no durational interruption of the speech signal, e.g. in the case of F_0 reset at the beginning of a new intonationally delimited chunk. In this respect, pauses not only serve the physiological necessity of breathing, but are clearly linked to the structure of an utterance since they segment the speech flow.

In addition to these functions which support listeners' comprehension, pauses can also have a disruptive effect on comprehension in the case of an excessive number of pauses (due to the speaker's emotional state, e.g. anxiety; Faure 1980, 290; Levin *et al.* 1960, 469) or when pauses occur unexpectedly within grammatical structures (e.g. Royé 1983), although in the latter case, pauses may also be used as a deliberate rhetorical means (e.g. Cruttenden 1997, 30).

Due to their complementary-compensatory functions, prosodic elements are interdependent, i.e. they occur in combination, or more than one feature serves the same function.

This holds true for structuring the acoustic continuum when speaking. Although pauses can be an indicator of chunks, intonation serves this purpose in an even more effective way.

Intonation is defined as the pitch contour of an utterance (Ahrens 2004). Changes in the pitch contour are cues for the intonational segmentation of the speech flow (Halliday 1966). These intonationally produced chunks are described as intonation units, which are "defined as a prosodic unit with a coherent F_0 contour and at least one pitch movement perceived as prominent" (Ahrens 2005, 53). Intonation units also have specific final pitch patterns and may be delimited by additional boundary signals, such as pauses. A prosodic universal found in all languages is *declination* (Vaissière 1983), i.e. the declining F_0 contour towards the end of an intonation unit, which is due to physiological reasons. The following intonation unit starts with an F_0 reset (Crystal 1969, 227), which is a strong boundary signal, too.

Closely connected to intonation is accent. Although accents are hybrid phenomena depending on the interplay of tonal, durational and dynamic parameters, the dominant parameter is usually F_0 (e.g. Crystal 1969; Günther 1999), the changes of which can be perceived as prominent, i.e. accents. Phonetically, accents are an important feature at word level because word accent has to be placed on the correct syllable according to the accent rules of each language. In some languages, word meaning can vary if the accent is shifted to another syllable. Phonologically, accents are distinctive at sentence or utterance level, since there the speaker can decide independently what element(s) s/he wants to emphasise. Generally, speakers choose those elements which are the most important parts of what they say. In this respect, accents are clearly related to one of the main functions of prosody, i.e. prominence.

Historical perspectives: Prosody in interpreting

As mentioned above, prosody is an integral part of an orally presented text and it is thus also important if the communicative event is bilingual and has to take place via interpreters. In interpreting, prosodic features in the source and in the target text are equally important.

Even in bilingual communication via an interpreter, the above-mentioned prosodic features and specificities of monolingual communication apply to source text production. The source text speaker uses his or her prosody for emphasising important elements in the message s/he wants to convey, thus making comprehension easier for the interpreter and those among the audience who listen to the original speech. Prosody is especially important in the case of irony in the source text (Kade 1963). Research has shown the impact of source text prosody on the interpreter's performance: monotonous or not very lively intonation and the lack of pauses result in comprehension problems and a less accurate target text (Gerver 1969, 1976).

Interpreters are professional speakers and, therefore, voice and the way of speaking are also important factors in their performance when it comes to delivering a comprehensible text (Alexieva 1990; Cartellieri 1983). In simultaneous interpreting where the target text is only perceived via headsets, the importance of the interpreter's voice and speaking skills is more than evident.

The importance of prosody in interpreters' performance has already been stressed in early publications on interpreting, but it took a relatively long time before it became a research topic in interpreting studies. For many years, authors have seemed to assume that prosodic features of an interpreted target text were just the same as in monolingual speech production (Déjean Le Féal 1990; Kirchhoff 1976). However, research confirmed that in simultaneous interpreting, the target texts sound "less smooth than 'natural' speech" (Barik 1975, 294), a fact that Shlesinger described later as intonation *sui generis*: "the intonational system used in simultaneous interpretation appears to be marked by a set of salient features not found in any other language use" (1994: 226). Despite her claim that interpreted texts sound like normal, spontaneous speech (Kirchhoff 1976, 67), Kirchhoff also acknowledged that hesitation phenomena in the target text delivery are conditioned by difficult processing conditions, like simultaneous listening and speaking (Kirchhoff 1976, 67). Thus, in bilingual communication, too, prosodic features of the target text can reflect underlying cognitive operations of speech processing.

In consecutive interpreting, delivery of the target text is less prone to be affected by the simultaneously incoming source text and can thus be regarded as being more like monolingual speech production. Research into prosody in consecutive interpreting, however, shows that pause and hesitation patterns can differ from typical monolingual speaking (e.g. Mead 2002). This phenomenon can be attributed to the simultaneous reading of notes and information retrieval from memory in the second phase of the consecutive interpreting process.

Core issues and topics: Research into prosody in interpreting

Research into prosody in simultaneous interpreting can be grouped according to the prosodic phenomena that were examined: (1) pauses, speech rate and segmentation, (2) intonation and fundamental frequency and (3) accentuation and stress.

Pauses, speech rate and segmentation

Early studies focused on pauses since they were regarded as the key factor for the simultaneous listening and understanding of the source language and speaking in the target language. Experimental study design in a laboratory setting was the rule, as applied by Barik (1973), Gerver (1969), Goldman-Eisler (1967, 1968, 1972, 1980) and Goldman-Eisler and Cohen (1974). Alexieva (1988), too, used student interpreters in a lab situation for her study on pause patterns in which she found fewer and shorter pauses in the interpreters' output, a finding later studies were not able to confirm.

The first researcher who used an authentic corpus (English–Hebrew and vice-versa) for her study of prosodic features was Shlesinger (1994). She set out from Halliday's categories of *tonality* (i.e. segmentation into intonation units), *tonicity* (i.e. the positioning and accentuation of the tonic syllable) and *tone* (i.e. pitch movement) (Halliday 1966, 1967). She added speech rate and duration to these categories. Her results led her to postulate an intonation *sui generis* for simultaneous interpreting (Shlesinger 1994, 226).

In an authentic English–Korean corpus, Lee (1999) was able to confirm Gerver's (1969) results and the crucial role of source text pauses for the cognitive processes underlying comprehension and monitoring.

Tissi (2000) identified different types of pauses and disfluencies in her experimental corpus with interpreting students in the German–Italian language combination. Her findings confirmed Lee's result of fewer pauses in simultaneously interpreted target texts. She also analysed the length of pauses and found that longer pauses tended to have a higher average duration in the target texts.

Cecot (2001) also analysed pauses and disfluencies quantitatively in her experimental study. She interviewed the interpreters about their perception of their own performance and was thus able to show that the majority of the interpreters in her study were not aware of their pauses during target text delivery, although Cecot's quantitative results confirmed an objectively significant number of pauses and disfluencies. Results like this are a first indicator of the role of pauses and disfluencies in the debate on perception of target text and their quality in general. Furthermore, the interpreters' erroneous self-perception of their own output is relevant for interpreting practice.

A few years later, Lee's (1999) results were also confirmed by Ahrens (2004, 2005, 2007) who in an authentic English–German corpus was able to link target text pause patterns to cognitive processes of source text comprehension and to the informational structure of the target text: the interpreters paused at the end of intonation units which, at the same time, were very often the end of an informational chunk, i.e. the interpreters used pauses for structuring their output in a way that enhanced the target text audience's comprehension.

Intonation and fundamental frequency

Darò (1990) considered F_0 to be an indicator of the emotion interpreters felt towards their native and working languages. Not surprisingly, the lowest degree of anxiety was measured in the interpreters' mother tongue. Since Darò tested F_0 only in reading but not when simultaneously interpreting, the question remains if F_0 would go up due to the complex speech processing involved in interpreting.

In her study, Shlesinger found that the "low-rise nonfinal pitch movement" (Shlesinger 1994, 231) was the dominant intonational contour at the end of intonation units. It was expected to hinder the audience's comprehension since falling pitch movements would have been likelier in the positions in question.

Ahrens (2004, 2005) was able to confirm the dominance of progredient final F_0 contours in her study. A typical intonational contour was the final "rise-level" (Ahrens 2005, 68), which in combination with level or rising final pitch movements resulted in a wave-like F_0 contour. These types of pitch movements are perceived as "singsong" and are found frequently in interpreters' performances, i.e. they are a characteristic feature in interpreting, thus supporting Shlesinger's (1994) observation of an intonation *sui generis*.

The "rise-level" contours have also been described for German monolingual speech production as the "left-hand pier of a bridge" typical for enumerations or lists, i.e. in positions where a speaker indicates intonationally that another or more elements will follow. In simultaneous interpreting with the linear incoming source text, processing of segments which have not been uttered completely by the speaker is inherent in the interpreting process itself and can thus result in this "list-like" intonation because the interpreter cannot be sure if further elements for the idea s/he is processing will follow or not.

Cognitive load and chunking were also an important aspect for Nafá Waasaf (2007) who, in her empirical analysis of an authentic corpus consisting of interpreters' performances in the European Parliament and the European Commission, focused on the structural organisation by means of intonation of the texts she analysed. She was not able to confirm the dominance of specific intonational patterns described by Shlesinger (1994) and Ahrens (2004, 2005), but rather observed intonational patterns and phenomena described in literature on prosody in general, such as intonational reset at the beginning of intonational phrases (e.g. Ahrens 2004, 2005) or declination and falling final contours (e.g. Vaissière 1983).

Accentuation and stress

Shlesinger (1994) also analysed the position of accentuated syllables in her corpus. She observed that accents and semantic contrasts were not always compatible, like in the case of accentuated prepositions without contrastive or emphatic value. This misaccentuation can result in misunderstandings, she concluded.

Williams (1995), too, described anomalous stress patterns in an authentic corpus of Swedish–English simultaneous interpreting. Anomalous stress in the target text was triggered by – correct – accents in the overlapping source text, resulting in a "misrendering of the original message" (Williams 1995, 48).

Without undertaking a phonological study herself, Kalina (1998) commented briefly on accentuation in interpreted target texts in the context of her research into interpreting strategies: in simultaneous interpreting, the target texts often sound *staccato* or "machine-gun" like, i.e. as if every word were stressed (Kalina 1998, 200). This auditive impression has not been underpinned by quantitative comparison so far. Ahrens (2004, 2005) correlated intonational segmentation and accentuation in her corpus. Since intonational units are defined as comprising at least one stressed word, i.e. at least one pitch movement that can be perceived as being prominent, short intonational units consisting of one or two words only result in every, or every second word being stressed. In the target texts she analysed, Ahrens found a considerably higher percentage of one- or two-word intonational units leading to a *staccato*-like stress pattern with all words having the same weight, which might be boring and tiring for the listener and detrimental to her or his comprehension.

Main research methods

Research into prosodic features in interpreting has always been corpus based. Early studies in the 1960s and 1970s focusing on speech rate and pause patterns worked with experimental study designs in a laboratory setting for recording and compiling the respective corpora (e.g. Barik 1973, 1975; Gerver 1969; Goldman-Eisler 1968).

The subsequent analyses of the recordings used technical equipment of that time for visualising the speech signal and the pauses in it. Apart from objectively measurable prosodic parameters, the general auditive impression of a recording was also used for formulating research hypotheses.

Until 1994, studies focusing on prosodic features in interpreting with experimental data were the state of the art. The advantage they provide is that they allow the control of variables and parameters that could influence the results. This is the reason why in studies undertaken in the late 20th and early 21st centuries, researchers have started to use experimental study designs again when they want to manipulate a specific parameter, such as intonation (e.g. Collados Aís 1998/2002, 2007; Holub 2010) or fluency (e.g. Pradas Macías 2004; Rennert 2010).

Shlesinger (1994) was the first to work with a corpus of recordings of authentic interpreting performances. Since research into prosody is extremely time-consuming, she only analysed a randomised selection of ten recorded passages with a duration of 90 seconds each that had been transcribed and after a lapse of three years minimum read again by the same interpreter who had once interpreted the target text in question. Auditive impression and a survey among a control group of listeners as regards comprehensibility of the interpreted texts complemented her data.

With her ground-breaking study design of manipulating the intonation and contents of a target text in order to record three different versions of the same text, Collados Aís (1998/2002) established a research paradigm and method that has become an indispensable part of the methodological repertoire of interpreting research. She also carried out an acoustic analysis of pitch and intensity of the digitised recordings by means of the software Visi-Pitch. At that time, digitisation of long recordings was still a problem, as reported by Ahrens (2004, 2005) who analysed an authentic corpus of one source text with a duration of 72 minutes and three target texts in dual-track quality. Digitisation was done by means of the software Wavelab 3.0, which allowed the parallel digitisation of the two time-aligned tracks of the recording and the subsequent separation of the channels for analysis. Since all target text recordings were time-aligned with the respective source text recording, it was possible to synchronise both channels again in the following acoustic analysis.

The analysis of the acoustic parameters F_0, intensity and duration was carried out using Praat, a software developed for phonetic and phonological analyses at the Department of Phonetics at the University of Amsterdam (Praat 2015). The software program is freeware and is being constantly updated and improved by its developers.

Digital recording, including of long events and in dual-track quality, has become very easy to make using modern programs such as Audacity, a free multi-track audio editor and recorder, and can be edited in any audio format that suits other software such as Praat or EXMARaLDA (Audacity 2015; EXMARaLDA 2015). Manipulating long recordings for research purposes is not prohibitively time-consuming thanks to these programs.

Transcribing, analysing, annotating and editing can also be done by EXMARaLDA, a tool being developed especially for working with oral corpora, which allows editing in a so-called "partitur" format (ExMARALDA 2015). A detailed description of editing experimental material for research into fluency using Audacity and EXMARaLDA is given by Rennert (2013).

Acoustic methodology supported by additional analyses, be it discourse analysis or/and surveys among different user groups, as well as the triangulation of the results obtained by these different methods is state-of-the-art methodology in studies related to phonetic and phonological features in interpreting.

Current debate

Since the turn of the century, research into prosody in interpreting has focused on prosody as an – often underestimated – parameter of interpreting quality.

The interdependence of intonation and quality assessment in simultaneous interpreting was made evident for the first time by Collados Aís (1998/2002) in a comprehensive study in the German–Spanish language pair. The contents and intonation of the simultaneously interpreted Spanish target text had been manipulated and the different text versions were then presented to different listener groups who had to answer questionnaires regarding contents and intonation in simultaneous interpreting. Collados Aís was able to demonstrate that intonation is one, if not the most, important factor when it comes to evaluating interpreters' actual performances, although many listeners say that voice and intonation are not important when asked beforehand about their expectations about an interpreter's performance.

With her innovative research methodology, Collados Aís (1998/2002) established the "expectation vs. actual evaluation" paradigm in the debate on quality in interpreting studies and practice. She was able to put voice and prosody at the centre of the quality debate although most earlier surveys on user expectations carried out among users of interpreters' services did not rank non-verbal parameters, such as pleasant voice or fluency of delivery, as being very important for interpreting quality as compared to sense consistency or completeness of the target text (e.g. Bühler 1986; Collados Aís 1998/2002; Gile 1990; Kurz 1989, 1993, 1997a, 1997b; Kurz and Pöchhacker 1995; Meak 1990; Moser 1996).

Many of the earlier studies on prosodic phenomena in interpreting concluded that these elements are important for the comprehensibility of the target text delivered by an interpreter (e.g. Ahrens 2004, 2005; Shlesinger 1994), since they give guidance to the listener about how to understand the message. Infelicitous choice of intonational patterns, excessive pausing and hesitations or hyperaccentuation are features that might make listeners' comprehension more difficult – or even impede it.

In the subproject "intonation" of a recent comprehensive research project on quality in simultaneous interpreting (QuaSI 2010), Holub (2010), too, showed that monotonous intonation has a strong impact on text comprehension and the evaluation of the target text. In her study, Holub applied Collados Aís' (1998/2002) method of producing different target text versions by computer-aided manipulation of F_0.

Fluency is another prosodic factor strongly influencing the evaluation of overall quality of an interpreter's performance, and was at the centre of a second subproject of QuaSI. Following Pradas Macías' (2004) concept of fluency, Rennert (2010) defined it as a temporal variable that results from the complex interplay of a number of constitutive parameters, such as pauses, tempo of speech, lengthening of vowels and consonants, audible breathing, hesitations, repairs, false starts and repetitions. Rennert (2010) showed that a lack of fluency is regarded as bad quality. Like Holub (2010), she also used an experimental study design with specifically manipulated target texts (Rennert 2013).

All in all, the debate on phonetics and phonology in interpreting focuses on the complex relationship between prosodic parameters and quality, since research has been able to prove that prosodic and other voice-related features influence strongly whether an interpreter's performance is regarded as good, professional and reliable (Collados Aís 2007, 217–219).

Future directions

Since the influence of prosodic features in the perception and evaluation of interpreters' performances has been confirmed by research, and since there is still no generally accepted definition of interpreting quality (Zwischenberger 2013, 17), this will be the direction future research will continue to follow. This will necessitate analyses of more data, including data in less frequent language combinations. The aim will be to come to a definition of interpreting quality, but at the same time to a description of an optimum prosodic delivery in specific settings.

In this context, findings from automatic speech recognition and synthesis as well as machine translation research offer interesting insights since these disciplines are involved in developing automatic interpretation systems. A first intent to develop such a speech-to-speech translation system was the *Verbmobil* project in the 1990s (Verbmobil 2000; Wahlster 2000). Another system designed for lecture translation was compared to human interpreting in an experimental study in cooperation between the Karlsruhe Institute of Technology and the Translation and Interpreting Faculty of Mainz University in Germersheim, Germany, in which the audience had to evaluate the performance of the machine and the human interpreter (Fünfer 2013; Stüker *et al.* 2014). In general, the human performance clearly received higher scores – e.g. due to better comprehensibility as compared to the output of the machine – but interestingly enough, in the voice- and prosody-related parameters in the evaluation, the difference between the scores for the machine and the human interpreter was less prominent. This means that speech synthesis had made considerable progress in the first decade or so of the 21st century. Although even the developers of this already rather mature machine interpreting system admit the superiority of human interpreting performance (Stüker *et al.* 2014, 277), they see a number of helpful applications for mobile systems installed on laptops, tablets or smart phones, as already tested and applied in a number of doctor–patient conversations in remote areas and less frequent language combinations, such as English–Thai, where interpreters are difficult to find (Fünfer 2013, 132–133).

Technological progress and an increased use of technology for, in and even instead of human interpreting will be an important field for research and the profession in the coming years; this should not only be seen as a threat, but also as an opportunity for researchers, students and practitioners.

Implications for interpreting practice

Since the effect of the speaker's voice is crucial for successful oral communication and since voice and prosody are important factors for creating confidence among communication partners, it is obvious that this also holds true in interpreted communication events. Interpreters have to be aware of the effect of their voice and the various ways of achieving flexible and adequate vocal modulation. Therefore, in the case of phonetics and phonology, implications for (interpreting) practice are of a very applied nature.

Interpreters need to be aware of the different requirements relating to their voice and speaking skills in all interpreting modes (consecutive, simultaneous, whispering), settings (conferences, court, public services, among others) and acoustic conditions (with or without microphone, small or big room, indoors or outdoors, surrounding noise, etc.). This implies that, like any member of a speaking profession, interpreters should have knowledge about voice care and vocal health.

Voice is extremely sensitive to physiological and psychological stress as well as to wrong breathing. Tension on the vocal cords, increased subglottal pressure or an uncomfortable bodily position, e.g. when interpreting in the whispering mode, have a direct impact on voice: F_0 becomes higher and the voice is thus perceived as shrill. Voice phenomena often occur without being noticed consciously by the speaker. Therefore, speakers in general, and interpreters in particular, have to train their awareness of these phenomena and problems.

Speaking skills and how to treat one's voice have to be internalised by interpreters since the interpreting task is demanding and cognitive resources are needed for processing source language input and target text output. Continuous training is needed in order to achieve internalisation. Nowadays, most interpreter training courses include classes in public speaking and rhetoric. Topics presented in such courses range from voice physiology and voice care to standard pronunciation and oral delivery of all kinds of texts in spontaneous as well as reproductive, i.e. interpretational communicative acts.

But voice training is a life-long process. Speaking habits, working conditions and aging have an important impact on the interpreter's voice. Typical voice disorders occurring because of wrong speaking habits and respiration include for example hoarse voice, vocal fatigue or even vocal nodules. Although these can be reversed by medical treatment and speech therapy, it is better to prevent damage to the voice from the very beginning of one's professional life as an interpreter. This implies continuous professional training in speaking skills: listening critically to one's own output on the basis of personal recordings even after having left the training institution should be a permanent part of the interpreter's quality assurance measures.

Seminars on voice care and training as well as speaking skills for interpreters offered by speech trainers and therapists also aim at awareness-raising and improving performance quality. Refreshing skills that had been learned once during training but then often seem to be forgotten during professional practice is highly recommended since it has become clear in a variety of studies (e.g. Collados Aís 1998/2002; Holub 2010) that interpreters and their performance are judged by their vocal and prosodic performance. Taking care of one's voice and prosodic skills is an essential part of quality assurance in interpreting.

Further reading

Collados Aís, A., Iglesias Fernández, E., Pradas Macías, E. M. and Stevaux, E., eds. 2011. *Qualitätspara-meter beim Simultandolmetschen. Interdisziplinäre Perspektiven*. Tübingen: Narr.
This commendable book deals with interpreting quality and 10 different, but highly interdependent criteria which define it, such as intonation, accent and voice, but also terminology and sense consistency, among others. Its bibliography is very valuable since it includes well-known contributions to the interpreting quality debate as well as a large number of fruitful contributions from other disciplines.

Pöchhacker, F., ed. 2015. *Routledge Encyclopedia of Interpreting Studies*. London: Routledge.
This volume brings together state-of-the-art key issues in interpreting studies in alphabetical order. Cross-references show the interdependence of the variety of topics, thus offering a structured comprehensive overview of interpreting studies as an increasingly diverse and fascinating field.

Pöchhacker, F. and Shlesinger, M., eds. 2002. *The Interpreting Studies Reader*. London: Routledge.
This book is a collection of 26 key articles in the field of interpreting research from its beginning in the 1950s until 2002. It presents interpreting in a multidisciplinary perspective, and since articles that originally had not been published in English have been translated, it also gives access to contributions in less frequently used languages.

Related topics

Non-verbal communication and interpreting.

References

Ahrens, B. 2004. *Prosodie beim Simultandolmetschen*. Frankfurt: Lang.
Ahrens, B. 2005. Prosodic phenomena in simultaneous interpreting: a conceptual approach and its practical application. *Interpreting* 7(1), pp. 51–76.
Ahrens, B. 2007. Pauses (and other prosodic features) in simultaneous interpreting. *Forum* 5(1), pp. 1–18.
Alexieva, B. 1988. "Analysis of the Simultaneous Interpreter's Output". In *Translation, Our Future. Proceedings, XIth World Congress of FIT*, edited by P. Nekeman, 484–488. Maastricht: Euroterm.
Alexieva, B. 1990. Creativity in simultaneous interpretation. *Babel* 36(1), pp. 1–6.
Audacity. 2015. Available from: http://sourceforge.net/projects/audacity/ [Accessed 17 December 2015].
Barik, H. C. 1973. Simultaneous interpretation: temporal and quantitative data. *Language and Speech* 16(3), pp. 237–270.
Barik, H. C. 1975. Simultaneous interpretation: qualitative and linguistic data. *Language and Speech* 18(3), pp. 272–297.
Behaghel, O. 1900. Geschriebenes Deutsch und gesprochenes Deutsch. Festvortrag, gehalten auf der Hauptversammlung des Allgemeinen Deutschen Sprachvereins zu Zittau am 1. Oktober 1899. *Wissenschaftlich Beihefte zur Zeitschrift des Allgemeinen Deutschen Sprachvereins* 17/18, pp. 213–232.
Bolinger, D. 1986. *Intonation and its Parts: Melody in Spoken English*. Stanford, CA: Stanford University Press.
Bühler, H. 1986. Linguistic (semantic) and extra-linguistic (pragmatic) criteria for the evaluation of conference interpretation and interpreters. *Multilingua* 5(4), pp. 231–235.
Cartellieri, C. 1983. The inescapable dilemma: quality and/or quantity in interpreting. *Babel* 29(4), pp. 209–213.
Catford, J. C. 2001. *A Practical Introduction to Phonetics*. 2nd ed. Oxford: Oxford University Press.
Cecot, M. 2001. Pauses in simultaneous interpretation: a contrastive analysis of professional interpreters' performance. *Interpreters' Newsletter* 11, pp. 63–85.

Clark, J., Yallop, C. and Fletcher, J. 2007. *An Introduction to Phonetics and Phonology*. 3rd ed. Malden, MA: Blackwell.

Collados Aís, A. 1998/2002. "Quality Assessment in Simultaneous Interpreting: The Importance of Nonverbal Communication". In *The Interpreting Studies Reader*, edited by F. Pöchhacker and M. Shlesinger, 326–336. London: Routledge. First published 1998 in A. Collados Aís, *La evaluación de la calidad en interpretación simultánea: La importancia de la comunicación no verbal*. Peligros (Granada): Comares.

Collados Aís, A. 2007. "La evaluación de la investigación". In *La evaluación de la calidad en interpretación simultánea: parámetros de incidencia*, edited by A. Collados Aís, E. Pradas Macías, E. Macarena, E. Stévaux and O. García Becerra, 213–224. Albolote (Granada): Comares.

Cruttenden, A. 1997. *Intonation*. 2nd ed. Cambridge: Cambridge University Press.

Crystal, D. 1969. *Prosodic Systems and Intonation in English*. Cambridge: Cambridge University Press.

Cutler, A. 1983. "Speakers' Conception of the Function of Prosody". In *Prosody: Models and Measurements*, edited by A. Cutler and D. R. Ladd, 79–91. Berlin: Springer.

Darò, V. 1990. Voice frequency in languages and simultaneous interpretation. *The Interpreters' Newsletter* 3, pp. 88–92.

Déjean Le Féal, K. 1990. "Some Thoughts on the Evaluation of Simultaneous Interpretation". In *Interpreting: Yesterday, Today and Tomorrow*, edited by D. Bowen and M. Bowen, 154–160. Binghamton, NY: SUNY.

Enkvist, N. E. 1982. "Introduction: Impromptu Speech, Structure, and Process". In *Impromptu Speech: A Symposium*, edited by N. E. Enkvist, 11–31. Åbo: Åbo Akademi.

EXMARaLDA. 2015. *EXMARaLDA: Tools for oral corpora*. Available from: http://www.exmaralda.org/en/ [Accessed 19 December 2015].

Faure, M. 1980. "Results of a Contrastive Study of Hesitation Phenomena in French and German". In *Temporal Variables in Speech: Studies in Honour of Frieda Goldman-Eisler*, edited by H. W. Dechert and M. Raupach, 287–290. The Hague: Mouton.

Fünfer, S. 2013. *Mensch oder Maschine? Dolmetscher und maschinelles Dolmetschsystem im Vergleich*. Berlin: Frank & Timme.

Gerver, D. 1969. "The Effects of Source Language Presentation Rate on the Performance of Simultaneous Conference Interpreters". In *Proceedings of the Second Louisville Conference on Rate and/or Frequency-Controlled Speech*, edited by E. Foulke, 162–184. Louisville, KY: Center for Rate-Controlled Recordings, University of Louisville.

Gerver, D. 1976. "Empirical Studies of Simultaneous Interpretation: A Review and a Model". In *Translation: Applications and Research*, edited by R. W. Brislin, 165–207. New York: Gardner Press.

Gile, D. 1990. "L'évaluation de la qualité de l'interprétation par les délégués: une étude de cas". *The Interpreters' Newsletter*, 3, pp. 66–71.

Goldman-Eisler, F. 1958. Speech analysis and mental processes. *Language and Speech*, 1, pp. 59–75.

Goldman-Eisler, F. 1961. A comparative study of two hesitation phenomena. *Language and Speech* 4, pp. 18–26.

Goldman-Eisler, F. 1967. Sequential patterns and cognitive processes in speech. *Language and Speech* 10, pp. 122–132.

Goldman-Eisler, F. 1968. *Psycholinguistics: Experiments in Spontaneous Speech*. London: Academic Press.

Goldman-Eisler, F. 1972. Segmentation of input in simultaneous translation. *Journal of Psycholinguistic Research* 1(2), pp. 127–140.

Goldman-Eisler, F. 1980. "Psychological Mechanisms of Speech Production as Studied Through the Analysis of Simultaneous Translation". In *Language Production* Vol. 1: *Speech and Talk*, edited by B. Butterworth, 143–153. London: Academic Press.

Goldman-Eisler, F. and Cohen, M. 1974. An experimental study of interference between receptive and productive processes relating to simultaneous translation. *Language and Speech* 17(1), pp. 1–10.

Günther, C. 1999. *Prosodie und Sprachproduktion*. Tübingen: Niemeyer.

Halliday, M. A. K. 1966. "Intonation Systems in English". In *Patterns of Language: Papers in General, Descriptive and Applied Linguistics*, edited by A. Mcintosh and M. A. K. Halliday, 111–133. London: Longmans.

Halliday, M. A. K. 1967. *Intonation and Grammar in British English*. The Hague: Mouton.

Henderson, A. I. 1980. "Juncture Pause and Intonation Fall and the Perceptual Segmentation of Speech". In *Temporal Variables in Speech: Studies in Honour of Frieda Goldman-Eisler*, edited by H. W. Dechert and M. Raupach, 199–206. The Hague: Mouton.

Heuft, B. 1999. *Eine prominenzbasiete Methode zur Prosodieanalyse und -synthese*. Frankfurt: Lang.

Holub, E. 2010. Does intonation matter? The impact of monotony on listener comprehension. *The Interpreters' Newsletter* 15, pp. 117–126.

Kade, O. 1963. Der Dolmetschvorgang und die Notation. Bedeutung und Aufgaben der Notiertechnik und des Notiersystems beim konsekutiven Dolmetschen. *Fremdsprachen* 7(1), pp. 12–20.

Kalina, S. 1998. *Strategische Prozesse beim Dolmetschen: Theoretische Grundlagen, empirische Fallstudien, didaktische Konsequenzen*. Tübingen: Narr.

Katamba, F. 1989. *An Introduction to Phonology*. London: Longman.

Key, M. R., ed. 1980. *The Relationship of Verbal and Nonverbal Communication*. The Hague: Mouton.

Kirchhoff, H. 1976. "Das Simultandolmetschen: Interdependenz der Variablen im Dolmetschprozeß, Dolmetschmodelle und Dolmetschstrategien". In *Theorie und Praxis des Übersetzens und Dolmetschens*, edited by H. W. Drescher and S. Scheffzek, 59–71. Frankfurt: Lang.

Kurz, I. 1989. "Conference Interpreting: User Expectations". In *Coming of Age: Proceedings of the 30th Annual Conference of the American Translators Association, Washington, DC, October 11–15, 1989*, edited by D. L. Harnmond, 143–148. Medford, NJ: Learned Information.

Kurz, I. 1993. Conference interpretation: expectations of different user groups. *The Interpreters' Newsletter* 5, pp. 13–21.

Kurz, I. 1997a. "Drahtseilakt ohne Netz? Live-Dolmetschen für die Medien". In *Berufsbilder für Übersetzer und Dolmetscher*, edited by I. Kurz and A. Moisl, 127–132. Wien: WUV.

Kurz, I. 1997b. "Getting the Message Across: Simultaneous Interpreting for the Media". In *Translation as Intercultural Communication: Selected Papers from the EST Congress, Prague 1995*, edited by M. Snell-Hornby, Z. Jettmarová and K. Kaindl, 195–205. Amsterdam: John Benjamins.

Kurz, I. and Pöchhacker, F. 1995. Quality in TV interpreting. *Translatio: Nouvelles de la FIT* 14(3/4), pp. 350–358.

Lee, T.-H. 1999. Speech proportion and accuracy in simultaneous interpretation from English into Korean. *Meta* 44(2), pp. 260–267.

Lehiste, I. 1970. *Suprasegmentals*. Cambridge, MA: The MIT Press.

Lehtonen, J. 1982. "Nonverbal Aspects of Impromptu Speech". In *Impromptu Speech: A Symposium*, edited by N. E. Enkvist, 33–45. Åbo: Åbo Akademi.

Levin, H., Baldwin, A. L., Gallwey, M. and Paivio, A. 1960. Audience stress, personality, and speech. *Journal of Abnormal and Social Psychology* 61(3), pp. 469–473.

Mead, P. 2002. *Évolution des pauses dans l'apprentissage de l'interprétation consécutive*. PhD Thesis. Université Lumière Lyon 2. Available from: http://theses.univ-lyon2.fr/documents/lyon2/2002/mead_p/download [Accessed 19 December 2015].

Meak, L. 1990. Interprétation simultanée et congrès medical: attentes et commentaires. *The Interpreters' Newsletter* 3, pp. 8–13.

Moser, P. 1996. Expectations of users of conference interpretation. *Interpreting* 1(2), pp. 145–178.

Nafá Waasaf, M. L. 2007. Intonation and the structural organization of texts in simultaneous interpreting. *Interpreting* 9(2), pp. 177–198.

Praat, 2015. *Praat: Doing phonetics by computer*. Available from: http://www.fon.hum.uva.nl/praat/ [Accessed 17 December 2015].

Pradas Macías, E. M. 2004. *La fluidez y sus pausas: enfoque desde la interpretación de conferencias*. Albolote (Granada): Comares.

Pétursson, M. and Neppert, J. 1996. *Elementarbuch der Phonetik*. 2nd ed. Hamburg: Buske.

QuaSI, 2010. *Quality in Simultaneous Interpreting.* Available from: http://quasi.univie.ac.at [Accessed 15 December 2015].

Rennert, S. 2010. The impact of fluency on the subjective assessment of interpreting quality. *The Interpreters' Newsletter* 15, pp. 101–115.

Rennert, S. 2013. "The Production of Experimental Material for Fluency Research". In *Quality in Interpreting: Widening the Scope.* Vol. 1, edited by O. García Becerra, E. M. Pradas Macías and R. Barranco-Droege, 175–200. Granada: Comares.

Royé, H.-W. 1983. *Segmentierung und Hervorhebungen in gesprochener deutscher Standardsprache. Analyse eines Polylogs.* Tübingen: Niemeyer.

Schönherr, B. 1997. *Syntax – Prosodie – nonverbale Kommunikation: Empirische Untersuchungen zur Interaktion sprachlicher und parasprachlicher Ausdrucksmittel im Gespräch.* Tübingen: Niemeyer.

Shlesinger, M. 1994. "Intonation in the Production and Perception of Simultaneous Interpretation". In *Bridging the Gap: Empirical Research in Simultaneous Interpretation,* edited by S. Lambert and B. Moser-Mercer, 225–236. Amsterdam: Benjamins.

Stüker, S., Cho, E., Fügen, C., Hermann, T., Kilgour, K., Mediani, M., Mohr, C., Niehues, J., Rottmann, K. and Waibel, A. 2014. "Ein System zur automatischen simultanen Übersetzung deutscher Vorlesungen". In *Translationswissenschaftliches Kolloquium. Beiträge zur Übersetzungs- und Dolmetschwissenschaft (Köln/Germersheim),* edited by B. Ahrens, S. Hansen-Schirra, M. Krein-Kühle, M. Schreiber and U. Wienen, 267–280. Frankfurt: Lang.

Tissi, B. 2000. Silent pauses and disfluencies in simultaneous interpretation: a descriptive analysis. *The Interpreters' Newsletter* 10, pp. 103–127.

Vaissière, J. 1983. "Language-independent Prosodic Features". In *Prosody: Models and Measurements,* edited by A. Cutler and D. R. Ladd, 53–66. Berlin: Springer.

Williams, S. 1995. Observations on anomalous stress in interpreting. *The Translator* 1(1), pp. 47–64.

Verbmobil. 2000. Available from: http://verbmobil.dfki.de [Accessed 17 December 2015].

Wahlster, W., ed. 2000. *Verbmobil: Foundations of Speech-to-Speech Translation.* Berlin: Springer.

Zwischenberger, C. 2013. *Qualität und Rollenbilder beim simultanen Konferenzendolmetschen.* Berlin: Frank & Timme.

Part II
Meaning making

Part II

Meaning making

Non-verbal communication and interpreting

Benoît Krémer and Claudia Mejía Quijano

Introduction and historical perspectives

Non-verbal communication has been explored from standpoints so varied that Poyatos (2003) maintains that it is best studied using an interdisciplinary approach. Poyatos explicitly includes interpretation among the disciplines which would stand to benefit from research in this area, but non-verbal communication has received scant attention in the specialist interpretation literature, or, more accurately, it has been discussed from various different angles, in a fragmented fashion.

As many scholars note (Gile 1995; Ahrens 2004, 14–46; Diriker 2004, 7–25; Seeber 2015), interpreting research has undergone many developments in terms of both its main focus (description, prescription, teaching) and its methods (scientific studies, models, inter-disciplinarity). Researchers have increasingly considered interpreting as an activity in context (Stenzl 1983; Pöchhacker 1994; Kalina 1998; Diriker 2004), and have therefore included non-verbal elements (prosody, intonation, situation) in their analyses. However, they have concentrated on these elements individually without integrating them into coherent acts of speech. We consider the act of speech that lies at the heart of the interpreting situation not as a simple juxtaposition or addition of discrete items that should be studied in isolation, but as parts of a whole which, as such, should be studied using an all-encompassing approach. This lack of theoretical coherence on the part of interpretation scholars is all the more surprising given that:

(a) non-verbal communication is one of the elements that sets interpretation most clearly apart from translation; as Seleskovitch observes (1968, 50) with unwitting relevance to our discussion here, "the interpreter is in the presence of people, not texts" (we shall come back to this below);

(b) since interpretation became a profession, interpreters themselves have stressed the importance of non-verbal aspects of communication for their work (Thiéry 1970, 1974);

(c) there has been a fervent debate among professionals about the use of technology for remote sound and image transmission, where interpretation takes place largely in the absence of non-verbal elements (AIIC 2011; Mouzourakis 2006).

In this chapter, we identify the key functions of non-verbal aspects of communication for the purposes of both the work of interpreters and the theoretical advancement of the field. This will allow us to shed further light on the role played by non-verbal aspects of communication in interpreter training, as well as in changes in the interpreting profession.

Interpretation as a transfer practice

The communication scenario with which we are concerned here exhibits a number of specific traits which set it apart from ordinary communication scenarios.

Firstly, the interpreter's role is unusual in that rather than merely listening to the speech, s/he is also its future co-sender (Thiéry 1970). Since the interpreter is not the original source of the meaning being conveyed (Prieto 1993; Chernov 2004), s/he must comprehend it and make it his/her own with a view to becoming the co-sender of this meaning in a language other than that of the original. This requires a level of comprehension which is much more thorough-going and exhaustive than that of a mere listener.

Secondly, the message is addressed to a (group of) listener(s) who, by definition, is equipped to understand the initial message only if the interpreter has performed his/her task to perfection. The interpreter carries out a *transfer practice* which is a crucial part of the communication (Mejía Quijano and Marmolejo 2010) and upon which the meaning shared between speaker and audience ultimately depends. This is the reason for our focus on the role, not of impromptu interpreters, but on professional interpreters who have the training and experience necessary to know how the profession works and where its pitfalls lie. We also look exclusively at simultaneous conference interpretation, though some of our findings are relevant to other types of interpretation.

Unlike listeners to a message being conveyed "directly", without transfer from one language to another, the interpreter is not merely a receiver of that message. Rather, s/he is actively involved in appropriating it and reformulating it. Due to the complexity of these tasks, which is heightened by the near-simultaneous manner in which they are performed, the interpreter is dependent upon any element that may assist with them, including non-verbal communication – the role of which we shall now explore.

Core issues and topics

Context of the interpretation scenario

For any speaker, ideas are a kind of magma from which s/he extracts the meaning that s/he wishes to express. Once the speaker has arranged these ideas in the right order, s/he selects the words in which s/he intends to clothe them and utters them aloud; this utterance marks the beginning of an act of speech. In a monolingual scenario, the speaker addresses the listeners directly. In a multilingual one, the original speaker needs the interpreter's assistance in order to reach all of the listeners present. Strictly speaking, then, the interpreter is not a listener but a co-speaker who must appropriate the oral message in its entirety (Seleskovitch 1968), picking up on all the aspects of the speaker's message (nuances, intentions), comprehending the content of the discourse and the meaning behind the act of speech, and also remaining receptive to any (potentially relevant) indications (see below) which may be spontaneously produced.

To these ends, the interpreter actively decodes the speaker's message. In so doing, in addition to his/her training, experience and practice, s/he calls firstly upon any general knowledge relevant to what is being said:

- Specific preparation for the conference: research on the subject in hand, terminology and key issues
- Knowledge of the content and topic of the conference
- Knowledge of the cultural context of the conference

Secondly, the interpreter calls upon his/her knowledge of the participants and contextual information about them:

- The speaker: origin, education, speaking habits (accent, idiolect, voice, pace), communicative and pedagogical skills
- The speaker's intentions: to inform, to persuade, to provoke, to influence
- Who the interlocutors are: specialist or non-specialist audience, level of preparation
- The audience's expectations
- The interaction between speaker and audience: unilateral communication, dialogue, questions and answers, number of participants

Finally, the interpreter takes into account the specific circumstances in which the meeting is taking place:

- Overall setting (conference, symposium, presentation, interview) and purpose (dialogue, exchange, uni- or multidirectional communication)
- Location (atmosphere, historical buildings, protected sites)
- Time (date, period of historical significance, time of day)

This is so as not to lose sight of the ultimate goal (*skopos*, Vermeer 1989) of the communication in which the interpreter is involved: despite the intricacies of each individual speaker's argument, their overall contributions move along "lines" which are intended to lead somewhere (exchange of scientific or technical information, general agreement on a position or specific agreement on a text, trade or diplomatic negotiations, etc.).

These components form the backdrop for the interpreter's work, but they are not necessarily elements of non-verbal communication. They are the pre-existing circumstances of the interpretation scenario. Since they may shape meaning, however, they can sometimes give rise to the use of non-verbal elements of communication.

The interpretation process (1): From speaker to interpreter, or active comprehension

During the act of interpreting, these pre-existing circumstances offer resources which the interpreter calls upon and applies to the utterance in context, combining his/her comprehension of the discourse with his/her assessment of the relevance of the codified or spontaneous non-verbal components which appear alongside it.

Naturally, the interpreter draws primarily on the part of the message consciously expressed by the speaker. This is made up of words, on the one hand, and all the other meanings conveyed by the speaker for the audience's discernment on the other: deliberate gestures (particularly when these function as the non-linguistic equivalents of indexical words), deliberate facial expressions, moving around, images, diagrams or other supporting material for the speech, and so on. Such voluntary output is often sufficiently culturally coded for the speaker to be able to use it in support of the spoken words and rely on the listener's ability to understand it (Buyssens 1943).

These elements have been expressly identified by those who generally underline the role of non-verbal communication in interpretation. However, most of the meanings conveyed by voluntary non-verbal elements very frequently prove superfluous in practice when compared with the verbal utterance itself (because the speaker reads diagrams out or explains images) or with the speaker's prosody (specific intonation for indexical words). This partly explains why they have tended not to be subject to a specific or more in-depth theoretical focus. As an example, Seleskovitch and Lederer (1986, 48) insist on "verbal context" ("*le contexte verbal*") and "cognitive context" ("*le contexte cognitif*") as playing a major part in the interpreter's comprehension process. Thiéry (1990, 43) identifies "situation analysis" as a useful tool for the interpreter, but limited to the "purpose of communication".

However, another part of the message is made up of indications within the act of speech which the speaker emits involuntarily. These come in many forms, but are often oral and acoustic, such as:

- Voice levels: volume may reveal stress; trembling may betray underlying emotions
- Tempo: an increase in the pace at which words are produced may, for example, allow the speaker to skip a controversial idea, or there may be a slowdown in the pace caused by hesitation over whether the words selected are the right ones
- Pronunciation: diction may become clearer in order to stress an important idea, or fatigue may lead to mumbling
- Coincidental noises: tongue or finger clicking in accordance with cultural habits, for instance

Such indications may also take on a visual or kinaesthetic form, such as:

- Spontaneous gestures: from micro-gestures, which are perceptible but discreet and betray suppressed emotion, to sweeping arm or body movements caused by irrepressible emotion
- Involuntary but culturally conditioned gestures: hands or fingers in a specific position or shape, usually appearing alongside a particular expression or state of mind
- Facial expressions: winking, frowning and other expressions which reveal the speaker's underlying mood, such as amusement, irony or disgust
- Deliberate glances towards a particular part of or person in the room while emphasising a specific idea or asking for corroboration from a particular individual

Lists of elements that may contribute to non-verbal communication, such as those offered by Poyatos (1985, 1986), suggest that there is an innumerable and perhaps even infinite array of these involuntary indications. Ferdinand de Saussure went so far as to assert that any object or occurrence perceptible to human beings may carry meaning:

> *En me promenant, je fais sans rien dire une encoche sur un arbre, comme par plaisir.*
> *La personne qui m'accompagne garde l'idée de cette encoche, et il est incontestable*

qu'elle associe deux ou trois idées à cette encoche dès ce moment, alors que je n'avais pas moi-même d'autre idée que de la mystifier ou de m'amuser. – Toute chose matérielle est déjà pour nous signe: c'est-à-dire impression que nous associons à d'autres, mais la chose matérielle paraît indispensable. [While out walking, without saying a word, I make a notch in the bark of a tree, as if for my own amusement. My companion records the memory of the notch and, from that very moment, undeniably links one or two other ideas with that of the notch, when in fact my sole purpose was just to mystify this person or to entertain myself. For us, any material thing immediately constitutes a *sign*, that is to say an impression that we associate with other impressions, but it would seem that the material thing is crucial.]

(Saussure 1974, 40; tr. Peter Clayburn)

The interpreter has to sift through this infinite range of involuntary indications, judging how relevant each is to the comprehension of the speech. Scholars have tried to identify objective criteria upon which this selection process is based; one possibility is that certain indications display a spontaneous, innate and natural quality that allows them to steer the interpreter reliably through the deduction process (Poyatos 1987; Besson *et al.* 2005; Seeber 2012). However, some indications are commonly deemed natural while also being recognised as stemming from cultural habit. These include the volume of a speaker's voice: as a natural indication, this would suggest emotion on the part of the speaker, but the bounds of this parameter also depend on cultural habits in the speaker's community.

Here, as elsewhere, interpreters are obliged to work on a case-by-case basis. But in so doing, they are fortunate enough to benefit from the guidance of two powerful beacons.

Coherence and redundancy: The two guides in active comprehension

The interpreter's task is not to imbibe these non-verbal elements in isolation and decide whether s/he should or should not interpret them for his/her audience (Poyatos 1987). Rather, interpreters must include whatever elements they deem pertinent to their overall comprehension in its entirety and thereby equip themselves to present that whole to the listener. As the interpretation scenario unfolds, one excellent guide to how relevant involuntary indications may be is their coherence, not only among themselves, but also with the voluntary information provided and, above all, with the pre-existing circumstances of the interpretation scenario. For instance, the likelihood that the index "muffled voice" will carry meaning is greater when it appears alongside the corresponding indications "speaker is emotional" and "account of tragic experiences" than when it is accompanied by the indications "speaker has a cold" and "microphone not working properly".

The interpreter must also beware of one of the foremost constants in communication, namely the redundancy of certain indications: a muffled voice may reveal nothing more than a hoarse speaker. One isolated indication is not enough to produce relevant meaning. As Chernov has it, the interpreter's anticipation is based on "the redundancy of discourse, both objective (linguistic) and subjective (extralinguistic) and the inferencing ability of the simultaneous interpreter" (Chernov 2004, 174).

Prosody performs a particular role in all of this due to its position at the halfway point between verbal elements (intonation, stress) and non-verbal ones (pace, volume, etc.): prosody often acts together with a gesture or a glance, and this sometimes leads efficiency-seeking interpreters to prioritise it as their only source of information, or even to deny themselves other inputs, by closing their eyes to concentrate solely on the speaker's voice and words. Interpreters should exercise caution in this regard, however, for certain unexpected and meaningful effects, such as irony, may result from this linguistic "double act" by dint of the undermining of redundancy between prosody and gesture: some in the audience may be laughing at a gesture on the speaker's part which was out of kilter with the explicit meaning of the speech, and if the interpreter misses this, s/he will be unable to include this information in his/her rendition.

The tool of redundancy requires skill. Interpreters cannot leave it completely aside, but nor can they depend on it wholly as a means of economising on work, for only the coherence of the information provided in its entirety reveals the true value of any redundancy in the speech. This coherence may allow the interpreter to "correct" the verbal speech being transmitted when this does not fulfil its communicative function but other functions which are key to the goal of the meeting. For instance, at one meeting, where the atmosphere was relaxed and the participants were agreeing on a particular point, a speaker (taking the floor in French, which was not his native tongue) smiled broadly while congratulating the French delegate who had taken the floor before him, saying, "*Je souscris à vos propos. Vous avez dit avant moi, mais moins bien que moi, ce que je voulais dire.*" ["I agree with you. You said what I wanted to say before I did, but *less well than I did*."] The interpreter recognised the relevance of the indications showing her that the words actually spoken were an involuntary slip (the difficulty of double negatives and litotes for non-native speakers, a distaste for irony on the part of the speaker, and so on) and thus corrected the idea, taking into account the backdrop of the interpretation scenario and allowing the aim of the meeting to have the final say in her decision. This example shows not that the interpreter was unfaithful to the speaker's intention but, on the contrary, that she paid heed to the overall intention, taking into account all the elements, including non-verbal elements, of the communication scenario.

Coherence between verbal aspects, non-verbal aspects and the circumstances of the interpretation scenario is thus pivotal in the specific interpretation processes of inference and anticipation.

The role of non-verbal communication in comprehending an act of speech

These elements of non-verbal communication perform several functions. As in the case of the usual process of comprehension:

- They allow interpreters to understand the verbal elements. In all languages, words are polysemous: they never have one single meaning, but rather a number of potential meanings. Once a word is combined with other words in a sentence, it becomes less polysemous; the communication scenario in which a sentence appears further determines its meaning, but one or several non-verbal elements sometimes allow a final decision to be made as to what the overall utterance means by clarifying which of the word's potential meanings is intended by the speaker. In a given act of speech, then, non-verbal elements are, first and foremost, necessary for accurately determining the meaning of elements of verbal communication.
- They allow interpreters to complete or nuance the information provided in the speaker's verbal message by adding, for instance, the underlying intentions behind the communication. Language is also ruled by an economy principle: an act of speech always involves the sharing of the information conveyed by the means concurrently available. Considerable economy can be achieved by virtue of the simultaneous employment of several means of communication, and speakers do not deny themselves such opportunities.
- They allow the non-communicative function of words to be revealed when personal circumstances involuntarily interfere with the speech (slips, emotions).

- They allow interpreters to ensure that they have understood the verbal message by confirming its content or by adding corroborating elements to it.
- They allow interpreters to anticipate relevant pieces of information before they are unveiled in full or completely confirmed. Gestures are known to precede words by a few fractions of a second; a clenched fist may thus herald a vehement assertion, a faltering voice may introduce a moving idea and a furrowed brow may announce a worrying thought.

This last function is a necessary part of the interpreter's message: in addition to his/her linguistic and grammatical anticipation of the speaker's message, the interpreter uses all available indications (including visual and kinaesthetic ones) to predict the direction in which the speech will proceed. This advance "information" is of considerable help to interpreters in preparing their strategic moves; their task is to ascertain (a) whether these indications are relevant to the meaning of the message, for which they rely on the overall coherence; (b) whether they will make the information gathered explicit in their version; and (c) if so, by what means.

The interpretation process (2): From comprehension to production, or transfer

Anticipation is crucial because it affords the interpreter enough time to transfer the semantic content of the original into another language. It can be assumed that this process is possible because all relevant information is synthesised at a functional level less abstract than that of language and closer to individual and sensory experience, which makes it less cumbersome and more reliable.

In the process of drawing as close as possible to the meaning of the speaker's message, the interpreter takes advantage of anything which may allow him/her to construct a specific type of mental image (Chernov 2004) which is to an extent detached from the words of any specific language (Krémer 2013, 2016).

These mental images, which interpreters use as the basic tool for the transfer process, are not photographs, mirrors or reflections of a given thing. They have meaning, but are not precise, established icons or symbols in a particular culture. Firstly, they are completely personal to interpreters themselves in each individual scenario: they allow a speech to elicit images linked to their own experience. For that speech, the images will take on a meaning at that point in time and in light of the circumstances of that scenario. The function of the non-verbal elements is to help create these mental images in the interpreter's mind; to the "direct" information provided by words and phrases, non-verbal elements add more "contextual" information which brings the situation being reported coherently to life. The message as assembled by the interpreter is thus no longer only a linear sequence of words to be translated, but rather a set of three-dimensional situations which can almost be visualised.

Such images have a certain semantic depth: they are a reduction of all the information gleaned in the comprehension phase, a kind of staging of the message akin to that of the poet recounting real-life experiences:

> When gathering legends, a poet collects for a particular scene only the *props* in the strictly theatrical sense of the term; once the actors have exited the stage, a particular object remains – a flower on the floor, perhaps – which lingers in one's memory and shows more or less what has occurred.
>
> (Saussure 1986, 220)

The most intense form of non-verbal communication is painting, where the lack of words and a third dimension does not prevent an event from being recounted, as in the work by Chardin in Figure 5.1, for instance. The name of the painting is "Boy with a spinning top". Bolens (2013) analyses it as follows: the image depicts a child in contemporary attire; before him is a flat surface upon which we see an object, and in the background appear a quill, some paper and a book. We see that the child's gaze is set upon the object in question: a spinning top. But we also know that the top is constantly moving, because it has not yet fallen over. Similarly, we know that the child is the one who spun the top in the first place because his right hand is still in a very specific position: the ends of his fingers are pressed together, having only a moment ago clasped the top of the toy and set it in motion. By portraying all of this so precisely, the painting allows our comprehension to go beyond what is actually depicted: from the objects in the background (books and writing implements), we can deduce that the child was supposed to be studying, but was more interested in playing. These conclusions are brought to us by our own experience. They are not expressly "stated" in the painting; we draw upon the knowledge we have acquired elsewhere to instill a meaning in the scene before us. That meaning may range from the thoroughly superficial (the depiction of a moment in the life of a child) to the thoroughly profound (a warning against the dangers of idleness).

For transfer to succeed, the interpreter will let his/her imagination summon to the surface similar images evoked by the speech. Unlike paintings, however, these images are not static: with each new idea, the image will be corrected, altered or perhaps completely reworked.

Figure 5.1   *Boy with a spinning top* by Jean-Baptiste-Siméon Chardin. Credit: L'Enfant au toton, Portrait d'Auguste Gabriel Godefroy (1728–1813), fils cadet du joaillier Charles Godefroy. Vers 1736 | Chardin Jean Baptiste Siméon (1699–1779) peintre | Photo © Musée du Louvre, Paris, Dist. RMN-Grand Palais – © Angèle Dequier

In this sense, there is a clear link between this process on the part of the interpreter and the oneiric activity: in dreams, we experience mental images which are constantly evolving, with characters who undergo transformations and situations which change without the described reality's losing its relevance. The phenomenon undergone by the interpreter listening attentively to a speech is similar to this except that, unlike the sleeper who forgets these images on emerging from slumber, the interpreter constructs this silent scene with the purpose of telling the story more deftly.

This honing of mental images, which the interpreter performs at a more sensory and almost latent level of conscious activity, allows transfer to take place more quickly. Listening and re-expressing content are complex and highly abstract mental processes so it is clearly economically profitable to call upon a more automatic type of cerebral function to assist with the transfer process. However, in terms of their role in communication, we might also compare these moving mental images with the magma of thought mentioned above (that is to say, the starting point which is in fact a prerequisite for any act of speech): one must be able to conceive initially what one wants to say before one can say it (Prieto 1975) and interpreters' mental images combine their comprehension of the speaker's message with their own experience and memorial record of reality, constructing the speaker's meaning on the basis of their own sensory experience. They can therefore conceive of the meaning to be transferred non-linguistically and thereby "take the floor" as an individual wishing to put a meaning into words, striving to ascribe linguistic form to their communicative intention, rather than as mere messengers parroting someone else's words.

The desire to adopt the role of co-speaker makes the interpreter a fully fledged contributor to the communication scenario by giving him/her the status of "participant" rather than a third party external to the act of speech. Only when s/he becomes a true co-sender of the message can s/he really address the audience in this other language which s/he shares with them. The interpreter's speech, now freed from the linguistic clothing in which it was received, benefits from the fluency which comes with spontaneity, and can easily leave room for creativity, which makes the task of speech production less burdensome and more pleasant for the interpreter.

Because non-verbal elements are more sensory and less abstract than verbal content and form a coherent whole, they are a crucial tool for the interpreter at this point in the transfer process.

The interpretation process (3): Co-sending

The interpreter is now equipped with the specific content to be re-expressed, which is in his or her mind in the form of images; this content is tantamount to what the speaker wanted to say. The interpreter can now turn to producing the speech in another language.

Even at this stage, however, non-verbal communication has an important role to play. Though barely, if at all, visible to their audience, interpreters do not deliver their speeches like emotionless robots; over the course of their work, they too become responsible for sending the message. For this reason, albeit in the artificial surroundings of a simultaneous interpretation booth and with no one there to witness it directly, they recreate a complete act of speech. This means that they do not limit themselves to verbal elements, but include non-verbal elements of communication. Changes in voice and prosody and physical movements and gestures, be they conscious or subconscious, can be observed at this stage because the interpreter is addressing the audience as a co-sender of the message.

We might assume non-verbal communication to be superfluous here, given that no one is able to witness the corresponding indications and the only link between the interpreter and the listeners is the sound of the interpreter's voice transmitted through the technical equipment (microphone, wires and earpieces). But this assumption overlooks, firstly, the role which non-verbal communication plays at this stage in the interpreter's own sense of conviction. Meaning is elusive, and interpreters must convince themselves before they can convince others. To achieve this, they must listen to and remain in control of the speeches they produce. The purpose of this is to monitor their language for formal accuracy and to ensure that the content they are expressing (a) tallies with the message as they have understood it and (b) forms a coherent whole, both as an idea in isolation and as one idea in a sequence of ideas.

Secondly, as we observed above, redundancy is a constant feature of communication, and within the interpreting booth, a furious hand gesture is inseparable from the agitated prosody of the spoken word which conveys the irritation discerned in the speaker. No speech is truly comprehensible without the prosodic features corresponding to the meaning being conveyed, and all prosodic features come with their own gestures in a kind of communicative synaes-thesia. Interpreters' voices are a unique combination of verbal and non-verbal traits, and their art involves using these traits in order to perform their role as co-senders and co-speakers. Non-verbal communication is their most useful accomplice in this task: the best way to try to convince an audience is by using tone, hesitation and suspense, controlling breathing, uttering some phrases more quickly and others more slowly, conveying a note of interrogation and including moments of silence.

In addition, because of the need for communicative synaesthesia, if interpreters exhibit a lack of non-verbal communication in the booth, their prosody becomes monotonous. This makes it seem to the listener that the interpreter is not addressing his or her speech to anyone in particular, akin to a speaker reading a "written" text aloud without having familiarised him- or herself with it first. The fact that the audience cannot see the interpreter's gestures and expressions does not mean that the interpreter is not addressing that audience in the usual way. Communication is usually established when a speech is addressed to a listener; when the listening is being done in a language other than the speaker's, the recipient is left in no doubt that the message is not being addressed directly to him or her if the prosody is that of a robot, and there is a chance that the listener will stop focusing on the speaker's message and give up his or her role as a recipient of it. It is therefore preferable for interpreters to accept the audience's surprise at their "antics" in the booth rather than run the risk of failing to achieve their foremost task.

The non-verbal communication of the listeners themselves is no less important for the interpreter at this stage in the process of co-sending: if, for instance, certain members of the audience nod, show signs of satisfaction or appear to be convinced while listening to the interpretation, this shows the interpreter that s/he has established a line of communication between the participants. In addition, by looking at the listeners, the interpreter can assess whether they have understood the speech. Finally, if the same non-verbal signals are coming from the entire audience, the interpreter has successfully conveyed the speaker's message. Non-verbal elements thus allow both the speaker and the interpreter to monitor the listeners' comprehension of the message and to correct, nuance and improve this if need be.

Current debates

The role of non-verbal communication in theorising and teaching interpretation as opposed to translation

In order to convey a speaker's message to an audience after having re-expressed it in a different language, the interpreter requires a thorough understanding of the initial message.

The same is true of translators, but for them the entire message is contained in the text being translated; all relevant information is to be found there, for otherwise the reader would be unable to reconstitute the message. A text is thus a canvas of words, but made up of language-bound discourse interwoven with non-verbal elements of the act of speech which may be made explicit using equivalent words or inserted in the text by other means (punctuation, syntax or layout, for example).

Poyatos (1994) partly developed his theory of non-verbal communication on the basis of literary characterisation (see, for instance, his 1994 work on Don Quixote). Similarly, a new wave of literary analysis is focusing on the existence of non-verbal, and especially kinaesthetic, elements in literary texts (Bolens 2008, 2013); this highlights authors' skill in including these elements of the reality being described. Rather surprisingly, then, non-verbal communication has been studied using essentially "linguistic" texts!

In interpretation, all elements of the message are delivered at the moment when the act of communication takes place and as a coherent whole. Actual words are only one part of this, and are inserted into the broader mass of non-verbal elements of communication. This explains why depictions of the interpretation profession have always involved throwing into relief certain non-verbal elements which feature in the interpretation scenario. Both in photos of interpreters at Nuremberg and in the celebrated Egyptian bas-relief, Horemheb and the Syrians/Nubians (see Figure 5.2), hand gestures and bodily posture need no assistance in informing the spectator of the interpretation scenario being portrayed. Yet, there is a lack of scholarly work on and theoretical coherence around non-verbal communication in interpreting, as though this were an optional addition to the theory of interpretation. Seleskovitch and Lederer, for instance, underscore the importance of what we above term the pre-existing circumstances of the interpretation scenario, but those circumstances are somewhat confused with non-verbal elements in the strictest sense, voluntary or otherwise, under the umbrella of "verbal interaction":

If the interpreting booth does not look out over the room, the interpreters must at least have some kind of view of it. The reasons for this are clear; the same prerequisites apply to all verbal interactions. In order to do their work properly, interpreters need not only to see the person speaking (this is frequently observed and widely understood); it is equally pivotal for them the see the person or people whom they themselves are addressing. The close-up view of the speaker provided by a screen is undoubtedly often superior in every respect to a direct view of the room, for facial expressions, movements and gestures are clearly perceptible in it. This is of undeniably significant assistance in elucidating the meaning of the speaker's words.

(Seleskovitch and Lederer 2002, 363)

Perhaps it is only with new technologies spurring major changes in the way in which some speakers prepare their speeches (PowerPoints, images and audio and video recordings) and new findings on non-verbal communication in general coming to light, that the need to uncover these non-verbal elements is becoming clear.

In any case, it is crucial to stress the distinction between theorisation in Translation Studies and in Interpretation Studies, and the differing roles which non-verbal communication plays in each of these. Unless work on interpretation takes into account the reality of the act of speech as a coherent, composite whole which includes elements of non-verbal communication in a simultaneous syntactic system, such scholarship will run the risk of becoming a study of translation, with its linear syntax. This will obstruct the path to research focusing on the theory of interpretation proper, and it will skew the work done on translation.

Figure 5.2   Ancient Egypt: Horemheb and the Syrians/Nubians (with the interpreter on the left)
Source: National Museum of Antiquities, Leiden.

Future directions

We have thus far adopted the term "non-verbal communication" to refer to the phenomenon being studied here. Having completed our discussion of the various functions which this performs in interpretation, however, we should consider this expression in the particular context of the field of interpretation.

Firstly, the label suffers the major disadvantage of being negative: *non*-verbal communication refers to all elements of the act of communication which do not involve oral expression of words or phrases. This paves the way for a number of different effects: one may include sociolinguistic aspects, visual or kinaesthetic considerations, or psychological and even neurological factors. These aspects are often merely listed without clear explanation, however, which makes the task of determining what they are supposed to cover difficult; each author includes whichever components s/he sees fit, according to his/her own custom, which leads to misunderstandings. Nor does this negated form allow a distinction to be made between the circumstances of the interpretation scenario and non-verbal elements in the stricter sense; this conflation of factors prevents the phenomenon from being accurately studied and, to an even greater extent, practice and teaching from being brought more into step with the findings.

The second drawback of the term "non-verbal communication" is that it includes the notion of "verbal", which refers to the fact that the message requires words, and that those words are uttered *orally*. We cannot restrict the notion of "verbal" to purely acoustic output, however, for the idea of "non-verbal" is also partly linked to prosody. Prosody does comprise non-linguistic features (geographically marked accents, emotions, pace, etc.) as well as linguistic ones (distinctive accents, intonation marking syntax). Prosody may thus be deemed at once "verbal" and "non-verbal", which means that it is as impossible to account for it in non-verbal communication as it is to omit it! In sum, the scope of the term "verbal" does not map onto the field of interpretation, and always roots theoretical work in predominantly "linguistic" concerns.

This leaves the term "communication", which is ambiguous here at the very least. Does "non-verbal communication" mean communicating without any recourse to words? If this is the case, the only true case of non-verbal communication is that which the deaf practise on a daily basis when they use various sign languages. While our focus here has not been on the "verbal", it goes without saying that we at no point considered examining communication in which no words were involved. To be more precise, then, "non-verbal communication" refers not to a type of "communication" but to the "non-linguistic" components of communication in general.

In this chapter, we have striven to focus upon the role played in simultaneous conference interpretation by a series of elements which, while distinct from linguistic aspects, are no less pivotal in communication. They may potentially appear against the backdrop of the interpretation scenario and its particular circumstances, ranging from the way in which words are uttered to the elements or features which are indeed present via all that a given speaker produces. But they only ever include features which carry meaning for the speaker. In other words, these are devices through which speakers deliberately, though not always consciously, manifest their ideas in a form perceptible to others.

Rather than their properties (acoustic, visual, kinaesthetic, objective, etc.), it is the fact that these features play a semantic role in the act of communication that makes them part of it. Their meaning may be pre-established, in the case of culturally coded items, or forged in the act when discourse converges with other elements, making them similar to indications. They are meaningful signs or interpretable indications which we can now term semiological, to give them a positive label in accordance with the tenets of Saussure's "semiology", a discipline which focuses on precisely these "non-verbal" elements (Buyssens 1943; Barthes 1964; Prieto 1975, 1991, 1993; Saussure 1957, 1974, 1986, 2006).

These semiological elements are key for interpreters because as co-senders of the message they require an active understanding of the speech through which they can furnish themselves with a "mental staging" of the message. This allows them to use a parallel act of speech to recreate their own version of the speech in another language. Without these semiological elements, the act of speech is incomplete, and the amount of information available to interpreters for comprehending the speaker's message fully and assuming their role as true co-speakers is subsequently reduced.

Implications for practice

Semiological elements and current developments in the interpreting profession

Recent technical developments allowing interpreters not to work in the meeting room, that is to say the setting in which the communication between speaker and audience is taking place, but to follow the debate remotely (see Mouzourakis 2006, 46) pose a problem where the interpreter's task is concerned.

Besides fatigue, which surfaces more quickly in such conditions (Moser-Mercer 2005) because less information is available to the interpreter, meaning that semantic uncertainty increases and the interpreter's task is more arduous, interpreters find themselves confronted with a fragmented view of the communication scenario. The screen conveying the image to the interpreters shows only part of what is going on in the room (speaker's face, PowerPoint slides), and not necessarily other elements which might feed into their perception of the overall act of speech (audience reactions, extraneous events, sufficient close-up of the podium). Interpreters are dependent upon the producers' or camera technicians' decisions, which are informed by those individuals' own objectives, as well as on the speed of their reactions when something which may lead the interpreters to require a different view occurs.

Only when the full importance of the act of speech, taken as an inseparable whole which combines semiological and linguistic elements, has been recognised will it be possible to draw conclusions about research on Interpretation Studies and about the conditions in which remote interpreting can be carried out.

We must also assess the psychological processes in play where the personality of the interpreter is concerned: the need to identify with first the speaker and then the audience engenders a sense of insecurity which triggers natural defence mechanisms. The most powerful of these is splitting, where the interpreter sees the various tasks which s/he is being asked to carry out not as a single whole but as a succession of separate operations, some of which s/he prioritises over others. In order to move beyond this fragmented approach, the mental images which form interpreters' real-life experiences reconstitute their own identity and, by allowing them to overcome the fragmentation, enable them to bask in the glory of the job (well done).

Finally, before a specific pedagogy of interpretation will be able to hone new teaching methods it is necessary to gain a more thorough understanding of (a) the semiological work behind the interpreter's selection of which content, out of all the voluntary signs and involuntary indications available, to retain to convey the message; (b) the role of coherence and redundancy between semiological and linguistic elements; and (c) the formation of the interpreter's mental staging of the message. These would ensure transfer of the highest quality and offer tools tailored to the different types of interpretation, the number of which is increasing. With audiovisual technologies becoming ever more present in daily life and work in our societies, and given the fragmentation of the interpreter's work to which this can give rise, those tools cannot come soon enough.

Further reading

Eco, U. 1977. *A Theory of Semiotics*. London and Basingstoke: Macmillan.
A general introduction to semiotics, which discusses signs and codes and is particularly interesting in its approaches of cultural influences, disambiguation, undercoding and overcoding.

Feyereisen, P. and de Lannoy, J.-D. 1991. *Gestures and Speech: Psychological Investigations*. Cambridge: Cambridge University Press.
This book gives a general approach of the role of gestures in speech and communication, including an analysis of "body language". Chapter 3 ("Autonomy of gestures and speech") analyses gestural cues to emotion, the interaction between verbal and non-verbal communication and the interpretation of discrepant messages.

Wadensjö, C. 1998. *Interpreting as Interaction*. London and New York: Longman.
Presents context, objectives and roles of the participants in interpreting interaction with a view to making sense of the utterances in a communicative and social perspective.

Related topics

Semiotics and translation.

References

AIIC. 2011. *Conference and Remote Interpreting: A New Turning Point?* Available from: http://aiic.net/page/3590/conference-and-remote-interpreting-a-new-turning-point/lang/1 [Accessed 3 February 2016].

Ahrens, B. 2004. *Prosodie beim Simultandolmetschen*, Publikationen des FASK GermersheimFrankfurt-am-Main/Berlin: Peter Lang.

Barthes, R. 1964. "Eléments de sémiologie". *Communications No. 4*. Paris, France, Seuil.

Besson, C., Graf, D., Hartung, I., Kropfhäusser, B. and Voisard, S. 2005. "The Importance of Non-Verbal Communication in Professional Interpretation". Paper prepared for a BA course at the FTI, University of Geneva. Available from: http://aiic.net/page/1662/the-importance-of-non-verbal-communication-in-professional-interpretation/lang/1.

Bolens, G. 2008. *Le style des gestes. Corporéite et kinésie dans le récit littéraire*. Lausanne: Editions BHMS.

Bolens, G. 2013. "La trace des signifiants et l'analyse littéraire". *Ferdinand de Saussure: neurosciences, psychanalyse et sémiologie*, workshop of the Research Group on Saussurean Semiology – SEMSA (University of Antioquia-Colombia) and the Agalma Foundation, 3 Oct. 2013. Geneva: Le Cénacle. Available from: http://www.youtube.com/watch?v=r3BGTHnj7ms [Accessed 3 February 2016].

Buyssens, E. 1943. *Les langages et le discours*. Brussels, Belgium: Office de Publicité.

Chernov, G. V. 2004. *Inference and Anticipation in Simultaneous Interpreting: A Probability-Prediction Model*. Amsterdam: John Benjamins.

Diriker, E. 2004. *De-/Re-Contextualizing Conference Interpreting: Interpreters in the Ivory Tower?* Amsterdam: John Benjamins.

Gile, D. 1995. *Regards sur la recherche en interprétation de conférence*. Lille: Presses Universitaires de Lille.

Kalina, S. 1998. *Strategische Prozesse beim Dolmetschen: Theoretische Grundlagen, empirische Fallstudien, didaktische Konsequenzen*. Tübingen: Günter Narr.

Krémer, B. 2013. The Importance of Mental Images in Interpretation. Conference, 30 August 2013. II Encuentro académico SEMSA. Universidad de Antioquia, Colombia, Medellín.

Krémer, B. 2016. *Introduction à l'interprétation*. Polycopié du cours donné à l'Université de Genève. Geneva: FTI.

Mejía Quijano, C. and Marmolejo Sánchez, S. 2010. Las prácticas de transferencia, laboratorio del habla. *Entornos* 23, pp. 93–103.

Moser-Mercer, B. 2005. Remote interpreting: the crucial role of presence. *Bulletin VALS-ASLA (Swiss Association of Applied Linguistics)* 81, pp. 73–97.

Mouzourakis, P. 2006. Remote interpreting: a technical perspective on recent experiments. *Interpreting* 8(1), pp. 45–66.

Pöchhacker, F. 1994. *Simultandolmetschen als komplexes Handeln*. Tübingen: Günter Narr.

Poyatos, F. 1985. The deeper levels of face-to-face interaction. *Language & Communication* 5(2), pp. 111–131.

Poyatos, F. 1986. Enfoque integrativo de los componentes verbales y no verbales de la interacción y sus procesos y problemas de codificación. *Anuario de psicología* 34, pp. 127–155.

Poyatos, F. 1987. Nonverbal communication in simultaneous and consecutive interpretation: a theoretical model and new perspectives. *Textcontext* 2, pp. 73–108.

Poyatos, F. 1994. *La comunicación no verbal*. Vol. 3. Madrid: Istmo.

Poyatos, F. 2003. Los comportamientos no verbales como contexto y entorno del discurso oral. *Oralia: Análisis del discurso oral* 6, pp. 283–307.

Prieto, L. J. 1975. *Pertinence et pratique*. Paris: Editions de Minuit.

Prieto, L. J. 1991. *Saggi di semiotica I*. 1993 *Saggi di semiotica II*. 1995 *Saggi di semiotica III*. Parma: Il Mulino.

Prieto, L. J. 1993. L'acte de communication traductif. *Cahiers Ferdinand de Saussure* 47, pp. 107–141.

Saussure, F. de. 1957. "Introduction au deuxième cours de linguistique générale de Ferdinand de Saussure". In *Cahiers Ferdinand de Saussure*, edited by Robert Godel. Vol. 15, 3–103. Geneva: Librairie Droz.

Saussure, F. de. 1974. *Cours de linguistique générale*. Critical edition by R. Engler, Vol. 2. Wiesbaden, Germany: O. Harrassowitz.

Saussure, F. de. 1986. "Le leggende germaniche: Scritti Scelti e annotati". BPU: Ms. fr. edited by Anna Marinetti and Marcello Meli, 3958–3959. Italy: Zielo-Este.

Saussure, F. de. 2006. "Edition des notes d'Emile Constantin du *Troisième Cours de Linguistique Générale (1910–1911)*". In *Cahiers Ferdinand de Saussure*, Vol. 58, edited by Claudia Mejía Quijano, Geneva: Droz.

Seeber, K. G. 2012. "Multimodal Input in Simultaneous Interpreting: An Eye-Tracking Experiment". In *Proceedings of the First International Conference TRANSLATA, Translation & Interpreting Research: Yesterday – Today – Tomorrow, May 12–14, 2011, Innsbruck*, edited by L. N. Zybatov, A. Petrova and M. Ustaszewski, 341–347. Frankfurt: Peter Lang.

Seeber, K. G. 2015. "Simultaneous Interpreting". In *Routledge Handbook of Interpreting*, edited by H. Mikkelson and R. Jourdenais, 79–95. Oxford: Routledge.

Seleskovitch, D. 1968. *L'interprète dans les conférences internationales: problèmes de langage et de communication*. Paris: Minard.

Seleskovitch, D. and Lederer, M. 1986. *Interpréter pour traduire*. Paris: Didier érudition.

Seleskovitch, D. and Lederer, M. 2002. *Pédagogie raisonnée de l'interprétation*. Commission européenne: Didier Erudition.

Stenzl, C. 1983. *Simultaneous Interpretation: Groundwork Towards a Comprehensive Model*. Unpublished MA Thesis. Birbeck College: University of London.

Thiéry, C. 1970. "Télévision et Contrats Directs". Author's manuscript.

Thiéry, C. 1974. Can simultaneous interpretation work? *Bulletin de l'AIIC* 2(1), pp. 3–5.

Thiéry, C. 1990. "The Sense of Situation in Conference Interpreting". In *Interpreting: Yesterday, Today and Tomorrow*, edited by D. Bowen and M. Bowen, 40–43. Binghampton, NY: SUNY.

Vermeer, H. J. 1989. *Skopos und Translationsauftrag*. Heidelberg: Universität Heidelberg.

Relevance Theory, interpreting, and translation

Magda Stroińska and Grażyna Drzazga

Introduction

During his 1977 visit to Poland, American president Jimmy Carter uttered the sentence: "I left the United States this morning", which was translated into Polish as a somewhat dramatic declaration: *porzuciłem Stany Zjednoczone* ("I abandoned the United States"), thus becoming one of best-known cases of misinterpretation in diplomatic relations (Macdonald 2015). While this particular mistranslation may have been accounted for by the interpreter's limited knowledge of one of the languages, the example illustrates that no type of translation or interpretation is a simple act of finding equivalents. If it were, the target language (TL) sentence could be deemed correct, because *left*, in some contexts, it can indeed be translated as *porzucić* ("abandon"). However, this was not the message that President Carter wanted to communicate to his audience. The interpreter's choice should have been *opuściłem* ("I left") or even *wyjechałem* ("I departed").

The framework of Relevance Theory allows one to pinpoint difficulties that translators and interpreters encounter in identifying the relevant message in the source text. This task appears to be particularly challenging in the context of oral interpretation, where limited time forces the interpreter to choose from a set of possible interpretations of the message very fast. In this chapter, after providing an overview of Relevance Theory, we shall use examples from courtroom interpretation to illustrate a number of problems that *explicatures* and *implicatures* may pose in interpreting and how Relevance Theory may be used in interpreters' training and work.

Historical perspectives

The simplest model of human communication involves two participants: a sender of a message and a receiver. In order for the communication to take place, the sender has to encode and send their message while the receiver has to receive and decode the message. This simplistic model, referred to as the *code model*, ignores intricate processes which take place during communication and assumes that the received and decoded message is a precise reproduction of the original message, with no distortions.

This obvious simplification of the process of communication has been noted by many scholars, who have proposed improved versions of the model, from Bühler's (1934/1990) Organon model and Shannon and Weaver's (1949) simple transmission model to Jakobson's (1960) model based on the functions of language.

The philosopher H. P. Grice shifted scholarly attention to the relationship between the participants and suggested that for successful communication to take place, both sides have to be aware of a set of maxims that constitute what he referred to as the Cooperative Principle, which governs everyday conversation. Grice formulated his Cooperative Principle as follows: "Make your conversational contribution such as is required, at the stage at which it occurs, by the accepted purpose and direction of the talk exchange in which you are engaged" (Grice 1975, 45). The four maxims that fall under this principle are: the maxim of Quality ("tell the truth"), Quantity ("say as much as required"), Relation ("be relevant"), and Manner ("be orderly and avoid ambiguity)". Because conversational participants know that these maxims and the Cooperative Principle generally govern conversation, they will be able to supply information that seems to be lacking or not to conform to the principle in other ways in some cases of conversational interaction. The maxims and the Principle of Cooperation ensure that in the process of decoding the message, the receiver is able to choose from among potentially many interpretations the one that conveys the message most likely intended by the sender. Gricean maxims prove particularly useful in the interpretation of figurative expressions and non-literal communication.

In 1987, Sperber and Wilson used Grice's idea that communication is based on intentions and interpretations to propose a framework for looking at communication from a cognitive perspective, starting with the assumption that people tend to pay most attention to what they perceive as most relevant in a given situation (Sperber and Wilson 1986/1995, 156). Instead of the simple process of encoding and decoding information, Sperber and Wilson postulated that the very act of sending a message implied that the sender assumed that the message was relevant. In other words, when someone says something, they must think that what they have to say is important enough to try to communicate it. The communicative principle of relevance (Sperber and Wilson 1986/1995, 266–78) states that "every act of ostensive communication communicates a presumption of its own optimal relevance". This implies that when the message has been received, the recipient should be able, with minimum effort, to choose from the set of possible interpretations the meaning that he or she believes was considered most relevant by the sender.

Sperber and Wilson propose the following definition of relevance: "An assumption is relevant in a context if and only if it has some contextual effect in that context" (Sperber and Wilson 1986/1995, 122), and Wilson (2014, 131) sums up the approach as follows:

> Relevance theory [. . .] treats utterance comprehension as an inferential process which takes as input the production of an utterance by a speaker, together with contextual information, and yields as output an interpretation of the speaker's meaning. Utterance comprehension is seen as essentially an exercise in mind-reading, and the challenge for relevance theorists attempting to build a psychologically plausible, empirically testable pragmatic theory is precisely to explain how the closed formal system of language provides effective pieces of evidence which, combined with contextual information, enable successful comprehension to take place.

It is worth noting that the proposed Relevance Theory-based model of communication is also capable of representing the interpretation of figurative language. While in Grice's framework, figurative expressions, such as metaphors would be considered a violation of the maxim of truthfulness, thus triggering a conversational implicature, Relevance Theory explains them with reference to weak implicatures (also called poetic effects). The main difference between a strong and a weak implicature is that the latter creates "common impressions rather than common knowledge" (Sperber and Wilson 1986/1995, 224).

Using this Relevance Theory-based model of communication, Ernst-August Gutt (1990) suggests that there is no need for a separate translation theory, because the act of translating or interpreting is just another act of communication ("secondary communication", c.f. Smith 2002) and, as such, can easily be fitted into the Relevance Theory framework. Gutt sees translation as an action based on the interpretive use of language, and postulates that the only difference between translation and other types of communication is that the original text and the translated text are in two different languages. Thus, the study of the process of translation, as viewed from the perspective of Relevance Theory, focuses "on the comparison of interpretations, not on the reproduction of words, linguistic constructions or textual features" (Gutt 1991/2000, 233). Its goal is to select the interpretation that offers the greatest amount of cognitive effect with a minimum of processing effort. Cognitive effects are understood as enhancements to an individual's knowledge, whether by adding new assumptions that strengthen existing ones, or by discarding assumptions that conflict with or are weaker than existing ones, or by combining an input stimulus with an existing assumption to yield a new cognitive effect called a contextual implication (Kliffer and Stroińska 2004, 166). As for the mental architecture of their theory, Sperber and Wilson (1986/1995) propose the co-existence of a rule-based linguistic code and an inferencing mechanism that takes the code as input in order to arrive at a full interpretation of an utterance. Understanding an utterance involves the formation of explicatures, i.e. inferences that spell out the additional information required for determining propositional truth value, and implicatures, i.e. inferences that enrich the interpretation by adding extra propositions. The formation of both explicatures and implicatures depends on two principles of relevance: the cognitive principle and the communicative principle. The cognitive principle states that human brains are pre-wired to favour stimuli, thoughts, and ways of reasoning that are most relevant, i.e. produce maximum cognitive effects with the least effort. The communicative principle, on the other hand, states that every ostensive stimulus creates in the hearer an expectation that it is the optimally relevant one in terms of the knowledge, abilities, and preferences of its producer. The notion of "abilities" is important here because the message produced (the ostensive stimulus) does not always match the speaker's communicative intention in cases where people communicate under various constraints, both physical and psychological.

In courtroom situations, both the speaker and the interpreter have to deal with a number of issues, including the psychological stress of appearing in front of the judge, talking about potentially stressful or traumatic experiences, and, in the case of the interpreter, having to translate utterances on the spot, without the benefit of full knowledge of the context and the speaker's background. Nevertheless, based on the Presumption of Optimal Relevance (Sperber and Wilson 1986/1995, 270), the hearer (and also the interpreter) may still assume that the ostensive stimulus used by the speaker (the message uttered) is relevant enough for it to be worth the addressee's effort to process it, and that it is the most relevant one given the communicator's abilities and preferences.

Core issues and topics

One of the fundamentals of Relevance Theory is the observation that the relationship between semantic representations of sentences and what is in fact communicated is not simple.

Sperber and Wilson suggest that this gap "is filled not by more coding, but by inference" (Sperber and Wilson 1987, 607). An inferential process has to take place, taking into account a context, the knowledge of which should be shared by the sender of the message and the receiver (or the speaker and the hearer). This inferential model, grounded in Grice's work, suggests that the intended meaning of the message may be inferred by using the context and the evidence of the speaker's intention to share the message.

In order to explain how information sharing happens, Sperber and Wilson propose two concepts: *manifest* and *cognitive environment*. They provide the following definitions:

> A fact is manifest to an individual at a given time if and only if he is capable at that time of representing it mentally and accepting its representation as true or probably true.

> A cognitive environment of an individual is a set of facts that are manifest to him.
>
> (Sperber and Wilson 1986/1995, 39)

A person's cognitive environment is not limited to facts that are part of the person's knowledge; rather, it represents the capability of a person to become aware of new facts. Therefore, mutual manifestness is crucial for communication to take place. Mutual manifestness, unlike mutual knowledge assumed in the code model, does not restrict communication to two people who know the same information, rather, it assumes that in order for communication to take place, two (or more) cognitive environments of the persons participating in an event of communication have to interact and become shared. Sperber and Wilson explain that "to say that people share a cognitive environment does not imply that they make the same assumptions: merely that they are capable of doing so" (Sperber and Wilson 1986/1995, 41).

Assuming that this *mutual cognitive environment* is already established, in order to decode the message, one has to distinguish between implicatures and explicatures. According to Sperber and Wilson, "The only difference between the explicit content of an utterance and its *implicatures* is supposed to be that the explicit content is decoded, while the *implicatures* are inferred" (Sperber and Wilson 1986/1995, 56). Implicatures are further divided into implicated premises and implicated conclusions (Sperber and Wilson 1986/1995, 195). Implicated premises are built by the hearer on the basis of their own memory, while implicated conclusions are built on explicatures and the context. To understand the text completely, one has to both understand the explicatures, and infer the implicatures.

Sperber and Wilson also offer a new perspective on context. In Relevance Theory, the context is not a stable construct, but rather is understood as "a subset of the individual's old assumptions, with which the new assumptions combine to yield a variety of contextual effects" (Sperber and Wilson 1986/1995, 132). Therefore, context is dynamic and changing over the course of a communicative event.

From the point of view of translation theory, the greatest achievement of this approach is, according to Gutt (1991/2000), the development of a universal definition of faithfulness, which has always been a problematic issue in Translation Studies. Gutt summarises his account of how to make translation decisions as follows:

> Thus if we ask in what respects the intended interpretation of the translation should resemble the original, the answer is: in respects that make it adequately relevant to the audience – that is, that offer adequate contextual effects; if we ask how the translation should be expressed, the answer is: it should be expressed in such a manner that it yields the intended interpretation without putting the audience to unnecessary processing effort.
>
> (Gutt 1991/2000, 107)

Gutt (1991/2000) argues that Relevance Theory is applicable to many types of translation, from travel brochures and rhymes to simultaneous interpretation. For the latter, he suggests that in the act of interpretation "the translator will often settle for renderings that resemble the original less closely but get across easily what he considers to be adequately relevant aspects of the original" (Gutt 1991/2000, 123). The translator's task is then "to understand at each point what contextual effects were inferred in the original context and thereby form a comprehensive hypothesis of the intended interpretation of the original, consisting of both explicatures and implicatures" (Gutt 1991/2000, 233).

Gutt introduces a distinction between *direct* and *indirect* translation. In indirect translation, there is no need to refer to the context of the source text, while direct translation requires the audience to be familiar with the context of the source text in order to interpret it. Gutt (1990) further explains this distinction as follows: "A receptor language utterance is a direct translation of a source language utterance if and only if it purports to interpretively resemble the original completely" (1990, 154). In other words, direct translation entails complete interpretive resemblance and it results from the assumption that the audience of the translated text has to be familiar with the *cognitive environment* of the source text. Indirect translation, on the other hand, allows the translator to be more flexible, because the target text has to resemble the source text only in its most relevant aspects. This also implies that the product of direct translation may require more effort to process.

Current debates

The applicability of Relevance Theory to the study of communication has been an object of intense discussion. The most prominent point of criticism is the unclear distinction between the notions of mutual knowledge and mutual manifestness. Sperber and Wilson (1986/1995) clearly rejected the appropriateness of the concept of mutual knowledge. However, it can be argued that in their own work Sperber and Wilson actually rely on the assumptions of mutual knowledge while introducing the concept of mutual manifestness. For instance, it appears that mutual manifestness is as recursive as mutual knowledge (as Yus Ramos (1998, 309–310) summarises it: "A knows p; B knows that A knows p; A knows that B knows that A knows p; ad infinitum"). Therefore, it can be argued that mutual knowledge and mutual manifestness are so similar that one cannot properly distinguish between them (for a more detailed discussion, see Yus Ramos 1998). In addition, Levinson (1989, 456), claims that the theory "is obscure and it is not clear how it could be made to have clear empirical application". He argues that the theory is not "data-driven" and that "the new paradigm offered here exists largely as manifesto" (1989, 469). Relevance Theory no longer attracts the same level of interest or debate in the literature but it continues to serve as a theoretical basis for multiple investigations.

In Translation Studies, the usefulness of Relevance Theory is no longer subject to heated debates. Gutt's (1990) proposal, even though it starts by emphasising the pointlessness of translation theory *per se*, is referenced in some sources on translation theory, not as a compendium of practical advice but rather for its attempt at defining the notion of equivalence (Pym 2010, 35, even refers to Gutt as "a theorist of equivalence") or for its discussion of the role of context in translation (Baker 2006). Lack of practical applications of Relevance Theory in translation practice is the strongest criticism in the literature. Most notably, Wendland (1996, 1997) points to many flaws of Relevance Theory as applied to the practice of Bible translation. While acknowledging some contributions made by Gutt, (e.g. the departure from the unrealistic attempt to translate the "full meaning"), Wendland (1996, 91) states that the approach "appears to be deficient in a number of other areas, particularly in its exclusivistic perspective and its idiosyncratic terminology, which leads to some confusion in its practical application". Wendland's criticism starts with the very principle of relevance which he considers impractical, because it "presupposes an *idealized* communicative situation" (Wendland 1996, 94). Malmkjær (1992, 308) adds to that criticism, stating that "an understanding of relevance theory will not by itself enable translators to predict the relevance of any particular turn of phrase to those individuals which they might see as the projected audience for their translations".

Regardless of this early criticism, Relevance Theory continues to be used as a tool in translation theory, because it seems to capture the complexity of translation and interpretation processes and "it may well prove to be the most reliable tool for handling the interpretive richness evinced by real-life data" (Kliffer and Stroińska 2004, 171).

Future directions

Over the early decades of the 21st century, the field of Translation Studies witnessed a steady departure from theoretical investigations in favour of the implementation of various types of empirical research to gain insights into the translation process. Scholars seem increasingly interested not only in the product of translation, but also in cognitive aspects of the process of translating (Drzazga 2013; Tirkkonen-Condit and Jääskeläinen 2000). Relevance Theory has been used as one of the frameworks in empirical investigations of translation (Alves and Goncalves 2003). The flexibility of the framework allows investigators to apply and adapt it to fit their research methodology. It may therefore be expected that Gutt's proposal will be used in a variety of future experimental studies on the translation process.

Implications for practice

The following section presents three case studies that illustrate authentic situations from the court interpretation practice of one of the authors of this chapter, who has been working as a certified court interpreter (for Polish and German) for over 25 years. They all took place in the courtrooms of the Province of Ontario, Canada. Canada offers court interpretation services by fully qualified court interpreters to all persons involved in court proceedings if they claim insufficient knowledge of English or French. Since the case studies described in this section reflect personal experience, we have first-hand insight into the decision-making processes that accompanied the translation choices. We have avoided reference to specific cases in order to protect the identities of the individuals involved.

Case study 1: Lexical choices

A man in his thirties, a native speaker of Polish with very limited English, was accused of stealing a packet of cigarettes from a department store. When testifying, he explained that he went into the store in order to purchase something else but decided to also get a packet of cigarettes. He obtained a packet of cigarettes and proceeded to the automobile section to look for *wycieraczki do samochodu* [literally, wipers for the car], which the court interpreter, without any hesitation, translated as "windshield wipers". The defendant argued that he put the packet of cigarettes into his pocket so that he could use both hands to select the "windshield wipers". The judge asked with some astonishment why the defendant was not able to handle windshield wipers with one hand. The man responded that he needed both his hands as the windshield wipers were heavy. The judge then asked whether the defendant purchased any windshield wipers to which the man responded that he could not find a pair in the colour he needed. The judge, with some disbelief, asked whether windshield wipers came in different colours, which the man confirmed. He then added that he wanted *wycieraczki* ("wipers") that would go with the colour of his car but could not find a matching pair. The court interpreter too was surprised to hear that windshield wipers came in different colours and was contemplating finding some to match her car's colour, but the disbelief on the part of the judge, along with the obviously inconsistent answers of the defendant (why would a young man find windshield wipers heavy?) triggered some second thoughts and made her reconsider the information assembled thus far. The interpreter realized that she had made a mistake: the defendant was using the term *wycieraczki do* to mean floor mats (i.e. mats on which one can wipe one's feet; the word *wycieraczka* is in fact used to describe any mat, e.g. a door mat) and not windshield wipers.

The reason why the interpreter selected windshield wipers over floor mats was the relative prominence of windshield wipers within the context of purchasing something for a car. At the initial point, the interpreter did not feel that there was any need to make a choice, as the only item that appeared to be a candidate for an equivalent for *wycieraczki do samochodu* was "windshield wipers". It was only when evidence of incompatibility between windshield wipers and the discourse developed by the defendant started to accumulate that the interpreter began to look for reasons and began considering whether there was another possible translation. It was at that point, taking into account all the information available – considerable weight, different colours – that the interpreter realized that there was another English candidate to translate *wycieraczki do samochodu*.

This points to the fact that the relevance of an equivalent may be built over time and does not have to be apparent from the onset of an exchange. In this case, at the start, one equivalent seemed to be the most relevant, in fact the only candidate for translation. But when more information was gathered about the object under discussion, i.e. as the context constructed over the course of the conversation expanded, another candidate emerged and took on more relevance in the context of the exchange. In this case, the interpreter had to stop the proceedings and explained to the judge her error in judgement and in interpretation.

In this case, the relevance-guided comprehension heuristic (Wilson and Sperber 2002) made the interpreter follow the path of greatest relevance and least effort in constructing an interpretation and in resolving ambiguity and referential indeterminacy once it became apparent to the interpreter. As the context was enriched by adding more information about the "wipers", the interpreter was able to adjust interpretation until the expectations of relevance were satisfied. She also had to explain her error.

Case study 2: Pragmatic choices

The following example is mentioned in Stroińska (2001, 13) in the context of translatability of worldviews and in Kliffer and Stroińska (2004, 167–168). A middle-aged Polish-speaking man was accused of murdering his estranged wife. The main argument that the judge quoted was that, when told by a police officer that his wife was dead, the man kept asking "What happened?" instead of asking "How did she die?" The fact that he never asked how his wife had died indicated, in the police officer's words, that he must have known and so must have been the murderer.

In similar circumstances, in English, the question "What happened?" is a perfectly possible way to make inquiries. However, it is also possible to ask *how* the person had died. In Polish, the question "How did s/he die?" could only be asked by a coroner or a forensic expert. It would not have been asked by a relative of the deceased, not even by an estranged spouse.

For the police officer, the question "What happened?" triggered an interpretation that went far beyond its actual meaning. Whereas for the accused (or for that matter any Polish speaker), "What happened?" would have meant: "Tell me more", for the police officer it also provided a piece of evidence against the suspect. The officer's interpretation was based on the fact that English offers a choice between a casual question "What happened?" and more specific questions, such as "How did they die?" or "What was the cause of death?" Polish and English offer different choices to speakers, and these choices can only be interpreted within the context of the respective languages.

While in any other situation the choice between asking "What happened?" and "How did the person die?" would have been inconsequential, in the police interrogation, the two choices had dramatically different implicatures. The recording of the police interview with the estranged husband was played in court. The interpreter asked to talk to the prosecutor and the judge to explain that the question "What happened?" asked repeatedly by the husband was an unmarked one and carried no implicatures.

Case study 3: Syntactic choices

One of the questions most often asked in Canadian courtrooms is "How do you plead to this charge?". It is posed by court clerks after they have read the charges to the defendant. The expected answers are either "Guilty" or "Not guilty". However, as it is a WH-question, other answers may also be logically possible, for example, "I could plead guilty to a lesser charge". The equivalent questions asked in Polish and German courts are "*Czy przyznaje się Pan/Pani do winy?*" and "*Bekennen Sie sich schuldig?*" (literally "Do you admit your guilt?"). As it is a Yes/No question, the expected answers are "Yes" or "No". Defendants who try to give any other answer are promptly admonished by the judge or the prosecutor and asked to enter their plea.

There are problematic issues related to the format of this question in Polish and German. For example, it presupposes that an offence had been committed, with no presumption of innocence until proven guilty, common in English and American law. In countries that have had the experience of authoritarian rule, as was the case for both Germany and Poland, people know that being charged does not always imply that an offence had indeed been committed. Based on their experience with the communist system, many Poles who immigrated to Canada before 1989 still show a high level of mistrust of the justice system, and this mistrust may also serve as an excuse for getting angry or emotional, or even for not telling the truth.

Originally, it seemed to the interpreter that using the standard Polish equivalent "Do you admit your guilt?" was the best option when rendering the question "How do you plead to this charge?". This was, after all, a question that was expected by the defendant. However, when the interpreter asked in Polish whether they admitted their guilt, Polish defendants often answered this crucial question in English themselves, making the exchange confusing. The judge and other English-speaking participants in the proceedings heard the WH-question "How do you plead to this charge?", followed by the defendant's answer "Yes" or "No". A confusing or illogical answer usually reflects poorly on the defendant, not the interpreter, as most of those present can only follow one language side of the exchange. Also, the interpreter should translate as closely to the original text as possible; thus, translating "yes" as "guilty" may seem to be an ethical stretch and translating "*tak*" or "*nie*" as "yes" or "no" would not help either.

In order to avoid the defendant giving an answer that was incongruous with the question, the interpreter switched from the "best" and contextually most relevant Polish and German equivalents to the second-best versions that were consistent with the syntax of the English question. It had to be a question to which the answers would be "Guilty" or "Not guilty." Thus the questions that the interpreter asks the defendants now are: "*Przy tak sformułowanych zarzutach, czy oświadcza Pan/Pani, że jest Pan/Pani winny/winna czy niewinny/niewinna?*" ("To the so stated charges, what plea do you wish to enter: guilty or not guilty?") in Polish, and "*Bekennen Sie sich schuldig oder unschuldig im Sinne dieser Anklage?*" ("Do you plead guilty or not guilty to this charge?") in German.

In the case described above, the best candidate for translation of the English question (most relevant and arrived at with least effort) had to be abandoned given the accumulated evidence that its use produced undesirable outcomes: incongruous answers and the impression of confusion on either the part of the defendant or the interpreter. The alternative, preferred translation is not literal and is not the formula used in Polish or German courts. However, it serves the purpose better as it evokes the same range of answers as the English question thus fulfilling the audience's expectation of relevance.

A summary of the case studies

The decision-making processes that the interpreter engages in differ in the three case studies presented above: however, in each situation, the most relevant translation, involving least effort, proved to be deficient. In case study 1, the choice of the right lexical equivalent was delayed because the interpreter initially chose what she considered the only translation of the item in question. It was selected with least effort due to its contextual prominence. When thinking about wipers for a car, floor mats are not the first association. Yet, as the evidence against windshield wipers mounted up, and based on the developing contextual knowledge, the interpreter had to re-evaluate her initial choice and reassign relevance. Within the new context, enriched by the new information (heavy and available in different colours), another object emerged as the best candidate.

In case study 2, the best translation seemed to be the literal translation. After all, the question "What happened?" seems easy to translate. However, the Polish equivalent has a much wider scope of application: it can be both a very casual and also a more neutral (even if not formal) question when inquiring about more details. As such, it corresponds to both the English question "What happened?" and the request "Tell me more" or "Give me more details". It can be assumed that the latter was the meaning that the husband intended when informed about the death of his estranged wife. In this case, the interpreter was facing a situation where a translation choice had already been made by the Polish-speaking police officer who interrogated the husband. As this interpretation seemed to trigger undesirable implicatures, the interpreter alerted the court to that fact.

However, even if the court interpreter were to translate the interrogation herself, it is most likely that she too would have translated "*Co się stało?*" as "What happened?". It was only when the prosecution began to argue that the question potentially implicated the husband as the murderer (because not asking about how his wife had died indicated that the accused already knew this fact) that the interpreter realised that this translation had to be re-evaluated. The decision-making process took place in two steps. Initially, literal translation seemed the best or even the sole choice. Only when the literal translation was misinterpreted was an explanation needed in order to show to the English-speaking court officials the different range of implicatures of the Polish question.

In case study 3, the pragmatically equivalent and contextually appropriate but not literal Polish and German translation of "How do you plead to this charge?" had to be dismissed because it produced incongruous answers from the defendants. Again, the decision-making process involved a gradual discovery of a problem and then a search for a solution: selecting a translation that followed the structure of the original question rather than the culture-specific, pragmatically appropriate equivalent.

In each case, the relevance of the best candidate for translation emerged gradually as the interpreter gathered more information through the clues offered by the speakers (cf. Zhonggang 2006). These clues were used to gradually construct the context and led the interpreter to the translation choices with optimal relevance.

Conclusions

In discussions of translation, the usual focus of attention has been the product rather than the process. One could evaluate the translated text in terms of its faithful rendition of the original's intentions, style, and/or artistic value. Relevance Theory added cognitive impact to this list of evaluation criteria, but it did not necessarily challenge the static approach to translation (Gutt 1990, 1991/2000, 1998, 2005). From the cognitive linguistics point of view, however, translation and interpretation can be viewed as processes of decision-making where solutions are made and then re-examined and modified, as new information is added in the construction of the context (Carston and Powell 2006; Shreve and Angelone 2010). The relative relevance of translation choices is constantly re-evaluated and so those choices are not final and may change. Our examples show that the decision-making processes and changes in translation may be taking place within one "conversation" (case study 1) or over a longer period of time when experience of poor comprehension of the translated text, and/or confusion about its relevance and its contextual effects lead the interpreter to new translation choices in order to keep the translated text relevant.

Viewing translation and interpretation as a clue-based interpretive use of language across language boundaries, as suggested by Zhonggang (2006), is particularly useful in analysing on the spot interpretation practices where interpreters have to navigate their way through text to be translated without the benefit of having knowledge of the context in which the speaker is operating. The clues provided by the speaker over time may lead interpreters to modify their initial choices even if this requires considerable processing effort on their part. The result of the interpreter's work is a text that can be processed by the L2 audience with minimal effort and which can be seen as having optimal relevance.

Further reading

Alves, F. and Goncalves, J. L. 2007. "Modelling translator's competence: Relevance and expertise under scrutiny". In *Doubts and Directions in Translation Studies*, edited by Y. Gambier, M. Shlesinger and R. Stolze, 41–55. Amsterdam: John Benjamins.
In this chapter, the authors use Relevance Theory and connectionist principles to propose and assess a model of translator competence. This source provides an example of how Relevance Theory may be used to redefine some key concepts in translation theory.

Edwards, A. B. 1995. *The Practice of Court Interpreting*. Amsterdam and Philadelphia: John Benjamins.
This book offers insights into the profession of a court interpreter. It provides practical guidelines for prospective interpreters by discussing various stages of the job – from case preparation to testifying as an expert witness.

Gutt, E.-A. 1992. *Relevance Theory: A Guide to Successful Communication in Translation*. Dallas and New York: Summer Institute of Linguistics Inc. and United Bible Societies.
This book provides five lectures which outline Gutt's perspective on Relevance Theory, as well as providing suggestions for how the theory can be applied to the translation of the Bible.

Hatim, B. and Munday, J. 2004. "Translation and relevance". In *Translation: An Advanced Resource Book*, edited by B. Hatim and J. Munday, 57–66. New York: Routledge.
This chapter provides a background for those readers who are unfamiliar with the framework of Relevance Theory in translation. The reader is guided through a number of tasks and questions to gain a deeper understanding of different aspects and key concepts of the theory.

Wałaszewska, E., Kiesielewska-Krysiuk, M., Korzeniowska, A. and Grzegorzewska, M. 2009. *Relevant Worlds: Current Perspectives on Language, Translation and Relevance Theory*. Newcastle upon Tyne: Cambridge Scholars Publishing.
The first part of this book focuses on Relevance Theory *per se*. In the second part, the theory is applied to translation of various kinds of texts – ranging from official documents to Polish soap operas.

Related topics

Semantics and translation; Implicature and presupposition in translation and interpreting.

References

Alves, F. and Goncalves, J. L. 2003. "A Relevance Theory Approach to the Investigation of Inferential Processes in Translation". In *Triangulating Translation: Perspectives in Process Oriented Research*, edited by F. Alves, 11–34. Amsterdam: John Benjamins.

Baker, M. 2006. Contextualization in translator-and interpreter-mediated events. *Journal of Pragmatics* 38, pp. 321–337.

Bühler, K. 1934/1990. *The Theory of Language: The Representational Function of Language (Sprachtheorie)*, trans. D. F. Goodwin. Amsterdam: John Benjamins.

Carston, R. and Powell, G. 2006. "Relevance Theory: New Directions and Developments". In *Oxford Handbook of Philosophy of Language*, edited by E. Lepore and B. C. Smith, 341–360. Oxford: Oxford University Press.

Drzazga, G. 2013. *The Puzzle of Grammatical Gender: Insights from the Cognitive Theory of Translation and the Nature of Polish Hybrid Nouns*. PhD Thesis. McMaster University.

Gutt, E. A. 1990. Theoretical account of translation – without a translation theory. *International Journal of Translation Studies*, 2, pp. 135–164.

Gutt, E. A. 1991/2000. *Translation and Relevance. Cognition and Context*. Oxford: Blackwell Publishing/Manchester: St Jerome Publishing.

Gutt, E. A. 1998. "Pragmatic Aspects of Translation: Some Relevance Theory Observations". In *The Pragmatics of Translation*, edited by L. Hickey, 41–53. Clevedon: Multilingual Matters.

Gutt, E. A. 2005. On the significance of the cognitive core of translation. *The Translator* 11(1), pp. 25–49.

Grice, P. 1975. "Logic and Conversation". In *Syntax and Semantics 3: Speech Acts*, edited by P. Cole and J. Morgan, 41–58. New York: Academic Press.

Jakobson, R. 1960. "Closing Statements: Linguistics and Poetics". In *Style in Language*, edited by T. A. Sebeok, 350–377. Cambridge MA: The MIT Press.

Kliffer, M. and Stroińska, M. 2004. Relevance theory and translation. *Linguistica Atlantica* 25, pp. 165–172.

Levinson, S. C. 1989. A review of relevance. *Journal of Linguistics* 25, pp. 455–472.

Macdonald, F. 2015. "The greatest mistranslations ever". [online]. BBC News. Available from: http://www.bbc.com/culture/story/20150202-the-greatest-mistranslations-ever [Accessed 3 March 2016].

Malmkjær, K. 1992. Review: E. A. Gutt, Translation and relevance: cognition and context. *Mind and Language* 7, pp. 298–309.

Pym, A. 2010. *Exploring Translation Theories*. London: Routledge.

Shannon, C. E. and Weaver, W. 1949. *The Mathematical Theory of Communication*. Urbana: University of Illinois Press.

Shreve, G. M. and Angelone, E. 2010. *Translation and Cognition*. Amsterdam: John Benjamins.

Smith, K. 2002. Translation as secondary communication: the relevance theory perspective of Ernst-August Gutt. *Acta Theologica Supplementum* 2, pp. 107–117.

Sperber, D. and Wilson, D. 1986/1995. *Relevance: Communication and Cognition*. Oxford: Blackwell.

Sperber, D. and Wilson, D. 1987. Précis of Relevance: Communication and Cognition. *Behavioral and Brain Sciences* 10(4), pp. 697–710.

Stroińska, M., ed. 2001. *Relative Points of View: Linguistic Reflections of Culture*. Oxford: Berghahn Books.

Tirkkonen-Condit, S. and Jääskeläinen, R. 2000. *Tapping and Mapping the Processes of Translation and Interpreting*. Amsterdam: John Benjamins.

Wendland, E. R. 1996. A review of "Relevance Theory" in relation to Bible translation in South Central Africa, part 1. *Journal of Northwest Semitic Languages* 22, pp. 91–106.

Wendland, E. R. 1997. A review of "Relevance Theory" in relation to Bible translation in South Central Africa, part 2. *Journal of Northwest Semitic Languages* 23, pp. 83–108.

Wilson, D. 2014. Relevance theory. *UCLWPL* 2014, pp. 129–148.

Wilson, D. and Sperber, D. 2002. Truthfulness and relevance. *Mind* 111(443), pp. 583–632.

Yus Ramos, F. 1998. Decade of relevance theory. *Journal of Pragmatics* 30, pp. 305–345.

Zhonggang, S. 2006. A relevance theory perspective on translating the implicit information in literary texts. *Journal of Translation* 2(2), pp. 43–60.

Implicature and presupposition in translation and interpreting

Ying Cui and Yanli Zhao

Introduction

Translation and interpretation both involve the transference of meaning between languages and cultures, the former in the written form and the latter in the oral or sometimes sign-language form. Translation is the conveyance of the meaning of a source-language text to the target-language text, and the translator usually has time and access to resources to produce an accurate translation. Interpretation is the facilitating of oral communication between users of different languages, and the interpreter has neither time nor access to resources when doing interpretation. While there are various kinds of interpretation depending on the occasion, such as court interpretation, conference interpretation, and escort interpretation, there are two major types of interpretation according to the mode of practice: namely consecutive interpretation and simultaneous interpretation. In consecutive interpreting, the interpreter speaks after the source-language speaker completes a few sentences. The interpreter listens and takes notes as the speaker progresses through the message, and when the speaker pauses or finishes speaking, the interpreter renders the portion of the message into the target language. In simultaneous interpretation, the source-language speaker speaks continuously, and the interpreter has to render the message into the target language as quickly as s/he can formulate it from the source language while listening to the speaker. In both of the two modes of interpretation, the interpreter needs to analyse the utterance, grasp the meaning, and transfer it to the target language. In this sense, interpretation is linked to translation. In other words, while translation and interpretation have their differences, as interpretation requires a more timely response on the part of the interpreter who does not have as much time to ponder upon the issues as translators do and has to make decisions then and there, they share some common features in that they both entail the analysis of the original text or utterance and the reproduction of the meaning and implications in the target language.

Analysing the original text or utterance and reproducing the meaning in the target language involves more than the semantic meaning, and translators and interpreters also need to take into account the meaning beyond the texts and read between the lines in order to produce translations that are both accurate and functional. Such extra-textual meaning is often conveyed by means of implicature and presupposition. The term "implicature" is derived from the verb "imply" and refers to what is implicit in actual language use (Mey 2001, 99–100). The term "presupposition", as the prefix "pre-" indicates, refers to something speakers assume to be case before making a statement; it is related to implicature in that it is also something not explicitly said in a text, but it is more complicated or even controversial partly because of its scope. While presupposition plays an important role in language comprehension, there has been little consensus concerning its nature or operations in textualisation. Different opinions and viewpoints have been proposed, and there is "more literature on presupposition than on almost any other topic in pragmatics (excepting perhaps speech acts)" (Levinson 1983, 167). Presupposition is regarded as "the least established and least uniform notion of pragmatics" (Segerdahl 1996, 185), for "virtually everything written about presupposition is challenged or contradicted by some authority on the subject" (Fawcett 1998, 114). In the next section, we will briefly review the literature on implicature and presupposition.

Historical perspectives

Implicature

The concept of implicature originates with H. P. Grice (Huang 2007, 23). The word, "implicature", cognate of "implication" which indicates a "narrowly defined logical relationship between two propositions", is derived from the verb, "imply" and refers to what is implicit in actual language use (Mey 2001, 99–100). Implicatures can be defined as what is conveyed minus what is said (Sandt 1988, 51). Two major types of implicatures exist: conventional and conversational implicatures (Thomas 1995, 57). Conventional implicatures "are non-truth-conditional elements of sentence-meaning" (Levinson 1983, 19). For example, the word, *manage* implies "trying (seriously)", which is one of its conventional implicatures (Mey 2001, 28). Such conventional implicatures associated with certain words or structures are regarded as semantic presuppositions (Green 1996, 116–119; Marmaridou 2000, 138), and the words or structures are considered to be presupposition triggers (for more details, see Levinson 1983, 181–185). More discussion on semantic presupposition will be provided below.

Unlike conventional implicature, conversational implicature is generated in the context of conversations and it can be analysed according to Grice's Cooperative Principle (CP). According to Grice, the CP expresses a set of unspoken guidelines for speaking that speakers observe under normal circumstances. The Cooperative Principle can be explicated in terms of the following maxims:

1. Quantity:

   - Make your contribution as informative as is required for the current purposes of the exchange.
   - Do not make your contribution more informative than is required.

2. Quality: Try to make your contribution one that is true.

   - Do not say what you believe to be false.
   - Do not say that for which you lack adequate evidence.

3. Relation: Be relevant.
4. Manner: Be perspicuous.

   - Avoid obscurity of expression.
   - Avoid ambiguity.

- Be brief (avoid unnecessary prolixity).
- Be orderly.

(Grice 1975, 47)

When speakers deliberately flout a conversational maxim, a conversational implicature is conveyed. For instance, a normal response to the question "How did you like the lecturer?" would concern one's feelings for or attitudes towards the lecturer as in "I liked him a lot" or "I didn't like him". If a speaker answers the question by saying "Well, I'm sure he was speaking English", the response is not directly relevant to the question, as it does not mention whether or how much the speaker liked the lecturer. Such violation of the relevance maxim carries the conversational implicature that the lecturer's speech was, for example, confusing or pointless. A possible explanation for indirectness of this kind may be considerations of politeness; the speaker may not want to directly say something negative about the lecturer.

Politeness, which concerns the consideration of others, is a basic guideline for human interaction. It is "a system of interpersonal relations" used to "facilitate interaction by minimizing the potential for conflict and confrontation inherent in all human interchange" (Lakoff, in Hickey 1998, 54). Leech (1983) proposes the following maxims of the Politeness Principle (PP):

1. Tact maxim: Minimize cost to other, maximize benefit to other;
2. Generosity maxim: Minimize benefit to self, maximize cost to self;
3. Approbation maxim: Minimize dispraise of other, maximize praise of other;
4. Modesty maxim: Minimize praise of self, maximize dispraise of self;
5. Agreement maxim: Minimize disagreement between self and other, maximize agreement between self and other;
6. Sympathy maxim: Minimize antipathy between self and other, maximize sympathy between self and other.

(Leech 1983, 131–133)

Taking into account a speaker's potential consideration of benefit, praise, sympathy, and agreement in communication helps to explain and interpret conversational implicatures. In many cases, the reason why speakers violate the maxims of the CP is that they are trying to be polite and observe the maxims of the PP. In the above example, where the speaker answers the question "How did you like the lecturer?" by saying "Well, I'm sure he was speaking English", the speaker tries to minimise dispraise of the lecturer and observe the approbation maxim, but violates the relevance maxim. All in all, it can be seen that while conventional implicature attaches to the semantic meaning of words or expressions, conversational implicature is generated by language in use in particular contexts which include speakers, speakers' intentions and attitudes, and the circumstances surrounding the discourse. Thus, conversational implicature is related to pragmatic presupposition which will be illustrated in the following section.

Presupposition

As noted in the previous section, implicatures are closely associated with presuppositions. Conventional implicatures and conversational implicatures are in fact types of semantic and pragmatic presuppositions respectively. In the field of linguistics, three major approaches to presupposition are identified: first, the semantic view considers presupposition to be a purely logical phenomenon characterised in terms of truth and entailment; second, the pragmatic view considers presupposition to derive from speakers' and hearers' background knowledge and beliefs, and explains the phenomenon with reference to the conversational maxims under the Gricean CP and notions from speech act theory; third, there is a view according to which presupposition is an empty and misleading label covering a variety of fundamentally different phenomena (Sandt 1988, 10). The first and second understandings of presupposition will be treated as semantic and pragmatic perspectives on presupposition. The third view, which is partly formed in response to problems with the semantic and pragmatic perspectives on presuppositions to be discussed below, underlies the experiential approach which resorts to context to explain phenomena that others seek to explain in terms of presupposition.

The semantic approach to presupposition is centred on the concept of truth, which is conceived as the relation between sentences and the world in standard mathematical logic (Keenan 1998, 8). The fundamental commitment is that presupposition is inherent in linguistic objects like words and sentences, and contextual elements are left out of discussion (Sandt 1988, 13). According to this view, proposition P presupposes proposition Q if and only if Q is necessitated both by P and by the negation of P (Van Fraassen, as noted in Stalnaker 1998a, 61). In other words, semantic presuppositions are defined by a binary relation between sentences in terms of truth value: "A presupposes B if the truth of B is a condition for the semantic value of A to be true or false" (Beaver 2001, 8–9). For example, in the sentence, "The man in the blue coat left", the expression "the man in the blue coat" carries the presupposition that there existed a man who was wearing a blue coat. The truth of this presupposition is the precondition for the sentence to have a truth value. The negation of the sentence, "The man in the blue coat did not leave", also carries the presupposition that there existed such a man, and semantic presupposition can be identified via this negation test. In many cases, semantic presuppositions are regarded as instances of conventional implicatures associated with certain words or structures (See Oh and Dinneen 1979, 3, 11–15). In this sense, semantic presuppositions are more concerned with presupposition triggers which have their own connotations. For instance, the word *manage*, as mentioned above, is a presupposition trigger, giving rise to a presupposition that people have tried. Triggers cover many types of words or linguistic structures, and both the positive and the negative forms of sentences that contain such triggers have the same presupposition. For example, as just mentioned, definite descriptions such as [the + noun] can be triggers. Other examples include particles, such as *too*, *either*, *also*, *even*, and *only*. In addition, some factive verbs can also trigger semantic presuppositions, such as *forget*, *realise*, and *take into account* (for more information about presupposition triggers, see Cui (2013, 195), Levinson (1983, 181–185)). Although presupposition triggers are discussed here under semantic presuppositions, they may be investigated in terms of pragmatic presuppositions as well, for the linguistic triggers are also used in communicative situations. Presupposition triggers for semantic presuppositions are actually linguistic means whereby pragmatic presuppositions are induced.

Although the semantic approach is often considered to be "relevant to giving a rigorous theoretical explanation" of presupposition, pragmatic accounts are closer to the ordinary sense of presupposition (Keenan 1998, 17). The pragmatic approach takes into account various contextual factors and does not focus on truth conditions. Stalnaker (1998b, 21–23) holds that in the pragmatic approach presupposition can be understood in different ways depending on contexts and explained in terms of general assumptions in communication. In this sense, presupposition can be regarded as something the speaker assumes to be true prior to making an utterance. Although truth is also involved, it is not considered in a logic sense, but in the light of communicative purpose and context. The pragmatic approach to presupposition mainly draws upon the theory of speech acts (see Austin 1962; Searle 1969), which concerns the felicity or appropriateness conditions of communication, and upon the theory of conversational implicatures (Marmaridou 2000, 136). With reference to felicity or appropriateness conditions, pragmatic presuppositions can be summarised as: "An utterance A pragmatically presupposes a proposition B iff A is appropriate only if B is mutually known by participants" (Levinson 1983, 205). The definition touches upon both properties of appropriateness, which reflects the relationship between an utterance and the relevant context, and mutual knowledge, which is shared by interlocutors about the world and the immediate situation. For instance, if a person who is illiterate asks a friend, "Could you read the letter for me", the speaker presupposes the following: the friend can read, he is available, he is willing to help, and the speaker can trust him. In other words, it is speakers, not sentences, who have presuppositions (Yule 1996, 25; Stalnaker 1998a, 61). It can be seen that the pragmatic conception of presupposition sees it as a propositional attitude that speakers have to their utterances rather than as a semantic relation. In this sense, presupposition focuses on interlocutors and their assumptions about each other's utterances, which can be analysed in relation to conversational implicatures (Green 1996, 116–119; Marmaridou 2000, 138; Oh and Dinneen 1979, 2–11). Presupposition related to conversational implicatures can be analysed according to the maxims of the CP and the PP as discussed above. In the example where the speaker answers the question "How did you like the lecturer?" by saying "Well, I'm sure he was speaking English", the speaker has the following pragmatic presuppositions: the lecturer's speech was confusing or pointless and it is impolite to dispraise the lecturer. Pragmatic presuppositions "not only concern knowledge, whether true or false: they concern expectations, desires, interests, claims, attitudes towards the world, fears etc." (Caffi 1994, 3324, cited in Mey 2001, 186). Therefore, pragmatic presuppositions are located in a wider communicative setting covering such factors as speaker, hearer, context, belief, appropriateness, and mutual knowledge (Segerdahl 1996, 190). Accordingly, a ternary relation between two sentences and one context is established (Beaver 2001, 8–9).

To generalise, the semantic approach to presupposition is mainly concerned with logical relations between sentences, and the pragmatic approach to presupposition takes into account contextual factors. The difference between semantic and pragmatic approaches is related to the fundamental division between semantics and pragmatics. There are two major contrasts between the two fields: first, semantics is more concerned with the conventional meaning of language, while pragmatics pays more attention to language use or conversational implicatures; second, semantics focuses on the content of text, particularly truth conditions, while pragmatics considers the context, such as attitudes or interests of participants (Stalnaker 1998b, 28). These differences have led to different approaches to the study of presupposition, and although the two approaches are sometimes opposed, presupposition is both semantic and pragmatic in nature. Language use implies belief on the speaker's part in the existence of referents, which is mainly a semantic issue; meanwhile, sentences are instruments used intentionally by participants who have beliefs and attitudes, which are mainly pragmatic issues (Green 1996, 112–113). As Sandt (1988, 26) expresses it, "a semantic presupposition of a sentence is a pragmatic presupposition of the users of the sentence". In other words, a semantic presupposition of a proposition will be a pragmatic presupposition of the people in that context (Segerdahl 1996, 189). Actually, "[n]o text of any kind would be comprehensible without considerable shared context and background" (Tannen 2007, 37). Context is also essential for understanding presuppositions in Translation Studies. More discussion in this regard will be provided in the following section.

Core issues and topics

The previous section has shown that implicature and presupposition are closely related concepts. In some approaches, implicatures have been seen as types of presuppositions, and exploration of presupposition can provide an expanded perspective on implicature. Both implicature and presupposition are relevant to translation and interpretation, as both concern the meaning of linguistic expressions and play a role in carrying semantic and pragmatic implications. For this reason, translators and interpreters are more likely to understand the meaning of their source texts and to produce an appropriate target text if they pay attention to implicature and presupposition when analysing the original text and when presenting the target text. However, while implicature and presupposition are relevant to translation and interpretation, conveying implicature and presupposition in translation and interpretation is not straightforward.

In the case of implicature, the translator and the interpreter can fall back on the lexical implications of words or expressions and the CP and PP. Any implicatures generated can be taken into account in the process of translation and interpretation and the target text can be formulated in such a way that similar implicatures are likely, in the translator's or interpreter's view, to be generated by the target text. However, considering that translation and interpretation involve linguistic, social, cultural, and even psychological factors, implicature is not easy to replicate, and there are more aspects that the translator and the interpreter need to consider than lexical meaning and communicative principles. When dealing with cultural gaps associated with certain words or expressions, the translator and the interpreter have to consider the reception by the target readers or audience and make adjustments or add explanations when necessary.

In the context of translation, presupposition is more complicated, as it requires identification of presupposition and of the part of presupposition that is most relevant to translation and interpretation. Presupposition is important for translation and interpretation because in order to be able to understand the original text and produce a translation or interpretation that is appropriate and has included all the original implications, it is essential for translators and interpreters to unpack the presuppositions connected with the original text. Yet exploration of presupposition in connection with translation and interpretation is rare. Generally speaking, the core issues for studying presupposition in translation and interpretation include the following. First, a systematic review of presupposition needs to be undertaken in order to identify what types of presuppositions have a bearing on translation and interpretation. We have briefly discussed semantic and pragmatic presuppositions above, and it is clear that the purely logical approach to presupposition cannot alone account for translation and interpretation, which take place in a context. The role that context plays in translation and interpretation and in connection with presupposition must be taken into consideration, both by theorists, so that new perspectives on presupposition in light of translation and interpretation can be explored, and by translation and interpreting practitioners who may draw on these insights during their decision-making. Finally, the functions of presupposition in translation and interpretation need to be investigated so that the translator and the interpreter can acquire a better understanding of their importance and application. In order to address these issues and explore the characteristics of presupposition that are especially applicable to translation and interpretation, we need to examine the key debates and issues in semantic and pragmatic studies of presupposition.

Current debates

Before discussing presupposition and translation and interpretation, we need to introduce debates regarding presupposition in the field of linguistics, because these will shed light on the importance of context. As noted above, presuppositions that are realised via linguistic triggers and which pass the negation test are usually regarded as semantic presuppositions. However, some presuppositions can be triggered by contextual conditions. Consider the following sentence: "If Mary gets this job, her salary will be very high" (Marmaridou 2000, 123). The presupposition underlying this sentence, that if people get the kind of job in question they will earn high salaries, is not triggered by linguistic expressions but by common sense. Such presuppositions are of a pragmatic nature. These two concepts of presupposition have been the topic of a great deal of debate.

There are some problems with presupposition for which neither the semantic approach nor the pragmatic approach can provide appropriate solutions. As mentioned above, semantic presuppositions have the property of remaining constant under negation; however, some presuppositions may in fact fail in certain contexts (Abbott 2006). For instance, in the sentence, "Jane cried before she left him", the word, *before* presupposes that Jane actually left him, which is also related to the conventional implicature of the word *before* that something has happened earlier. By comparison, the sentence, "Jane dreamed that she was angry before she left him", does not presuppose that Jane left him. Rather, it implies that she did not leave him, because if something is dreamed, it is not real. In other words, our knowledge about the implications of *dreamed* has cancelled the presupposition that she left him. Such sensitivity to background assumptions is not restricted to before-clauses, and it can be detected in many other linguistic structures or contextual situations (for further information about defeasibility of presuppositions, see Levinson 1983, 186–191; Marmaridou 2000, 125–127). In addition to the defeasibility problem, there is also the so-called projection problem, which concerns whether a presupposition of an embedded sentence can pass through and become a presupposition of the complex sentence. It was originally suggested that the set of presuppositions of a complex sentence is the simple sum of the presuppositions of the clauses of which it is composed. In other words, if S_0 is a complex sentence containing sentences $S_1, S_2, S_3, \ldots S_n$, then the presuppositions of S_0 = the presupposition of S_1 + the presupposition of $S_2 \ldots$ + the presupposition of S_n (Levinson 1983; Soames 1998). However, this rule presents a number of compositional problems. For example, in the sentence, "Mary didn't stop smoking cigars, because in fact she never started", the trigger *stop* presupposes that Mary once smoked, but this cannot be transferred to the whole sentence, because the whole sentence makes it clear that Mary never smoked.

In summary, the defeasibility problem illustrates that there are cases where presupposition fails to be projected. Therefore, the defeasibility problems can be considered to boil down to the projection problem. While "any comprehensive theory of presupposition must resolve the projection problem" (Horn 1997, 307), neither the semantic nor the pragmatic approach can properly explain how and why presupposition fails to be projected. The projection of presupposition is essentially an issue of logic, and investigation of it is not directly relevant to translation and interpretation, which may involve analysis of logical relations and presentation of information in logical or comprehensible ways but is not merely a matter of pure truth-conditional calculation. We can see that presuppositions are cancellable or defeasible or fail to be projected whenever they are not compatible with people's background assumptions about the world or specific communicative situations. In other words, presuppositions can be triggered by linguistic expressions, but they survive only when our knowledge about the world and the immediate context allows it. Such observations highlight the role context plays, and, indeed, it has been proposed that whenever a sentence presupposes something, it must be considered in a context entailing it (Heim 1992). When it comes to discourse analysis, a broader comprehension of text is closely connected with contextual knowledge (Sbisà 1999).

Translation and interpretation are even more closely related to context, for a proper transfer from one language and culture to another inevitably involves consideration of the original contextual conditions, the target readers, and the target context.

Future directions

Introduction of context

As mentioned above, the semantic approach has demonstrated that the tools of formal logic fail when confronted with the full range of natural language phenomena, and similarly the pragmatic approach has not provided satisfactory explanations concerning the projection problem either. Unlike semantic and pragmatic frameworks, the experiential approach abandons the algorithmic means and truth-conditional view of semantics (Fauconnier 1994); instead, it seeks to construct a framework where "our experience of and through language" may explain issues such as presupposition (Marmaridou 2000, 149). In other words, language use is considered in context, and various contextual factors are taken into account. The pragmatic approach to presupposition is also of a contextual nature, as it touches upon such aspects as background information and speakers' intentions and attitudes; however, context is not specified in pragmatic explorations and the relationship between context and presupposition is not clarified.

In the experiential approach, sentences are regarded as mental spaces and presuppositions are thought to be moving between the spaces. The basic idea is that, as we talk and think, mental spaces are set up via space-builders, and get structured and linked under grammatical, contextual, and cultural conditions thus creating a network of spaces through which discourse unfolds (Fauconnier and Sweetser 1996). The term "space-builder" refers to such grammatical expressions as may establish a new space or refer back to one already set up. For example, in the sentence, "I believe it will be ok", the word *believe* sets up the mental space, "my belief world", which may or may not be the same as the real world. During the unfolding of a discourse, mental spaces are created via linguistic expressions. It is context that determines whether presuppositions in these spaces can be satisfied and inherited or projected from one space to another. For illustration, in the sentence, "Mary believes that it will not stop raining until tomorrow", the trigger *stop* presupposes that it is raining. However, this presupposition is subject to a world made up of Mary's beliefs. In this case, the presupposition is filtered. When it is the case that it is raining, the presupposition can pass through, for it goes from the real world to Mary's belief world, which is less basic than the real one; however, if it is not raining, when this presupposition moves from the belief world to the real world, it will be blocked. In other words, whether the presupposition in this example can pass to the whole sentence is not determined in the space of Mary's beliefs but by the real context. Thus, this experiential approach holds that contextual conditions in reality determine what kind of presuppositions there are and how such presuppositions can move.

To generalise, the mental space perspective offers an explanation of how presuppositions move between subordinate clauses and complex sentences. In the theoretical framework of mental spaces, the projection problem can be reworded as whether a presupposition in space M, which represents a part of a complex sentence, can be satisfied in parent space R, which is the whole sentence. Whether the presupposition in M can be projected to R depends on the context, and when the presupposition is in accord with the real contextual situation, it can be projected to the whole sentence. While it may be objected that the experiential explanations are subjective, subjectification is "closely related to our existing list of ways in which information contextually migrates upwards in a space network" (Ferrari and Sweetser 2012, 55). Such analysis provides explanations of why presuppositions get blocked and under what conditions they are inherited. We can see that the projection of presupposition is essentially a matter of contextual compatibility. In other words, the experiential illustration of presupposition, which focuses on what is going on in people's minds, is in nature a contextual one, and the movement of presuppositions is decided by context, although the factor of context is not explicitly discussed or given a great deal of overt emphasis.

Contextual presupposition in translation and interpretation

So far we have reviewed three approaches to presupposition; the semantic, the pragmatic, and the experiential. The experiential approach addresses the projection problem and demonstrates the importance of including context in the exploration of presupposition, but the presupposition discussed is still semantic in nature. Therefore, there are two basic categories of presupposition: semantic presupposition that is based on logical relations, and pragmatic presupposition that is more concerned with speakers and the communicative situation.

The term "presupposition" is composed of two parts, "pre-" and "supposition", and in ordinary language use, the word denotes anything we believe to be the case and relevant to an utterance we are about to make. Semantic presuppositions form only "a small proportion of the usages associated with the ordinary language term" and have the property of remaining constant under the negation test (Levinson 1983, 168). It has been observed that semantic presuppositions triggered by linguistic structures are unlikely to be affected in translation or interpretation, for linguistic items which give rise to semantic presuppositions are very similar in different languages, even when comparing various language groups (Levinson 1983, 216). For example, we can find equivalence regarding presupposition triggers between different language groups, such as English, a European language, and Chinese, a Sinitic language. To illustrate, the sentence, "She regretted going to Las Vegas", is usually translated as "她后悔去了拉斯维加斯" (*ta hou hui qu le la si wei jia si*, She regretted going to Las Vegas) in Chinese. The trigger *regret* presupposes that something has been done, and the Chinese term used to translate it has the same triggering properties. Therefore, semantic presupposition is not regarded as focal in the field of Translation Studies. In addition, considering the nature of translation and interpretation, which involve various contextual factors, the purely logical or truth-value oriented nature of the semantic approach is not sufficient to account for them. However, as we will discuss below, semantic presuppositions can be useful tools to help the translator and the interpreter to package information.

While the pragmatic approach covers more than logic and truth value, and in this sense is more relevant to translation and interpretation, it has not identified a framework that can serve as a reference point for translators and interpreters. In fact, in connection with research on presupposition, it has been claimed that the elements of interest to Translation Studies are often "those which the linguists would like to put beyond the pale" (Fawcett 1998, 123). The practice of translation and interpretation takes place in a context, and the translator and the interpreter need to consider the reception of their works by the target readers or audience in the target context. The point of view of context as a source for presuppositions is also found in Givón (1989, 135–137), and such presuppositions are considered to be based on "contextual assumptions" (Levinson 1983, 167). Viewed from the contextual perspective, presupposition in the field of translation and interpretation can be regarded as translators' and interpreters' assumptions about the target context and the target readers or audience, especially their needs and expectations.

The identification of presuppositions can be difficult, for "even with the best of wills and the cleverest techniques, sometimes it is impossible to work out all the presuppositions in a text" (Mey 2001, 188). This is particularly the case with contextual presuppositions in translation. Context covers almost everything involved in communication, from the readers' knowledge and social background to the co-text, and investigation of this is potentially endless, as there is always more to notice in terms of readers' knowledge than has been discovered (Cui and Zhao 2014, 35). The framework for presupposition in translation established by Cui and Zhao (2014) specifies three categories of presuppositions related to translation, including needs analysis, the CP and PP for communication, and textualisation principles. Texts and their translations are intended to address readers' needs. Translators have their own presuppositions about the target readers' needs as well as about how these needs can be gratified, and it is against the background of such presuppositions that translators make decisions about how to design their translations. Communicative principles are means by which the various types of needs of others, such as the cognitive need to know and understand a text and the esteem need to win others' respect and acceptance, can be satisfied. Although the CP has been developed with the analysis of spoken language in mind, it is also relevant to written language and therefore to translation (Fawcett 1997, 130). For Translation Studies, the CP can work as a general theory of the act of translation or "intercultural cooperation" and as an instruction to translators to act appropriately (Fawcett 1997, 130). Normally, text receivers have expectations about the amount of information they should be provided with, the quality of the information, and the manner in which the information should be presented. Correspondingly, writers or translators presuppose that the right amount of information should be given, the information should be true and relevant, and be presented in a clear, brief, and orderly manner, as receivers' expectations need to be respected. Leech's maxims of politeness are more flexible than the CP although participants in communications have expectations concerning benefit, cost, praise, dispraise, sympathy, and disagreement. Text producers or translators presuppose that listeners or text receivers should be provided with more benefit, less cost, more praise, less dispraise, less disagreement, and more sympathy. The third category of presuppositions is related to the textualisation of the first and second categories and involves the organisation of texts. There are four basic principles in textual rhetoric, namely the processbility principle, the clarity principle, the economy principle, and the expressibility principle. Processibility is the fundamental condition for readers to be able to read a text; clarity helps receivers to work out textual implications; being brief makes a text easier to remember; and expressibility enhances the text's effectiveness and aesthetic value. Generally speaking, both text receivers and translators and interpreters expect that a text should be processible, clear, economical, and expressible.

While the framework outlined above is formulated with translation in mind, it also applies to interpretation, for, as mentioned at the beginning of this chapter, translation and interpretation both involve the analysis of the original text and transference between languages and cultures. To be more specific, in doing interpretation, the interpreter is supposed to be clear about the recipients' needs in order to interpret in a way that meets their goals and purposes. Under normal circumstances, for both consecutive interpretation and simultaneous interpretation, the recipients need to acquire the information which the speaker is conveying in a timely and accurate fashion. In order to present the information properly and efficiently, the interpreter is expected to pay attention to the maxims of the CP and the PP, especially in such modes of consecutive interpretation as liaison interpretation where the interpreter works with the recipients face to face. The interpreter needs to respect recipients' customs and values, and be flexible and make adjustments according to recipients' reception of the information and their reactions. The interpreter is a coordinator in the communication between the speaker and the recipients. If the recipients have difficulty understanding a subject matter, the interpreter should provide more explanation or ask the speaker for elaboration or clarification. The degree to which this is possible depends on the occasion – for example, an interpreter may not have much flexibility at a formal press conference; nevertheless, the interpreter has to keep the target recipients' needs in mind, and to present the interpretations with the target recipients' expectations in mind. As to the quality of interpretations, the principles of processibility, clarity, economy, and expressibility are particularly relevant. Recipients expect the interpretation to be processible, clear, and expressible, and the interpreter needs to be economical because there is always time pressure during interpretation. This is especially the case for simultaneous interpretation, where the interpreter is multitasking and does not have time to take notes and organise the text as consecutive interpreters do. The simultaneous interpreter is listening, thinking, and speaking at the same time, and the coherence of their interpretations is often at stake. Therefore, during simultaneous interpretation, the interpreter needs to pay special attention to ensuring that what they present is processible, clear, and expressible, and their wording needs to be economical and concise in order to save time and follow the speaker's pace.

Implications for practice

The contextual presuppositions related to translation and interpretation as outlined above are of a semantic nature in that they relate to the organisation of a text as well as the presentation of semantic meaning such as the presuppositions about the processibility and clarity of a text. However, such semantic implications have nothing in common with what is studied in semantic presupposition, which is truth-conditional and based on logic. The semantic aspect of presupposition in connection with translation and interpretation is more concerned with the organisation of information in textualisation. In this sense, semantic presupposition and implicature are useful tools for translators and interpreters to use when analysing the implications of the original text and presenting information in an effective and efficient way. First, making a conscious effort to reveal the claims implied in the original text by analysing the semantic presuppositions and implicatures can help translators and interpreters to understand the original text; and complete and accurate comprehension is fundamental for translation and interpretation. Second, transferring some information in the form of semantic presuppositions or implicatures can make a text concise, because space can be saved when not all claims need to be expressed overtly. Third, textualising information in implied ways can increase a text's persuasion power. People make various inferences when reading or listening to a speech, and when some information is implied via semantic presuppositions or implicatures it leads to more receiver involvement and the recipients will reflect on and work out the implications. People's perception of what is asserted and what is implied in a text is an interesting issue, and as studies in psychology and psycholinguistics have shown, people tend to confuse implications and assertions when recalling a passage (Carroll 2004, 148–149; Cohen, Eysenck and Le Voi 1986, 41). If readers accept implications which are not expressly asserted, the persuasion of the text is enhanced, and this phenomenon is known as subliminal persuasion (Lakhani 2008, 152).

Like semantic presuppositions, pragmatic presuppositions are also often relevant to translation and interpretation. These involve various contextual factors such as the target readers' needs and expectations. Exploring such contextual presuppositions that the original author may have about the text recipients can help the translator and the interpreter to grasp the author's or speaker's intentions and attitudes better, which can help guide their translation and interpretation choices. In addition, the presuppositions that translators and interpreters have about the target readers and context play an essential role in their decision-making process when they decide what information to provide and how to provide it. Such presuppositions cover a wide range of categories, for they involve almost anything that may be related to translation and interpretation, such as the general knowledge target recipients have and the information that is shared between translators and interpreters and target recipients. In carrying out the translation and interpretation activity, translators and interpreters must estimate to what extent the target readers are likely to share their presuppositions, which is "a difficult judgement to make and involves a delicate balancing act" (Fawcett 1997, 125). In most cases, translators and interpreters have to rely on their own intuition or impressionistic judgement. However, since the presuppositions translators and interpreters have influence their decision-making and therefore the translations and interpretations that they produce, exploring such presuppositions can help to explain various issues in translation and interpretation. Therefore the presupposition perspective is also relevant to research on translation and interpretation.

It is possible to argue that there are three major types of research models in Translation Studies: comparative models aim to explore language-pair translation guidelines or language-system contrasts; process models focus on cognitive factors influencing the process of translation; and causal models explore why translations are produced in the way they are (Saldanha and O'Brien 2014, 6). The investigation of contextual presuppositions can shed light on the processes and causes of translation and interpretation and can therefore be applied in the process and causal models of research. One of the major challenges is that it is difficult to be exhaustive in identifying such presuppositions, as noted above. What we have said about the contextual presuppositions that are thought to be relevant to translation and interpretation is mainly pertinent to presuppositions that can serve as a general framework for the investigation of translation and interpretation, and further analysis and discussion is required in contexts involving different languages and cultures. Despite the possible universality of presuppositions about people's needs, communicative principles, and textualisation, there are likely to be cultural nuances and differences, the investigation of which will be invaluable for explaining why adjustment is often made in translation and interpretation.

Further reading

Ahmed, M. and Shazali, M. 2011. Presupposition as a pragmatic inference toward a new conceptualization of the term. *International Journal of Business and Social Science* 2(7), pp. 63–68.
This study explores the pragmatic inference of presupposition as an external and cultural linguistic item which can always help extend the discourse analysis of interlocutors.

Baker, M. 2006. Contextualization in translator- and interpreter-mediated events. *Journal of Pragmatics* 38, pp. 321–337.
This article explores context and contextualisation in translation and interpreting. It proposes that contextualisation in both translation and interpretation can reveal the goals and ideological positioning of participants.

Cui, Y. and Zhao, Y. 2014. "Mediation of Cultural Images in Translation of Advertisements: Alterations and Cultural Presuppositions". In *Media and Translation: An Interdisciplinary Approach*, edited by D. Abend-David, 315–334. London: Continuum.

This chapter focuses on the translation of advertising in newspapers and magazines and aims to investigate the reasons for such mediation from the perspective of presupposition. It discusses semantic and pragmatic presupposition in the light of advertisement translation.

Haugh, M. 2007. The co-constitution of politeness implicature in conversation. *Journal of Pragmatics* 39, pp. 84–110.
This article studies politeness and implicature, two key concepts in the field of pragmatics, and explores the notion of politeness implicature.

McNally, L. 2013. Semantics and pragmatics. *WIREs Cognitive Science* 4, pp. 285–297.
This article analyses the major distinctions between semantics and pragmatics, such as context-invariant versus context-dependent content, truth-conditional versus non-truth-conditional content, language-centred versus speaker-centred perspectives on meaning, and proposes the integration of the two.

Related topics

Semantics and translation; Relevance Theory, interpreting and translation.

References

Abbott, B. 2006. "Where Have Some of the Presuppositions Gone?" In *Drawing the Boundaries of Meaning: Neo-Gricean Studies in Pragmatics and Semantics in Honor of Laurence R. Horn*, edited by B. J. Birner and G. Ward, 1–20. Philadelphia: John Benjamins.
Austin, J. L. 1962. *How to Do Things with Words*. Oxford: Clarendon.
Beaver, D. I. 2001. *Presupposition and Assertion in Dynamic Semantics*. Stanford: CSLI.
Caffi, C. 1994. "Pragmatic Presupposition". In *Encyclopedia of Language and Linguistics*, edited by R. E. Asher and J. M. Y. Simpson, 3320–3327. Oxford: Pergamon.
Carroll, D. W. 2004. *Psychology of Language*. Belmont: Wadsworth/Thomson Learning.
Cohen, G., Eysenck, M. W. and Le Voi, M. E. 1986. *Memory: A Cognitive Approach*. Milton Keynes: Open University.
Cui, Y. 2013. Presupposition revisited: the role of context. *Linguistics Journal* 7(1), pp. 189–208.
Cui, Y. and Zhao, Y. 2014. A contextual perspective on presupposition: with reference to Translation Studies. *Stellenbosch Papers in Linguistics Plus* 43, pp. 31–42.
Fauconnier, G. 1994. *Mental Spaces: Aspects of Meaning Construction in Natural Language*. Cambridge: Cambridge University Press.
Fauconnier, G. and Sweetser, E. 1996. *Spaces, Worlds and Grammar*. Chicago: The University of Chicago Press.
Fawcett, P. 1997. *Translation and Language: Linguistic Theories Explained*. Manchester: St Jerome.
Fawcett, P. 1998. "Presupposition and Translation". In *The Pragmatics of Translation*, edited by L. Hickey, 114–123. Clevedon: Multilingual Matters.
Ferrari, L. and Sweetser, E. 2012. "Subjectivity and Upwards Projection in Mental Space Structure". In *Viewpoint in Language: A Multimodal Perspective*, edited by B. Dancygier and E. Sweetser, 47–64. Cambridge: Cambridge University Press.
Givón, T. 1989. *Mind, Code, and Context: Essays in Pragmatics*. Hillsdale, NJ: Lawrence Erlbaum.
Green, G. M. 1996. *Pragmatics and Natural Language Understanding*. 2nd ed. Mahwah, NJ: Erlbaum.
Grice, H. P. 1975. "Logic and Conversation". In *Syntax and Semantics, Vol. 3: Speech Acts*, edited by P. Cole and J. L. Morgan, 41–58. New York: Academic Press.
Heim, I. 1992. Presupposition projection and the semantics of attitude verbs. *Journal of Semantics* 9, pp. 183–221.
Hickey, L., ed. 1998. *The Pragmatics of Translation*. Clevedon: Multilingual Matters.
Horn, L. R. 1997. "Presupposition and Implicature". In *The Handbook of Contemporary Semantic Theory*, edited by S. Lappin, 209–319. Oxford: Blackwell.

Huang, Y. 2007. *Pragmatics*. Oxford: Oxford University Press.

Keenan, E. L. 1998. "Two Kinds of Presupposition in Natural Language" In *Pragmatics: Critical Concepts*, edited by A. Kasher, 8–15. London: Routledge.

Lakhani, D. 2008. *Subliminal Persuasion: Influence and Marketing Secrets They Don't Want You to Know*. Hoboken, NJ: John Wiley and Sons.

Leech, G. N. 1983. *Principles of Pragmatics*. London: Longman.

Levinson, S. C. 1983. *Pragmatics*. London: Cambridge University Press.

Marmaridou, S. A. 2000. *Pragmatic Meaning and Cognition*. Amsterdam: John Benjamins.

Mey, J. 2001. *Pragmatics: An Introduction*. Oxford: Blackwell.

Oh, C.-K. and Dinneen, D. A., eds. 1979. *Syntax and Semantics: Presupposition*. Vol. 11. New York: Academic Press.

Saldanha, G. and O'Brien, S. 2014. *Research Methodologies in Translation Studies*. London: Routledge.

Sandt, R. A. van der 1988. *Context and Presupposition*. London: Croom Helm.

Sbisà, M. 1999. "Presupposition, implicature and context in text understanding". In *Modeling and Using Context*, edited by P. Bouquet, L. Serafini, P. Brézillon, M. Benerecetti and F. Castellani, 324–338. Berlin: Springer. Available online at http://citeseerx.ist.psu.edu/viewdoc/download?doi=10.1.1.100.2538&rep=rep1&type=pdf [Accessed 13 July 2012.]

Searle, J. R. 1969. *Speech Acts: An Essay in the Philosophy of Language*. Cambridge: Cambridge University Press.

Segerdahl, P. 1996. *Language Use: A Philosophical Investigation into the Basic Notions of Pragmatics*. London: Macmillan.

Soames, S. 1998. "How Presuppositions are Inherited: A Solution to the Projection Problem". In *Pragmatics: Critical Concepts*, edited by Asa Kasher. Vol. IV, 69–137. London: Routledge.

Stalnaker, R. C. 1998a. "Pragmatics". In *Pragmatics: Critical Concepts*, edited by A. Kasher. Vol. IV, 55–70. London: Routledge.

Stalnaker, R. C. 1998b. "Pragmatic presuppositions". In *Pragmatics: Critical Concepts*, edited by Asa Kasher. Vol. IV, 16–31. London: Routledge.

Tannen, D. 2007. *Talking Voices: Repetition, Dialogue, and Imagery in Conversational Discourse*. Cambridge: Cambridge University Press.

Thomas, J. 1995. *Meaning in Interaction: An Introduction to Pragmatics*. London: Longman.

Yule, G. 1996. *Pragmatics*. Oxford: Oxford University Press.

8

Rhetoric, oratory, interpreting and translation

James Luke Hadley and Siobhán McElduff

Introduction and definitions

Rhetoric is traditionally understood as "the systematic study of using language to influence others" (Schiappa and Hamm 2007, 5), rather than an ability to persuade, or an understanding that good oratory has a significant public impact, something which is a clear concern in the earliest European texts. In Homer's epic poems the *Iliad* and *Odyssey* (8th century BCE), an ability to speak well in public goes hand in hand with an ability to act as necessary for a member of the elite. The important role of public speech in elite life led to the development of training in, and writing on, rhetoric in Classical Athens, the Hellenistic kingdoms that ruled the Near East and Egypt after the conquests of Alexander the Great, and in ancient Rome.

The terminologies used in English and other European traditions to discuss, describe, and dissect rhetorical practices are historically and culturally loaded. They are directly influenced by their origins in ancient Greece and Rome, and the contexts in which they were found in these same cultures as requisite factors in the education of elite males. It is important to note this cultural legacy when considering rhetoric and oratory in global terms, especially in conjunction with fundamentally intercultural activities such as translation and interpreting. The very word "rhetoric" is Greek (*rhetorike*), created by adding *-ike* to *rhetor*, a word used in Classical Athens for those who tabled motions in courts and assemblies: its first use is found in the philosopher Plato's (c. 428–348 BCE) *Gorgias*, a philosophical dialogue which attacks the Sophist Gorgias, a Sicilian rhetorician. Partly as a result of the influence of Classical terminology, and the implications this has over classification, rhetoric was once viewed as "an entirely Western phenomenon" (Murphy 1972, 1), which had only been spread across the world by waves of European migration and colonisation. However, this narrow view tends to ignore the fact that Asian traditions of rhetorical analysis and debates on oratory have been in existence for millennia, that the important roles in formulating rhetorical models of Greek colonies and Roman cities in Asia Minor mean that no clear line can be drawn between European and non-European traditions, and that no single tradition can be identified, unifying Europe. The Chinese were formulating rhetorical terminology and schemata, especially for the codification of their complex poetical systems, by the 4th century BCE, the lifetime of Aristotle (384–322 BCE), and the Indian literary rhetorical theory tradition reaches back to around five centuries before then (Gangal and Hosterman 1982). In what follows, the Greco-centrism that has historically coloured much global scholarship on rhetoric and oratory, together with alternative perspectives, and the implications of each for the study of translation and interpreting, will be explored.

Historical perspectives

Unlike the Romans, who enthusiastically and openly incorporated Greek culture into their own, even pointing to the start of Latin literature as an act of translation, the Greeks resisted translation, at least openly. They referred to all non-Greek speakers as barbarians, meaning that their words were meaningless sounds – like "barbarbar". Such languages might also be assimilated to the sounds of animals, such as the twittering of birds (e.g. Herodotus, *Histories* 2.57; Aeschylus, *Agamemnon* 1050–1052; Aristophanes *Frogs* 680–682), and serious interest in them and their linguistic traditions, even with literate cultures, was limited. The arrival of the Romans as a Mediterranean power changed matters, of course, as their power and conquests presented the Greeks with a language whose authority had to be recognised to some degree, even if only by creating a new category to complicate the binary of Greek and barbarian: Roman. One Greek attempt to deal with the rise of Rome and Latin was to argue that Latin was a dialect of Greek, a theory called Aeolism (on which see Stevens 2006); a parallel attempt to draw the two cultures together came via mythology: one story of the origin of Rome had it founded by a son of Odysseus, Rom, rather than Romulus (Dionysius of Halicarnassus 1.72.2 and 5).

The rise of rhetoric as a field of study in Athens is often connected with the arrival of the Sicilian Sophist and rhetor Gorgias there in 427 BCE (Sophists were teachers of rhetoric and other arts who were paid directly for their teaching). The precise study of rhetoric before then is highly controversial: the traditional view has been that rhetoric began in 5th-century Sicily with the mysterious (and possibly legendary) figures of Corax and Tisias. That said, our evidence for the rise of rhetoric is heavily Athenian, and connected to the rise of direct democracy there, after the reforms of the legislator Ephialtes in 461/462 BCE. Rhetoric was embraced by those who made use of the courts or needed to sway popular opinion – and by philosophers, such as Plato and Aristotle (384–322 BCE). Despite his clear dislike for Gorgias and Sophists in general, Plato's writings show the early conjunction of rhetoric and philosophy in Athens, but translation and translation theory were not part of Greek rhetorical theory and training (see Robinson 1992, 13–5 for a discussion of its absence). Despite the enormous expansion of Greek culture and peoples under the conquests of Alexander the Great and the successor Hellenistic kingdoms of the Near East and Egypt, Greek rhetoric remained – with some rare exceptions – curiously uninterested in issues of foreign language and translation.

Latin rhetoric is entirely different. It has its roots in Greek rhetoric and in the Roman conquest of the Italian peninsula (which contained many Greek cities) and the Mediterranean from the 4th century BCE to the defeat of Cleopatra and Antony in 31 BCE. In this period the rewards of empire flooded into Rome: this included cultural spoils in the forms of statues, art, literature, and educated Greek slaves who were employed enthusiastically by an increasingly wealthy and Hellenised Roman elite. Much of what we know about earlier Latin rhetoric comes from *On the Orator* (54 BCE), *Orator* (46 BCE), and *Brutus* (46 BCE) by Cicero (106–43 BCE), the most famous Latin orator and the best-known Roman orator to talk about translation. His most famous work on translation, *On the Best Type of Orator* – a preface to a translation of two Greek speeches of 4th-century Athens – was also written in 46 BCE, in the dying days of the Roman Republic. However, despite its significance for the history of translation, it is likely that *On the Best Type of Orator* is an abandoned draft, never widely circulated, and it is also important to realise that it is a *rhetorical* treatise that must be read in conjunction with Cicero's other rhetorical and philosophical works.

Even before Cicero, the first extant Latin speeches we have – from the 2nd century BCE – show the influence of Greek oratory and rhetorical systemisation. Earlier traces of a native tradition can be found, but are hard to track and are irrelevant for this chapter. However, while Roman rhetoric borrowed heavily from Greek rhetoric, especially in "the formal system of classification and organization that Greek rhetoric applies to language" (Connolly 2007, 140), it constantly kept a distance between Latin and Greek rhetoric (*ibid.*; see also Stroup 2006). One of our two earliest Latin rhetorical treatises, the anonymous *Rhetoric for Herennius* (80s BCE; the other is Cicero's youthful *On Invention*, which went on to be extremely influential in the Middle Ages) opens by taking stabs at self-aggrandising Greeks who talk about irrelevant matters when compared with the straight-speaking Latin author.

The arrival of Greek oratory in Rome was not without controversy: in 161 BCE the Senate ordered the praetor M. Pomponius to expel all the Greek rhetoricians and philosophers from the city of Rome, and Cato the Elder (243–149 BCE) bitterly attacked the influence of Greek culture on Rome – all while keeping a Greek tutor at home for his son (Plutarch, *Cato the Elder* 20.3). Despite hiccups like these, training in Greek as well as Latin became part of the process of elite male training for Roman public life. So ingrained did it become that the Censors once issued an edict seeking to have Latin schools of rhetoric closed in 89 BCE, due to anxieties about radical policies they might be teaching – Greek schools of rhetoric were apparently safer places to acculturate and train elite Roman youth (see Kaster 1997, 272–4; Gruen 1990). In the Late Republic some Romans travelled widely for training in Greek: Cicero studied in Athens (at the New Academy) and in Rhodes; the poet Horace also studied in Athens. But it was not necessary to leave Rome, as it was filled with Greek teachers of rhetoric; Cicero's *On the Orator* 1.14 tells us that the earliest teachers of rhetoric in Rome were Greek speakers, while Quintilian (35–90s CE), the first imperially appointed professor of rhetoric, praised Greek rhetoricians who attracted Roman politicians as their students (3.1.16–18)). Romans might learn Greek and through Greek from these, but training in translation from Greek was critical in Latin oratorical training. Thus, translation theory in Rome and for much of the Middle Ages is conjoined with and is a subset of rhetorical training and theory, rather than poetics. This is not to say that one cannot find traces of discussion in Roman poets, such as the comic authors Plautus (fl. 205–184 BCE) and Terence (fl. 160s BCE), but even in Horace's (65–8 BCE) famous discussion of translation in his *Art of Poetry* we see the traces of rhetorical theory and practice: in Rome rhetoric "supplies a hermeneutic model for translations" (Copeland 1991, 37).

It is in Cicero's *On the Orator* where we see our first clear and explicit discussion of translation practices and purposes in Rome, and it is articulated as a part of rhetorical training, a part that enables the Roman orator to escape the influence of *Latin* texts by turning to Greek ones. This dialogue features as one of its speakers, Lucius Licinius Crassus (140–91 BCE), one of the great orators of the generation before Cicero, and briefly his teacher. In Book I, he tells his internal audience that he began translating from Greek at a young age because he realised that working with Latin orators (*and* poets) meant he was too affected by their voices and word choices to write in an independent style. In turning to translation he aimed to increase both the vocabulary and resources of Latin for himself and others (1.154–155) and become a better and more successful orator with his own, mature voice. The rhetorical tradition produced translators who explicitly turned to translation from Greek not out of a desire to replicate the Greek original, but out of a desire to improve their own speech and to create new, blended works that would bring the translator praise for their originality and improve Latin (sometimes at the expense of Greek texts: see e.g. Cicero, *Tusculan Disputations* 2.5–6). Thus, when Cicero claimed to draw on Greek Stoic sources not as an interpreter, but according to his own desires – that is without consideration for the intent of the original source (*On Moral Duties* 1.6; 45 BCE) – he was articulating what seems to have been a common attitude for Roman translators. Translation might be called in part an imperial art in Rome and it is significant that discussions of translation in practice elide the role of Greek instructors and helpers.

One constant debate in Rome on translation revolves around where it lies as a subject of education, that is, where it sits on the line between grammarians and rhetoricians and in the stages of an elite education, and whether it is something that should be taught at the middle or final stages of that education (see further Copeland 1991, 11–21). As we move forward in time we also, of course, hit the increasing presence of Christianity and religious writings on translation that privilege the source text and the new issue of Hebrew and translations from the Hebrew Bible. Such perspectives place additional burdens on rhetoric and require it to reshape its approach to translation, but do not spin it into the area of poetics.

Under the empire, rhetoric remained integral to the shaping of the elite Roman male, and command over Latin *and* Greek was essential for those who wanted to wield power and authority. As such, translation remained linked to rhetorical teaching and theory, and most of our extant discussion of translation reflects that. Quintilian's *Institutes of Oratory* (mid 90s CE) places translation within the early stages of rhetorical training (1.9.2–30); other sources show its continuing role among elite adults. Pliny the Younger (61–112 CE) discusses it at some length in a well-known letter (7.9) to a fellow senator, Fuscus, advising it as a way for him to improve his style by competing with his source texts. Pliny ends by telling Fuscus to bring his translation work back to his peers in Rome for their approval. As Pliny's letters were all written for publication and are generally read as attempts to represent and model ideal elite modes of behaviour, his advice was meant to reach far more people than Fuscus. We see shifts in the Roman conception of translation in Aulus Gellius (2nd century CE), where the source text becomes of more significance. This shift is unconnected to the rise of Christianity and the Christian absorption of Roman and Greek rhetorical practices, but suggests that even before Christian authors like Saint Jerome (c.347–420 CE) articulated their concepts of translation, the rhetorical tradition was shifting to a new conception of the authority of the source text. Although Jerome borrows much Ciceronian language for translation (he was a committed Ciceronianist, once dreaming that he was accused of being that rather than a Christian), he does not share Cicero's assumptions about translation as displacement and he "and other patristic translators removed translation from the realm of rhetorical performance, and urged instead an unchanging, immanent signified that would be immune from the accidents of actual linguistic difference" (Stanton 1997, 141). If translation was to reflect the word of God it must reflect the power of the original, and it must not constantly shift with each generation. In other words, a religious text could not have multiple translations by a range of authors and it would not be acceptable to carve chunks of it off to form part of a new text with one's own name attached as author. Such thought was not necessarily new, even if it was new to the Roman tradition. In the *Letter of Aristaeus* (2nd century BCE), the translation of the *Septuagint*, the Greek version of the Torah, the translation is described as divinely inspired, with 72 selected translators producing their translations in 72 days. The Greek pseudo-translations of Egyptian magical texts, such as the *Hermetic Corpus*, struggle in some similar ways with the difficulty of translating what is supposedly divine speech, and moving from a non-Classical language into Greek – such concerns also bedevilled those translating Hebrew texts into Latin and Greek.

It would be impossible to discuss in any real sense the rhetorical traditions and authors of the Middle Ages, either in the Greek Eastern Roman Empire or in the various kingdoms that arose out of the collapse of the Western Empire. But it can be said that in Late Antiquity and the Middle Ages translation straddles rhetoric, and grammar is not seen as an offshoot of the poetic, but the grammatical, arts (Copeland 1991). That much remains. The more complex discussions of translation in Cicero, such as in *On the Orator* or *On the Best Type of Orator* fade, as does the influence of those texts, which are eclipsed by his *On Invention*. In the West direct access to the Greek tradition vanishes as language skills in Greek dissipate and texts gradually faded from circulation. One can posit a more decisive break, though, in terms of the Roman and Late Antique articulation of rhetoric and translation with the rise of vernacular translation traditions, the reappearance of Greek scholarship in Western Europe after the fall of Constantinople, and the rise of post-Classical ideas about the importance of originality.

In the above we have not touched much on interpreting and interpreters. Linguistic interpreters were not of much interest to Greeks or Romans, except under exceptional circumstances. A good example of this is the case of the Aetolians in 191 BCE, where someone, most likely an interpreter, mistranslated the Latin word *fides* with Greek *pistis*, resulting in the Aetolians accidentally agreeing to *total* surrender to the Romans (Livy 36.28; Polybius 20.9–10). The words are very similar in meaning, both connoting roughly "trust" or "faith". However, surrendering into the *fides* of the Roman people meant unconditional surrender, something which the Aetolians apparently did not realise. When they complained about the situation, the Roman commander told them to stop acting so Greek about the situation or he'd throw them in chains.

When discussing the orator as translator, Cicero will sometimes contrast him (the ideal Roman orator was always a man) to an interpreter, but it is important to realise that the interpreter for Cicero is a straw man, a convenient polar opposite to the orator (McElduff 2013, 115–120) rather than a representation of an individual or historical group. We see this in *On the Laws* where Cicero claims that it would be easy to "translate as an interpreter" (*interpretari*), that is, literally translate, Plato, but that he translates as he does out of a desire to speak as himself (2.17). His most famous articulation of the split between the orator as translator and the interpreter as translator appears in *On the Best Type of Orator* where he writes that he translated,

> not as an interpreter, but as an orator, with the same ideas, forms and, as it were, shape, and with language fitted to our usage. In this I did not think that I should render word for word, but instead preserved every category and the force [*vis*] of the words.
> (14; see e.g. *On Moral Ends* 3.15 for an almost identical formulation)

In this text Cicero aimed to use translation to defend himself and his oratory from attacks by other Roman elites, who were embracing a so-called Attic (Athenian) style, and claiming that he was an Asianist orator: he responded by translating (or planning to translate) two famous *Athenian*, that is Attic, speeches and to use that translation to prove his attackers wrong, and terrible orators to boot (McElduff 2013, 106–114). In a highly charged and politically important debate over what style of Greek rhetoric to imitate in Latin and how to imitate it, interpreters are mainly used by Cicero as a way to mark his competitors' style of speech as inadequate and mistranslations of the force [*vis*] of their Greek originals (Cicero is concerned about the *vis*, not the lexical content of translations here).

These figures of the Classical world have traditionally coloured scholarship focused on oratory and rhetoric, influencing the ways the phenomena are perceived and defined.

This colouring for many years led to the view that rhetoric and oratory in contexts such as Asia and Africa are introduced notions with no native or antecedent analogues. In these contexts, therefore, oratory and rhetoric become subjects of translation, and national rhetorical systems are seen as developing both in response to their importation, and also as a means of making the translation of these ideas possible. Several examples in East Asia illustrate this point well. Ancient and Classical China exert a legacy over the modern Chinese, Japanese, Korean, and Vietnamese cultures that is comparable to the legacy held by the Classical Mediterranean world over modern Europe and much of the Americas. Japan, as the most enthusiastically outward-looking nation in the region in the latter half of the 19th century, acted as the main vehicle through which many facets of European society, including rhetorical traditions, entered and spread throughout East Asia. In an effort to ward off the spectre of European colonisation that had already overwhelmed many of the country's neighbours, the Japanese authorities during the Meiji era (1868–1912) overturned the inward-looking, agriculture-based, feudal societal structure that had historically characterised the country, and created one of the most technologically advanced, and wealthiest nation states in the world.

Much of this reworking of the Japanese nation was driven by direct importation of technology, artefacts, notions, and even expertise in the form of the *O-yatoi Gaikokujin* [foreign experts], who were invited to the country in huge numbers (Gooday and Low 1998). With this focus on the theme of importation, the introduction of the foreign concepts of rhetoric and oratory is traditionally ascribed to Fukuzawa Yukichi. Traditionally, official communication between the authorities and the people had been one-way, top-down, and predominantly written, with little or no place for discussion. Fukuzawa compared this situation with those of the modern nation states of Europe and North America, and concluded that dialogue should be added to Japanese politics and academia (Okabe 1973, 189). This position was controversial at the time, since spoken Japanese was widely held by leading scholars such as Mori Arinori to be a language unsuited for technical discourse because of its large numbers of homophones (Okabe 1973, 194). For similar reasons, Mori famously argued for the abandonment of the Japanese language for the purposes of education, in favour of either English or French. Fukuzawa set out to prove this position wrong by presenting a talk in Japanese to the Meirokusha, Japan's first academic society, and then ascertaining whether the audience had understood and been compelled by it (Okabe 1973, 194). In this way, he convinced some of the Meiji era's most influential characters of the power of the foreign arts of oratory and rhetoric. From this moment on, the two notions were spread throughout Japan and East Asia.

Core issues and topics

As is also the case in countless other aspects of intercultural communication in recent scholarship, the narrow definition of rhetoric and oratory as essentially homogenous inventions of Classical Antiquity has been attacked to varying degrees, and compared to Edward Said's notions of Orientalism (Lu 1998, 14–15). Said argues that perceptions of cultures outside Europe and North America are distorted by the lens of academia, which tends to perceive these cultures as peripheral and subordinate. Partly in reaction to this theorem, much recent scholarship, especially that focusing on Asian contexts, has turned away from the assumption that practices and modes of thought such as rhetoric and oratory were wholly absent in these contexts prior to their introduction from outside.

It is somewhat ironic, perhaps, then, that this very issue has also been one of contention in the study of Greek and Roman rhetoric. Led by Italian scholars such as Nevio Zorzetti (1990, 1991), more has been written recently on the pre-Hellenistic traditions of Rome and their possible continuance in later, Hellenised Roman culture (see e.g. Zorzetti 1990; McElduff and Sciarrino 2011; Habinek 2005) and on how the Romans struggled to shape Latin as a language that could rival Greek as a literary and oratorical language. In the Late Republic such concerns were particularly to the fore, but out of all that was written in the period, including Julius Caesar's *On Analogy* (dedicated to Cicero), little survives. We have sections (6 of its 25 books) of the polymath Varro's (116–27 BCE) *On the Latin Language*, also dedicated to Cicero, which gives us a window on the concerns of the Late Republic as it tried to create *Latinitas*, correct Latinity, and forge Latin into a language capable of competing with Greek on the world stage. Varro's work is hard to describe: it resembles an encyclopaedia more than a collection of etymologies, as it is sometimes read (see Spencer forthcoming), but its overall aim might be described as an attempt "to examine the matter of what unites Latin speakers" (*ibid.*) and the forces that threaten that unity. This is a text about Romanness – Cicero once said that Varro taught Romans who and where they were (*Academica* 1.9): while it does acknowledge (often inaccurately) the influence of Greek on the vocabulary of Latin for some common words (e.g. 6.88), Varro consistently privileges Latin over Greek origins for even obscure Latin words.

Just as the study of Latin oratory has shifted from seeing it uncomplicatedly as an imitation of Greek oratory with, as Horace described it, "captive Greece capturing its savage conqueror" (*Epistles* 2.1.156–157), and Rome's native traditions and concerns swept away before the power of Hellenistic influence, scholarship on Asian rhetorical research has reconstructed native Asian rhetorical traditions that were largely eclipsed by the European tradition that had previously been equated with modernity. As part of this reconstructive effort, scholars have rejected the use of Greek and Latin terminology for the description of phenomena that are native to Asia, arguing that, for example, only a Classical Chinese purview is apt for the description of Classical Chinese rhetorical phenomena (Lu 1998, 23). While this sentiment is undeniably idealistic, imagining that contemporary observers are able to perceive the perspective of prior generations in anything other than retrospect, it has prompted scholars to adopt culture-specific terminology, rather than reinterpreting established European terms. From the East Asian perspective, perhaps the most important of these terms is *bian* (辯) [eloquence], which is compounded with characters such as 士 (*shi*) and 者 (*zhe*) to describe practitioners of rhetoric in Classical China and the cultures over which it exerted a strong influence. However, in defining the nuances of these notionally culture-specific terms, scholars advocating their use most frequently fall back on equating them with their better-known counterparts in the Greek tradition, *rhetor* and *sophist* respectively (Lu 1998, 26).

Similarly, when categorising and analysing the nature of Classical Chinese rhetoric, much scholarship (e.g. Garrett 1983; Jensen 1987) has tended to add definition to the tradition as self-contained by using the Greek tradition as a counterpoint for comparison. Almost inevitably, this approach has produced a number of generalisations characterising Chinese rhetoric, normally based on comparisons with fundamental aspects of the Greek tradition. These generalisations include an emphasis on "harmony" or a lack of logic in Chinese rhetoric when compared to Greek. In turn, these generalisations have, in recent years, been systematically challenged or heavily nuanced with detailed textual analysis of Chinese classics, and scholarship has tended away from considering traditions such as the Classical Chinese as isolates, and more as parts of the long tradition of intercultural communication that, through translation and interpreting, has transported religions, philosophies, and stories across Eurasia for millennia.

Main research methods

Classics has a very long disciplinary history stretching back hundreds of years. As such it is not that receptive to change, and maintains a style of referring to and citing scholarship that is very different from Translation Studies and related, younger disciplines. In particular, Classics' love of footnotes and narrating the genealogy of knowledge (see Nimis 1984) can strike outsiders to the discipline as bizarre and overwrought, but still that love is best taken seriously. Scholarship that only cites one *European* language is often not considered acceptable, which can be frustrating for those working on comparative studies from a range of traditions, as they may find those traditions are afforded different amounts of respect. Close, philologically intensive reading is also a feature of Classics. Latin has a very small vocabulary for such a successful language, meaning that understanding the locus-specific meaning of words is very important. This issue is especially acute for rhetorical and translation terms, as Latin does not have a single, or even predominant term for translation, and all terms for translation have a wide diversity of meanings. Classical Chinese too, with its extreme economy with words, can create challenges in interpretation, especially in texts written in the variations of Classical Chinese that remained standard for academic discourse in Japan, for example, until the late 19th century, but vary significantly from the written language as codified at the end of the Han dynasty (206–220 CE).

Current debates

Translation as an area of study in Classics was traditionally approached from a comparative and philological focus, with an interest in searching for lost Greek originals via Latin adaptations or translations. It was also not a topic that had any Greek antecedent, and thus was considered, somewhat ironically, inferior to others that did. The study of translation was also traditionally seen as a subset of intertexuality, the study of the traces of Greek texts in Roman ones, and how those traces affect their meaning. This view has shifted with a wider focus on translations and translators as culturally situated, with more than literary pressures affecting their work (see Dupont, Valette-Cagnac and Auvray-Assayas 2005; Bortolussi *et al.* 2007). The range of translating cultures addressed has also risen, with intense discussion over the ways in which Herodotus and other Greek authors accessed information about the Near East, for example (McElduff and Sciarrino 2011). In terms of translation, only recently have we had significant interest in Cicero as a creative translator, especially his translation of philosophy, and in how much his translation practice and theory is influenced by external circumstances such the collapse of the Roman Republic (Baraz 2012). Another author of the Late Republic who is currently generating intense interest is Varro; much current work approaches *On the Latin Language* as a complex text that reveals much about the cultural and political concerns of his period in the subjects it covers and its shape. In addition, as the range of translating cultures (even those that resisted translation like the Egyptians and the Greeks) in the ancient Mediterranean being studied has increased, the idea of a single Western ideal of translation that reaches back to the Classical past is increasingly being challenged (McElduff and Sciarrino 2011).

Thus, the study of ancient Greek and Roman rhetorical traditions, which were once narrowly focused on their geographical centres, are in the process of broadening significantly to consider interactions, and comparisons with a broader range of contemporaneous cultures. At precisely the same time, translation scholars have become increasingly aware of the Euro-centrism that has historically characterised much translation theorisation, and scholars working on historical Asian traditions of rhetoric and translation have increasingly come to focus more on inter-Asian interactions than the Euro-Asian interactions. In this way, the study of rhetoric, oratory, translation, and interpreting are all becoming less about the focused study of the phenomena per se, and more about the roles and impacts each has had in and across a range of contexts.

The transmission from the 3rd century BCE of Buddhism across the Indian subcontinent, westwards towards the Hellenistic kingdoms, eastward to Burma and Thailand, and northward to East Asia via China is a key example of this historical phenomenon of a pan-Eurasian movement of ideas, and a multitude of cultural contexts in which a highly variable range of impacts remain tangible (see Neelis 2011; Mizuno 1982). Buddhism arrived in China in around the 1st century CE, having already spread across much of Asia. Over the course of half a millennium between the death of the historical Buddha (~400 BCE) and the transmission of Buddhism along the silk roads to Han dynasty China, it had developed a sophisticated rhetoric for the formulation of its hundreds of sutras and commentaries (Mizuno 1982). These sutras are customarily attributed to the historical Buddha, and the commentaries to towering figures such as Nagarjuna whose work has impelled them to obtain semi-divine status in their own right. The so-called Mahayana Buddhism that established itself in China in particular, developed a distinct rhetorical style in which *dhāraṇī* [memory] and *pratibhāna* [eloquence] are held up as ideals, though linguistic snobbery and sophism are strongly discouraged (Braarvig 2012, 97). This rhetorical style is based on Indian logic, especially the *catuṣkoṭi* or *tetralemma* [fourfold negation], and was translated and incorporated into the traditions of East Asia along with the Buddhist doctrines. Somewhat paradoxically, the same tradition argues that ultimate truths cannot be reached through logic and rhetoric, but only through realisation of the apparent *tathātā* [suchness] of reality, an ideal that is highly reminiscent of Plato. In the Buddhist tradition, it is perhaps most strongly exemplified in the 拈華微笑 (Jp. *nengemishō*) foundation story of the 禪 [*Chan*] school, known as *Thiền* in Vietnamese, *Seon* in Korean, and *Zen* in Japanese, in which the Buddha is depicted giving a wordless sermon by simply holding up a white flower, emphasising the efficacy of direct experience over language-based, intellectual analysis.

The translation of this highly advanced logical and rhetorical tradition into Classical Chinese, through which it proliferated across East Asia, took place over many centuries. However, possibly because of the vast spans of time in question and the multitude of languages involved, current research linking Buddhist logic as a sub-stratum of Indian logic, together with rhetoric, oratory, and translation, and their effects on East Asian target cultures remains extremely scarce and preliminary.

Future directions

As Translation Studies and studies of rhetoric and oratory continue to broaden in their focus to include more research on the intersections of these phenomena in non-European, and especially Asian, contexts, it appears highly likely that all three fields will see a dramatic increase in available data. To date, research on the interplay of rhetoric and oratory in, for example, the Japanese context remains somewhat impeded by the traditional view that rhetoric and oratory are fundamentally European constructs that were introduced to Japan. Similarly, in Chinese contexts, a recent trend in research has examined uses of rhetoric during and since the Cultural Revolution (Lu 2004; Leese 2011). While these are extremely valuable and important research topics, they maintain the focus on rhetorical models that are perceived as European inventions that were reworked in East Asia, as opposed to the ancient or indigenous forms of rhetorical practice that shaped East Asia and its translations for centuries.

The religious aspect, in particular, is one that has received relatively little focus in English-language scholarship. It is common knowledge that figures such as Xuanzang and Kumarajiva each translated large numbers of Buddhist texts from Indian languages to Classical Chinese in radically different ways; the first relying to a greater extent on mapping new concepts to terminology already extant in the Chinese language, while the latter relied more on calquing and coining terminology (see Sharma, Huijiao and Lokesh 2011; Tanahashi 2014). However, very little has been written about the rhetorical effects of each of these strategies, and their ultimate cultural, literary, and linguistic impacts on large swathes of East Asia, where these translations have circulated for well over a millennium. Given that the Chinese Buddhist canon was shared between the nations of East Asia for much of their history, and consists of such a huge amount of material (the *Taishō Tripiṭakai* (大正新脩大藏經) is 85 volumes in length), it appears that research on the rhetorical mechanics of the Chinese Buddhist translation project constitutes a very substantial source of research data that is currently under-researched or un-researched, especially in scholarship in European languages.

In Classics, concentration will likely be increasingly focused on the multilingual nature of the ancient Mediterranean, on the diverse linguistic and cultural traditions that interacted and affected each other. Scholarship is also concentrating on translation as a particularly Roman practice and Roman translation theory as formulated to fit particular historical and cultural circumstances rather than as general pronouncements that fit all later European traditions. Cicero as a translator – and as a theorist on translation – is receiving renewed attention, especially in the area of his philosophical dialogues. Some Ciceronian contemporaries, such as Catullus and Lucretius, are also being re-evaluated as translators or through the lens of Translation Studies.

Implications for practice

Rhetoric and oratory are frequently overlooked in current research on translator and interpreter practice, in favour of the closely related stylistics, possibly as a result of the common roots of stylistics and contemporary Translation Studies in the work of such figures as Saussure and Jakobson (1959/2004). Even following the downfall of equivalence as the defining paradigm of Translation Studies, the use by translators of rhetorical devices not directly inherited from the source text appears to raise ethical concerns with many. There remains a sense that the structure of a translated text is, or ought to be, fundamentally defined by the source author. Thus, stylistics may be used to cater to such concerns as "naturalness of expression" or "domestication", but adding or altering the existing rhetorical structure of a text may appear to be going too far. Nonetheless, a solid understanding of rhetorical practices and devices allows for the identification of strategies when they occur, and the attempted recreation of these in their target texts, should this be translators' perceived intention. For the European tradition, an understanding of the origin of translation theory, especially Roman translation theory, in the field of rhetoric is vital for understanding many Classical and Medieval discussions of translation; it is also critical for understanding debates over how one should translate (as an interpreter or an orator).

Further reading

Baraz, Y. 2012. *A Written Republic: Cicero's Philosophical Politics*. Princeton: Princeton University Press.
This book provides a clear introduction to Cicero's philosophical translation and its connections to the collapse of the Roman Republic.

Copeland, R. 1991. *Rhetoric, Hermeneutics and Translation in the Middle Ages: Academic Traditions and Vernacular Texts*. Cambridge: Cambridge University Press.
Essential reading for anyone interested in translation and rhetoric from the Romans through the Middle Ages.

Lipson, C. and Binkley, R. A. 2009. *Ancient Non-Greek Rhetorics*. West Lafayette, IN: Parlor Press.
Essential reading for those interested in the topic of rhetoric beyond the Greek tradition.

McElduff, S. N. 2013. *Roman Theories of Translation: Surpassing the Source*. London: Routledge.
This book discusses Roman translation theory from the 3rd century BCE through the 2nd century CE.

Tomasi, M. 2004. *Rhetoric in Modern Japan: Western Influences on the Development of Narrative and Oratorical Style*. Honolulu: University of Hawaii Press.
Should be consulted by those interested in the replacement of Asian rhetorical traditions in Japan with the adoption of European counterparts.

Related topics

Text linguistics, translation and interpreting; Stylistics and translation.

References

Baraz, Y. 2012. *A Written Republic: Cicero's Philosophical Politics*. Princeton: Princeton University Press.
Bortolussi, B., Keller, M., Minon, S. and Sznajder, L. 2007. *Traduire, transposer, transmettre: dans l'antiquité gréco-romaine: textes, images et monuments de l'antiquité au haut moyen âge*. Paris: Picard.
Braarvig, J. 2012. "Rhetoric of Emptiness". In *Zen Buddhist Rhetoric in China, Korea, and Japan*, edited by C. Anderl. Leiden and Boston: Brill.
Connolly, J. 2007. "The New World Order: Greek Rhetoric in Rome". In *A Companion to Greek Rhetoric*, edited by I. Worthington. Oxford: Blackwell Publishing.
Copeland, R. 1991. *Rhetoric, Hermeneutics and Translation in the Middle Ages: Academic Traditions and Vernacular Texts*. Cambridge: Cambridge University Press.
Dupont, F., Valette-Cagnac, E. and Auvray-Assayas, C. 2005. *Façons de parler grec à rome*. Paris: Belin.
Gangal, A. and Hosterman, C. 1982. Toward an examination of the rhetoric of ancient India. *Southern Speech Communication Journal* 47, pp. 277–291.
Garrett, M. M. 1983. *The "Mo-Tzu" and the "Lü-Shih Ch'un-Ch'iu": A Case Study of Classical Chinese Theory and Practice of Argument*. Berkeley: University of California.
Gooday, G. J. and Low, M. F. 1998. Technology transfer and cultural exchange: Western scientists and engineers encounter late Tokugawa and Meiji Japan. *Osiris* 13, pp. 99–128.
Gruen, E. S. 1990. *Studies in Greek Culture and Roman Policy*. Leiden: Brill.
Habinek, T. 2005. *The World of Roman Song: From Ritualized Speech to Social Order*. Baltimore: Johns Hopkins University Press.
Jakobson, R. 1959/2004. "On linguistic aspects of translation". Reprinted in Venuti, L. (ed.), *The Translation Studies Reader*. London: Routledge, from Brower, R. A. (ed.) *On Translation*. Cambridge, MA: Harvard University Press, pp. 232–239.
Jensen, J. V. 1987. Rhetorical emphases of taoism. *Rhetorica* 5, pp. 219–229.
Kaster, R. A. 1997. *Guardians of Language: The Grammarian and Society in Late Antiquity*. Berkeley: University of California Press.
Leese, D. 2011. *Mao Cult: Rhetoric and Ritual in China's Cultural Revolution*. Cambridge and New York: Cambridge University Press.

Lu, X. 1998. *Rhetoric in Ancient China, Fifth to Third Century BCE: A Comparison with Classical Greek Rhetoric*. Columbia, SC: University of South Carolina Press.

Lu, X. 2004. *Rhetoric of the Chinese Cultural Revolution: The Impact on Chinese Thought, Culture, and Communication*. Columbia, SC: University of South Carolina Press.

McElduff, S. N. 2013. *Roman Theories of Translation: Surpassing the Source*. London: Routledge.

McElduff, S. N. and Sciarrino, E. 2011. *Complicating the History of Western Translation: The Ancient Mediterrannean in Perspective*. Manchester, UK and Kinderhook, NY: St Jerome.

Mizuno, K. 1982. *Buddhist Sutras: Origin, Development, Transmission*. Tokyo: Kosei Publishing.

Murphy, J. J. 1972. *A Synoptic History of Rhetoric*. New York: Random House.

Neelis, J. E. 2011. *Early Buddhist Transmission and Trade Networks: Mobility and Exchange Within and Beyond the Northwestern Borderlands of South Asia*. Leiden and Boston: Brill.

Nimis, S. 1984. Fussnoten: das Fundament der Wissenschaft. *Arethusa* 17, p. 105.

Okabe, R. 1973. Yukichi Fukuzawa: a promulgator of western rhetoric in Japan. *Quarterly Journal of Speech* 59, pp. 186–195.

Robinson, D. 1992. The ascetic foundations of western translation theory: Jerome and Augustine. *Translation and Literature* 1, pp. 3–25.

Schiappa, E. and Hamm, J. 2007. "Rhetorical questions". In *A Companion to Greek Rhetoric*, edited by I. Worthington, 1–15. Oxford: Blackwell Publishing.

Sharma, N., Huijiao and Lokesh, C. 2011. *Kumarajiva: The Transcreator of Buddhist Chinese Diction*. New Delhi: Niyogi Books.

Spencer, D. Forthcoming. *Varro's Guide to being Roman: Reading "De Lingua Latina"*. Athens, OH: Ohio University Press.

Stanton, R. 1997. Rhetoric and translation in Ælfric's prefaces. *Translation and Literature* 6(2), pp. 135–148.

Stevens, B. 2006. Æolism: Latin as a dialect of Greek. *Classical Journal* 102(2), pp. 115–144.

Stroup, S. C. 2006. "Greek Rhetoric Meets Rome: Expansion, Resistance, and Acculturation". In *A Companion to Roman Rhetoric*, edited by W. Dominik and J. Hall. Malden, MA: Blackwell Publishing.

Tanahashi, K. 2014. *The Heart Sutra: A Comprehensive Guide to the Classic of Mahayana Buddhism*. Boston, MA: Shambhala Publications Inc.

Zorzetti, N. 1990. "The Carmina Convivalia". In *Sympotica: A Symposium on the Symposion*, edited by O. Murray, 289–307. Oxford: Clarendon Press.

Zorzetti, N. 1991. Poetry and ancient city: the case of Rome. *Classical Journal* 32(April–May), pp. 311–329.

Part III
Texts in speech and writing

9

Discourse analysis, interpreting and translation

Stefan Baumgarten and Melani Schröter

Introduction and definitions

This chapter differentiates between discourse analysis (DA) and Critical Discourse Analysis (CDA), and reviews the impact and possible uses of both for Translation Studies (TS). DA deals with the study of language as a social practice by explicitly taking into account discursive, situational and (inter)textual dimensions of communicative exchanges (Brown and Yule 1983; cf. Paltridge 2006). CDA highlights the ideological dimensions and implications of language by casting a "critical" eye over ideologically significant meanings and unequal power relations in hegemonic and exploitative settings, especially with reference to the way discourse shapes and is shaped by naturalised manipulative and discriminatory practices (Fairclough 1995; van Dijk 1998, 2008a). Defining and differentiating DA and CDA remains, however, problematic owing to diverging conceptualisations of the notion of discourse in different academic settings and disciplines. Significantly, both approaches tend to concentrate on ideologies embedded within structures and processes pertaining to intracultural (patterns of) communication. Whilst comparative discourse analyses across languages exist, and some studies have become incorporated into work in intercultural communication (Scollon, Wong Scollon and Jones 2000), neither DA nor CDA have integrated perspectives more immediately relevant for crosscultural communication, that is, for the study of translation as a social and ideological phenomenon circumscribed by its own distinctive sociotextual parameters. Since for scholars working with methods drawn from DA and CDA the default mode of analysis has been the investigation of intracultural communication, it is useful to differentiate between intercultural and crosscultural communication. If intercultural communication as a mode of linguistic contact is based on encounters between members of different discourse communities, we can think of crosscultural communication as based on linguistic mediations through sociotextual transformations. Translation and interpreting (T&I) are not solely based on textual contact, as there exists a large debate about where to draw the line between textual and other forms of crosscultural communication. A recent debate has centred around the notion of cultural translation (Buden *et al.* 2009), which stems from work in anthropology and ethnography that focuses on crosscultural encounters involving the shifting of identities, as Carbonell (1996, 81) puts it, "whenever an alien experience is internalized and rewritten in the culture where that experience is received". We will confine ourselves to textual instances of T&I, since (C)DA is most beneficial in providing insights into sociocultural and ideological implications through textual mediations. In this sense, (C)DA may provide useful and sometimes decisive evidence for research in the (critical) social sciences. In this chapter, we regard T&I as a process that may be instrumental in bringing about social and ideological transformations. T&I may include paraphrasing within one language, mediating across languages and traversing across semiotic systems, e.g. the translation of a book into a film (Jakobson 1959/2000). Considering that T&I constitute instances of crosscultural mediation, (C)DA has not sufficiently acknowledged the existence of translational processes in (patterned) communicative exchanges, so there remains much work to be done in bringing these processes to the fore in discourse-analytical research. Conversely, TS is in the process of establishing a comprehensive body of studies that avail themselves of tools and methods from (C)DA (Schäffner 2004; Munday and Zhang 2015). Given that (C)DA does not have a strong philosophical and historical outlook, it appears reasonable to consider it as a method and analytical toolkit rather than as a fully fledged research paradigm. In any case, both TS research that applies (C)DA as a method and (C)DA approaches themselves could benefit from a more comprehensive philosophico-historical perspective, which would render their critical potential more convincing.

T&I constitute two different forms of textual mediation and both are instances of crosscultural communication. Within TS, there has been growing interest in accommodating analytical concepts from (C)DA, for instance with regard to the study of literary translation (Munday 2008), political discourse in translation (Schäffner 2004) and translation in the European Union (Calzada-Pérez 2006). Whilst some of these studies draw on Hallidayan systemic linguistics, there has also been a growing interest in looking at translation from the perspectives of (global and regional) power asymmetries, (cultural) politics and (institutional) ideologies (Venuti 1995; Cronin 2003). Textual research in TS has followed shifting trends in synchronic linguistics since around the middle of the 20th century, beginning with Chomskyan generative grammar via text-linguistic approaches, pragmatics and sociolinguistics. Today, CDA approaches have become an established mode of textual research (Munday and Zhang 2015).

Historical perspectives

The evolution of (C)DA is endebted to three large-scale developments in linguistics. First, since around the 1950s synchronic linguistics in the structuralist paradigm has increasingly acknowledged that textual elements within clauses and sentences are not the only units connected by grammatical means, but that there also exists grammaticality beyond sentence borders, for example through text cohesion. From the 1970s onwards, developments within text linguistics triggered interest in a systematic description of structural characteristics of entire texts as more complex units of language use. In particular, the notion of genre provided a link to extratextual domains, since many genres display specific generic conventions and only occur in certain contextual domains. A focus on genre also provided a bridge to the question of how texts relate to each other, given that the relation between different tokens (individual texts) of a type (genre) can be considered a form of intertextuality. Second, the development of pragmatics shifted the emphasis from the systematic and conventional structure of language to what speakers try to achieve when using language, and how the enveloping speech situation proves essential to decoding the meaning of an utterance, for instance through speakers' use of politeness strategies and implicatures. Third, the development of sociolinguistics and the sociology of language with their interest in language use in relation to social categories such as class, gender and language policies established the significance of sociohistorical and ideological context as analytical dimensions. The links between (C)DA, text linguistics, pragmatics and sociolinguistics can be observed across publications such as Brown and Yule (1983), Schiffrin (1994), Paltridge (2006) and Jaworski and Coupland (2006).

Paradigm shifts in synchronic linguistics, the development of pragmatics, and socio-linguistic approaches have also been closely reflected in TS research. First, Chomskyan linguistics influenced research on Bible translation from the 1960s onwards, work which relied on the idea of grammatical units as valid equivalents across languages (Nida 1964). With the onset of text-linguistic approaches, a sharper focus on units beyond the sentence level emerged, with work by Czech and German scholars featuring prominently (Levy 1967; Neubert 1985). Systematic research on text types, genres and genre conventions was pioneered in Germany from the 1970s onwards (Reiss 1977), with comprehensive studies on intertextuality and translation following around the 1980s (House 1977/1981; Hatim and Mason 1990). Second, insights from pragmatics began to be taken up from the 1980s onwards, when more nuanced attention began to be paid to contextual and interpersonal parameters. Gutt's (1991, 376, 393) application of relevance theory (Sperber and Wilson 1986) was foundational, especially his concept of "translation as interlingual interpretive use" that aimed "to develop a concept of faithfulness that is generally applicable and yet both text- and context-specific". Whilst Gutt's cognitive account ignores crucial issues of power and ideology, Hatim and Mason (1997; also Mason 1194/2010) paved the way for a context-sensitive pragmatics open to the identification of ideological meaning relations in cross-cultural communication, and Munday (2008, 2012) employed (C)DA to establish a method and analytical framework for the analysis of translational communication. Based on a corpus-linguistic methodology, Munday investigates how translator styles relate to ideology and how translator attitudes may be unearthed through the observation of semantic prosodies. Finally, sociolinguistic approaches have always been implicitly present in TS research, with register analysis having become a mainstay in accounting for social variation in translated material and interpreted encounters. Other research ranges from the translation of social dialects to the deliberate exposure of female identities when translating male-based literary canons (von Flotow 1997). Moreover, sociological approaches have studied translation in relation to language contact, multilingualism and language planning, and to questions concerning major and minor languages (Cronin 2003).

The politically engaged strand of DA is indebted to the same developments in the empirical study of language in social contexts, but went beyond these with an even more explicit emancipatory agenda than in TS, with the aim of uncovering power relations and ideologies in language use in order to achieve change through criticism. Early examples of this approach include the work of "critical linguists" such as Kress and Hodge (1979) and Fowler *et al*. (1979). Both Fairclough (2001) in the preface to the second edition of his seminal book *Language and Power* (1st edition 1989) and van Dijk (2006) in the preface to the second edition of *Discourse Studies: A Multidisciplinary Introduction* (1st edition 1997) observe that CDA became increasingly and rapidly popular from the late 1990s onwards. Since then, CDA has seen a notable diversification with the integration of a range of preexisting as well as new concepts and methodological approaches from linguistics, but also from the social sciences and media and communication studies. TS has evolved in parallel to the flourishing of CDA as a methodological innovation for much text-based research, and following its inception around the 1970s (Holmes 1988) TS has become firmly institutionalised since around the late 1990s. Significantly, however, TS remains a less politically engaged and much more diversified and heterogeneous academic discourse than CDA. Nevertheless, TS went through various paradigmatic "turns", beginning with a cultural turn during the 1990s that helped to emancipate the field from a certain overreliance on linguistic methodologies (Bassnett and Lefevere 1990). The cultural turn was a leap forward in understanding the role of T&I as a social practice in an increasingly globalising world. A further significant development concerns the suggestion of a power turn (Tymoczko and Gentzler 2002), which reminded scholars "that the explanations of the shifts that occur in translation are not to be found in the nature of culture itself, but in the power relations that govern in any culture" (Nergaard 2007, 39–40). This latest development in TS is equipping the field with a new transdisciplinary ethos, opening up the terrain for an increasing adoption of paradigms, methods and concepts from philosophy, sociology, psychology, literary studies and the cognitive sciences.

Core issues and topics

DA engages with the use of language beyond individual sentences or utterances and, hence, beyond the domains of grammar and semantics (cf. Brown and Yule 1983; Schiffrin 1994). Its key notions are text and genre, and its key areas of investigation are the analysis and description of different genres, text structure and composition, text grammar (cohesion) and text semantics (coherence). DA investigates the way elements within texts build up and contribute to constitute texts, the features that allow texts to be grouped into genres and the way texts refer to and interact with each other through intertextuality (cf. Paltridge 2006; Bax 2011). In TS, Neubert and Shreve (1992, 25) transcend grammatical and semantic categorisations by regarding translations as "text-induced text productions", while Reiss (1977) emphasised the significance of the concepts of text type (a text's rhetorical drift) and genre (a text's social patterning) both for the activity and study of translation. Toury (1995, 23) moved away more decisively from a text-centred approach by introducing the concept of translation norms into TS, which indeed established a paradigmatic shift, given that now translations came to be seen mainly as "facts of a 'target' culture". Translators, who tend to work within a target cultural context, are constrained by sociocultural norms that (sub)consciously govern their behaviour and in turn their textual output, so translation research became inspired to proceed from a target-cultural and target-text perspective rather than the other way around. The concept of norms has to be considered by any student of T&I, yet it remains problematic to establish empirical (textual) evidence, because norms can only be identified by means of intertextual relations across a diversity of genres, texts and individual styles. Hatim and Mason (1997, 18), on the other hand, accompanies and prefigures more power-sensitive research in that they envisage translation as a discursive and sociotextual practice that embodies "attitudinal expression, with language becoming the mouthpiece of societal institutions (sexism, feminism, bureaucratism, etc.)".

   CDA is interested in how discourse constructs and reflects sociopolitical issues, how discourse reproduces social relations and the performance and negotiation of power, and how ideologies are encoded in discourse. CDA's key notions are power and ideology, and its key areas of investigation are the systematic identification of language use, especially in the ways it echoes or supports power relations, and dominant ideologies encoded in texts. CDA has produced a multitude of studies based on English and other languages, albeit hardly ever in comparison. Topics range from gendered discourse and heteronormativity, stereotyping, othering or racist discourse towards the discursive inscriptions of socioeconomic conditions, e.g. in view of globalisation, poverty or economic crisis. Especially since the cultural turn, TS has produced many insightful studies on the ways in which translation has fostered the creation of discourses that serve specific ideological interests, for instance related to translation's role in colonial and hegemonic power relations (Niranjana 1992; Venuti 1998), nationalist agitation (Brisset 1989) and the politics of resistance (Tymoczko 2010). The construction of new social identities and literary canons through translational strategies and the role of translation in large multinational institutions have become focal points of investigation. These studies, however, are based on divergent philosophical premises, methodologies and analytical tools, which makes it difficult to identify a strand in TS that systematically adopts ideas from CDA. Hence, whilst we can observe an increasing cross-fertilisation between TS, the social sciences and cultural studies, a clearly identifiable strand of CDA-informed TS research would help to refine our understanding of the involvement of T&I in the generation and maintenance of unequal power relations and social inequalities.

Translation research has evolved from static, language-centred approaches towards approaches that explicitly account for contexts, ideologies and power relations. It is therefore not surprising that work in the relatively static area of contrastive discourse analysis has not informed recent research in TS, given that the former is largely meant to inform language typology and second-language acquisition. Whilst a number of text-grammatical, text-structuring and cohesive features have been studied in detail for different language pairs (cf. as a recent example Taboada, Suárez and Álvarez 2013), there has never been a recognisable research programme to contrast genre conventions systematically (but see e.g. Bhatia and Bhatia 2011; Connor 1996; Paltridge 1997; Swales 1998; cf. Barton, Dickson and Kinloch 2015). In DA, at least there is a set of recognised text-grammatical and cohesive features with functions that can generally be described fairly clearly, and there is a consensus about what the determining features are that enable description and differentation between genres. For CDA, the picture is more complicated, since it is more difficult to determine a set of features that constitute and reflect power or ideology, or hegemonic versus subversive discourse; nor is it the aim of CDA to develop such an inventory.

Against this backdrop, and especially when the focus is not on one individual language, it is useful to distinguish between contrastive, intercultural and crosscultural discourse analysis. Whilst any contrastive mode of analysis would be usefully employed in theoretical and pedagogic research on language *per se* and on language learning, an intercultural mode of analysis would focus more strongly on the speakers and on how they negotiate their linguistic interactions with members of other discourse communities. Crosscultural discourse analysis, in turn, would be devoted to T&I, in particular to studying the ways in which this form of crosscultural communication is circumscribed by its own communicative parameters and constraints. Empirical analyses by M. Baker (1996) have shown that translations may display specific structural and lexicogrammatical features, for instance tendencies towards explicitating or semantically disambiguating source-text information. Whereas Baker's corpus-analytical research, however, has not accounted for the pervasiveness of power relations and ideological significations, Venuti's (1995, 1998) extended discussion of the ongoing "invisibility" of the translation profession explicitly condemns market-driven and hegemonic translation strategies in the Anglo-American world. According to him, and inspired by Schleiermacher's concept of foreignising and domesticating translation strategies, literary translations into English tend to domesticate the foreign text by eradicating its cultural specificities in order to provide a smooth reading experience, whereas translations out of English into other languages tend to do the opposite by maintaining Anglo-American cultural characteristics, and in the process they help to bolster the (inter)national power of Anglo-American values.

Such strategies can also be described as sociocultural norms at work in crosscultural communication, and they are related to the pressures of socioeconomic patterns of globalisation.

Main research methods

Research in (C)DA and TS employs a large variety of methodologies (cf. van Dijk 2006; Wodak and Meyer 2009; Saldanha and O'Brien 2013). Owing to the inflationary employment of the notion of discourse in the arts and humanities and the social sciences since around the 1970s, it is no surprise that (C)DA and TS are both heavily reliant on this analytical construct. The methodological heterogeneity of (C)DA and TS is also reflected in an increasing interest in DA within the social sciences, triggered by scholars such as, among others, Michel Foucault, Pierre Bourdieu, Jacques Derrida and Mikhail Bakhtin. This reliance on seminal thinkers with interests in questions about language and communication distinguishes both (C) DA and TS from the large array of more empirically orientated research in sociolinguistic and (applied) linguistics. In general, it is possible to differentiate between more theory-centred and more empirical research methodologies.

First, it became increasingly obvious that it was crucial to focus on the notion of discourse as a *theoretical* construct, not least due to the advent of the internet and the phenomenon of hypertext, which came to highlight other-than-language-based modes of communication. In (C)DA, and following Kress and van Leeuwen (2001, 2006), there is increasing interest in combinations of text, text design, images and sound in what came to be known as multimodal discourse analysis (cf. Machin 2010). Methodological pluralism is also related to conceptual innovations concerning different aspects of language use in diverging social contexts. Concepts from cognitive linguistics, for instance, have been increasingly utilised in DA, mostly regarding the role of frames and scripts in the interpretation of discourse (cf. Brown and Yule 1983, 223ff.). CDA, in turn, has emphasised the role of cognition in theorising the relation between discourse and context (van Dijk 2008b; Hart 2011), and the role of metaphor in discourse, especially concerning the potential of pervasive metaphors to sustain ideologies (e.g. Musolff 2004; Charteris-Black 2005).

In view of its increasing institutionalisation since the 1970s, TS has given rise to a large diversity of research methodologies and analytical models. Following on from early comparative models that focused on structural differences between source texts and their translations, House's (1977/1981) and Hatim and Mason's (1997) register models and Chesterman's (2000) causal model paved the way for sociologically minded translation comparisons. In its wake, discourse-analytical models have slowly begun to proliferate. Of particular note is Schäffner's method of linking translational choices to "strategic functions" (2004: 144–145; based on Chilton and Schäffner 2002, also Chilton 2004), which was adapted in Baumgarten's study of different English translations of Hitler's *Mein Kampf* (Baumgarten 2009, 28–29; cf. also Baumgarten and Gagnon 2016, 10–13). Also noteworthy are M. Baker's (2006) typology of narrative in translation, and Marais' (2014) study of translation in multilingual South Africa which relied on complexity theory and semiotics. Caimotto's (forthcoming) study of deictic markers in a speech by Barack Obama that was translated for several Italian newspapers avails itself of proximisation theory (Cap 2013), showing that unavoidable differences in deictic positioning between English and Italian help to foreground the source text's ideological contradictions. All these approaches have in common that they are mindful of the significance of norm-based behaviour in translation, whilst they also acknowledge that no examination of text and context variables can ever reach definite causal conclusions, given that sociocultural values and identities are to be investigated against the backdrop of historical and spatial constraints.

Second, an increasing focus on the notion of discourse in *empirical* methodologies stems from a generally large methodological diversity as well as growing availability of user-friendly corpus technology in (applied) linguistics. In the first instance, DA embraces a variety of empirical approaches to the analysis of language use in context, such as conversation analysis and interactional sociolinguistics, ethnographic models, pragmatics, as well as narrative, argumentation and content analysis. In addition, CDA has seen a number of innovative proposals for new research methods, such as the "discourse historical approach" (Reisigl and Wodak 2009) and the "sociocognitive approach" (van Dijk 1998), which often integrate elements of preexisting concepts and methodologies (e.g. topoi and argumentation in the case of the former, mental models in the case of the latter). In the Anglophone world, many scholars have adopted systemic functional linguistics (Halliday 1978, 1985) in order to investigate the relationship between highly context-sensitive linguistic features (e.g. modality) and their functions in discourse contexts (e.g. Fairclough 1995, 2001). In TS, a special issue of *Target* testified to an increasing diversification of empirical discourse-analytical studies, with Munday and Zhang (2015, 328) summarising the main models and themes (see Table 9.1)

Research exists on each category but at the time of writing no comprehensive overview of work in DA and translation exists in the form of a monograph. In (C)DA, the development and growing availability of corpus-linguistic tools have led to an increasing popularity of corpus-assisted discourse studies (CADS; cf. P. Baker 2006; Partington, Duguid and Taylor 2013). The attraction of CADS lies in its potential to uncover repeated patterns in language use that are unlikely to be noticed when analysing small amounts of text. This approach offers the

Table 9.1 Based on Munday and Zhang's (2015, 328) categorisation of research in discourse analysis and translation

1st level category	2nd level category	3rd level category
Extralinguistic factors	*Culture*	Context of culture and translation
	Ideology	Power, ideology and translation (including a second-level subtheme of CDA)
Linguistic factors	*Communicative dimension*	*User:* idiolect, dialect, etc. (including translation shifts caused by user difference; crosslinguistic difference)
		Use: genre and register analysis (including field, tenor and mode and context of situation)
	Pragmatic dimension	Speech act and translation; implicature (the cooperative principle and Gricean maxims); coherence in translation; narrative analysis and translation
	Semiotic/textual dimension	Texture and textuality in translation; textual scale (word, clause, sentence, text) and translation units; cohesion in translation; thematic and information structure in translation; transivity in translation; modality in translation; semiotics and multimodality; intertextuality; appraisal and translator attitude; paratexts in translation

possibility of cross-tabulating large text corpora and a remedy to claims about the imbalanced and limited choice of material for (critical) analyses (cf. the section on "Current debates" below). In TS, valuable corpus-driven research has appeared since the 1990s, and there exist various overviews (e.g. Olohan 2004; Zanettin 2012). Taking Table 9.1 as a rough guideline, and beginning with M. Baker's (1996; cf. the section on "Core issues and topics" above) foundational work on typical patterns of translated language, research has recently progressed further from pragmatic and communicative factors into the realms of culture and ideology, which makes it possible to speak of the slow evolution of a new context-sensitive empirical paradigm in TS that integrates corpus methodology with the analysis of cultural and ideological dimensions.

Current debates

DA is not particularly prone to controversy. Rather than searching for social explanations, it is a field of enquiry that largely rests on an ethos of scholarly descriptivism. DA has moved beyond the study of written text and spoken conversation to devote increasing attention to online communication in a new research area known as computer-mediated discourse studies (CMDS). Issues arising from this for the study of text structures, genre conventions and intertextuality go beyond the ever more blurring lines between oral and written or casual and formal communication. They also concern the ever changing attitudes to and methods of generating texts, especially in view of communicative interactions between and across users, hypertexts and recipients. Here, new possibilities and conventions arise for the structuring of texts (hyperlinks, modularisation), for collective authorship, instant feedback and content that is determined by user history. It is not surprising, on the other hand, that in CDA current debates first and foremost relate to its "critical" and thus engaged stance towards its objects of investigation, with further discussions centring around the reliability of empirical results, CDA's Eurocentrism and the predominance of research in English. Blommaert, while embracing CDA, emphasises its reliance on certain approaches to linguistic analysis, in particular systemic functional linguistics (2005, 35; cf. Widdowson 2004, 90–103), and what he identifies as its unwillingness to look beyond available linguistic data, for instance at "discourses that are absent" and at "the ways in which society operates on language users and influences what they can accomplish in language long before they open their mouths". There are also unresolved issues centring around the lack of interest, especially in Anglophone CDA, in countries and societies that do not belong to "the core of the world's system" (Blommaert 2005) and the false Western assumption of "universal validity for our ways of life" (*ibid.*, 36), especially when it comes to discourses of globalisation and late modernity.

There is, however, a growing interest in numerous countries, with many emerging studies on a variety of languages. Contributions to the journal *Discourse & Society* since 2014, for instance, include work from Israel, Brazil, Switzerland, Nigeria, Iran, Malaysia, Sweden, Portugal, Japan and Morocco. These contributions nonetheless follow methods and models established in Anglophone CDA research, and they are published in an Anglophone journal, translating their material into English. For a decidedly critical and reflective discipline like CDA, there is indeed a notable absence of a self-reflective debate about the hegemonic status of Anglophone CDA and its academic gatekeepers in conjunction with the implications of the hegemonic status occupied by English in research and higher education around the globe. Another point of criticism made by Blommaert (2005, 37; italics original) is CDA's lack of historical depth, since "to the extent that CDA attempts to launch a critique of *systemic* features of contemporary societies . . . , a synchronic approach will not do". And Widdowson (2004) criticises the empirical approaches in many CDA studies for focusing on a selection of textual features that are determined by the researchers' previous assumptions about the text. One might add that such studies are often based on a rather limited and obvious choice of texts; a classical example would be studying xenophobic or homophobic discourse on the basis of *Daily Mail* reporting. However, while CDA is still dominated by analyses of news media discourse, the genres used within CDA have become more diversified, albeit with a notable focus on power and ideology in hegemonic rather than subversive or counter-hegemonic discourse.

It is reasonable to argue that since the cultural turn in the 1990s, TS simultaneously underwent a kind of "critical turn". Translation Studies since then began to increasingly focus on what might be termed an "ethics of globalisation" (cf. Bielsa and Hughes 2009), given that the production, dissemination and consumption of translations happens in divergent socio-cultural and socioeconomic environments. Such contexts are both defined through unequal relations of power, and through a general redefinition of concepts such as selfhood, nation-hood or territoriality, especially in the wake of (entrepreneurial) globalisation. Questions of ideology and power became increasingly foregrounded, whilst TS remains in need of a more finely nunanced theoretical apparatus in analysing these questions with regard to the context of crosscultural communication. Innovations, for instance, could be drawn from critical globalisation studies or critical theory, especially regarding an analysis of translation under the conditions of today's globalised capitalism. Whereas a debate on the fate of translation in today's era of advanced consumer capitalism has barely begun, there exist lively debates on news translation (Bielsa and Bassnett 2009), on the dominance of English in translational encounters, on the fate of minor, or non-state, languages in translation (Branchadell and West 2005) and on the employment of translation as a counter-hegemonic discourse in activist movements (Boéri and Maier 2010). Such research is driven by an increasing need to con-ceptualise the practice of translation as involving numerous social actors – publishers, editors, translators, etc. – which implies a move away from questions of systemic structure to questions of agency. It is important to note, however, that such shifts in analytical priorities need to be linked to historical (dis)continuities and to larger philosophical debates within a discipline.

Future directions

It is not unreasonable to argue that (C)DA needs to be informed by more historical depth, especially given its predilection for systemic structures and personal interactions in con-temporary societies. A closer engagement with concepts and methods from critical and economic theory remains desirable, as evident in the more openly historicising and political approaches of Marxist or anarchist persuasions. (C)DA's focus on power relations and ideological positions may also be enhanced through a renewed contrastive cultural per-spective on language as social action. A contrastive cultural discourse analysis (CCDA) may be fruitfully differentiated along intercultural dimensions (focusing on interpersonal encounters and thus agency) and crosscultural dimensions (focusing on recontextualisations and thus translation; cf. "Introduction and definitions" above). CCDA as a whole could describe power-induced and ideological similarities and differences across discourse com-munities (cf. Wierzbicka 1997, 2006, 2010), for instance in relation to discourses about authority, love, money, gender, ethnicity, etc. Such contrastive culture studies could underpin arguments about inter- and crosscultural (translational) linguistic patterns embedded in discursive constellations of power and ideology (cf. Widdowson 2004), in the sense of how patterns of linguistic representation are intertextually and interdiscursively linked across languages and discourse communities (cf. Fairclough 1992).

A CCDA approach would help to remedy (C)DA's persistent bias towards intracultural discourse along national lines and its continuous Eurocentrism, especially its overreliance on hegemonic languages, above all English. Most importantly, CCDA would further accentuate a pending comprehensive account of rising socioeconomic inequalities across cultural domains. In the face of growing capitalist globalisation, simmering political, ethnic and religious controversies, and in the face of forced population displacements on an unprecedented scale, a method of contrastive cultural analysis would be well placed to highlight ever more alarming socioeconomic discrepancies world-wide. Over the years, (C)DA has offered numerous studies on localised interactions across power differentials and on more openly hierarchical large-scale discursive settings, i.e. discourse in entrepreneurial and (non-)governmental institutions. (C)DA has not, however, related its findings to a comprehensive account of global power relations within current international arrangements of state power, and we will hopefully also see more research on the ever growing pseudo-democratisation, commodification and technologisation of language use in the political and cultural domains (Fairclough 1999).

The *intercultural* dimension of CCDA would focus on international encounters and interactions between people, on internalisations of cultural premises, on the dangers of culture-blind misunderstanding and on resolutions to overcome cultural essentialism (cf. Jackson 2012; Dervin and Machart 2015). Such an approach would also proactively promote intercultural, i.e. cosmopolitan, citizenship through creating enhanced sensitivity towards the "other", i.e. all that is initially foreign, in communicative interactions. Much work on intercultural communication has focused on cultural norms of politeness in terms of face-saving or face-threatening behaviour, using concepts that emerged from pragmatics (e.g. Scollon, Wong Scollon and Jones 2000). But cultural premises and culture-specific forms of linguistic practice are enshrined in discourse in multifarious ways, as Wierzbicka's work (1997, 2006, 2010) illustrates by investigating only a small number of cultural key words. An intercultural dimension could play a significant role in highlighting discourse-determined variations across genre conventions and semantic content that may become problematic in intercultural encounters. Considering an increasingly globalising (and thus homogenising) news media discourse, for instance, an intercultural dimension would flag up questions related to cultural agency, recipient anticipation, selectivity, content production and consumption. The issue of globalising media discourse also relates to the communicative norm of using English as a foreign language in intercultural encounters (cf. Pennycook 2007; Cagliero and Jenkins 2010), a custom that moreover tends to gloss over cultural alterity and the manifold realities inscribed in linguistic practices, particularly in view of discourse-determined meanings and genre conventions that speakers bring into global Englishes. CCDA's intercultural dimension may also highlight the cultural residues of English and the ways in which its use as lingua franca, especially in academia, potentially limits engagement with socioeconomic conceptualisations that are not enshrined in the English language and its associated, yet ever shifting, sociocultural landscapes (Wierzbicka 2014).

The *crosscultural* dimension of CCDA would focus on translation and interpreting as text-induced phenomena, as instances of crosscultural communication based on linguistic mediations through cultural recontextualisations. A novel crosscultural perspective for (C)DA would foreground T&I as communicative and semiotic phenomena in their own right. A crosscultural perspective would probe into the historical and political impact of cultural essentialism in relation to translational products and practices, for instance in the ways in which T&I are embedded in crosscultural networks of power, influence and authority. Sociological questions concerning text selection and norm-governed behaviour will have to be triangulated with the resulting sociotextual profiles, patterns of audience reception as well as culture-specific and historical contexts. Against the backdrop of hierarchical power relations and their associated ideological significations, relevant research questions could ask: Which texts are assigned cultural significance and therefore get selected for translation? What norms govern the textual profiles of specific translations, in other words which notions of correctness concerning style, lexicogrammar and genre conventions determine the behaviour of T&I producers? Inasmuch as translations are influenced by dominant discourses and ideologies, particularly in the target language, what may the resulting intertextual patterns tell us about power, domination and hegemony in today's globalised world? And generally, what are the stakes of T&I in relation to technology, neoliberal geopolitics, migration and social movement politics? Investigations of crosscultural discourse patterns, however, must not sidestep an equally important focus on discursive silence, on those never verbalised but nonetheless ideologically relevant communicative features that continue to have a bearing on crosscultural events. Work in the sociology of globalisation is relevant in this regard, for instance the "sociology of absence" proposed by Santos (2006), where silences and gaps, e.g. non-translations, are considered as discursively constructed and thus ideologically meaningful.

Implications for practice

Research and text production are activities shaped by historical and cultural circumstance. Researchers and text producers have the option of adopting a disinterested or engaged approach, of being unconcerned about the wider social implications of their activities or of being mindful about the world's suffering and potential ways out of current predicaments. Consequently, academic researchers, in any domain of sociocultural enquiry, might opt for a descriptive approach that is mainly geared towards understanding social and semiotic phenomena (e.g. Marais 2014), or they could pursue a critical agenda that attempts to lay bare the underlying dynamics of power, conflict and struggle that are constitutive of every social situation. On the other hand, producers of texts, be it "originary" or translational communication, all bring their own conscious and unconscious ideological agendas and interests to the table. Most text producers are located in non-democratic and thus hierarchically structured workplace settings, which themselves are embedded in local and global networks of power. By and large, text producers construct their (shifting) identities within these parameters of discursive influence and political authority. Their location in the web of power inevitably influences their interpersonal alliances and ideological positions, which in turn flow into the textual output produced.

People in general and text producers in particular often do not have the opportunity to stick to their own ethical agenda. Translators who accept commissions from the armaments industry might be in financial distress, but they might also be fervent believers in military rule and trigger-happy self-defence. They might be pacifists or warmongers, anti-authoritarians or disciplinarians. When it comes to an *engaged* and thus critical account of their activities, the only thing researchers can do is lay bare their own ideological leanings and to engage in a critical examination of translators' discursive moves. From a perspective informed by notions of power, hegemony and domination, and with Blommaert's demand to look beyond existing and easily identifiable interactional and linguistic manifestations of discourse, it seems vital to bring issues of selection into sharp relief. Which texts get selected for translation, and hence, represent "symbolic power" (Bourdieu 1991)? Equally, making the arrangements and processes of T&I more visible and transparent will allow for a critical assessment, for instance in the media, and encourage a more critical distance from the translated text as the end product of this process (cf. Schäffner 2012). Ultimately, however, any practical implication surrounding the theme of "discourse analysis, interpreting and translation" depends on people's attitudes, beliefs and ideological views concerning the world's geopolitical disparities and socioeconiomic injustices. Do we really care, or shall we just accept things as they are?

Further reading

Baumgarten, S. and Gagnon, C. 2016. *Translating the European House: Discourse, Ideology and Politics – Selected Papers by Christina Schäffner.* Newcastle: Cambridge Scholars Publishing.
This edited volume offers a cross-section of Christina Schäffner's seminal work on translation and politics, written between 1996 and 2012. With a focus on translation in the European context, this article collection illuminates various points of contact between translation research and CDA, including numerous case studies and translation examples. The book may serve as a valuable blueprint for future studies that seek to build on Schäffner's CDA-inspired investigations, methods and conclusions.

Jaworski, A. and Coupland, N., eds. 2006. *The Discourse Reader.* 2nd ed. London: Routledge.
This reader provides a collection of key texts that illustrate the developments, key issues and concepts in DA and CDA. It is divided into six parts, including part 3 on "Sequence and Structure" pertinent to DA, and part 6 on "Power, Ideology and Control" pertinent to CDA. Each part is preceded by a brief introduction by the editors, contextualising key texts in the development of the study of discourse.

Mason, I. 2010/1994. "Discourse, Ideology and Translation". In *Critical Readings in Translation Studies*, edited by M. Baker, 83–96, 2010. London: Routledge (also in Hatim and Mason 1997, chapters 2 and 9).
Mason's linguistic analysis of an article on Mexican colonial history can be seen as a piece of "classic" CDA-inspired translation research. Mason shows how underlying value orientations can be highlighted through a contrastive analysis of lexis and text structure in a Spanish text and its English translation, and how the resulting discursive shifts reveal a target text ideology that depicts native historical actors as less actively involved in shaping their own destiny than the Spanish colonisers.

Munday, J. 2012. *Evaluation in Translation: Critical Points of Translator Decision-making.* Abingdon: Routledge.
Many of Jeremy Munday's investigations into translation are underpinned by key principles and methods from systemic functional linguistics. Even though this study does not explicitly adopt a CDA approach, Munday's focus on appraisal theory, an innovation in CDA that scrutinises subtle markers of attitude in language, might bode well for future studies of translation that choose to adopt a critical linguistic stance.

Paltridge, B. 2006. *Discourse Analysis: An Introduction.* London: Continuum.
This introduction includes chapters that cover the main ground of DA (chapters 4, 5 and 6), and provide links between DA, pragmatics and sociolinguistics (chapters 2 and 3), and it includes a chapter about CDA which highlights concisely the main aspects that CDA adds to DA.

Related topics

Genre analysis and translation; Text linguistics, translating and interpreting; Narrative analysis and translation; Sociolinguistics, translation and interpreting; Translation, interpreting and new technologies.

References

Baker, M. 1996. "Corpus-based Translation Studies: The Challenges that Lie Ahead". In *Terminology, LSP, and Translation: Studies in Language Engineering in Honour of Juan Sager*, edited by H. Somers, 175–187. Amsterdam: John Benjamins.

Baker, M. 2006. *Translation and Conflict: A Narrative Account*. London: Routledge.

Baker, P. 2006. *Using Corpora in Discourse Analysis*. London: Continuum.

Barton, E., Dickson, B. and Kinloch, V. 2015. Discourse research in applied linguistics: contrastive rhetoric and genre analysis. *Word* 50(3), pp. 375–386.

Bassnett, S. and Lefevere, A., eds. 1990. *Translation, History and Culture*. London: Pinter.

Baumgarten, S. 2009. *Translating Hitler's "Mein Kampf": A Corpus-Aided Discourse-Analytical Study*. Saarbrücken: VDM Verlag Dr. Müller.

Baumgarten, S. and Gagnon, C. 2016. *Translating the European House: Discourse, Ideology and Politics: Selected Papers by Christina Schäffner*. Newcastle: Cambridge Scholars Publishing.

Bax, S. 2011. *Discourse and Genre: Analysing Language in Context*. Basingstoke: Palgrave Macmillan.

Bhatia, V. and Bhatia, A. 2011. Legal discourse across cultures and socio-pragmatic contexts. *World Englishes* 30(4), pp. 481–495.

Bielsa, E. and Bassnett, S. 2009. *Translation in Global News*. London: Routledge.

Bielsa, E. and Hughes, C., eds. 2009. *Globalization, Political Violence and Translation*. Basingstoke: Palgrave Macmillan.

Blommaert, J. 2005. *Discourse: A Critical Introduction*. Cambridge: Cambridge University Press.

Boéri, J. and Maier, C., eds. 2010. *Compromiso Social y Traducción/Interpretación* [*Translation/ Interpreting and Social Activism*]. Granada (Spain): ECOS Traductores e Intérpretes por la Solidaridad.

Bourdieu, P. 1991. *Language and Symbolic Power*. Cambridge: Polity Press.

Branchadell, A. and West, L. M., eds. 2005. *Less Translated Languages*. Amsterdam & Philadelphia: John Benjamins.

Brisset, A. 1989. In search of a target language: the politics of theatre translation in Quebec. *Target* 1(1), pp. 9–27.

Brown, G. and Yule, G. 1983. *Discourse Analysis*. Cambridge: Cambridge University Press.

Buden, B., Nowotny, S., Simon, S., Bery, A. and Cronin, M. 2009. Cultural translation: an introduction to the problem, and responses. *Translation Studies* 2(2), pp. 196–219.

Cagliero, R. and Jenkins, J., eds. 2010. *Discourses, Communities, and Global Englishes*. Bern: Peter Lang.

Caimotto, C. (forthcoming). "Proximization amidst Liquidity: Osama bin Laden's Death Translated". In *Translation and Power in a Globalized World*, edited by S. Baumgarten and J. Cornellà-Detrell. Bristol: Multilingual Matters.

Calzada-Pérez, M. 2006. *Transitivity in Translating: The Interdependence of Texture and Context*. Bern: Peter Lang.

Cap, P. 2013. *Proximization: The Pragmatics of Symbolic Distance Crossing*. Amsterdam: John Benjamins.

Carbonell, O. 1996. "The Exotic Space of Cultural Translation". In *Translation, Power, Subversion*, edited by R. Alvarez and M. Vidal, 79–98. Clevedon: Multiingual Matters.

Charteris-Black, J. 2005. *Politicians and Rhetoric: The Persuasive Power of Metaphor*. Basingstoke: Palgrave Macmillan.

Chesterman, A. 2000. "A Causal Model for Translation Studies". In *Intercultural Faultlines: Research Models in Translation Studies I. Textual and Cognitive Aspects*, edited by M. Olohan, 15–27. Manchester: St Jerome Publishing.

Chilton, P. A. 2004. *Analysing Political Discourse: Theory and Practice*. London: Routledge.

Chilton, P. A. and Schäffner, C., eds. 2002. *Politics as Text and Talk: Analytic Approaches to Political Discourse*. Amsterdam: John Benjamins.

Connor, U. 1996. *Contrastive Rhetoric: Cross-cultural Aspects of Second-language Writing*. Cambridge: Cambridge University Press.

Cronin, M. 2003. *Translation and Globalization*. London: Routledge.

Dervin, F. and Machart, R., eds. 2015. *Cultural Essentialism in Intercultural Relations*. Basingstoke: Palgrave Macmillan.

Fairclough, N. 1992. *Discourse and Social Change*. Cambridge: Polity Press.

Fairclough, N. 1995. *Critical Discourse Analysis: The Critical Study of Language*. London: Longman.

Fairclough, N. 1999. Global capitalism and critical awareness of language. *Language Awareness* 8(2), pp. 71–83.

Fairclough, N. 2001. *Language and Power*. 2nd ed. Harlow: Pearson Education.

Fowler, R., Kress, G., Hodge, R. and Trew, T. 1979. *Language and Control*. London: Routledge and Kegan Paul.

Gutt, E. A. 1991. "Translation as Interlingual Interpretive Use". In *The Translation Studies Reader*, edited by L. Venuti, 2000, 376–396. London: Routledge.

Halliday, M. A. K. 1978. *Language as Social Semiotic: The Social Interpretation of Language and Meaning*. London: Edward Arnold.

Halliday, M. A. K. 1985. *Introduction to Functional Grammar*. London: Edward Arnold.

Hatim, B. and Mason, I. 1990. *Discourse and the Translator*. London: Longman.

Hatim, B. and Mason, I. 1997. *The Translator as Communicator*. London: Routledge.

Hart, C., ed. 2011. *Critical Discourse Studies in Context and Cognition*. Amsterdam: John Benjamins.

Holmes, J. S. 1988/2004. "The Name and Nature of Translation Studies". In *The Translation Studies Reader*, 2nd ed., edited by L. Venuti, 180–192. London: Routledge.

House, J. 1977/1981. *A Model for Translation Quality Assessment*. Tübingen: Gunter Narr Verlag.

Jackson, J., ed. 2012. *The Routledge Handbook of Language and Intercultural Communication*. Abingdon: Routledge.

Jakobson, R. 1959/2000. "On Linguistic Aspects of Translation". In *On Translation*, edited by R. A. Brower, 232–239. Cambridge, MA: Harvard University Press. Reprinted 2000 in *The Translation Studies Reader*, edited by L. Venuti, 113–118. London: Routledge.

Jaworski, A. and Coupland, N., eds. 2006. *The Discourse Reader*. 2nd ed. London: Routledge.

Kress, G. and Hodge, R. 1979. *Language as Ideology*. London: Routledge and Kegan Paul.

Kress, G. and van Leeuwen, T. 2001. *Multimodal Discourse: The Modes and Media of Contemporary Communication*. London: Arnold.

Kress, G. and van Leeuwen, T. 2006. *Reading Images: The Grammar of Visual Design*. London: Routledge.

Levy, J. 1967. "Translation as a Decision Process". In *To Honor Roman Jakobson*. Vol. 2, 1171–1182. The Hague: Mouton. Reprinted in *The Translation Studies Reader*, edited by L. Venuti, 2000, 148–159. London: Routledge.

Machin, D. 2010. *Analysing Popular Music: Image, Sound, Text*. Los Angeles: SAGE.

Marais, K. 2014. *Translation Theory and Development Studies: A Complexity Theory Approach*. London: Routledge.

Munday, J. 2008. *Style and Ideology in Translation: Latin American Writing in English*. London: Routledge.

Munday, J. 2012. *Evaluation in Translation: Critical Points of Translator Decision-making*. Abingdon: Routledge.

Munday, J. and Zhang, M. 2015. Discourse Analysis in Translation Studies. Special issue of *Target* 27(3).

Musolff, A. 2004. *Metaphor and Political Discourse: Analogical Reasoning in Debates about Europe*. Basingstoke: Palgrave Macmillan.

Nergaard, S. 2007. *Translation and Power: Recent Theoretical Updates*. Universita Studi di Firenze.

Neubert, A. 1985. *Text and Translation*. Leipzig: VEB Verlag Enzyklopädie.

Neubert, A. and Shreve, G. 1992. *Translation as Text*. Kent, OH: Kent State University Press.

Nida, E. A. 1964. *Toward a Science of Translating with Special Reference to Principles and Procedures Involved in Bible Translating*. Leiden: E. J. Brill.

Niranjana, T. 1992. *Siting Translation: History, Post-Structuralism, and the Colonial Context*. Berkeley: University of California Press.

Olohan, M. 2004. *Introducing Corpora in Translation Studies*. London: Routledge.

Paltridge, B. 1997. *Genres, Frames, and Writing in Research Settings*. Amsterdam: John Benjamins.

Paltridge, B. 2006. *Discourse Analysis: An Introduction*. London: Continuum.

Partington, A., Duguid, A. and Taylor, C. 2013. *Patterns and Meanings in Discourse: Theory and Practice in Corpus-Assisted Discourse Studies (CADS)*. Amsterdam: John Benjamins.

Pennycook, A. 2007. *Global Englishes and Transcultural Flows*. London: Routledge.

Reisigl, M. and Wodak, R. 2009. "The Discourse-Historical Approach (DHA)". In *Methods for Critical Discourse Analysis* (2nd rev. ed.), edited by R. Wodak and M. Meyer, 87–121. Sage, London.

Reiss, K. 1977/1989. "Text-types, translation types and translation assessment", trans. A. Chesterman. In *Readings in Translation Theory*, edited by A. Chesterman, 1989, 105–115. Helsinki: Oy Finn Lectura Ab.

Saldanha, G. and O'Brien, S. 2013. *Research Methodologies in Translation Studies*. Manchester: St Jerome.

Santos, B. de Sousa. 2006. *The Rise of the Global Left: The World Social Forum and Beyond*. London: Zed Books.

Schäffner, C. 2004. Political discourse analysis from the point of view of translation studies. *Journal of Language and Politics* 3(1), pp. 117–150 [republished in Baumgarten and Gagnon 2016].

Schäffner, C. 2012. Unknown agents in translated political discourse. *Target* 24(1), pp. 103–125.

Schiffrin, D. 1994. *Approaches to Discourse*. Malden: Blackwell.

Scollon, R., Wong Scollon, S. and Jones, R. H. 2000. *Intercultural Communication: A Discourse Approach*. 3rd ed. Malden: Wiley Blackwell.

Sperber, D. and Wilson, D. 1986. *Relevance: Communication and Cognition*. Oxford: Blackwell. (2nd ed. 1995.)

Swales, J. 1998. *Other Floors, Other Voices: A Textography of a Small University Building*. Hillsdale, NJ: Lawrence Erlbaum.

Taboada, M., Doval Suárez, S. and González Álvarez, E., eds. 2013. *Contrastive Discourse Analysis: Functional and Corpus Perspectives*. Sheffield: Equinox.

Toury, G. 1995. *Descriptive Translation Studies – and Beyond*. Amsterdam: John Benjamins.

Tymoczko, M., ed. 2010. *Translation, Resistance, Activism*. Amherst: University of Massachusetts Press.

Tymoczko, M. and Gentzler, E., eds. 2002. *Translation and Power*. Amherst: University of Massachusetts Press.

Van Dijk, T. A. 1998. *Ideology: A Multidisciplinary Approach*. London: SAGE.

Van Dijk, T. A., ed. 2006. *Discourse Studies: A Multidisciplinary Introduction*. 2nd ed. Los Angeles: SAGE.

Van Dijk, T. A. 2008a. *Discourse and Power*. Basingstoke: Palgrave Macmillan.

Van Dijk, T. A. 2008b. *Discourse and Context: A Sociocognitive Approach*. Cambridge: Cambridge University Press.

Venuti, L. 1995. *The Translator's Invisibility: A History of Translation*. London: Routledge.

Venuti, L. 1998. *The Scandals of Translation: Towards an Ethics of Difference*. London: Routledge.

Von Flotow, L. 1997. *Translation and Gender: Translating in the "Era of Feminism"*. Manchester: St Jerome.

Widdowson, H. 2004. *Text, Context, Pretext: Critical Issues in Discourse Analysis*. Malden: Blackwell.

Wierzbicka, A. 1997. *Understanding Cultures through their Key Words: English, Russian, Polish, German, and Japanese*. New York: Oxford University Press.

Wierzbicka, A. 2006. *English: Meaning and Culture*. Oxford: Oxford University Press.

Wierzbicka, A. 2010. *Experience, Evidence, and Sense: The Hidden Cultural Legacy of English*. Oxford: Oxford University Press.

Wierzbicka, A. 2014. *Imprisoned in English: The Hazards of English as a Default Language*. Oxford: Oxford University Press.

Wodak, R. and Meyer, M., eds. 2009. *Methods of Critical Discourse Analysis*. 2nd ed. Los Angeles: SAGE.

Zanettin, F. 2012. *Translation-driven Corpora*. Manchester: St Jerome.

10

Genre analysis and translation

Łucja Biel

Introduction and definitions

The term *genre* [Brit. /ˈʒɒ̃rə/, /ˈʒɒnrə/, /ˈʒɑːnrə/] was borrowed in the early 19th century from French and its literal meaning is "a kind" (OED, Oxford English Dictionary [online], 2016). It is one of the key terms of both literary studies and language studies, in particular in various strands of functional linguistics, such as discourse analysis, Critical Discourse Analysis, Systemic Functional Linguistics, rhetorical studies, the New Rhetoric, English for Specific Purposes and applied linguistics. It reflects long-standing attempts to categorise texts into larger groups and to look for regularities and abstraction above the text level. Examples of genres include: a novel, a poem, a CV, an annual report, a contract, a user manual, a TV commercial.

The meaning of "genre" has evolved significantly over the decades and differs depending on the theoretical framework. First, genre was associated with text types, that is a group of texts which share a similar form, style and content. One of the well-known definitions of genre, proposed by Swales, stresses the importance of a communicative purpose: "a class of communicative events, the members of which share some set of communicative purposes which are recognized by the expert members of the parent discourse community" (Swales 1990, 58). What is often evoked in the definitions of genre is a conventionalised use of language – the habitual repeated use of a set of conventions. The fixedness of patterns varies across genres; for example, a genre of legislation is ritualised and shows a high fixedness of form and routine formulae, while a genre of TV commercials is much less predictable, more unconventional and creative. More recent approaches stress that genres tend to be dynamic, evolving and subject to hybridisation. They are viewed as "flexible macrostructures" in which obligatory and optional elements occur in a predefined order (cf. Cap and Okulska 2013, 4). Current approaches to genre have shifted focus from a product to a process and associate genres strongly with the social context in which they are used. A genre is thus viewed as a "way of *acting and interacting* linguistically" (Fairclough 2003, 17, emphasis added), a social process which is staged and fulfils a specific goal (cf. Martin and Rose 2007, 8) and as social action which consists in typified ways of acting in recurring social situations (Miller 1984). What these definitions have in common is a strong emphasis on a repeated use of relatively stable, recognisable patterns in a particular discourse community for a specific communicative purpose to realise a social goal. One of the consequences of the conventional use of language in genres is that it sends recognisable signals of being "in a genre" and creates expectations in the discourse community about communicative purpose, form and content. Within Translation Studies the term, "genre", is often used interchangeably with the term "text type", and indeed, the two concepts are related; however, "genre" evokes the social context of use and associated concepts such as agency, power and ideology, while text types group texts at a higher level of abstraction, e.g. rhetorical purpose (Hatim and Mason 1990), cognitive categories (Trosborg 1997, 16) or force of a text (Tsiplakou and Floros 2013). Text types are also referred to as prototypical text categories, text prototypes and deep structure genres (see further Tsiplakou and Floros 2013, 121).

Genres enter into relationships and interact with each other. They tend to form larger hierarchical and non-hierarchical clusters, known under a number of names – most notably, systems of interdependent genres (cf. Bazerman 1994), genre chains (cf. Fairclough 2003, 216), constellations of genres (Swales 2004, 12), networks of genres (Fairclough 2006, 34) or genre colonies (Bhatia 2004, 57). A genre cluster may be exemplified with: an invitation to speak at the symposium, an acceptance, promotional materials with the speaker's abstract and biography, the speech itself, slides and handouts and an article submitted to conference proceedings (cf. Swales 2004, 18). Genres comprised within clusters are interrelated and linked to each other by a communicative purpose. They are arranged in a more or less fixed chronological order or in a ranking order (cf. Swales 2004, 13) where one genre is transformed into another. Such transformations may be perceived as "intralingual translation" or "transgeneric translation" from more to less specialised genres (Ezpeleta Piorno 2012, 168, 174). Take for example the medicinal product information genre system, which includes the central genre of the summary of product characteristics (SPS) with instructions of use for the discourse community of healthcare professionals; this specialised document is a basis for preparing readable documents, such as a patient information leaflet (PIL) and advertising materials addressed to the lay community of patients (Ezpeleta Piorno 2012, 172). Some genres within a cluster may control the form and content of other genres or of the entire cluster – they are known as meta-genres, i.e. "genres about genres" (Giltrow 2001, 190) and "atmospheres surrounding genres" (Giltrow 2001, 196). An example of a meta-genre is the EU Interinstitutional Style Guide, which introduces uniform stylistic rules to be applied by the EU institutions and translators across various genres in the institutional context, e.g. legal acts, reports, monographs. Finally, hierarchical clusters of genres may involve evaluations – for instance, in the humanities, monographs tend to be valued more than other academic genres, such as research papers or reviews.

Two other types of relations which are of interest in genre analysis are intertextuality and interdiscursivity. Intertextuality shows the relationship of a text to other texts: "how texts draw upon, incorporate, recontextualize and dialogue with other texts" (Fairclough 2003, 17). Interdiscursivity analyses embeddings of a text in other genres, genre mixing and hybridisation: it explores "the particular mix of genres, of discourses, and of styles upon which it draws, and how different genres, discourses or styles are articulated (or 'worked') together in the text" (Fairclough 2003, 218). Thus, to be complete, genre analysis should account not only for the structural components of a genre and its conventions, but also for the sociocultural context, that is, a discourse community and its expectations, communicative purpose, social goal, as well as relationships with other texts and genres.

The term "genre" should be differentiated from the related term "register", even though the concepts which these terms denote overlap to a certain degree and the terms are sometimes used interchangeably. Genre and register are two perspectives on analysing texts (Biber and Conrad 2009, 15). Register may be defined as a functional variety of language associated with a given situation type (Halliday 2004, 27; see also Biber and Conrad 2009, 6), but there are differing views on what should be comprised in register analysis as opposed to genre analysis. Within Systemic Functional Linguistics, register analysis is based on three situational variables: a field (what is going on), tenor (who is taking part) and mode (the role that the language is playing) (Halliday 1978). In Biber and Conrad's corpus-linguistic approach, genre analysis focuses on the rhetorical structure and formatting of the *whole* texts, while register analysis focuses on lower-level pervasive lexico-grammatical patterns in text *excerpts* (Biber and Conrad 2009, 16). It is worth noting that the latter would be included as a component of genre analysis in Bhatia's approach grounded in discourse analysis (2004, 164–167; see also Biber and Conrad 2009, 21–22 for an overview of approaches).

Historical perspectives

Genre analysis and genre as such have generally been less prominent in Translation Studies than within linguistics, but have been gaining in importance since the 1990s. As mentioned in the previous section, the terms "genres" and "text types" are frequently used interchangeably by translation scholars.

Text types appear in Holmes's map of Translation Studies as one of the strands within "pure" theoretical Translation Studies, that is "text-type (or discourse-type) restricted theories", which study translations within specific domains, such as legal translation or medical translation (Holmes 2004 [1972], 187). Translation-related research into text types coincides with the emergence and growth of the discipline of Translation Studies in the 1970s. Interest has been particularly strong in Germany within functional theories of translation, especially Katharina Reiss's (2000 [1971]) work on text types (*Texttyp*) and text varieties (*Textsorte*), which correspond to Anglo-Saxon genres (cf. Schäffner 2002, 4), in the context of translation criticism. Reiss (2000 [1971], 17) argues that a text type is the primary determinant of translation strategies (though not the only one). The relation between text types and translation strategies was observed by St Jerome as early as in the 4th century CE. Jerome noted that non-religious texts should be translated more freely than religious texts (Chesterman 1997, 23). Reiss's work is based on Bühler's three functions of language, which she relates to the following text types: informative/content-focused (communication of facts, i.e. a press release), expressive/form-focused (aesthetic, creative content, i.e. a poem), operative/appeal-focused (persuasive content, i.e. an advertisement) and audiomedial (a complementary "hyper-type" – audiovisual texts). According to Reiss, translations should respect the function of the source text (ST) type. Thus, translations of informative texts should completely transfer the information content of the ST ("invariance"), translations of expressive texts should transfer artistic aspects of the ST and translations of operative texts should have the same psychological effect on target readers' behaviour as they have on ST readers' behaviour (Reiss 2000[1971], 24–47). Although Reiss's contribution is important in that it brought the communicative purpose of translations into the spotlight and stimulated discussion about text types, it has been criticised for a number of reasons. Above all, given the hybrid and mul-tifunctional nature of texts, Reiss's classification of text types is far too rigid and general and, hence, it has limited applicability in practice (see Hatim and Mason 1990, 138; Fawcett 1997, 104–111; and Munday 2001, 77 for a more detailed overview of the criticism of Reiss's approach).

Research into text types was undertaken in the following decades by a number of scholars who proposed more refined categorisations based on varied criteria. For example, Mary Snell-Hornby's integrated approach places text types (prototypes) along a continuum without discrete boundaries, especially between literary and non-literary translation (Snell-Hornby 1995 [1988], 31). With genres being one of the prominent markers of lexicographical literature on specialised (LSP) translation texts (cf. Rogers 2015, 31), text typologies and genre-based classifications have been especially prolific in specialised translation. One of these is Göpferich's (1995) pragmatic text typology applicable to the translation of scientific and technical texts. Göpferich (1995, 320) criticises "the invariance requirement" to fully transfer the information content in informative texts in so far as they apply to scientific and technical domains. She argues that translation strategies should not be recommended for global text categories but for text types with similar communicative functions (1995, 322).

With genre being one of the main analytical tools in discourse analysis, the growing interest in genre (rather than text type) was a natural consequence of the application of discourse analytical methods to Translation Studies in the late 1980s and 1990s (James 1989; Hatim and Mason 1990; 1997; Neubert and Shreve 1992; Trosborg 1997; 2002). James (1989) was among the first to promote the use of the concept of genre in Translation Studies, in particular in translator training. The application of genre analysis to translation intensified, following rapid developments stimulated by seminal books within the English for Specific Purposes approach by Swales (1990; 2004) and Bhatia (1993; 2004). The growing interest in research on genres is confirmed by Zhang *et al.*'s (2015, 229) bibliometric study of discourse-analysis research on translation in eight major translation journals in the period 1990–2013. The study shows that interest in genre and register analysis peaked between 1996 and 2005, before being overtaken by interest in such extralinguistic factors as power, ideology and context. Overall, the 1990s mark a shift in research into cross-linguistic differences between comparable genres in the source language (SL) and the target language (TL), especially for specialised translation purposes.

Hatim and Mason (1990; 1997), UK-based translation scholars, applied discourse analysis and Critical Discourse Analysis to their model of translation based on the genre-text-discourse triad which reflects the socio-textual practices of discourse communities. For Hatim and Mason (1990, 69; 1997, 18), texts realise users' rhetorical purposes, genres are "conventionalised forms of texts" adjusted to the goals of social occasions, while discourses reflect attitudes. Even though they note that genre may be a less important variable than the social context of translation (1990, 13), Hatim and Mason (1990, 69–70) identify genre and genre membership as key factors which affect the translator's decision-making process. Generic conventions are indices of cultures and the translator is bound by "generic constraints" in translation related to communicative purposes, rhetorical mode and intentionality behind a specific genre in the source and target language. Hatim and Mason (1990, 140) propose their own typology of texts, seeing text types as "the translator's focus" and "a conceptual framework which enables us to classify texts in terms of communicative intentions serving an overall rhetorical purpose". Hatim and Mason's (1990, 153–160) typology is based on a continuum from "extremely detached and non-evaluative" texts to texts which are "extremely involved and highly evaluative". Their classification of texts (text types) for translation purposes is based on the notions of rhetorical purpose and dominant contextual focus: "argumentation" (which involves evaluation), "exposition" (presentation in a non-evaluative way) and "instruction" (which intends to evoke certain behaviour; contracts, legislation).

The concept of genre was also used in translation quality assessment models, most notably in Juliane House's functional-pragmatic model of translation evaluation, based on Halliday's

Systemic Functional Linguistics and discourse analysis. House's (1977; 2001, 247) model involves the assessment of the ST and target text (TT) according to the four-tiered analytical model at the level of language/text, register, genre and textual function. As House (2001, 248) notes, genre allocates a given ST to a higher-level category of texts with a common communicative purpose and provides information on "deeper" structures: "While register captures the connection between texts and their 'microcontext,' Genre connects texts with the 'macrocontext' of the linguacultural community in which a text is embedded". Chesterman (1997, 65) links the concept of genre with expectancy norms, arguing that evaluations of translations are based on expectancy norms which, in turn, are shaped by target readers' expectations about genre and discourse conventions.

Another wave of interest in genre analysis was brought about by work on corpora in the 2000s, following the rapid development of corpus linguistics in the 1980s and its introduction to Translation Studies in the 1990s. Corpora are large electronic collections of texts which are studied with dedicated software. Corpora show high sensitivity to genres and other categorisations of texts as, in most cases, corpus design is genre based and is guided by the criterion of representativeness; that is, a corpus must be representative of a genre its creator intends to study (cf. Olohan 2004, 45–47). Translation Studies rely on two types of corpora: comparable corpora, which are monolingual corpora of translated and non-translated texts; and parallel corpora, which are corpora with STs aligned with their translations. Research comparing translations against non-translations in the same language was pioneered by Baker (1995) with a view to identifying distinctive features of translations (see also "Current debates" section below). It inspired a number of scholars to engage in corpus-based studies which have started to produce quantitative data on how translations differ from non-translations in terms of generic conventions in various domains, e.g. in localisation (Jiménez-Crespo 2012) or in legal translation (Biel 2014). Corpora are also applied in practically oriented research into genres: for example, contrastive genre analyses conducted by the GENTT (Textual Genres in Translation) research group (Borja Albi 2013). Overall, genre-based corpus studies are still an emerging field, which has brought genre analysis into the spotlight again.

Core issues and topics

While the main preoccupation of genre analysis in linguistics is to identify how genres differ from one another, translation-oriented genre analysis has focused on identifying differences in generic structures, conventions and expectations across languages and cultures. This area is sometimes referred to as contrastive rhetoric, contrastive textology and contrastive analysis of genres and it is supported by ample evidence that conventions differ not only across genres but also within the same genre across languages and cultures as they are shaped by distinct discourse communities (cf. Hatim and Mason 1990, 97; Nord 1991, 19; Baker 1992, 183, 186; Colina 1997, 336). Genres may be differently realised linguistically across cultures and, hence, generic conventions are culture-specific to some extent: "For the translator it is important to be aware of the fact that although the same genres may exist in different cultures, they may in fact be – and often are – structured or composed in different ways" (Trosborg 2002, 14). Differences may for example concern cohesive devices (Baker 1992, 190), conjunctions (Baker 1992, 196), tolerance of repetitions (Hatim and Mason 1990, 97), routine formulaic phrases in patents (Göpferich 1995, 321), referencing patterns as regards the use of pronouns instead of full names (Baker 1992, 183) or personal forms of address in school books (Göpferich 1995, 322), to name but a few. Differences have also been noted at higher levels of generic organisation, that is the conceptual organisation of content and functional stages known as moves (Rogers 2015, 34, see also the section "Main research methods" below). For example, the genre of legislation contains only normative provisions in some countries (e.g. in Poland), while in other legal systems it may also contain the enacting formula (the UK – *BE IT ENACTED by the Queen's most Excellent Majesty, by and with the advice and consent of the Lords Spiritual and Temporal, and Commons, in this present Parliament assembled, and by the authority of the same, as follows*), lengthy non-normative preambles which include citations with legal grounds (*Having regard to the Treaty establishing the European Union*) and recitals with political considerations to legitimise enactments (cf. Biel 2014, 77–78). Finally, some genres do not have any formal counterparts in a target culture, e.g. the Arabic verse form, the qasidah, and may "resist" translation (Bassnett 2006, 90). Some genres are not only remote culturally from the target discourse community, but may also be remote in time – see Bassnett (2006, 92) on the problem of translating a "dead genre", e.g. an epic poem such as the *Iliad*, for a new generation of readers.

A related topic is how generic differences between the SL and the TL are approached in translation. As Baker (1992, 188) notes, the standard situation is to adjust the translation to TL textual conventions, in order to ensure "genre-fidelity" (James 1989). However, the recommendation to adjust to TL conventions depends on the level of generic organisation. Hatim (2001, 123) observes that "the translator has limited scope to modify genres in translation, possibilities nevertheless exist at the level of genre-upholding lexical selection (collocations, imagery, etc.)". Thus, adjustments may be expected at the level of phraseology and routine formulae; translators are less likely to intervene to rearrange the original information flow and moves. It is however argued that if the translator fails to adapt the TT to generic conventions, including changes in textual organisation, it may have an adverse impact on comprehension: "the text's rhetorical purpose will not be achieved, and ultimately, processing of the text as a coherent, cohesive whole may be difficult" (Colina 1997, 337). Research into how text types are skewed or shifted in translation was identified by Holmes (2004 [1972], 188) as early as in 1972 as an important question to be explored by translation scholars. This topic was also raised by James (1989, 31) as "genre violation", resulting from distortions of the ST rhetorical structure in the translation process and by Hatim and Munday (2004, 88) as "genre shifts".

The degree of adaptation to TL conventions will certainly vary across genres. While certain relatively fixed genres, such as contracts or school diplomas, do not permit much adaptation above the phrase level, promotional genres, such as company websites or commercials, might require a much higher degree of adaptation above the phrase level, including the omission or reduction of some stages (functional elements of content) which are irrelevant to the target audience. These adaptations are also referred to as transediting, i.e. a combination of translation and editing (cf. Stetting 1989, 371). They involve what House refers to as covert translation, that is the application of a cultural filter so as to ensure that texts are not recognised as translations but may function as independent texts in the target culture (cf. House 1977; 2001). Some genres, e.g. political speeches, require the opposite – overt translation (House 1977). If a genre does not exist in the target culture, the translator may opt for introducing a new genre or make adaptations to existing, similar genres. As Bassnett (2006, 90) notes, such adaptations may be assessed negatively in literary translation as they would "subvert the source to fit into the horizon of expectation of the target readers".

This takes us to the topic of how genres impact the translator's decision-making process. As noted by Reiss in the early 1970s, text types affect the translator's behaviour. With the attention shifting from text types to genres, genres have been found to be among the key determinants of the translator's decision-making process and the choice of translation strategies and techniques. This may be illustrated by the role of genre in journalistic translation. Informative genres, such as a news report, where the personal style is reduced, allow ample space for rearrangement and changes vis-à-vis the ST while argumentative genres – such as the opinion article, the column – require more faithful renderings (Bielsa 2007, 48).

An important area of studies includes the link between translation and genre hybridity, genre transformations, as well as the transfer of new genres via translation. As Bassnett notes, translation has been a carrier of new genres throughout centuries, such as the sonnet or the haiku, and has contributed to genre shifts, which may be exemplified by the 12th- and 13th-century shift from epic to lyric and romance: "[t]he history of genre shifts is intimately bound up with translation" (Bassnett 2006, 89). Translation may also trigger genre transformations in the target culture. It may be illustrated with the popularity of the Harry Potter books, which "resurrected a genre that educationalists felt was totally unacceptable for contemporary children" (Bassnett 2006, 94), namely the school story. Another example is a CV: up till the mid 1990s a standard Polish CV was called "*Życiorys*" [lit. "life story"] and was a first-person narrative (*I was born on ... in ...*). This was transformed, influenced by the inflow of Western European CVs, into a depersonalised bulleted template called "CV" with a partially different selection of personal information.

Another area of interest is the use of genre analysis as a pedagogical tool in translator training, especially as regards domain-restricted specialised translation. This topic will be addressed in more detail in the section on "Implications for practice".

The final topic to be covered in this section is translation, both literary and specialised, as genre. Literary translation is regarded as a distinct literary genre governed by its own norms and purposes (Ortega y Gasset 2004 [1937], 61; see also James 1989, 35); literary translation implies loss and it "is not the work, but a path toward the work" (Ortega y Gasset 2004 [1937], 61). Within specialised translation a related concept of transgenre was introduced, that is a genre which is "exclusive to translation" and differs from the source genre and target genre (Borja, García Izquierdo and Montalt 2009, 62, 68).

Main research methods

Genre analysis describes distinctive features of genres, known as generic conventions, generic structure, as well as social, communicative, cultural, cognitive and ideological factors behind the use of genres. Genres are researched in discourse analysis and Critical Discourse Analysis within three main approaches: English for Specific Purposes (ESP), the Sydney School and the New Rhetoric (Flowerdew and Wan 2010, 79). The ESP approach, which is represented by Swales (1990; 2004) and Bhatia (1993; 2004), is oriented towards preparing learning resources for non-native speakers of English. It has developed a multi-perspective model of genre analysis linking moves (stages) to communicative purposes of a genre. The Sydney School, which shows similarities to the ESP approach, emerged from Hallidayan Systemic Functional Linguistics (Martin and Rose 2007; 2008) and was also interested in the identification of "generic staging". The New Rhetoric, which developed in North America with interest in native writing, focuses on social purposes, shifting attention from linguistic to ethnographic methodologies (cf. Flowerdew and Wan 2010, 79–81 for a more detailed overview of these approaches).

Genre analysis is conducted with the use of mainly qualitative and, more recently, with quantitative corpus methods, depending on the aspect of genre organisation to be studied. The traditional qualitative approach applies top-down analysis: it starts with the conceptual macrostructure of a genre and moves towards the microstructure, lower-level realisations in the form of fixed patterns. The more recent quantitative approaches proceed in a bottom-up fashion, starting with the analysis of lexico-grammatical patterns and moving towards larger units.

Genre analysis focuses on "the conventional, formulaic, routine labour-saving aspect of language use" as opposed to creative aspects (James 1989, 32). One of the main goals of genre analysis is to uncover the generalisable structure/format of genres (cf. Hatim and Mason 1990, 171) which they impose on texts. The conceptual structure of a genre consists of functional stages known as "moves" and their steps, which were proposed as basic units of a genre by Swales (1990). Working on research articles, Swales introduced the CARS (Create a Research Space) model with three moves in article introductions: Move 1: Establishing a territory; Move 2: Establishing a niche; Move 3: Occupying the niche (Swales 1990, 140–141). Moves and their steps realise the communicative purpose of a genre and they appear in a certain order in a text. They may be organised in a chronological or spatial order or from general to specific or as problems-methods-solutions structures; the conventional arrangement of content may differ across cultures (cf. Rogers 2015, 33). Some genres may have a well-defined predictable generic structure, while less ritualised genres may be more flexible with optional and varied stages (cf. Fairclough 2003, 72–74).

Unless we study stable fixed formulaic genres, the level of lexico-grammatical patterns of a genre is best explored quantitatively with electronic corpus analysis software rather than through manual analysis. The advantage of electronic analysis is that it is faster, more reliable and accurate, and can be conducted on a much larger corpus than manual analysis allows. While discourse analysis methods involve close reading of usually a very limited number of texts, corpus methods involve computer-assisted vertical readings of many texts. One of the basic methods is keywords analysis, which identifies lexemes with a markedly higher frequency in a specific genre against a reference corpus. Keywords are thus a useful tool in identifying distinctive features of a genre (cf. Scott 2013, 199). Corpora are also efficient in identifying genre-unique regularities at the phrase level – recurrent lexico-grammatical patterns which are typical of a given genre. These include collocations, routine formulae and lexical bundles (n-grams). A comprehensive framework for corpus-driven analyses of lexico-grammatical patterns across registers/genres was proposed by Biber and Conrad (2009, 215–246) under the name of Multi-Dimensional (MD) register analysis. The method compares: (1) the distribution of vocabulary (common versus rare nouns), (2) part-of-speech classes (e.g. nouns, verbs, adjectives, personal pronouns, prepositions), (3) semantic categories for word classes (e.g. activity verbs, mental verbs), (4) grammatical features (nominalisations, past and present tense verbs, passive voice), (5) syntactic structures (relative clauses, complement clauses) and (6) lexico-grammatical combinations (Biber and Conrad 2009, 226–227).

It should be remembered though that corpus-based genre analysis has been criticised for its preoccupation with lexico-grammatical patterns at the sentence level and its failure to sufficiently address certain textual, pragmatic, rhetorical or discursive phenomena, such as interdiscursivity, intertextuality or genre hybridisation, which require qualitative rather than quantitative analysis (cf. Olohan 2004, 425 for a more detailed overview of criticism). Despite some attempts to annotate corpora, these aspects still pose technical and methodological challenges and the analysis of features which go beyond the sentence level needs to be complemented with traditional qualitative analysis.

Borja, García Izquierdo and Montalt (2009) propose a useful template of genre description for researching specialised translation. The template covers both the lexico-grammatical patterns, the macrostructure, relations to other genres and the communicative situation:

1. Name of a genre, e.g. EU legislation
2. Subgenre(s), if any, and their structure: e.g. (a) primary legislation – treaties; (b) secondary legislation – regulations, directives, decisions, soft law (opinions, recommendations)
3. Communicative situation: register, domain, mode, participants and the discursive community, function, social goal
4. Lexico-grammatical patterns: lexemes, terminology, collocations, typical grammatical patterns (nouns and nominalisations; the verb group: modal verbs, auxiliaries, tenses, passives, impersonal constructions, mood; adverbials, deixis; cohesion)
5. Macrostructure: composition of the text, moves and steps
6. Relation to other genres: systems of genres, genre chains, meta-genres
7. Comments: bibliography, websites.

(cf. Borja, García Izquierdo and Montalt 2009, 65)

This template is a basis for further analysis of three complementary dimensions of genre analysis in this model: the formal level (conventionalised forms), the communicative and sociocultural level and the cognitive level (the participants' purposes) (Borja, García Izquierdo and Montalt 2009, 65; Borja Albi 2013, 36–37).

A much more extensive model of genre analysis, proposed by Bhatia, is the multi-perspective model of applied genre analysis (1993, revised version 2004). Bhatia's model consists of the following seven steps:

1. placing the given genre-text in a situational context (a genre-text is a representative example of the genre studied) on the basis of the researcher's prior experience and background knowledge;
2. surveying existing literature;
3. refining the situational/contextual analysis through the following steps: defining the author of the text, its audience, their relationship and goals; defining the historical, socio-cultural, philosophical, and occupational situation of the discourse community; identifying the network of related texts and linguistic traditions which influence the genre; identifying the topic, domain and extra-textual reality of a text;
4. corpus design: defining a genre and subgenre; defining criteria for selecting texts for the corpus;
5. textual, intertextual and interdiscursive perspective: analysis of lexico-grammatical patterns; analysis of text-patterning or textualisation, cognitive or discourse structuring (moves), analysis of intertextuality and interdiscursivity;
6. ethnographic analysis (observations, narrative accounts, etc.) of practices in the discourse community: physical circumstances that affect the nature and structure of genre; critical moments of engagement and interaction; the social structure, history, beliefs and goals of the discourse community;
7. studying the institutional context and rules.

(Bhatia 1993, 22–36; 2004, 164–167)

This holistic model applies varied methodological tools to account for the complexity of genres and incorporates the multi-dimensional perspective which includes the textual perspective, the ethnographic perspective, the socio-cognitive perspective (integrity of the system of genres) and the socio-critical perspective (ideology and power) (Bhatia 2004, 163). Since translation-oriented genre analysis usually involves time-consuming cross-cultural contrasts of use of the same genre in the SL and TL culture, it may not be feasible to apply the multi-perspective model fully in practice. Nevertheless, if the analysis is selective, a researcher should be aware of its limitations and aspects which are left out.

Current debates

The major debate involving genre analysis concerns translation universals. It was proposed by Baker in the 1990s that translations are marked by distinctive universal features ("translation universals") which may be products of translation process constraints and which are independent of language pairs, genres, cultures and translation norms. The features were hypothesised to include: explicitation, simplification, disambiguation, normalisation/conservatism, standardisation and levelling out (Baker 1995). The major contested aspect is the universality of the features of translated texts and their resulting independence of other variables. It has been suggested that cross-genre comparisons are needed to determine how features of translations are influenced by genres and text types (cf. Olohan 2004, 191). Recent studies (Delaere, De Sutter and Plevoets 2012; De Sutter, Delaere and Plevoets 2012) seem to confirm that genre is one of the important determinants of variation which impact features of translations: for example some genres may trigger the use by translators of more explicitation (e.g. leaflets), while others may be more prone to standardisation (legal genres).

Future directions

The main future direction of genre analysis is likely to be further work on genre variation and contrastive genre analysis using electronically analysable corpora, which have already brought new life and foci into genre analysis. This direction was suggested as early as 1995 by Kussmaul (1995, 83): "it would be very helpful if ... conventions and the differences between conventions in the source and target language were known. For this reason we should encourage corpus-based contrastive studies". Some empirical data have been provided across different genres over the years; however, this has mainly been for language pairs involving English, and a great deal of work still needs to be done, especially within specialised translation and for different language pairs. House (2013, 56) observes that such empirical data are needed if Translation Studies are to advance theoretically: "there is a deplorable lack of systematic contrastive pragmatic work on register and genre variation, which renders a solid theoretical underpinning of translation studies in this respect next to impossible".

Implications for practice

Genres are of relevance not only for translation theory but also for translator training and practice. The translator's specialisation may be limited to certain genres within the specialised domain, e.g. some translators may translate only novels, poems, drama, financial statements, press releases or financial statements. In reality, however, most translators handle more than one genre.

The pedagogical value of genres has been promoted within the English for Specific Purposes approach (Swales 1990, 213; Bhatia 1993, 18) and transplanted into Translation

Studies. Genre analysis and, in particular, analysis which enhances the knowledge of generic conventions, has been a key component of (specialised) translator training for many years. The knowledge of ST generic formats is useful for interpretative purposes while the knowledge of TT generic formats is important for production purposes (Rogers 2015, 32). James (1989) argues for genre analysis to be integrated into translator training programmes. He recommends the "text-typological" approach to syllabus design to ensure that trainees have sufficient exposure to both central and hybrid genres. Knowledge of genres and trainees' expectations about generic formats will help them to shift from bottom-up to more advanced top-down textual processing during the translation process (1989, 36). Trainees should also learn how to conduct genre identification and ST and TT genre analysis, which should take place at the beginning of the translation task (1989, 36–37). The importance of genres (text types) as didactic tools in translator training has been emphasised by a number of translation scholars since the 1990s (cf. Emery 1991; Kussmaul 1995, 149; Göpferich 1995, 322; Hatim and Mason 1997, 179–198; Chesterman 1997, 161; Colina 1997; García Izquierdo 2000; Hatim 2001, 171–183; Borja Albi 2013, 33). Göpferich (1995, 322–323) argues that being grouped according to similar communicative-pragmatic features, text types offer similar translation difficulties, which can be covered systematically in this approach. Experimenting with the translation of cookbook recipes, Colina (1997) has demonstrated that trainees exposed to explicit instruction on generic conventions ("contrastive rhetoric") show a substantial improvement in their translations. Borja Albi (2013, 34) emphasises that competence in genres and genre systems enables trainees to socialise as "communication agents" in the specialised domain and to avoid being perceived as outsiders in the professional discourse community.

The internalisation of genre knowledge is seen as an important component for professional translators to perform effectively (cf. Trosborg 1997, 17; Rogers 2015, 32). The need to incorporate genre analysis into training is reflected in the incorporation of genres as an integral component of translation competence subsumed under various sub-competences:

- In the European Master's in Translation (EMT) model of competences for professional translators, experts in multilingual and multimedia communication, it is part of the textual dimension of the intercultural competence which reflects the translator's ability to compare discursive practices in the SL and TL, "Knowing how to compose a document in accordance with the conventions of the genre and rhetorical standards" (Gambier 2009).
- In the PACTE (2003, 91) model, it is part of bilingual sub-competence which comprises the textual knowledge of the SL and the TL, including knowledge of genres and their conventions.

Genre analysis is also used in the preparation of resources for translators. These include genre-based corpora and generic templates to be used during the translation process. A special type of resource is DIY (ad hoc, disposable) corpora, which are genre-based and which are built quickly by translators through web harvesting, and analysed to complete a translation assignment (Varantola 2002). Much more complex and targeted tools based on genre analysis were developed within the practically oriented action project, the JudGENTT online knowledge management system for court translators. The project applies genres as reusable tools "for accessing and reusing conceptual, textual and linguistic information for managing specialised communication" (Borja Albi 2013, 37). The project is grounded in corpus-based genre system analysis and individual genre analysis in four legal systems. The value of the project lies in the integration of all resources, including the corpora, genre matrices (templates), glossaries, bibliographies and contextual information on criminal procedure, in one place on an online searchable platform (Borja Albi 2013).

Further reading

Chapter 2, "Criticism and the source language text" in: Reiss, K., 2000 [1971]. *Translation Criticism – the Potentials and Limitations: Categories and Criteria for Translation Quality Assessment*. Translated by E. F. Rhodes. Manchester: St Jerome.
A classic text which proposes a translation-oriented text typology as a prerequisite of translation criticism and a determinant of translation method.

Chapter 4 "Translating and Language as Discourse" and Chapter 8 "Text Type as the Translators' Focus" in: Hatim, B., and Mason, I., 1990. *Discourse and the Translator*. Harlow: Longman.
This influential book introduced discourse analysis methods to Translation Studies. Chapter 4 discusses the text-genre-discourse triad, as well as generic constraints in translation. Chapter 8 proposes a new text typology based on a predominant contextual focus.

Chapter 4 "Genres and generic structure" in: Fairclough, N., 2003. *Analysing Discourse. Textual Analysis for Social Research*. London: Routledge.
This chapter focuses on how genres structure texts and links genre analysis to social action. It analyses the relationship between a text and a genre and illustrates the analysis of generic structure.

Chapter 6 "Integrating research methods" in: Bhatia, V. K., 2004. *Worlds of Written Discourse*. London: Continuum.
This chapter discusses the goals of genre analysis, proposes a holistic multi-perspective model of genre analysis with a step-by-step procedure and integrates varied research methods to account for the complexity of genres. The final section illustrates how the model may be applied to analyse publishers' blurbs.

Borja, A., García Izquierdo, I. and Montalt, V. 2009. "Research Methodology in Specialized Genres for Translation Purposes". *The Interpreter and Translator Trainer*, 3(1), pp. 57–77.
This article presents a model of genre analysis which is adjusted to research on specialised translation. It describes three complementary dimensions of genre analysis: the formal dimension, the communicative dimension and the cognitive dimension, both from the monolingual and multilingual (contrastive) perspective, and contains useful advice and ideas for researching genres for translation purposes.

Related topics

Theories of linguistics and of translation and interpreting; Semantics and translation; Rhetoric, oratory, interpreting and translation; Discourse analysis, interpreting and translation; Text linguistics, translating, and interpreting; Narrative analysis and translation; Stylistics and translation; Language for Specific Purposes and translation; Sociolinguistics, translation and interpreting; Language, interpreting, and translation in the news media; Corpus linguistics, translation and interpreting.

References

Baker, M. 1992. *In Other Words: A Coursebook on Translation*. London: Routledge.
Baker, M. 1995. Corpora in translation studies: an overview and some suggestions for future research. *Target* 7(2), pp. 223–243.
Bassnett, S. 2006. "Translating Genre". In *Genre Matters: Essays in Theory and Criticism*, edited by G. Dowd, L. Stevenson and J. Strong, 85–89. Bristol: Intellect.
Bazerman, C. H. 1994. "Systems of Genres and the Enactment of Social Intentions". In *Genre and the New Rhetoric*, edited by A. Freedman and P. Medway, 79–101. London: Taylor and Francis.
Bhatia, V. K. 1993. *Analysing Genre: Language Use in Professional Settings*. London: Continuum.
Bhatia, V. K. 2004. *Worlds of Written Discourse*. London: Continuum.
Biber, D. and Conrad, S. 2009. *Register, Genre and Style*. Cambridge: Cambridge University Press.

Biel, Ł. 2014. *Lost in the Eurofog: The Textual Fit of Translated Law.* Frankfurt am Main: Peter Lang.

Bielsa, E. 2007. Translation in global news agencies. *Target,* 19(1), pp. 35–55.

Borja Albi, A. 2013. "A Genre Analysis Approach to the Study of the Translation of Court Documents". In *Linguistica Antverpiensia 12,* special issue on Research Models and Methods in Legal Translation, edited by Ł. Biel and J. Engberg, 34–53. Available from: https://lans-tts.uantwerpen.be/index.php/LANS-TTS/article/view/235 [Accessed 2 January 2016].

Borja, A., García Izquierdo, I. and Montalt, V. 2009. Research methodology in specialized genres for translation purposes. *The Interpreter and Translator Trainer* 3(1), pp. 57–77.

Cap, P. and Okulska, U. 2013. "Analyzing Genres in Political Communication: An Introduction". In *Analyzing Genres in Political Communication,* edited by P. Cap and U. Okulska, 1–26. Amsterdam: John Benjamins.

Chesterman, A. 1997. *Memes of Translation: The Spread of Ideas in Translation Theory.* Amsterdam: John Benjamins.

Colina, S. 1997. Contrastive rhetoric and text-typological conventions in translation teaching. *Target* 9(2), pp. 335–353.

De Sutter, G., Delaere, I. and Plevoets, K. 2012. "Lexical Lectometry in Corpus-Based Translation Studies. Combining Profile-Based Correspondence Analysis and Logistic Regression Modelling". In *Quantitative Methods in Corpus-Based Translation Studies: A Practical Guide to Descriptive Translation Research,* edited by M. P. Oakes and M. Ji, 325–346. Amsterdam: John Benjamins.

Delaere, I., De Sutter, G. and Plevoets, K. 2012. Is translated language more standardized than non-translated language? Using profile-based correspondence analysis for measuring linguistic distances between language varieties. *Target* 24(2), pp. 203–224.

Emery, P. 1991. Text classification and text analysis in advanced translation teaching. *Meta: Translators' Journal* 36(4), pp. 567–577.

Ezpeleta Piorno, P. 2012. An example of genre shift in the medicinal product information genre system. *Linguistica Antverpiensia New Series – Themes in Translation Studies* 11, pp. 139–159.

Fairclough, N. 2003. *Analysing Discourse: Textual Analysis for Social Research.* London: Routledge.

Fairclough, N. 2006. *Language and Globalization.* London: Routledge.

Fawcett, P. 1997. *Translation and Language: Linguistic Theories Explained.* Manchester: St Jerome.

Flowerdew, J. and Wan, A. 2010. The linguistic and the contextual in applied genre analysis: The case of the company audit report. *English for Specific Purposes* 29, pp. 78–93.

Gambier, Y., ed. 2009. *Competences for Professional Translators, Experts in Multilingual and Multimedia Communication* [online]. Available from: http://ec.europa.eu/dgs/translation/programmes/emt/key_documents/emt_competences_translators_en.pdf [Accessed 25 September 2015].

García Izquierdo, I. 2000. The concept of text type and its relevance to translator training. *Target* 12(2), pp. 283–295.

Giltrow, J. 2001. "Meta-Genre". In *The Rhetoric and Ideology of Genre: Strategies for Stability and Change,* edited by R. M. Coe, L. Lingard and T. Teslenko, 187–206. Cresskill, NJ: Hampton.

Göpferich, S. 1995. A pragmatic classification of LSP texts in science and technology. *Target* 7(2), pp. 305–326.

Halliday, M. A. K. 1978. *Language as a Social Semiotic: The Social Interpretation of Language and Meaning.* London: Edward Arnold.

Halliday, M. A. K. 2004. *An Introduction to Functional Grammar.* Revised by Ch. M. I. M. Matthiessen. London: Hodder Education.

Hatim, B. 2001. *Teaching and Researching Translation.* Harlow: Longman.

Hatim, B. and Mason, I. 1990. *Discourse and the Translator.* Harlow: Longman.

Hatim, B. and Mason, I. 1997. *The Translator as Communicator.* London: Routledge.

Hatim, B. and Munday, J. 2004. *Translation: An Advanced Resource Book.* London: Routledge.

Holmes, J. S. 2004[1972]. "The Name and Nature of Translation Studies". In *The Translation Studies Reader.* 2nd ed., edited by L. Venuti, 180–192. New York: Routledge.

House, J. 1977. A model for assessing translation quality. *Meta: Translators' Journal* 22(2), pp. 103–109.

House, J. 2001. Translation quality assessment: linguistic description versus social evaluation. *Meta: Translators' Journal* 46(2), pp. 243–257.

House, J. 2013. Towards a new linguistic-cognitive orientation in translation studies. *Target* 25(1), pp. 46–60.

James, C. 1989. Genre analysis and the translator. *Target* 1(1), pp. 29–41.

Jiménez-Crespo, M. A. 2012. Loss in translation: a contrastive genre study of original and localised non-profit US websites. *The Journal of Specialised Translation* 17, pp. 136–163.

Kussmaul, P. 1995. *Training the Translator*. Amsterdam: John Benjamins.

Martin, J. R. and Rose, D. 2007. *Genre Relations: Mapping Culture*. London: Equinox.

Martin, J. R. and Rose, D. 2008. *Working with Discourse: Meaning Beyond the Clause*. London: Bloomsbury.

Miller, C. R. 1984. Genre as social action. *Quarterly Journal of Speech* 70, pp. 151–167.

Munday, J. 2001. *Introducing Translation Studies: Theories and Applications*. London: Routledge.

Neubert, A. and Shreve, G. M. 1992. *Translation as Text*. Kent, US: Kent State University Press.

Nord, C. 1991. *Text Analysis in Translation: Theory, Methodology, and Didactic Applications of a Model for Translation-Oriented Text Analysis*. Translated by C. Nord and P. Sparrow. Amsterdam: Rodopi.

OED Oxford English Dictionary [online]. 2016. Oxford University Press. Available from: www.oed.com [Accessed 2 February 2016].

Olohan, M. 2004. *Introducing Corpora in Translation Studies*. London: Routledge.

Ortega y Gasset, J. 2004[1937]. "The misery and the splendor of translation" [Translated by E. Gamble Miller]. In *The Translation Studies Reader*, edited by L. Venuti, 2000, 49–53. New York: Routledge.

PACTE, 2003. "Building a Translation Competence Model". In *Triangulating Translation*, edited by F. Alves, 43–66. Amsterdam: John Benjamins.

Reiss, K. 2000[1971]. *Translation Criticism – The Potentials and Limitations: Categories and Criteria for Translation Quality Assessment*. Translated by E. F. Rhodes. Manchester: St Jerome.

Rogers, M. 2015. *Specialised Translation: Shedding the "Non-literary" Tag*. Basingstoke: Palgrave Macmillan.

Schäffner, C. 2002. "Editorial". In *The Role of Discourse Analysis for Translation and in Translator Training*, edited by C. Schäffner, 1–8. Clevedon: Multilingual Matters.

Scott, M. 2013. *WordSmith Tools 6.0*. Liverpool: Lexical Analysis Software.

Snell-Hornby, M. 1995[1988]. *Translation Studies: An Integrated Approach*. Revised ed. Amsterdam: John Benjamins.

Stetting, K. 1989. "Transediting: A New Term for Coping with the Grey Area between Editing and Translating". In *Proceedings from the Fourth Nordic Conference for English Studies*, edited by G. Cale, K. Haastrup and A. Lykke Jakobsen, 371–382. Copenhagen: University of Copenhagen.

Swales, J. M. 1990. *Genre Analysis: English in Academic and Research Settings*. Cambridge: Cambridge University Press.

Swales, J. M. 2004. *Research Genres: Explorations and Applications*. Cambridge: Cambridge University Press.

Trosborg, A. 1997. "Text Typology: Register, Genre and Text Type". In *Text Typology and Translation*, edited by A. Trosborg, 3–23. Amsterdam: John Benjamins.

Trosborg, A. 2002. "Discourse Analysis as Part of Translator Training". In *The Role of Discourse Analysis for Translation and in Translator Training*, edited by C. Schäffner, 9–52. Clevedon: Multilingual Matters.

Tsiplakou, S. and Floros, G. 2013. Never mind the text types, here's textual force: towards a pragmatic reconceptualization of text type. *Journal of Pragmatics* 45, pp. 119–130.

Varantola, K. 2002. Disposable corpora as intelligent tools in translation. *Cadernos de Tradução IX – Tradução e Corpora* 1(9), pp. 171–189.

Zhang, M., Pan, H., Chen, X. and Luo, T. 2015. Mapping discourse analysis in translation studies via bibliometrics: a survey of journal publications. *Perspectives: Studies in Translatology* 23(2), pp. 223–239.

11

Text linguistics, translating, and interpreting

Gregory M. Shreve

Introduction

Any attempt to explicate the relationship of text linguistics to translation and interpreting has to proceed from an understanding of the nature of text, and of the key features that distinguish texts from non-texts. This is no mean undertaking, but without engaging in an extensive review of the scholarship on this issue some aspects of texts – features that make a text a text – can be identified.

Texts are commonly understood as units of language larger than a single sentence, typically comprised of several written sentences or spoken utterances grouped together in a particular sequence. In this contribution we do not make a significant distinction between the notion of text and the notion of discourse, using the former term to refer to both. Similarly, one could substitute the word "utterance" for the word "sentence" in the rest of this contribution, and hereafter we use "sentence" to mean both.

The grouping of sentences we call a text is non-random; the sentences have been brought together deliberately for communicative purposes by a text producer in order to carry out a "definable communicative function" (Crystal 2008, 260). The properties of the grouping can vary according to the communicative setting in which it is used; variation in these properties can be used to classify texts into different types for instance, an endeavour called *text typology* pursued both in text linguistics and Translation Studies.

Some of the properties of a text that distinguish it from texts of other types are related to the nature of structural or formal connections across sentence boundaries. Other properties are semantic, involving the meanings evoked by individual sentences in the text and how those meanings are connected to one another to produce a coherent whole. Texts also have pragmatic properties; they are articulated in a socio-cultural setting between social actors enacting definable social roles. Texts can thus be seen as "interaction structures" (Neubert and Shreve 1992, 43) where the formal and semantic elements of a text are intentionally structured in alignment with the communicative purposes of situated social interactions. This extended definition brings together the crucial elements of the notion of text as understood by linguists who have delved into the nature of text over the past several decades (van Dijk 1972; 1977; Werlich 1976; Halliday and Hasan 1976; de Beaugrande and Dressler 1981), founding a discipline called text linguistics, whose influence on translation and interpreting studies we investigate in this contribution.

Historical perspectives

Text linguistics was not the origin of Translation Studies' concern with the relationship between text and translation. Relatively early on in the history of Translation Studies, scholars such as Reiss (1971) were arguing that the proper object of Translation Studies was not the word or sentence, but the connected sequence of sentences used in written communication, the text. The movement towards a textual focus in Translation Studies, particularly in Germany in the 1970s and early 1980s, was part of an explicit recognition that translation was a pragmatically bound communicative activity. We can see a growing theoretical concern with communicative and functional issues in translation (e.g., the *skopostheorie* of Katharina Reiss and Hans Vermeer and the *translatorisches handeln* – translational action – theories of Justa Holz-Mänttäri) throughout those decades, and the textual turn in Translation Studies is part of that development.

The early adoption of the text as an object of study in translation is related to a similar movement in linguistics to include the pragmatic, communicative, and social aspects of language. Thus, it is no surprise that the concern with texts in Translation Studies develops to some degree in parallel with similar concerns in text linguistics – and from some of the same underlying theoretical sources (see Snell-Hornby 2006 for an excellent discussion of the pragmatic turn in Translation Studies). However, in this contribution, we will not be focusing on the history of the broader textual concern in Translation Studies, but rather on the specific intersection of Translation Studies with text linguistics, understood as a specific theoretical framework that developed from the same roots and with the same motivations as the pragmatic and textual turn in Translation Studies.

Text linguistics arose in the 1970s as a sub-discipline of linguistics; it was the result of a shift of perspective among some language scholars from the *sentential* to the *textual*. This shift was motivated by several factors. First, as in Translation Studies, there was an increasing recognition that isolated sentences were not generally natural units of communication. When people use language in speech and writing, they use connected sequences of sentences. Next, it was apparent that many important concerns of linguistic research (e.g., pragmatics and semantics) could not be fruitfully studied without also studying the *context* of sentences (Carstens 2001). By context here we mean (1) the structural and semantic relationships of a sentence in a group of sentences to the sentences that precede and follow it, and (2) the pragmatic situational context surrounding the production of sentences. These two meanings of context have defined two directions in text linguistics broadly considered, one concerned with formal description of the relationships between sentences in texts as an extension of formal grammars (text grammars), and the other with how texts are related to their situational and social contexts. The latter has had the greatest influence on translation and interpreting studies.

Discourse analysis is closely related to text linguistics, in that the object of study is also language use beyond the boundaries of discrete sentences. Both are concerned with the social contexts of language use, with the social purposes and functions of language in social interaction. It is, in fact, difficult to make a clear distinction between the concerns of discourse analysis and those of text linguistics without making a distinction between discourse and text. Some scholars have argued for a distinction based on modality (spoken vs. written). Others have said that texts are non-interactive while discourses are interactive. But, for the most part there has been no consensus, and one is inclined to agree with Crystal (2011, 1) that discourse analysis and text linguistics are more or less the same.

In this chapter, for clarity of argument as well as limitations of space, we focus quite narrowly on text linguistics as associated with the work of specific scholars whose frameworks have been adopted broadly into translation and interpreting studies: Teun van Dijk, M. A. K. Halliday and Ruqaiya Hasan, and Robert de Beaugrande and Wolfgang Dressler. A common thread among these authors is the idea that speakers or writers of texts make deliberate, patterned language choices from a potential set of available choices (the language system) and that those choices are related to the situation in which the language is used. The pattern of choices is recognisable in the linguistic and semantic structures of a text.

Within text linguistics broadly, so-called "text grammatical" approaches emphasise that the "selection" of sentences that appear in a text (and their lexical and structural properties) can be described in a formal manner as a rule system. The recourse to the notion of rules places text grammars in the context of formal models of sentence grammars, but with a broader scope – where the focus is not on the syntactical arrangement of words in sentences (traditional syntax), but on the arrangement of sentences within the larger construct of the text itself and of the semantic and lexical relationships between sentences. The earliest well-known proponent of this perspective is van Dijk, who was central in early attempts to specify the kinds of relationships that might exist between sentences; he focused on global textual meaning relationships between sentences as well as formal organisational ones – these patterns of relationship were called "macrostructures" and "macropropositions" (van Dijk 2004).

Text grammatical approaches had great utility in the development of text linguistics, because they were among the first language models to emphasise the "connectedness" of sentences in texts, especially at the semantic level (van Dijk 2004), what text linguistics later came to refer to as textual coherence. Van Dijk himself saw text grammars becoming a part of and being informed by developments in text processing, and his later work (van Dijk 1977; van Dijk and Kintsch 1983) reflects this evolution. We take up the relationship between text linguistics and text processing again later in this chapter. Today text grammars are seen as a specific active field of research within text linguistics, but they are no longer on the main line of inquiry. Text grammatical approaches have had some influence on translation theory, as for instance Neubert and Shreve's (1992) placement of van Dijk's notions of macroproposition and macrosructure, as well as macrorules, in the context of translated texts.

Where text grammatical approaches were to a great extent concerned with the explication of formal properties of texts, the main direction of theory development in text linguistics emphasised to a much greater extent how the form of a text is a reflection of its functional role in situated communication. This direction of study is an outgrowth of the rise of sociolinguistics and, particularly, of systemic functional linguistics associated with the work of figures such as J. R. Firth and M. A. K. Halliday. Functional linguistics emphasises the notion of choice, e.g., that there is a pool of language (the language system) from which a writer or speaker makes deliberate choices. Those choices are non-random – structured – and reflect the socio-cultural functions that a language production has to serve.

In text linguistics the central concern with the situational context of communication derives from the systemic functional linguistic idea of "context of situation" with its three related sub-elements: "field of discourse", "mode of discourse", and "tenor of discourse". Field generally refers to the topic or subject matter of a text and also the particulars of the "total event in which the text is functioning" – e.g., the pragmatic context of the text, including the time and place where it is used (Halliday and Hasan 1976, 22). Mode focuses on the purposes and function of a text, including what the text author intends the text to achieve and what use the text reader is expected to make of it (function). Mode also implies a particular way of achieving purpose – whether by use of written or spoken language, for instance, and is thus related to the idea that particular forms of language are associated with particular purposes. Tenor emphasises the social relationships surrounding the use of a text and realised by the text; the notion recognises that a text is a specific and deliberate language "structure" that manifests a particular kind of interaction between social actors. As we look later at the "core issues" of text linguistics in translation we can see how each of them proceeds from these fundamental notions.

A particular combination of field, mode, and tenor, e.g., a certain context of situation, can be associated with a specific deliberate selection of meanings and lexico-grammatical choices. Said another way, the context of situation determines the language we use when we speak or write: what we mean, and how we indicate in speech or writing what we mean. Functional linguistics defines a register as those "linguistic features which are typically associated with a configuration of situational features – with particular values of the field, mode and tenor" (Halliday and Hasan 1976, 22). A register is a "text variety" that captures the relationship between situational factors and the linguistic features of language in use (Halliday 1978, 32) and is the conceptual foundation of text typology in text linguistics.

It is not our purpose in this chapter to review systemic functional linguistics or socio-linguistics, but to argue that systemic functional linguistics is the historical background to what we commonly call text linguistics proper – a movement that is to a great extent associated, as we have indicated, with the work of Halliday and Hasan, and de Beaugrande and Dressler.

As indicated earlier, Translation Studies and text linguistics as disciplines developed in parallel; both had early and continuing relationships to systemic functional linguistics. For instance Manfredi (2008) points out that J. C. Catford based some of his early translation theory on the work of Firth and Halliday. Manfredi particularly identifies Halliday's impact on Peter Newmark (1987) and strong influence on Juliane House's systemic-functional model of translation. She also prominently cites *Discourse and the Translator* (1990) by Basil Hatim and Ian Mason, who usefully brought much of Halliday's framework into Translation Studies. In fact, there is a very clear line of interest in Halliday and systemic functional linguistics running through Translation Studies up until this day (see for instance the work of Steiner 2005; Steiner and Webster 2015).

However, if we define the topic of our contribution more strictly, to text linguistics as we have introduced it, then the area of intersection with Translation Studies is much narrower. Only a few works, Hatim and Mason's volume among them, actually address topics most closely identified with text linguistics. Many works in Translation Studies that purportedly deal with "text linguistics" end up only focusing on specific issues such as text types or text analysis – concerns that exist both within and outside of text linguistics – and these concerns are not sufficient to mark such work as departing from a text-linguistic framework (Reiss' original interest in text types, for instance, derives from earlier work by Karl Bühler). Discussing texts, text types, and the communicative nature of texts is not, in and of itself, sufficient to imply a text-linguistic basis of argument.

Hatim (1998) argues that text linguistics in translation is concerned primarily with register analysis – which leads to a text-linguistic perspective on text typology because it departs from specific theoretical foundations – "texture" (which concerns itself with coherence and cohesion) and theme–rheme analysis, related to the informativity of texts, but at the sentential level. With this in mind only a few major early scholarly works in Translation Studies engaged with text linguistics in a comprehensive way. Hatim and Mason's (1990) volume certainly engages fully with text linguistics, as does a body of work by Albrecht Neubert of the

University of Leipzig. Neubert was a major proponent of the de Beaugrande and Dressler framework. After de Beaugrande and Dressler published their *Introduction to Text Linguistics* in 1981, Neubert began to incorporate its ideas, most notably in the mid 1980s with the publication of "Textlinguistik des Übersetzens" (Neubert 1985b) and *Text and Translation* (Neubert 1985a) – this latter book was republished and revised with Gregory M. Shreve in 1992 as *Translation as Text*. In interpreting studies, early work with a text-linguistic slant is quite sparse, although Alexieva (1994) recognised early on that there were important connections between interpreting and text linguistics.

In the remainder of this chapter we will look at some of the core issues of translation, interpreting, and text linguistics identified in these works. This short historical foray is not, of course, intended to cite every article bringing together text linguistics, translation, and interpreting, and will be confined to a few main bodies of influential thought. We have recognised the role of systemic functional linguistics in translation, and of a broader arena of discussion in discourse analysis (e.g., Critical Discourse Analysis), but those are worthy of their own discussion.

Core issues

Texture, cohesion, and coherence

A fundamental idea of text linguistics is that sentences in a group of sentences exhibit connectedness at the structural and semantic levels. Sentences have relationships to one another at the level of the language forms employed (lexis and syntax) as well as at the level of meaning. It is the presence of these relationships that allows the processing of texts as coherent carriers of meaning. Halliday and Hasan (1976, 2) called this property "texture", arguing that "a text has a texture, and this is what distinguishes it from something that is not a text. It derives this texture from the fact that it functions as a unity with respect to its environment". The notion of functioning as a unity is important, because it emphasises that a text is perceived by its readers or hearers as a holistic communicative event and not as a disjointed random sequence of sentences.

Halliday and Hasan (1976) argue that texture arises solely from the linguistic mechanisms of cohesion (Fulcher 1989). De Beaugrande and Dressler (1981) agree that cohesion is a critical property of texture, but add to it the idea of coherence. Cohesion, as understood by Halliday and Hasan, is created through mechanisms of lexical and grammatical cohesion. Lexical cohesion uses devices such as repetition and collocation to mark the relatedness of words in a text, and grammatical cohesion uses grammatical mechanisms such as reference (specifically anaphoric and cataphoric reference), substitution, ellipsis, and conjunction. The primary notion here is that a text (as opposed to a non-text) exhibits "explicit clues that make a text a text" and those markers are grammatical and lexical – not semantic, per se – in nature (Sanders and Maat 2006, 591). The linguistic markers are connected and sequentially interdependent – cohesion arises "when the interpretation of some element in the discourse is dependent on that of another" (Halliday and Hasan 1976, 4). Thus the sense of connectedness of a text is created solely from the presence of language-dependent cohesive devices. Halliday and Hasan's concept of cohesion had a tremendous influence on text linguistics, but was not without its critics. They felt that something more was required to understand texture: coherence.

The sense of the connectedness of text – what we have called texture – has itself also been called coherence by some scholars, creating some ambiguity about the actual scope of the term coherence (and indeed Halliday and Hasan also use the term, but in ways not specifically pertinent to the present argument). For clarity, when we use the term in this contribution, we refer not to a more general sense such as is also covered by the word "texture", but to a more specific notion that recognises the contribution the reader brings to constructing the semantic connectedness of the text. From a text-processing point of view, critics argue that previous knowledge stored in long-term memory interacts with cohesive devices and other textual mechanisms like tense to help the reader construct the global meaning and semantic connectedness of a text. Critics of "cohesion-only" views argued that more fruitful approaches to texture should recognise that linguistic mechanisms work in concert with a reader's prior knowledge to construct texture. Texture is therefore a result of both cohesion and coherence.

In this chapter, cohesion and coherence are used primarily in the sense meant by de Beaugrande and Dressler (1981, 84). They said coherence "concerns the ways in which the components of the textual world, i.e., the configuration of concepts and relations which underlie the surface text, are mutually accessible and relevant" (1981, 4). If one unpacks this statement, coherence is a framework for talking about the propositional and conceptual unity of a text and how that unity is built up via interaction between the language of a text and the knowledge the reader brings to the text. A coherent text, in this sense, is one that enables the reader to understand the text by building up a mental model of what it means, or, as Neubert and Shreve (1992, 94) put it: "A coherent text has an underlying logical structure that acts to guide the reader through the text".

Hatim (1998) noted that cohesion and coherence have attracted the greatest amount of attention in Translation Studies. It is no surprise that a large number of translation scholars have investigated the role of cohesion and coherence in translation and interpreting. We cannot possibly discuss all of them, but of notable mention is the work of Baker (1992) who usefully discusses the implications of cohesion and coherence using practical examples. Hatim and Mason (1990) also take up the two topics and deal extensively with them using de Beaugrande and Dressler's framework; they also apply concepts of texture to interpreting (1997) – adding to the sparse literature in that area. Neubert and Shreve (1992) similarly adopt that framework and provide an extensive discussion of the relevance of cohesion and coherence to the translator's task. Niska (1999) discusses the implications of cohesion and coherence in simultaneous interpreting at length – in fact, his work is an explicit application of de Beaugrande and Dressler's text linguistics to interpreting studies. A useful summary of coherence and cohesion in Translation Studies approaches is contained in Mubenga's (2010) article on their role in interlingual subtitling.

Perhaps the greatest insight into the core issues of coherence and cohesion in translation was given by Blum-Kulka (1986; 2000). Blum-Kulka describes so-called "shifts" in cohesion and coherence as part of the translation process. Shifts in cohesion are often necessitated by differences in the source and target grammatical systems, and as the translator accommodates those differences it can lead to what she called "shifts in levels of explicitness" and "shifts in text meaning". Shifts of cohesion can result in a target text that indicates underlying semantic relations to a greater or lesser degree than the original. But Blum-Kulka (2000, 300) makes the important point that it is not just linguistic system differences that lead to these shifts. She argues that they result from the "constraints" of the translation process itself, something she calls the "explicitation hypothesis". Shifts in text meaning, on the other hand, happen when the "explicit and implicit meaning potential" (2000, 299) of the source is changed by the translator's use of particular target-side cohesive devices; her argument here is that a translator's choice of cohesive device in the target language can intentionally (or unintentionally) alter the meaning of the target relative to the source – thus the translator needs to be aware of the potential for meaning shift.

Blum-Kulka also looks at shifts in coherence, relating them to alterations in the "interpretability". Here she distinguishes between reader-focused shifts and text-focused shifts of coherence. The former are precipitated by the nature of the translational act – because the situation and readership of the target relative to the source has changed. The latter kind of shift is, similar to her argument about shifts in explicitness – again, the result of the translation process and choices made or not made by the translator.

Blum-Kulka cuts to the core of the issue of coherence and cohesion in translation. We have to be aware that there will be shifts, some of them derive from differences in the language systems of source and target, and some derive from the translation process itself and the translator's accommodations to changes in the context of situation. Some shifts are deliberate and others are not, but the process of translation introduces changes in the cohesion and coherence of the target text relative to the source – and that is quite probably an inescapable derivative of the act. The texture of the target text is induced by the source text, but is not identical to it.

Textuality and the seven standards

So far we have been grappling with the notion of what makes a text a text, citing some key notions such as texture, coherence, and cohesion. De Beaugrande and Dressler also introduced an additional concept, that of "textuality". Textuality turned out to be quite an influential notion, so much so that, the contributions of Halliday and Hasan notwithstanding, much of what is understood today as text linguistics is associated with this seminal notion. As Carstens (2001, 589) says, "it appears as if the approach put forward by de Beaugrande and Dressler (1981) (in their well-known Introduction to text linguistics) is favoured by many linguists when they claim to be text linguists as such".

Where texture is essentially a text-focused concept, because coherence and cohesion are experienced as a function of reading or hearing a text, textuality expands the notion of textness, or being a text, to include other factors. A text does not just have texture. De Beaugrande and Dressler (1981, 3) argue that a text is "a communicative occurrence which meets seven standards of textuality. If any of these standards is not considered to have been satisfied, the text will not be communicative". Cohesion and coherence, already discussed, are included in the seven standards, but five additional properties are specified: intentionality, acceptability, informativity, situationality, and intertextuality. Each of these standards has implications for translation and interpreting. Simply put, if these "standards" are necessary to establish the communicative viability of a source text, then they apply equally to target texts.

Intentionality and acceptability are two sides of the same coin (Carstens 2001). Intentionality refers to the fact that when writing a text an author "intends" to accomplish something, has a purpose in mind. A text is a linguistic strategy for achieving an end; intentionality implies that a text is structured (e.g., coherent and cohesive) in such a way as to achieve that intent. On the other side of the textual coin, a text reader expects that a text has been structured in such a way that the producer's intentions can be fulfilled, or, conversely, the user's purpose for reading the text can be addressed. Acceptability refers in some sense to the "fitness for purpose" of the received text. An author's objective in writing a text, or a translator's in translating it, cannot be achieved if the reader cannot understand what the text in question is intended to do (Neubert and Shreve 1992, 73). Intentionality and acceptability are a kind of cooperation between reader and writer (or hearer and listener) in the interests of communicative success. In the context of translation the author's intent may or may not be identical to the purpose for which a translation is commissioned. Thus, authorial intent and translational purpose may diverge. It is part of the translator's task to understand such divergences – but in all cases the translator has to act to support the target text's functionality in its new environment.

Informativity has to do with what the text communicates. It refers not just to the content of the text, but specifically to the way that "information occurrences" (de Beaugrande and Dressler 1981, 8–9) are presented. Texts present new or novel information in the context of old or known information. The informativity of a text is calibrated by the writer at least partially on the basis of an appreciation of what knowledge the reader and writer share (mutual knowledge) and what authors expect readers already know (prior knowledge). In addition, some information occurrences in a text have more significance or "communicative weight" than others, something that de Beaugrande and Dressler called "orders of informativity". A simple example is, for instance, that terms (specialised vocabulary) in a text have a higher information value than non-terms in the same text. The translator grapples with issues of informativity all of the time, when deciding what can, for instance, be omitted from a text. Issues of informativity surround decisions about what to explicitate (or alternatively implicitate) depending on assessments of the knowledge differences between source audiences and target audiences.

It was mentioned earlier that Hatim (1998) identified theme–rheme analysis as a central concern of text linguistics in translation. Regarding theme and rheme, Hatim (1998, 265) says "the basic premise here is that sentences consist of themes, which present known, context-dependent information, and rhemes, which present new, context-independent information". Themes and rhemes are components of informativity, but considered at the sentential level. Thematic choice involves selecting a clause element as the theme in a sentence, but different language systems may preferentially select different clause elements. So a thematic clause choice may be unmarked or usual in a source language text but become marked and unusual in the target text during translation. It may assume an importance it does not actually have, or sound foreign and awkward. Conversely if the original choice is marked, for instance selected by the author to be unusual (e.g., for emphasis), and when translated it becomes unmarked and quite typical, it may lose meaning.

Situationality recognises explicitly that texts are produced and read in communicative contexts (situations). As such, this standard recognises that a text is above all a communicative event and not just a product (cf. de Beaugrande 1997 and his use of the phrasing "text event"). There is a connection between the text event and its situation – texts are expected to be relevant to their situations of occurrence. That is to say, texts are reflective of their contexts of use, their time and place of production, the intentions of their producers, and indeed the totality of what Halliday and Hasan (1976) called the "context of situation".

The translator's concern with situationality proceeds from the realisation that the translational activity is also a text event, a situated, contextualised communicative activity. In fact, one can see translation as a process where a particular text produced for a source culture audience in the source language by an author is re-contextualised for a target culture audience in the target language (Kvam 2014). The original text has a specific situationality, but in translation, that original situationality is replaced by a new one that dislocates the text from its source circumstance. The text-aware translator proceeds in the production of the target text by understanding the new context in which the translation has to operate and how it is the same or different from the source text's context and conditions of use. In a textual view of translation, successful translation involves not just the successful conversion of source sentences to the conventions of the target linguistic system, but also attention to those aspects of the textual whole – formal, semantic, pragmatic – that have to be modified to meet a new communicative circumstance.

Finally, intertextuality, the last standard, is an explicit recognition of the idea that texts are not written or read in a textual vacuum. When we read a text we do so with a previous experience of texts, and particularly of texts associated with the specific situation in which we are using the text. We always process texts in the wider context of other texts experienced in our cultural milieu (cf. Neubert's (1984) introduction of the term, "text world"). Thus, intertextuality is a reference to the way a given text relates to other texts that are (or have been) relevant in a particular kind of situation or to a specific kind of purpose. This notion of "related texts" or "similarly useful" texts allows us to make an important connection between intertextuality and the notion of text types, in the sense that situations and purposes are held in common condition texts in such a way that they have similar configurational properties – we often capture this notion in Translation Studies with the concept of a "parallel text". The translator needs to be exquisitely aware of the intertextual "demand" on the target text s/he produces by understanding how that demand will require transformations of the target text in line with linguistic and textual properties that target readers expect from a particular type of text. To this extent, there is a clear relationship between intertextuality and acceptability.

The translator's concern with textuality

Thus, in de Beaugrande and Dressler's terms, the translator has to fully understand the textuality of the source text and how it will resemble or differ from the textuality of the target text. Of course, this all proceeds from the assumption that the translator wants to produce a text on the target side that functions as, is perceived as, a text by the target reader. Albrecht Neubert (1985a, 18) called translation, "text-induced text production", and this formulation quite accurately captures the text-linguistic view of translation – that we do not really translate languages (because languages are systems, and communication proceeds via socially embedded selection from the potential forms of the system) – and that we do not really translate just words and sentences (because these cannot be translated independently without concern for the textual and communicative context). Thus, the object of translation is a text and the product of translation is a text, with all that implies about coherence, cohesion, and the other standards of textuality.

Text linguistics is a scholarly means to examine and illuminate the transformations that a text undergoes when it is translated, beyond the scope of the rendition of individual words and sentences. As mentioned earlier, texts have structural and semantic features that reflect relationships between sentences. To what extent does translation preserve, alter, or destroy those relationships? Text linguistics in translation places our focus squarely on the nature of texts – textuality – and how the textuality of a source text is related to the textuality of its target. Where do they or must they coincide? Where can they or must they differ? How does an understanding of the nature of text inform the translation process? How does translation (as Blum-Kulka points out) precipitate changes, necessary or otherwise, to the texture and textuality of a target relative to its source?

Current debates

Text linguistics (and a concern with texts in general) has a relatively long history in Translation Studies, as we have seen. It is not easy to identify any strong thread of contemporary debate at their intersection. For instance, while there has always been some contention about the theoretical status of text types in text linguistics – and how one defines and recognises them – and that concern can bleed over into Translation Studies, it is not clear that this qualifies as a debate. Rather more interesting, and perhaps more thorny a question, is how Translation Studies' concerns with textuality can be integrated with its parallel interest in the cognitive nature of the translation or interpreting process.

To a surprising extent these two lines of thought have developed rather independently in our discipline; we have clear lines of research and teaching that are text-focused, and textual issues, often from an explicitly text-linguistic perspective, are addressed quite commonly in the translation classroom of today. But we have not really looked at the translated or interpreted text as a complex cognitive event. Target texts have to be produced and they have to be read or heard; text linguistics deals with this from a product-oriented point of view, but less so from a process-oriented point of view.

Van Dijk realised early on that text linguistics would have to grapple with how we understand and produce texts – with text processing – hence his collaboration with Walter Kintsch (Kintsch and van Dijk 1978; van Dijk and Kintsch 1983). While text linguistics has focused on the structure and properties of texts as a kind of socio-communicative product, text processing has focused on how the structures of the text (e.g., Kintsch's "textbase") are processed to construct a mental representation of the meaning of a text ("situation model") – see Kintsch (1988; 1992). Text processing has turned out to be a powerful, influential theory in sub-disciplines of psychology, especially in the arena of text comprehension and reading theory.

Is this a current debate in our discipline? No. The problem is actually that it is not being discussed. We have not yet begun to try to integrate the cognitive science of translation with the cognitive science of text. And while this topic might not currently be a disciplinary issue, it should certainly be one.

Future directions

The integration of text linguistics and text processing in the context of translation is the next logical step in translation and interpreting studies. As early as the turn of this century, Blum-Kulka (2000, 313) recognised the importance of this future direction, arguing that "the analysis of texts should be followed by an investigation of text effects. In other words I advocate a psycholinguistic approach to the study of translation effects". Tellingly, she explicitly cites the work of van Dijk and Kintsch (1983) as a foundation for the integration she calls for. House (2012, 180) also calls for this integration when she (referring to de Beaugrande and Dressler) argues that:

> Several of these textuality standards reveal that in producing and understanding texts in translation one must go beyond linguistic analysis and look at a text's psychological and social basis. In doing this one views the text in terms of the cognitive processes underlying its production and comprehension.

Niska (1999) quite presciently understood that many of the central concerns of interpreting – especially given its early concerns with process – could only be addressed by integrating text linguistics and text processing; this topic is explicitly addressed in his work. Shreve and Lacruz (2014), more recently, have looked at translation from the text-processing perspective, trying to integrate text comprehension (and theories of reading) with text production (and theories of writing). They argue that we have to understand the legacy notion of "transfer" in Translation Studies not only by looking at the mechanics of a bilingual's lexico-semantic system, but at how processes of reading and writing across languages work in the context of translation, where the situationality, acceptability, and informativity of a text are greatly modified because of pragmatic circumstances, but also due to differences in the prior knowledge of target readers of a translation as against those of source readers of a source text. They conclude their exposition by arguing that translation, rather than being Neubert's "text-induced text production" is better viewed as "situation model induced situation model production" via the translator's manipulation of the target text's textbase.

Implications for practice

As a practical matter, and we have alluded to this before when speaking of the text-aware translator, text-linguistic approaches to translation have the potential to broaden the horizons of the translator. In the section on core issues, we have discussed specific ways that concepts from text linguistics impinge on the translation activity, shifting the translator's focus from the narrowly lexical and sentential, to include the textual.

Specifically, text linguistics implies that there is an obligation on the part of the translator to "recreate" or rather "create anew" the textual properties of the source text for the target text. If we want the target text to be a text – fully fledged and processed as a proxy for the source text by the target audience – then the seven standards have to be addressed. The implications for practice seem clear: if we pay attention to textual properties in an informed way, there will be a corresponding improvement in the "textuality" of the translation, a quantum leap if you will, in the "textual quality" of the translation.

However, there are complications. For instance, to what extent does the way we process texts as translators or interpreters (e.g., sequential, step-like, sentence-by-sentence, translation unit by translation unit) preclude us from considering the more global, textual issues? Our current understanding of cognitive processes in translation makes it all too clear that the very way that translation proceeds brings the translator's focus, necessarily, down to the sentential level, maybe even clausal level. Does this sentential dominance then necessarily push textual concerns to pre-translation activities or post-translation revision using some kind of text analysis as in Christiane Nord's (1988) work, *Text Analysis and Translation*? How much time will then actually be given to text analysis?

This raises the issue that I will refer to as the "good enough" syndrome. What this means is that for any given practical translation, factoring in all of the constraints and the economics of the translational transaction, at what point is the translation "sufficient for purpose" or "fit for purpose" and satisfactory given the client's requirements and the translation brief? There is probably a tipping point beyond which pursuing the translation to the extent of trying to address all of the aspects of textuality becomes a "losing proposition" in an economic sense, even if the case can be made that the quality of the translation is improved. This seems crass and mercenary, but is nevertheless true as practical matter. And in interpreting, the practical matters and cognitive constraints of "real-time" performance preclude much target-side attention to textual features.

Since we have raised the issue of quality and have assumed that appropriate attention to textual issues in translation would improve translation quality at least along the textual dimension, how would we characterise that improvement? What are the dimensions of textuality that are most likely to bring about a discernible improvement in quality if addressed? In some cases, as for instance the effective and appropriate use of target language cohesive devices, one could readily argue that target-text coherence is demonstrably improved – and therefore acceptability is enhanced. Similarly, as we discussed earlier, appropriate understanding of informativity issues can assist in identifying when explicitation is necessary or not. Intertextuality can be brought into play by focusing on the utility of parallel texts in translation practice. Situationality emerges in an emphasis on the translation brief, intentionality in the emphasis on understanding the purpose of one's target text and how it relates to the function of one's translation. This is a lot to bring to the translation activity without explanation, example, and practice in application.

Ultimately, it seems most likely that the influence of text linguistics on translation practice must necessarily be indirect, interpreted through a text-aware translation pedagogy. Decoding the seven standards of textuality, understanding the components of texture, or realising the utility of text typology and parallel texts, is best conferred in the translation classroom where those notions can be unpacked and illustrated in guided practice. We want students to understand that how we judge a translation is not just a result of whether the meanings of words and sentences have been transferred. There are more global concerns. We might want to teach students that we can look at the success of translation from the perspective of accuracy (the extent to which meaning has been preserved), adequacy (the extent to which the required function and purpose have been achieved), and acceptability (the extent to which the text user accepts our text in his or her communicative circumstance). We have to extend notions of accuracy in translation to include the semantic structure and content of the text as a whole – its coherence and informativity. We have to extend adequacy to deal with situationality and intentionality, and we have to extend acceptability to include considerations of cohesion and intertextuality.

Further reading

de Beaugrande, R.-A. and Dressler, W. U. 1981. *Introduction to Text Linguistics*. London: Longman. One of the seminal works in text linguistics, explaining the nature of textuality and introducing the seven standards.

Halliday, M. A. K. and Hasan, R. 1976. *Cohesion in English*. London: Longman. A seminal work in text linguistics, but also the foundation of our understanding of cohesion and its mechanisms.

Hatim, B. and Mason, I. 1990. *Discourse and the Translator*. London: Longman. An important work that brings the work of Halliday and Hasan into Translation Studies.

Neubert, A. and Shreve, G. M. 1992. *Translation as Text*. Ohio: Kent State University Press. The text-linguistic framework of de Beaugrande and Dressler is introduced at length and placed in a translational context.

Related topics

Discourse analysis, interpreting and translation; Genre analysis and translation; Sociolinguistics, translation and interpreting; Language processing, interpreting and translation.

References

Alexieva, B. 1994. "Types of Texts and Intertextuality in Simultaneous Interpreting". In *Translation Studies: An Interdiscipline*, edited by M. Snell-Hornby, F. Pöchhacker and K. Kaindl, 179–187. Amsterdam: John Benjamins.
Baker, M. 1992. *In Other Words*. London: Routledge.

Beaugrande, R.-A. de. 1997. *New Foundations for a Science of Text and Discourse: Cognition, Communication, and the Freedom of Access to Knowledge and Society.* Norwood, NJ: Ablex.

Beaugrande, R.-A. de and Dressler, W. U. 1981. *Introduction to Text Linguistics.* London: Longman.

Blum-Kulka, S. 1986. "Shifts of Cohesion and Coherence in Translation". In *Interlingual and Intercultural Communication: Discourse and Cognition in Translation and Second Language Acquisition Studies*, edited by J. House and S. Blum-Kulka, 17–35. Tübingen: Gunter Narr. Reprinted 2000 in *The Translation Studies Reader*, edited by L. Venuti, 298–313. London: Routledge.

Carstens, W. 2001. "Text Linguistics: Relevant Linguistics?" In *Poetics, Linguistics, and History: Discourses of War and Conflict, PALA Conference Papers 1999*, edited by I. Bierman and A. L. Combrink, 588–595. Potchefstroom: Potchefstroom University.

Crystal, D. 2008. *Dictionary of Linguistics and Phonetics.* Hoboken, NJ: Blackwell Publishing.

Crystal, D. 2011. *Language and Discourse* [WWW Document]. Available from: http://cw.routledge.com/textbooks/9780415602679/pdfs/synopsis6.pdf [Accessed 1 June 2016].

Fulcher, G. 1989. Cohesion and coherence in theory and reading research. *Journal of Research in Reading* 12, pp. 146–163.

Halliday, M. A. K. 1978. *Language as Social Semiotic: The Social Interpretation of Language and Meaning.* London: Edward Arnold.

Halliday, M. A. K. and Hasan, R. 1976. *Cohesion in English.* London: Longman.

Hatim, B. 1998. "Text Linguistics and Translation". In *Routledge Encyclopedia of Translation Studies*, edited by M. Baker, 262–265. London: Routledge.

Hatim, B. and Mason, I. 1990. *Discourse and the Translator.* London: Longman.

House, J. 2012. "Text Linguistics and Translation". In *Handbook of Translation Studies*, edited by Y. Gambier and L. van Doorslaer, 178–183. Amsterdam: John Benjamins.

Kintsch, W. 1988. The role of knowledge in discourse comprehension: a construction-integration model. *Psychological Review* 95, pp. 163–182.

Kintsch, W. 1992. "How Readers Construct Situation Models for Stories: The Role of Syntactic Cues and Causal Inferences". In *From Learning Processes to Cognitive Processes: Essays in Honor of William K. Estes*, edited by A. F. Healy, S. M. Kosslyn and R. M. Shiffrin, 261–278. Hillsdale, NJ: Lawrence Erlbaum.

Kintsch, W. and van Dijk, T. A. 1978. Toward a model of text comprehension and production. *Psychological Review* 85, pp. 363–394.

Kvam, S. 2014. Text linguistics and the translation brief: on the relevance of conversation analysis as an operational tool in a pragmatic text linguistic approach to translation. *Perspectives: Studies in Translatology* 22, pp. 21–38.

Manfredi, M. 2008. *Translating Text and Context: Translation Studies and Systemic Functional Linguistics.* Bologna: Dupress.

Mubenga, K. S. 2010. Towards an integrated approach to cohesion and coherence in interlingual subtitling. *Stellenbosch Papers in Linguistics PLUS* 40, pp. 39–54.

Neubert, A. 1984. "Text-Bound Translation Teaching". In *Translation Theory and Its Implementation in the Teaching of Translating and Interpreting*, edited by W. Wilss and G. Thome, 61–70. Tübingen: Gunter Narr.

Neubert, A. 1985a. *Text and Translation*, Übersetzungswissenschaftliche Beiträge, Vol. 8. Leipzig: Verlag Enzyklopädie.

Neubert, A. 1985b. "Textlinguistik des Übersetzens". In *Beiträge Zur Englischen Textlinguistik, Linguistische Studien*, 15–24. Leipzig: Akademie der Wissenschaften der DDR.

Neubert, A. and Shreve, G. M. 1992. *Translation as Text.* Kent, OH: Kent State University Press.

Newmark, P. 1987. "The Use of Systemic Linguistics in Translation Analysis and Criticism". In *Language Topics: Essays in Honour of Michael Halliday*, edited by R. Steele and T. Threadgold. Amsterdam: John Benjamins.

Niska, H. 1999. *Text Linguistic Models for the Study of Simultaneous Interpreting.* Stockholm: Stockholm University.

Nord, C. 1988. *Text Analysis and Translation: Theoretical Foundations, Method and Didactic Use of a Translation-Related Text Analysis.* Heidelberg: Groos.

Reiss, K. 1971. *Möglichkeiten und Grenzen der Übersetzungskritik.* Munich: Huber.

Sanders, T. and Maat, H. P. 2006. "Cohesion and Coherence: Linguistic Approaches". In *Encyclopedia of Language and Linguistics*, edited by K. Brown, 591–595. Amsterdam: Elsevier.

Shreve, G. M. and Lacruz, I. 2014. "Translation as a Higher-Order Text Processing". In *A Companion to Translation Studies*, edited by S. Bermann and C. Porter, 107–118. Hoboken, NJ: Wiley Blackwell.

Snell-Hornby, M. 2006. *The Turns of Translation Studies: New Paradigms or Shifting Viewpoints.* Amsterdam: John Benjamins.

Steiner, E. 2005. "Halliday and Translation Theory: Enhancing the Options, Broadening the Range and Keeping the Ground". In *Continuing Discourse on Language: A Functional Perspective*, edited by R. Hasan, C. Mathiessen and J. J. Webster, 481–500. London: Equinox.

Steiner, E. and Webster, J. 2015. "Halliday's Contributions to a Theory of Translation". In *The Bloomsbury Companion to M. A. K. Halliday*, edited by J. J. Webster, 412–426. London: Bloomsbury.

van Dijk, T. A. 1972. *Some Aspects of Text Grammars.* The Hague: Mouton

van Dijk, T. A. 1977. *Text and Context.* London: Longman.

van Dijk, T. A. 2004. *From Text Grammar to Critical Discourse Analysis: A Brief Academic Bibliography* [WWW Document]. Available from: http://www.discourses.org/From%20text%20grammar%20to%20critical%20discourse%20analysis.html [Accessed 1 April 2016].

van Dijk, T. A. and Kintsch, W. 1983. *Strategies of Discourse Comprehension.* New York: Academic Press.

Werlich, E. 1976. *A Text Grammar of English.* Heidelberg: Quelle and Meyer.

12

Narrative analysis and translation

Mona Baker

Interest in narrative has a long and complex history that spans centuries and a diverse range of modern disciplines. Herman, Jahn and Ruyan (2005, 344) date the concept back "a couple of millennia, both in Western and non-Western cultures", but credit French structuralists, especially Roland Barthes and Claude Bremond, with emancipating it from the restricted bounds of literature and elevating it to "a semiotic phenomenon that transcends disciplines and media". Lyotard's work further expanded the definition of narrative beyond any form of textual realisation with the claim that Grand Narratives "may exist as collective beliefs rather than the message of particular texts" (Herman *et al.* 2005, 344), thus paving the way for the now widespread use of the term in this diffuse sense, as in 'gendered narratives' and 'narratives of race'.

Among the many definitions and uses of narrative adopted by scholars in various disciplines today, the strand that has taken root in Translation Studies draws on developments in social theory, and has come to be known as socio-narrative theory (Harding 2012a). To date, the most detailed exposition of socio-narrative theory and its application in Translation Studies remains *Translation and Conflict: A Narrative Account* (Baker 2006). Case studies that have developed the approach or some aspect of it include Boéri (2008), Pérez-González (2010), Morales-Moreno (2011), Harding (2012b; 2014), Erkazanci Durmus (2014) and Bassi (2015), among others, and a detailed engagement with the theoretical underpinning of the approach can be found in Robinson (2011). This chapter focuses on the analysis of translated texts and interpreted events across different media using the tools afforded by socio-narrative theory, and begins with an outline of the theory's assumptions and the difference between narrative, as understood in this approach, and discourse, especially as defined in Critical Discourse Analysis (CDA).

Basic assumptions

A narrative is a story with a perceived beginning and a projected end, and with a pattern of emplotment that allows both narrator and audience to make sense of the events depicted. Narratives are populated by protagonists, whether animate or inanimate, configured in relation to each other and the unfolding story. Socio-narrative theory takes as its point of departure the idea that narrative is *the* principal mode by which we experience the world, rather than merely a genre or particular type of text. The claim is not that everything comes to us already configured in narrative form, hence the distinction between narrative and chronology, list or database (White 1987; Herman 2013). Rather, our minds construct narratives out of various types of input in order to comprehend and make sense of the world; Herman (2013) refers to this process as storying the world. Texts of different types and in different media feed into this process, and Herman (2013, 9) includes translations and other types of retellings among the network of narratives that mediate our understandings and memories of specific experiences.

A related assumption is that the narratives we tell ourselves and others about the world(s) in which we live construct rather than represent reality. Translation can then be understood as a form of (re)narration that participates in constructing the world rather than merely a process of transferring semantic content from one language to another, accurately or otherwise. This raises the question of the status of "the real" in narrative theory, and the related question of the limits of neutrality in the context of translation and interpreting. The claim is not that there is no reality, nor that translators necessarily do or should set out to disregard the source text and re-narrate from their own perspective. Rather, what socio-narrative theory suggests is that "real events do not offer themselves as stories" (White 1987, 4), and that in order to make sense of them we have to narrativise them, to bestow a structure and an order of meaning on them. This order of meaning is informed by our own location within a variety of public and personal narratives and reflects the inescapable prejudices and limitations of that location. The same argument holds for physical entities as it does for events. As Harding (2012b, 23) argues, drawing on Sarbin (1998), while it is not possible to deny the reality of a brick wall given that we cannot walk through it, whether we assign that wall the function of protection or imprisonment is part of the process of narrativisation and reveals one of the ways in which the narratives we weave inform how we act in the world and hence constitute reality for us and others.

To complicate matters further, deliberate fabrications are widespread, and we do not always recognise them as such. A powerful example is the case of the Syrian-American LGBT blogger Amina Abdallah Arraf al Omari, better known as the "Gay Girl from Damascus", whose story captured extensive media attention in 2011 and generated widespread sympathy on social media, until *The Electronic Intifada* exposed her as a hoax (Abunimah 2011). She turned out to be a fictitious character created by Tom MacMaster, a doctoral student at the University of Edinburgh. By then the fictitious Amina had developed a romantic relationship with a real-life French-Canadian gay blogger, and her alleged abduction by three men working for the Syrian President's family had mobilised various groups to lobby the US government to use its influence to set her free. Despite many clues that should have raised doubts about her authenticity, such as the fact that she was never available on Skype or on the phone and the nude pictures she sent her lover never showed her face (O'Hehir 2015), she was real because she had a real-life girlfriend and because *The Guardian*, a highly respected British newspaper, interviewed her and included a photograph she provided in the report (Marsh 2011). While this example does not involve translation, it reveals the same kind of logic that underpins the phenomenon of pseudotranslation, which has attracted much scholarly attention. In both cases, and irrespective of their status as real or fictitious, the narratives we weave about events, people and texts actively construct the world because they generate responses and consequences that may or may not be anticipated by those who play a role in elaborating and disseminating these narratives, and these consequences cannot simply be written off when a narrative turns out to be fictitious. Hence, as Rambelli (2009, 211) explains, James Macpherson's pseudotranslation of the Ossianic poems "supported the romantic hypothesis that poetry was not a matter of rhetorical devices but a natural and primitive form of expression", and the poems eventually came to constitute "a major point of reference for Scottish national pride [and] served as a model for other cultures which sought epic cycles of foundation, such as Finland". The impact of the Ossianic poems on the development of poetic or national traditions remains, irrespective of their fictitious status.

Narrative and discourse

Narrative and discourse are both key notions in the humanities, and scholars continue to define them in a variety of ways. They also overlap, as evident in the fact that narrative analyses frequently refer to hegemonic and other types of discourse, and discourse-oriented analyses often feature references such as corporate narratives. Despite the overlaps and diversity of definitions, however, the two concepts remain distinct in terms of the underlying assumptions of the theoretical frameworks in which they are embedded and, consequently, the types of analysis they support. Given the growing popularity of CDA among scholars of translation and interpreting, this section will focus on the partly overlapping concepts of discourse, as defined in CDA, and narrative, as used in socio-narrative theory, in order to address the question of whether narrative analysis can offer alternative insights that a CDA framework does not already afford us.

The starting point for definitions of discourse, including its definition in CDA, is Michel Foucault's work, but as Mills (2003) points out, Foucault himself offered various and often contradictory definitions of this concept. Nevertheless, practically all definitions of discourse, including its conceptualisation in CDA and CDA-informed studies of translation and interpreting, share a focus on abstract forms of knowledge and the way knowledge is constructed and mediated, primarily through text. Importantly, knowledge is understood as institutionally generated and sanctioned, as evident in Mason's (1994/2010, 86) definition of discourse as "systematically organised sets of statements which give expression to the meanings and values of an institution". The emphasis on text and institutions has important consequences for the types of analysis that can be supported by CDA, as opposed to socio-narrative theory.

First, although a number of scholars who work with the notion of discourse have attempted in recent years to extend its purview beyond verbal material, the emphasis continues to be placed on text, hence Wodak and Meyer's (2001/2009, 6) distinction between discourse as "structured forms of knowledge" and text as "concrete oral utterances or written documents". A narrative, by contrast, is assumed to be "realisable across a variety of media", such as "written and spoken text, images, diagrams, colour, layout, lighting in theatre and film, choice of setting, and style of dressing" (Baker 2014, 159–160). This lends narrative greater versatility in analysing complex instances of translation, such as web-based material (Baker 2007; 2010a; McDonough-Dolmaya 2010) and illustrated children's literature (Sinbaldi 2011). Narrative also lends itself much more readily to the analysis of paratextual material such as book covers (Al-Herthani 2009; Summers 2012), and to relating their verbal and non-verbal features to the wider cultural and political context in which the translation is embedded. For example, Al-Herthani explains that the front cover of the 1993 English edition of Edward Said's *Culture and Imperialism* shows a large faded globe, with a crowd underneath, including an Asian officer wearing a turban and bowing to a white man who is dressed as a high-ranking official. Here, as Al-Herthani (2009, 152) explains,

The globe may serve as a frame that evokes several narratives, including complicity between scholars and imperialism, since it is scholars who produce scientific and systematic means of controlling the other, such as maps and globes. The globe, a map of the world, may also signal the expansionist nature of imperial powers which have the whole world as a target, ultimately seeking to rule both the natives and "the waves", as Said (1993, 378) puts it. The way the Asian man is portrayed reminds the reader of the imperial narratives of "subject races" (Said 1995) who are happy to pay obeisance to their Western masters.

The cover of Kamal Abu-Deeb's Arabic translation, on the other hand, depicts a picture taken from the Palace of Versailles, which shows two large Roman statues lying helpless and defeated on the ground "with a rope coiled around the neck of each statue" (Al-Herthani 2009, 150). Al-Herthani (2009, *ibid.*) interprets this image as "symbolising the defeat of imperial powers at the hands of resistant communities", and argues that it "hints at one facet of Said's intellectual project, namely the decolonisation of symbols of colonial heritage, which are depicted here as lifeless statues, with no power and no legitimacy". Thus, while the image on the cover of the English text "evokes and anchors the narrative of imperial hegemony" which is the focus of the first part of the book, the image on the cover of the translation "elaborates a narrative that challenges imperialism and declares its defeat" (2009, 157), the topic of the second part of the book. Each image gives salience to a different element of the overall narrative elaborated by Said, in the same way as foregrounding and backgrounding textual elements through omission, addition and reordering are a facet of one of the key dimensions of narrativity, namely selective appropriation.

Second, CDA's emphasis on textual material and abstract structures of knowledge is rendered more restrictive by a tendency to downgrade the individual text in favour of repeated occurrences across a large body of material produced by institutional actors, because individual texts are assumed to have "minimal effects, which are hardly noticeable and almost impossible to prove", while "a discourse, with its recurring contents, symbols and strategies, leads to the emergence and solidification of 'knowledge' and therefore has sustained effects" (Wodak and Meyer 2001/2009, 38). A corollary to the dismissal of individual texts is that "individual resources" and "the specifics of single-exchange situations" are not deemed relevant to CDA analyses – only "the overall structural features in social fields or in overall society" (Wodak and Meyer 2001/2009, 10). This has important implications for the types of genre that lend themselves to productive analysis using CDA, with obvious restrictions relating to literature and any form of creative endeavour. By definition, much literature deliberately breaks away from recurrent discursive patterns, which makes it difficult to isolate textual patterns repeated across many literary texts. Media texts, on the other hand, lend themselves extremely well to CDA analysis and continue to attract considerable attention from CDA scholars.

Socio-narrative theory is not hampered by assumptions relating to the value of individual texts and resources, nor by the highly deterministic claim that "it is not the subject who makes the discourses, but the discourses that make the subject" (Jäger and Maier 2001/2010, 37). Unlike CDA scholars who argue that "[t]he subject is of interest not as an actor, but as a product of discourses" (2001/2010, 37), narrative theory recognises the role that individuals can play in shaping the world around them to varying degrees and pays equal attention to the personal and the public, the hegemonic and the resistant. Although some types of narrative – specifically meta narrative – tend toward the abstract and the hegemonic, and in this sense overlap more clearly with the notion of discourse as structures of knowledge and the emphasis on institutional power, narrative theory also pays considerable attention to the detailed, concrete stories of everyday life and the personal dimension of experience. It further acknowledges that individuals can and do exercise agency and are not mere products of discourses nor of dominant narratives. This attention to the personal and the non-mainstream is reflected in the typology of narratives that informs studies of translation and interpreting which have adopted the socio-narrative approach to date, as explained in the following section.

Finally, narrative and discourse seem to generate different resonances, irrespective of the claims made about their relative epistemological status by leading scholars in each field. While discourse is associated with knowledge, and hence objective reality, narrative is associated with stories and hence with fictional accounts. Herman (2013, 344) thus argue that an expression such as 'narratives of science' now,

> carries the implication that scientific discourse does not reflect but covertly constructs reality, does not discover truths but fabricates them according to the rules of its own game in a process disturbingly comparable to the overt working of narrative fiction.

At the same time, in the context of the epistemological crisis that has come to define our contemporary world, many increasingly see narrative as all that is left "when belief in the possibility of knowledge is eroded" (2013, 344).

A fluid typology

Revisited and adapted to different contexts by scholars such as Boéri (2008) and Harding (2012a; 2012b), the typology of narratives that informs socio-narrative studies consistently pays equal attention to personal and institutional narratives, however labelled. The typology was first proposed by social theorists Somers and Gibson (1994) and later elaborated in Baker (2006) with specific reference to translation and interpreting. It initially consisted of four categories: ontological (personal), public, conceptual (disciplinary) and meta narratives, discussed in more detail below. Boéri's (2008, 26) study of conference interpreting introduced an additional category, professional narratives, to cover "stories and explanations that professionals elaborate for themselves and others about the nature and ethos of their activity". Harding's (2011; 2012a; 2012b) revision of the typology is more substantial: instead of a flat model, she proposes a more detailed taxonomy that foregrounds the difference between personal and collective narratives at the top level, with subcategories under each. In both cases the position of personal narratives within the typology remains intact; indeed, personal narratives are specifically foregrounded in Harding's typology, and the studies themselves draw on the tension between the personal and the public to explain important aspects of the data. While all theoretical models are open to extension and adaptation as scholars apply them in different contexts, socio-narrative theory is particularly amenable to this type of intervention because of its underlying assumption that all narratives are constructed, and hence "where we choose to draw any boundaries, including boundaries between theoretical categories, is part of the narrative world we are constantly engaged in constructing for ourselves and others" (Baker 2010a, 351–352).

To return to the original typology proposed by Baker (2006), ontological narratives, referred to in subsequent publications as personal narratives, were first defined restrictively as "personal narratives that we *tell ourselves* about our place in the world and our personal history" (2006: 28; emphasis added). This definition unduly confined them to the domain of cognition and was later refined to strengthen the interpersonal dimension, allowing the category to further encompass the narratives an individual tells others and those that others elaborate about the individual, with the main criterion being that a given individual "is located at the centre of narration ... is the subject of the narrative" (Baker 2010a, 350). Personal narratives in this expanded definition include genres such as autobiographies as well as biographies, eyewitness accounts and courtroom testimonies, whether delivered by the defendant or a witness. In all cases what is disseminated is an account of events that explicitly features either the narrator or another individual at the centre of the narrative.

The attention paid to personal narratives reflects socio-narrative theory's interest in discordant voices and how they challenge streamlined, reductionist accounts of the world or some aspect of it. The role played by translation in foregrounding or occluding such voices has been the subject of several studies. Harding's (2012b) extended study of media reporting on the 2004 Beslan hostage crisis found that eyewitness reports which figured to varying degrees in the original reporting in Russian practically disappeared in all English versions offered by state-controlled as well as independent news outlets. The effect of translation was ultimately to "emphasise and reinforce simplistic, reductionist framing narratives and to weaken or even eliminate complex and multivalent narratives" of a major trauma in modern Russian and Chechen history (2012b, 223). Similarly, van Rooyen (2011) cites an example of a radio news item translated from English for the South African Broadcasting Corporation's Afrikaans service, which omitted a long stretch where a township resident explains why he wants to see an end to coal mines in his area. Van Rooyen (2011, 26) explains this example partly in socio-narrative terms, as reflecting "obscured patterns of domination and oppression". People living in townships, she argues, "did not have a voice" in apartheid South Africa, but now they are "given the opportunity to speak but [are] silenced once more in the Afrikaans news bulletin".

Like all categories proposed by socio-narrative theory, the boundaries between personal and other types of narrative are porous and the categories themselves highly interdependent. Unless a personal narrative remains locked in the mind of a single individual, as the initial definition of the category unintentionally implies, it simultaneously constitutes a public narrative, to a greater or lesser degree. Public narratives are "stories elaborated by and circulating among social and institutional formations larger than the individual" (Baker 2006, 33), obvious examples of the overlap being the personal-cum-public narratives of high-profile individuals such as Nelson Mandela and Simone de Beauvoir.

Conceptual narratives are "the stories and explanations that scholars in any field elaborate for themselves and others about their object of inquiry" (Baker 2006, 39). Said's (1978) critique of the narratives produced by orientalists is a good example, but this critique is itself a conceptual narrative. Similarly, in the context of translation and interpreting studies, Baker (2008, 22) argues elsewhere, Skopos theory constitutes a conceptual narrative that evokes representations of "an industrialized, affluent society populated by clients and highly professional translators"; the latter are projected as "highly trained, confident young men and women [who] ... go about their work in a conflict-free environment and live happily ever after". This corporate narrative of the world of translation clearly does not accommodate locally sourced, trained translators and interpreters, let alone untrained taxi drivers and doctors who often have to scrape a living in various conflict zones by working for military forces and media outlets. The US military forces in Iraq and Afghanistan, for instance, narrated not only locally sourced interpreters but also American interpreters of Iraqi or Afghan origin as potential sources of threat and denied them basic rights of protection, including "enter[ing] the Green Zone through the priority lane in order to avoid being easy targets for suicide bombers as they stood in long queues" (Baker 2010b, 210). As with any narrative, Skopos theory foregrounds certain aspects of experience and downplays others, with consequences for those excluded from its purview. The corporate account of the world it elaborates is shared by many other approaches in the professional and academic worlds and has been extremely influential. In recent years it has been challenged by both professionals and scholars, however, leading to significant developments in the way professional associations such as the International Association of Conference Interpreters (AIIC) position themselves. Kahane's (2008) article in the *AIIC Webzine*, which frames the argument in socio-narrative terms, called on AIIC members to acknowledge the predicament of interpreters in war-riven countries (Kahane 2008). On the scholarly side, Boéri (2008) mounted a similar challenge in the same year, and one year later the AIIC launched a project to support "Interpreters in Conflict Areas" irrespective of their professional or membership status. Attention to such dynamic processes that involve individuals and small groups challenging and adjusting powerful mainstream narratives, be they public, professional or conceptual, has rendered socio-narrative theory particularly attractive to scholars interested in the activist dimension of translation and interpreting.

Meta narratives are "particularly potent public narratives that persist over long periods of time and influence the lives of people across a wide range of settings" (Baker 2010a, 351). They are characterised by "a sense of inescapability" (Baker 2010a, 351) and a high level of abstraction (Harding 2012b, 39). Examples include religious narratives such as Buddhism, Judaism, Christianity and Islam, as well as political narratives such as the Cold War and the so-called War on Terror. The latter has attracted particular attention in socio-narrative studies of translation and interpreting (Baker 2007; 2010a; Harding 2012a; 2012b; Bassi 2015).

The porosity of the boundaries between personal, public, conceptual and meta narratives does not compromise an analysis that draws on this typology, because the idea is not to identify the types of narrative evoked in a given text or set of materials mechanistically, but to capture the interplay and tensions between them in order to explain meaningful differences that can be observed over time or between different sets of data. For example, Bassi (2015) draws on socio-narrative theory in a detailed analysis of the way in which Roberto Saviano, author of the Italian non-fiction best seller *Gomorra* (2006), was branded in his home country and internationally through translation. The book is a first-person account of the criminal organisation Camorra, which is involved in the disposal business and considered responsible for the widely publicised rubbish crisis that started in Naples in 1994. Its publication angered the organisation, whose bosses were reported to have issued threats against Saviano's life. Umberto Eco's 2006 broadcast message, in which he urged the state to offer Saviano protection and compared him to well-known figures killed by the Mafia in 1992, set the scene for branding the author domestically and "plac[ing] his personal story within the public narrative of the national struggle against organized crime" (Bassi 2015, 53). When an Italian newspaper broke the news in October 2008 that an ex-Camorra boss had revealed details of a plot to kill Saviano, a series of events began to unfold that included six Nobel Prize Winners signing a letter expressing solidarity with the author. Saviano's high-profile appearances with Salman Rushdie outside Italy paved the way for branding him as "Italy's Salman Rushdie" and for his association internationally with the meta narrative of the War on Terror and, more broadly, of "a meta-narrative of history as a coherent movement towards 'democracy' and 'freedom'" (2015, 58). Bassi's (2015, 57) meticulous analysis shows that over time, and with the intervention of various narrators, this branding became "part of a coherent timeline linking the 'Rushdie affair' with 9/11" and the War on Terror. Ironically, Saviano's own narrative of *Gomorra* explains it "as a modern organization perfectly integrated within capitalism and democratic Europe", but this explanation is undermined by the narratives in which the author is embedded internationally. As Bassi (2015, 59) explains,

> in Saviano's narrative, the "global threat" comes from the Western project of capitalism; in the narrative of the label "Italy's Salman Rushdie" and "writer under threat", a good West is threatened by something that is located outside Europe and on its borders, and which is imagined as culturally distant.

An interdependent set of dimensions

Socio-narrative studies investigate translation as a form of mediation with a complex relationship to other forms of mediation assumed to precede and directly inform it to varying degrees. From close translations of sacred texts to the transediting of news items, fansubbing, volunteer interpreting, theatre translation and even pseudotranslation, the focus is not on establishing the degree of match between a putative original and a putative target text but on what dimensions of narrativity are deployed and how they impact the new context of narration. According to Baker (2006), who draws on both Somers and Gibson (1994) and Bruner (1991), the eight dimensions of narrativity are temporality, relationality, selective appropriation, causal emplotment, particularity, genericness, normativeness/canonicity and breach, and narrative accrual. The most important of these are discussed and exemplified here.

Temporality has received the most sustained level of attention from scholars of narrative. White (1987, 177), following Paul Ricoeur, distinguishes between "the experience of time as mere seriality and an experience of temporality in which events take on the aspect of elements of lived stories, with a discernible beginning, middle, and end". The emplotment of stories along a timeline not only projects a certain pattern of coherence onto a set of events but also endows the narrative with moral force, allowing us to attribute blame, responsibility, victimhood or credit to various protagonists. The order in which a story develops is therefore an intrinsic part of the narrative being told and is meaningful in its own right. For example, a non-chronologically ordered narrative may allow the narrator to complicate the perspective from which the story is told, which explains Milan Kundera's outrage at the first English translation of *The Joke*, an intricate narrative told in a different way from the perspective of each key protagonist. The translators, David Hamblyn and Oliver Stallybrass, apparently "found the lack of strict chronological order in the book misleading" and "decided to introduce chronology by cutting, 'pasting' and shifting the chapters around" (Kuhiwczak 1990, 125). A polyphonic narrative about the ambiguity and complexity of human experience thus became a flat, localised story about the relationships between specific protagonists.

The passage of time impacts the meanings assigned to verbal, visual and behavioural signs deployed in articulating a narrative, in ways that cannot be anticipated or controlled by narrators, including translators. Abdel Nasser (2016) offers several examples of the impact of the changing context of the Egyptian revolution on the way poems written and (re)translated before or during 2011–2012 are reread after the military takeover in 2013. One example, not discussed in these terms by Abdel Nasser (2016, 119), comes from her own translation of Amin Haddad's poem "Freedom is from the Martyrs", written to commemorate the massacre of demonstrators in October 2011 and later published in 2013 as part of a collection of the same title. The translation follows the original closely in referring to "the blood of martyrs *on the asphalt*" (my emphasis) which "blooms flowers and blooms light". The expression, "on the asphalt", acquired a particular resonance following the military takeover in June 2013, and especially after the issuing of a protest law in November of the same year that continues to allow the authorities to imprison very large numbers of activists. Whatever the intention of the poet and the translator, this phrase now strongly evokes public narratives of the long-awaited release of some of the many youths arrested on Egyptian streets, and the cheering of other activists at the end of each protracted trial as a prisoner is announced free and "on the asphalt". This new meaning does not invalidate the initial reading of the poem and its translation, but it evokes other layers of experience – other public and personal narratives – unlikely to have been anticipated by the poet or the translator.

Like other dimensions of narrativity, temporality is not necessarily or solely realised in textual form, so that "even where explicit verbal indicators about the temporal position of events are absent, the rendering of a character's appearance or of the setting can suggest the position of a given scene or occurrence on an overarching timeline" (Herman 2013, 126). Moreover, as Herman's comment makes clear, the concept of temporality extends to spatiality in narrative theory, with time and space being regarded as deeply interdependent notions. Translations can then relocate source narratives not only temporally but also spatially, and can do so through verbal as well as non-verbal means, as demonstrated in Karunanayake's (2015) study of theatre translation in the context of recent conflicts in Sri Lanka (1983–2009). *Saakki,* the 1986 Sinhala translation of Dario Fo's *The Accidental Death of an Anarchist,* relocates the events of the play in Sri Lanka partly through verbal means, such as introducing references to Buddhism alongside the original references to Christianity (2015, 214). This strategy proved successful, Karunanayake (2015, 213) argues, because "both religions are familiar to the target audience". At the same time, the Sinhala translation anchors the new setting within *Kolam,* "an early 20th century community or non-urban theatre form that made extensive use of masks" (2015, 215). The director of *Saakki* drew on the *Kolam* tradition of engaging with space by using the auditorium for performance and situating the audience on the stage of a formal theatre space in Colombo (2015, 221), in a reversal of canonical practices that reconfigures the relationship between actors and audiences. This reversal of norms reminds us that breach is "part of the inherent potentiality of narrative" that allows it to "disrupt the legitimacy of a canonical storyline or genre" (Baker 2006, 98). All these choices cumulatively relocate the events narrated in the source text within the temporal and spatial context of 1990s Sri Lanka, with important implications for the way the audience interprets the unfolding political narrative.

Relationality is a dimension of narrativity that translators and interpreters can easily relate to: it means that individual elements acquire meaning and value from the way they are configured within a narrative and cannot mean in the same way once transformed into a different narrative environment. Translation scholars have traditionally treated this issue as a facet of culture specificity, but the notion of relationality covers much more and is not tied to verbal elements of a narrative. One example which allows us to think beyond the semantic meaning of lexical items is the occurrence of typographical and grammatical errors in activist subtitling, as in Figures 12.1 and 12.2.

Unpolished output such as the subtitles shown here is traditionally considered unprofessional and, from the perspective of the corporate world, would not inspire confidence in the film makers or subtitlers involved in the two Egyptian collectives. Babels, the network of volunteers who provide interpreting at World Social Forum events, have come under heavy attack from some professional interpreters precisely on the basis that their output fails to meet the standards of high-quality, polished performance, as set by the AIIC (Boéri 2008). In the world of contemporary activism and citizen media reporting, however, and given the attendant pressures and precariousness associated with these contexts, "unpolished" and "polished"

Figure 12.1 Typographical error in *Freedom for Hassan Mostafa*

Source: The Mosireen Collective https://www.youtube.com/watch?v=NQH3LCebMJU (accessed 16 May 2016).

acquire reverse values. Thus, for instance, "images produced via the use of mobile camera phones" during such crises as the London bombings in July 2007 have now become iconic "because of – rather than despite of – their shaky, grainy look" (Cross 2016, 228). Typographical and minor grammatical errors are an intrinsic element of what Selim (2016, 83) refers to as "'crisis translation', . . . done in the urgency of the moment, when a specific event or series of events require immediate dissemination to the outside world", and are thus not only tolerated but may suggest a greater degree of authenticity and commitment. Indeed, as Cross (2016, 229) argues, "the amateur" now "forms a point of resistance for the professional" and authenticity is gradually acquiring greater value than expertise, to the point where the professional world itself is beginning to appropriate some of the features associated with unpolished, "authentic" output.

Relationality combines with other narrative dimensions to elaborate specific narratives, as exemplified in Baker's (2010a) study of the Middle East Media Research Institute. A pro-Israel advocacy group that claims its work "directly supports fighting the U.S. War on Terror" and boasts "providing thousands of pages of translated documents of . . . print media, terrorist websites, school books, and tens of thousands of hours of translated footage from Arab and Iranian television" (the Middle East Media Research Institute (MEMRI), "About Us" page), MEMRI's narrative of the world is partly elaborated through its choice of source and target languages and the strictly uni-directional flow of its translation. Source languages always include Arabic and Persian, with other languages like Turkish, Daru, Pashtu and Hindi being included or excluded at different points in time. These are "index . . . societies that are depicted as sources of threat" and therefore have to be monitored (Baker 2010a, 355). Target languages consistently feature English, French, Spanish, German and Hebrew, with languages such as Russian and Chinese included or excluded according to the political climate of the day. They "index those [communities] that must

Figure 12.2 Grammatical error in *Episode 2: Sabah Ibrahim*

Source: Words of Women from the Egyptian Revolution https://www.youtube.com/watch?v=
M9aXkZCr5hE (accessed 16 May 2016).

police the world and fight terrorism", that are entrusted with monitoring sources of threat
(2010a, 355). This pattern of selective appropriation, together with the flow of translations
in one direction only, are in keeping with the meta narrative of the "War on Terror", with its
non-negotiable "us" and "them" binary. Speakers of the source languages do not need to be
informed of what speakers of the target languages say to each other, "they simply need to be
monitored" (2010a, 356). The source language group is emplotted as aggressor and the
target language group as bearing the burden of monitoring these sources of threat and,
importantly, as victim. The implication is that in invading other countries "the victims are
merely responding to the aggression being visited on them" (2010a, 356). In terms of
relationality, "[e]ach language accrues a specific value by virtue of its positioning within the
narrative" at any given moment in time (Baker 2010a, 356). Russian and Chinese appeared
as target languages in 2007, part of the community entrusted with policing the world, but by
2016 they were no longer included in this category. Turkish began life as a target language
in 1999 and became a source language in 2006. These changes in the choice of target and
source languages, Baker (2010a, 356) argues, signal "a change, or an attempt to effect
change, in political reality". The value accrued to each at different points in time is specific
to this unfolding narrative.

Baker (2006, 85–98) discusses and exemplifies various aspects of genericness at length. An
important aspect of genericness is how a given narrative signals its factual versus fictional
status. Genres understood or presented as factual, such as autobiographies and films presented
as based on true stories, invite questions about their truth from critical recipients of the
narrative, though uncritical recipients often accept the version of reality they depict. Baker
(2014, 172) argues that translation is a genre in its own right which, like media reporting, "is
naively thought of as a matter of objective recounting of factual material", of a prior reality,
and therefore "indirectly bestows a factual character on the representations it generates". The

entire MEMRI project plays on this assumption: MEMRI claims to simply report, through translation, what the sources of threat are saying to each other, which is quite different from what they tell "us" in English or other languages. Translation, as a genre, thus derives its status as objective reporting from its association with texts assumed to pre-exist it. The highly contested *Tiananmen Papers* is a case in point. Published in January 2001 and presented as an English translation by Andrew Nathan and Perry Link, it purported to be based on a pre-existing Chinese document that included transcripts of secret conversations among China's political elite during the 1989 Tiananmen events. The Chinese "original" appeared later, in April 2001. Moody (2002, 150) suggests that "even in the Chinese text the raw data have already been considerably massaged", and points out that there are differences between the English and Chinese versions, irrespective of the authenticity of the latter: in length, style and the attribution of statements to specific politicians, among other things. And yet, on 8 January 2001 the BBC casually reported extracts from the purported English translation, presented as a set of "secret Chinese official documents on the 1989 ... uprising" (BBC News 2001), without any reference to its contested status. The extracts included statements such as "The spear is now pointed directly at you and the others of the elder generation of proletarian revolutionaries", attributed to Li Peng.

Baker (2014) discusses a US political commercial entitled *Chinese Professor* aired on CNN in October 2011 in similar terms. The commercial, she argues, chooses to have the Chinese-looking actor speak in Chinese, rather than English, in part because "the presence of subtitles constitutes the Chinese speech as an 'original', a source text, and therefore indirectly constructs it as 'authentic'" (2014, 173). Many (uncritical) viewers will get the impression that the foreign speech came first, that it is a prior, original communication, and hence "accept the illusion" that the subtitles are there simply to report what the Chinese are saying behind our back, so to speak, "despite the fact that the speech itself is constructed to suit the producers' agenda and the subtitles may indeed have been written before, rather than after, the Chinese monologue" (2014, 173).

Future directions

One of the difficulties of working with socio-narrative theory is that it goes against the grain of established research traditions in Translation Studies. It refrains from streamlining translator choices into types of strategy; does not focus on identifying recurrent linguistic patterns as in norm theory and corpus-based studies; and assumes – indeed requires – the embeddedness of the researcher in the narrative world under analysis, both as a theoretical premise and as a prerequisite to making sense of the data. This makes the theory challenging for those who are used to thinking of research analysis as a matter of identifying categories, patterns or types of strategy and drawing "objective" conclusions about the motivations behind systematic choices. The challenge is exacerbated by the relative dearth of existing studies of translation and interpreting that draw on socio-narrative theory. The field would therefore benefit from more extended case studies that address a broader range of contexts and genres, including interpreting and translating asylum narratives, autobiographies, testimonies and children's literature – all of which lend themselves very readily to narrative analysis. It would also benefit from studies that examine how communities of translators and interpreters, whether professional or non-professional, elaborate narratives of who they are and how they relate to the public, conceptual and meta narratives of the day. Boéri (2008) offers an excellent starting point in this respect, but narrative studies of this type can go further, to examine areas of dissonance or coherence between the public narrative of a community and the actual strategies its members adopt as they translate and interpret in specific contexts.

Further reading

Baker, M. 2006. *Translation and Conflict: A Narrative Account*. London: Routledge.
This book introduced socio-narrative studies and hence remains a central reference point for scholars in the field. It does not include extended case studies, but it offers a detailed exposition of the theoretical assumptions and conceptual tools needed to apply socio-narrative theory, with examples from a wide range of genres and contexts.

Baker, M. 2010. Narratives of terrorism and security: "accurate" translations, suspicious frames. *Critical Studies on Terrorism* 3(3), pp. 347–364.
A detailed case study of an entire programme of translation that offers examples of socio-narrative analysis of a wide range of data, including choice of source and target languages, directionality of translation, the grouping of translations under specific categories, the selection of material to be translated, and paratextual framing through choice of titles for individual translations.

Bassi, S. 2015. Italy's Salman Rushdie: the renarration of "Roberto Saviano" in English for the post-9/11 cultural market. *Translation Studies* 8(1), pp. 48–62.
An extremely detailed and sophisticated application of socio-narrative theory, this article analyses the branding of authors in their home countries and internationally, the movement of cultural products across highly charged political territories, and the type of representations this dynamic generates.

Boéri, J. 2008. A narrative account of the Babels vs. Naumann controversy: competing perspectives on activism in conference interpreting. *The Translator* 14(1), pp. 21–50.
A very well-argued socio-narrative analysis of an encounter between two communities of conference interpreting with vastly different values, this detailed case study addresses important controversies relating to professionalism and volunteer work and reveals the narrative dynamism of a fast-changing area of practice.

Harding, S.-A. 2012a. How do I apply narrative theory? *Target* 24(2), pp. 286–309.
Offering a detailed, extended case study of mainstream and non-mainstream news reporting of the 2004 Beslan hostage crisis, this article is particularly useful for its overview of some studies informed by socio-narrative theory, and its focus on exemplifying how the theory can be applied and extended to accommodate concepts from narratology.

Related topics

Discourse analysis, interpreting and translation.

References

Abdel Nasser, T. 2016. "Revolutionary Poetics and Translation". In *Translating Dissent: Voices from and with the Egyptian Revolution*, edited by M. Baker, 107–122. London: Routledge.
Abunimah, A. 2011. "New Evidence about Amina, the 'Gay Girl in Damascus' Hoax". *The Electronic Intifada*, 12 June. Available from: https://electronicintifada.net/blogs/ali-abunimah/new-evidence-about-amina-gay-girl-damascus-hoax [Accessed 20 April 2016].
Al-Herthani, M. M. 2009. *Edward Said in Arabic: Narrativity and Paratextual Framing*. PhD Thesis. Manchester: Centre for Translation & Intercultural Studies, University of Manchester.
Baker, M. 2006. *Translation and Conflict: A Narrative Account*. London: Routledge.
Baker, M. 2007. Reframing conflict in translation. *Social Semiotics* 17(1), pp. 151–169.

Baker, M. 2008. Ethics of renarration: Mona Baker is interviewed by Andrew Chesterman. *Cultus* 1(1), pp. 10–33.

Baker, M. 2010a. Narratives of terrorism and security: "accurate" translations, suspicious frames. *Critical Studies on Terrorism* 3(3), pp. 347–364.

Baker, M. 2010b. Interpreters and translators in the war zone: narrated and narrators. In *Translation and Violent Conflict*, special issue of *The Translator*, 16(2), edited by M. Inghilleri and S.-A. Harding, 197–222.

Baker, M. 2014. "Translation as Renarration". In *Translation: A Multidisciplinary Approach*, edited by Juliane House, 158–177. Basingstoke: Palgrave Macmillan.

Bassi, S. 2015. "Italy's Salman Rushdie: the renarration of 'Roberto Saviano' in English for the Post-9/11 cultural market". *Translation Studies* 8(1), pp. 48–62.

BBC News, 2001. *Extracts from Tiananmen Papers*. 8 January. Available from: http://news.bbc.co.uk/1/hi/world/asia-pacific/1106614.stm [Accessed 20 May 2016].

Boéri, J. 2008. A narrative account of the Babels vs. Naumann controversy: competing perspectives on activism in conference interpreting. *The Translator* 14(1), pp. 21–50.

Bruner, J. 1991 The narrative construction of reality. *Critical Inquiry* 18(1), pp. 1–21.

Cross, K. 2016. "Memory, Guardianship and the Witnessing Amateur in the Emergence of Citizen Journalism". In *Citizen Media and Public Spaces: Diverse Expressions of Citizenship and Dissent*, edited by M. Baker and B. B. Blaagaard, 225–238. London: Routledge.

Erkazanci Durmus, H. 2014. A habitus-oriented perspective on resistance to language planning through translation. *Target* 26(3), pp. 385–405.

Harding, S.-A. 2011. Translation and the circulation of competing narratives from the wars in Chechnya: a case study from the 2004 Beslan Hostage disaster. *Meta* 56(1), pp. 42–62.

Harding, S.-A. 2012a. How do I apply narrative theory? *Target* 24(2), pp. 286–309.

Harding, S.-A. 2012b. *Beslan: Six Stories of the Siege*. Manchester: Manchester University Press.

Harding, S.-A. 2014. "But we don't read, professor!": Translation, Bloomsbury Qatar Foundation Publishing, and building a "vibrant literary culture". *Perspectives* 22(4), pp. 511–533.

Herman, D. 2013. *Storytelling and the Sciences of Mind*. Cambridge, MA: The MIT Press.

Herman, D., Jahn, M. and Ruyan, M.-L., eds. 2005. *Routledge Encyclopedia of Narrative Theory*. London: Routledge.

Jäger, S. and Maier, F. 2001/2010. "Theoretical and Methodological Aspects of Foucaldian Critical Discourse Analysis and Dispositive Analysis". In *Methods of Critical Discourse Analysis*. 2nd ed., edited by R. Wodak and M. Meyer, 34–61. Los Angeles: Sage.

Kahane, E. 2008. "Interpreters in Conflict Zones: The Limits of Neutrality". *AIIC Webzine*, English version by Phil Smith. Available from: http://aiic.net/page/2691/interpreters-in-conflict-zones-the-limits-of-neutrality/lang/1 [Accessed 1 May 2016].

Karunanayake, D. 2015. *Theatre Translation, Communities of Practice and the Sri Lankan Conflicts: Renarration as Political Critique*. PhD Thesis. Manchester: Centre for Translation and Intercultural Studies, University of Manchester.

Kuhiwczak, P. 1990. "Translation as Appropriation: The Case of Milan Kundera's *The Joke*". In *Translation, History and Culture*, edited by S. Bassnett and A. Lefevere, 118–130. London: Pinter Publishers.

Marsh, K. 2011. *A Gay Girl in Damascus Becomes a Heroine of the Syrian Revolt*. 26 May. Available from: http://www.theguardian.com/world/2011/may/06/gay-girl-damascus-syria-blog [Accessed 20 April 2016].

Mason, I. 1994/2010. "Discourse, Ideology and Translation". In *Critical Readings in Translation Studies*, edited by M. Baker, 83–95. London: Routledge.

McDonough-Dolmaya, J. 2010. (Re)imagining Canada: projecting Canada to Canadians through localized websites. *Translation Studies* 3(3), pp. 302–317.

Middle East Media Research Institute (MEMRI). Available from: http://www.memri.org [Accessed 19 May 2016].

Mills, S. 2003. *Michel Foucault*. London: Routledge.

Moody, P. R. 2002. Tiananmen: the papers and the story. *Review of Politics* 64(1), 149–165.

Morales-Moreno, M. 2011. Displacing the "slum-line": a narrative approach. *Social Semiotics* 21(1), pp. 1–13.

O'Hehir, A. 2015. "A Gay Girl in Damascus": behind the twisted tale of a blogger who "catfished" the whole world. *Salon*, 23 July. Available from http://www.salon.com/2015/07/23/a_gay_girl_in_damascus_behind_the_twisted_tale_of_a_blogger_who_catfished_the_whole_world/ [Accessed 20 April 2016].

Pérez-González, L. 2010. "Ad-hocracies of Translation Activism in the Blogosphere: A Genealogical Case Study". In *Text and Context: Essays on Translation and Interpreting in Honour of Ian Mason*, edited by M. Baker, M. Olohan and M. Calzada Pérez, 259–287. Manchester: St Jerome Publishing.

Rambelli, P. 2009. "Pseudotranslation". In *Routledge Encyclopedia of Translation Studies*, edited by M. Baker and G. Saldanha. 2nd ed., 208–211. London: Routledge.

Robinson, D. 2011. *Translation and the Problem of Sway*. Amsterdam: John Benjamins.

Said, E. 1978. *Orientalism*. New York: Pantheon.

Said, E. 1993. *Culture and Imperialism*. London: Vintage.

Said, E. 1995. Orientalism: an afterword. *Raritan* 14, pp. 32–60.

Sarbin, T. 1998. "Poetic Construction of Reality". In *Believed-in Imaginings: The Narrative Construction of Reality*, edited by J. de Rivera and T. R. Sarbin, 297–307. Washington, DC: American Psychological Association.

Selim, S. 2016. "Text and Context: Translating in a State of Emergency". In *Translating Dissent: Voices from and with the Egyptian Revolution*, edited by M. Baker, 77–87. London: Routledge.

Sinbaldi, C. 2011. Pinocchio, a political puppet: the fascist adventures of Collodi's Novel. *Italian Studies* 66(3), pp. 333–352.

Somers, M. R. and Gibson, G. D. 1994. "Reclaiming the Epistemological 'Other': Narrative and the Social Constitution of Identity". In *Social Theory and the Politics of Identity*, edited by C. Calhoun, 37–99. Oxford: Blackwell.

Summers, C. 2012. Translating the author-function: the (re)narration of Christa Wolf. *New Voices in Translation Studies* 8, pp. 170–187. Available from: http://www.iatis.org/images/stories/publications/new-voices/Issue8-2012/IPCITI/article-summers-2012.pdf.

van Rooyen, M. 2011. A mediation model for the translation of radio news texts in a multicultural newsroom. *Southern African Linguistics and Applied Language Studies* 29(1), pp. 17–29.

White, H. 1987. *The Content of the Form: Narrative Discourse and Historical Representation*. Baltimore: The John Hopkins University Press.

Wodak, R. and Meyer, M. 2001/2009. *Methods of Critical Discourse Analysis*. 2nd ed. Los Angeles: Sage.

13

Stylistics and translation

Jean Boase-Beier

Introduction

In order to begin a discussion of the various ways in which translation and stylistics interact, and to outline what might be involved in both a stylistic approach to translation and a translational approach to stylistics, we must first – and especially in the overall context of this handbook – consider the role and position of stylistics with respect to linguistics.

To assess where to locate stylistics as a discipline, a good place to start is with the definition of style, since stylistics is the study of style (Wales 2001, 372). Wales defines "style" straightforwardly as "the perceived distinctive manner of expression in writing or speaking" (Wales 2001, 371). People write in many different contexts, and speak in a non-literary context most of the time (unless, of course, they are characters in a novel or play), so this definition of itself suggests that stylistics cannot be confined to literary texts. This is indeed the position taken by many scholars of stylistics, who would argue that its analytical procedures apply equally to non-literary texts (see, for example, Jeffries 2014, 408). Jeffries (*ibid.*) calls the stylistics of non-literary texts, especially when it focuses on ideology, "critical stylistics". The assumption that literary and non-literary texts can be studied using similar tools and methodologies is also common in discourse analysis (see van Dijk 1985, 1–9).

Turning now to translation, we note that, whether literary or non-literary texts are involved, the style of the text is of central importance (cf. Boase-Beier 2011, 12), and at least since Roman times (see Boase-Beier 2006, 10–12) translation and style have been linked, even though the link has not always been made explicit. Stylistics has only been a recognised discipline since about the 1960s (see Wales 2001, 269) and the origins of Translation Studies are often dated to James Holmes' use of the term in the early 1970s (see Holmes 2005, 67–80; Malmkjær 2013, 31); thus the view that the two disciplines interact in important ways is necessarily a recent one.

Historical perspectives

The question of how stylistics and translation interact is closely related to the interactions of stylistics with both linguistics and literary studies. Trying to decide whether stylistics is a branch of one or the other suggests we regard the two areas as in opposition, but such a view risks ignoring the origins of modern stylistics. If we locate those origins, prior to the 1960s, in early work by the scholars of the Moscow Linguistic Circle (often called the Russian Formalists) – whose founding members in 1915 included poetics scholar Boris Eichenbaum, literary theoretician Viktor Shklovsky, narrative theorist Mikhail Bakhtin and Roman Jakobson, linguist, poet and scholar of translation – we can see that linguistic and literary study were not treated separately (see Lemon and Reis 1965). Of particular importance to the subject of this chapter is the fact that the study of translation was naturally regarded as an area for both linguistic and literary study. The same applies to the Prague Linguistic Circle (often referred to as the Prague Structuralists), of which Jakobson was again, in 1926, a founding member, together with Jan Mukařovský, who wrote on poetic language and Czech verse, and Vladimír Procházka, a translator and translation scholar (see Garvin 1964).

Both the Russian Formalists and the Prague Structuralists devoted part of their work to establishing the place of literary language alongside other uses of language in a functionally based view. And for both groups of scholars, translation was one of the key areas that helped them gain an understanding of meaning and how it related to structure. Translation influenced the view these early scholars of style and language shared that one could find what Jakobson calls "the essence of language" (Jakobson 1971) or "a common language" (Toman 1999).

Structuralist thinking – thinking based on an understanding of underlying and often unconscious structures in society, culture, language and literature – which influenced the Moscow and Prague scholars, and the developing discipline of stylistics, as well as literary and philosophical scholars such as Jacques Derrida or Roland Barthes, was always tied to the sense of what happens when language crosses linguistic and cultural boundaries; and translation, especially to the extent that it calls into question both nationalism and universalism, thus lay at its heart (cf. Derrida 1985, 93–161).

If we try to trace the development of stylistics we see, then, that not only were linguistics and literature intimately connected, but both were intrinsically linked with translation.

Core issues and topics

In sum, it makes sense to say that stylistics is part of both literary studies and linguistics, but neither subsumed under nor limited to either area. For this reason Leech (2008, 1–4) calls it an "interdiscipline".

Much the same can be said of Translation Studies (cf. Holmes 2005, 68). Some have considered the area to be more allied to linguistics (Catford 1965; see also Fawcett 1997 and Malmkjær 2005), some consider it more allied to literary studies, especially Comparative or World Literature (Apter 2013, 2–6) and universities, ever at loss when it comes to interdisciplinary work, are quite likely to locate it (if anywhere) in languages.

Translation Studies and stylistics seem, then, natural allies, since both work with the same raw materials and address similar core issues (texts, language, ways of saying, different text-types), both are by nature interdisciplinary and both have been areas of intense scholarly engagement and academic growth since the late 1950s (cf. Lambrou and Stockwell 2007, 1; Arrojo 2013, 118).

However, stylistics, as the study of style in texts, has more clearly defined borders than does Translation Studies, which can be defined very broadly, to cover such aspects as the translation market, the overall modelling of the movement of texts between cultures and languages (for example in polysystem theory; see e.g. Hermans 1999) or the consideration of how philosophy and translation interact (see Large 2014). Yet in many of the areas with which Translation Studies typically concerns itself it would be very difficult to pursue meaningful research without at least a consideration of stylistics. This is particularly the case where literary translation is concerned. Thus, for example, Jones (2011), in his detailed study of political and practical issues involved in the translation of poetry into English, emphasises the importance of style to the poetry translator's work (Jones 2011, 93–97) and hence to the academic study of their work (2011, 13). Other studies discuss the importance of stylistics for understanding how translated poetry is read (Boase-Beier 2015) and how prose translations are read (Malmkjær 2004).

In order to explore the various ways in which stylistics and Translation Studies interact we must now consider what we mean by "translation" and "Translation Studies". Up to now I have not always made a clear distinction. Yet they are obviously not the same, even if they can quite reasonably be used interchangeably in certain contexts, as in the titles of books such as *Linguistics and the Language of Translation* (Malmkjær 2005), where "language of translation" could arguably be said to mean both the aspects of language involved in translation and the language we use to speak about translation. In most cases, however, they are not used interchangeably: the word "translation" can be regarded as a superordinate term, or hyperonym, which has two subordinate terms or hyponyms: (i) "translation" and (ii) "Translation Studies". The latter is clear enough: it is the study of translation, defined more broadly or narrowly, depending on the context. Ignoring its general, superordinate sense, the term "translation", both as a hyponym (i), and as the subject of Translation Studies (ii), has itself several meanings: the act of translation, on the one hand, or a translated text, on the other, are the most obvious ones.

These distinctions are presented as a simple diagram in Figure 13.1. It should be noted by those readers familiar with James Holmes' overview of Translation Studies (Holmes 2005), or Toury's understanding of it (Toury 1995, 10), or with Malmkjær's addition to it of translating as a branch of applied Translation Studies (Malmkjær 2005, 18–20), that my very simple diagram is not intended to contradict any of these because it does not aim to convey the structure of a field or discipline, but rather of the use of particular terms: we use the *word* "translation", I would argue, as both a superordinate term and as a hyponym in the ways just described.

The distinction just made at the level of hyponyms: (i) translation and (ii) Translation Studies is fundamental to a consideration of stylistics and translation. This is so because the role of stylistics in actually performing a translation, on the one hand, or in reading a translation, on the other (these are the two uses of "translation" at the bottom level on the left of Figure 13.1), seems likely to be different from its role in the scholarly consideration of either (on the bottom right of Figure 13.1). But in practice the difference cannot always be maintained. Of course, performing a translation is not the same as studying how people perform it. Nor is, on the face of it, reading texts the same as studying how people read them. The distinction seems obvious: the position of the English reader of Müller's (1997) *Heute wär ich mir lieber nicht begegnet*, in Hulse and Boehm's (2001) translation *The Appointment* is not the same as the position of a Translation Studies scholar commenting on the style of the translation (for example, Boase-Beier 2013). On that basis, one could reasonably argue that stylistics has no place in the reading of translated texts by the general reader but only when they are read by the scholar. This distinction, between a supposed "general" reader and the reader who is also a stylistician, is one which has been the subject of many debates in stylistics (see Stockwell 2013). I have argued elsewhere that, when the text being read is a translation, an increased awareness of style, and of the stylistic shifts that

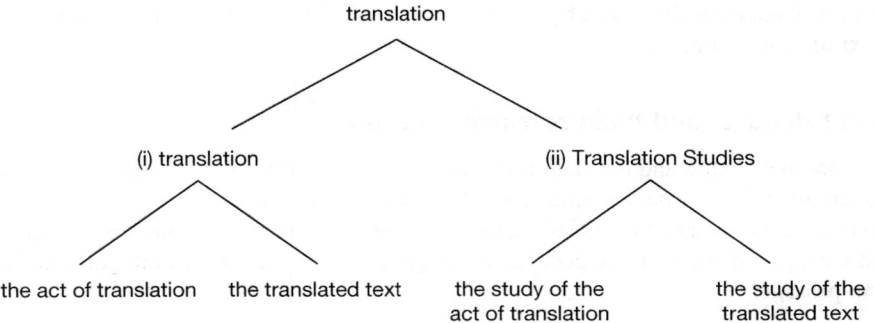

Figure 13.1 The use of the word "translation" as a superordinate term and as a hyperonym

the text is likely to have undergone, is especially desirable, so that the gap between the general and the academic reader might diminish; this is the notion of "analytical reading" (see Boase-Beier 2015, 72–85).

But I shall not pursue this question here. To avoid undue complexity, I assume on the whole that readers are readers, and that the role of stylistics in reading translated texts is not very different from its role in studying how they are read.

That translation and Translation Studies have an important role in stylistics is in part, as I suggested above, because of the multilingual Eastern European context in which the latter developed. In those early stylistic studies, different genres and registers within a language were seen to have much in common with different languages and to that extent thinking about text-types, styles, genres and registers arose naturally in a context in which different languages were at play. This is an important point, and one which is sometimes forgotten in contemporary stylistics, which can appear too resolutely monolingual, in spite of the occasional exception such as Nigel Fabb's 1997 book, which, like the earliest structuralist work I mentioned above, discusses many different linguistic and literary traditions, not merely incidentally, but as a way of approaching a "unified account" (Fabb 1997, 1) of linguistic form in literature.

It is common for linguistics scholars to be able and willing to consider languages other than the one or ones they happen to speak, to think it important to do so and to have a good system of glosses (such as the Leipzig glossing rules; see Lehmann 1982) that make such consideration both possible and useful. The problem is far greater for literary scholars, who are often unfamiliar with systems of glossing and so can assume, somewhat bizarrely, that languages other than their own are inaccessible (cf. Corbett 2014, 290).

A belief that other languages are by nature inaccessible leads in turn to a view of translation as an act which has the primary function of facilitating access to the strange and the foreign. The contrasting view of translation as textual enhancement (cf. Benjamin 2012, 77; Boase-Beier 2015, 51–85), or as a way to deeper understanding of texts (Felstiner 1995, 20), or a means to both enrichment (cf. Benjamin 2012, 82) and greater understanding of language (cf. Jakobson 2012, 127), will be more likely to arise in a multilingual context, or in a multilingual view of translation (cf. Pym 1998, 181). In such a view, translation and the questions it raises are by nature closely tied up with the questions that motivate stylistics. These are such questions as: How do we express different nuances of meaning? Can two different forms have the same meaning? Will different readers ever read the same text in the same way? What is the role of linguistic, cultural and cognitive context in reading a text?

Such questions, typically asked by stylistics, can often be considered more fruitfully in the context of translation.

Current debates and main research methods

Most work in stylistics and translation involves one of two perspectives: what translation can tell us about style, or what stylistics can tell us about translation.

Both require close analytical reading of texts, and a comparison of source and target texts. As an example of the first perspective, we might consider the use of ambiguity in the following passage:

> Ah, love, let us be true
>
> . . .
>
> To one another! for the world, which seems
>
> To lie before us like a land of dreams,
>
> So various, so beautiful, so new,
>
> Hath really neither joy, nor love, nor light,
>
> . . .

These lines are taken from Matthew Arnold's famous poem "Dover Beach", written around 1851 (see Arnold 1998, 78). I have not here supplied any further context, either in terms of the rest of the poem, or in terms of the background against which Arnold was writing, and which can be considered part of his cognitive context – that which Arnold knew, thought and felt, at the time he was writing. Even without either of these wider contexts, it is possible to see that the phrase "seems to lie" is ambiguous, because the word "lie" is ambiguous. In one sense, the phrase means that the land which does indeed lie before us seems new and beautiful and dreamlike when in fact it is not. Thus it may actually lie before us, but it only *seems* to do so in this particular dreamlike way: the reality is different. But there is another meaning: let *us* be true because the land we are looking at seems (to the speaker) to lie, it seems to have the appearance of a beautiful dream when in fact it is not. This meaning of "lie" is further suggested by the precariousness of the land, a shingle beach, constantly being shifted by the sea, however stable it might appear to be.

Of course, there is a great deal more going on in this poem, and even in these few lines, than I could possibly discuss here. But it is interesting, and helpful to the stylistician, to consider the translation. Aue (n.d.) has translated "the world, which seems / To lie before us" as "*dieser Weltraum, der aufzutun sich scheint*". The interesting thing here is that "*sich auf(zu)tun*" ((to) rise up, to open out, to emerge) does not suggest the second meaning of "lie".

Rather than criticising Aue's translation (after all, *aufzutun* rather wonderfully suggests the opening up of a world of ambiguity), a much more productive way of thinking about the difference is to see that many aspects of the meaning of the original word "lie" start to become clearer when we confront it with the expression "*sich auftun*", "rise up", "open out" or "emerge". The interesting point is not the difference between lying and rising up or emerging, but the difference between a word that sends us off on at least two different ways of thinking about the state of the world described, and one that does so less obviously. The differences in the ways of reading the original and translated poems highlight an aspect of the style of the original, and therefore of the choices that led to it, with particular clarity.

It is also interesting, from the point of view of stylistics, to consider what happens when writers translate their own work or write different versions of a text in different languages. For example, we can compare a line of Ausländer's (2012, 304) German poem *"Das Weißeste"* with her English poem "The Whitest" (Ausländer 2008, 207). The poems are close in meaning and form, and use similar assonances: *"weißest . . . weißer . . . Zeichen . . . Einsiedler . . . Einsamkeit . . . schreibt . . . Weißeste . . . Zeit . . ."* in the German poem and "whitest . . . whiter . . . cry . . . fright . . . dry . . . writes . . . signs . . . isolation . . . whitest . . . time . . ." in the English. In the German, 7 words are linked by assonance in a 17-word poem, and the proportion is very similar in English. To the stylistician this comparison suggests several things. For one thing, it suggests that the repetition is an important source of meaning in the poem and that therefore it is to be regarded as an instance of "iconicity" (see Boase-Beier 2006, 101–106), that is, of language that in form suggests its content: repetition suggests both the passage and the static nature of time. For another, it suggests that those words which carry the same sound in both languages, namely *"weiß"*/"white", *"Zeichen"*/"sign", *"schreiben"*/"write" and *"Zeit"*/"time" are being linked, both within and across languages. The links of sound suggest that those ties that work to form patterns within a language also do so between different languages. The poem can thus, when considered together with its counterpart, be seen as a meditation not only on time, but also on the connectedness of languages.

Translation, then, lies at the heart of stylistics not only because of the way stylistics developed historically, but also because translation is a particularly useful tool in understanding and analysing a text. Elsewhere (Boase-Beier 2015, 77) I have argued that this is so even if no translation exists, because the consideration of what would happen if certain words, phrases or ideas were to cross linguistic and cultural boundaries is not limited to the availability of translated versions (see also Venuti 2008, 21).

Conversely, stylistics lies at the heart of Translation Studies, and it is for this reason that the second perspective given earlier is possible. It depends upon the question of what stylistics can tell us about the ways in which textual detail is affected by translation. This is especially the case when stylistics is taken in its narrower sense of literary stylistics, which is often referred to as poetics (see Boase-Beier 2015, 15–16 for a discussion of the differences). It is particularly in the style of novels, plays and poems that we are most likely to meet stylistically complex figures, such as ambiguity, and furthermore, in literary texts such stylistic figures tend to be tied in to a repeated pattern of images and structures throughout the text. Just as, in order to see what translation can tell us about style, we need to look at the differences between original and translated text as givens, and consider as equivalences those equivalences chosen by the translator, so, too, when considering what stylistics can tell us about translation, the point is not generally to use stylistic non-equivalence as a means to judge the translation. Instead, where stylistics is particularly useful is in analysing and describing what changes the translation has made, and how these affect the reading of the text. It is essential that the stylistics of translated texts takes account of the relationship of target text to source text. Malmkjær (2004) refers to stylistics that does this, noting the patterns in that relationship, as "translational stylistics".

Translational stylistics presupposes, at least in so far as we are considering how texts are translated, rather than how they are read (see the following section), that there is a direct link between style and choice, a link highlighted by many stylisticians; see, for example, Short (1996, 68–69) or Leech (2008, 59–60).

To say that the link between style and choice is direct is not to imply that it is always recoverable. Stylistic analysis will only allow a reconstruction of what translators have done, just as the stylistic analysis of an untranslated text will only allow reasoned reconstruction of the choices a writer made. But, on the assumption that such reconstructions are possible and interesting, it makes sense to argue that, in addition to the translational stylistics of the target text, we need to have an awareness of its poetics. That is our link with the translator's practice. I mentioned above that poetics is often assumed to be the stylistics of literary texts, as opposed to non-literary texts. But this is not the only, or indeed the most useful, distinction. Many works of cognitive poetics (poetics that considers how the mind works) are based on the assumption that the "literary mind" (Turner 1996) is the basis of all our thinking. On this view, the distinction between literary and non-literary texts is not absolute, just as it is not (as I noted above) for many critical stylisticians and discourse analysts. A more useful distinction for Translation Studies between stylistics and poetics is that, where stylistics focuses on the elements of a text that make us read the way we do, poetics takes into account the process of writing. When studying the translation of literary texts in particular, the poetics of the translator are influenced to a very great extent by the poetics of the source-text author, that is, by the system of choices the translator ascribes to the source-text author. Another way of putting this is to say that the translator's understanding of the poetics that informed the source text forms part of her or his cognitive context (the sum total of her or his knowledge, beliefs and attitudes). As I have argued elsewhere (Boase-Beier 2015, 90–91), we need, therefore, to supplement translational stylistics with "translational poetics": the poetics that gave rise to the translated text and that includes (via the translator's knowledge and interpretative and critical abilities) the reconstructed poetics of the source-text author.

While the fact that the writer of the translated text was the translator, and not the original writer, is often ignored by reviewers of translations as well as by literary critics (see Venuti 2008, 1–13), it is obvious to the translation scholar that such questions about choice, and the motivations that analysis seeks to reconstruct, are primarily questions about the translator's choices, motivations and background knowledge, when the text to be analysed is a translation.

The question of the translator's motivation and choices – of the translator's poetics – may seem to apply mainly to translations of literary texts, but in fact all types of texts translated by human agency will be partly driven by their translator's choices, against the background of her or his cognitive context. However, the constraints may be different. For many non-literary texts, constraints such as the function (for example if the text is an advertisement) or the register, that is, the set of conventional forms of expression pertaining to a particular text-type, will also form part of the translator's cognitive context. Other factors, particularly in the case of literary texts, may be literary conventions, as in rhymed poetry, different degrees of censorship in the source and target culture or various aspects of the publication process (cf. Jones 2011, 51–83). Because stylistic analysis, like all critical analysis of texts, usually has no direct access to the practice behind them, it may be supplemented by questionnaires or studies of the scholar's own translation practice, as is done by Jones (2011).

Future directions

It has often been argued recently that stylistics is primarily concerned with reading. For example, Stockwell (2002, 2) says that stylistics is primarily the study and analysis of how what we find in the text makes us read the text in the way we do. It is clear that the consideration of a translator's choices and motivations must also be concerned with how these choices relate to what the translator assumes about the readers. This also holds true for the original writer's choices. It should be borne in mind that, as I mentioned above, there are different types of reader. It is almost certainly not the reader *qua* literary critic or translation scholar with whom the writer of original or translated texts is concerned, but the general reader. Stylistics, especially in recent years, has been greatly influenced by theories of reading and reception within literary studies, such as those of Iser (see Iser 1974); in conjunction with Translation Studies this is likely to lead to a greater emphasis on the reader's engagement with the stylistic detail of the translated text (cf. Boase-Beier 2006, 31–43) and on how the reader's engagement with the source text differs. Though this is an area in which there has not been very much work as yet, there are some exceptions, such as Hermans (2014) or Boase-Beier (2015).

As an example, consider the following lines from a 1947 novel by Fallada (2011) and its translation by Michael Hofmann, in which a postwoman, Eva Kluge, is delivering letters to addresses in Berlin during the Second World War:

> *Sie ist politisch gar nicht interessiert, sie ist einfach eine Frau, und als Frau findet sie, daß man Kinder nicht darum in die Welt gesetzt hat, daß sie totgeschossen werden.*
>
> (Fallada 2011, 9)

> Not that she's a political animal, she's just an ordinary woman, but as a woman she's of the view that you don't bring children into the world to have them shot.
>
> (Hofmann 2007, 3)

The German and English texts are semantically quite similar, but there are many differences of style, especially in the representation of thought. For example, "*politisch gar nicht interessiert*" (politically not at all interested) is neutral, does not contain an idiom and might represent the way the postwoman would characterise herself. On the other hand "not ... a political animal" is a contemporary idiom, and suggests that the narrator is a speaker of contemporary English; this changes the perspective from that of the woman within the early 1940s Berlin world of the novel to that of a present-day narrator describing the woman, a narrator who is not quite taking the woman's point of view. We know that readers tend to associate narrators with the implied or inferred author, that is the person they imagine to be the author (cf. Stockwell 2002, 42), and the reader of the English version is likely, because of the idiomatic English, to associate the narrator with the translator rather than the author. Furthermore, the German uses the perfect tense for "*Kinder ... in die Welt gesetzt hat*" (has put children into the world), suggesting that the postwoman's thoughts are being represented and that she has borne children (who might then play a role later in the novel), or that she is putting herself "as a woman" in the position of a woman who has borne children. The English version uses the present tense and so has the form of a general principle.

Overall we can see from this brief comparison that the narrator of the source text is, as it were, in Eva Kluge's head and is able to give us her thoughts. The narrator of the translated text is not, and so we are aware, as readers of the English version, of an extra layer of story-telling. It is interesting to consider here a suggestion by Hermans (2014) that translation can always be seen as a type of echoic report on something said, whereby an echoic utterance is one which communicates to the reader the attitude of the speaker to what is being said (cf. Sperber and Wilson 1986, 239). Using concepts such as echoic utterance, or also the categories of indirect speech as suggested by, for example, Gutt (2000), can allow us to gain a better sense of how a reader will process a translation such as Hofmann's, where the analyst may note a change in register between the original and the translation, but where the reader will not normally have access to the original.

Another aspect of reading that a stylistic description might engage with is foregrounding, that is, the situation in which the stylistic pattern in a text serves to draw the reader's attention to a particular word, expression or feature. Foregrounding, a term based on the Prague Structuralists' term *aktualisace* (see Garvin 1964, viii; Leech 2008, 18), can be quite different in original and translated texts. Compare, for example, the following line and its translation:

to steal from it (R. S. Thomas 1993, 436)

dort zu stehlen (Perryman 1998, 49)

This is line 6 of a 10-line poem, that begins with Baudelaire's grave, and the narrator's grave, goes on to use an image of the tree of science, and finishes with an image of the tree of poetry. "It" is ambiguous: it could refer to any of these four things. Because "it" is at the end of the line, and therefore foregrounded, the English reader is more likely to consider exactly what it refers to, that is, what is stolen from, than the German reader, where the word "*dort*" (there) is vague of reference, rather than ambiguous, and is not at the end of the line, so less foregrounded. However, it is foregrounded in a different way: the notion of stealing in a particular location rather than stealing something or from someone, is in itself unusual enough to draw the reader's attention. The difference between the original text and the translation draws attention to Thomas' concern, in all his poetry, with the nature of "it", both as a referring pronoun and as a theological concept (see Boase-Beier 2014). Indeed, it could be argued that the foregrounded use of "it" (in titles of poems and even of collections) with ambiguous reference is an element of Thomas' mind-style, the way a "mental self" is presented stylistically (Fowler 1977, 103). By describing patterns of foregrounding to arrive at a description of an original author's mind-style, as manifested in the text, we are able to show how readers of original and translated texts are likely to read differently.

The fact that the number of stylistic studies of how we read translated texts is relatively small suggests that, when stylisticians use translated texts as the subject of stylistic analysis, drawing conclusions about the way we read, they are inclined to do so without realising that the fact that they are translated "changes everything", as the title of Venuti's book (Venuti 2013, 109–115) puts it. Indeed, even quite recent stylistic analysis will sometimes discuss words and phrases of a text, ascribing them to the author when in fact they are the words and phrases of a (usually unnamed) translator. Thus, for example, Hamilton (2012) discusses the words of translator E. J. Richards as though they were those of the original author Christine de Pizan, and Neary (2014, 187) analyses words that are probably those of David Wyllie as though they were Kafka's. This is not to say that such analyses are invalid – after all, the English texts exist – but only to note that the analyst might reach different conclusions if the existence of a source text had been taken into account; this is the point that Malmkjær (2004) makes, as mentioned above.

It could reasonably be expected that stylisticians, like linguists more generally, since they have the terminology and the traditions at their disposal to explain how textual detail gives rise to effects on the reader, would want to engage with the reading of translated texts, and would not be held back by a lack of knowledge of the source language. After all, most translated texts are read by readers who do not know the source language. When we discuss the reading of translated texts, then, we are concerned with what the knowledge of their translated status means just as much as with the sort of actual comparison (as in the case of the examples from Ausländer, Fallada and Thomas above) that not everyone is in a position to carry out. Stylistics can help us to describe what it is we do when we read a translated text, and how the effects of the text are achieved.

For example, if I read Rose Ausländer's poetry in English translation, without access to the original, I am made aware that I am reading a translation in part by elements of style. Consider, for example, the following lines (cf. Boase-Beier 2015, 83):

I speak

. . .

of weeping willows
blood-beeches

If we were analysing the style we would assume that "blood-beech" designates the same tree as the English "copper beech". "Blood" we would assume to be the substance used as a comparison for the red leaves of the copper beech in German. Furthermore, knowing the poem to be translated from German, we would assume that the choice of "blood" is not merely an arbitrary echo of the German but perhaps has some resonance in the poem, maybe linked to the "weeping willows", and so on.

There will of course be a distinction in this case between a reader who is versed in stylistics and one who is not. But this is true of any text, translated or not.

Implications for practice

It would be a mistake to assume that, just because stylistics is a useful tool in describing how translation happens and how translations are read, it is automatically also a useful tool for the translator. It is certainly the case that a great deal of the translator's art (just as that of any writer) takes place intuitively, without recourse to theoretical descriptions or tools. And yet, because of the influence of the source text, and the translator's need to understand how it achieves its effects, stylistics can in fact be very helpful for the translator.

Jones, for example, discussing the use of many studies which either "rely on translators' memories" or on the use of a "think-aloud protocol" in which choices are recorded in real time (see Jones 2011, 10–11), and considering his own translation as an example, provides a detailed analysis of the stylistic features of the work he is translating, that of Bosnian poet Mak Dizdar (Jones 2011, 30). These include features such as metre and rhythm, deviation from syntactic norms, images and metaphors, ambiguity, and so on.

Iconicity is another stylistic feature that often plays a role in literary texts. Consider, for example, the following line from a poem by Volker von Törne, which is followed by my translation:

Den Flug der Taube kreuzte der Habicht

(von Törne 1981, 162)

The flight of the dove cut across by the hawk

(Boase-Beier and Vivis, 2017)

This is a very simple example: the iconicity of the original lies in its use of slightly unusual word order in which the object ("*Flug der Taube*", "flight of the dove") precedes the verb "*kreuzte*" ("crossed") and the subject, "*Habicht*" (hawk) comes last. This is possible in

German because the form of the definite article, "*den*" ("the") is clearly accusative and therefore must belong to the object noun phrase. This syntactic order echoes what one might see: first the dove flying, and then the hawk cutting across its flight. My English translation keeps to a similar word order, bearing in mind the importance of iconicity, even though using it means that no finite verb is possible, if the rhythm is also considered important enough to keep. That is, the iconicity of the syntax, and the rhythm, are deemed more important than the form of the verb, even though this means that the English is not a complete sentence, whereas the German is.

As some of the examples discussed above indicate, many instances of translated poems and novels can be found where the translation differs quite substantially in its stylistics from the source text. It might be tempting in such cases to say that the translator has failed to take the style of the original adequately into account. And yet we cannot just assume that this is the case. Both stylistics and Translation Studies generally tend to be descriptive rather than prescriptive, and also usually try to avoid being evaluative when describing the details of a text: what the scholar wants to know is what such textual detail, including differences between a translated text and its original, might tell us.

Nevertheless, it could be argued that greater attention to style might be useful for translators. This is not a question of a translator being expected to know the terms that stylisticians use to describe texts. It is more a question of awareness. And if translations are judged not to be good on stylistic grounds (cf. Berman 2012, 248–249), this is not because of a simple lack of stylistic equivalence with the original. It is, rather, that a translator who has little awareness of style (which includes for Berman "underlying networks of signification"; Berman 2012, 248), will be unlikely to be able to write a target text which contains similar structures and patterns.

A stylistically aware translation, on the other hand (cf. Boase-Beier 2006, 112–113) will include awareness of at least the following:

(i) The importance of context in influencing meaning. Thus, Walter Aue, translating Matthew Arnold's poem cited above, needed to know how the image of shifting shingle earlier in the poem relates to a larger historical context and how both relate to the ambiguity of "lie". Such awareness helps the translator decide whether and how to keep the ambiguity.

(ii) The fact that stylistic features of the source text reflect choices. Thus a translator of Arnold's "Dover Beach" can make reasonable assumptions about the significance of "lie" in the original poem.

(iii) The importance of mind-style and its influence on how to translate in cases such as that of R. S. Thomas' poem.

(iv) The importance of narratological distinctions like those we saw in the example from Hofmann's translation of Fallada, such as that between a narrator, an author, and the inferred author that the reader of a text constructs; these are essential to the translator in deciding which voice and perspective to take.

(v) How we represent speech and thought, as in the Fallada example.

(vi) Familiarity with common stylistic figures such as foregrounding, repetition, ambiguity, indirect speech and iconicity.

A translator might of course make many of these decisions without having any awareness that stylisticians speak of "mind-style" or "inferred author" or "iconicity". But what such awareness can do is to make the translator more likely to realise what is happening in the original and to have a basis for judging the extent to which such stylistic features represent the choices of the author of the source text. Stylistics thus has an important part to play in the training of translators, especially literary translators.

Further reading

Boase-Beier, J. 2006. *Stylistic Approaches to Translation*. Manchester: St Jerome Publishing.
This work examines how translation can be described, read and carried out using stylistics and the concept of style as a basis.

Boase-Beier, J. 2014. "Using Translation to Read a Poem". In *Literary Translation: Redrawing the Boundaries*, edited by J. Boase-Beier, A. Fawcett and P. Wilson, 241–252. London: Palgrave Macmillan.
This chapter is one of a small number of current studies that explain how comparing an original text with its translation can enhance our stylistic analysis and understanding of the original.

Boase-Beier, J. 2015. *Translating the Poetry of the Holocaust*. London: Bloomsbury.
This book is a study of how the stylistic and poetic elements of the text affect, involve and engage the reader and how this interaction with the reader differs in the translated text.

Hermans, T. 2014. Positioning translators: voices, views and values in translation. *Language and Literature* 23(3), pp. 285–301.
From the point of view of narrative and narratology, this article examines the role of the translator in the translated text and how translation affects the way the narrative structures are understood.

Malmkjær, K. 2004. Translational stylistics: Dulcken's translations of Hans Christian Andersen. *Language and Literature* 13(1), pp. 13–24.
This article explains the need for translational stylistics, that is, the stylistic study of a translated text that takes into account the text's relation to its original.

Related topics

Relevance Theory, interpreting, and translation; Tropes and translation; Wordplay and translation.

References

Apter, E. 2013. *Against World Literature: On the Politics of Untranslatability*. London: Verso.
Arnold, M. 1998. *Matthew Arnold*. London: Dent.
Arrojo, R. 2013. "The Relevance of Theory in Translation Studies". In *The Routledge Handbook of Translation Studies*, edited by C. Millán and F. Bartrina, 117–128. Abingdon: Routledge.
Aue, W., trans. n.d. *Matthew Arnold: Der Strand von Dover*. Available from http://myweb.dal.ca/waue/Trans/Arnold-Dover.html.
Ausländer, R. 2008. *The Forbidden Tree*. Frankfurt am Main: S. Fischer Verlag.
Ausländer, R. 2012. *Gedichte*. Frankfurt am Main: S. Fischer Verlag.
Benjamin, W. 2012. "The Translator's Task", trans. S. Rendall. In *The Translation Studies Reader*, edited by L. Venuti. 3rd ed., 75–83. Abingdon: Routledge.
Berman, A. 2012. "Translation and the Trials of the Foreign", trans. L. Venuti, in *The Translation Studies Reader*, edited by L. Venuti. 3rd ed., 240–253. Abingdon: Routledge.
Boase-Beier, J. 2006. *Stylistic Approaches to Translation*. Manchester: St Jerome Publishing.
Boase-Beier, J. 2011. *A Critical Introduction to Translation Studies*. London: Continuum.
Boase-Beier, J. 2013. "Herta Müller in Translation". In *Herta Müller*, edited by B. Haines and L. Marven. Oxford: Oxford University Press.

Boase-Beier, J. 2014. "Using Translation to Read a Poem". In *Literary Translation: Redrawing the Boundaries*, edited by J. Boase-Beier, A. Fawcett and P. Wilson, 241–252. Basingstoke: Palgrave Macmillan.

Boase-Beier, J. 2015. *Translating the Poetry of the Holocaust*. London: Bloomsbury.

Boase-Beier, J. and Vivis, A., trans. 2017. *Volker von Törne: Memorial to the Future*. Todmorden: Arc Publications.

Catford, J. C. 1965. *A Linguistic Theory of Translation*. Oxford: Oxford University Press.

Corbett, J. 2014. Review of *Literary Translation: Redrawing the Boundaries*, ed. J. Boase-Beier, A. Fawcett and P. Wilson. *Translation and Literature* 24(2), pp. 287–290.

Derrida, J. 1985. *The Ear of the Other*, trans. P. Kamuf; ed. C. McDonald. Lincoln, NE: University of Nebraska Press.

Fabb, N. 1997. *Linguistics and Literature*. Oxford: Blackwell.

Fallada, H. 2011. *Jeder Stirbt für Sich Allein*. Berlin: Aufbau Verlag.

Fawcett, P. 1997. *Translation and Language: Linguistic Theories Explained*. Manchester: St Jerome Publishing.

Felstiner, J. 1995. *Paul Celan: Poet, Survivor, Jew*. New Haven, CT: Yale University Press.

Fowler, R. 1977. *Linguistics and the Novel*. London: Methuen.

Garvin, P., trans. and ed. 1964. *A Prague School Reader on Esthetics, Literary Structure, and Style*. Washington, DC: Georgetown University Press.

Gutt, E.-A. 2000. *Translation and Relevance*. 2nd ed. Manchester: St Jerome Publishing.

Hamilton, C. 2012. "Conceptual Integration in Christine de Pizan's 'City of Ladies'". In *Cognitive Stylistics: Language and Cognition in Text Analysis*, edited by E. Semino and J. Culpeper, 1–22. Amsterdam: John Benjamins.

Hermans, T. 1999. *Translation in Systems: Descriptive and System-oriented Approaches Explained*. Manchester: St Jerome Publishing.

Hermans, T. 2014. Positioning translators: voices, views and values in translation. *Language and Literature* 23(3), pp. 285–301.

Hofmann, M., trans. 2007. *Hans Fallada: Alone in Berlin*. Harmondsworth: Penguin.

Holmes, J. 2005. *Translated! Papers on Literary Translation and Translation Studies*. 2nd ed. Amsterdam: Rodopi.

Hulse, M. and Boehm, P., trans. 2001. *Herta Müller: The Appointment*. New York: Picador.

Iser, W. 1974. *The Implied Reader: Patterns of Communication in Prose Fiction from Bunyan to Beckett*. Baltimore, MD: Johns Hopkins University Press.

Jakobson, R. 1971. "Quest for the Essence of Language". In *Selected Writings II*, edited by S. Rudy, 21–37. The Hague: Mouton.

Jakobson, R. 2012. "On Linguistic Aspects of Translation". In *The Translation Studies Reader*, edited by L. Venuti. 3rd ed., 126–131. Abingdon: Routledge.

Jeffries, L. 2014. "Critical Stylistics". In *The Routledge Handbook of Stylistics*, edited by M. Burke, 408–420. Abingdon: Routledge.

Jones, F. R. 2011. *Poetry Translating as Expert Action*. Amsterdam: John Benjamins.

Lambrou, M. and Stockwell, P., eds. 2007. *Contemporary Stylistics*. London: Continuum.

Large, D. 2014. "On the Work of Philosopher-Translators". In *Literary Translation: Redrawing the Boundaries*, edited by J. Boase-Beier, A. Fawcett and P. Wilson. Basingstoke: Palgrave Macmillan.

Leech, G. 2008. *Language in Literature: Style and Foregrounding*. Edinburgh: Pearson Longman.

Lehmann, C. 1982. Directions for interlinear morphemic translations. *Folia Linguistica* 16, pp. 199–224.

Lemon, L. L. and Reis, M. J., eds. 1965. *Russian Formalist Criticism: Four Essays*. Lincoln, NE: University of Nebraska Press.

Malmkjær, K. 2004. Translational stylistics: Dulcken's translations of Hans Christian Andersen. *Language and Literature* 13(1), pp. 13–24.

Malmkjær, K. 2005. *Linguistics and the Language of Translation*. Edinburgh: Edinburgh University Press.

Malmkjær, K. 2013. "Where Are We? (From Holmes's Map Until Now)". In *The Routledge Handbook of Translation Studies*, edited by C. Millán and F. Bartrina, 31–44. Abingdon: Routledge.

Müller, H. 1997. *Heute wär ich mir lieber nicht begegnet*. Munich: Carl Hanser Verlag.

Neary, C. 2014. "Stylistics, Point of View, and Modality". In *The Routledge Handbook of Stylistics*, edited by M. Burke, 175–190. Abingdon: Routledge.

Perryman, K. trans. 1998. *R. S. Thomas: Die Vogelscheuche Nächstenliebe*. Denklingen: Babel.

Pym, A. 1998. *Method in Translation History*. Manchester: St Jerome Publishing.

Short, M. 1996. *Exploring the Language of Poems, Plays and Prose*. London: Longman.

Sperber, D. and Wilson, D. 1986. *Relevance: Communication and Cognition*. 2nd ed. Oxford: Blackwell.

Stockwell, P. 2002. *Cognitive Poetics: An Introduction*. London: Routledge.

Stockwell, P. 2013. The positioned reader. *Language and Literature* 22(3), pp. 263–277.

Thomas, R. S. 1993. *Collected Poems 1945–1990*. London: Phoenix.

Toman, J. 1999. *The Magic of a Common Language: Jakobson, Mathesius, Trubetzkoy and the Prague Linguistic Circle*. Cambridge, MA: The MIT Press.

Toury, G. 1995. *Descriptive Translation Studies and Beyond*. Amsterdam: John Benjamins.

Turner, M. 1996. *The Literary Mind: The Origins of Thought and Language*. Oxford: Oxford University Press.

van Dijk, T. A., ed. 1985. *Discourse and Literature: New Approaches to the Analysis of Literary Genres*, Amsterdam: John Benjamins.

Venuti, L. 2008. *The Translator's Invisibility: A History of Translation*. 2nd ed. London: Routledge.

Venuti, L. 2013. *Translation Changes Everything: Theory and Practice*. Abingdon: Routledge.

von Törne, V. 1981. *Im Lande Vogelfrei: Gesammelte Gedichte*. Berlin: Klaus Wagenbach Verlag.

Wales, K. 2001. *A Dictionary of Stylistics*. 2nd ed. London: Longman.

14

Tropes and translation

James Dickins

Introduction and definitions

Following the Western classical tradition, we can define a trope as a "deviation from the ordinary and principal signification of a word [or phrase]" (Corbett and Connors 1999, 379) or "transference" of meaning (Murphy 2001, 22–23; Strachan and Terry 2011, 112–117). Burke (1941) proposed four master tropes: metaphor, metonymy, synecdoche, and irony. However, irony does not involve deviation from an ordinary or principal meaning, but, rather a divergence between the situation referred to and the meaning of the utterance of a type intended to be evident to both speaker/writer and listener/reader – a particular kind of "shared lie" (cf. Dickins 1998, 296–300). Given this difference from other tropes, I will exclude irony from further discussion. I will, however, include simile, given its similarity to metaphor. The following are traditional definitions:

Metaphor

Trope "in which a name or descriptive word or phrase is transferred to an object or action different from, but analogous to, that to which it is literally applicable" (*Oxford English Dictionary (OED)* Online); e.g. "The past is *a foreign country*; they do things differently there" (from L. P. Hartley, *The go-between*).

Simile

Trope "that expresses the resemblance of one thing to another of a different category" (*Collins English Dictionary (CED)*); e.g. "The past is *like a foreign country*; they do things differently there".

Metonymy

Trope characterised by "the action of substituting for a word or phrase denoting an object, action, institution, etc., a word or phrase denoting a property or something associated with it"

(*OED* Online); e.g. "*Table three* wants to pay his bill", meaning "the man at table three wants to pay his bill".

Synecdoche

Trope "in which a more inclusive term is used for a less inclusive one or vice versa, as a whole for a part or a part for a whole" (*OED* Online); e.g. "*The bald head* wants to pay his bill", meaning "The man with a bald head wants to pay his bill".

Basic principles

Expression, sense, and reference (ascription and referent)

I will first present a model of "wording" and meaning, comprising three main elements: expression, sense, and reference. An expression is a word, phrase, or sentence. A sense is a particular "abstract meaning" this expression has. A referent is what an expression in a particular sense refers to in a particular "speech/writing event". An ascription is the category to which this referent is related. Referent and ascription together constitute reference. Thus, I can use the expression "the baker" in the sense "the one who bakes" (*OED* Online) with the referent on a particular occasion of a particular individual, in which case I have ascribed the individual to the category "baker(s)". This person (referent) could also be referred to in any number of other ways ("your dad", "her husband", etc.) – these other ways being different ascriptions of the same referent (cf. Dickins 2014; 2016).

Lexicalisation and non-lexicalisation

A fundamental distinction is made between lexicalised and non-lexicalised tropes. In a lexicalised trope, the relevant figurative sense is delimited by the basic semantic conventions of the language, i.e. the range of "entities" which this figurative sense has is limited in specifiable ways. An example of a lexicalised metaphor is "rubbish" in "That argument's rubbish", where "rubbish" has a secondary lexicalised metaphorical sense "Worthless or absurd ideas, talk, or writing; nonsense", contrasting with its basic lexicalised sense "Waste material; refuse, debris, litter; rejected and useless matter of any kind, household waste" (definitions from *OED* Online). By contrast, in "The past is a foreign country; they do things differently there", "foreign country" is a non-lexicalised metaphor; there are no basic semantic conventions of English which limit and specify the range of "entities" to which "foreign country" can apply in the non-literal sense.

Non-lexicalised tropes

Non-lexicalised metaphor

The traditional Western view of metaphor, going back to Aristotle (cf. Levin 1982), defines metaphor in terms of topic, vehicle, and grounds. Other terms are also used, e.g. "tenor" (following Richards 1937) or "target" (Lakoff and Johnson 1980) instead of "topic", and "base" (Lakoff and Johnson 1980), "figure", or "basis" instead of "vehicle" (cf. Ritchie 2013, 10). The topic is the entity referred to, the vehicle is the notion to which this entity is being compared, and the grounds the respect in which this comparison is made. In "The past is another country; they do things differently there" (cf. also Goatly 1997, 9) "the past" is the topic which the phrase "another country" refers to. "Another country" is the vehicle to which "the past" is being compared. And "they do things differently there" is the grounds, on which the past can be said to be like another country.

Table 14.1 integrates the topic–vehicle–grounds model with the expression–sense–reference model (see above).

Example 1 is explained as follows:

Immediately relevant text

All text immediately relevant for understanding the occurrence of the trope in question, including the figurative expression itself.

Immediately relevant co-text

Everything which is part of the immediately relevant text excluding the figurative expression. Here, the immediately relevant co-text is "The past is _____; they do things differently there".

Figurative expression or trope or figure of speech

Word, phrase, or sentence used figuratively. Here, "another country".

Topic

Here, "The past". This can be analysed in terms of the elements topic expression, topic sense, and topic reference, with sub-elements topic referent and topic ascription. The topic referent is the same referent as the figurative expression (here "another country"). The topic ("The past") and the figurative expression ("another country") are, however, ascribed to different categories (see further discussion of "ascription" under "grounds" below).

Vehicle

The more basic ("literal") sense of that expression. In the case of "another country", the sense "foreign nation (etc.)".

Referent of figurative expression

The "entity" referred to by both "The past" and "another country", i.e. past time, the past, etc.

Grounds (ascription to sub-sense)

Ascription to the category of entities which are like another country, on the grounds that they do things differently there (etc.), involving a *sub-sense* of the *sense* of entities which are like another country. Ascriptions to sub-senses are frequently vague even where the ascription is signalled by an explicit grounds as in "they do things differently there".

Sense and sub-sense involve two types of ascription. If I say, "a water molecule consists of three atoms", I am using "atom[s]" in a way that relates to the entire category of atoms in the relevant sense. If, however, I say "Joan of Arc was a beautiful woman", I may not be claiming that she was physically beautiful, but rather that she was spiritually beautiful. There is, however, no categorical distinction between "beautiful" meaning "physically beautiful" and "beautiful" meaning "spiritually beautiful". There is a single sense with a range of "sub-senses", such that I can say of somebody that they are "beautiful" to mean "physically beautiful" or "spiritually beautiful" or even both simultaneously. In singling out "spiritually

Table 14.1 Non-lexicalised metaphor

	Non-lexicalised metaphor			
	Example 1	*Example 2*	*Example 3*	*Example 4*
Immediately relevant text = *immediately relevant co-text, plus figurative expression*	"The past is another country; they do things differently there."	"I have just remembered another country."	"Big questions bruised my mind."	"The sun set angrily."
Figurative expression (or ***trope*** or ***figure (of speech)***) **Topic** = *co-referent of figurative expression, plus ascription of this co-referent (plus sense)*	*Metaphor* "another country" the past	*Metaphor* "another country" NONE	*Metaphor* "bruised" NONE	*Metaphor* "angrily" NONE
Vehicle = *operative more basic sense of figurative expression*	"another country" in operative more basic sense "foreign state, etc."	"another country" in operative more basic sense "foreign state, etc."	"bruise[d]" in more basic sense "injure by a blow which discolours the skin but does not lacerate it"	"angrily" in more basic sense "in an enraged, wrathful, irate, etc. manner"
Sense of figurative expression	Category of entities like another country (in some non-basic respect)	Category of entities like another country (in some non-basic respect)	Category of actions like bruise[d] (bruising) (in some non-basic respect)	Category of circumstances like angrily (in some non-basic respect)

(Continued)

Table 14.1. (continued)

		Non-lexicalised metaphor			
		Example 1	*Example 2*	*Example 3*	*Example 4*
Reference of figurative expression	**Referent of figurative expression**	The "entity" referred to by "The past" (and also "another country"; i.e. past time, the past, etc., however categorised)	The "entity" referred to by "another country", i.e. the past	The "entity" referred to by "bruised", i.e. the event which might also be referred to by "damaged (mentally)", "caused temporary harm to", etc.	The "entity" (circumstance) referred to by "angrily", i.e. the manner in which the sun set, which might also be referred to as "having a vivid red colour", etc.
	Grounds = ascription of figurative expression to sub-sense — *Explicit grounds (mentioned in co-text)*	*Comparison/Analogy* Category of entities like another country in that/on the *grounds* that they do things differently there (etc.)	NONE	NONE	NONE
	Implicit grounds (not mentioned in co-text)		*Comparison/Analogy* Category of entities like another country in that/on the *grounds* that e.g. people did things differently then (etc.)	*Comparison/Analogy* Category of actions like bruise[d] (bruising) in that/on the *grounds* that e.g. they caused temporary but noticeable harm	*Comparison/Analogy* Category of circumstances like/as if "angrily" in that/on the *grounds* that e.g. they have a vivid red colour

beautiful" or "physically beautiful" I am not ascribing the person/entity referred to as "Joan of Arc" to the category covered by "beautiful" in its full (relevant) sense, but only the sub-sense "spiritually beautiful" (see further Dickins 1998, 210–211).

Example 2 in Table 14.1 "I have just remembered another country" illustrates that the topic is not an essential part of a figurative expression. By providing an explicit co-referent for the figurative expression, a topic helps make plain what the referent of the figurative expression is. Example 2 also shows that there is no need for an explicit grounds. Again, features of the context can provide this. Example 3 (from Elizabeth Jennings' poem "Answers"; see Semino 2008, 47) and Example 4 illustrate that metaphors are not limited by word-class category.

As Example 1 in Table 14.2 shows, non-lexicalised simile has roughly the same meanings as non-lexicalised metaphor. The comparison/analogy element, "like", is not only part of the figurative expression, but is the entirety of the figurative expression in a simile. "Another country" is used in a non-figurative sense. "Like" is used in its standard sense, but in a non-basic sub-sense, namely the grounds that "they do things differently there".

The fact that literal comparisons operate in the same way as similes and that there is no difference in the sense in these examples shows that there is no categorical distinction between literal comparisons and similes. In expressions involving "like", "literalness (and its comp-lement metaphoricity [non-literalness]) is a matter of degree" (Ortony 1979 [1993], 164).

Non-lexicalised metonymy

While non-lexicalised simile is like non-lexicalised metaphor semantically, metonymy and synecdoche correspond more directly to metaphor analytically.

Example 1 in Table 14.3 parallels the examples "The past is another country" and "The past is like another country". Example 2 in this table is a more standard example. For a discussion of explicit grounds with metonymy, see the section on "Purposes of metonymy and syn-ecdoche" below.

Example 1 in Table 14.4 parallels the equative examples "The past is another country" and "The past is like another country". Example 2 parallels "Table three wants to pay his bill". In the case of non-lexicalised synecdoche, the ascription is to the overall sense, rather than a sub-sense. See below for a discussion of explicit grounds with synecdoche.

Table 14.5 summarises non-lexicalised tropes.

As Table 14.6 shows, the sense of a lexicalised figurative expression is the relevant non-basic lexicalised sense. The grounds of lexicalised tropes do not "construct" the semantic interpretation of the figure: they are not denotative. They only allow us to "reconstruct" a plausible "account" of the nature of the relationship between the sense of the expression and its more basic sense. In lexicalised tropes, therefore, the grounds are connotative.

Core–periphery–approximation–transfer: Categorical differences or continuum?

Goatly (1997, 17–22) recognises four categories of meaning for a word/phrase in a particular sense of relevance to tropes:

Core–periphery–approximation–transfer

These can be considered in relation to the word "chair", in the sense "seat with a back on which one person sits, typically having four legs and often having arms" (*CED*). According to this definition a core chair has four legs and arms, while a peripheral chair lacks one or both of these features. For approximation, Goatly (1997, 17) gives the example of a person climbing a

Table 14.2 Non-lexicalised simile

	Non-lexicalised simile	
	Example 1	*Example 2*
Immediately relevant text = *immediately relevant co-text, plus figurative expression*	"The past is like another country; they do things differently there."	"Cigarettes are like pacifiers."
Figurative expression (or *trope* or *figure (of speech)*)	**Simile** "like another country"	**Simile** "like pacifiers"
Topic = *co-referent of figurative expression, plus ascription of this co-referent (plus sense)*	the past (*i.e. what the phrase "the past" refers to); and the category to which the phrase "the past" ascribes this referent – its ascription, i.e. past time*)	cigarettes (*i.e. what the word "cigarettes" refers to); and the category to which the word "cigarettes" ascribes this referent, i.e. short tightly rolled cylinders of tobacco*)
Vehicle = *operative more basic sense of figurative expression*	NOT APPLICABLE	NOT APPLICABLE
Sense of figurative expression		
Reference of figurative expression	Category of entities like another country (in some non-basic respect)	Category of entities like cigarettes (in some non-basic respect)
Referent of figurative expression	The "entity" referred to by "The past" (and also by "like another country"; i.e. past time, the past, etc, however categorised)	The "entity" referred to by "Cigarettes" (and also by "like pacifiers"; i.e. short tightly rolled cylinders of tobacco, etc, however categorised)
Grounds = *ascription of figurative expression to sub-sense*	***Comparison/Analogy***	***Comparison/Analogy***
Explicit grounds (*mentioned in co-text*)	Category of entities like another country on the grounds that they do things differently there	
Implicit grounds (*not mentioned in co-text*)		Category of entities like pacifiers on the grounds that they have a calming effect

Table 14.3 Non-lexicalised metonymy

			Non-lexicalised metonymy	
			Example 1	*Example 2*
Immediately relevant text = *immediately relevant co-text, plus figurative expression*			"The unhappy customer is table three."	"Table three wants to pay his bill."
Figurative expression			**Metonym** "table three"	**Metonym** "table three"
Topic = *co-referent of figurative expression, plus ascription of this co-referent (plus sense)*			the unhappy customer (*i.e. what the phrase "the unhappy customer" refers to and the category to which the phrase "the unhappy customer" ascribes this referent i.e. the category of unhappy customers*)	**NONE**
Vehicle = *operative more basic sense of figurative expression*			"table three" in operative more basic sense "piece of furniture with a flat top and one or more legs, providing a level surface for eating, writing, or working at, numbered as three"	"table three" in operative more basic sense "piece of furniture with a flat top and one or more legs, providing a level surface for eating, writing, or working at, numbered as three"
Sense of figurative expression			Category of entities associated with table three	Category of entities associated with table three
Reference of figurative expression	**Referent of figurative expression**		The person referred to by "the unhappy customer" and also "table three"	The person referred to by "table three"
	Grounds	**Explicit grounds** (*mentioned in co-text*)	**Association** Category of entities associated with table three, in that they are sitting there	
		Implicit grounds (*not mentioned in co-text*)		**Association** Category of entities associated with table three, in that they are sitting there

Table 14.4 Non-lexicalised synecdoche

	Non-lexicalised synecdoche	
	Example 1	*Example 2*
Immediately relevant text	"The unhappy customer is the bald head."	"The bald head wants to pay his bill."
Figurative expression	**Synecdoche** "the bald head"	**Synecdoche** "the bald head"
Topic *= co-referent of figurative expression, plus ascription of this co-referent (plus sense)*	the unhappy customer *(i.e. what the phrase "unhappy customer" refers to – (a particular individual); and the category to which the phrase "the unhappy customer" ascribes this referent, i.e. the category of bald-headed people/entities)*	**NONE**
Vehicle *= operative more basic sense of figurative expression*	"the bald head" in operative more basic sense	"the bald head" in operative more basic sense
Sense of figurative expression	"upper part of human body above the neck lacking hair on top"	"upper part of human body above the neck lacking hair on top"
Reference of figurative expression — **Referent of figurative expression**	Category of entities having a bald head The person referred to by "the unhappy customer" and also "the bald head"	Category of entities having a bald head The person referred to by "the bald head"
Grounds = *ascription of figurative expression to sub-sense* — *Explicit grounds (mentioned in co-text)* / *Implicit grounds (not mentioned in co-text)*	**Meronymy** Category of entities having a bald head *[The ascription is to the sense, rather than the sub-sense]*	**Meronymy** Category of entities having a bald head *[The ascription is to the sense, rather than the sub-sense]*

Table 14.5 Types and features of non-lexicalised tropes

Type of trope → / Feature of trope ↓	Comparative/Analogical		Associative	Meronymic (involving part-whole relationship)
	Complex (with explicit figurative marker)	**Simple** (no explicit figurative marker)		
	Non-lexicalised simile	Non-lexicalised metaphor	Non-lexicalised metonymy	Non-lexicalised synecdoche
Immediately relevant text = immediately relevant co-text, plus figurative expression	"The past is like another country; they do things differently there."	"The past is another country; they do things differently there."	"The unhappy customer is table three."	"The unhappy customer is the bald head."
Figurative expression (or **trope** or **figure (of speech)**) **Topic** = co-referent of figurative expression, plus ascription of this co-referent (plus sense)	**Simile** "like another country" the past (i.e. what the phrase "the past" refers to; and the category to which the phrase "the past" ascribes this referent – its ascription, i.e. past time)	**Metaphor** "another country" the past (i.e. what the phrase "the past" refers to; and the category to which the phrase "the past" ascribes this referent – its ascription, i.e. past time)	**Metonym** "table three" the unhappy customer (i.e. what the phrase "the unhappy customer" refers to; and the category to which the phrase "the unhappy customer" ascribes this referent, i.e. the category of unhappy customers)	**Synecdoche** "the bald head" the unhappy customer (i.e. what the phrase "unhappy customer" refers to; and the category to which the phrase "the unhappy customer" ascribes this referent, i.e. the category of bald-headed people/entities)

(Continued)

Table 14.5. (continued)

Type of trope →	Comparative/Analogical		Associative	Meronymic (involving part-whole relationship)
	Complex (with explicit figurative marker)	*Simple* (no explicit figurative marker)		
Feature of trope →	Non-lexicalised simile	Non-lexicalised metaphor	Non-lexicalised metonymy	Non-lexicalised synecdoche
Vehicle = operative more basic sense of figurative expression	**NOT APPLICABLE**	"another country" in operative more basic sense "foreign state, etc."	"table three" in operative more basic sense "piece of furniture with a flat top and one or more legs, providing a level surface for eating, writing, or working at, numbered as three"	"the bald head" in operative more basic sense "upper part of human body above the neck lacking hair on top"
Sense of figurative expression	Category of entities like another country (in some non-basic respect)	Category of entities like another country (in some non-basic respect)	Category of entities associated with table three	Category of entities having a bald head

(Continued)

Table 14.5. (continued)

Feature of trope → / Type of trope →	Comparative/Analogical		Associative	Meronymic (involving part-whole relationship)
	Complex (with explicit figurative marker)	*Simple* (no explicit figurative marker)		
Reference of figurative expression	*Non-lexicalised simile*	*Non-lexicalised metaphor*	*Non-lexicalised metonymy*	*Non-lexicalised synecdoche*
Referent of figurative expression	The "entity" referred to by "the past" (and also by "like another country"; i.e. past time, the past, etc., however categorised)	The "entity" referred to by "the past" (and also "another country"; i.e. past time, the past, etc., however categorised)	The person referred to by "the unhappy customer" and also "table three"	The person referred to by "the unhappy customer" and also "the bald head"
Grounds = ascription of figurative expression to sub-sense — **Explicit grounds** (*mentioned in co-text*)	**Comparison/Analogy** Category of entities like another country on the *grounds* that they do things differently there	**Comparison/Analogy** Category of entities like another country on the *grounds* that they do things differently there (etc.)		
Implicit grounds (*not mentioned in co-text*)			**Association** Category of entities associated with table three, in that they are sitting at table three	**Meronymy (part–whole relationship)** Category of entities having a bald head [The ascription is to the sense, rather than the sub-sense]

Table 14.6 Types and features of lexicalised tropes

Type of trope → Feature of trope ↓	Comparative/Analogical		Associative	Meronymic (involving part-whole relationship)
	Complex (with explicit figurative marker)	Simple (no explicit figurative marker)		
	Lexicalised simile	Lexicalised metaphor	Lexicalised metonymy	Lexicalised synecdoche
Immediately relevant text = *immediately relevant co-text, plus figurative expression*	"That joke's as old as the hills."	"I never expected such a sharp rebuke."	"Use your head."	"Have you got wheels?"
Figurative expression (or *trope* or *figure (of speech)*) **Topic** = *co-referent of figurative expression, plus ascription of this co-referent (plus sense)*	**Simile** "as old as the hills" "That joke"	**Metaphor** "sharp" "rebuke" **None**	**Metonym** "head" **None**	**Synecdoche** "wheels" **None**
Vehicle = *operative more basic sense of figurative expression*	"as old as the hills" in operative more basic sense "equally old as a natural elevation of the earth's surface rising more or less steeply above the level of the surrounding land"	"sharp" in operative more basic sense "having an edge or point"	"head" in operative more basic sense of "uppermost part of the body"	"wheels" in operative more basic sense of "solid discs or circular rings joined to hubs"
Sense of figurative expression	Category of exceedingly old entities	Category of non-blunt entities	Category of entities classifiable as "intelligence, etc."	Category of wheeled vehicles

(Continued)

Table 14.6. (continued)

Feature of trope ↓ \ Type of trope →		Comparative/Analogical — Complex (with explicit figurative marker): Lexicalised simile	Comparative/Analogical — Simple (no explicit figurative marker): Lexicalised metaphor	Associative: Lexicalised metonymy	Meronymic (involving part-whole relationship): Lexicalised synecdoche
Reference of figurative expression	**Referent of figurative expression**	The "entity" referred to by "That joke" (and also "as old as the hills"; i.e. the joke etc., however categorised)	The "entity" referred to by "sharp" (and also by "rebuke"), however categorised	The "entity" referred to by "head", i.e. intelligence	The "entity" referred to by "wheels", i.e. a wheeled vehicle
	Grounds = ascription of figurative expression to sub-sense — **Explicit grounds** (mentioned in co-text) / **Implicit grounds** (not mentioned in co-text)	**Not properly operative, but "reconstructable" as: Comparison/Analogy** Category of entities that are as old as the hills on the grounds that they are exceedingly old	**Not properly operative, but "reconstructable" as: Comparison/Analogy** Category of entities that are sharp, on the grounds they cause significant hurt	**Not properly operative, but "reconstructable" as:** Category of activities associated with the head, in that they take place in the head	**Not properly operative, but "reconstructable" as: Meronymy (part-whole relationship)** Category of entities having wheels

mountain who is tired. His friend points to a boulder and says, "Why don't you sit on that chair?", using "chair" in a sub-sense extending its standard (core + peripheral) sub-sense. An example of *transfer* is "chair" as used in an utterance "Tom is a chair" (see also below), where the meaning of "chair" is figurative (metaphorical).

There is clearly no categorical distinction between core and periphery meanings (sub-senses), nor, apparently, between periphery and approximation: we can imagine chairs which progressively become less and less like "core chairs" and more and more like approximations to chairs. Is there, however, a categorical distinction between approximation and transfer, or does approximation shade into transfer? Since the approximation sub-sense derives from central features of the core sub-sense (i.e. the use of a chair for sitting), and since the transfer sub-sense derives from non-central features of the core sub-sense, the issue is whether there is any categorical distinction between central and non-central features of the core sub-sense.

Consider: a country house host says to a group of guests, having discovered that one of the other guests has been murdered, "I have some shocking news; please all take a chair". One guest, Angelina, who is already sitting on her boyfriend's lap, says "Tom's my chair; he'll give me all the physical support I need". This is an example of approximation: Tom is not a real chair, but he is functioning equivalently to a real chair, as made plain by "he'll give me all the physical support I need". If, however, Angelina says, "Tom's my chair; he'll give me all the emotional support I need", this is transfer (metaphor); Tom is being described as a "chair" supporting Angelina emotionally analogously to the way a chair supports someone physically. Finally, if Angelina says "Tom's my chair; he'll give me all the support I need both physically and emotionally", we have an utterance which is at once an approximation ("physically") and a metaphor ("emotionally").

Metaphor–metonymy–synecdoche: Categorical differences or continuum?

Are metaphor, metonymy, and synecdoche categorically distinct, or merely "arbitrary but appropriate" (Hjelmslev 1953, 24–25) points on a continuum, such that different divisions could have been used?

The easiest pair to deal with are metonymy and synecdoche. A wheel is clearly part of a car. However, is a spare wheel part of a car? What if the owner foolishly decides to drag it behind the car attached by a rope to the towing bar? Part–whole relationships (e.g. wheel to car) shade into associative relationships (e.g. wheel dragged along behind car): non-lex-icalised metonymy and non-lexicalised synecdoche form a continuum. This is consistent with a long tradition which regards synecdoche as a sub-type of metonymy (cf. Lakoff and Johnson 1980, 36).

The relationship between metaphor and metonymy/synecdoche is also continuous. Consider a restaurant manager who says "Margaret Thatcher wants to pay his bill". Asked why he referred to the male customer in question as "Margaret Thatcher", he explains that, "he talked all the time about Margaret Thatcher, had very similar views to hers, and even looked a bit like her". The first grounds given by the manager is a kind of metonymy, with an association through the customer's topic of conversation between himself and Margaret Thatcher. The second grounds is a kind of metaphor: the customer is like Margaret Thatcher in some non-basic aspect (her views, rather than, say, her appearance). The third grounds, however is an approximation rather than a metaphor, using a basic-aspect likeness (physical appearance) rather than the non-basic likeness aspect traditionally used to define metaphor. The lack of tension between all of these as grounds for the "figurative" usage "Margaret

Thatcher" suggests that there is no categorical distinction between metonymy/synecdoche and metaphor.

Categorical differences vs. continua: Summary and implications

In Figure 14.1, double-headed arrows indicate continua, rather than categorical differences.

Figure 14.1 shows why, in non-lexicalised cases, (i) we cannot always tell where metaphor, metonymy, and synecdoche begin, and (ii) we cannot always tell which is being instanced. It also suggests that instead of three separate senses, "like (etc.)" for metaphor, "associated with (etc.)" for metonymy, and "part of" for synecdoche, all three tropes are united under a single global sub-sense category of "transfer".

Table 14.7 provides a revised analysis of non-lexicalised tropes taking into account the continua arguments presented earlier.

Metaphorical force

Metaphorical force is a matter of the salience of metaphor perception (Newmark 1985; Dickins 2005; Semino 2008; Knowles and Moon 2006). Goatly (1997, 31–35) distinguishes dead, sleeping, tired, and active metaphors:

Dead metaphor

"either the former non-metaphorical sense is rarely used, or the connection between the two senses has become so distant with time that it is no longer recognized by most speakers" (Deignan 2005, 38), e.g. "pupil" in the senses "young student" and "opening in the iris".

Sleeping metaphor

"the metaphorical meaning is conventional. The literal meaning is still in use and may be evoked by the metaphorical sense on occasion" (Deignan 2005, 38), e.g. "crane" in the senses "species of marsh bird" and "machine for moving heavy weights".

Tired metaphor

"the metaphorical sense is more likely to evoke the literal sense here than in the previous category [sleeping metaphor]" (Deignan 2005, 38). An example is "fox" in the sense "cunning person" (Goatly 1997, 33).

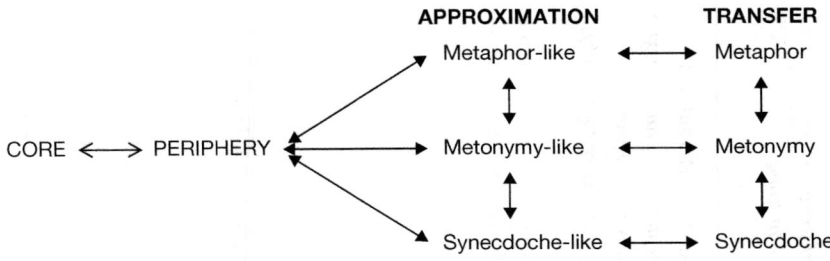

Figure 14.1 Non-lexicalised tropes

Table 14.7 Revised analysis of non-lexicalised tropes

Type of trope → Feature of trope →	Transfer on core–periphery–approximation–transfer *continuum*		
Immediately relevant text = *immediately relevant co-text, plus figurative expression*	"The past is another country; they do things differently there."	"The unhappy customer is table three."	"The unhappy customer is the bald head."
Figurative expression (or *trope* or *figure (of speech)*)	"another country"	"table three"	"the bald head"
Topic = *co-referent of figurative expression, plus ascription of this co-referent (plus sense)*	the past (*i.e. what the phrase "the past" refers to; and the category to which the phrase "the past" ascribes this referent, i.e. past time*)	the unhappy customer (*i.e. what the phrase "the unhappy customer" refers to; and the category to which the phrase "the unhappy customer" ascribes this referent, i.e. the category of unhappy customers*)	the unhappy customer (*i.e. what the phrase "unhappy customer" refers to; and the category to which the phrase "the unhappy customer" ascribes this referent, i.e. the category of bald-headed people/entities*)
Vehicle = *operative core subs-sense of figurative expression*	"another country" in operative core sub-sense "foreign state, etc."	"table three" in operative core sub-sense "piece of furniture with a flat top and one or more legs, providing a level surface for eating, writing, or working at, numbered as three"	"the bald head" in operative core sub-sense "upper part of human body above the neck lacking hair on top"

(Continued)

Table 14.7. (continued)

Type of trope → Feature of trope →	Transfer on core–periphery–approximation–transfer *continuum*		
Sense of figurative expression	Category of entities in "transfer relationship" with another country	Category of entities in "transfer relationship" with table three	Category of entities in "transfer relationship" with a bald head
Reference of figurative expression — **Referent of figurative expression**	The "entity" referred to by "The past" (and also "another country"; i.e. past time, the past, etc., however categorised)	The person referred to by "the unhappy customer" and also "table three"	The person referred to by "the unhappy customer" and also "the bald head"
Grounds = ascription of figurative expression to core sub-sense — ***Explicit grounds*** (*mentioned in co-text*)	Category of entities in "transfer relationship" with another country on the *grounds* that they do things differently there (etc.)		
Implicit grounds (*not mentioned in co-text*)		Category of entities in "transfer relationship" with table three, in that they are sitting at table three	Category of entities in "transfer relationship" with a bald head *[The ascription is to the sense, rather than the sub-sense]*

Active metaphor

"the metaphorical sense is evoked entirely through the literal sense. There is no established lexical relationship between the two senses" (Deignan 2005, 38), e.g. "icicles" to refer to "fingers" in Larkin's "He had five icicles on each hand" (Goatly 1997, 33).

Conceptual metaphor theory

Conceptual metaphor theory (Lakoff and Johnson 1980) proposes that many metaphors fit into coherent metaphorical patterns, or "schemata" (my term), ultimately grounded in human physical and social experience. Being grounded in human reality, metaphorical schemata tend towards language-universality (Kövecses 2010, 195–214). Thus, the ANGER IS A PRESSURISED CONTAINER schema is found in English, Hungarian, Japanese, Chinese, Zulu, Polish, Wolof, and Tahitian (Kövecses 2010, 197–206). Time expressions in apparently all languages can involve the schema TIME IS MOTION: e.g. English "The time will *come*" (Kövecses 2010, 38). There are, however, significant differences between languages, demonstrating that conventionality is also at play. While in most of the world's languages, the future is conceptualised as being in front of oneself and the past behind, in Aymara, the past is ahead and the future behind (Núñez and Sweetser 2005).

Purposes of metaphor and simile

The purposes of metaphor and simile are of two types: denotative-oriented and connotative-oriented (Dickins 2005, 234–235).

The denotative-oriented purposes are:

i   "*[T]o describe a mental process or state, a concept, a person, an object, a quality or action more comprehensively and concisely than is possible in literal or physical language*" (Newmark 1988, 104).
   "Obama slams Putin" is a concise way of saying Obama severely criticises Putin. With non-lexicalised metaphors and similes, this purpose is paramount where it is felt impossible to express the intended meaning in non-figurative language, a common usage in everyday speech being when people talk about strong emotions.

ii *To express an open-ended denotation or potential range of denotations*
   Non-lexicalised metaphors and similes often express an open-ended denotation. This open-endedness results when the grounds are not defined precisely enough by the context to enable a reader to say exactly what the metaphor means. Thus, "a man is (like) a tree" may have any number of interpretations and in many contexts it will be impossible to identify which grounds is most appropriate.

The connotative-oriented purpose of metaphors and similes is "to appeal to the senses, to interest, to clarify 'graphically', to please, to delight, to surprise" (Newmark 1988, 104). Metaphors and similes are frequently used for humorous aesthetic purposes, e.g. from a football summary on British radio: "Tottenham were a marshmallow of a team: sweet, expensive – and downright soft in the middle", where the effect is achieved by metaphorical "manipulation" within the grounds.

A further purpose of metaphors and similes, common in popular science (Pramling and Säljö 2007), is to explain specialist notions in terms accessible to non-specialists. However, "certain metaphorizations can cause severe theoretical problems" (Goschler 2007, 17), obfuscating features of the theory.

Purposes of metonymy and synecdoche

One purpose of metonymy and synecdoche is efficiency (brevity) of communication. "Table three" is shorter than "The person sitting at table three". Another purpose is vocabulary variation for stylistic purposes; e.g. "The Whitehouse has refused to respond" for "The American President has refused to respond".

Major works on translation of tropes

Works on metaphor translation include: Alvarez (1993), Broeck (1981), Dagut (1976; 1987), Dickins (2005), Dobrzynska (1995), Fernández, Sacristán, and Olivera (2005), Fuertes-Olivera and Pizarro-Sánchez (2002), Gentzler (2000), Kurth (1995; 1999), Maalej (n.d.), Mandelblit (1995), Merakchi and Rogers (2013), Monti (2009), Newmark (1985; 1988, 106–122), Samaniego (1996; 2013), Schaffner (2004), Toury (1995). Almost the only other tropes which have received attention in Translation Studies are simile and metonymy. Recent works on translation of metonymy include Vandepitte and Hartsuiker (2011), Brdar and Brdar-Szabó (2013; 2014), and Denroche (2015, 153–179). The relative lack of focus on tropes other than metaphor in Translation Studies reflects that metaphor poses the greatest translation problems, and in the remainder of this chapter I will focus these.

Approaches to the translation of metaphor

Early works on metaphor translation (Dagut 1976) often focused on original metaphors. Newmark (1985; 1988) adopts the topic–vehicle–grounds approach to metaphor (terming these "object", "topic", and "image"). Newmark recognises five categories of metaphor: dead, cliché, stock, recent, and original.

Newmark's dead metaphors (Newmark 1988, 106) correspond roughly to Goatly's dead metaphors. Newmark's stock metaphors are similar to Goatly's sleeping metaphors. Newmark's cliché metaphors are "'metaphors that have perhaps temporarily outlived their usefulness, that are used as a substitute for clear thought, often emotively, but without corresponding to the facts of the matter" (Newmark 1988, 107), e.g. "The County school will in effect become not a *backwater*, but a *break through* in educational development which will *set trends* for the future" (Newmark 1988, 107). Newmark's original metaphors are equivalent to Goatly's active metaphors, and considered to have most metaphorical force.

Newmark's recent and adapted metaphors do not fit into a metaphorical-force scale. Recent metaphors are metaphorical neologisms, whether slang forms, e.g. "sick" meaning "good, wonderful" (assuming this is a metaphor), or technical terms such as "port" ("logical circuit for the input or output of data": *CED*). Adapted metaphors manipulate existing metaphorical idioms, e.g. "the ball is *a little in their court*". They are non-lexicalised, because they are not standard parts of the language, but draw on existing idioms in both their form and meaning.

Newmark's work has a strongly pedagogical orientation; his categories of metaphor are unified more by their attempt to address translation problems than by their theoretical coherence. The discussion of metaphor translation procedures is strongly prescriptive: the reader is told not only what procedures are available, but which ones to use in particular circumstances. In addition to the translation of source text (ST) metaphor by target text (TT) metaphor, Newmark recognises also translation of ST metaphor by TT simile and sense (grounds).

Toury's (1995, 107–109) account of metaphor translation is, by contrast, purely descriptive, in accordance with his focus on norms: what translators do, not what they should do. His categorisation of metaphors is simpler, and less intrinsically interesting, than that of either Goatly or Newmark. He does, however, recognise the possibility of ST non-metaphors being translated by TT metaphors, as well as other tropes, such as simile (Toury 1995, 109).

Dickins (2005) produces a model for metaphor translation along the lines of that discussed above. He adopts a descriptive approach, but assumes that descriptive norms resulting from statistical analysis can be recast as pedagogical guidelines.

Since Mandelblit (1995) and particularly since Schaffner (2004), a significant amount of work on metaphor translation has made use of conceptual metaphor theory. Other approaches to metaphor such as Gricean analyses and relevance theory are much less well represented.

While metaphor translation is not normally difficult where metaphorical force is weak (cf. Dickins 2005, 229–230 for an extended Arabic–English example), there are cases where it can prove problematic, as discussed in the following sections.

Metaphorical congruence and incongruence

Metaphorical congruence: occurs when a series of metaphors in a text belong to the same schema (or compatible schemata), as in the following from *The Independent* newspaper (5 December 2007) – relevant metaphors in italics:

> The *storm clouds* are *gathering over* the jobs market; the *climate* on the high street is growing distinctly *chilly*; a *typhoon* of bad debt is *buffeting* the banks. Could a *"perfect storm"* be about to *hit* the British economy?

All these metaphors belong to the schema ADVERSITY IS ADVERSITY DUE TO BAD WEATHER (Lakoff, Espenson, Schwartz 1991, 74), and are deployed in such a way that their reflected meanings do not clash. Where metaphors in a text do not belong to the same or compatible schemata, there is metaphorical incongruence – "mixed" metaphors. Incongruent metaphors can happily co-occur when they are not particularly forceful (see Kimmel 2010; also Dickins 2005, 229–230).

Metaphorical congruence can be a translation issue, particularly where there is a high density of non-lexicalized metaphors. Consider the following from مدينة البغي *madīnat al-baġy* "The City of Oppression" by the Palestinian writer عيسى بشارة *ʿīsā bišāra* (Brown 1996, 50; discussed in Dickins, Hervey, and Higgins 2002, 157; Dickins 2005, 253–255):

[...] { تمنى صابر لو أنه يستطيع ان {يفجر} هذا الصوت و{يفجر} معه {بركان} الحرية الذي {لا يصحو له جفن} و{لا تثور له ثائرة}.

This can be translated fairly literally as:

> Saber wished that he could {explode} his voice and {explode} with it the {volcano} of freedom at which {an eyelid does not wake up} nor {does a tumult arise}.

The overall metaphorical image of the outpouring of unrestrained emotion as volcanic violence is fairly schematic in both Arabic and English, and this image is maintained congruently throughout the extract except in the phrase جفن له يصحو لا "an eyelid does not wake up". This does not seem to matter in Arabic, which in some text-types seems to accept mixing of even fairly forceful metaphors (cf. Dickins 2005, 256–264). In English, however, "an eyelid does not wake up" jars, and the metaphorical incongruence is not significantly improved by a more idiomatic alternative preserving the same general metaphorical image such as "no-one bats an eyelid". The situation is remedied by using a non-metaphorical alternative, such as "attracted", to give a TT (with various other changes) along the lines:

> Saber wished that he could make this voice {burst forth} and that in turn the {volcano} of freedom would {erupt}, which had never once {flared up in rage} nor even {attracted} people's attention.

Metaphorical exuberance and density

Some languages accept a greater degree of metaphorical density than others, at least in some text-types. Newmark (1988, 112–113) claims that English editorials typically use more metaphors than those in other European languages. Arabic seems to allow even greater "metaphorical exuberance" than English, particularly where the author is being emotive. Accordingly, Arabic ST metaphors not infrequently appear too strong or too dense for equivalent forms of English writing and there is some need to tone down the metaphors of the Arabic ST in the English TT.

The following is the opening sentence of a short story البنفسج حقل *ḥaql al-banafsaj* "The violet field" by the Syrian writer تامر زكريا *zakariyā tāmir*. ST metaphors and their TT equivalents are noted by curly brackets and a following superscript number:

عاش محمد أعواماً {مديدة[1]} في مدينة صغيرة {تقبع[2]} {بذل[3]} عند {أقدام[4]} جبل شاهق {ترتطم[5]} السحب بصخوره الصفراء.

This can be translated fairly literally as follows:

> Mohammed lived for {extended[1]} years in a small town which {squatted[2]} {with ignominy[3]} at the {foot[4]} of a lofty mountain against whose yellow rocks the clouds {crashed[5]}.

A more idiomatic translation of this (St John 1999, 4) reads:

> Mohammed had lived for {many[1]} years in a small town. It {squatted[2]} {insignificantly[3]} at the {foot[4]} of a towering mountain whose pale rocks {touched[5]} the sky.

Here, the number of ST metaphors has been reduced (e.g. TT "many" vs. ST مديدة "extended"), and retained metaphors are sometimes made weaker (e.g. TT "touched" instead of ST ترتطم "crashed"). The operative factor in this "downtoning" seems to be that despite the rhetorical and textual purposes of the ST metaphors, the relatively neutral emotive context of the start of a story does not easily support such metaphorical exuberance in English (see further Dickins 2005, 256–258).

James Dickins

Further reading

Brdar, M. and Brdar-Szabó, R. 2014. Metonymies we (don't) translate by. *Argumentum* 10, pp. 232–247.
This is one of the few published works to focus on the translation of metonymy.

Goatly, A. 1997. *The Language of Metaphors*. London: Routledge.
This wide-ranging book presents metaphor analysis from numerous perspectives. Many of the examples given are particularly intriguing, challenging existing approaches and providing the basis for future research.

Kövecses, Z. 2010. *Metaphor*. 2nd ed. Oxford: Oxford University Press.
This is an authoritative introduction to conceptual metaphor theory.

Lakoff, G. and Johnson, M. 1980. *Metaphors We Live by*. Chicago: University of Chicago Press.
The original book on conceptual metaphor theory, this is still worth reading.

Ritchie, L. D. 2013. *Metaphor*. Cambridge: Cambridge University Press.
This is an up-to-date introduction to metaphor, with application to domains such as conversation, politics, and literature.

Related topics

Semantics and translation; Relevance Theory, interpreting, and translation; Implicature and presupposition in translation and interpreting.

References

Alvarez, A. 1993. On translating metaphor. *META* 38(3), pp. 479–490.
Brdar, M. and Brdar-Szabó, R. 2013. "Translating (by Means of) Metonymy". In *Cognitive Linguistics and Translation: Advances in Some Theoretical Models and Applications*, edited by A. Rojo and I. Ibarretxe-Antuñano, 199–226. Berlin: Mouton de Gruyter.
Brdar, M. and Brdar-Szabó, R. 2014. Metonymies we (don't) translate by. *Argumentum* 10, pp. 232–247.
Broeck, R. 1981. The limits of translatability exemplified by metaphor translation. *Poetics Today* 2(4), pp. 73–87.
Brown, C. 1996. Translation of Extracts from مدينة البغي ("The City of Oppression"), بشارة عيسى. (Eissa Bishara). BA Translation Project: University of Durham.
Burke, K. 1941. The four master tropes. *The Kenyon Review* 3(4), pp. 421–438.
Corbett, E. P. J. and Connors, R. J. 1999. *Classical Rhetoric for the Modern Student*. 4th ed. Oxford: Oxford University Press.
Dagut, M. B. 1976. Can metaphor be translated? *Babel* 12(1), pp. 21–33.
Dagut, M. B. 1987. More about the translatability of metaphor. *Babel* 33(2), pp. 77–83.
Deignan, A. 2005. *Metaphor and Corpus Linguistics*. Amsterdam: John Benjamins.
Denroche, C. 2015. *Metonymy and Language: A New Theory of Linguistic Processing*. London: Routledge.
Dickins, J. 1998. *Extended Axiomatic Linguistics*. Berlin: Mouton de Gruyter.
Dickins, J. 2005. Two models for metaphor translation. *Target* 17(2), pp. 227–273.
Dickins, J. 2014. Associative meaning and scalar implicature: a linguistic-semiotic account. *Linguistica Online*. Available from: http://www.phil.muni.cz/linguistica/art/dickins/dic-003.pdf.
Dickins, J. 2016. Construction of a linguistic theory from first principles and confrontation with crucial data. *Linguistica Online*. Available from: http://www.phil.muni.cz/linguistica/art/dickins/dic-004.pdf.

Dickins, J., Hervey, S. G. J. and Higgins, I. 2002. *Thinking Arabic Translation*. London: Routledge.

Dobrzynska, T. 1995. Translating metaphor: problems of meaning. *Journal of Pragmatics* 24, pp. 595–604.

Fernández, E. S., Sacristán, M. S. V. and Olivera, P. A. F. 2005. "Translations We Live by: The Impact of Metaphor Translation on Target Systems". In *Lengua y Sociedad: Investigasiones Resientes an Linguistca Aplicada*, edited by P. A. Fuertes Olivera, 61–81. Valladolid: University of Valladolid.

Fuertes-Olivera, P. A. and Pizarro-Sánchez, I. 2002. Translation and similarity-creating metaphors in specialised languages. *Target* 14(1), pp. 43–73.

Gentzler, E. 2000. "Translating Metaphor: Beyond the Western Tradition." In *Beyond the Western Tradition*, edited by M. Gaddis Rose, 11–24. Binghamton: State University Press of New York.

Goatly, A. 1997. *The Language of Metaphors*. London: Routledge.

Goschler, J. 2007. Metaphors in cognitive and neurosciences: which impact have metaphors on scientific theories and models? In *Metaphorik.de* (online journal). Available from: www.metaphorik.de/12/goschler.pdf.

Hjelmslev, L. 1953. *Prolegomena to a Theory of Language*, trans. F. Whitfield. Madison: University of Wisconsin.

Kimmel, M. 2010. Why we mix metaphors (and mix them well): discourse coherence, conceptual metaphor, and beyond. *Journal of Pragmatics* 42, pp. 97–115.

Knowles, M. and Moon, R. 2006. *Introducing Metaphor*. London: Routledge.

Kövecses, Z. 2010. *Metaphor*. 2nd ed. Oxford: Oxford University Press.

Kurth, E.-N. 1995. *Metaphernübersetzung*. Frankfurt: Peter Lang.

Kurth, E.-N. 1999. "'Altered Images': Cognitive and Pragmatic Aspects of Metaphor Translation". In *Translation and the (Re)location of Meaning*, edited by J. Vandaele, 97–116. Leuven: The Leuven Research Centre for Translation, Communication and Cultures.

Lakoff, G., Espenson, J. and Schwartz, A. 1991. *Master Metaphor List*, 2nd ed. California: University of Berkley. Available from: araw.mede.uic.edu/~alansz/metaphor/METAPHORLIST.pdf.

Lakoff, G. and Johnson, M. 1980. *Metaphors We Live by*. Chicago: University of Chicago Press.

Levin, S. R. 1982. Aristotle's theory of metaphor. *Philosophy and Rhetoric* 15(1), pp. 24–46.

Maalej, Z. n.d. *Translating Metaphor between Unrelated Cultures: A Cognitive Perspective*. Available from: http:simsim.rug.ac.be/Zmaalej/transmeta.html.

Mandelblit, N. 1995. "The Cognitive View of Metaphor and its Implications for Translation Theory". In *Translation and Meaning*, Part 3, edited by M. Thelen and B. Lewandowska-Tomaszczyk, 482–495. Maastricht: Maastricht University Press.

Merakchi, K. and Rogers, M. 2013. The translation of culturally bound metaphors in the genre of popular science articles: a corpus-based case study from *Scientific American* translated into Arabic. *Intercultural Pragmatics* 10(2), pp. 205–374.

Monti, E. 2009. Translating the metaphors we live by. *European Journal of English Studies* 13(2), pp. 207–221.

Murphy, T. 2001. *Nietzsche, Metaphor, Religion*. New York: SUNY.

Newmark, P. 1985. "The Translation of Metaphor". In *The Ubiquity of Metaphor*, edited by W. Paprotte and R. Dirven, 295–326. Amsterdam: John Benjamins.

Newmark, P. 1988. *A Textbook of Translation*. London: Prentice Hall.

Núñez, R. E. and Sweetser, E. 2005. With the future behind them: convergent evidence from Aymara language and gesture in the crosslinguistic comparison of spatial construals of time. *Cognitive Science* 30, pp. 401–450.

Ortony, A., ed. 1979 [1993]. *Metaphor and Thought*. Cambridge: Cambridge University Press.

Pramling, N. and Säljö, R. 2007. Scientific knowledge, popularisation, and the use of metaphors: modern genetics in popular science magazines. *Scandinavian Journal of Educational Research* 51(3), pp. 275–295.

Richards, I. A. 1937. *The Philosophy of Rhetoric*. Oxford: Oxford University Press.

Ritchie, L. D. 2013. *Metaphor*. Cambridge: Cambridge University Press.

Samaniego, F. E. 1996. *La Traducción de la Metáfora*. Valladolid: Secretariado de Publicaciones de la Universidad de Valladolid.

Samaniego, F. E. 2013. "Translation Studies and the Cognitive Theory of Metaphor". In *Metaphor and Metonymy Revisited: Beyond the Contemporary Theory of Metaphor*, edited by F. Gonzálvez-García, M. S. P. Cervel and L. P. Hernández, 265–282. Amsterdam: John Benjamins Publishing Company.

Schaffner, C. 2004. Metaphor and translation: some implications of a cognitive approach. *Journal of Pragmatics* 36, pp. 1253–1269.

Semino, E. 2008. *Metaphor in Discourse*. Cambridge: Cambridge University Press.

St John, J. 1999. *Translation of* حقل البنفسج *and* النار والماء *by* زكريا تامر (In دمشق الحرائق. 1973. Damascus: دار الانوار). BA Translation Project: University of Durham.

Strachan, J. and Terry, R. 2011. *Poetry*. 2nd ed. Edinburgh: Edinburgh University Press.

Toury, G. 1995. *Descriptive Translation Studies and Beyond*. Amsterdam: John Benjamins.

Vandepitte, S. and Hartsuiker, R. J. 2011. "Metonymic Language Use as a Student Translation Problem: Towards a Controlled Psycholinguistic Investigation". In *Methods and Strategies of Process Research: Integrative Approaches in Translation Studies*, edited by C. Alvstad, A. Hild and E. Tiselius, 67–92. Amsterdam: John Benjamins.

15

Wordplay and translation

Ida Klitgård

Traduttore – traditore!

A pun is the lowest form of wit. It does not tax the brain a bit. One merely takes a word that's plain. And picks one out that sounds the same.

(Samuel Johnson 1709–1784)

The translation of puns is of marginal importance and of irresistible interest

(Newmark 1988, 217)

Introduction and definitions

This chapter opens with a number of long-standing paradoxes concerning the translation of wordplay. The famous play on words in the Italian expression "traduttore – traditore" is widely quoted in Translation Studies and carries the crux of the matter here as when translating the wordplay into English, for instance, the pair "translator – traitor" in fact loses the very play on words, and only a feeble alliteration and assonance survive. The English translation commits treason as it were on the original Italian saying, and in the same vein, translating wordplay is generally considered impossible.

A large number of types of language manipulation may be included under the umbrella term of "wordplay": acrostic, malapropism, palindrome, rhyming slang, tongue twisters, spoonerism, riddle, chiasmus, etc. Here I will, however, focus on the type of wordplay which causes the most problems to translators and which has received the greatest attention in the field of Translation Studies: the pun. That is, the manipulation of sounds and meanings of words with the intent of being witty.

Unfortunately, such wordplay is often considered of lesser value than fancy metaphors or other stylistically sophisticated ways of expressing profundity. The great lexicographer Samuel Johnson coined the second famous saying above that "A pun is the lowest form of wit", forever pushing double meaning witticisms into the shadows of bad taste as there is no significant sapience in them. And here the Italian saying appears as a perfect testimony to his claim that you merely pick a word that is plain and then take another that sounds the same: "traduttore – traditore".

It is, however, not that simple. Wordplay may not only be a despised feature due to its apparent plainness. True, Johnson criticised the amusement of the pun as it only relies on homonymy in his view. He scorned the form and cared not for the multiple opportunities of rhetorical layers of meaning embedded in wordplay. But even though we today recognise wordplay as capable of giving rise to multiple humorous meanings – or maybe exactly because of this recognition – the pun is still a hated feature to some people. In China, for example, there has been an attempt to ban the use of puns as it breaches "the law on standard spoken and written Chinese, makes promoting cultural heritage harder and may mislead the public – especially children" (Branigan 2014). The State Administration for Press, Publication, Radio, Film and Television believes in purifying the language in order to avoid cultural and linguistic chaos, but according to Branigan this is an attempt to eliminate the possibilities of joking at the expense of the country's leadership and their policies. So puns are in reality not that plain. They enable us to say things that cannot otherwise be said, and that is why they are both repulsive and attractive at the same time, as Peter Newmark notes in the third epigraph of this chapter.

But how does wordplay achieve that power? In the online *Oxford English Dictionary (OED)* and the online *Merriam-Webster Dictionary* we find the following definitions of "wordplay" and "pun", which seem to be used interchangeably:

OED:

wordplay n. [compare German Wortspiel (17th cent.), and also play n. 8c] (a) the action of playing with words; witty use of words, esp. of verbal ambiguities; (b) an instance of this, a play on words (see play n. 8c), a pun.

Merriam-Webster:

wordplay: playful or clever use of words

OED:

pun n. Etymology: Origin unknown. Perhaps shortened < punctilio n. or its etymon Italian puntiglio. The use of a word in such a way as to suggest two or more meanings or different associations, or of two or more words of the same or nearly the same sound with different meanings, so as to produce a humorous effect; a play on words.

Merriam-Webster:

pun: the usually humorous use of a word in such a way as to suggest two or more of its meanings or the meaning of another word similar in sound

It appears that "wordplay" is a more broad term for the action of trifling with words, whereas a "pun" expresses a more specifically ambiguous meaning based on words with similar forms and sounds. A pun may also be referred to as a *paronomasia* in rhetoric. These conceits are widely used in literature, advertisement, jingles, slogans, brand names, organisations, journalism, politics, songs, comedy and everyday language, but in this chapter I will restrict my illustrations to literature.

Since the above definitions rest on such words as "meanings", "use of a word" and "same sound" – words and expressions that may themselves be perceived as ambiguous or at least imprecise – we need to outline a typology of wordplay and puns from a linguistic point of view. This will enable a qualified discussion of the reasons to shun the pun in the context of translation.

A lexical-grammatical description of wordplay

If we turn to the field of lexical grammar, we get an idea of how language patterns elicit meaning: we get both a typology and a description of the capacity of wordplay. In his article "A linguistic account of wordplay: The lexical grammar of punning", Partington (2009) tries to fill a lacuna in research on wordplay, as the prevalent taxonomic approach with lists of kinds of puns is unable to explain the underlying structure and function of wordplay in authentic discourse. In his use of various concepts from lexical grammar based on corpus linguistics, Partington allows for a wider understanding of what happens in the construction of wordplay and why it may be so (un)funny – or as Newmark (1988, 217) puts it: "of marginal importance and of irresistible interest". But it must be noted that even though the title of Partington's article speaks of "wordplay" and "punning", it is the latter he in fact analyses.

Partington quotes Koestler's (1964) definition of the pun as a bisociation formed through an acoustic knot, i.e. a simultaneous mental association of one idea with two different fields not normally associated with it by way of sound similarity. This can be expressed through the equation SS1(M1) and SS2(M2) (SS = sound sequence and M = meaning) (Partington 2009, 1795). And rather than only speaking of either homonymic or homophonic puns, he speaks of a more fundamental distinction between "near" puns and "exact" puns:

1. Near puns – $SS1(M1) \approx SS2(M2)$ – resemblance:
   Here two sound sequences are involved which resemble each other phonologically, such as in the before-mentioned pun on "traduttore - traditore".
2. Exact puns – $SS1(M1) = SS2(M2)$ – identity:
   Here two sound sequences are involved which are identical. They may be split into either homonymy (words alike in sound and spelling) or homophony (words alike in sound only):

   2.a. Homonymic exact pun:

   "Do you believe in *clubs* for young people?"
   "Only when kindness fails."

   The word "club" here means both a place for people to hang out and a kind of weapon to hit young people with when good upbringing fails.

   2.a. Homophonic exact pun:

   "Why is a defective condom called a Welsh letter?"
   "Because it has a *leak* in it."

   A "leak" is a hole, but the homophone "leek" is the national symbol of Wales.

In both examples there is a combination of something expected and something which is unexpected. Clubs to hang out in and holes in condoms would be what we expect the respective question to be about, and so the second association takes us by surprise and evokes humour. But why do we expect one meaning over the other? This aspect is what Partington refers to as lexical priming, a term which he borrows from Hoey (2005). But to understand that concept, we need to understand the concept of collocation.

A collocation is a specific sequence or arrangement of words that seems to occur more often than randomly, and when such arrangements turn into conventional set combinations, they become predictable phraseological collocations – such as "blonde hair". We conventionally speak of blonde hair, not yellow hair – as in the corresponding "red hair", "brown hair" and "black hair." Hoey explains:

> The subversiveness of collocation has rarely been noted, but it is as important a property as its pervasiveness and stems from it. The ubiquity of collocation challenges current theories of language because it demands explanation, and the only explanation that seems to account for the existence of collocation is that each lexical item is primed for collocational use. By primed, I mean that as the word is learnt through encounters with it in speech and writing, it is loaded with the cumulative effects of those encounters such that it is part of our knowledge of the word that it co-occurs with other words.
>
> Collocation priming is not a permanent feature of the word. Each use we make of the word, and each new encounter, either reinforces the priming or loosens it, if we use it in defiance of the priming. It may accordingly shift in the course of an individual's life-time, and if it does so, and to the extent that it does so, the lexical item shifts slightly in meaning and/or function. This may be referred to as drifts in the priming.
>
> Collocational priming is sensitive to the domain in which the lexical item is encountered. Part of our knowledge of a lexical item is that it is used in certain combinations in certain kinds of text. So the phrase in winter is primed for use in travel writing whereas the phrase during the winter months, which means more or less the same thing, is primed for use in gardening writing.
>
> (Hoey 2004)

To this can be added the tendency for lexical items to either attract or avoid certain grammatical categories, which is called colligation, or certain grammatical positions, which is called *textual* colligation (Partington 2009, 1797). Partington explains that "in winter" primes an occurrence of the present tense and "timeless truths" as well as a position in the beginning of a sentence. The complete array of such combinatorial expectancies is called a priming prosody (Partington 2009, 1798). In extension to this, I propose that such grammatical preferences or expectancies may explain the translation teacher's all too habitual urge to tell students that this or that translation just "sounds better" or that one's "intuition" tells one that this or that solution is to be preferred, while being quite unable to explain why.

According to Hoey, the fluency of native speakers originates in the subconscious process of language learning that includes noticing and recording lexical priming:

> More specifically, whenever a native speaker encounters a word, he or she makes a mental note, quite subconsciously, of:
>
> - the words it occurs with
> - the grammatical patterns it occurs in
> - the meanings with which it is associated.
>
> They also make a subconscious note of:
>
> - whether it is used to be polite (or rude)
> - what kind of style it tends to occur in

- whether it occurs more often in speech or writing
- whether the speaker is someone younger or older.

They also notice where the person who has used the word comes from and whether he or she was being humorous or serious. They notice, too, whether the word or phrase is typically used in particular kinds of text, in academic writing, for example, rather than novels, advertisements or newspaper writing. They even notice whether it is associated with the beginnings or ends of sentences or with paragraph boundaries.

(Hoey 2009)

That is why it is crucial for foreign or second language learners to immerse themselves in or expose themselves as much as possible to the foreign language to get a feel for lexical priming.

To return to wordplay, or puns, they function as a combination of words and meanings that are both expected and unexpected at the same time. The conventional semantic expectancies are disrupted. In the homonymic exact pun above, our first favoured reading, or what we hear at first, is the meaning of the word "club" as a society for young people, presumably because the combination "clubs for" tend to lead to that conclusion. The secondary meaning of a weapon used for hitting is what is unexpected and thus lays a filter of shocking ambiguity on top of the word, eliciting laughter. The same is the case with the homophonic exact pun above where we expect the meaning of a hole at first as it is primed to collocate with a container, here a condom, whereas vegetables are not.

Partington then consequently speaks of two basic principles of language organisation, referring to Sinclair's (1987) distinction:

1. The collocational (idiomatic/phraseological) principle: discourse is constructed by way of a series of (semi-)preconstituted blocks chosen at a time
2. The open-choice (terminological) principle: discourse is a series of open-ended choices of empty slots having to be filled by a word chosen one by one.

(Partington 2009, 1798)

According to psycholinguistic studies, the collocational (idiomatic/phraseological) mode is the dominant, default mode of interpreting discourse because it is the fastest way to comprehend communication. Thus, readers or listeners access idiomatic interpretations of preconstituted blocks before literal interpretations. And it is the very interplay, "the enforced switching from one mode of interpretation to another, from the idiom to the open-choice, which is at the heart of a great part of wordplay" (Partington 2009, 1799). When readers or listeners are forced to (also) use the open-choice analytical mechanism instead of purely interpreting the priming prosody of the idiomatic block, they encounter a kind of relexicalisation: "The effect achieved is a general revitalisation of the language at that point in the text. Novelty breathes life into the discourse" (Partington 2009, 1799). Or as Walter Redfern puts it: "extracting the maximum juice of words" (Redfern 1997, 267). Of course such interpretation only works if the receiver shares the lexical primings due to the same knowledge of the world, and that is one of the reasons why humour often travels very badly across cultures and languages.

The same may be said of the sub-category of the so-called delexicalised puns where the reverse is happening. The key word in such puns is in conventional everyday use emptied of its full literal meaning, such as the verb "take" in "take a bath", but in delexicalised puns the full meaning has returned as in "taking a bath" interpreted as removing or stealing a bath.

That is, the distinct contribution of the word to the meaning of the utterance has been reduced to an unexpected literal meaning. This may also be termed a zeugma.

Another kind of interpretation is the reworked/reconstruction pun. This is the case with near puns where the nearness of two different meanings through sound resemblance (M1 and M2) as in "traduttore – traditori" forces the receiver to couple the surprise effect with a piecing together of the actually expected blocks. So, in relexicalised puns a surprise effect occurs through a true sense of novelty and revitalisation, whereas in reworked puns, the surprise effect is coupled with the receiver's active contribution in seeing the unexpected connection between the lexical items.

Partington concludes his study by trying to explain what makes a good pun and what makes a bad pun. The good, or justified/motivated pun relies on a kind of kinship or similarity between the combined ideas or senses, whereas the bad, or unmotivated/hollow pun rests on a missing link, so to speak, between the two meanings which unite it. We may smile, but not burst into laughter, when hearing a bad pun. Or we may say that that was a poor joke. As psychologists searching for the world's best joke have concluded: the necessary ingredients in a good joke are shock and surprise – but more importantly "the kick of the discovery" that you are suddenly turning your thinking around and shifting your perceptions (Weems 2014). That is why wordplay is both of marginal importance and irresistible interest. It combines the expected mundane world with an unpredicted sensation of freshness.

So far we have dwelled on wordplay as a play on words in single phrases or full sentences – except for the by now exhausted "traduttore – traditore". This, however, may be an example of an elliptical sentence saying that a translator is like a traitor. Furthermore, Partington also speaks of "lexical cascading" which is an accumulation of words and phrases from the same lexico-grammatical class which together form a kind of extended wordplay as in "*Food* features large on summit *menu*" or "Novel *voting system*: Literature *at the polls*: *New* and *retiring candidates* choose their favourite" (Partington 2009, 1808). But is wordplay only possible as an acoustic knot incorporated into a collocational arrangement of words? What about single words in themselves? Partington says that "puns generally do not play with single words but phrases, larger units of discourse" (Partington 2009, 1795). Admittedly, the word "club" on its own, for example, does not give rise to any surprise effect or the slightest laughter even though it has more than one meaning. But so-called neologisms or blends do.

When it comes to word formation, a kind of revitalisation, playfulness and (amusing) double meanings may, however, indeed be applied to achieve a witty effect. We speak in general of neologisms, but this broad term is misleading as only very few words may be said to be actual new coinings. Instead we may speak of lexical innovation in word formation and break this down into a variety of morphological processes such as derivation, compounding, semantic change, functional shifts, initialisms, borrowings, back-formations, blends and coinings (Ayto 1996, 65), from which only blends and coinings (true neologisms) are relevant in this context.

A neologism is a word which is newly coined and thus new to the language, such as the Martian word "grok" denoting life, water and an experience of ultimate empathy where the observer becomes part of the observed as invented in Robert A. Heinlein's 1961 science fiction novel *Stranger in a Strange Land*; or James Joyce's "quark" for the cry of a duck in *Finnegans Wake* (1939). Such words fill a lexical gap in a particular literary sphere and sometimes even in a subsequent broader context. The physicists George Zweig and Murray Gell-Mann, for example, deliberately borrowed Joyce's "quark" to denote an elementary particle in matter. Gell-Mann explains:

> In 1963, when I assigned the name "quark" to the fundamental constituents of the nucleon, I had the sound first, without the spelling, which could have been "kwork".

Then, in one of my occasional perusals of *Finnegans Wake*, by James Joyce, I came across the word "quark" in the phrase "Three quarks for Muster Mark." Since "quark" (meaning, for one thing, the cry of the gull) was clearly intended to rhyme with "Mark", as well as "bark" and other such words, I had to find an excuse to pronounce it as "kwork." But the book represents the dream of a publican named Humphrey Chimpden Earwicker. Words in the text are typically drawn from several sources at once, like the "portmanteau" words in "Through the Looking-Glass." From time to time, phrases occur in the book that are partially determined by calls for drinks at the bar. I argued, therefore, that perhaps one of the multiple sources of the cry "Three quarks for Muster Mark" might be "Three quarts for Mister Mark", in which case the pronunciation "kwork" would not be totally unjustified. In any case, the number three fitted perfectly the way quarks occur in nature.

(Gell-Mann 1995, 180)

However, striking literary neologisms most often remain so-called nonce words, i.e. words which are only used once and never catch on in a wider circulation of language.

A blend, on the other hand, is the merging of parts of words into a new word, as in "brunch" coined by "breakfast" and "lunch"; and as in "cyborg" coined by "cybernetic" and "organism". Such cases of clipping of splinters of words and packing them into one word is also known as "portmanteau words", which in itself is a new word originating in Lewis Carroll's novel *Through the Looking-Glass, and What Alice Found There* (1871).

Both neologisms and blends may have an extreme freshness and image-making power, as with wordplay in phrases. But the blend is closer to the pun in nature than the neologism. As the pun was a simultaneous mental association of one idea with two different fields not normally associated with it by way of sound similarity, the blend, I suggest, is a simultaneous mental association of one idea with two different fields derivatively associated with it by way of hybridity. The blend is more free than the pun as all sense-making parts of words may be put together to form entirely new words as long as they follow general morphological, syntactic and phonetic rules in language. The pun is dependent on the acoustic knot which ties two meanings together. This may be explained thus:

- the pun: one word with two meanings primarily based on the collocational principle, as in "club" in the above-mentioned sequence of sentences
- the blend/portmanteau: one meaning depending on two words primarily based on the open-choice principle, as in "brunch" as mentioned above.

Main research methods

The distinctions between puns and portmanteaux have been thoroughly discussed in Delabastita's vast studies on wordplay and translation on which a number of subsequent studies draw significantly (e.g. Klitgård 2005; Pérez 2008; Marco 2010; Low 2011). His definition of wordplay is often quoted in Translation Studies:

Wordplay is the general name indicating the various *textual* phenomena in which *structural features* of the language(s) used are exploited in order to bring about a *communicatively significant confrontation* of two (or more) linguistic structures with *more or less similar forms* and *more or less different meanings*.

(Delabastita 1996, 128)

Delabastita explains the pun as contrasting linguistic structures with different meanings based on formal identity in terms of four specifications: homonymy (identical sounds and spelling), homophony (identical sounds, but different spelling), homography (identical spelling, but different sounds) and paronomy (slight variation in both sounds and spelling). The two contrasting linguistic structures – what Partington called an "acoustic knot" – may exist concurrently in the same portion of text (vertical wordplay – cf. Partington's exact puns) or one after another in the text (horizontal wordplay – cf. Partington's near puns). The grid of the eight typologies in Table 15.1 is often quoted in the literature relying on Delabastita's work (here I provide explanations of the four categories in square brackets).

As with Partington's lexical grammar, Delabastita also speaks of punning as a textual phenomenon relying on specific textual settings, such as either verbal or situational contexts, and based on either the collocational or open-choice principle, even though these are not the exact terms he uses. The verbal contexts originate in our expectations of (a) grammatical well-formedness; (b) thematic coherence; (c) conventional sequence of phrases (Partington and Hoey's "priming") such as titles, collocations, proverbs, etc. The situational contexts refer to dialogue situations and multimedia texts (Delabastita 1996, 129). The revitalisation which Partington speaks of is here described as always already existing in tangles of potential ambiguities and associations in the punster's deliberate exploitation of the following linguistic features:

1. The phonological and graphological structure, such as soundplay in alliteration
2. The lexical structure, such as polysemy and idioms
3. The morphological structure, such as "Is life worth living? It depends on the liver." This type of pun is structured as a compound/derivative which is etymologically incorrect, but semantically effective
4. The syntactic structure, such as "Players please" which can be read as a praise of the cigarette brand or as a request in a shop

(Delabastita 1996, 130–131)

Table 15.1 The eight typologies of pun (after Delabastita 1993, 81)

Homony [same spelling and pronunciation, but different meaning]	*Homophony* [same pronunciation, but different spelling and different meaning]	*Homography* [same written form, but different pronunciation and different meaning]	*Paronymy* [derivative word with related meaning]
VERTICAL Pyromania: a burning passion	VERTICAL Wedding belles	VERTICAL MessAge [name of mid-1990s rap band]	VERTICAL Come in for a faith lift [slogan on church]
HORIZONTAL Carry on dancing carries Carry to the top [article on ambitious young dancer called Carry]	HORIZONTAL Counsel for Council home buyers	HORIZONTAL How the US put US to shame	HORIZONTAL It's G.B. for the Beegees [article on pop band touring Britain]

And "For this massive dormant associative power of words and structures to become effective, they need to be employed in specifically contrived textual settings" (Delabastita 1996, 129).

Delabastita's typology, however, does not leave room for morphological puns such as blends/portmanteaux which are single-word wordplay not necessarily disrupting the textual structure. Here Lladó's rhetorical typology may supplement Delabastita's. Besides wordplay based on either consonance (defined as phonetic similarity), polysemy and homophony, Lladó also proposes wordplay based on transformation "which includes all figures based on the alteration of the phonetic and graphic structure of a word in order to create a different one, such as anagram, *portmanteau* word, metathesis, metagram, heterogram and palindrome" (Lladó 2002 translated and quoted in Marco 2010, 267).

Since wordplay is always already there in the covert associative power of language, or as Hofstaedter (1997) says, "there are hidden puns lying around at all times" (Hofstaedter quoted in Low 2011, 63), one might assume that the translation of both phraseological puns and morphological puns is a simple matter. But the pun is the lowest form of wit, Johnson said, maybe because it is exactly not artfully constructed but just lying around everywhere only waiting to rise and shine: "The pun [. . .] is not just an ambiguity that has crept into an utterance unawares, to embarrass or amuse before being dismissed; it is ambiguity *unashamed of itself*, and this is what makes it a scandal and not just an inconvenience" (Attridge 1988, 141).

One major problem in translating puns is that the "covert associative power of language" is not the same across time and socio-linguistic cultures. The power of primed "hidden puns lying around" is not shared between different time periods and different languages if the codes and cultural references differ. As Chiaro for instance has demonstrated, in the interlingual translation of sexual and political jokes, problems of equivalence and thus understanding arise when the source and target cultures do not share the same views on for example what is taboo and what is not, or the same sociocultural knowledge of historical or topical events (Chiaro 1992, 77–84).

According to Delabastita, however, this does not mean that wordplay is untranslatable. The various translation strategies he lists testify to a number of legitimate techniques which are at the translator's disposal. Here I quote Delabastita's famous list of strategies at length with added numbers:

1. PUN → PUN: the source-text pun is translated by a target-language pun, which may be more or less different from the original wordplay in terms of formal structure, semantic structure, or textual function
2. PUN → NON-PUN: the pun is rendered by a non-punning phrase which may salvage both senses of the wordplay but in a non-punning conjunction, or select one of the senses at the cost of suppressing the other; of course, it may also occur that both components of the pun are translated "beyond recognition"
3. PUN → RELATED RHETORICAL DEVICE: the pun is replaced by some wordplay-related rhetorical device (repetition, alliteration, rhyme, referential vagueness, irony, paradox, etc.) which aims to recapture the effect of the source-text pun
4. PUN → ZERO: the portion of the text containing the pun is simply omitted
5. PUN ST = PUN TT: the translator reproduces the source-text pun and possibly its immediate environment in its original formulation, i.e. without actually "translating" it
6. NON-PUN → PUN: the translator introduces a pun in textual positions where the original text has no wordplay, by way of compensation to make up for source-text puns lost elsewhere, or for any other reason

7. ZERO → PUN: totally new textual material is added, which contains wordplay and which has no apparent precedent or justification in the source text except as a compensatory device

8. EDITORIAL TECHNIQUES: explanatory footnotes or endnotes, comments provided in translators' forewords, the "anthological" presentation of different, supposedly complementary solutions to one and the same source-text problem, and so forth.

(Delabastita 1996, 134)

Furthermore, all these strategies can be combined in various ways, such as a pun being suppressed (PUN → NON-PUN) with a footnote explaining why (EDITORIAL TECHNIQUES) and perhaps with a compensatory pun elsewhere (NON-PUN → PUN). So – and this may come as a surprise to some – shunning the pun in (2) and (4) is a valid translation strategy according to Delabastita. This is supported by Pérez who says "Claiming that puns are untranslatable implies considering that those strategies are not good enough to qualify as genuine translation" (Pérez 2008, 36).

Current debates

Deciding which strategy to use depends on a number of factors impinging on the translation situation. In his corpus study of the translation of wordplay in English literary texts by Oscar Wilde and Graham Swift into Catalan, Marco takes Delabastita's methods a step further. Reviewing the literature on wordplay, he makes a list of such factors:

1. Isomorphism: Kinship between the languages. The closer the languages, the greater chance of equivalence
2. Degree of cultural specificity of the elements in the pun
3. Translator-related subjected factors, such as talent, proficiency and willingness to work on solving the problems
4. Objective factors, such as working conditions
5. Translation norms of the target system
6. Textual genre/text-type
7. Intended target readership. E.g. differences in relevance to adults and children
8. Kind of linguistic structures played upon, such as the phonological, graphological, lexical, morphological and syntactic levels
9. Stylistic function and motivation, such as (a) the functions of humour (entertainment, social criticism, pedagogical moralising intention); (b) mental state or attitude (bitterness, cynicism, irony, etc.); (c) scope (local or global in the text); (d) relationship between the wordplay and the composition of the text (plot, characters, themes, etc.)
10. The relative frequency of wordplay in the text
11. Type of wordplay, e.g. horizonal and vertical
12. Domain(s) of experience and knowledge/isotopies: "the greater the distance between the two (or more) isotopies activated by wordplay, the more surprising the effect".

(Marco 2010, 271–73)

Even though Marco revises Delabastita's techniques slightly in this study, he finds that the various ways in which punning activity are lost in translation from English to Catalan are the most prevalent strategies, including translating a pun into zero puns or a pun into a non-pun. They account for 62.72% of his cases, whereas the techniques that constitute a neutral approach, such as translating a pun to a similar or different pun, account for around half of that, 31.82%. There are no cases of a positive balance, such as a non-pun translated into a pun or zero pun translated into a pun, and the most recurrent factors behind these strategies seem to be (in this order taken from the above list):

9. stylistic function
8. the kind of linguistic structure
2. cultural specificity
12. domain of experience
1. degree of isomorphism

To this he adds the factor of *skopos* which includes (6) textual genre and (7) target audience. One is left to wonder whether there is no author-related factor, i.e. taking the author's habitual, characteristic or famed use of wordplay into consideration. Oscar Wilde, for instance, is an equilibrist writer who puts Johnson's scorn for puns to shame, and since this is such a strong characteristic of Wilde's voice, the translator is forced to put extra effort into making translation equivalence happen.

As I have previously argued (2005), on a par with Marco's later finding of the most prevalent translation factor, the stylistic function of punning is indisputable. But not only does the translator have to make isolated qualified choices with both vertical and horizontal singular puns, s/he may also have to consider wider syntagmatic contextual patterns, networks or clusters of related wordplay throughout a literary text – and this approach validates a greater focus on the author factor in future research on the translation of wordplay. A poignant case is James Joyce's novel *Ulysses* (1922) as it is a vast playful fabric of interconnected multilingual imagery, motifs and extensive "cascades" of wordplay, as Partington calls it (Klitgård 2007), which includes both vertical, horizontal and single-word puns (portmanteaux). The examples in the following section have been taken from *Ulysses*.

Examples

In the "Sirens" episode of *Ulysses*, the main character Leopold Bloom writes a letter to his admirer Martha Clifford while listening to music in a bar. His pondering thoughts about her previous letter to him are telling of the problems in translating puns: "How will you pun? You punish me?" (Joyce 1922/1986, 11.890–891 – referring to episode and line number.) His stream of thoughts is interrupted rendering only half of the word "punish", which I jokingly suggest turns into a question from James Joyce to the reader-translator: How will you pun – and thereby punish me? I.e. being a "traditore" to his art. The reader is immediately presented with the surprise effect as "pun" is not typically primed with "How will you". And then we are presented with the originally intended word "punish" which reassures us that everything is back to normal – but not without having planted in us the novel relexicalised feeling that punning and punishment may be associated with each other which makes this a case of constructed paronymy. As Herman explains: "The text itself reflects on the formation of puns via the transposition of morphemes". It is "a procedure that at the limit furnishes the logic of puns – roots itself in the phonic substance of a given material language" (Herman 1995, 76). But how do you translate that into a different language where there may be no shared derivation?

The recent much-celebrated Danish retranslation of *Ulysses* by Karsten Sand Iversen retorts to the strategy of translating a pun into a non-pun as he writes: "*Hvordan vil du straf? Du straffe mig?*" (Joyce 2015, 300) which uses the translation of "punish" into the Danish equivalent *"straffe"*. No pun intended in this strategy. The last of three attempts at the first Danish translation by Boisen (1949, 1970 and 1980) has *"Hvordan vil du smæ? Du smække mig?"* (Joyce 1980/1990, vol. 1, 329) which translates into the English *spanking*. Boisen interprets the punishment in a certain way and renders this without modesty. But again, the pun on the linguistic structures between punning and punishment is lost.

An example of the contiguous use of a vertical homophone in *Ulysses* is the expression in the "Wandering Rocks" episode: "Tell him I'm Boylan with impatience" merging the similar (Irish) pronunciations of the character Blazes Boylan's name with the verb, "boiling". This is cunningly repeated twice in a completely different context in the subsequent musical "Sirens" episode: "With patience Lenehan waited for Boylan with impatience" and "I'm off, said Boylan with impatience". These two examples have been stripped from their punning content and turned into jesting nonsense in the second example and a literal meaning in the third example where Boylan has actually entered the bar and is about to leave. This network has been translated thus [back-translations are provided in square brackets]:

1. "Tell him I'm Boylan with impatience" (Joyce 1922/1986, 10.486)

   Mogens Boisen:
   "Sig til ham, at jeg er Boylan af utålmodighed" [Tell him I'm Boylan with impatience]
      (Joyce 1949, 239)

   Strategy: PUN ST = PUN TT
   "Sig til ham, at I am Boylan af utålmodighed" [Tell him *I am Boylan* with impatience]
      (Joyce 1980/1990, vol. 1, 275)

   Strategy: PUN ST = PUN TT

   Karsten Sand Iversen:
   "Sig til ham han får med boylan hvis han ikke" [Tell him he's going to get beaten with the hanger if he doesn't] (Joyce 2015, 250)

   Strategy: PUN → NON-PUN

2. "With patience Lenehan waited for Boylan with impatience" (Joyce 1922/1986, 11.289–290)

   Mogens Boisen:
   "Med tålmodighed ventede Lenehan på Boylan *af utålmodighed"* [With patience Lenehan waited for *Boylan* with impatience] (Joyce 1980/1990, vol. 1, 310 – the same in 1949)

   Karsten Sand Iversen:
   "Med tålmodighed ventede Lenehan på Boylan med utålmodighed" [With patience Lenehan waited for Boylan with impatience] (Joyce 2015, 283)

3. "I'm off, said Boylan with impatience". (Joyce 1922/1986, 10.426)

   Mogens Boisen:
   "Jeg går, sagde Boylan *med utålmodighed"* [I'm leaving, said Boylan with impatience] (Joyce 1949, 274)
   "Jeg er gået, sagde Boylan med utålmodighed" [I'm out of here, said Boylan with impatience] (Joyce 1980/1990, vol. 1, 314)

Karsten Sand Iversen:
"Jeg går, sagde Boylan med utålmodighed" [I'm leaving, said Boylan with impatience]
(Joyce 2015, 287)

As we can see in the first example, Boisen reproduces the difficult source text homophone in its original formulation without actually translating it, hoping that this will lend the sentence an unexpected local aura. Sand Iversen, on the other hand, manages to translate the pun into a Danish expression *"få med bøjlen"* [get beaten with a coat hanger] as the word *"bøjlen"* has almost the same pronunciation as "Boylan". This is of course clever, but the Danish reader has no idea that the original reads "Boylan" as the context does not help us here, and is thus unable to link the two into a pun. The punning quality is thus lost. In the subsequent two examples where Joyce plays with the literalised expression "with impatience" and "with patience", the Danish translators have been unable to link them to the pun in the "Wandering Rocks" episode and thus maintain the contiguous nature of much wordplay in the novel.

Elsewhere Bloom amuses himself by making a cascade of horizontal homonymic puns on the words "waiter" and "waits" in the senses of serving at a table in a restaurant and pausing/delaying:

> Pat is a waiter who waits while you wait. Hee hee hee hee. He waits while you wait. Hee hee. A waiter is he. Hee hee hee hee. He waits while you wait. While you wait if you wait he will wait while you wait. Hee hee hee hee. Hoh. Wait while you wait.
>
> (Joyce 1922/1986, 11.916–19)

This passage is obviously a challenge to any translator into a language which does not contain any words with the ambiguity carried by "wait" in English. This is the case with Danish where a waiter in a restaurant is called *"tjener"*, and the verb for "waiting" in the sense of serving is *"betjene"* while the verb for "waiting" in the sense of pausing is *"vente"*. Someone who waits – "a waiter" – would be literally called *"en der venter"* [someone who waits] or perhaps playfully "en venter" [a waiter]. Thus there are no concurrences between serving and waiting in Danish in any of the cases. Here are the Danish translations:

Mogens Boisen:
"Pat er en tjener som henter mens man venter. Hi hi hi hi. Han henter, mens man venter. Mens man venter, hvis man venter vil han hente, mens man venter. Hi hi hi hi. Ho. Henter mens man venter" (Joyce 1980/1990, vol. 1, 330 – the same in 1949)

Strategy: PUN → RELATED RHETORICAL DEVICE.

Karsten Sand Iversen:
"Pat er en opvarter som varter mens man venter. Hi hi. En varter er han. Hi hi hi hi. Han varter mens man venter. Hi hi hi hi. Hoho. Varter mens man venter" (Joyce 2015, 301)

Strategy: PUN → RELATED RHETORICAL EFFECT

Boisen's translation is amusing as he compensates for the homonymic punning by playing with the tongue-twisting rhymes in *"venter"* [waits] and *"henter"* [fetches] throughout the passage, which both recaptures the effect and makes good sense as a waiter is someone who fetches things for the customers.

Sand Iversen also struggles with the puns as he changes the word "waiter" into the Danish "opvarter" which is archaic Danish for a waiter and today more or less synonymous with "servant", etymologically related to the German *Aufwärter*. The derived Danish verb "opvarte" [serve] – related to the German *aufwarten* – has been cut short into "varte" which is archaic Danish for *serve* as the verb "opvarte" can be split into "varte op" meaning *to serve, attend*. As an extra benefit, the word "varte" alliterates with "vente", and thus the original phnonological effect is achieved but at the cost of an exact homonym.

An example of the difficulties of translating the morphological one-word pun – i.e. a blend/portmanteau – is the title "Father Cantekissem" (Joyce 1922/1986, 14.816) blending "catechism" with the Irish pronunciation of "can't he kiss them". The Danish translations are the following:

Mogens Boisen:
"fader maaikkekysses" (Joyce 1949, 413) [father maynotbekissed]

Strategy: PUN → NON-PUN OR PUN → RELATED RHETORICAL DEVICE
"fader Seul-i-bed" (Joyce 1980/1990, vol. 2, 31) [father alone in bed]

Strategy: PUN → PUN

Karsten Sand Iversen:
"Fader Katekusmis" (Joyce 2015, 431) [Father Catecukitty]

Strategy: PUN → PUN

Boisen's 1949 translation strips the word of its transforming blend, spells out one of the meanings and rejects the other meaning. However, by splicing the words "maa ikke kisses" [may not be kissed] he achieves the effect of a blend nevertheless. In his second translation, he couples the French word "seul" [alone, on his own] with the English "bed" which together with the Danish "i" [in] happen to be phonologically almost identical with the Danish word "cølibat" [celibacy]. In this way Boisen maintains the kinship between the Catholic isotopy and the meaning referring to the celibacy rule of priest abstinence. This is a highly successful and teasing multilingual solution which forces the Danish reader to actively construct the pun. There is no collocational priming disruption which gives rise to a surprise effect as there is no underlying, ready logic behind the components of this portmanteau. It is truly artfully crafted and thus takes a toll on the Danish reader's patience.

Sand Iversen's suggestion is closer to the original as the Catechismus isotopy has been preserved, now coupled with references to the first part of the Danish word "kusse" [cunt] and "mis" [kitty] which is Danish slang for the vagina equivalent to the English "pussy". This also works very well in the context, and thus both translators demonstrate that they do not shun the morphological pun but contribute to a creative, revitalised and surprising expansion of language. As Attridge says in a poststructuralist vein:

The portmanteau shatters any illusion that the systems of difference in language are fixed and sharply drawn, and reminds us that signifiers are perpetually dissolving into one another: in the neverending diachronic development of language; in the blurred edges between speech and writing; in errors and misunderstandings, unfortunate and fruitful; in riddles, jokes, games and dreams.

(Attridge 1988, 151)

Conclusion and future directions

The marginally important and irresistibly interesting pun – both the phraseological and the morphological one – defies all kinds of simple equivalence in translation. It may be the lowest form of wit, but it tells us something about lexical priming, about the collocational processes of discourse and about the heart of humour. Wordplay is not just an isolated feature to be put into tables and boxes of stringent typology. Future studies would do well to undertake contrastive lexical-grammatical or psycholinguistic analyses of underlying primed collocational structures in source text wordplay and target text translations in order to reach a deeper understanding of the strategies applied and the factors involved.

Further reading

Delabastita, D. 1994. Focus on the pun: Wordplay as a special problem in translation studies. *Target* 6(2), pp. 223–243.
This is a review article surveying the historical landmarks and crucial debates in the research on the translation of wordplay.

Delabastita, D., ed. 1997. *Traductio: Essays on Punnning and Translation*. Manchester: St Jerome Publishing.
A collection of essays on the translation of puns from a wide variety of perspectives, including linguistic, cognitive linguistic, cultural, feminist and post-structuralist, on a number of different genres, such as Bible translation, literature and television comedy.

Heibert, F. 1992. *Das Wortspiel als Stilmittel und seine Übersetzung*. Tübingen: Gunter Narr Verlag.
This is an extensive, groundbreaking and stringent linguistic study on the translation of wordplay in James Joyce's *Ulysses* combining descriptive approach with evaluative criticism and prescriptive norms.

Vandaele, J. 2010. "Wordplay in Translation". In *Handbook of Translation Studies*. Vol. 2., edited by Y. Gambier and L. van Doorslaar. Amsterdam: John Benjamins Publishing Company.
Gives a brief overview of main concerns, people and results in the field of translation and wordplay.

Related topics

Stylistics and translation; Tropes and translation.

References

Attridge, D. 1988. "Unpacking the Portmanteau, or Who's Afraid of *Finnegans Wake?*". In *On Puns: The Foundation of Letters*, edited by J. Culler. Oxford: Basil Blackwell.
Ayto, J. 1996. "Lexical Innovation: Neologism and Dictionaries". In *Words, Words, Words: The Translator and the Language Learner*, edited by G. Anderman and M. Rogers. Clevedon: Multilingual Matters.
Branigan, T. 2014. "China Bans Wordplay in Attempt at Pun Control". *The Guardian*, 28 November. Available from: http://www.theguardian.com/world/2014/nov/28/china-media-watchdog-bans-wordplay-puns [Accessed 18 February 2015].
Chiaro, D. 1992. *The Language of Jokes: Analysing Verbal Play*. London: Routledge.
Delabastita, D. 1993. *There's a Double Tongue: An Investigation into the Translation of Shakespeare's Wordplay, with Special Reference to Hamlet*. Amsterdam: Rodopi.
Delabastita, D. 1996. "Introduction". In *Wordplay and Translation*. Special issue of *The Translator: Studies in Intercultural Communication*, edited by D. Delabastita 2(2), 127–139.

Gell-Mann, M. 1995. *The Quark and the Jaguar: Adventures in the Simple and the Complex*. New York: Henry Holt and Co.

Herman, D. 1995. *Universal Grammar and Narrative Form*. Durham, NC: Duke University Press.

Hoey, M. 2004. *Lexical Priming and the Properties of Text*. Available from: http://www.monabaker.com/tsresources/LexicalPrimingandthePropertiesofText.htm [Accessed 27 February 2015].

Hoey, M. 2005. *Lexical Priming: A New Theory on Words and Language*. London: Routledge.

Hoey, M. 2009. "Language Awareness: Lexical Priming". *MED Magazine* 52, January. Available from: http://www.macmillandictionaries.com/MED-Magazine/January2009/52-LA-LexicalPriming.htm [Accessed 27 February 2015].

Hofstaedter, D. 1997. *Le Ton beau de Marot*. New York: Basic Books.

Joyce, J. 1922/1986. *Ulysses*, edited by H. W. Gabler. London: The Bodley Head.

Joyce, J. 1949/1970. *Ulysses*, transl. by Mogens Boisen. Copenhagen: Martins Forlag. Revised ed. 1970.

Joyce, J. 1980/1990. *Ulysses*. Vols 1 and 2, transl. Mogens Boisen. Copenhagen: Gyldendal.

Joyce, J. 2015. *Ulysses*, transl. Karsten Sand Iversen. Copenhagen: Rosinante.

Klitgård, I. 2005. Taking the pun by the horns: the translation of wordplay in James Joyce's *Ulysses*. *Target* 17(1), pp. 71–92.

Klitgård, I. 2007. *Fictions of Hybridity: Translating Style in James Joyce's "Ulysses"*. Odense: University Press of Southern Denmark.

Koestler, A. 1964. *The Act of Creation*. London: Hutchinson.

Lladó, R. 2002. *La paraula revessa. Estudi sobre la traducció dels jocs de mots*. Bellaterra: Servei de Publicacions de la Universitat Autònoma de Barcelona.

Low, P. A. 2011. Translating jokes and puns. *Perspectives: Studies in Translatology* 19(1), pp. 59–70.

Marco, J. 2010. The translation of wordplay in literary texts: typology, techniques and factors in a corpus of English-Catalan source text and target text segments. *Target* 22(2), pp. 264–297.

Newmark, P. 1988. *A Textbook of Translation*. New York: Prentice Hall.

Partington, A. S. 2009. A linguistic account of wordplay: the lexical grammar of punning. *Journal of Pragmatics* 41, pp. 1794–1809.

Pérez, F. J. D. 2008. Wordplay in film titles: translating puns into Spanish. *Babel* 54(1), pp. 36–58.

Redfern, W. 1997. "Traduction, Puns, Clichés, Plagiat". In *Traductio: Essays on Punning and Translation*, edited by D. Delabastita. Manchester: St Jerome Publishing.

Sinclair, J. 1987. "Collocation: A Progress Report". In *Language Topics: Essays in Honour of Michael Halliday*, edited by R. Steele and T. Threadgold. Amsterdam: John Benjamins.

Weems, S. 2014. "The Science Behind Why We Laugh, and the Funniest Joke in the World". *Huffington Post*. Available from: http://www.huffingtonpost.com/scott-weems/joke-book_b_4892644.html [Accessed 27 February 2015].

Part IV

Individuals and their interactions

16

Bilingualism, translation, and interpreting

John W. Schwieter and Aline Ferreira

Introduction

A human's ability to translate and interpret languages has intrigued linguists, philosophers, psychologists, and bilingual experts for decades. Indeed, it is a rather frequent occurrence: non-professional translation happens in everyday circumstances among bilinguals with no training (Harris 1976), and, at the same time, is carried out by a vast number of highly-qualified professional translators. In both cases, understanding and describing how bilinguals are able to produce output in one language from input in a different language has led to rich, dynamic approaches to researching translation, interpreting, and bilingualism (see Schwieter & Ferreira, 2017 for an overview). In this chapter, we will discuss some of these approaches.

Defining translation, and interpreting, competence, and bilingualism

We begin by asking the question: What is translation? Translation can be seen as an activity between languages to express the same reality (Vinay and Darbelnet 1958) although it has been defined in various ways. Hurtado Albir (2011) perhaps describes translation best by characterising it as: a textual operation, an act of communication, and a cognitive activity. As a textual activity, the meaning of the message is translated: it is not simply a matter of converting the source language into another language. In this case, translation is understood as a communication act, not a linguistic act (Seleskovitch and Lederer 1984) which occurs in a social context (Hatim and Mason 1990). According to Seleskovitch and Lederer's Interpretive Theory of Translation, translation is divided into three processes: comprehension, deverbalisation, and re-expression (for a review, see Hurtado Albir and Alves 2009). Translation is also a cognitive activity, in which a translator performs a complex mental process that consists of comprehending the meaning of a text and subsequently formulating it using the resources found in another language, all while considering the needs of the recipient and the purpose of the translation (Hurtado Albir 2011).

We can also identify translation as a skill which involves knowing how to solve translation problems that arise in each occurrence (Hurtado Albir 2011). It is a kind of language production that can be analysed in terms of process and product (Mossop *et al.* 2005). Translation is also viewed as a form of communication through a change of language: it is an interlingual interpretive use that can be explained by relevance principles (Gutt 1991/2000) in which what is intended to be conveyed and how it is conveyed must be adequate to a specific audience.

Although interpreting is carried out in different contexts, the most common type is conference interpreting, which encompasses consecutive (CI) and simultaneous (SI). In both cases, communication is exclusively oral. Consecutive interpreting is that which is done after the utterance is complete: the speaker makes an utterance, stops for the interpreter to translate it, and so on (Gile 2006). Although consecutive interpreting is still much in demand (Gile 2006), it has been largely replaced by simultaneous interpreting (SI), which is carried out while the delegate is speaking. This mode of interpreting is commonly used in courts and legal contexts (for a review of SI, see Seeber 2015).

The increased presence of SI has aroused interest among researchers in explaining this complex task. Studies on SI have been well informed by psycholinguistic research on how languages are processed. This resulted in simplistic descriptions of this complex task, in terms of transcoding, or a simple replacement of a language units from one language to the other (see Gile 2006 for a review).

Although the research questions investigated in Translation Studies (TS) and interpreting studies (IS) are different, they intersect with their common denominator: bi/multilingualism. A topic that has yet to be extensively discussed is the role of bilingualism in translation and interpreting, when a high level of proficiency in two languages is indispensable. In TS, the PACTE (2003) research group's model of translation competence suggests that bilingual competence, which comprises pragmatic, socio-linguistic, textual, grammatical, and lexical knowledge, is a procedural knowledge required to communicate in two languages. Along with four other competences (extra-linguistic, knowledge about translation, instrumental, and strategic plus psycho-physiological components), bilingual competence plays an important role in solving translation problems (Ferreira 2013).

Wilss (1976) defines translation competence as a union of three partial competences: receptive competence, productive competence, and super-competence. The first is related to how translators understand the target text while the second competence refers to writing abilities. The third relates to the ability to transfer messages between two different linguistic systems. Under these assumptions, as discussed by Shreve (2012, 1), "knowing how to translate" is also related to having linguistic knowledge in L1 and L2 (e.g., being *bilingual*). According to Harris and Sherwood (1978, 155), "all bilinguals are able to translate, within the limits of their mastery of the two languages; therefore translating is coextensive with bilingualism." However, this "natural translation" is different from translation competence. The former is only one aspect of bilingual competence possessed by all bilinguals, while the latter is one which professional translators have (Lörscher 2012). Professional translators can translate not only because they are bilinguals but because they are trained to efficiently transfer meanings and forms from one language into the other.

Situating bilingualism in TS and IS can help to establish a better understanding of these competences. Lörscher (2012) presents an overview of bilingualism and translation competence. One interpretation of bilingualism he offers is that an individual is *bilingual* when s/he can be considered a native speaker in both languages, in each of the respective communities, which would imply rare cases of bilingualism. A second interpretation of bilingualism is broader and assumes that a bilingual is anyone who possesses one of the four language skills (listening, reading, speaking, and writing) in two languages (Macnamara 1967), or an individual who can produce "complete meaningful utterances in the other language" (Haugen 1956). However, a more contemporary view of bilingualism occupies a medial position between these two definitions. Based on work by Grosjean (2001), Lörscher argues that individuals are *bilingual* if they are capable of using two languages in the context of their daily lives. Competence in each context can vary with respect to the four language skills (speaking, writing, reading, and listening) and to the domain of the communication. Although the notion of bilingualism still remains complex, the fact that it is discussed by experts from various research areas (second language (L2) acquisition, psycholinguistics, sociology, psychology, international education, etc.) who use different methods to operationalise bilingualism, helps us to get closer to refining and capturing what it truly entails.

Historical perspectives

Translation activities have been conducted for some four or five thousand years (Santoyo 2006), and probably follow the consolidation of writing (Hurtado Albir 2011). As for interpreting, even though it became widespread in the post-war period, it has existed since Ancient Egypt. Santoyo (1987) refers to four periods through which translation has passed: oral translation, written translation, a reflection period, and translation theory. Hurtado Albir presents a rich review of the stages in the history of translation, from the first thoughts and manifestations on translation to modern theories which consider translation as a discipline of its own. This overview presents diverse theoretical approaches that are linguistic, textual, communicative, sociocultural, philosophical, and cognitive in nature. These approaches have been informed by topics focusing on, among others, translation processes and practical issues such as training and professional practice. Strategies, quality perception, translation competence, bi(multi)lingualism, and proficiency are a few of the variables that have been tested in scholarly venues dedicated to cognitive perspectives on translation (Ferreira and Schwieter 2015; Schwieter and Ferreira 2014a; Shreve and Angelone 2010).

Although research in TS is relatively new, the body of work that describes the translation process, translation product, and training has increased since the 1980s. Prior to this, research was based on philosophical or philological discussions in which theories were developed mainly based on experience (Orozco-Jutorán 2003). Methodologically speaking, early work consisted of corpus analyses or self-observations (Neunzig 1999). Similarly, research in IS has increased, even though it is "less mature and may be facing more fundamental questions about its identity and the way ahead" (Gile 1998, 69; see also Gambier, Gile, and Taylor 1997). In its early stages, work in IS was conducted by psychologists and educators. Perhaps one of the first publications to combine both fields was Sanz's (1930) report on observations and interviews with conference interpreters (Pöchhacker 2009). Prior to this, however, Herbert (1952), a former interpreter during the Paris peace negotiations of 1919, published *The Interpreter's Handbook: How to Become a Conference Interpreter*, anticipating a future for research in IS, and although research on interpreting was scarce until the 1960s, the momentum increased when experimental psychologists such as Oléron and Nanpon (1964) got involved. Soon after, several PhD dissertations were defended throughout the 1970s and 1980s.

By the time psychologists and conference interpreters began working on research on interpreting, there was also an interest in cognitive aspects of interpreting. Scientific studies were firstly carried out by psycholinguists and cognitive psychologists, but interpreting practitioners also carried out studies using methods different than those typically used in cognitive science. In the late 1980s, "practisearchers" (Gile 2015, 42) showed interest in cognitive psychology and it became apparent that there was a need for more scientific, objective studies, in light of the "speculative theorizing vs. empirical research" dichotomy (Gile 1990).

While we cannot go so far as to say that there was a shift in TS and IS towards cognitive science (Pöchhacker 2009), we also cannot deny that there were research implications for TS and IS upon the birth of community-based interpreting and the application of new technologies (e.g., remote interpreting). Because research approaches widened their scope, there has been an increase in the number of studies on a variety of topics such as memory, attentional control, performance, aptitude, teaching, history, the interpreter's role, and technology (for a review see Pöchhacker 2009). In the next section, we outline some of the key issues from research in cognitive bilingualism that have interfaced with TS and IS.

Core issues and topics

Language proficiency and directionality in translation

Several variables exploring cognitive aspects of bilingualism such as language comprehension and production, discourse processing, memory, attention, and expertise contribute to our understanding of translation and interpreting (Christoffels and De Groot 2005). Commonly, linguists are interested in processing differences between the first language (L1) and L2, and researchers in interpreting focus on competence and L2 proficiency (Gile 2015). In TS, we have seen an increased interest among psycholinguists to investigate the architecture and functionality of the bilingual memory and among translation experts to analyse both the translation processes and product.

Even though it is clear that being *proficient* is necessary in translation and interpreting, the exact definition of *proficiency* is still being debated. Defining levels of proficiency in both languages and the role of each language during translation performance might be related to how professionals carry out the task at hand (Ferreira 2013, 2014). L2 proficiency is influenced by several factors such as age of acquisition, similarity between languages, personality, motivation, L1 proficiency, and social economic status, among others (Ferreira *et al.* 2016). Most professional interpreters and translators are highly proficient in more than two languages, even though finding a perfectly-balanced bilingual is rare and, as a consequence, translators and interpreters are usually trained to translate from a passive to an active language (Hamers and Blanc 2000), or from the L2 to the L1 (Ferreira 2013), even though decoding from a passive language might impair the process required for the reconstruction of the text in the target language.

Interestingly, SI used to be carried out exclusively from the L1 into the L2 in the former Soviet Union (Seeber 2015). This practice was supported with reference to the fact that only a native speaker of the input language would be able to understand every nuance of the input, and it is clear that highly-developed language skills in both languages are crucial for translators and interpreters. However, those skills are not only related to specific aspects of language (e.g., grammar), but also to cognitive variables, verbal intelligence, general culture, and verbal-fluency factors (Carroll 1978).

Mental representations in the bilingual memory

How are is a concept that has two translation equivalents represented in the bilingual mind? Early explanations of lexical and conceptual representations in the bilingual memory entertained two possibilities: word association and concept mediation. Subsequent explanations were more developmental in nature. In Figure 16.1, we show three hypotheses about the bilingual memory and explain each below.

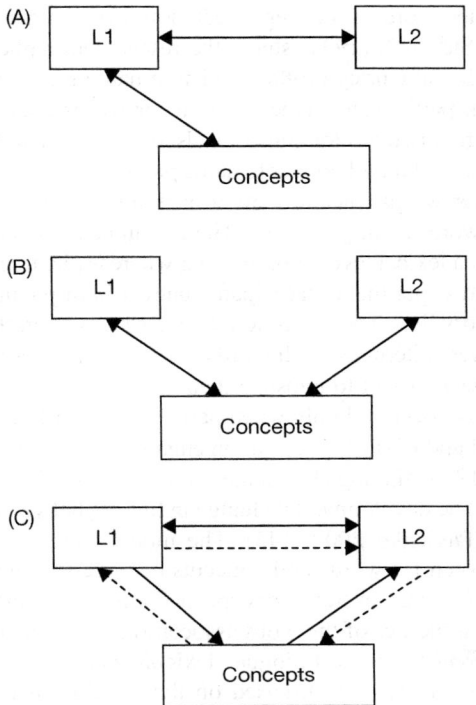

Figure 16.1 Three depictions of lexical and conceptual mediation in the bilingual memory: the word association model (A), the concept mediation hypothesis (B), and the Revised Hierarchical Model (C), adapted from Schwieter and Ferreira (2014b)

In Figure 16.1a, the word association hypothesis posits that a direct association exists between words in both languages but that access to the conceptual store must occur through L1 words. Putting it differently, according to the word association hypothesis, an L2 word is understood and produced by first retrieving its L1 word equivalent. However, other studies suggest that words in both languages may have direct access to the common conceptual store as can be seen in the concept mediation hypothesis (see Figure 16.1b). Support for the concept mediation hypothesis came from Potter *et al.* (1984) who carried out a study in which bilingual word translation performance was compared to picture naming. Results showed that it took longer to name pictures and the researchers argued that in bilingualism, access to concepts is required before a word is articulated.

Kroll and Curley (1988) tested the concept mediation hypothesis and found support for a developmental explanation in which there appeared to be a shift from reliance on word-to-word connections (at lower proficiency levels) to reliance on conceptual links (at higher proficiency levels). In order to assess whether conceptual access is influenced by the type of words to be translated or pictures to be named in both L1 and L2, the researchers predicted that the semantic organisation of the words and concepts would benefit only relatively fluent bilinguals. Results showed that more proficient participants took longer to translate the words into the L2 only when the words were of mixed categories, whereas it took longer to name pictures in the L1 when the list consisted of pictures of the same category.

As more research tested word vs. concept mediation, developmental explanations became favoured. In Kroll and Stewart's (1994) study, the researchers replicated the category interference effect from Kroll and Curley (1988) in picture naming and word translation in three experiments. In the first, participants named pictures or words only in their L1 in two conditions: in the same category (fruits, clothing, animals, etc.) or in mixed categories. Words were named faster than pictures and it took longer to name pictures in the categorised lists than in the randomised lists. In other words, picture naming was influenced by belonging to the same semantic category, but word naming was not. The researchers argued that word naming primarily reflects activity at a lexical level of processing whereas picture naming requires concept mediation. In the second experiment, participants named both pictures and words in same-category or mixed-category lists. There was no longer a category interference effect for picture naming when pictures were alternated with words. In the third experiment, instead of naming the words, participants were asked to translate them from L2 to L1 and from L1 to L2. The category interference effect occurred only when participants translated from the L1 to the L2, suggesting that L1-to-L2 and L2-to-L1 translation engage different interlanguage connections.

Kroll and Stewart's (1994) findings led to the proposal of the Revised Hierarchical Model (RHM) which captures "the developmental change in linking between L2 and L1 word forms and lexical concepts" (Pavlenko 2009, 143). The model suggests that as L2 proficiency increases, the links between L2 words and concepts become stronger, allowing for a direct link to the conceptual store and in turn, concept mediation. In some ways, we can see the RHM as a developmental merger of the word association and concept mediation models.

Cross-linguistic differences in the bilingual lexicon were described in the Distributed Feature Model (De Groot 1992, 1993), based on the conclusion that concrete words and cognates were translated faster than abstract words. Several studies (De Groot 1992, 1993; De Groot, Dannenburg, and Van Hell 1994; Kroll and Stewart 1994) have shown that while the representations of concrete words and cognates are shared across languages, abstract words share fewer semantic features. In fact, Dong, Cui, and MacWhinney's (2005) study revealed that conceptual representations of translation equivalents can be shared or partially separate for L1 and L2 and that links between words and concepts are stronger in the L1 compared to the L2, a finding also documented in translation experiments at the discourse level with proficient bilinguals (Ferreira 2013, 2014).

A dynamic view of the bilingual memory

Recently, researchers have begun to look at the architecture of the bilingual memory as a dynamic system which involves conceptual restructuring and overlapping. As seen in Figure 16.2a, the Modified Hierarchical Model (MHM; Pavlenko 2009) suggests that conceptual representations can be either: fully shared, partially overlapping, or not shared (i.e., language specific). Concepts are activated depending on the linguistic and social contexts in a two-way interaction between the mind and the environment. The model also recognises the importance of conceptual transfer, which relies on the differentiation between semantic and conceptual levels of representation. Semantic representation is related to knowledge of the number of concepts that are expressed by a specific word, and also to knowledge of the connections and relationships between words. A core element of the MHM is that the conceptual restructuring and development of linguistic categories in the target language is a main goal of bilingualism and is a gradual process.

Given that many professional translators and interpreters have knowledge of more than two languages, the Trilingual Modified Hierarchical Model (TMHM) (Benati and Schwieter

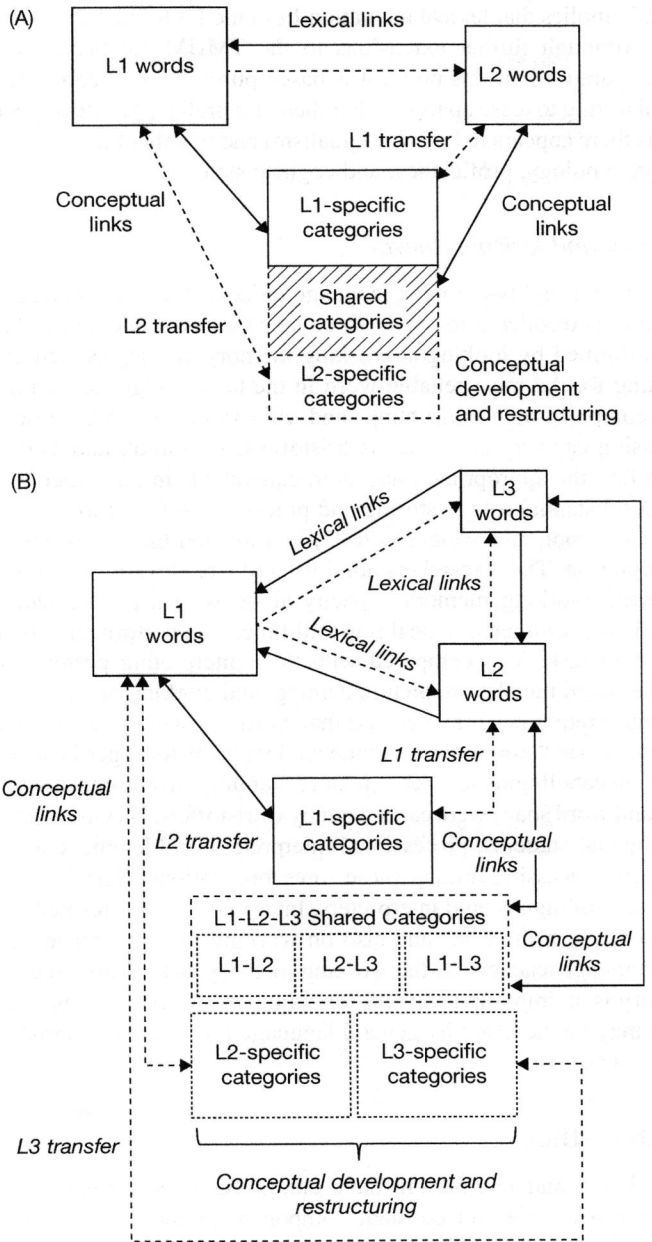

Figure 16.2 Dynamic views of bilingual and trilingual memory: the Modified Hierarchical Model (A) (Pavlenko 2009) and the Trilingual Modified Hierarchical Model (B) (Benati and Schwieter 2017)

2017), shown in Figure 16.2b, is particularly important to discuss. The addition of a third language implies that concepts can be shared between any two or all three of the languages. While maintaining the developmental strengths of the RHM, and the dynamic characteristic of conceptual overlapping and restructuring of the MHM, the TMHM proposes that the addition of an L3 implies that lexical mediation from the L3 to the L2 and from the L3 to the L1 can occur. Although further extensions to the TMHM are being made (Libben and Schwieter, in preparation), at this point, it is based purely upon theoretical speculation and merits empirical testing to tease apart whether there is a preferred route of lexical mediation in trilingualism (as there appears to be in bilingualism) and whether this is modulated by factors such as language typology, proficiency, and cognate status.

Working memory and lexical retrieval

In studies that analyse highly-complex language tasks such as interpreting, word-level analyses are sometimes considered too basic to be taken into consideration. However, research has been well informed by looking at working memory and lexical retrieval during interpreting. Searching for the most reliable word in the target language during translation and interpreting is complex, time consuming, and vulnerable to "break down due to loss of valuable processing capacity and time" (Christoffels, De Groot, and Waldorp 2003, 202). While trying to find the appropriate translation equivalents in the target language, working memory plays a substantial role in storing and processing information.

Christoffels, De Groot, and Waldorp (2003) investigated the role of memory and lexical retrieval in interpreting. The researchers administered a reading span task and a verbal digit span task to assess working memory capacity along with a picture naming and a word translation task which estimated lexical retrieval time. The performance by untrained bilinguals on these four tasks was compared with their interpreting performance. The results demonstrated that word translation, picture naming, and working memory to a lesser degree, correlate with interpreting performance and that word translation performance and working memory capacities form "(conditionally) independent paths to SI performance" (2003, 208).

A battery of psycholinguistic tasks (picture naming, word translation, reading span, speaking span, and word span) were carried out by Christoffels, De Groot, and Kroll (2006) in a study with bilingual students, professional interpreters, and language teachers in order to compare language processing among these three populations. Results showed significant differences between bilinguals and interpreters. Interpreters outperformed bilingual students in speed and accuracy in the tasks and also on working memory capacity. They only outperformed the language teachers on the working memory tasks. The researchers argued that "working memory is an important subskill for simultaneous interpreting whereas the role of lexical retrieval may be mediated by general language proficiency" (Christoffels, De Groot, and Kroll 2006, 343).

Main research methods

Studies on translation and interpreting have employed diverse methodologies. However, language has been a critical, yet constant component in each, albeit seen from different perspectives. Word span and reading span tasks, for instance, are commonly carried out in bilingual studies and have also been used to explain differences between bilinguals' and professional interpreters' working memory capacities (Christoffels, De Groot, and Kroll 2006). Studies on bilingual children normally use standardised measures of receptive vocabulary such as the Peabody Picture Vocabulary Test (Dunn and Dunn 1997) and its adaptations for languages other than English (e.g., the Spanish version *Test de Vocabulario en Imágenes Peabody* by Dunn *et al.* 1986), as well as measures of productive vocabulary (Expressive One Word Picture Vocabulary Test, Brownell 2000). These tasks are normally carried out as part of a series of tasks (e.g., language questionnaires, reading comprehension, reading fluency, etc.) and correlational analyses between vocabulary and other variables are conducted to explain variations in language and cognitive development in bilinguals (Ferreira, Schwieter, and Gile 2015).

TS and IS have been using methodologies from linguistics, literacy research, and cognitive and developmental psychology, among other disciplines, for decades. While tasks such as the Verbal Fluency Measure (Gollan, Montoya, and Werner 2002), commonly used in research on bilingualism, might not tell us much about a translator's or interpreter's language profile (Ferreira *et al.* 2016), there are a number of other tasks that have explanatory power for translation processes, across a spectrum of language learners, bilinguals, and novice and expert translators and interpreters. In the 1990s, the use of quantitative measures in TS and IS increased as psycholinguists and psychologists became interested in TS and IS (Gile 1991). Recent advancements in technology have further increased the presence of these measures. IS has particularly moved away from formal linguistic approaches (reflection, theory, and critique) towards empirical approaches (Ferreira, Schwieter, and Gile 2015). Whereas studies on bilingualism comprise a range of participant types, translation and interpreting research focuses mainly on highly proficient bi/multilinguals. Furthermore, in both TS and IS, the use of multiple data collection methods to elicit different types of data (e.g., triangulation) is a common practice that helps to strengthen the conclusions drawn from data analyses and to assure validity in research design.

SI is one of the most complex language processing tasks imaginable (Frauenfelder and Schriefers 1997). Few other language tasks combine the need to comprehend and produce speech simultaneously, and to concurrently command and control two languages. Understanding SI may be of great interest to cognitive psychologists and psycholinguists because of the demanding nature of SI in terms of online processing and control. Word translation and word- or picture-naming tasks have been used to investigate language control, suppression, and lexical retrieval. Language direction and cognate status are a few examples of variables that have been under scrutiny (Gernsbacher and Shlesinger 1997; Macizo and Bajo 2006; Ibáñez, Macizo, and Bajo 2010; Schwieter and Ferreira 2014b; among others). In these experiments, words, pictures, or sentences are randomly presented on a computer screen and participants are asked to simply name or translate what appears in front of them. Reaction time (in ms) and accuracy (in %) are usually the variables measured and analysed. In addition, it is common practice to ask participants to fill in self-rating language questionnaires and participate in tasks that measure working memory.

In research on translation processes, several methods have been employed including keystroke and mouse logging, screen recording, eye tracking, retrospection, interviews, and quality revision. Mouse and keyboard activities, pause patterns, and visual replay functions have been broadly investigated (Göpferich 2009; Ferreira 2014) using Translog (Jakobsen and Schou 1999) as a research tool. Screen recording is used to analyse how translators deal with a particular segment (editing processes, mouse clicks, etc.), to estimate the external resources relied on during a task (e.g., internet browser), and even to record facial expressions. One of the most popular softwares for screen recording is TechSmith's Camtasia Studio which has been used in a number of studies (O'Brien 2006; Göpferich, Alves, and Mees 2009; Angelone 2010).

Studies using eye-tracking technology have also gained popularity (O'Brien 2006, 2009; Pavlović 2009; Ferreira *et al.* 2016). This approach tracks eye movements and maps them onto what is displayed on a screen. This allows the researcher to analyse several aspects of fixations such as gaze time, average fixation duration, total task length, pupil dilation, etc., in each area of interest presented on the screen (source text, target text, external support) (Ferreira *et al.* 2016). Neuroimaging techniques have also been highly useful in TS and IS through positron emission tomography (PET) (Rinne *et al.* 2000; Tommola *et al.* 2000); functional magnetic resonance imaging (fMRI) and event-related potentials (ERPs) in electroencephalography (EEG) have also been employed (Kraushaar and Lambert 1987; Gran and Fabbro 1988; Grabner *et al.* 2007).

Retrospections and think aloud protocols offer a qualitative approach to investigating translation processes. While retrospections are assumed to be less cognitively demanding and to not affect the translation process because they are carried out after the task, think aloud protocols are conducted while translators are working on the task, which slows down the translation process (Krings 2001; Jakobsen 2003). In order to assess translator profiles and to homogenise participant groups, researchers commonly gather descriptive data that detail participant characteristics (Ferreira 2013; Michael *et al.* 2014). Questionnaires such as the Language Product Evaluation Tool (LPET) can also be used to measure text quality. The LPET combines rubric- and check-list-approaches to analyse the factors that comprise translation quality (Michael *et al.* 2014). Several dimensions of quality can be evaluated such as significance, completeness, accuracy, omission of irrelevant information, organisation, and writing (Michael, Massaro, and Perlman 2009).

Regarding the quality of translation produced by bilinguals, case studies are commonly conducted, usually employing indirect observation (e.g., an analysis of audio- or video-recorded data) and interviews. Some studies also analyse descriptive data, in which certain parameters are met and coded into quantitative data and statistically analysed (Dam 2004; Szabo 2006). Overall, questionnaires, observations, tests, and individual and group interviews (face-to-face and phone) are among the most common data collection methods in measuring quality in TS and IS. Quantitative analyses are commonly carried out through descriptive, inferential, and correlational statistics, along with speech data (for audio-recorded data). Qualitative measures focus on aspects such as the role of the interpreter, specificities of each mode (community interpreting, healthcare interpreting, court interpreting, etc.), linguistic variation (discourse analysis), adaptation, and strategies.

Current debates

TS and IS have expanded in very different ways and as detailed above, many theories and models have been proposed and new research methods have been developed and improved due to the collaborative nature of TS, IS, and research on bilingualism. Technology is constantly bringing new approaches and questions to research and has changed the way translators and interpreters approach the profession. Post-editing machine translation is now a common practice that has evolved considerably since the late 1960s (see Sin-wai 2015 for a review). In SI, interpreting booths are still used, but are now equipped with video screens. Personal computers and the internet are also commonly used to access documents and terminology databases (Seeber 2015). Technology has also made remote medical interpretation a common practice, raising concerns about perceptions of quality (Locatis *et al.* 2010).

Quality is key not only in educational programmes in translation and interpreting, but also in the development of instruments for professional certifications and the creation of research methods and procedures. Models of translation quality that have attempted to explain *how* quality should be measured have not come to an agreement (e.g., in terms of reader response, acceptability, function) (see Angelelli and Jacobson 2009, for a review). Similarly, researchers in IS are still debating whether quality is related to an interpreter's performance and/or role (Angelelli 2001), and very likely debates in bilingualism, translation, and interpreting will continue to focus on translation quality and the role of technologies in TS and IS.

High-level language proficiency is essential in cross-cultural language communication, and language education can benefit from faster and better language tools which can speed up the process of bi/multilingual communication. The way in which organisations and people interact in real time around the world has drastically changed in the last decade as a result of the use of digital technologies which have diversified and developed bilinguals' communication abilities and increased the need for interaction among translation and interpreting professionals.

Future directions

As discussed above, new technologies in instantaneous, bilingual communication emerge, research on several areas related to bilingualism, translation, and interpreting has developed. These new technologies have changed the way in which research in TS and IS is conducted. Machine translation (MT) is a cost-effective way to translate, even though it requires high-quality human revision. Because MT has improved in terms of quality and accessibility (e.g., it is free and available on many websites), it has become very popular among users and researchers. As for interpreting, the use of technologies such as VoIP (Voice or Video over Internet Protocol) and video-link for remote interpreting is up-and-coming. With regard to language learning, students benefit from search engines and access to an infinite amount of material.

Researchers have discussed how bilingual dominance and directionality in translation affect the way interpreting and translation are carried out. While it has been argued that translators and interpreters should only work into their L1 (Newmark 1988; Bros-Brann 1976), this is not realistic in many settings and is an issue for future research so that this controversial topic is not based on assumptions rather than empirical evidence (Gile 2005; Ferreira 2014). Analysing the effects of directionality in translation might shed light on the development of training strategies to rectify deficiencies in translation and interpreting tasks into a non-native language (Gile 2005).

Implications for practice

Debates have focused on the fact that translation and interpreting competences are different from bilingual competence, and that bilingual competence is an important prerequisite for translation and interpreting training. Because translating and interpreting into the L2 is a common practice, European training courses are taught on a regular basis in the L2. Technology has played an important role in these courses as they offer translation practice in several languages using MT, localisation tools, and translation memories. Technology and innovative methodologies have also helped to investigate how processing of two languages from the word to discourse level takes place. As discussed throughout the chapter, developmental theories of bilingualism have helped to explain mental representations and presented a "wealth of fruitful information that can be quite revealing for studies in translation processes" (Schwieter and Ferreira 2014b, 88). They explain oral word translation as either a lexically or conceptually mediated procedure as modulated by the translation direction and proficiency level. Studying how an L2 develops during the transformation of language learner to bilingual, translator, or interpreter – especially with innovative, new technologies – will help to refine our understanding of what it means to be bilingual and how the translation and interpreting processes cognitively function.

Further reading

Christoffels, I. and De Groot, A. 2005. "Simultaneous Interpreting: A Cognitive Perspective". In *Handbook of Bilingualism: Psycholinguistic Approaches*, edited by J. Kroll and A. De Groot, 454–479. New York: Oxford University Press.
This chapter discusses possible cognitive subskills of simultaneous interpreting and asks whether experience in interpreting is related to specific capabilities.

Gile, D. 2005. "Directionality in Conference Interpreting: A Cognitive View". In *Directionality in Interpreting. The "Retour" or the Native?*, edited by R. Godijns, and M. Hindedael, 9–26. Ghent: Communication and Cognition.
This chapter outlines relevant factors in interpreting studies and explains how directionality and other variables explain (ir)regularities in conference interpreting.

Hurtado Albir, A. 2011. *Traducción y traductología. Introducción a la traductología*. Madrid: Cátedra.
The book is a well-compiled introduction to TS. Chapter 3 in particular brings a critical examination on how the field has evolved.

Schwieter, J. W. and Ferreira, A., eds. 2014a. *The Development of Translation Competence: Theories and Methodologies from Psycholinguistics and Cognitive Science*. Newcastle upon Tyne: Cambridge Scholars Publishing.
This book presents original studies from perspectives in psycholinguistics and cognitive science with the common goal of better understanding the development of linguistic competence that translators need to be effective professionals.

Related topics

Language disorders, interpreting, and translation; Language processing in translation.

References

Angelelli, C. 2001. *Deconstructing the Invisible Interpreter: A Critical Study of the Interpersonal Role of the Interpreter in a Cross-Cultural/Linguistic Communicative Event*. PhD Thesis. Stanford University.
Angelelli, C. V. and Jacobson, H. E. 2009. "Introduction. Testing and Assessment in Translation and Interpreting Studies. A Call for Dialogue Between Research and Practice". In *Testing and Assessment in Translation and Interpreting Studies* (American Translators Association Scholarly Monograph Series XIV), edited by C. Angelelli and H. E. Jacobson, 1–10. Amsterdam: John Benjamins.
Angelone, E. 2010. Uncertainty, uncertainty management and metacognitive problem solving in the translation task. *Translation and Cognition* 15, pp. 17–40.
Benati, A. and Schwieter, J. W. 2017. "Input Processing and Processing Instruction: Pedagogical and Cognitive Considerations for L3 Acquisition". In *L3 Syntactic Transfer: Models, New Developments, and Implications*, edited by T. Angelovska and A. Hahn, 253–275. Amsterdam: Benjamins.
Bros-Brann, E. 1976. Critical comments on H. C. Barik's article "Interpreters talk a lot, among other things". *AIIC Bulletin* 4(1), pp. 16–18.
Brownell, R. 2000. *Expressive One-Word Picture Vocabulary Test*. 3rd ed. Novato: Academic Therapy Publications.
Carroll, J. B. 1978. "Linguistic Abilities in Translators and Interpreters". In *Language Interpretation and Communication*, edited by D. Gerver and H. W. Sinaiko, 119–130. New York: Plenum Press.
Christoffels, I. and De Groot, A. 2005. "Simultaneous Interpreting: A Cognitive Perspective". In *Handbook of Bilingualism: Psycholinguistic Approaches*, edited by J. Kroll and A. De Groot, 454–479. New York: Oxford University Press.

Christoffels, I., De Groot, A. and Kroll, J. 2006. Memory and language skills in simultaneous interpreters: the role of expertise and language proficiency. *Journal of Memory and Language* 54(3), pp. 324–345.

Christoffels, I., De Groot, A. and Waldorp, L. 2003. Basic skills in a complex task: a graphical model relating memory and lexical retrieval to simultaneous interpreting. *Bilingualism: Language and Cognition* 6, pp. 201–211.

Dam, H. V. 2004. Interpreters' notes: on the choice of language. *Interpreting* 6(1), pp. 3–17.

De Groot, A. M. B. 1992. "Bilingual Lexical Representation: A Closer Look at Conceptual Representations". In *Orthography, Phonology, Morphology, and Meaning*, edited by R. Frost and L. Katz, 389–412. Amsterdam: Elsevier.

De Groot, A. M. B. 1993. "Word-Type Effects in Bilingual Processing Tasks: Support for a Mixed Representational System". In *The Bilingual Lexicon*, edited by R. Schreuder and B. Weltens, 27–51. Amsterdam: John Benjamins.

De Groot, A. M. B., Dannenburg, L. and Van Hell, J. G. 1994. Forward and backward word translation by bilinguals. *Journal of Memory and Language* 33, pp. 600–629.

Dong, Y., Cui, S. and MacWhinney, B. 2005. Shared and separate meanings in the bilingual mental lexicon. *Bilingualism: Language and Cognition* 8, pp. 221–238.

Dunn, L. M. and Dunn, L. M. 1997. *Peabody Picture Vocabulary Test*. 3rd ed. Circle Pines, MN: American Guidance Service.

Dunn, L. M., Lugo, D., Padilla, E. and Dunn, L. M. 1986. *Test de Vocabulario en Imágenes Peabody*. Circle Pines, MN: American Guidance Service.

Ferreira, A. 2013. *Direcionalidade em tradução: o papel da subcompetência bilíngue em tarefas de tradução L1 e L2*. PhD Thesis. Federal University of Minas Gerais.

Ferreira, A. 2014. Analyzing recursiveness patterns and retrospective protocols of professional translators in L1 and L2 translation tasks. *Translation and Interpreting Studies* 9(1), pp. 109–127.

Ferreira, A. and Schwieter, J. W., eds. 2015. *Psycholinguistic and Cognitive Inquiries into Translation and Interpreting*. Amsterdam: John Benjamins.

Ferreira, A., Schwieter, J. W. and Gile, D. 2015. "The Position of Psycholinguistic and Cognitive Science in Translation and Interpreting: An Introduction". In *Psycholinguistic and Cognitive Inquires into Translation and Interpreting*, edited by A. Ferreira and J. W. Schwieter, 3–16. Amsterdam: John Benjamins.

Ferreira, A., Schwieter, J. W., Gottardo, A. and Jones, J. A. 2016. Cognitive effort in direct and inverse translation performance: insight from eye-tracking technology. *Cadernos de Tradução* 36(3), pp. 60–80.

Frauenfelder, U. and Schriefers, H. 1997. A psycholinguistic perspective on simultaneous interpreting. *Interpreting* 2, pp. 55–89.

Gambier, Y., Gile, D. and Taylor, C., eds. 1997. *Conference Interpreting: Current Trends in Research*. Amsterdam: John Benjamins.

Gernsbacher, M. A. and Shlesinger, M. 1997. The proposed role of suppression in simultaneous interpretation. *Interpreting* 2, pp. 119–140.

Gile, D. 1990. "Scientific Research vs. Personal Theories in the Investigation of Interpretation". In *Aspects of Applied and Experimental Research on Conference Interpretation*, edited by L. Gran and C. Taylor, 28–41. Udine: Campanotto Editore.

Gile, D. 1991. Methodological aspects of interpretation and translation research. *Target* 3(2), pp. 154–174.

Gile, D. 1998. Observational studies and experimental studies in the investigation of conference interpreting. *Target* 10(1), pp. 69–93.

Gile, D. 2005. "Directionality in Conference Interpreting: A Cognitive View". In *Directionality in Interpreting: The "Retour" or the Native?*, edited by R. Godijns and M. Hindedael, 149–158. Ghent: Communication and Cognition.

Gile, D. 2006. Conference interpreting. *Encyclopedia of Language and Linguistics* 2(3), pp. 6–9.

Gile, D. 2015. "The Contributions of Cognitive Psychology and Psycholinguistics to Conference Interpreting". In *Psycholinguistic and Cognitive Inquires into Translation and Interpreting*, edited by A. Ferreira and J. W. Schwieter, 41–66. Amsterdam: John Benjamins.

Gollan, T. H., Montoya, R. I. and Werner, G. A. 2002. Semantic and letter fluency in Spanish-English bilinguals. *Neuropsychology* 16(4), pp. 562–576.

Göpferich, S. 2009. "Towards a Model of Translation Competence and Its Acquisition: The Longitudinal Study TransComp". In *Behind the Mind: Methods, Models and Results in the Translation Process Research*, edited by S. Göpferich, A. L. Jakobsen and I. M. Mees, 11–37. Copenhagen: Samfundslitteratur.

Göpferich, S., Alves, F., and Mees, I. M., eds. 2009. *New Approaches in Translation Process Research*. Copenhagen Studies in Language 39. Copenhagen: Samfundslitteratur.

Grabner, R. H., Brunner, C., Leeb, R., Neuper, C., Pfurtscheller, G. 2007. Event-related EEG theta and alpha band oscillatory responses during language translation. *Brain Research Bulletin* 72(1), pp. 57–65.

Gran, L. and Fabbro, F. 1988. The role of neuroscience in the teaching of interpretation. *The Interpreters' Newsletter* 1, pp. 23–41.

Grosjean, F. 2001. "The Bilingual's Language Modes". In *One Mind, Two Languages: Bilingual Language Processing*, edited by J. L. Nicol, 1–22. Oxford: Blackwell.

Gutt, E.-A. 1991/2000. *Translation and Relevance. Cognition and Context*. Oxford: Blackwell; Manchester: St Jerome.

Hamers, J. F. and Blanc, M. H. A. 2000. *Bilinguality and Bilingualism*. Cambridge: Cambridge University Press.

Harris, B. 1976. The importance of natural translation. *Working Papers on Bilingualism* 12, pp. 96–144. Reprinted as *Working Papers in Translatology 2*. Ottawa: University of Ottawa.

Harris, B. and Sherwood, B. 1978. Translating as an innate skill. *Language Interpretation and Communication* 6, pp. 155–170.

Hatim, B. and Mason, I. 1990. *Discourse and the Translator*. London: Longman.

Haugen, E. 1956. *Bilingualism in the Americas: A Bibliography and Research Guide*. Alabama: University of Alabama Press.

Herbert, J. 1952. *The Interpreter's Handbook: How to Become a Conference Interpreter*. Genève: Libraire de l'université, Georg & Cie S.A.

Hurtado Albir, A. 2011. *Traducción y traductología. Introducción a la traductología*. Madrid: Cátedra.

Hurtado Albir, A. and Alves, F. 2009. "Translation as a Cognitive Activity". In *The Routledge Companion to Translation Studies*, edited by J. Munday, 54–73. New York: Routledge.

Ibáñez, A. J., Macizo, P. and Bajo, M. T. 2010. Language access and language selection in professionaltranslators. *Acta Psychologica* 135(2), pp. 257–266.

Jakobsen, A. L. 2003. "Effects of Think Aloud on Translation Speed, Revision and Segmentation". In *Triangulating Translation: Perspectives in Process Oriented Research*, edited by F. Alves, 69–95. Amsterdam: John Benjamins.

Jakobsen, A. L. and Schou, L. 1999. "Translog Documentation". In *Probing the Process in Translation*, edited by G. Hansen, 151–186. Copenhagen: Samfundsliteratur.

Kraushaar, B. and Lambert, S. 1987. Shadowing proficiency according to ear of input and type of bilinguality. *Bulletin of the Canadian Association of Applied Linguistics* 9(1), pp. 17–31.

Krings, H. 2001. *Repairing Texts: Empirical Investigations of Machine Translation Post-Editing Processes*, edited by S. Koby. Ohio: Kent State University Press.

Kroll, J. F. and Curley, J. 1988. *Picture Naming and Bilingual Translation*. Unpublished manuscript. South Hadley, MA: Mount Holyoke College.

Kroll, J. and Stewart, E. 1994. Category interference in translation and picture naming: Evidence for asymmetric connections between bilingual memory representations. *Journal of Memory and Language* 33, pp. 149–174.

Locatis, C., Williamson, D., Gould-Kabler, C., Zone-Smith, L., Detzler, I., Roberson, J, Maisiak R. and Ackerman, M. 2010. Comparing in-person, video, and telephonic medical interpretation. *Journal of General Internal Medicine* 25(4), pp. 345–350.

Lörscher, W. 2012. Bilingualism and translation competence. *SYNAPS: A Journal of Professional Communication* 27, pp. 3–15.

Macizo, P. and Bajo, M. T. 2006. Reading for understanding and reading for translation: do they involve the same processes? *Cognition* 99, pp. 1–34.

Macnamara, J. 1967. The bilingual's linguistic performance: A psychological overview. *Journal of Social Issues* 23, pp. 58–77.

Michael, E. B., Massaro, D. and Perlman, M. 2009. What's the bottom line? Development of and potential uses for the Summary Translation Evaluation Tool (STET). *The Next Wave* 18, pp. 42–49.

Michael, E. B., Sarner, L., Massaro, D., Bailey, B., de Terra, D., Messenger, S., Rhoad, K., Castle, S. and Campbell, S. G. 2014. "Establishing Standards and Metrics for Translation: Experiments to Validate the Language Product Evaluation Tool". In *The Development of Translation Competence: Theories and Methodologies from Psycholinguistics and Cognitive Science*, edited by J. W. Schwieter and A. Ferreira, 166–199. Newcastle upon Tyne: Cambridge Scholars Publishing.

Mossop, B., Gutt, E., Peeters, J., Klaudy, K., Setton, R. and Tirkkonen-Condit, S. 2005. Back to translation as language. *Across Languages and Cultures* 6(2), pp. 143–172.

Neunzig, W. 1999. *Sobre la investigación empírica en traductología cuestiones epistémicas y meto-dológicas*. Trabajo de investigación inédito. Universitat Autònoma de Barcelona, Departament de Traducció i d'Interpretació.

Newmark, P. 1988. *A Textbook of Translation*. New York: Prentice Hall.

O'Brien, S. 2006. Eye-tracking and translation memory matches. *Perspectives: Studies in Translatology* 14(3), pp. 185–203.

O'Brien, S. 2009. "Eye Tracking in Translation-Process Research: Methodological Challenges and Solutions." In *Methodology, Technology and Innovation in Translation Process Research* (Copen-hagen Studies in Language 38), edited by I. M. Mees, F. Alves and S. Göpferich, 251–266. Copenhagen: Samfundslitteratur.

Oléron, P. and Nanpon, H. 1964. Recherches sur la repetition orale de mots presents audivement. *L'Annee Psychologies* 64, pp. 397–410.

Orozco-Jutorán, M. 2003. "Review of Empirical Research in Written Translation." Dipòsit Digital de Documents de la UAB [online]. Available from: <http://gent.uab.cat/marianaorozco/sites/gent.uab.cat.marianaorozco/files/Review_Orozco_DDD.pdf> [Accessed 25 August 2015].

PACTE. 2003. "Building a Translation Competence Model". In *Triangulating Translation: Perspec-tives in Process Oriented Research*, edited by F. Alves, 43–66. Amsterdam: John Benjamins.

Pavlenko, A. 2009. "Conceptual Representation in the Bilingual Lexicon and Second Language Vocabulary Learning". In *The Bilingual Mental Lexicon: Interdisciplinary Approaches*, edited by A. Pavlenko, 125–160. Bristol: Multilingual Matters.

Pavlović, N. 2009. "More Ways to Explore the Translating Mind: Collaborative Translation Protocols". In *Behind the Mind*, edited by S. Gopferich, A. L. Jakobsen and I. M. Mees, 81–105. Copenhagen: Samfundslitteratur.

Pöchhacker, F. 2009. "The Turns of Interpreting Studies". In *Efforts and Models in Interpreting and Translation Research: A tribute to Daniel Gile*, edited by G. Hansen, A. Chesterman and H. Gerzymisch-Arbogast, 25–46. Amsterdam: John Benjamins.

Potter, C. M., Kwok-Fai So, K., von Eckart, B. and Feldman, L. B. 1984. Lexical and conceptual representation in beginning and proficient bilinguals. *Journal of Verbal Learning and Verbal Behav-iour* 23, pp. 23–38.

Rinne, J. O., Tommola, J., Laine, M., Krause, B. J., Schmidt, D. and Kassinen, V. 2000. The translating brain: cerebral activation patterns during simultaneous interpreting. *Neuroscience Letter* 294, pp. 85–88.

Santoyo, J. C. 1987. *Traducción, Traducciones, Traductores. Ensayo de bibliografía española*. León: Universidad de León, Secretariado de Publicaciones.

Santoyo, J. C. 2006. "Blank Spaces in the History of Translation". In *Charting the Future of Translation History*, edited by G. L. Bastin and P. F. Bandia, 11–44. Ottawa: University of Ottawa Press.

Sanz, J. 1930. *Le travail et les aptitudes des interpreters*. Washington, DC: Gallaudet University Press.

Schwieter, J. W. and Ferreira, A., eds. 2014a. *The Development of Translation Competence: Theories and Methodologies from Psycholinguistics and Cognitive Science*. Newcastle upon Tyne: Cambridge Scholars Publishing.

Schwieter, J. W. and Ferreira, A., eds. 2014b. "Underlying Processes of L1 and L3 Word Translation: Exploring the Semantic Relatedness Effect". In *The Development of Translation Competence: Theories and Methodologies from Psycholinguistics and Cognitive Science*, edited by J. W. Schwieter and A. Ferreira, 87–106. Newcastle: Cambridge Scholars Press.

Schwieter, J. W. and Ferreira, A., eds. 2017. *The Handbook of Translation and Cognition*. Malden, MA and Oxford: Wiley-Blackwell.

Seeber, K. G. 2015. "Simultaneous Interpreting". In *The Routledge Handbook of Interpreting*, edited by H. Mikkelson and R. Jourdenais, 79–95. New York: Routledge.

Seleskovitch, D. and Lederer, M. 1984. *Interpréter pour traduire, Col. Traductologie, 1*. París: Didier Érudition.

Shreve, G. 2012. "Bilingualism and Translation". In *Handbook of Translation Studies*, edited by Y. Gambier and L. van Doorslaer, 1–6. Amsterdam: John Benjamins.

Shreve, G. and Angelone, E., eds. 2010. *Translation and Cognition*. Amsterdam: John Benjamins.

Sin-wai, C. 2015. "The Development of Translation Technology". In *Routledge Encyclopedia of Translation Technology*, edited by C. Sin-wai, 3–31. New York: Routledge.

Szabo, C. 2006. Language choice in note-taking for consecutive interpreting. *Interpreting* 8(2), pp. 129–147.

Tommola, J., Laine, M., Sunnari, M and Rinne, J. O. 2000. Images of shadowing and interpreting. *Interpreting* 5(2), pp. 147–157.

Vinay, J. P. and Darbelnet, J. 1958. *Stylistique comparée du français et de l'anglais*. Paris: Didier.

Wilss, W. 1976. "Perspectives and Limitations of a Didactic Framework for the Teaching of Translation." In *Translation applications and research*, edited by R. W. Brislin, 117–137. New York: Gardner.

17

Language disorders, interpreting, and translation

Alfredo Ardila

Introduction

The study of the language disorders associated with brain pathology (aphasias) represents the real beginning of cognitive and behavioural neurosciences. The analysis of aphasia as a matter of fact is a crucial question not only for neurology and related clinical areas, but also for linguistics, neuropsychology, psychology, and speech therapy. Throughout contemporary history, aphasia has been and continues as one of the most significant and extensively analysed brain syndromes.

Aphasia can be defined as the loss or impairment of language caused by brain damage (Benson and Ardila 1996). The modern conception of aphasia was introduced in 1861 at the Anthropological Society of Paris when Paul Broca presented the case of an individual who suffered a loss of language associated with brain pathology; the patient had a very limited expressive language (virtually limited to a syllable: "tan"), produced with effort; language grammar was absent. Thirteen years later Karl Wernicke described a second type of language disorder characterised by defects in language understanding.

In this chapter three different questions will be approached. Initially, a clinical description of the language disorders associated with brain pathology will be presented. A distinction will be introduced between the fundamental or major aphasic syndromes (Wernicke's and Broca's aphasia) impairing language phonology, lexicon, semantics and, grammar, on the one hand; and other aphasic syndromes affecting the ability to produce language or the executive control of the language, on the other. In the following section, the brain organisation of language in bilinguals will be examined; it will be emphasised that there are some crucial variables (such as the age of acquisition of the second language) that significantly affect the pattern of organisation of the language in the brain. In the last section the question of aphasia in bilinguals will be approached; different patterns of clinical manifestation and recovery will be distinguished. Disturbances in the translation ability observed in bilinguals will be considered.

Language disorders associated with brain pathology

Since the 19th century, it has been well established that there are two major and fundamental aphasic syndromes, named in different ways, but roughly corresponding to Wernicke-type aphasia and Broca-type aphasia (e.g., Albert *et al.* 1981; Ardila 2014; Benson and Ardila 1996; Head 1926; Hécaen 1972; Kertesz 1979). These two major aphasic syndromes have been related to two basic linguistic operations: selecting (language as paradigm) and sequencing (language as syntagm) (Jakobson 1971; Jakobson and Halle 1956; Luria 1972/ 1983). In cases of brain pathology it can be observed that an individual may lose the ability to use language in two rather different ways: the language impairment can be situated on the paradigmatic axis (similarity disorder) (found in Wernicke's aphasia), or the syntagmatic axis (contiguity disorder) (found in Broca's aphasia). Thus, in cases of brain pathology language can be impaired in two different ways: at the lexical/semantic level (in Wernicke's aphasia) or at the grammatical level (in Broca's aphasia). Consequently, so-called Wernicke's and Broca's aphasia represent the major (or fundamental) aphasic syndromes

Major aphasic disorders

Wernicke's aphasia

Wernicke's aphasia (also known as sensory or receptive aphasia) results from pathology in Wernicke's area. Wernicke's area corresponds to the auditory association area of the left hemisphere of the brain. The primary auditory area corresponds to Brodmann's area (BA) 41 (Heschel's gyrus, or the transverse temporal gyrus), and some authors also include BA42. It can be assumed that Wernicke's area (the auditory association area of the left hemisphere) corresponds to BA22, BA21, and BA37; frequently BA39 is also included (see Figure 17.1).

In Wernicke's aphasia word-finding difficulties are evident, the patient's vocabulary is decreased, and language-understanding disturbances are significant. Wernicke's aphasia patients may not fully discriminate the acoustic information contained in speech, that is, they may fail to recognise the language phonemes (a defect known as auditory verbal agnosia). Lexical (word) and semantic (meaning) associations may also become deficient. In Wernicke's aphasia the language deficit can consequently be situated at three different levels: at the level of language sound (phonemes) recognition, at the level of vocabulary use and understanding (lexicon), and finally at the level of semantic associations (word meaning comprehension). Phoneme and word selection are deficient, but language syntax is well preserved and even overused.

Speech is produced without effort. No articulatory defects (dysarthria) are observed. Fluency is normal and frequently there is excessive language output. Often extra syllables in words and extra words in sentences are found; this excessive amount of language without a clear meaning is referred to as logorrhoea. Because of the relative absence of meaningful words (so-called "empty speech") and the excessive language output, an overuse of grammatical words (frequently incorrectly selected) is found; this phenomenon is known as paragrammatism (or dyssyntaxis). Dyssyntaxis has been defined as "Pathological linguistic productions in which are observed a fairly large number of sentences that transgress one or more of the normative rules of the community's morphosyntactic convention" (Berube 1991, 62).

Paraphasias (i.e., incorrectly produced words) are abundant. Paraphasias can be both phonological (i.e., the phonological sequence is incorrect because of phoneme substitutions, additions, or omissions) and verbal (a word is replaced by another – usually semantically related – word), even though phonological or verbal paraphasias can predominate in a specific patient. Frequently, neologisms (understandable pseudo-words) are also found. When a patient presents abundant (even excessive) verbal output that is difficult to understand due to

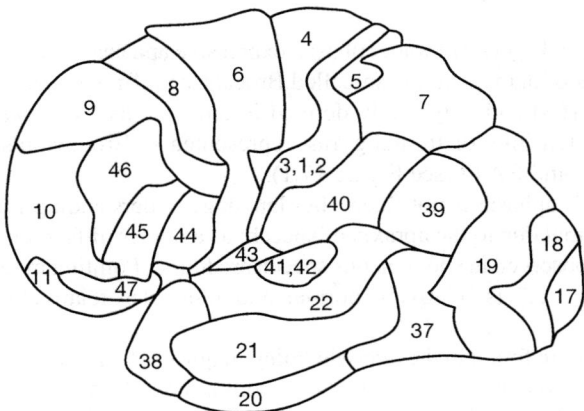

Figure 17.1 Wernicke's area roughly corresponds to Brodmann's areas 22, 21, and 37, although 39 is also frequently included

the significant amount of paraphasias and neologisms and a relative absence of meaningful words (nouns), the term jargonaphasia is frequently used.

These patients present significant difficulties in language understanding. However, language-understanding impairments present significant variations according to different contextual conditions. When short sentences are used, it is notoriously easier for the patient to understand; increasing the number of words in speech results in more severe language-understanding defects. Language understanding requires an increased attention and continuous effort (similar to the attention and effort required to understand a foreign language). Usually at the beginning of the conversation the patient has very remarkable language comprehension defects, but progressively language understanding increases. The language understanding remains relatively high for some short time (maybe 15 or 20 minutes), but later it begins to decrease (this is known as the "fatigue phenomenon"). Furthermore, if changes in the conversational topic are introduced, language understanding immediately decreases. So, language-understanding difficulties are variable according to the specific conversational conditions.

It is assumed that there are two major defects accounting for the language-understanding defects in Wernicke's aphasia. (1) Defects in phoneme discrimination; the extreme situation (i.e., complete inability to discriminate speech phonemes) corresponds to the so-called "pure word-deafness" syndrome. Usually, patients with Wernicke's aphasia have some defects in phoneme discrimination; in severe cases, the patient can suggest that s/he is unable to understand the phonological composition of speech (for instance, s/he may state that other people seem to be speaking using a foreign language, or even that they are not really speaking but making noises). (2) Defects in verbal memory: the patient cannot recall the previously learned verbal information, such as words, sentences, and in general verbal knowledge (i.e., there is a retrograde verbal amnesia); and the patient also has significant difficulties in memorising new verbal information (i.e., there is an anterograde verbal amnesia). For instance, repetition of sentences is limited to sentences consisting of three or four words. However, for understanding conversational language, it is required that an individual is able to keep in operative (working) memory some seven to eight words, and hence, to be able to repeat sentences consisting of seven to eight words. It is consequently obvious that patients with Wernicke's aphasia cannot correctly understand spoken language.

Broca's aphasia

Broca's aphasia – also known as motor aphasia, expressive aphasia, or kinetic motor aphasia – is observed in cases of damage to the so-called Broca's area. Broca's area corresponds to the third frontal gyrus (F3) and is typically defined in terms of the *pars opercularis* and *pars triangularis* of the left inferior frontal gyrus, represented in Brodmann's cytoarchitectonic map as areas BA44 and BA45 (see Figure 17.1).

Speech in Broca's aphasia is not fluent, but language understanding is relatively normal. Repetition is abnormal due to the apraxia of speech; as a matter of fact, during repetition, the same disturbances observed in spontaneous speech are found. Pointing in response to requests like "show me the . . . ." is relatively normal and illustrates relatively normal language understanding.

Motor difficulties are found in the overwhelming majority of patients with Broca's aphasia. A right hemiparesis (weakness in the right hemi-body), more distal (the hand) than proximal (the shoulder) is usually found. Hemiparesis varies in severity but frequently corresponds to a hemiplegia (inability to move the right hemi-body). The hemiparesis is observed in the right arm and face, but it is milder in the right leg. Because of the motor disturbance, dysarthria is almost invariably found; the dysarthria corresponds to a spastic type of dysarthria charac-terised by an increased muscle tone. Depending on the extent of the damage in the parietal lobe, somatosensory abnormalities can be found, such as right hemi-body hypoesthesia (decreased sensibility in the right hemi-body), two-points discrimination (ability to discern that two nearby objects touching the skin are truly two distinct points, not one) defects, difficulties in localising tactile stimuli in the right hemi-body, etc.

Aphasic individuals presenting Broca-type aphasia (a continuity or syntagmatic disorder according to Jakobson 1971) lose the ability to combine linguistic elements. Their grammar is restricted or absent, and they can produce and understand only isolated meaningful words. Words with purely grammatical function (such as articles and prepositions) tend to be omitted. Affixes may be substituted one for another, but more likely they are simply not produced. These patients thus tend to use only very short sentences containing mostly meaningful words (nouns). In severe cases, sentences can be as short as a single word (e.g., "dog") and in general, there is a reduction in resources available for syntactic processing (Caplan 2006). This disturbance in the use of grammar is known as agrammatism. Agrammatism is also observed in language understanding; so, these patients have difficulties understanding sentences whose meanings depend on their syntax (e.g., "The dog was bitten by the cat"; who was bitten, the dog or the cat?).

Stereotypes (restricted expression repeatedly used by the patient, as if it were the only language form available) are frequently found (for instance, the initial patient described by Broca in 1863 had a single stereotyped utterance ("tan") that he repeated when attempting to speak). Stereotypes can be short (for instance, a syllable, as in Broca's patient's "tan"), or long (for instance, "/beintisinko/"); can be meaningful (e.g., "pencil") or meaningless (e.g., "sood"). Occasionally, the stereotype corresponds to a profanity (that obviously becomes particularly embarrassing not only for the patient but also for other people!). The origin of the specific stereotype is not well understood, but it has been suggested that it corresponds to some language information existing exactly before the onset of the aphasia.

Patients with Broca's aphasia present a defect in making precise articulatory movements; that results in a significant amount of phonetic deviations (inaccurate production of pho-nemes), occasionally resulting in so-called "foreign accent in aphasia" ("perceived" foreign accent in speech).

In addition to phonetic deviation, patients with Broca's aphasia present a significant amount of phonological paraphasias. Phonological paraphasias in this type of aphasia are mostly due to phoneme omissions and phoneme substitutions. As a matter of fact, patients can have significant difficulties in producing certain phonemes (e.g., fricative phonemes) and complex syllables (e.g., consonant-consonant-vowel as in "tree"); fricative phonemes are replaced by stop phonemes (e.g., /s/ becomes /t/) and complex syllables become basic syllables (that is, consonant-vowel; for instance, "tree" becomes "tee"). These verbal articulatory defects in Broca's aphasia are known as apraxia of speech. Phonological paraphasias are a result of the apraxia of speech.

It is usually recognised that Broca's aphasia has two different distinguishing characteristics: (a) a motor component (lack of fluency, disintegration of the speech kinetic melodies, verbal-articulatory impairments, etc. that is usually referred as apraxia of speech); and (b) agrammatism (e.g., Benson and Ardila 1996; Goodglass 1993; Kertesz 1985; Luria 1976). A large part of the fronto-parieto-temporal cortex has been observed to be involved with syntactic-morphological functions (Bhatnagar *et al.* 2000). Apraxia of speech has been specifically associated with damage in the left precentral gyrus of the insula (Dronkers 1996; but see Hillis *et al.* 2004).

Other aphasic disorders

In addition to the two major aphasic syndromes (Broca's aphasia and Wernicke's aphasia), different aphasia classifications generally include a diversity of language disturbances, such as conduction aphasia, transcortical (extrasylvian) aphasia, anomic aphasia, etc. Indeed, some aphasic syndromes can be considered as variants of Broca's and Wernicke's aphasias. For instance, amnesic or anomic or nominal aphasia (usually due to damage in the vicinity of BA37) can be interpreted as a subtype of Wernicke's aphasia in which the semantic associations of words are significantly impaired. By the same token, extrasylvian (transcortical) sensory aphasia can also be regarded as a subtype of Wernicke's aphasia, and indeed, that is the interpretation proposed by some authors (e.g., Lecours, Lhermitte, and Bryans, 1983).

Conduction aphasia

Conduction aphasia was initially described by Wernicke in 1874, and interpreted as a disconnection between the left superior temporal gyrus (Wernicke's area) and the left inferior frontal gyrus (Broca's area) (Wernicke 1874). Wernicke's interpretation was supported by Geschwind during the 1960s (resulting in the so-called Wernicke–Geschwind model of language), who put it in terms of modern anatomic nomenclature, attributing to the arcuate fasciculus the main role in the speech repetition disturbances. According to Geschwind (1965), disconnection syndromes were higher-function deficits that resulted from white matter lesions or lesions of the association cortices; conduction aphasia was usually presented as the prototypal example of a disconnection syndrome. This remains its most frequent interpretation (e.g., Damasio and Damasio 1980): conduction aphasia is usually due to a lesion affecting the arcuate fasciculus (Yamada *et al.* 2007) and sporadically an indirect pathway passing through the inferior parietal cortex and the insula (Catani, Jones, and Ffytche 2005) (see Figure 17.2).

According to Benson *et al.* (1973), conduction aphasia has three fundamental and five secondary characteristics; so-called secondary characteristics are frequently but not necessarily found in conduction aphasia. The three basic characteristics are: (1) fluent conversational language; (2) comprehension almost normal; and (3) significant impairments in repetition. Secondary characteristics include: (1) impairments in naming; (2) reading impairments; (3) variable writing difficulties (apraxic agraphia); (4) ideomotor apraxia; and

Alfredo Ardila

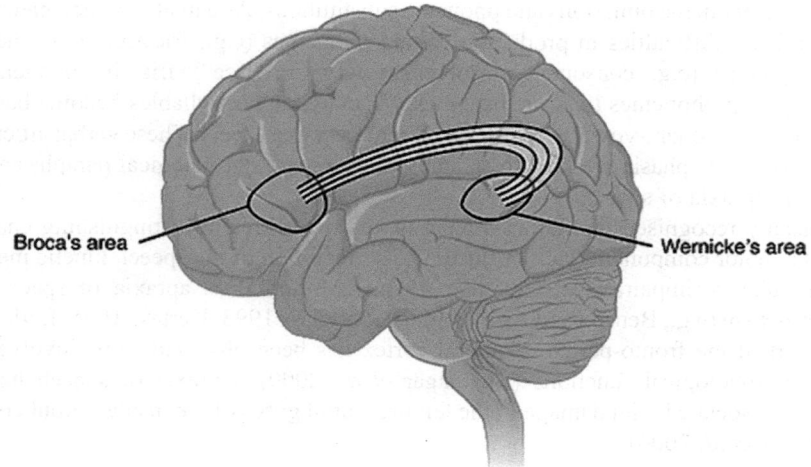

Figure 17.2 Explanation of conduction aphasia as a disconnection between Wernicke's area and Broca's area

(5) additional neurological impairments. Bartha and Benke (2003) report that conduction aphasia patients present as relatively homogenic in their aphasic manifestations: severe impairment of repetition and fluent expressive language functions with frequent phonemic paraphasias, repetitive self-corrections, word-finding difficulties, and paraphrasing. Repetitive self-corrections frequently result in so-called *conduit d'approche* (behaviour of approximation). Language comprehension (auditory and reading) is only mildly impaired.

When attempting to repeat (but also on occasion in spontaneous language), a patient with conduction aphasia presents successive approaches to the target word (*conduit d'approche*); every time s/he produces the word, the patient recognises it has been incorrectly produced (because language understanding is preserved), and attempts to correct it. A significant amount of phonological paraphasias are observed and, from time to time, verbal paraphasias are also found. Sometimes it is impossible to produce the word during repetition, but not in spontaneous language.

Transcortical (extrasylvian) sensory aphasia

Transcortical (or extrasylvian) sensory aphasia (TSA) has been a polemic syndrome; frequently it is considered as a subtype of Wernicke's aphasia. The polemic is related to the way TSA is defined and the elements included in its definition. Some authors have even simply denied the existence of such a syndrome. Two integrative revisions of TSA are available (Berthier 1999; Boatman *et al.* 2000).

In general, it is considered that TSA includes the following elements: (1) good repetition (the patient repeats words and sentences presented by the examiner, regardless of whether they are incorrect and even in a foreign language); (2) fluent conversational language; (3) significant amount of verbal paraphasias and neologisms; and (4) empty speech. TSA presents similar deficits as in Wernicke's aphasia, but repetition ability is spared and phoneme discrimination impairments are not found. Some authors also include a semantic jargon in the definition of TSA (Goodglass 1993; Kertesz 1982), but jargon is not a required symptom for the diagnosis of TSA. By the same token, other language impairments can also be found, such as poor naming, and preserved oral reading with impaired reading comprehension, but their presence is not essential to establish the diagnosis of TSA (Berthier 1999).

Transcortical (extrasylvian) motor aphasia

Transcortical (or extrasylvian) motor aphasia (also known dynamic aphasia; Luria 1966, 1980), is associated with left convexital prefrontal damage. It is characterised by nonfluent language, good comprehension, and good repetition. Prosody, articulation, and grammar are preserved. The patient presents long latencies in language when beginning to speak or when answering questions. Answers to open questions are slow and incomplete, and the patient tends to repeat the words included in the question. Expressive language is limited with some tendency to echolalia and perseveration; occasionally verbal paraphasias are observed. This type of aphasia could be interpreted as a language disturbance at the pragmatic level (use of the language according to the specific social context).

Extrasylvian (transcortical) motor aphasia could be interpreted as an executive function defect specifically affecting language use. The ability to actively and appropriately generate language appears impaired while the phonology, lexicon, semantics, and grammar are preserved. Simply speaking, the question is: should the ability to correctly generate language be regarded as a linguistic ability (i.e., a cognitive ability)? Or rather, should it be considered as an executive function ability (i.e., a metacognitive ability)? Consequently, extrasylvian (transcortical) motor aphasia does not necessarily have to be interpreted as a primary aphasic syndrome, but rather as a language disturbance due to a more general intellectual impairment (dysexecutive syndrome). In this regard, it is a secondary – not primary – aphasia syndrome. Extrasylvian (transcortical) motor aphasia could indeed be referred to as "dysexecutive aphasia" (Ardila 2010).

Aphasia of the supplementary motor area

In 1940, Brickner reported that electrocortical stimulation of the supplementary motor area (SMA) (mesial aspect of BA6) resulted in continuous perseveration (Brickner 1940). Penfield and Welch (1951) observed arrest of speech associated with stimulation of this cortical region. However, language disturbances associated with SMA pathology were reported relatively late in the aphasia literature. Clinical characteristics of this type of aphasia were described by Rubens (1975, 1976). Jonas (1981) later referred to the participation of the SMA in speech emission.

The occlusion of the left anterior cerebral artery (that irrigates the SMA) represents its most frequent aetiology, but it has also been reported in cases of tumours and traumatic head injury (e.g., Ardila and López 1984). Speech is characterised by (1) an initial mutism lasting about 2–10 days; (2) later, a virtually total inability to initiate speech; (3) nearly normal speech repetition; (4) normal language understanding; and (5) absence of echolalia. A right leg paresis and right leg sensory loss are observed; a mild right shoulder paresis and Babinski sign are also found. Language recovery is outstanding and it is usually observed during the following few weeks or months. Spontaneous language is limited, but language understanding and language repetition are normal; there is a significant difficulty in initiating and maintaining speech, even if the patient makes significant effort to speak; reading aloud is defective but reading understanding is nearly normal; writing is slow and painstaking. It is noteworthy that this type of aphasia has sometimes been interpreted as an extrasylvian (transcortical) motor aphasia.

The SMA is a mainly mesial premotor area involved in the ability to sequence multiple movements performed in a particular order (Tanji and Shima 1994). SMA participates in initiating, maintaining, coordinating, and planning complex sequences of movements; it receives information from the posterior parietal and frontal association areas, and projects to the primary motor cortex (Kandel, Schwartz, and Jessell 1995). SMA damage is also associated with slow reaction time (Alexander *et al.* 2007). It has been observed that activation of the SMA precedes voluntary movement (Erdler *et al.* 2000); a crucial role in the motor expression of speech processing has also been assumed (Fried *et al.* 1991). Evidently, the SMA is a complex motor cortical area, not primarily a language-related brain area. Its role in language seemingly refers to the motor ability to initiate and maintain voluntary speech production.

Brain organisation of language in bilinguals

It has been suggested that in bilingual individuals the brain representations of L2 differ in comparison with those of L1; this dissociation in the brain organisation of L1 and L2 is considered to be particularly evident in late bilinguals (people who have learnt L2 after L1 has been acquired; that is, after the age of about 12 years) (Fabbro 2001; Mouthona, Annonia, and Khatebc 2013). Evidently, when L2 is acquired late in life, it is generally mediated by L1; and even the language-learning strategies and mechanisms can be different. For instance, grammatical knowledge and processing is usually associated with procedural memory in L1 (that is, it is a kind of automatic learning), but it is more dependent on declarative memory for L2 (that is, it is more consciously controlled).

So, potentially L1 and L2 can have different brain representation (divergent representation), or coincident brain organisation (convergent representation). Divergent representation means that each language has at least a partially different cerebral organisation than the other. Convergent representation refers to a similar brain organisation of L1 and L2.

The question of language representation in the brain was originally raised on the basis of clinical observations of bilingual aphasic patients. Severity of impairment and recovery characteristics for L1 and L2 were taken into consideration. Several of these reports showed an unequal pattern of impairment in the two languages (selective impairment) (e.g., Fabbro and Paradis 1995), whereas others suggested an unequal pattern of recovery of the two languages (selective recovery) (Paradis 1993), congruent with a different (divergent) brain organisation of L1 and L2.

At a certain point in the history of this question, it was proposed that whereas L1 was organised in the left hemisphere, L2 was more bilaterally represented, indicating an increased involvement of the right hemisphere in L2 (e.g., Wesche and Schneiderman 1982). As for this hypothesis of a more bilateral language representation for L2, clinical studies have shown that the incidence of aphasia with a right hemisphere lesion (in what is commonly called "crossed aphasia") in bilingual subjects is similar to that observed in monolinguals, thereby infirming the assumption of a different representation of languages for L1 and L2.

Clinical observations suggested that different languages might rely on distinct neural substrates (Fabbro, Naatanen, and Kujala 1999). As a matter of fact, electrocortical brain stimulation studies also provided evidence for distinct representation of the different languages in the brain. Various reports indicated that the stimulation of different cerebral locations, during neurosurgery monitoring, interfered unequally with the patients' languages (Giussani *et al.* 2007). These data suggested that some cortical sites might selectively be involved in one of the languages but not the others. By the same token, some functional neuroimaging investigations reported different brain activation between L1 and L2, with different experimental paradigms in regions such as Broca's area, the cerebellum, supramarginal gyri, and others (Dehaene *et al.* 1997).

The alternative possibility, that the different languages converge into the same brain regions and that linguistic knowledge of L1 and L2 are processed by the same neural network, also finds support in both clinical and experimental data. The theory of convergence proposes that the acquisition of L2 even in late learners involves the same brain network used for the L1 as in monolingual speakers, including the processing of semantic, syntactic, phonological, but also grammatical information (Mouthona *et al.* 2013). A common language representation for the different languages in bilinguals had been supported by other clinical studies that reported *similar impairments* in both languages after brain damage (and a *parallel recovery*) (Fabbro 2001).

So, contrary to some functional studies that supported the hypothesis of a differential brain representation for L1 and L2, other studies suggested that the first and second languages use the same neural circuits (e.g., Illes *et al.* 1999). Support for the language representation convergence theory was reported in picture naming, and semantic judgement tasks, where overlapping brain activation was observed for L1 and L2 (Mouthona *et al.* 2013).

Nowadays, the discrepancy between the data provided by the different fields of research or from different studies from the same field (e.g., functional imaging research) are thought to result either from factors inherent to the populations studied (low vs. high proficiency, early vs. late, or balanced vs. unbalanced bilinguals) or from a bad definition of the question addressed.

In conclusion, contemporary research supports both points of view: L1 and L2 have a coincidental brain organisation; and also, L1 and L2 have a partially different brain organisation; L2 uses more extended brain circuits, even involving the right hemisphere. Age of acquisition of L2 and proficiency in L1 and L2 are supposed to represent the two most crucial variables accounting for this difference in brain organisation (Fabbro 2001; Mouthona *et al.* 2013). In early balanced bilinguals both languages have a coincident brain organisation; in late unbalanced bilinguals, brain organisation of L1 and L2 is partially different.

Aphasia in bilinguals

Worldwide, some 6,800 different languages are spoken (http://www.ethnologue.com), and over half of the world's population is bilingual or multilingual. This means that over half of the cases of aphasia are bilingual aphasias.

Parallel and dissociated aphasia

Different clinical observations have demonstrated that bilingual aphasics do not necessarily manifest the same language disorders with the same degree of severity in both languages (Albert and Obler 1978). Aphasia can be parallel (both languages are impaired in a similar way) or dissociated (there is a different aphasia profile for each of the languages). Fabbro (2001) observed, in a sample of 20 bilingual aphasics, parallel aphasia in 65% of the subjects; in the rest (35%) aphasia was dissociated: 20% showed a greater impairment of L2, while 15% of the patients showed a greater impairment of L1. These percentages can be considered relatively typical.

It is assumed that parallel aphasia is usually found in early bilinguals, whereas dissociated aphasia is characteristic of late bilinguals. As a matter of fact, language representation of both languages can be regarded as coincidental in early bilinguals, whereas language representation of L1 and L2 is not completely coincidental in late bilinguals. L2 seems to be acquired through the same neural structures responsible for L1 acquisition; that means that language understanding is related to the left temporal lobe (Wernicke's area) whereas language production is based on left inferior frontal gyrus activity (Broca's area); however, neural differences may be observed, in terms of more extended activity of the neural system mediating L2 processing (Abutalebi 2008). Indeed many studies have reported that later acquired languages may involve broader activation locations than the first acquired language; largely overlapping, but sometimes distinct cortical areas are involved in the comprehension and production of first and second languages (Obler *et al.* 2007).

In cases of dissociated aphasia, usually the most impaired language is L2, but sometimes, it can be L1. For instance, Ardila (2008) reported the case of a 63-year-old right-handed female native Spanish speaker, who had been living in the USA for 38 years. She never studied English in a formal way, but after years of having been exposed to it, she had learned some English. Suddenly, she presented an extensive left temporal intracerebral haemorrhage. A significant language-understanding defect was found, associated with severe impairments in verbal memory (Wernicke's aphasia), difficulties in language repetition, severe anomia with phonological and semantic paraphasias and neologisms, alexia, and aphasic agraphia. The naming defect was more severe in Spanish than in English; furthermore, there was also a clear tendency to answer in English, to switch to English, and mixing English and Spanish. The patient presented a dissociated aphasia with a better conservation of L2 (English) than L1 (Spanish).

Occasionally, it has been reported that bilinguals can present a different pattern of aphasia in L1 and L2. For example, Silverberg and Gordon (1979) reported two cases of dissociated aphasia; following a left parietotemporal lesion, moderate nonfluent aphasia was found in the native language of the first patient, in contrast to less severe, fluent aphasia in the patient's L2. Conversely, mild anomia was found in L1 of a second patient, while global aphasia was found in L2. His lesion was located in the left posterior frontal area.

Patterns of L1 and L2 recovery

Two opposite points of view were proposed during the 19th century to explain language recovery in bilingual aphasics.

- Ribot's law or Ribot's (1883) rule. This states that the language best recovered by polyglot aphasics is the mother language.
- Pitres' law or Pitres' (1895) rule. Pitres described seven cases of bilingual aphasics presenting differential recovery of the two languages. He suggested that patients tended to better recover the language that was *most familiar* to them prior to the aphasia onset, even if it was not the mother tongue.

Paradis (1977) refers to six different patterns of aphasia recovery in bilinguals.

1. Differential. Each language is impaired separately and recovered at the same or different rate
2. Parallel. Different languages are similarly impaired and restored at the same rate.
3. Antagonistic. Recovery of one language progresses, while the other regresses.
4. Successive. One language does not show any recovery until another has been restored.
5. Selective. One language is not recovered at all.
6. Mixed. Both languages are used in some combinations.

However, most patients present the first (differential) or second (parallel) recovery pattern. The other patterns are indeed unusual. Fabbro *et al.* (1999) report a parallel recovery in about 40% of cases, a better recovery of L1 in 32% of patients, and a better recovery of L2 in about 28% of cases.

How translating ability can be affected

Translation ability represents a crucial ability in bilinguals. It is generally thought that translation is easier from L2 to L1 than in the opposite direction. Translation can be difficult in early bilinguals, because the words in both languages can have different semantic associations; that is, early bilinguals are coordinate bilinguals (Weinreich, 1953). Translation can be included as a specific task in testing bilingual aphasics; and as a matter of fact, it is a subtest in the Bilingual Aphasia Test (Paradis and Libben 2014; www.mcgill.ca/linguistics/research/bat). The preserved ability to translate can be regarded as an index of complex language control.

In bilingual aphasics, mixing of the languages has been frequently observed (Ardila 2008; Perecman 1984). Patients may become unable to separate their languages and to use each one in the appropriate circumstances. Patients can present mixing of languages within a single utterance, or pathological switching, alternating their languages across different utterances; language mixing is most frequently observed in cases of left temporo-parietal pathology. Reports about pathological language switching are not frequently found; Fabbro, Skrap, and Aglioti (2000) described a patient with a lesion to the left anterior cingulate and to the frontal lobe – also marginally involving the right anterior cingulate area – who presented with pathological switching between languages in the absence of any other linguistic impairment.

Idiosyncratic disturbances in the ability to translate have been documented in aphasic patients. Paradis, Goldblum, and Abidi (1982) analysed two patients presenting a pattern of recovery yet unreported. Both patients alternately suffered severe word-finding difficulties in one language while remaining relatively fluent in the other. They retained good comprehension in both of their languages at all times. They were able to translate correctly and without hesitation from the language they could speak well at the time into the language unavailable for spontaneous use, but were unable to translate from their temporarily poor language (which they understood well) into the language they could speak quite well at the time. Aglioti *et al.* (1996) reported a bilingual patient who presented with an uncommon pattern of aphasic deficit consequent to subcortical lesions mainly involving the left basal ganglia. The patient's mother tongue was Venetian, whereas her L2 was standard Italian. The patient had more difficulties when translating into her mother tongue than into her second language; this asymmetrical pattern in translating is not expected; as mentioned above, translating is generally considered to be much more difficult from L1 to L2 than from L2 to L1

Finally, it should be mentioned that the ability to translate between languages represents a complex linguistic ability that potentially could be used in aphasia rehabilitation with bilingual patients. In language therapy it has been documented that recovery of a word in one language usually generalises to the other language for cognate words (e.g., English "fruit", Spanish "*fruta*"), but not for non-cognate terms (e.g., English "pencil", Spanish "*lápiz*") (Roberts and Deslauriers 1999) suggesting that cognate words have a common brain representation in bilinguals. However, this cognate effect is variable across patients (Hughes and Tainturier 2015), probably depending upon the specific patient's bilingualism characteristics.

Alfredo Ardila

Further reading

Ardila, A. 2010. A proposed reinterpretation and reclassification of aphasia syndromes. *Aphasiology* 24(3), pp. 363–394.
This journal article is a review of the different aphasia syndromes and a proposed interpretation of aphasia.

Ardila, A. and Ramos, E., eds. 2007. *Speech and Language Disorders in Bilinguals*. New York: Nova Science Publishers.
A collection of articles about the manifestation of speech and language disorders in bilinguals.

Benson, D. F. and Ardila, A. 1996. *Aphasia: A Clinical Perspective*. New York: Oxford University Press.
This is a basic aphasia textbook.

Papathanasiou, I., Coppens, P. and Potagas, C. 2012. *Aphasia and Related Neurogenic Communication Disorders*. Burlington: Jones & Bartlett Learning.
This work presents an integrated review of different speech and language disorders.

Related topics

Bilingualism, translation, and interpreting; Language processing in translation.

References

Abutalebi, J. 2008. Neural aspects of second language representation and language control. *Acta Psychologica* 128, pp. 466–478.

Aglioti, S., Beltramello, A., Girardi, F. and Fabbro, F. 1996. Neurolinguistic and follow-up study of an unusual pattern of recovery from bilingual subcortical aphasia. *Brain* 119(5), pp. 1551–1564.

Albert, M. L., Goodglass, H., Helm, N. A., Rubers, A. B. and Alexander, M. P. 1981. *Clinical Aspects of Dysphasia*. New York: Springer-Verlag.

Albert, M. L. and Obler, L. K. 1978. *The Bilingual Brain: Neuropsychological and Neurolinguisitic Aspects of Bilingualism*. New York: Academic Press.

Alexander, M. P., Stuss, D. T., Picton, T., Shallice, T. and Gillingham, S. 2007. Regional frontal injuries cause distinct impairments in cognitive control. *Neurology* 68, pp. 1515–1523.

Ardila, A. 2008. Anomia disociada en un bilingüe tardío con mejor conservación de L2. *Neuropsicología, Neuropsiquiatría y Neurociencias* 8(2), pp. 91–95.

Ardila, A. 2010. A proposed reinterpretation and reclassification of aphasia syndromes. *Aphasiology* 24(3), pp. 363–394.

Ardila, A. 2014. *Aphasia Handbook*. Miami: Florida International University.

Ardila, A. and López, M. V. 1984. Transcortical motor aphasia: one or two aphasias? *Brain and Language* 22, pp. 350–353.

Bartha, L. and Benke, T. 2003. Acute conduction aphasia: an analysis of 20 cases. *Brain and Language* 85(1), pp. 93–108.

Benson, D. F. and Ardila, A. 1996. *Aphasia: A Clinical Perspective*. New York: Oxford University Press.

Benson, D. F., Sheremata, W. A., Bouchard, R., Segarra, J. M., Price, D. and Geschwind, N. 1973. Conduction aphasia: a clinicopathological study. *Archives of Neurology* 28(5), pp. 339–346.

Berthier, M. 1999. *Transcortical Aphasias*. Hove: Psychology Press.

Berube, L. 1991. *Terminologie de neuropsychologie et de neurologie du comportement*. Montréal: Les Éditions de la Chenelière Inc.

Bhatnagar, S. C., Mandybur, G. T., Buckingham, H. W. and Andy, O. J. 2000. Language representation in the human brain: evidence from cortical mapping. *Brain and Language* 74, pp. 238–259.

Bilingual Aphasia Test (BAT). www.mcgill.ca/linguistics/research/bat [Accessed 25 November 2015].

Boatman, D., Gordon, B., Hart, J., Selnes, O., Miglioretti, D. and Lenz, F. 2000. Transcortical sensory aphasia: revisited and revised. *Brain* 123, pp. 1634–1642.

Brickner, R. M. 1940. A human cortical area producing repetitive phenomena when stimulated. *Journal of Neurophysiology* 3, pp. 128–130.

Broca, P. 1861. Remarques sur le siège de la faculté du langage articulé; suivies d'une observation d'aphémie. *Bulletin de la Société d'Anthropologie* 2, pp. 330–357.

Caplan, D. 2006. Aphasic deficits in syntactic processing. *Cortex* 42, pp. 797–804.

Catani, M., Jones, D. K. and Ffytche, D. H. 2005. Perisylvian language networks of the human brain. *Annals of Neurology* 57, pp. 8–16.

Damasio, H. and Damasio, A. 1980. The anatomical basis of conduction aphasia. *Brain* 103, pp. 337–350.

Dehaene, S., Dupoux, E., Mehler, J., Cohen, L., Paulesu, E., Perani, D. and LeBiran, D. 1997. Anatomical variability in the cortical representation of first and second language. *Neuroreport* 8(17), pp. 3809–3815.

Dronkers, N. F. 1996. A new brain region for coordinating speech articulation. *Nature* 384, pp. 159–161.

Erdler, M., Beisteiner, R., Mayer, D., Kaindl, T., Edward, V. and Windischberger, C. 2000. Supplementary motor area activation preceding voluntary movement is detectable with a whole-scalp magneto-encephalography system. *Neuroimage* 11, pp. 697–707.

Ethnologue: The Languages of the World. www.ethnologue.com [Accessed 25 November 2015].

Fabbro, F. 2001. The bilingual brain: cerebral representation of languages. *Brain and Language* 79(2), pp. 211–222.

Fabbro, F., Naatanen, R. and Kujala, T. 1999. The neurolinguistics of bilingualism. *Nature* 398(6728), pp. 577–577.

Fabbro, F. and Paradis, M. 1995. "Differential Impairments in Four Multilingual Patients with Subcortical Lesions". In *Aspects of Bilingual Aphasia*, edited by M. Paradis, 139–176. Oxford: Pergamon.

Fabbro, F., Skrap, M. and Aglioti, S. 2000. Pathological switching between languages after frontal lesions in a bilingual patient. *Journal of Neurology, Neurosurgery and Psychiatry* 68(5), pp. 650–652.

Fried, I., Katz, A., McCarthy, G., Sass, K. J., Williamson, P. and Spencer, S. S. 1991. Functional organization of human supplementary motor cortex studied by electrical stimulation. *Journal of Neurosciences* 11, pp. 3656–3666.

Geschwind, N. 1965. Disconnection syndromes in animals and man. *Brain* 88, pp. 237–294.

Giussani, C., Roux, F. E., Lubrano, V., Gaini, S. M. and Bello, L. 2007. Review of language organization in bilingual patients: what can we learn from direct brain mapping? *Acta Neurochirurgica* 149(11), pp. 1109–1116.

Goodglass, H. 1993. *Understanding Aphasia*. New York: Academic Press.

Head, H. 1926. *Aphasia and Kindred Disorders of Speech*. London: Cambridge University Press.

Hécaen, H. 1972. *Introduction à la neuropsychologie*. Paris: Larousse.

Hillis, A. E., Work, M., Barker, P. B., Jacobs, M. A., Breese, E. L. and Maurer, K. 2004. Re-examining the brain regions crucial for orchestrating speech articulation. *Brain* 127, pp. 1479–1487.

Hughes, E. and Tainturier, M. 2015. "The cognate advantage in bilingual aphasia: Now you see it, now you don't". *Frontiers in Psychology. Conference Abstract: Academy of Aphasia 53rd Annual Meeting*.

Illes, J., Francis, W. S., Desmond, J. E., Gabrieli, J. D., Glover, G. H., Poldrack, R. and Wagner, A. D. 1999. Convergent cortical representation of semantic processing in bilinguals. *Brain and Language* 70(3), pp. 347–363.

Kertesz, A. 1979. *Aphasia and Associated Disorders*. New York: Grune and Stratton.

Kertesz, A. 1982. *The Western Aphasia Battery*. New York: Grune and Stratton.

Kertesz, A. 1985. "Aphasia". In *Handbook of Clinical Neurology*, Vol. 45: *Clinical Neuropsychology*, edited by J. A. M. Frederiks. Amsterdam: Elsevier.

Jakobson, R. 1971. *Studies on Child Language and Aphasia*. New York: Mouton.

Jakobson, R. and Halle, M. 1956. *Two Aspects of Language and Two Types of Aphasic Disturbances*. New York: Mouton.

Jonas, S. 1981. The supplementary motor region and speech emission. *Journal of Communication Disorders* 14, pp. 349–373.

Kandel, E. R., Schwartz, J. H. and Jessell, T. M. 1995. *Essentials of Neural Science and Behavior*. Norwalk, CT: Appleton and Lange.

Lecours, A. R., Lhermitte, F. and Bryans, B. 1983. *Aphasiology*. London: Baillere-Tindall

Luria, A. R. 1966. *Human Brain and Psychological Processes*. New York: Harper and Row.

Luria, A. R. 1972/1983. "Sobre las dos formas básicas del alteraciones afásicas en el lenguaje [On the Two Basic Forms of Aphasic Disturbances]". In *Psicobiologõa del Lenguaje*, edited by A. Ardila. Mexico: Trillas.

Luria, A. R. 1976. *Basic Problems of Neurolinguistics*. New York: Mouton.

Luria, A. R. 1980. *Higher Cortical Functions in Man*. 2nd ed. New York: Basic Books.

Mouthona, M., Annonia, J. M. and Khatebc, A. 2013. The bilingual brain. *Swiss Archives of Neurology and Neuropsychiatry* 164, pp. 266–274.

Obler, L. K., Hyun, J. M., Conner, P. S., O'Connor, B. and Anema, I. 2007. "Brain Organization of Language in Bilinguals". In *Speech and Language Disorders in Bilinguals*, edited by A. Ardila and E. Ramos, 21–46. New York: Nova Science Publishers.

Paradis, M. 1977. "Bilingualism and Aphasia". In *Studies in Neurolinguistics* Vol. 3, edited by H. Whitaker and H. A. Whitaker, 65–121. New York: Academic Press.

Paradis, M. 1993. *Foundations of Aphasia Rehabilitation*. New York: Pergamon Press.

Paradis, M., Goldblum, M. C. and Abidi, R. 1982. Alternate antagonism with paradoxical translation behavior in two bilingual aphasic patients. *Brain and Language* 15(1), pp. 55–69.

Paradis, M. and Libben, G. 2014. *The Assessment of Bilingual Aphasia*. Hove: Psychology Press.

Penfield, W. and Welch, K. 1951. The supplementary motor area of the cerebral cortex: a clinical and experimental study. *AMA Archives of Neurology and Psychiatry* 66, pp. 289–317.

Perecman, E. 1984. Spontaneous translation and language mixing in a polyglot aphasic. *Brain and Language* 23(1), pp. 43–63.

Pitres, A. 1895. Etude sur l'aphasie chez les polyglottes. *Revue de médecine* 15, pp. 873–899.

Ribot, T. 1883. *The Diseases of Memory*. New York: J. Fitzgerald.

Roberts, P. M. and Deslauriers, L. 1999. Picture naming of cognate and non-cognate nouns in bilingual aphasia. *Journal of Communication Disorders* 32(1), pp. 1–23.

Rubens, A. B. 1975. Aphasia with infarction in the territory of the anterior cerebral artery. *Cortex* 11, pp. 239–250.

Rubens, A. B. 1976. "Transcortical Motor Aphasia". In *Studies in Neurolinguistics*. Vol. 1, edited by H. Whitaker and H. A. Whitaker. New York: Academic Press.

Silverberg, R. and Gordon, H. W. 1979. Differential aphasia in two bilingual individuals. *Neurology* 29(1), pp. 51–55.

Tanji, J. and Shima, K. 1994. Role for supplementary motor area cells in planning several movements ahead. *Nature* 371, pp. 413–416.

Weinreich, U. 1953. *Languages in Contact: Findings and Problems*. The Hague: Mouton.

Wesche, M. B. and Schneiderman, E. I. 1982. Language lateralization in adult bilinguals. *Studies in Second Language Acquisition* 4(2), pp. 153–169.

Wernicke, C. 1874. *Der Aphasiche Symptomencomplex*. Breslau: Cohn and Weigert.

Yamada, K., Nagakane, Y., Mizuno, T., Hosomi, A., Nakagawa, M. and Nishimura, T. 2007. MR tractography depicting damage to the arcuate fasciculus in a patient with conduction aphasia. *Neurology* 68, pp. 789–790.

18

Language processing in translation

Moritz Schaeffer

Introduction and definitions

There are a number of cognitive models which aim at describing linguistic processing during translation, and a large number of studies which investigate aspects of the source or target text (ST or TT). A selection of each of these kinds of studies will be reviewed here.

Within Translation Studies (TS), the use of empirical methods is relatively recent (see below). Many of the studies which investigated a particular source or target language (SL or TL) aspect and its effect on linguistic processing during translation did not integrate their findings with existing models, theories and hypotheses regarding cognitive aspects of translation; they rarely attempted to confirm or refute existing hypotheses, and focused more often on isolated phenomena. They were often aimed at testing empirical methods, and provided preliminary findings which required replication before they could be argued to apply to translation in general: if a particular aspect of a ST has an effect on linguistic processing during translation, it remains to be seen whether this effect is restricted to the two texts and languages involved in the study or whether the same kind of aspect can also be shown to have a similar effect on linguistic processing during translation of a different text involving a different language pair. One further complication makes experimental design difficult: the tools which are used to describe linguistic processing during translation need to be language independent. For example, in Danish, if a sentence starts with an adverb, the verb has to be placed before the subject while different languages (such as English or Spanish) do not require this inversion – in fact, in a declarative sentence in English, the subject is always placed before the verb. It might be more difficult to translate a declarative sentence that starts with an adverb from Danish into English than a sentence which starts with a subject, because the former requires a change in word order, while the latter does not. This is exactly what Jensen, Sjørup and Balling (2009) found. However, it might be that the difficulty observed is associated with aspects which are specific to the two languages or the two language types involved, which would mean that the resulting claims would only apply to what has been observed, and it would be difficult to extend the findings to other language combinations or to translation in general. It is therefore important to find tools which are language independent. Jensen, Sjørup and Balling (2009) and Ruiz *et al.* (2008) (for the language combination English–Spanish) used two types of sentences – critical sentences, which required a word order change when being translated; and control sentences, which could be translated using the same word order as in the source sentence. Ruiz *et al.* (2008) used Spanish sentences with a postnominal adjective (the adjective is placed after the noun) and compared this with sentences where the adjective was placed before the noun (prepositive). When translating into English, the adjective has to be placed before the noun. Participants took longer to process sentences with postnominal adjectives than prepositive adjectives. Although unlikely, it is possible that the effects observed by Ruiz *et al.* and Jensen *et al.* are related to contrastive differences between English and Spanish or Danish involving adjectives and adverbs. Schaeffer *et al.* (2016) therefore operationalised these contrastive differences by measuring the word order differences between ST and TT sentences in number of words in order to have a language-independent measure which can be correlated with associated behaviour. Schaeffer *et al.* (2016) used a measure called *Cross* which counts the word order differences between source and target sentences; i.e., if the first ST word is aligned to the fifth TT word, it has a Cross value of 5. They found that it is more difficult to translate words which have a different place in the TT sentence than in the ST sentence, and the larger these differences are, the more difficult it is to translate the words. The data on the basis of which this claim was made consisted of translations from English into Danish, Spanish, Estonian, Chinese, Hindi and German. While this is a limited number of language combinations, it shows that the effects observed apply to more than one language combination.

In sum, the challenge for Translation Process Research (TPR) is to find language-independent tools with which to describe linguistic processing during translation and to design replicable experiments in order to explain and predict behaviour during translation, so that inferences can be made concerning the cognitive processes at play during translation in general.

Historical perspectives

Much of what we know about linguistic processing during translation is based on experimental studies involving the presentation of single words. The influential study by De Groot (1992) may serve as an example. De Groot employed three translation-related tasks using single words as stimuli: "normal translation", "cued translation" and "translation recognition". In the normal translation condition, participants were presented with a single word and were asked to say out loud what this word meant in the target language. In the cued translation task, in addition to the source word participants also saw the first letter of the intended target word and had to say out loud what the target word was. Finally, in the translation recognition task, participants were shown the source and the target word and were asked to press different keys on a computer keyboard indicating whether the target word was a correct translation of the source word or not. In all three tasks, reaction times were measured, for example, the time from the moment when the source word appeared on the screen until the participant started to say the translation out loud.

In designing the stimuli, De Groot (1992) made sure that the source words either only had one translation in the TL, or had a very clearly dominant equivalent. This is important because De Groot manipulated the cognate status of the target word (how similar a target word is to its source in terms of orthography and/or phonology). Also, if there is more than one possible translation for a source word, the cue (first letter) could cause unintended confusing effects if it was not the first letter of the word the participant has in mind.

De Groot (1992) found that a number of potential characteristics of words had an effect on reaction times. These included frequency of the source and the target word (how often a word appears in a large collection of texts), imageability (the degree to which the referent of the word can evoke a mental image – it is easier to imagine *table* than *justice*), familiarity (how familiar people are with a given word – similar to frequency, though subjective), context availability (how easy it is to think of a context for a particular word), definition accuracy (how easy it is to think of a definition of a particular word) and cognate status. The more frequent, imaginable and familiar a word is, the higher its context availability, the easier it is to think of a definition and the more similar source and target words are in terms of orthography/ phonology, the faster participants reacted to the stimuli. On the basis of these results, De Groot developed a model of the bilingual lexicon known as the Distributed Features Model (see Figure 18.1).

Three considerations led researchers in TS to use different methods to investigate linguistic processing during translation. Firstly, there was resistance in TS to adopting the kind of research methods De Groot was using because, it was argued, seeing a single word and saying out loud its equivalent is not what a translator normally does, so the results could not represent the cognitive processes which normally occur when a translator translates a complete text. The main and original driving force behind the development of the keylogging software Translog (see below), Arnt Lykke Jakobsen argued in 1999, was that "experiments run with Translog have ecological validity" (Jakobsen and Schou 1999, 15). Within Translog, participants normally translate longer texts while their keystrokes (and often also eye movements) are being recorded. Ecological validity relates to how representative the stimuli in an experiment are of the environment in which the mechanism under study naturally occurs. Muñoz Martín (2010, 181) argues, referring to Neisser (1976, 1987), that "results from non-ecological testing are doubtful in science", a statement that illustrates the importance that representativeness of the experimental setting has acquired in TS. Secondly, it was argued that

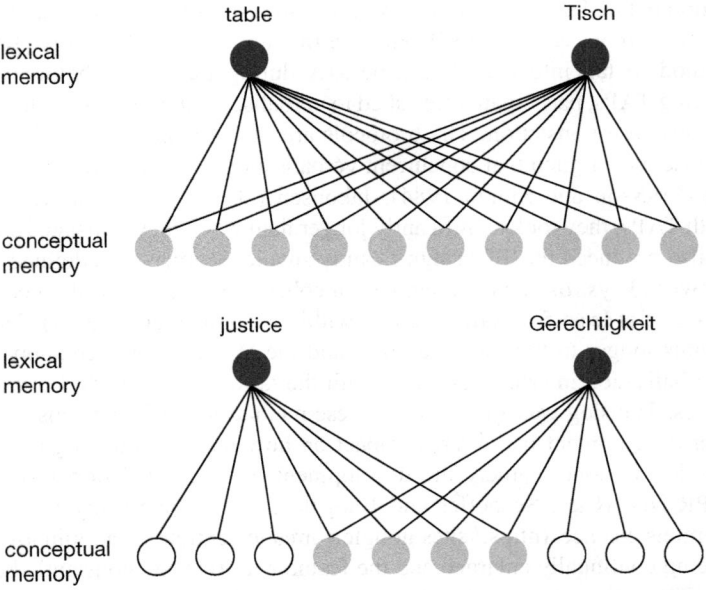

Figure 18.1   The Distributed Features Model

a bilingual who happens to have some knowledge of a second language does not engage in the same processes that a professional translator engages in when translating. The approach by researchers such as De Groot (1992, 1002) was that "word translation on its own is a useful tool to study bilingual representation and processing". De Groot (1992) therefore used bilinguals with no formal training or experience in translation. In TS, the emphasis was clearly on studying professionals or experts. Sirén and Hakkarainen (2002), echoing Krings (1986, 2001, 72) before them, argued that professional or expert translators should be studied because in that way "the pursuit of knowledge of the translation process in general, and of a successful translation process in particular, gains additional weight" (Sirén and Hakkarainen 2002, 71). In other words, the study of expert translators should be the focus given that, presumably, their processes are more successful than those of non-expert bilinguals and more relevant for translator education and theoretical insights into the translation process more generally. Thirdly, experience told TS researchers that under normal conditions, if a given text is translated by, say, 20 translators, these 20 translations are likely to differ in a number of ways. While translations for single words might be relatively stable, as soon as context plays a role, variation in the product of the process is to be expected as, e.g., Campbell (2000) and Dragsted (2012) have shown. Variability in the target texts when they are longer was one of the considerations which led to the development of Translog.

The development of Translog (Jakobsen and Schou 1999; Carl 2012) had arguably the largest effect on TPR and was, in many ways, the driving force behind what is known today as TPR. Initially, Translog could only record which keystrokes are made when, but later, eye movements and keystrokes were integrated and aligned in time and in terms of equivalence. This alignment makes it possible to, e.g., investigate a particular TT aspect and its effect on ST reading times. A number of small-scale experiments were carried out, many of which were published in the Copenhagen Studies in Language series (Göpferich, Jakobsen and Mees 2008; Alves, Göpferich and Mees 2009; Jakobsen, Mees and Göpferich 2009; Göpferich, Alves and Mees 2010; Sharp et al. 2011).

The development of Translog also occurred in response to a method which had been used extensively earlier (e.g., Krings 1986). The use of Think Aloud Protocols (TAPs) was the standard method to tap into cognitive processes during translation before Translog was available. During TAPs, participants are asked to verbalise their thoughts while engaged in an activity – in this case translation. The protocols are then labelled and analysed. However, contrary to those who argued that concurrent verbalisation does not interfere with the actual task at hand (Ericsson and Simon 1984), Jakobsen (2003) found that when participants translated with TAPs, they took significantly longer than when they translated without TAPs. Participants also produced the TT in significantly smaller segments, as defined by pauses of 5 seconds between keystrokes, i.e., a segment of coherent keystrokes is defined as occurring between pauses of at least 5 seconds (pauses within a segment are shorter). The fact that it took participants longer to translate the texts, and the effect on segmentation, suggest that concurrent verbalisation interferes not only with the task, but also with the associated cognitive processes. Translog was an answer to these methodological problems.

One further development had a large impact on how research into cognitive processing during translation is done, namely the development of the Translation Process Research Database (TPR-DB) (Carl, Schaeffer and Bangalore 2016), publically available under a creative commons licence (https://sites.google.com/site/centretranslationinnovation/). This database is being continually enlarged and the features it offers are constantly being refined. In 2016, the TPR-DB contained data from more than 300 different translators and more than 500 hours of text production (translation, post-editing of machine-translated text, monolingual editing of machine-translated text, monolingual copying, and more). These data were gathered in more than 1,400 sessions and contain over 600,000 translated words in 10 different TLs. Since the 2016 publication by Carl *et al.*, new target languages (Japanese) and tasks (translation with speech recognition) have been added (Carl, Aizawa and Yamada 2016). It is the only resource of its kind and offers the potential to answer a large number of questions. A number of problems which hampered earlier research are resolved with the TPR-DB: the number of participants had sometimes been rather limited and often, the lack of significant effects was attributed to the small number of participants. This is not a problem in the TPR-DB. Participants in the database all translated longer texts, unlike in the single word studies referred to earlier. Effects found in one language combination can easily be tested in a different language combination and this, together with the large number of participants, means that generalisability is less of a problem. Given that Translog is minimally invasive, it is likely that participants engage in processes they would normally engage in. There is a large and growing number of studies using the TPR-DB (https://sites.google.com/site/centretranslationinnovation/tpr-db-publications), some of which will be discussed below.

Core issues and topics

The ultimate aim of TPR is to produce a model of the cognitive processes which can explain and predict behaviour during translation. It can therefore be argued that one core issue is the role of the bilingual lexicon during translation, given that it plays a central role in bilingual language processing. Most researchers (De Groot and Starreveld 2015) now accept that language processing in bilinguals is generally non-selective: when a bilingual perceives, e.g., a word in one language, representations related to its counterpart are also activated. Possibly the most convincing study which supports this is by Wu and Thierry (2012). In this study, Chinese–English bilinguals had to press different keys on a response box depending on whether the images on the screen were squares or circles. Participants were told to ignore the English words which appeared on the screen. Unbeknown to the participants, some of the English words, when translated into Chinese, were homophones – in Chinese, they sounded like, but did not mean *circle* or *square*. Wu and Thierry recorded electro-physiological data and found an N200 effect (see below): when participants perceived the English homophones there was no effect on their behaviour – they did not press any keys; however, around 200 milliseconds after perceiving the homophones, the ERP (Event Related Potential) amplitude was larger for homophones than when participants perceived words where the translation of which was not a homophone and hence unrelated to *circle* or *square*. In other words, the brain reacted more strongly to homophones than to non-homophonic words. This kind of effect, which typically occurs after around 200 milliseconds and is called the N200 effect, is normally associated with processes involving cognitive control, i.e., participants automatically activated the Chinese equivalent and suppressed this activation immediately. Studies of bilingualism therefore focus on the mechanisms which allow multilinguals to keep their languages apart when the goal of this processing is to produce or comprehend text in one language only (Kroll *et al.* 2015).

The role of co-activation during translation was investigated by Macizo and Bajo (2004, 2006) and by Ruiz *et al.* (2008). Participants in these studies translated single sentences, and reaction times per word (during ST reading) were measured. In particular the later studies (Macizo and Bajo 2006; Ruiz *et al.* 2008) manipulated aspects of the TT which were shown to have an effect on reaction times. Bajo and colleagues aimed at testing an early and rudimentary model of the translation process proposed by Seleskovitch (1976), who argued that translation is normally carried out sequentially in that the first step is ST comprehension and only when this is complete and only once the source material is "deverbalised" can reformulation in the TL begin. Opposed to this sequential view is the assumption that representations specific to the TL are activated at the same time as SL representations are activated (horizontally and in parallel). All three studies found clear evidence against Seleskovitch's model: the evidence in these studies suggests that the TL is activated during ST reading. This might not be surprising now, though, given the overwhelming evidence there is for co-activation of the two linguistic systems in bilinguals.

Seleskovitch's early model, which was mainly designed for didactic purposes, is only one among many other attempts to produce a model of the cognitive processes that take place during translation (see Carl and Schaeffer 2017). Another such model is Halverson's (2003). This model finds its empirical validation partly in the research into the differences between translated text and original text in the same language. The focus here has been on what are called translation universals. This kind of research uses text corpora (large collections of text). Several universals have emerged from corpus-based research, such as normalisation or conventionalisation (the tendency to very frequently use linguistic patterns which are typical for the TL) (Baker 1993; but see also Malmkjær 2011). The unique items hypothesis (Tirkkonen-Condit 2004), for instance, posits that TL items which do not have a clear and obvious equivalent in the source language (SL) are less likely to be used in translated text, because "there is nothing in the source text that would trigger them off as immediate equivalents" (Tirkkonen-Condit 2004, 183). Tirkkonen-Condit (2004) found that unique items are less frequent in translated text as compared to non-translated text.

Halverson (2003) developed a model which can account for many of the findings in these corpus-based studies in terms of linguistic processing. Halverson refers to cognitive grammar (Langacker 1987) and De Groot's (1992) DFM when articulating the gravitational pull hypothesis. According to the DFM, the semantic representations of lexical items in two languages overlap to varying degrees, and words with a high degree of overlap are easier to translate. Halverson (2003) postulates that the degree of overlap has two effects: the greater the overlap, the more entrenched and the more cognitively salient these items are. Unique items in the sense described by Tirkkonen-Condit (2004) are therefore predicted to be less entrenched and less cognitively salient than words which are not unique to the TL.

In line with Langacker (1987), Halverson (2003) argues that the grammar and the lexicon form networks and the more often particular representations are used the more entrenched they become, forming proto-types. The relation between related categories of representations are also organised hierarchically, in so-called schemas. Halverson (2003, 209) explains that the networks are "characterized by global and/or local centres of gravity or prominence (prototypes and high-level schemas) that originate in various ways and that have numerous linguistic effects". Halverson further argues that during translation, "highly salient structures will exert a gravitational pull, resulting in an overrepresentation in translation of the specific TL lexical and grammatical structures that correspond to those salient nodes and configurations in the schematic network" (2003, 218). The predictions of the gravitational pull hypothesis explain, e.g., the finding from corpus-based research that translated text is more conventional than originally produced text: the salience and entrenchment of particular representations or networks makes them more likely to be used in translation than those which are less salient and entrenched. In sum, Halverson says that various translation universals "designate essentially the same thing, and represent the effects of gravitational pull exerted by category prototypes" (2003, 221). Of course, more or less implicitly underlying this theory is the assumption that SL items are co-activated with their associated TL items. However, corpus-based research has no way of making claims about the time course of the observed effects, given that the only data they use are the original and the final TT.

A study which used the TPR-DB (Schaeffer *et al.* 2016) was designed to test a model proposed by Schaeffer and Carl (2013). This model posited both early (parallel) and late (sequential) processes. Schaeffer and Carl (2013) argued that early automatic processes activate semantic and syntactic representations which are shared by the SL and the TL and that, later, monolingual vertical processes monitor the output from the early processes. Shared syntactic representations are defined in terms of the shared syntax account (Hartsuiker, Pickering and Veltkamp 2004), and shared semantic representations are defined in terms of the DFM. The shared syntax account posits that each lemma of a bilingual's languages is connected to what Hartsuiker, Pickering and Veltkamp (2004) call category nodes (such as *verb*). In addition, they are connected to combinatorial nodes (such as *active* or *passive*) and conceptual nodes (which are not language specific). Lemmas are further connected to language tags in order to allow for selective activation. However, when e.g., the Spanish word *golpear* [hit] is activated in a Spanish passive sentence, the combinatorial nodes for verb and passive are activated and hence make it more likely that subsequent language use in the other language of the bilingual will also use a passive verb – if the other language has similar syntactic structures. In sum, what the model posits is that syntax is shared across languages. The hypothesis in Schaeffer and Carl's model was that "shared representations are accessed very early during the process" (Schaeffer and Carl 2013, 174) and that during the early stages "there is no conscious control over how source and target are aligned cognitively" (Schaeffer and Carl 2013, 173).

An early, automatic effect of the TL on ST reading would be provided by an effect of, e.g., word order differences on first fixation durations. During reading, the eyes move from word to word and remain relatively stationary for certain periods of time. These stationary periods are called fixations. A first fixation duration is the time a reader spends looking at a word before either re-fixating the current word or before fixating a different word. The average fixation during normal reading is around 250ms and a great deal happens in this short period of time (Rayner 1998, 2009; Reichle, Warren and McConnell 2009), much of it thought to occur relatively automatically. The metric termed *Cross* (Carl, Schaeffer and Bangalore 2016, 26) has already been mentioned above. It denotes the word order differences between the ST and the TT segments. If the ST segment has exactly the same word order as the TT segment, then all words have a Cross value of 1. If, however, the first ST word is aligned to the sixth TT word, then the Cross value is 6. If the sixth ST word is aligned to the first TT word, then the Cross value is –6. As mentioned earlier, this feature of the TPR-DB is language independent and can therefore be used across languages. One other feature of the TPR-DB is called word translation entropy (HTra). It is computed by counting how many different TT items, which are aligned to the same ST item, there are in a corpus of a number of translations of the same ST. On the basis of the probabilities of each of these TT realisations, the distribution of these probabilities is calculated (Carl, Schaeffer and Bangalore 2016, 31). The more different TT realisations there are in a given sample of translations of the same ST, the larger the HTra value and the more likely it is that the overlap in terms of semantics is smaller. Schaeffer *et al.* (2016) found that both HTra and syntactic distortion (Cross) had a significant positive effect on first fixation durations and total reading time. Total reading time is the sum of all fixations on a particular word – irrespective of when they occur. The effect of Cross and HTra on first fixation durations probably represents early, automatic cognitive alignment, which is less effortful in the case of ST items for which the overlap between ST and TT representations in terms of syntax and semantics is greater (low HTra and Cross values). The data for the study by Schaeffer *et al.* (2016) consisted of 42,211 English ST words translated into six different target languages. While the large number of languages and the sizeable amount of data encourage confidence in the results, it should be stressed that a non-negligible amount of variation could not be explained with the predictors in the model presented by Schaeffer *et al.* (2016). In other words, while the model could make predictions with a certain degree of confidence, a possibly large number of variables which impact eye movements during translation remain unknown.

Main research methods

The principal research methods in TPR are eye tracking and keylogging. However, researchers are starting to use brain imaging techniques such as electroencephalography (EEG) and functional Magnetic Resonance Imaging (fMRI). The use of these imaging techniques is promising, although it is in its early stages within TS. One other fundamental distinction needs to be made: there are corpus-based eye movement or keylogging studies and those which tightly control stimuli and manipulate a (small number of) variable(s). Eye movement or keylogging corpus studies such as the one discussed above by Schaeffer *et al.* (2016) or the one by Balling and Carl (2014) normally control variables statistically, while experimental studies such as those by Bajo and colleagues (Macizo and Bajo 2004, 2006; Ruiz *et al.* 2008), the one by Wu and Thierry (2012) or the one by De Groot (1992) control variables in the design of the stimuli and the task. This is an important distinction and some advantages and disadvantages have already been discussed. In a typical experimental study, participants carry out one task and the stimuli consist of filler, critical and control items. Critical and control items are identical in many ways apart from one aspect or a small number of aspects. This makes it possible to make relatively strong claims regarding the effect of the manipulated variable on the dependent variable (reaction times, eye movement or keylogging measures, or ERP waveforms). Particular care is taken to make sure that the critical stimuli do not differ in any way apart from in the independent variable(s) of interest. The disadvantage of this kind of research is that, because stimuli and tasks are so highly controlled, and because sample sizes are often small, laborious replication is required to extend the results to other language combinations and participant samples – in addition to the fact that some tasks are unnatural: if, e.g., single sentences are presented one at a time in an eye tracking study, participants can normally not re-read earlier sentences and effects of the larger context cannot be measured. The dangers of corpus-based research are that a very large number of variables can have an effect on the dependent variable – many of which may be unknown. It may be that the hypothesised effect is in the data, but that it is buried under many other factors which are not included in the statistical model and which obscure the hypothesised effect. It may also be that the hypothesised effect is found, but that one or a number of unknown factors underlie the observed effect and the claim made on the basis of the observed effect should actually be attributed to (a) different (number of) aspect(s) of the data. Translation Studies is not alone in this conflict: there are a number of studies which investigate eye movements during normal reading on the basis of a corpus, such as the studies by Kennedy and Pynte (2005) or, more recently, by Cop, Drieghe and Duyck (2015). In the Cop *et al.* study, 19 bilinguals and 14 monolinguals read a whole novel while their eye movements were recorded. There are a very large number of experimental studies which investigate the effects of a particular, and highly controlled, aspect on eye movements (Rayner 1998, 2009). Ideally, findings from controlled experimental studies are tested in more natural settings and vice versa. The findings from single word studies such as the one by De Groot (1992) have been tested in studies involving single sentences (e.g., Schwartz and Kroll 2006) and in reading of a long text (e.g., Cop *et al.* 2015).

The dependent variables in eye tracking used in TPR have been imported from Psychology. The kind of research from which TPR has imported these eye movement measures was mainly interested in the early processes during reading. However, possibly the largest and most obvious difference between normal reading and reading while translating is that translation takes much longer than normal reading. Translation of course involves writing (in a different language) while normal reading does not. Kliegl *et al.* (2004) report a mean total reading time per word during reading for comprehension of 245ms (SD = 48). However, an examination of the data in the TPR-DB shows that during (monolingual) copying the mean total reading time per word on the source text is 797ms (SD = 1068), while during translation the mean total reading time per ST word is 1577ms (SD = 5824). Both latter tasks involve reading and producing a text and, on average, participants spend twice as long reading an ST word when they are translating it than when they are copying it and six times as long as when they are reading for comprehension. The co-ordination of reading and writing in addition to having to manage the demands of interlinguistic reformulation therefore requires a different set of eye movement measures than those that are currently used in Psychology and TPR. Dragsted (2010) suggests one such measure, the eye–key span (EKS) which measures the time between first fixation of a word and the first keystroke which contributes to the translation of the equivalent target word(s). This is similar to the ear–voice span in simultaneous interpreting. Schaeffer and Carl (Forthcoming) propose to use the probability with which the ST is read while the TT is being typed. Schaeffer and Carl (2013) argued that this could be used as an indicator of the degree to which processes are automated, and Schaeffer and Carl (Forthcoming) find evidence to support this claim. However, given the strong effect of the task (translation) on the late eye movement measures such as total reading time, and given that traditional eye movement studies offer very few measures which can adequately describe these late processes, TPR is in need of more suitable tools to describe eye movements on a whole text while the subject is typing the translation.

The way keylogging contributes to TPR has traditionally been by either giving access to interim solutions of a translator (e.g., Tirkkonen-Condit, Mäkisalo and Immonen 2008) or by making use of the time delay between individual keystrokes, i.e., pauses in the flow of typing (e.g., Immonen 2006). Interim solutions consist of text which is typed and then deleted. This kind of data are not accessible on the basis of the final TT, but keylogging allows the analysis of these deleted keystrokes. There are a number of features in the TPR-DB, which are unique to it, unlike the traditional eye movement measures imported from Psychology. Two will be described in detail.

The *InEff* feature (Carl, Schaeffer and Bangalore 2016, 26) describes the inefficiency with which a translation is produced. It is calculated by dividing the number of keystrokes which contributed to the production of a translation by the number of characters in the final TT. If the translator did not revise the translation in any way, *InEff* is 1; but if, say, the word was completely rewritten once, *InEff* is 2 – the higher this value, the more editing went into the translation.

The *Munit* feature (Carl, Schaeffer and Bangalore 2016, 25) indicates how many Micro Units (Alves and Vale 2011) a translator needs in order to produce a particular item. A Micro Unit is defined as a continuous typing activity between pauses (no typing) of 1 second or more. The information in the TPR-DB for a *Munit* is its duration, the duration of the typing pause that preceded it, the number of fixations that occurred (on the ST and the TT) during this *Munit*, and the time that the participant spent reading the ST while typing the TT. All durations are in milliseconds, so it is possible to analyse typing and eye movement behaviour in a fairly detailed manner. The rich features that the TPR-DB offers make it an ideal resource for the modelling of the cognitive processes during translation.

Current debates

Possibly the most well-studied model of the bilingual lexicon is the Revised Hierarchical Model (RHM) (Kroll and Stewart 1994). There are other, more recent models (Dong, Gui and MacWhinney 2005), in addition to the DFM (De Groot 1992) referred to earlier. Studies in TPR rarely base predictions on these models or attempt to test the predictions made by these models. This is partly because these models focus on lexical equivalence and are typically based on single word studies. However, García (2015, 21) argues that

> Accessing lexical equivalents of source-text words is just one of multiple mental activities during translation, and a most basic one at that. However, the basic nature of this skill does not render it trivial. On the contrary, it underscores the importance of studying lexical equivalence to understand more complex translation processes, since they will necessarily imply such a skill.

Given that the RHM makes very clear predictions regarding the impact of directionality on linguistic processing during translation – predictions which have been extensively tested – and given that basic factors such as cognate status, concreteness and L2 proficiency have been found to have reliable effects on behaviour during translation, it seems odd that these factors very rarely find their way into the design of experiments in TPR. It seems that, because of the lack of ecological validity (natural tasks and stimuli) in the many single word studies, researchers in TPR have rejected these findings. However, the reverse is also true: authors of single word studies do not tend to refer to studies which employ more natural texts and tasks – presumably because these researchers distrust results from studies which lack the kind of control employed in single word studies. Neutralising the tension between controlled experimental studies and studies which use more ecologically valid designs, and cross-fertilisation between findings from the two camps, promises to yield interesting findings and could lead to solid, generalisable results which will find their way into pedagogical and commercial applications.

Future directions

Three research trends which have already been highlighted above are likely to play an important role in future TPR. The findings from corpus-based research, i.e., studies of large corpora of translated texts (e.g., Hansen-Schirra, Neumann and Steiner 2012) could relatively easily be tested in TPR, but this has not happened to date. The model by Halverson (2003) may provide a good framework for the generation of hypotheses. Secondly, the incorporation of models and the testing of hypotheses generated on the basis of single word studies in the context of bilingualism research has not happened either and is likely to lead to interesting findings. Thirdly, the testing of findings from corpus-based TPR in controlled experiments is likely to lead to more solid models. In addition, machine learning has been used with TPR data (e.g., Martinez-Gomez et al. 2014). Martinez-Gomez et al. automatically classify process data (eye movement and keystroke records) in terms of whether and to what degree participants are professionals or not. Martinez-Gomez et al. were able to tell – with a reasonable degree of confidence – whether a participant was an expert or not and how many years' experience a translator had (with a margin of error of 4.15 years). This approach is likely to be exploited in future studies, because it has the potential to be useful in a number of applications (see below).

Implications for Practice

The challenge for TPR is to produce results which are relevant for the translation-related industries and the teaching of translation. So far, the findings from TPR have not achieved this aim. In the context of the post-editing of machine translation, there has been research which is more likely to be relevant for industry (e.g., Doherty, O'Brien and Carl 2010; Lacruz, Denkowski and Lavie 2014; Vieira 2014; O'Brien 2005, 2006, 2007). However, most of these studies investigate the relationship between cognitive effort and the quality of the machine-translated text – linguistic processing is subsumed under the generic term "cognitive effort" without necessarily specifying the actual processes which take place.

Further Reading

Carl, M., Bangalore, S. and Schaeffer, M. J. 2016. *New Directions in Empirical Translation Process Research: Exploring the CRITT TPR-DB*. Berlin: Springer.
Chapter 2 in this book gives a good overview of all the features in the TPR-DB. It also contains accounts of a large number of studies – all of which use the TPR-DB in one way or another.

Ferreira, A. and Schwieter, J. W. 2015. *Psycholinguistic and Cognitive Inquiries into Translation and Interpreting*. Amsterdam: John Benjamins.
This book gives a good overview of more current studies into the cognitive aspects of translation (and interpreting).

Shreve, G. M. and Angelone, E. 2010. *Translation and Cognition*. Amsterdam: John Benjamins.
This book is a good source for earlier studies and contains accounts of both empirical and more theoretical investigations.

Related topics

Corpus linguistics, translation and interpreting; Translation, interpreting and new technologies.

References

Alves, F., Göpferich, S. and Mees, I. M., eds. 2009. *Methodology, Technology and Innovation in Translation Process Research: A Tribute to Arnt Lykke Jakobsen*. Copenhagen: Samfundslitteratur.
Alves, F. and Vale, D. C. 2011. On drafting and revision in translation: a corpus linguistics oriented analysis of translation process data. In *Parallel Corpora: Annotation, Exploitation, Evaluation*. Special issue of *Translation: Corpora, Computation, Cognition* 1(1), pp. 105–122.
Baker, M. 1993. "Corpus Linguistics and Translation Studies". In *Text and Technology: In Honour of John Sinclair*, edited by M. Baker, G. Francis and E. Tognini-Bonelli, 233–250. Amsterdam: John Benjamins.
Balling, L. W. and Carl, M. 2014. "Production Time Across Languages and Tasks: A Large-Scale Analysis Using the CRITT Translation Process Database". In *The Development of Translation Competence: Theories and Methodologies from Psycholinguistics and Cognitive Science*, edited by J. W. Schwieter and A. Ferreira, 239–268. Newcastle upon Tyne: Cambridge Scholars Publishing.

Campbell, S. 2000. "Choice Network Analaysis in Translation Research". In *Intercultural Faultlines: Research Models in Translation Studies I – Textual and Cognitive Aspects*, edited by M. Olohan, 29–42. Manchester: St Jerome.

Carl, M. 2012. "Translog-II: A Program for Recording User Activity Data for Empirical Reading and Writing Research". In *The Eighth International Conference on Language Resources and Evaluation, 21–27 May 2012*, 2–6. Istanbul, Turkey: Department of International Language Studies and Computational Linguistics.

Carl, M., Aizawa, A. and Yamada, M. 2016. "English-to-Japanese Translation vs. Dictation vs. Postediting: Comparing Translation Modes in a Multilingual Setting". In *The LREC 2016 Proceedings: Tenth International Conference on Language Resources and Evaluation*, edited by N. Calzolari, K. Choukri, T. Declerck, M. Grobelnik, B. Maegaard, J. Mariani, A. Moreno, J. Odijk and S. Piperidis, 4024–4031. Portorož: ELRA.

Carl, M. and Schaeffer, M. J. 2017. "Models of the Translation Process". In *The Handbook of Translation Studies and Cognition*, edited by J. Schwieter and A. Ferreira, 50–70. Amsterdam: John Benjamins.

Carl, M., Schaeffer, M. J. and Bangalore, S. 2016. "The CRITT Translation Process Research Database". In *New Directions in Empirical Translation Process Research: Exploring the CRITT TPR-DB2*, edited by M. Carl, S. Bangalore and M. Schaeffer, 13–54. Cham: Springer.

Cop, U., Drieghe, D. and Duyck, W. 2015. Eye movement patterns in natural reading: a comparison of monolingual and bilingual reading of a novel. *PLoS ONE* 10(8), pp. 1–38.

Doherty, S., O'Brien, S. and Carl, M. 2010. Eye tracking as an MT evaluation technique. *Machine Translation* 24(1), pp. 1–13.

Dong, Y., Gui, S. and MacWhinney, B. 2005. Shared and separate meanings in the bilingual mental lexicon. *Bilingualism: Language and Cognition* 8(3), pp. 221–238.

Dragsted, B. 2010. "Coordination of Reading and Writing Processes in Translation: An Eye on Uncharted Territory". In *Translation and Cognition*, edited by G. M. Shreve and E. Angelone, 41–62. Amsterdam: John Benjamins.

Dragsted, B. 2012, Indicators of difficulty in translation: correlating product and process data. *Across Languages and Cultures* 13(1), pp. 81–98.

Ericsson, K. A. and Simon, H. A. 1984. *Protocol Analysis: Verbal Reports as Data*. Cambridge, MA: MIT Press.

García, A. M. 2015. Psycholinguistic explorations of lexical translation equivalents: thirty years of research and their implications for cognitive translatology. *Translation Spaces* 4(1), pp. 9–28.

Göpferich, S., Alves, F. and Mees, I. M., eds. 2010. *New Approaches in Translation Process Research*. Copenhagen: Samfundslitteratur.

Göpferich, S., Jakobsen, A. L. and Mees, I. M., eds. 2008. *Looking at Eyes: Eye-Tracking Studies of Reading and Translation Processing*. Copenhagen: Samfundslitteratur.

De Groot, A. M. B. 1992. Determinants of word translation. *Journal of Experimental Psychology: Learning, Memory, and Cognition* 18(5), pp. 1001–1018.

De Groot, A. M. B. and Starreveld, P. A. 2015. "Parallel Language Activation in Bilinguals' Word Production and its Modulating Factors: A Review and Computer Simulations". In *The Cambridge Handbook of Bilingual Processing*, edited by J. Schwieter, 389–415. Cambridge: Cambridge University Press.

Halverson, S. 2003. The cognitive basis of translation universals. *Target: International Journal of Translation Studies* 2(15), pp. 197–241.

Hansen-Schirra, S., Neumann, S. and Steiner, E. 2012. *Cross-Linguistic Corpora for the Study of Translations: Insights from the Language Pair English-German*. Berlin: de Gruyter.

Hartsuiker, R. J., Pickering, M. J. and Veltkamp, E. 2004. Is syntax separate or shared between languages? Cross-linguistic syntactic priming in Spanish-English bilinguals. *Psychological Science* 15(6), pp. 409–414.

Immonen, S. 2006. Translation as a writing process: pauses in translation versus monolingual text production. *Target: International Journal of Translation Studies* 18(2), pp. 313–336.

Jakobsen, A. L. 2003. "Effects of Think Aloud on Translation Speed, Revision and Segmentation". In *Triangulating Translation: Perspectives in Process Oriented Research*, edited by F. Alves, 69–95. Amsterdam: John Benjamins.

Jakobsen, A. L., Mees, I. M. and Göpferich, S., eds. 2009. *Behind the Mind: Methods, Models and Results in Translation Process Research*. Copenhagen: Samfundslitteratur.

Jakobsen, A. L. and Schou, L. 1999. "Translog Documentation". In *Probing the Process in Translation: Methods and Results*, edited by G. Hansen, 1–36. Frederiksberg: Samfundslitteratur.

Jensen, K. T. H., Sjørup, A. C. and Balling, L. W. 2009. "Effects of L1 Syntax on L2 Translation". In *Methodology, Technology and Innovation in Translation Process Research: A Tribute to Arnt Lykke Jakobsen*, edited by F. Alves, S. Göpferich and I. M. Mees, 319–336. Copenhagen: Samfundslitteratur.

Kennedy, A. and Pynte, J. 2005. Parafoveal-on-foveal effects in normal reading. *Vision Research* 45, pp. 153–168.

Kliegl, R., Grabner, E., Rolfs, M. and Engbert, R. 2004. Length, frequency, and predictability effects of words on eye movements in reading. *European Journal of Cognitive Psychology* 16(1–2), pp. 262–284.

Krings, H. P. 1986. *Was in den Köpfen von Übersetzern vorgeht: eine empirische Untersuchung zur Struktur des Übersetzungsprozesses an fortgeschrittenen Französischlernern*. Tübingen: Günter Narr Verlag.

Krings, H. P. 2001. *Repairing Texts: Empirical Investigations of Machine Translation Post-Editing Processes*. Kent, OH: The Kent State University Press.

Kroll, J., Gullifer, J., Mcclain, R. and Martin, M. C. 2015. "Selection and Control in Bilingual Comprehension and Production". In *The Cambridge Handbook of Bilingual Processing*, edited by J. W. Schwieter, 485–507. Cambridge: Cambridge University Press.

Kroll, J. F. and Stewart, E. 1994. Category interference in translation and picture naming: evidence for asymmetric connections between bilingual memory representations. *Journal of Memory and Language* 33(2), pp. 149–174.

Lacruz, I., Denkowski, M. and Lavie, A. 2014. "Cognitive Demand and Cognitive Effort in Post-Editing". In *Proceedings of the AMTA 2014 Workshop on Post-Editing Technology and Practice*, edited by S. O'Brien, M. Simard and L. Specia, 73–84. Vancouver: Canada.

Langacker, R. 1987. *Foundations of Cognitive Grammar 1*. Stanford, CA: Stanford University Press.

Macizo, P. and Bajo, M. T. 2004. When translation makes the difference: sentence processing in reading and translation. *Psicológica* 25, pp. 181–205.

Macizo, P. and Bajo, M. T. 2006. Reading for repetition and reading for translation: do they involve the same processes? *Cognition* 99(1), pp. 1–34.

Malmkjær, K. 2011. "Translation Universals". In *The Oxford Handbook of Translation Studies*, edited by K. Malmkjær and K. Windle, 83–94. Oxford: Oxford University Press.

Martinez-Gomez, P., Minicha, A., Huang, J., Carl, M. and Aizawa, A. 2014. "Recognition of Translator Expertise Using Sequences of Fixations and Keystrokes". In *ETRA '14: Proceedings of the Symposium on Eye Tracking Research and Applications*, edited by P. Qvarfordt and D. Witzner Hansen, 299–302. New York: Association for Computing Machinery.

Muñoz Martín, R. 2010. "On paradigms and cognitive translatology". In *Translation and Cognition*, edited by G. Shreve and E. Angelone, 169–187. Amsterdam: John Benjamins.

Neisser, U. 1976. *Cognition and Reality*. San Francisco: Freeman.

Neisser, U. 1987. *Concepts and Conceptual Development: Ecological and Intellectual Factors in Categorization*. Cambridge: Cambridge University Press.

O'Brien, S. 2005. Methodologies for measuring the correlations between post-editing effort and machine translatability. *Machine Translation* 19(1), pp. 37–58.

O'Brien, S. 2006. Pauses as indicators of cognitive effort in post-editing machine translation output. *Across Languages and Cultures* 7(1), pp. 1–21.

O'Brien, S. 2007. Eye-tracking and translation memory matches. *Perspectives* 14(3), pp. 185–205.

Rayner, K. 1998. Eye movements in reading and information processing: 20 years of research. *Psychological Bulletin* 124(3), pp. 372–422.

Rayner, K. 2009. Eye movements and attention in reading, scene perception, and visual search. *Quarterly Journal of Experimental Psychology* 62(8), pp. 1457–1506.

Reichle, E. D., Warren, T. and McConnell, K. 2009. Using E-Z reader to model the effects of higher level language processing on eye movements during reading. *Psychonomic Bulletin and Review* 16(1), pp. 1–21.

Ruiz, C., Paredes, N., Macizo, P. and Bajo, M. T. 2008. Activation of lexical and syntactic target language properties in translation. *Acta Psychologica* 128(3), pp. 490–500.

Schaeffer, M. J. and Carl, M. 2013. Shared representations and the translation process: a recursive model. *Translation and Interpreting Studies* 8(2), pp. 169–190.

Schaeffer, M. J. and Carl, M. Forthcoming. "Translation and Non-Translational Language Use". In *Empirical Modelling of Translation and Interpreting*, edited by S. Hansen-Schirra, O. Čulo, S. Hofmann and B. Meyer. Berlin: Language Science Press.

Schaeffer, M. J., Dragsted, B., Hvelplund, K. T. and Balling, L. W. 2016. "Word Translation Entropy: Evidence of Early Target Language Activation During Reading for Translation". In *New Directions in Empirical Translation Process Research: Exploring the CRITT TPR-DB*, edited by M. Carl, S. Bangalore and M. Schaeffer, 183–210. Berlin: Springer.

Schwartz, A. I. and Kroll, J. F. 2006. Bilingual lexical activation in sentence context. *Journal of Memory and Language* 55(2), pp. 197–212.

Seleskovitch, D. 1976. "Interpretation: A Psychological Approach to Translating". In *Translation: Applications and Research*, edited by R. W. Brislin, 92–116. New York: Gardner.

Sharp, B., Zock, M., Carl, M. and Jakobsen, A. L., eds. 2011. *Human–Machine Interaction in Translation: Proceedings of the 8th International NLPCS Workshop*. Copenhagen: Samfundslitteratur.

Sirén, S. and Hakkarainen, K. 2002. Expertise in translation. *Across Languages and Cultures* 3(1), pp. 71–82.

Tirkkonen-Condit, S. 2004. "Unique Items: Over- or Under-Represented in Translated Language?" In *Translation Universals: Do they Exist?*, edited by A. Mauranen and P. Kujamäki, 177–184. Amsterdam: John Benjamins.

Tirkkonen-Condit, S., Mäkisalo, J. and Immonen, S. 2008. The translation process: interplay between literal rendering and a search for sense. *Across Languages and Cultures* 9, pp. 1–15.

Vieira, L. N. 2014. Indices of cognitive effort in machine translation post-editing. *Machine Translation* 28(3–4), pp. 187–216.

Wu, Y. J. and Thierry, G. 2012. Unconscious translation during incidental foreign language processing. *NeuroImage* 59(4), pp. 3468–3473.

19

Sociolinguistics, translation, and interpreting

Federico M. Federici

Introduction

Translating and interpreting are sociolinguistic activities. Language mediations through interpreters and translators happen as part of normative social practices and are dictated by social and language behavioural rules that continuously evolve. Any language mediation occurs in this type of social communicative interaction, whether the agents in the communication are present (interpreting) or meet through the mediation (translation). No other discipline studies the interrelations established between message senders and receivers to create meaning through the interactive social context as closely as sociolinguistics. The same focus on how the factors influencing this interrelation organise meaning represents a priority for any language mediator. From the creation of machine-readable controlled texts to *ad-hoc* interpreting in the aftermath of an avalanche in a mountainous destination for international tourists, few processes are as concerned as translation and interpreting are with register, channel of communication, tenor, field, function of the message, and social relationships between interactants. These tend to be more complex than in cases of monolingual communication, since the sender of the message is typically from a different speech community than the receiver's, although the two may have several similarities in terms of sociolinguistic features that make it possible to achieve the task of mediating between cultures and languages, difficult though it may be.

Translation and interpreting studies (henceforth T&I) are two disciplines with many concerns in common but also several differences in the priority research areas they investigate (Gile, Hansen, and Pokorn 2010). As Gile (2004, 30) puts it, "translation and interpreting share much, both as professional activities and as research activities [making them] natural partners in development". Hence, in this chapter, T&I is used to refer to studies in either discipline that have acknowledged that sociolinguistic methods, concerns, and findings have much to offer to, and much to learn from, studies focused on interpreting and translation acts (Bayley, Cameron, and Lucas 2013b). The chapter maps concepts, ideas, and scholarly work that emphasise the natural relationship between T&I and the study of communication as pursued by sociolinguistics. More than a "natural and fruitful friend to translation studies" (Ramos Pinto 2012, 161), an essential understanding of sociolinguistic concepts is intrinsically beneficial to professional and trainee translators, whilst also offering counter-arguments to any claims about the untranslatability of dialects, minority, or regional languages (Federici, F. M. 2011).

This overview is divided into four sections. Firstly, it looks at classical and recent definitions of sociolinguistics that enable the conceptual mapping of its relationship with T&I; eliciting the epistemological concerns of the discipline shows their proximity with the discourse on interpreting and translating processes. Secondly, it considers the relationships between interpreting and sociolinguistics and those between translation and sociolinguistics. Thirdly, the notion that the act of communication is genre, context, and text-specific will be discussed in relation to sociolinguistic key terms (such as register and language variety). Finally, this overview suggests that recent, relevant research in T&I, focused on sociolinguistic positions, shows that an understanding of sociolinguistics is likely to become an intrinsic part of the competence of translators and interpreters of the 21st century, as they operate in an ever more technologically competitive context.

Historical perspectives

Independently of the many twists and turns of debates surrounding translation, most researchers and scholars in the field would agree that there is a natural relationship between linguistics, translation, and interpreting (Şerban 2013, 216). Independently of the length, complexity, and level of automation in the creation of the source message, intercultural language mediators and scholars of sociolinguistics share a concern with the concept of the "audience" for communicative acts. They also share the certainty that neither the description of language use in a speech community (sociolinguistics) nor the attempt to render a message from that language into another language in writing (translation) or orally (interpreting) can be discussed through monolithic, prescriptive, and unchangeable concepts. This section elicits the embeddedness of sociolinguistic concepts in acts of translation and interpreting.

Sociolinguistics as a discipline developed through work by linguists in the late 1960s, and is defined as follows by Crystal (2008, 440–441):

> sociolinguistics (n.) A branch of linguistics which studies all aspects of the relationship between language and society. Sociolinguists study such matters as the linguistic identity of social groups, social attitudes to language, standard and non-standard forms of language, the patterns and needs of national language use, social varieties and levels of language, the social basis of multilingualism, and so on. [. . .] In Hallidayan linguistics, the term sociosemantics has a somewhat broader sense, in which the choices available within a grammar are related to communication roles found within the speech situation, as when a particular type of question is perceived in social terms to be a threat. The term overlaps to some degree with ethnolinguistics and anthropological linguistics, reflecting the overlapping interests of the correlative disciplines involved – sociology, ethnology and anthropology. The study of dialects is sometimes seen as a branch of sociolinguistics, and sometimes differentiated from it, under the heading of dialectology, especially when regional dialects are the focus of study.

The definition indicates that where philosophical differences in positioning the relationship of language and society change, they engender a shift in perspective, as happens in several European linguistic traditions (e.g. in France, Italy, Germany, and Spain). Here, the term sociological linguistics is used to emphasise the integration of the study of language within the broader theoretical framework of sociological theories (drawing on Gramsci's reflections on language, see Boothman 2008). Another definition is found in Hudson (1980/1996, 3; italics in the original): "We can define sociolinguistics as *the study of language in relation to society*". Hudson goes on to discuss sociolinguistics as a dynamic phenomenon. Translating and interpreting are dynamic acts; traditional linguistics predominantly perceived meaning as stable within language systems, whilst Hudson (1980/1996, 10) emphasises that "society consists of individuals, and both sociologists and sociolinguists would agree that it is essential to keep individuals firmly in the centre of interest, and to avoid losing sight of them while talking about large-scale abstractions and movements". The centrality of speakers as actors in the generation of meaning concerns T&I scholars in more ways than one, as shown in work on sociolinguistics and gender (e.g. Federici, E. 2011; Ergün 2010), on social stereotypes in audiovisual translation (e.g. González Vera 2012), on literature (e.g. Sánchez 2007; Klaudy 2007), on journalistic genres (e.g. Marques Santos 2012), on songs (Al-Azzam and Al-Quran 2012) – in fact on any language feature considered by sociolinguists; and work within T&I which adopts sociolinguistic approaches in relation to identity (Cronin 2006; Gerbault 2010), conflict and narratives (Baker 2006; Harding 2013), and discourse (Hatim and Mason 1990, 1997; Munday 2012) developed in parallel with the opening up of new research directions in sociolinguistics (see also Ramos Pinto 2009).

Sociolinguistics is closely connected to T&I because even the most experienced practitioners know that no text is ever identical to a previous or later text. The more stylistically dense the texts, the more language mediators can agree with some of the tenets of sociolinguistics, such as that "we can be sure that *no two speakers have the same language, because no two speakers have the same experience of language*" (Hudson 1980/1996, 11; italics in the original). Among disciplines related to T&I, sociolinguistics is significant because it engages with individual manifestations of language as much as unifying categories that describe language phenomena.

Malmkjær (2011, 60–62) introduces the work of Catford (1965) as one of the first linguists interested in systemic functional grammar to contribute to adopting a systemic functional approach to debates in translation. Catford viewed translation as an event to be studied within applied linguistics. It may similarly be suggested that one of the concepts with the longest-lasting impact in T&I emerged from the London School of Sociolinguistics, initiated by J. R. Firth in the late 1960s, namely that:

> speech has a social function, both as a means of communication and also as a way of identifying social groups, and to study speech without reference to the society which uses it is to exclude the possibility of finding social explanations for the structures that are used.
>
> (Hudson 1980/1996, 3)

Halliday's systemic functional linguistics (SFL) with its reflections on the interrelations between registers and functions of utterances in meaning-making stems from the London School, and his sociolinguistics has had the most extensive and consistent influence in T&I (see also the Chapter 1 in this volume). Halliday considers language phenomena part of a sociosemiotic interrelationship that creates meaning. Incorporating semiotics into linguistics, his approach to studying languages radically reconceptualised all the parameters of language systems that enable linguists to study how and why meaning is made within the infinite potential of permutations that allows any language to express concepts in innumerable different ways. This conceptualisation of language enables translators and interpreters to communicate concepts and ideas that are culturally alien to a social group in distant and unrelated social contexts, expressed by distant and incompatible languages. By combining well-established considerations of languages as systemic entities, Halliday (1994, 16) posits language as a "network of systems, or interrelated sets of options for making meaning", which is functional both diachronically (any language develops as it is because of what it has evolved to do) and synchronically (any utterance in a language performs a function). Halliday's definition of language acts as a catalyst in which semiotic approaches and social approaches based on studying language as a multidimensional interaction converge to consider language phenomena as "reflect[ing] the multidimensional nature of human experience and interpersonal relations" (Halliday 2003, 29).

Core issues and topics

According to Nida (1976, 1979, 1993), sociolinguistics offers tools for the interpretation of the communicative act, thus enabling scholars and practitioners to analyse texts as communicative entities. Textual and extra-textual information supports the meaning-making process of any text, and Nida concludes that "only a sociolinguistic approach to translation is ultimately valid" (Nida 1976, 77; see also Pergnier 1978). In the 1970s, Halliday and Hasan's work on register exerted a strong influence on House (1977, 1997) and had, by the 1980s, become dominant among the concepts of the (then) newly-named discipline of Translation Studies. Snell-Hornby (1988/1995), Hönig and Kußmaul (1982), and Gerzymisch-Arbogast (1986) embedded sociolinguistic reflections on register in their work, which became dominant in the 1990s. After Baker's (1992) textbook and Bassnett and Lefevere's edited collection (1990), neither practical nor theoretical discussions in Translation Studies could exclude the sociolinguistic dimension with its emphasis on culture, context, individuality, and other "linguistic" dimensions of translations. The move to an interdisciplinary field of study included a sense of continuum that sociolinguistic perspectives on language and translation facilitated, in place of the 1960s and 1970s debates on the tension between language and culture (discussed in Șerban 2013). Halliday himself engaged with translation (1987) and recognised that sociolinguistic theories would benefit its practice; Yallop (1987) lamented the limited impact of Hallidayan work in translation, and Newmark (1987, 293) affirmed that "Hallidayan linguistics which sees language primarily as a meaning potential should offer itself as a serviceable tool for determining the constituent parts of a source language texts and its network of relations with its translation". During what was termed the "Cultural Turn" in Translation Studies, new emphasis on the interrelation between cultures and languages also came from the broader impact of Eco's semiotics and from cultural studies. Semiotic codes, as language systems were considered by semioticians, related directly to sociocultural behaviours. At the end of the 1990s, Katan (1999, 2004/2014) further underpinned the conceptual shifts, by linking notions emerging from anthropology (Giglioli 1972), anthropological linguistics (Ahearn 2011; Duranti 1997, 2001), and evolutionary linguistics to established sociolinguistic perspectives.

Discussions on register enabled translation and interpreting scholars to draw direct links between "language in use" as described in pragmatics and social practices, anthropology, and ethnography (Hudson 1980/1996, 10–11). The links can be made on the basis of anthropological and cultural concepts such as those of identity, belonging, status, norm, gender, power, positioning, marginality, environment, age, race, and many more aspects of human nature that are characteristics of sociolinguistic studies of language and society (see Trudgill 1992). One of the core features of systemic functional linguistics is its focus on concepts that have become central to current sociolinguistics (be they variationist or otherwise), including Halliday and Hasan's seminal work on "register". The term register (initially used by Reid

1956, 32) became the keyword to discuss language variety in relation to social constructs, as changes of register generate variations in language in relation to the characteristics of the user and related to their use, "in the sense that each speaker has a range of varieties and choices between them at different times" (Halliday, McIntosh, and Strevens 1964). The range correlates complex scenarios of choice of meaning depending on the function and social context of the communication, "If different types speak differently we can use our own speech to signal this choice. In other words, at each utterance our speech can be seen as an act of identity in a multidimensional space (Le Page and Tabouret-Keller 1985)" (Hudson 1980/1996, 12). Individuals' linguistic choices depend on the complexity of social relations. Hence, the relationship between meaning and context becomes central, and undeniably a conceptual tool for any translator or interpreter. Halliday and Hasan (1976, 22) understand register to be "the linguistic features which are typically associated with a configuration of situational features – with particular values of the field, mode and tenor", and House (1997, 2015, 64–65) discusses the relevance of these notions to achieving quality in translation. The three values of field, mode, and tenor are determining factors for significant linguistic features of the text: "The register is the set of meanings, the configuration of semantic patterns, that are typically drawn upon under the specified conditions, along with the words and structures that are used in the realization of these meanings" (Halliday and Hasan 1976, 23).

"Register" is a term that indicates specific values for words in relation to a speech community and a purpose. The concept is so significant and useful from a practical point of view that it has become integrated in a (market-driven) standard, the ISO Standard 12620:2009 (originally of 1999 and revised in 2009) on the Data Category Registry. The standard categorises a number of registers (bench level, dialect, facetious, formal, in-house, ironic, neutral, slang, taboo, technical, vulgar) in the Hallidayan sense. These categorisations, which emerge from descriptive studies of the fluid dynamics of meaning-making found in any language in use, become "standardised" codes to support translation technologies, computational linguistics, and natural language processing (see Bononno 2000). The applicability of register as a sociolinguistic concept to the most applied areas of T&I professional supports (terminology) is evidence of the recognisability of specific speech communities as receivers and senders of messages controlling and controlled by their own "sociolects" and varieties of the language. These are varieties of specialist language as much as sociolects of specific geographical areas (dialectal groupings) are, but most importantly are recognisable features of specialist language that translators and interpreters cannot ignore when working for the speech community that uses that language.

Halliday's (1990) analysis of two paragraphs of Darwin's *The Origin of the Species* (1859) suggests a system that allows translators and interpreters to discuss registers in relation to all textual genres. Through the definition of "register", Halliday explains translatability and untranslatability in simple terms: "we can translate different registers into a foreign language. We cannot translate different dialects: we can only mimic dialect variation" (Halliday 1990, 169). Here, Halliday distinguishes between register and dialect in the following terms: registers are "ways of saying different things" (*ibid.*) whereas "prototypically, dialects differ in expression; our notion of them is that they are 'different ways of saying the same thing'" (Halliday 1990, 168). Register is a flexible yet complex system, central to language, and a powerful tool that enables practitioners and theorists to compare completely different texts, from oral interactions to written forms of regional varieties.

One variety for which the study of its registers seems to be particularly useful for translation and interpreting is the broader concept of the term sociolect, "used by some sociolinguists to refer to a linguistic variety (or lect) defined on social (as opposed to regional) grounds, e.g. correlating with a particular social class or occupational group" (Crystal 2008, 440). This definition is comprehensive and can be used to criticise a literary or creative translation as, often, recognisable characters "exist" in the world outside the pages; it arguably works for some areas of oral interactions as well (legalese, court language, bureaucratese, police interpreting, and so on). The references within this definition to social components, social classes, and social status allow us to recognise a variety of speakers of a community (from mathematicians and scientists, to workers, to politicians). Their *lect* is a variety of discourse and language as well, with syntax and vocabulary shared by the group but not necessarily by non-members or all of the members of the group. Translators and interpreters operate on these very features to render a source text for a similar speech group in the target language.

In Hudson's (1980/1996) definitions of sociolinguistics, the relationship between the individual speaker (and her unique use of the language) and the speech community (and their recognisable set of shared features of register as a community of individuals) speak to interpreters and translators, who often deal with unique voices – however poor, good, authoritative, prescriptive, loose – in the source texts. In this perspective, an idiolect can be considered as the ensemble of linguistic features belonging to a person which is affected by geographical, educational, and even physical factors including class, gender, race, and historical influences that contribute to shaping one's ideological persona. This category is therefore relevant beyond stylistics, as illustrated in Wales's definition (2001, 197):

> The usage of an individual may well be constrained by his or her place of origin, but idiolect covers those features which vary from register to register, medium to medium, in daily language use; as well as the more permanent features that arise from personal idiosyncrasies, such as lisping, monotone delivery, favourite exclamations, etc. Idiolect thus becomes the equivalent of a finger-print: each of us is unique in our language habits. Such "voice-prints" are of great value to dramatists or novelists as a ready means of characterization, along with physical attributes.

These definitions blur and overlap, confirming "that society is structured, from a socio-linguistic point of view, in terms of a multi-dimensional space" (Hudson 1980/1996, 11). This space could be physical, involving globalised languages, or virtual as in the case of speech communities that operate on the incorporeal dimension of the internet.

In terms of translational activity, Hatim and Mason's (1990, 44) views on the definition of idiolect are interesting. They cite O'Donnell and Todd's definition of idiolect (1980, 62) that distinguishes between dialect and style: "'dialect', as the kind of variety which is found between idiolects, and 'style' as the kind of variety found within idiolects". Be they dialectal or stylistic, ephemeral, oral, or written down, these are challenges that are shared by interpreters and translators. The blurring of sociolinguistic definitions reflects the complexity of sociolinguistic research and of language as human interaction. For translators and interpreters, either consciously or unconsciously, the more abstract conceptualisations may not necessarily matter, but the sociolinguistic features of any act of communication contribute significantly to the creation of a message for a specific audience and initiate the offer of communication. The "varieties" of a codified grammar and syntax that we can know inside-out can yet throw at us unexpected constructions and formulae that make rendering their meaning a challenge. Trainee language mediators for translation and interpreting professions in the 21st century need to understand the complexity of language acts that presupposes relationships between meaning and speakers, relationships between speech communities and institutional or linguistic powers, relationships between correctness and idiomaticity, and relationships between gender, education, age, cultural beliefs, religious beliefs, sociocultural norms, and meaning-making.

Newmark (1988, 206) explains the importance of sociolectal features as follows:

> On the whole the quirks and sports of idiolect are normalised by the translator: in particular, rather exaggerated or exuberant metaphors and extravagant descriptive adjectives. [...] In some cases, it is not easy to distinguish between poor writing and idiolect [...] but the translator does not have to make the distinction, and merely normalises.

Although this point on the sociolinguistic rendering of idiolectal features may be valid for translators, the same context necessitates different reactions from interpreters, because in speech situations idiolectal features signify specific emotional states (in medical interpreting for instance) or deferential interactions (in police interrogations or legal interpreting). The two main macro-strategies, or norms in Toury's sense (1995/2012), may well be a standardisation or neutralisation, reducing the relevance and significance of the idiolect features, or a creative impetus to solve the impasse in entirely different ways; but many varieties of the language in use do not allow interpreters or translators to simply deploy them without jeopardising the quantity (let alone quality) of the information to be conveyed.

Current debates

The relationship between interlingual mediations, be they translation or interpreting acts, and sociolinguistics is undeniably close. Communicative acts happen in the language in use in a society, independently of the size of this "society" – be it made up of thousands or of a few members. This immediacy became the focus of much research in interpreting in the early 1980s, and was consolidated in work by Cecilia Wadensjö. Her work was influenced by interactional linguistics, a discipline which gradually came to affect the whole spectrum of research conducted in Interpreting Studies, from consecutive interpreting to liaison and dialogue interpreting in the community. Due to the immediate contextualisation of interpreting within an interactional speech act, the text mutates as part of the mediation in dialogue interpreting as well as in forms of conference interpreting where source speakers work on the basis of a prepared speech, but do not strictly speaking read it out. A speech community can include just one speaker per language plus the interpreter, in the interpreting triangle of dialogue interpreting; hence, the pertinence of sociolinguistics to debates in interpreting studies was recognised early in the life of sociolinguistics as a discipline. The predominant difference compared to Translation Studies is that the significance of sociolinguistics for interpreting studies is also acknowledged in works aimed at audiences interested in sociolinguistics, such as *The Oxford Handbook of Sociolinguistics*. The entry on interpreting in that handbook focuses far more clearly on the relationship between the disciplines than the entry on translation (Grin 2013), which focuses on relationships between issues in translation and issues in language policy and language contact, an ancillary position compared to the "equal" positioning of interpreting and sociolinguistics.

In Interpreting Studies, especially in texts for training (Allioni 1989), but also in the wider domain of community and dialogue interpreting, the relationship with sociolinguistics appeared entirely natural. It is worth noting that sociolinguistics is overwhelmingly monolingual, although Bayley, Cameron and Lucas (2013a, 1), editors of the *Oxford Handbook of Sociolinguistics*, note the need to consider "sociolinguistics as an interdisciplinary exercise, emphasizing new methodological developments, particularly the convergence of linguistic anthropology and variationist sociolinguistics", whilst also editorially challenging their discipline's status quo by inviting "contributors [who] have worked in a range of languages and address sociolinguistic issues in bi- and multilingual contexts" (*ibid.*). The issue of comparing translations to use their textual differences as "evidence" for sociolinguistic studies has been noted before (see Şerban 2013), and it is promising that the mutual relevance of research questions and concerns within closely related disciplines such as T&I studies and sociolinguistics has finally been perceived.

In their discussion of sign interpreting as a sociolinguistic activity, pioneers of the field of applying sociolinguistics to interpreting Metzger and Roy (2013, 736) emphasise that a number of years separate the growth of sociolinguistics in the 1960s and 1970s and pioneering research in interpreting. Sign interpreting was among the first areas to adopt sociolinguistic approaches (Cokely 1985, 1992; Roy 1989; Metzger 1995). Early work in interpreting (Gerver 1969/2002; Goldman-Eisler 1967) considered consecutive interpreting an object of study (Pöchhacker 2010b, 5) as part of research on psycholinguistics, given the cognitive load imposed by the task on the interpreters. For Pöchhacker, a more sociological approach was ushered in with the first research in medical interpreting (Cicourel 1981) by sociologists engaged with the social aspects of interaction rather than its linguistic impact. He observes that:

> only in relatively recent times, interpreting scholars have come to stake out their claim on the scientific landscape for the study of interpreting. By doing so, they are addressing a basic human (epistemological) need, taking charge of a phenomenon at the intersection of language, cognition, interaction and culture that is socially relevant and therefore clearly worth studying.
>
> (2010b, 7)

The delay may reflect a definition of interaction that was much more dominant in early studies of sign language interpreting, possibly a branch of interpreting that was less integrated in the spectrum from conference to dialogue interpreting until recently. For Metzger and Roy (2013, 76) the link between interpreting and sociolinguistics is self-evident: "Each interpreted interaction undertaken by a professional interpreter is situated within the sociolinguistic context of a relevant aspect of interpretation as a profession, but also the larger sociolinguistic context in which interpreters work" (2013, 376). It seems that this perspective reached interpreting researchers from a Translation Studies background, illustrating what Pöchhacker (2010a, 153) refers to as the "dual conceptual status of interpreting", as a discipline "at once subsumed under the broader notion of translation and set apart by its unique features". Mason's work on pragmatics, which was also significant in extending the notion of discourse in translation, extended to research in interpreting: Mason and Stewart (2001) posit a link between interactional linguistics and interpreting. Though Hallidayan ideas permeate many works in interpreting from the 1990s (Gile 1991; Shlesinger 1994, 1995), it is arguably in the areas of dialogue interpreting (Berk-Seligson 1990/2002) and especially in sign language interpreting that the sociolinguistic approach first flourished and produced a range of applicable findings. This context is considered by Metzger and Roy (2013, 376) as part of a reciprocity of focus between sociolinguistics and interpreting studies:

> Each interpreted interaction undertaken by a professional interpreter is situated within communities that harbor their own unique multilingual, bilingual, and language contact phenomenon; within a setting that represents a snapshot of what may be a long history of

language policies and planning; and in a social environment beset with language attitudes about one or both of the languages involved.

From the perspective introduced above, it seems almost tautological to say that core features of studies in interpreting tally with sociolinguistic approaches to the study of communication in society. Distinctions were drawn between conference interpreting and dialogue interpreting, with the latter emerging as an important area of training and research from the late 20th century, whilst with the Nuremberg trials the visibility of conference interpreters became embedded in high-level institutional, multilingual interactions. This visibility-focused research on the cognitive efforts of performing tasks in simultaneous conference interpreting.

The duality of focus corresponds also to a different relationship with power. Dialogic and typically illustrating an "unequal distribution of knowledge and power" (2010a, 155), for Pöchhacker there is a growing need for community-based interpreting in multicultural societies that strive for inclusivity and access to services for the multicultural and multilingual general public. The spectrum is not fixed but dynamic and interactions vary considerably across a range of contexts (see Pöchhacker 2004; Hale 2007). Positioning conference interpreting at one end of a spectrum of social interactions involved in interpreting and liaison interpreting (diplomatic, military, business settings with whispering as a variant of the simultaneous mode), and "community interpreting" at the other end of the spectrum, it is easy to see the importance of mode, tenor, and field of communication to power relations and domains of operation for interpreters. The fundamental concerns of sociolinguistics, such as changes in message constructions (discourse), are intrinsic in any modality of interpreting. In Wadensjö (1992, 1998), theorising interpreting within interactional sociolinguistics, a portrayal of the community interpreter emerged that shows the natural linkage of interpreting studies with sociolinguistics more clearly than had been the case in earlier work, although around the same time Moser-Mercer (1997) considered interpreting at the crossroads of interdisciplinary research approaches necessary to cognitive psychology. Pöchhacker (2010a, 157) considers this to be a different perspective to Wadensjö's, although, arguably, both theoretical positions have a focus on behavioural traits intrinsic to the activity of professional interpreters. Within sociolinguistics (and in particular in anthropological linguistics) behaviour traits explain processes of meaning-making as linguistic activities in a social setting independently of their conscious or unconscious psychological nature (see Giglioli 1972).

One similarity between translation, interpreting, and sociolinguistics therefore lies in the dominant descriptivism of the actual, authentic "acts" of interpreting, translation, and communication respectively. They are all focused on the intentional nature of constructing meaning as a dynamic rather than stable concept, from Toury's (1995/2012) influential drive towards a descriptive Translation Studies, which Gile (2004) considers equally applicable to interpreting studies, to recent redefinitions of the field in House (2014). Translation and interpreting studies are research areas that deal with socially driven and socially contextualised communication environments. They work with the same non-reductionist approach as sociolinguistics, which seeks to describe with comprehensible yet flexible categories vastly complex phenomena of language. For instance, this is the case with the relationship between a "speech community" and their variety of use, underpinned by specific functions and traditionally by some geographical interconnection, which is being reconsidered. Translators and interpreters operate within boundaries that would be considered core in sociolinguistics; it could be argued that a thorough understanding of sociolinguistics should be an intrinsic part of language mediator competence.

One of the theoretical strongholds of sociolinguistics is that this discipline embraces the complexity of realia. Rather than embracing reductionist models or systems, sociolinguists study the endless flows of infinite linguistic permutations connected with real speakers and their linguistic behaviours. It is impossible to generalise or simplify them into stable "structures". Even in the case of simplified languages as input for machine-translated texts, texts remain individual and dependent on context to create meaning, as well as anchored to a time of production and consumption in the case of literary texts (fiction, poetry, and plays). This distinguishing feature of communication acts applies to oral and written mediators alike. Discussing literature, Hofstadter (2009, 6) offers an emotive depiction of the uniqueness of idiolect when he becomes "aware of just how strange, even paradoxical, it was to use my native language – and, more specifically, my own deeply personal style of crafting, manipulating, and savouring phrases in my native language – to rewrite someone else's book". This individuality also relates to the notion of language variety that applies to the macro- as well as the micro level of analysis. Any speaker belongs to a speech community; this is the default position, however because language varieties are coagulations of different registers used by groups of speakers, it is better expressed by saying that any speaker belongs to a number of speech communities. Authentic conversations and interactions, authentic texts, retain the characteristics of belonging to a specialised language of sorts, hence the appropriateness of discussing texts in relation to language varieties. These language varieties share features within speech groups and retain different levels of uniqueness in the individual member of that group, the idiolect. Interpreting and translation attempt transmission of specific varieties to suitable, adequate, specialist, intermediate, and/or "equivalent" speech communities in the target language, which share comparable sociolinguistic features with the source speech community, or that the language mediators involved in the transmission consider as sharing similar features.

Sociolinguistic concepts of register and variety were reconsidered in the early decades of the 21st century in relation to global communication. House (2015, 99) refers to Blommaert's (2005, 73) concept of "orders of indexicality" as one that should make language mediators who strive for quality renderings in global communicative acts wary of *where* meaning is being created, and ultimately of the very notion of the variety of a "speech community". A further relevant observation is that these orders of indexical meanings continue to create sociolinguistic connections between linguistic signs and contexts, although such contexts may not necessarily be physical. If they are virtual, the functions of a community of speakers are not interpretable as sociolects of a *geophysical* nature: as "some of the biggest errors (and injustices) may be committed by simply projecting locally valid functions onto the ways of speaking of people who are involved in transnational flows" (Blommaert 2005, 72). From this perspective, House (2015, 99) warns that:

> classic sociolinguistic notions like "speech community" can no longer legitimately be held to be true. The focus needs to be on language in motion, with various spatiotemporal frames simultaneously interacting. Increasingly problematic is also the idea of a maintenance of functions: when linguistic items travel across time, space and indexical order, as they always do in translation, in transnational flows, they may well take on different locally valid functions.

Implications for practice

The transnational flow represents the death of concepts such as "lingua-culture" that offered useful points of departure for simplified discussions of culture and language interactions in translation from one national language into another, thus considering only dialects, minority languages, and regional sociolects as translation problems. Notions such as lingua-culture were in fact problematic from the outset (in any sociolinguistic perspective, no national language is entirely monolingual; and where tribal languages can be as remote and isolated as the speech community that uses them, diachronic discourse of language in contact still applies). Nevertheless, it could be argued that distinguishing virtual and global speech communities from local speech communities remains possible: the problematic nature of the global perspective does not invalidate the usability of the notion of speech community. A global speech community may use varieties of languages, such as the well-known international business English or commercial Chinglish; they are spatiotemporally distant from a South Frisian speech community but they can be considered as sociolects of a speech community, regardless of their virtual or global spatiality. Speech communities have become spatially different but not necessarily an obsolete category of thought, especially when such categories are used as analytical tools by language mediators.

Linguistic varieties and diachronic as well as synchronic variations are what make languages potentially able to express, in infinite permutations, infinite amounts of thoughts and feelings. The contrastive use of translations to discuss language behaviour as criticised by Şerban (2013, 215) fails because translation and interpreting are decision-making activities driven by the expectations, social norms, and individual behaviours expressed within the language variety and the idiolects used to create meaning in the target language. These reflect meaning in a similar variety as the one used in the source language, with the fluid imperfections of a crystal-clear surface of water mirroring one's face. The varieties can be very proximately within the linguistic system of departure and very distantly in the linguistic system of arrival; these distances in meaning, though immeasurable, nevertheless present the universal difficulty of translation, which has led to translation being deemed an impossible act from the perspective of prescriptive linguistics but a successful act – excluding concerns of equivalence – within the descriptive perspectives of sociolinguistics.

The main points to be considered are that sociolinguistic concepts should be the bread and butter of any language mediator (as communicative competence, Lung 1998); theoretically they help to organise practical tools (terminology) and to address the most unpredictable aspects of the mediation (pitching to an audience). As a conceptual tool, the sociolinguistic notion of variety covers anything from utterances of a simplistic functional nature in an unrepeatable context to the overall study of a dynamically evolving "standard" language, encompassing all the rules and potential grammatical categories of that system deemed as correct and just. Interpreters and translators do not mediate between language systems (Source Languages and Target Languages written with initial capitals), they mediate between speakers of a multi-layered variety.

The fluidity and complexity of every unique act of communication are unrepeatable, even when the act manifests in the form of a re-readable literary piece. Linguistics as a discipline may in the past have considered translation as a sub-branch, and many current institutional framings of academic and research activities in translation and interpreting continue to prevent the positioning of translation and interpreting as part of a broader disciplinary area of linguistics. However, the debate is irrelevant if we remove notions of disciplinary boundaries and consider the practical realities of translating: a basic understanding of sociolinguistics aids interpreters and translators in understanding the elusive notion of a source audience so as to enable them to consider rendering and reframing, narratives, and forms of transfer of meaning that are acceptable for a target audience.

Additionally, we translate and interpret in and out of dialects, contradicting Halliday's afore-mentioned assumption. By contradicting Halliday, the professional practices of translators and interpreters show that idiolects, dialects, sociolects, and any form of linguistic variety in an act of communication finds a successful linguistic mediation through the efforts of practitioners. This suggests that the theoretical postulations of connexions between T&I and sociolinguistics could go further, because the practice goes further than the potential cul-de-sacs of some extreme registers and language varieties. Undeniably, the use of professional or non-professional interpreters or translators in many circumstances (e.g. in emergencies, see Moser-Mercer *et al.* 2014; Federici 2016) introduce further "active" varieties influencing the process of rendering any form of communication into different languages with some (admittedly variable) degrees of success, thus ensuring that language mediators attempt to deal with any variety and register.

Latin authors and medieval writings in Latin about vernacular versions of the classics distinguished translation and interpreting as separate practices, one noble and one operational, one hermeneutic and one commercial. This distinction influenced a normative tradition that divided approaches to translating into a simplified yet influential binary opposition of word-for-word and sense-for-sense. The sociolinguist sees an opportunity to describe language mediation processes as a spectrum in which a non-linear progression word-for-word and sense-for-sense exist within the fluctuation of language, in the dynamic of meaning-making, in a continuum and not in isolation. The diversity within and between sociolinguistics, translation, and interpreting is essential to a wide and rich understanding of meaning-making in its many dimensions and interactions; however, a grounding in sociolinguistics equips translators and interpreters with the critical and analytical skills that complement domain specialisms and the technological supports available to them.

Further reading

Cokely, D. R. 1992. *Interpretation: A Sociolinguistic Model.* Burtonsville, MD: Linstok Press.
A complete sociolinguistic model of sign language interpreting.

Neubert, A. and Shreve, G. M. 1992. *Translation as Text.* Kent, OH: Kent State University Press.
Presents perspectives on sociolinguistic approaches to texts as whole entities and describes translation studies as the empirical study of the relationship among the translator, the process of translation, and the text.

Nida, E. A. 1993. The sociolinguistics of translation. *Sendebar* 4, pp. 19–27.
Repositions and reconceptualises Nida's earlier work within sociolinguistics.

Ramos Pinto, S. 2012 "Sociolinguistics and Translation." In *Handbook of Translation Studies.* Vol. 3, edited by Y. Gambier and L. van Doorslaer, 156–162. Amsterdam: John Benjamins.
A recent mapping of sociolinguistics and translation which suggests a different and complementary approach to the one offered in this chapter.

Wadensjö, C. 1998. *Interpreting as Interaction.* London: Longman.
Discusses interpreting behaviour in terms of interactional sociolinguistics.

References

Ahearn, L. M. 2011. *Living Language: An Introduction to Linguistic Anthropology.* Malden, MA: Wiley-Blackwell.
Al-Azzam, B. and Al-Quran, M. 2012. National songs in Jordan: a sociolinguistic and translational analysis. *Babel* 58(3), pp. 339–358.

Allioni, S. 1989. "Towards a Grammar of Consecutive Interpretation." In *The Theoretical and Practical Aspects of Teaching Conference Interpretation*, edited by L. Gran and J. Dodds, 191–197. Udine: Campanotto.

Baker, M. 1992. *In Other Words: A Coursebook on Translation*. London: Routledge.

Baker, M. 2006. *Translation and Conflict*. London: Routledge.

Bassnett, S. and Lefevere, A., eds. 1990. *Translation, History and Culture*. London: Cassell.

Bayley, R., Cameron, R. and Lucas, C., eds. 2013a. *The Oxford Handbook of Sociolinguistics*. Oxford: Oxford University Press.

Bayley, R., Cameron, R. and Lucas, C. 2013b. "The Study of Language and Society." In *The Oxford Handbook of Sociolinguistics*, edited by R. Bayley, R. Cameron and C. Lucas, 1–8. Oxford: Oxford University Press.

Berk-Seligson, S. 1990/2002. *The Bilingual Courtroom: Court Interpreters in the Judicial System*. Chicago, IL: University of Chicago Press.

Blommaert, J. 2005. *Discourse: A Critical Introduction*. Cambridge: Cambridge University Press.

Bononno, R. 2000. Terminology for translators: an implementation of ISO 12620. *Meta: Journal des Traducteurs* 45(4), pp. 646–669.

Boothman, D. 2008. The sources for Gramsci's concept of hegemony. *Rethinking Marxism* 20(2), pp. 201–215.

Catford, J. C. 1965. *A Linguistic Theory of Translation: An Essay in Applied Linguistics*. Oxford: Oxford University Press.

Cicourel, A. V. 1981. "Language and Medicine." In *Language in the USA*, edited by C. A. R. Ferguson and S. B. Heath, 407–429. Cambridge: Cambridge University Press.

Cokely, D. R. 1985. *Towards a Sociolinguistic Model of the Interpreting Process: Focus on ASL and English*. PhD Dissertation. Georgetown University.

Cokely, D. R. 1992. *Interpretation: A Sociolinguistic Model*. Burtonsville, MD: Linstok Press.

Cronin, M. 2006. *Translation and Identity*. London: Routledge.

Crystal, D. 2008. *Dictionary of Linguistics and Phonetics*. 6th ed. Oxford: Blackwell.

Duranti, A. 1997. *Linguistic Anthropology*. Cambridge: Cambridge University Press.

Duranti, A., ed. 2001. *Linguistic Anthropology: A Reader*. Malden, MA: Blackwell.

Ergün, E. 2010. Bridging across feminist translation and sociolinguistics. *Language and Linguistics Compass* 4(5), pp. 307–318.

Federici, E., ed. 2011. *Translating Gender*. Bern: Peter Lang.

Federici, F. M., ed. 2011. *Translating Dialects and Languages of Minorities*. Oxford: Peter Lang.

Federici, F. M., ed. 2016. *Mediating Emergencies and Conflicts: Frontline Translating and Interpreting*. London: Palgrave MacMillan.

Gerbault, J. 2010. "Localisation, traduction et diversité sociolinguistique en Afrique sub-saharienne: stratégies et perspectives" [Localization, Translation and Sociolinguistic Diversity in Sub-Saharan Africa: Strategies and Perspectives]. In *De la localisation à la délocalisation. Le facteur local en traduction/From Localization to Delocalization: The Local Factor in Translation*, special issue of *Meta: Journal des traducteurs*, edited by J.-R. Ladmiral and N. Froeliger, 55(4), pp. 817–844.

Gerver, D. 1969/2002. "The Effects of Source Language Presentation Rate on the Performance of Simultaneous Conference Interpreters." In *The Interpreting Studies Reader*, edited by F. Pöchhacker and M. Shlesinger, 53–66. London: Routledge.

Gerzymisch-Arbogast, H. 1986. "Zur Relevanz der Thema-Rhema-Gliederung für den Übersetzungsprozeß." In *Übersetzungswissenschaft – Eine Neuorientierung*, edited by M. Snell-Hornby, 160–183. Tübingen: Francke.

Giglioli, P. P. 1972, *Language and Social Context: Selected Readings*. Harmondsworth: Penguin Books.

Gile, D. 1991. "A Communication-Oriented Analysis of Quality in Non-Literary Translation and Interpretation." In *Translation: Theory and Practice. Tension and Interdependence*, edited by M. L. Larson, 188–200. Binghamton, NY: SUNY.

Gile, D. 2004. "Translation Research Versus Interpreting Research: Kinship, Differences and Prospects for Partnership." In *Translation Research and Interpreting Research: Traditions, Gaps and Synergies*, edited by C. Schäffner, 10–34. Clevedon: Multilingual Matters.

Gile, D., Hansen, G. and Pokorn, N. K., eds. 2010. *Why Translation Studies Matters*. Amsterdam: John Benjamins.

Goldman-Eisler, F. 1967. Sequential temporal patterns and cognitive processes in speech. *Language and Speech* 10(3), pp. 122–132.

González Vera, P. 2012. The translation of linguistic stereotypes in animated films: a case study of DreamWorks. *JoSTrans* 17, pp. 104–123.

Grin, F. 2013. "Language Policy, Ideology, and Attitudes: Key Issues in Western Europe." In *The Oxford Handbook of Sociolinguistics*, edited by R. Bayley, R. Cameron and C. Lucas, 629–651. Oxford: Oxford University Press.

Hale, S. 2007. *Community Interpreting*. Basingstoke: Palgrave Macmillan.

Halliday, M. A. K. 1990. "The Construction of Knowledge and Value in the Grammar of Scientific Discourse: With Reference to Charles Darwin's *The Origin of the Species*." In *Linguistic Studies of Text and Discourse*, edited by M. A. K. Halliday, 168–192. London: Continuum.

Halliday, M. A. K. 1994. *An Introduction to Functional Grammar*, 2nd ed. London: Arnold.

Halliday, M. A. K. 2003 "On the Architecture of Human Language." In *On Language and Linguistics*. Vol. 3 in *The Collected Works of M. A. K. Halliday* edited by J. Webster, 1–32. London: Continuum.

Halliday, M. A. K. and Hasan, R. 1976. *Cohesion in English*. London: Longman.

Halliday, M. A. K., McIntosh, M. and Strevens, P. 1964. *The Linguistic Sciences and Language Teaching*. London: Longman.

Harding, S.-A. 2013. "Narratives and Contextual Frames." In *Handbook of Translation Studies*. Vol. 4, edited by Y. Gambier and L. van Doorslaer, 105–110. Amsterdam: John Benjamins.

Hatim, B. and Mason, I. 1990. *Discourse and the Translator*. London: Routledge.

Hatim, B. and Mason, I. 1997. *The Translator as Communicator*. London: Routledge.

Hofstadter, D. 2009. *That Mad Ache: A Novel/Translator, Trader: An Essay*. Philadelphia: Basic Books.

Hönig, H. G. and Kußmaul, P. 1982. *Strategie der Übersetzung. Ein Lehr- und Arbeitsbuch*. Tübingen: Narr.

House, J. 1977. *A Model for Translation Quality Assessment*. Amsterdam: John Benjamins.

House, J. 1997. *Translation Quality Assessment: A Model Revisited*. Tübingen: Gunter Narr Verlag.

House, J., ed. 2014. *Translation: A Multidisciplinary Approach*. Houndshill: Palgrave MacMillan.

House, J. 2015. *Translation Quality Assessment: Past and Present*. London: Routledge.

Hudson, R. A. 1980/1996. *Sociolinguistics*. 2nd ed. Cambridge: Cambridge University Press.

Katan, D. 1999/2004/2014. *Translating Cultures: An Introduction for Translators, Interpreters and Mediators*. 2nd ed. London: Routledge.

Klaudy, K. 2007. Sociolinguistics of translation. *Studia Slavica* 52(1–2), pp. 229–234.

Le Page, R. B. and Tabouret-Keller, A. 1985. *Acts of Identity: Creole-Based Approaches to Language and Ethnicity*. Cambridge: Cambridge University Press.

Lung, R. 1998. Sociolinguistics and translators' communicative competence. *Perspectives* 6(1), pp. 35–46.

Malmkjær, K. 2011. "Linguistic Approaches to Translation." In *The Oxford Handbook of Translation Studies*, edited by K. Malmkjær and K. Windle, 57–70. Oxford: Oxford University Press.

Marques Santos, M. T. 2012. Normas em tradução: algumas considerações sobre os fatores extralinguísticos incidentes sobre a tradução jornalística [Norms in translation: some considerations about extralingual factors in journalistic translation]. *In-Traduções* 4(6), pp. 29–41.

Mason, I. and Stewart, M. 2001. "Interactional Pragmatics, Face and the Dialogue Interpreter." In *Triadic Exchanges*, edited by I. Mason, 51–70. Manchester: St Jerome.

Metzger, M. 1995. *The Paradox of Neutrality: A Comparison of Interpreters' Goals with the Reality of Interactive Discourse*. PhD Dissertation. Georgetown University.

Metzger, M. and Roy, C. B. 2013. "Sociolinguistic Studies of Signed Language Interpreting." In *The Oxford Handbook of Sociolinguistics*, edited by R. Bayley, R. Cameron and C. Lucas, 735–753. Oxford: Oxford University Press.

Moser-Mercer, B. 1997. "Beyond Curiosity." In *Cognitive Processes in Translation and Interpreting* (Applied Psychology 3: Individual, Social and Community Issues), edited by J. H. Danks, G. M. Shreve, S. B. Fountain and M. K. McBeath. London: Sage.

Moser-Mercer, B., Kherbiche, L. and Class, B. 2014. Interpreting conflict: training challenges in humanitarian field interpreting. *Journal of Human Rights Practice* 6(1), pp. 140–158.

Munday, J. 2012. *Evaluation in Translation: Critical Points of Translator Decision-Making.* London: Routledge.

Newmark, P. 1987. "The Use of Systemic Linguistics in Translation Analysis and Criticism." In *Language Topics: Essays in Honour of Michael Halliday.* Vol. 2, edited by R. Steele and T. Threadgold, 293–304. Amsterdam: John Benjamins.

Newmark, P. 1988. *A Textbook of Translation.* New York: Prentice-Hall.

Nida, E. A. 1976. "A Framework for the Analysis and the Evaluation of Theories of Translation." In *Translation: Applications and Research*, edited by R. Brislin, 47–91. New York: Gardner Press.

Nida, E. A. 1979. Translating means communicating: a sociolinguistic theory of translation. *Technical Papers for the Bible Translator* 30(1), pp. 101–107.

Nida, E. A. 1993. The sociolinguistics of translation. *Sendebar* 4, pp. 19–27.

Pergnier, M. 1978. Language-meaning and message-meaning: towards a sociolinguistic approach to translation. *Language Interpretation and Communication* 6, pp. 199–204.

Pöchhacker, F. 2004. *Introducing Interpreting Studies.* London: Routledge.

Pöchhacker, F. 2010a. "Interpreting." In *Handbook of Translation Studies.* Vol. 1, edited by Y. Gambier and L. van Doorslaer, 153–157. Amsterdam: John Benjamins.

Pöchhacker, F. 2010b. "Why Interpreting Studies Matters." In *Why Translation Matters*, edited by D. Gile, G. Hansen and N. K. Pokorn, 3–13. Amsterdam: John Benjamins.

Ramos Pinto, S. 2009. How important is the way you say it? A discussion on the translation of linguistic varieties. *Target* 21(2), pp. 289–307.

Ramos Pinto, S. 2012. "Sociolinguistics and Translation." In *Handbook of Translation Studies.* Vol. 1, edited by Y. Gambier and L. van Doorslaer, 156–162. Amsterdam: John Benjamins.

Reid, T. B. 1956. Linguistics, structuralism and philology. *Archivum Linguisticum* 8(11), pp. 28–37.

Roy, C. B. 1989. *A Sociolinguistic Analysis of the Interpreter's Role in the Turn Exchanges of an Interpreted Event.* PhD Dissertation. Georgetown University.

Sánchez, M. T. 2007. Translation and sociolinguistics: Can language translate society? *Babel* 53(2), pp. 123–131.

Şerban, A. 2013. "Linguistic Approaches in Translation Studies." In *The Routledge Handbook of Translation Studies*, edited by C. Millán and F. Bartrina, 213–227. London: Routledge.

Shlesinger, M. 1994. "Intonation in the Production and Perception of Simultaneous Interpretation." In *Bridging the Gap: Empirical Research in Simultaneous Interpretation*, edited by S. Lambert and B. Moser-Mercer, 225–236. Amsterdam: John Benjamins.

Shlesinger, M. 1995. Shifts in cohesion in simultaneous interpreting. *The Translator* 1(2), pp. 193–214.

Snell-Hornby, M. 1988/1995. *Translation Studies: An Integrated Approach.* Amsterdam: John Benjamins.

Toury, G. 1995/2012. *Descriptive Translation Studies and Beyond.* Amsterdam: John Benjamins. Rev. ed. 2012.

Trudgill, P. 1992. *Introducing Language and Society.* London: Penguin.

Wadensjö, C. 1992. *Interpreting as Interaction: On Dialogue Interpreting in Immigration Hearings and Medical Examinations.* PhD Dissertation. Linköping University.

Wadensjö, C. 1998. *Interpreting as Interaction.* London: Longman.

Yallop, C. 1987. "The Practice and Theory of Translation". In *Language Topics: Essays in Honour of Michael Halliday*, edited by R. Steele and T. Threadgold, 347–352. Amsterdam: John Benjamins.

Part V

Translation, interpreting, media and machines

20

Language and translation in film

Rocío Baños and Jorge Díaz-Cintas

Introduction

Ever since the advent of cinema at the end of the 19th century, audiovisual productions have been not only a major source of entertainment for audiences all over the world but they have also been used as an innovative way to communicate ideas, to sell products, to promote artistic material and to transmit all sorts of information. From the very beginning, films and other audiovisual products (television series, documentaries, videogames and the like) have crossed borders and travelled across countries to reach global audiences, thus overcoming cultural and linguistic differences. Given that not all viewers can enjoy the audiovisual material as originally envisaged by its director or creator, successful communication in this regard has only been possible thanks to translation.

Although a wide range of terms has been used in the past to refer to the translation of audiovisual productions (screen translation, film translation and multimedia translation, among others), audiovisual translation (AVT) seems to be the term most widely used both in the industry and in academia, and will also be used throughout this chapter. In line with current research in this field, AVT is here understood as an umbrella term referring to a wide range of practices related to the translation of audiovisual content. On occasions, such practices might entail making audiovisual programmes accessible to viewers who do not speak the language of the original text, therefore requiring interlingual translation in the form of dubbing or subtitling, for example. However, they might also involve providing access for audiences with sensory (e.g. hearing/visual) impairment to audiovisual material, often requiring intralingual or intersemiotic translation. In this respect, AVT also encompasses practices such as sign language interpreting (SLI), subtitling for the deaf and the hard-of-hearing (SDH), and audio description (AD) for the blind and the partially sighted. As the title makes clear, the focus of this chapter is on dubbing and subtitling, the two most widespread AVT interlingual modes used for the translation of films. Nonetheless, an overview of the different AVT modes will be provided below and the reader can investigate the literature cited further. References to other modes will also be made throughout the chapter as necessary.

As far as language transfer of audiovisual material is concerned, Díaz-Cintas and Orero (2010, 41) distinguish between two fundamental approaches: revoicing and subtitling. In the former, oral output is transferred aurally in the target language by inserting a new soundtrack; in the latter, there is a change from spoken to written mode, and dialogue and other verbal elements are transferred as written text on screen. Within these two umbrella approaches, further classifications of AVT techniques or modes can be established. Díaz-Cintas and Remael (2007, 8) define subtitling as a transfer mode which:

> consists of presenting a written text, generally on the lower part of the screen, that endeavours to recount the original dialogue of the speakers, as well as the discursive elements that appear in the image (letters, inserts, graffiti, inscriptions, placards and the like), and the information that is contained on the soundtrack.

Within subtitling, it is common to distinguish between interlingual and intralingual modes, the latter including subtitling in the same language as the original dialogue for foreign language learning and SDH. When subtitling live programmes, SDH can be produced through respeaking, a technique in which speech recognition software is used to convert the original dialogue – which is respoken by a respeaker – into subtitles (Romero-Fresco 2011). In addition to these, classifications of subtitling modes also include surtitling, whereby subtitles for opera and theatre performances are projected above the stage, and fansubbing, which is subtitling done by fans for fans and normally distributed for free over the internet.

As far as revoicing is concerned, dubbing and voiceover are the two most widely used interlingual modes. Chaume (2012, 1) defines dubbing as a type of AVT which "consists of replacing the original track of a film's (or any audiovisual text) source language dialogues with another track on which translated dialogues have been recorded in the target language". Dubbing is often associated with lip synchronisation, emphasising the need to synchronise the translated dialogue with the lip movements of the characters on screen. However, not all cases of dubbing require lip synch, as when a character (e.g. a narrator) is off screen. As a result, a distinction is often made between offscreen dubbing and lip synch dubbing. Unlike dubbing, in voiceover there is no replacement of audio tracks, but an overlapping: the original and the translated tracks of dialogue are presented simultaneously to the target viewer, with the volume of the former lowered, though still audible, to avoid confusion. In this AVT mode, which is often associated with non-fictional programmes such as documentaries but also used to translate fictional material in certain East European countries, the translated dialogue track usually starts and finishes a few seconds after and before the original dialogue (Franco, Matamala and Orero 2010, 43).

Chaume (2013, 107–111) also includes the following AVT modes in the revoicing category: simultaneous interpreting (often restricted to film festivals and film clubs), free commentary (a rather free revoicing, closer to journalism than to translation, frequently used in sport programmes or for comic purposes), fandubbing (home-made dubbings of audiovisual texts that have not yet been released in the target language country) and audio description, which, in Díaz-Cintas's (2008, 7) words, involves "transforming visual images into words, which are then spoken during the silent intervals in audiovisual programmes or live performances". In this special case of revoicing, the source text is not the original dialogue, but images and sounds which are translated into words for the blind and the partially sighted.

The classification provided above illustrates the variety and complexity of AVT, and yet, it is by no means exhaustive. Indeed, the different forms of audiovisual translation have multiplied over time, and although their main function remains the same, i.e. to allow audiovisual programmes to travel across linguistic communities, their impact on viewers is becoming increasingly more far reaching. AVT has recently found synergies with multimedia translation (video games, online newspapers, fansubs, fandubs) and especially with accessibility (SDH, AD), thus opening up new horizons and possibilities for certain groups of audience, and creating unforeseen potential in the field of audiovisual communication in general.

Historical perspectives

At the time of the invention of cinema, many thought that silent films would become a sort of Esperanto thanks to the "unequivocal" universality of the image. And yet, the language issue has always been present in the film industry as most silent productions made systematic use of intertitles that needed to be translated when the film was distributed abroad (Díaz-Cintas and Remael 2007). These dreams of unrestrictive communication would soon be shattered by the arrival of sound and the talking movies in the 1920s. The spoken word thus became an inseparable ally of the image and new translational practices had to be developed if distribution companies were to conquer new audiences around the world. Multilingual versions, subtitling and dubbing were the methods initially explored as a way to overcome the language barrier, and whereas the first was short-lived and died out towards the mid-1930s, the remaining two have survived and continue to be part of the contemporary AVT landscape.

From its very beginnings, AVT has been closely linked to technological developments. First cinema and then, after World War II, TV sets started to become commonplace in homes to such an extent that by the 1950s television was already the main source of entertainment and the primary medium for influencing public opinion. Since then, analogue technology has become digital and, by the mid-1990s, the Video Home System (VHS) tape had given way to the then revolutionary Digital Versatile/Video Disc (DVD), which, in turn, is being phased out and overtaken by movie streaming services on the web, known in some countries as "internet cinemas". The way in which we consume audiovisual productions has also been altered significantly, from the early large public spaces represented by cinemas, to the family experience of watching the television in the relative privacy of the living room, to the more individualistic approach of watching our favourite programmes in front of our personal computer, tablet or smartphone. Today's viewers tend to be more independent and impatient when it comes to their watching habits and expectations and want to be able to enjoy their preferred programmes whenever they choose and on any of the devices they possess. Video-on-demand services are a commercial response to meet the needs of this new breed of viewers by allowing them to watch what they want, when they want and in the quantities that they want. This evolution has brought along a shift from the printed paper to the digital screen, foregrounding the audiovisualisation of communication in our society and triggering a similar boom in the practice of audiovisual translation that can only continue to expand and flourish in the foreseeable future.

Despite being a well-established professional practice, AVT has been a relatively unknown field of research until recently. The first studies written on the topic were brief and published in a wide range of outlets, from cinema magazines and newspapers to translation journals, which has the adverse effect of making any attempt at dipping into the historiography of AVT a rather complex venture. Laks's (1957) *Le sous-titrage de films* can be considered a pioneering work for its comprehensive overview of this professional practice. The 1960s and 1970s were characterised by a lethargic approach to subtitling, though some works appeared on the topic of dubbing, with the journal *Babel* publishing a special issue on cinema translation in 1960, the monograph by Hesse-Quack (1969) on the process of dubbing, and the book authored by Fodor (1976) on the phonetic, semiotic, aesthetic and psychological aspects of dubbing.

In 1987, the first ever *Conference on Dubbing and Subtitling* was organised in Stockholm, under the auspices of the European Broadcasting Union, triggering an unprecedented interest in AVT that materialised in the publication of new articles and books in the field, among which the ones by Pommier (1988), Luyken *et al.* (1991), Ivarsson (1992) and Ivarsson and Carroll (1998) are perhaps the most important. Coinciding with digitalisation, the golden age of AVT can be traced to the 1990s, when the field became the object of more systematic research from a translational perspective and saw the publication of collective volumes, monographs and doctoral theses, along with the organisation of domain-specific international conferences and the development of university curricula specialising in AVT. Since then, we have witnessed an exponential increase in the number of contributions and scholarly activities on AVT, signalling a move from the margins to the centre of academic debates and highlighting the fact that the field has gained social significance and visibility, has finally come of age academically and has a most promising and inspiring future.

Core issues and topics

When investigating AVT, it is essential to first reflect on the specificity of audiovisual texts, which is determined by the way in which information is communicated. In films, meaning is conveyed not only through the dialogue exchanges between characters, but also through images, gestures, camera movements, music, special effects, etc. Information is thus transmitted simultaneously through the acoustic and the visual channels, and conveyed through a wide range of signifying codes, articulated according to specific filmic rules and conventions. As such, Chaume (2012, 100) defines the audiovisual text as "a semiotic construct woven by a series of signifying codes that operate simultaneously to produce meaning", which can be transmitted through the acoustic (linguistic, paralinguistic, musical, special effects and sound position codes) and the visual channels (iconographic, photographic, shot, mobility, graphic and montage/editing codes).

Many of the challenges faced by audiovisual translators result from the interaction of the various codes and from the fact that, in most cases, the only code they can work with is the linguistic one in the form of dialogue or background conversations. For instance, when an audiovisual translator decides to substitute a cultural reference in the film with another reference, more familiar to the target culture, it is imperative to consider the rest of the codes at play before making a decision and ascertain that no visual references to the culture-specific item being substituted can be seen on screen. These challenges have prompted authors like Titford (1982) to coin the term "constrained translation". Further developed by Mayoral, Kelly and Gallardo (1988), this concept highlights the complexity of AVT and foregrounds that the translator's task is constrained by the interaction of a wide range of communication elements (images, music, dialogue, etc.). Constraints in AVT can be of a different nature depending on the audiovisual genre being translated and the AVT mode being used. In both dubbing and subtitling particular attention is often paid to technical constraints, imposed by the need to synchronise the translation with the original text.

Technical constraints in subtitling

The two main constraints that impinge on the delivery of subtitles are spatial (governed by the amount of space available on screen for the text) and temporal (dictated by the time that a given subtitle remains on screen). Although there is no universal agreement on the way in which the subtitles should appear on screen, a number of trends can be discerned. The situation is one of change within a generally accepted practice, mainly triggered by the untapped potential released by digital technology and the uncontested prevalence of subtitling as the preferred AVT transfer on the internet to cater for all sorts of programmes, be they political, educational, fictional or commercial.

To guarantee that the text stays within the screen safety area and that it does not spill over the edges, and depending on the type and size of the font chosen (Arial, point 30, is frequently used), subtitles on screen tend to consist of a maximum of two lines of text, and each of the lines tends to contain a maximum of between 35 and 42 characters in the case of Latin-based alphabets, Arabic and Cyrillic languages. When it comes to Far Eastern languages like Chinese, Japanese and Korean, the maximum number of characters per line is set at around 14 to 16. In theatrical releases, the subtitles tend to be white, like the screen onto which they are projected, as they are usually laser-burnt onto the celluloid. In terms of positioning, the subtitles are usually displayed centred at the bottom of the screen, unless some important diegetic information occurs there, in which case they are usually displaced to the top of the screen.

One of the golden rules, from a temporal perspective, is that subtitles must appear in synchrony with the dialogue and the image. The synchronisation process, also known as spotting, cueing, timing or originating, consists of deciding the exact moment that a subtitle should appear on screen (in-time) and when it should disappear (out-time), while keeping temporal synchrony with the original utterances. The spotting has to mirror the rhythm of the film and the performance of the actors, and be mindful of any prosodic features such as interruptions and pauses. This process is undertaken with the help of bespoke subtitling programs and may be carried out by the translators themselves or by specialists who know the intricacies of the software.

The amount of time that a subtitle stays on screen depends on the delivery of the original exchanges and it is generally agreed that a subtitle of two full lines, containing around 37 characters in each line (i.e. a total of 74 characters), can be comfortably read in 6 seconds. This is known in the industry as the "6 second rule" (Díaz-Cintas and Remael 2007, 96–99). For shorter periods of time, proportional values are automatically calculated by the subtitling software, and under no circumstances should a subtitle stay on screen for less than 1 second (or $^5/_6$ of a second) to guarantee that the viewer can register its presence. Finally, the amount of text that can be projected on screen in a given period of time between 1 and 6 seconds is calculated according to the viewers' assumed reading speed, which will of course vary depending on literacy levels and age of viewers. In this respect, being able to read 160 words per minute (wpm) or 15 characters per second (cps) is considered to be standard while a reading speed of 180 wpm or 17 cps is considered fast.

Although these parameters still enjoy some currency in the industry, viewers' increased familiarity with reading text on screen and expedited technical developments witnessed in recent decades have brought along considerable changes. The sacred rule of having a maximum of two lines in a subtitle to minimise their impact on the photography is being broken daily by the emergence of three-, four- and even five-liners, notably in the subtitling being done on the internet; and the traditional positioning of the subtitles at the bottom of the screen is also being challenged as they begin to be displayed on different parts of the screen.

Likewise, restricting the number of characters per line to 35, 39 or even 42 is not an important factor any more. Most subtitling programs now make the most of proportional lettering, which means that within the safety area, subtitlers can write more text, depending on the font size being used and the actual letters that make up the message (e.g. an "i" takes less space than an "m"). It is therefore not uncommon to find subtitles that contain up to 70 characters in just one line. In addition to the aesthetic implications that so much text can have on the film, the issue remains as to whether viewers are given sufficient time to read such long subtitles.

Professional practice is rapidly evolving with the entrenchment of digital technology, the mushrooming of screens around us and the proliferation of audiovisual productions, with some of the most apparent changes materialising in the increase of the number of lines, the lengthening of lines, shorter exposure times and faster reading speeds, which, of course, have had a significant impact on the way the actual language transfer is carried out.

Technical constraints in dubbing

In film dubbing, when replacing the original dialogue track with the translated one, the accurate synchronisation between the new track and the rest of the components (original images, existing music and sound effects track, shot changes) is of paramount importance. Whereas translators should always be alert to the composite nature of the audiovisual production, they might not be responsible for the actual lip synchronisation as the dubbing process is characterised by the many professionals who take part in it.

Once the dialogue exchanges have been translated, they are adapted and synchronised by the dialogue writer or adapter. In some countries, it is common for translators to also act as dialogue writers, though this is not always the case. This is why, as pointed out by Whitman-Linsen (1992, 105), the work done by the translator is often referred to as a "rough translation", which undergoes many changes during the adaptation process. Dialogue writers adapt this draft translation to fit the articulatory movements of the onscreen characters, ensuring that the translation respects the open vowels as well as the bilabial and labiodental consonants uttered on screen (Chaume 2012, 73). Known as "phonetic synchrony", this process is only relevant in shots where the character's face and mouth are clearly visible (2012). Another type of synchrony that needs to be observed in dubbing is isochrony, which refers to the fact that the duration of the translation should be identical to that of onscreen characters' utterances: if the translation is too long or too short, the illusion could be broken, and the audience might realise or be reminded that the actors on screen are not pronouncing the translated lines and are in fact speaking a different language. Chaume (2012, 70) also refers to a third type of synchrony, "kinesic synchrony", whereby the translation needs to be synchronised with the actors' body movements. Once they are synchronised, translated dialogue exchanges are interpreted by dubbing actors or voice talents, under the supervision of the dubbing director, and then mixed and recorded by sound engineers in a dubbing or recording studio.

Assumptions about the critical importance that synchrony has in the dubbing process have not been substantiated by systematic research. Furthermore, the specificities of dubbed texts and the dubbing process do not solely rely on synchronisation. For instance, when considering which dubbing aspect has the greatest impact upon the audience and should thus take precedence over the others, Whitman-Linsen (1992, 54) highlights that "researchers and professional dubbers alike lend the greatest priority to a believable, convincing dialogue", which directly relates to the translational challenge of having to deal with prefabricated orality.

Further challenges in AVT: Prefabricated orality

The concept of prefabricated orality is determined by the specificities of the discourse found in audiovisual texts: spoken and seemingly spontaneous, yet planned and elaborated.

Dialogue originates in a script that has been carefully planned and written by a scriptwriter to be interpreted later by actors as if it were spontaneous and had not been written in advance. Film dialogue differs notably from spontaneous conversation and does not feature so many dysfluencies (hesitations, false starts, repeats and reformulations, which would distract and even annoy viewers), nor does it rely so heavily on phonetic and prosodic features and contextual information. Nevertheless, scriptwriters and actors use certain linguistic features that are typical of naturally occurring conversation in order to achieve realistic dialogues so that audiences can identify what they are watching with spontaneous speech and thus immerse themselves in the cinematic illusion. Done in a careful and purposeful manner, this is one of the reasons why the orality of films and other audiovisual texts is considered to be prefabricated (Chaume 2012) and its spontaneity is deemed to be pretended (Baños 2014a).

The orality of film dialogue should be dealt with equally carefully and purposefully in AVT, considering that translated films are governed by different conventions and influenced by a wide range of factors and constraints: the involvement of many agents and stakeholders in the translation process, the heterogeneous make-up of the target audience, professional issues, the constraints imposed by the source text and the above-mentioned space and temporal constraints. As highlighted by Whitman-Linsen (1992), mirroring spontaneous conversation is of paramount importance in dubbing, where the translator/dialogue writer takes the role of the scriptwriter and is expected to master the linguistic features available in the target language to produce convincing dialogue. Such an imitation is nevertheless a matter of compromise since, whereas the verisimilitude of dialogues is one of the criteria used to ascertain whether a dubbed production meets quality standards (Chaume 2012, 15), research has shown that the language of dubbing is very normative and not as spontaneous as we might think (Pavesi 2008; Baños 2014b).

In the case of subtitling, as a result of the change of medium from speech to writing, many of the typical features of spontaneous oral conversation tend to be the first to disappear in the subtitles. Omission and standardisation of orality markers are more prominent in subtitling than in dubbing due to the need to comply with writing conventions and to the difficulty of reflecting some features of spoken speech in writing. Yet, this is not the only reason why these features are lost in subtitles and, as Díaz-Cintas and Remael (2007, 63) contend, "quite a few can be salvaged in writing, but rendering them all would lead to illegible and exceedingly long subtitles". Subtitling priorities and constraints make it difficult for spoken features to be reflected in subtitles. Whereas this has an impact on the orality of the subtitles, it cannot be forgotten that subtitles are a supplement to the original production and that some orality markers which might be recognisable by the target audience (e.g. prosodic features, repetitions, hesitations) are still present in the original soundtrack and can be picked up by (some of) the viewers.

Main research methods

Given AVT's heterogeneous and interdisciplinary nature, scholars working in the field have looked for inspiration in related disciplines in their search for theoretical frameworks and methodological approaches that can also be exploited to account for AVT practices and processes (Bogucki 2013; Pérez-González 2014).

When it comes to investigating the different professional practices, the trend has been to study them together under the umbrella term of audiovisual translation, even though their study would gain in depth and substance if approached individually. Although they share some commonalities, the differences that separate them justify more targeted analyses. For instance, the shift from oral to written does not occur in dubbing; the strategies of condensation and deletion are pivotal to subtitling but not so much to dubbing; the transfer of discourse markers, exclamations and interjections is not a challenge in subtitling, but it is critical in dubbing; the representation of linguistic variation is virtually impossible to achieve in written subtitles; and the presence of the source language as well as its cohabitation with the target language in the subtitled version straightjackets the potential solutions in a way that does not happen in dubbing.

Early scholarly debates on the topic tended to consist of value-laden comparisons contrasting dubbing and subtitling, to focus exclusively on the linguistic code to the detriment of the remaining signifying audio and visual codes, and to describe the role of the various professionals involved as well as the actual translation processes. Although it is understandable in an emerging discipline that so much attention was paid to these particular themes, and although the results certainly contributed to the advancement of the discipline, the concern was that this type of research failed to embrace the communicative richness of audiovisual texts in their entirety. To correct this imbalance, scholars have advocated the use of "autochthonous models" (Pérez-González 2014, 96) for the study of AVT built on interdisciplinary and integrative methodological and theoretical foundations.

The work of Mayoral, Kelly and Gallardo (1988, 356) was pioneering in this regard, promoting a paradigm that went beyond the unilateral linguistic focus typical of previous approaches to translation and which took into account "those aspects which are characteristic of translation as a communication process and also those which depend on the relation of the linguistic message to other messages conveyed by non-linguistic systems". Another early attempt to provide an integrative and more complex framework for the study of audiovisual texts is that proposed by Delabastita (1989), who presents an organised inventory of questions and hypotheses to guide AVT research, inspired by Descriptive Translation Studies (DTS) principles. Delabastita's article suggests ways to unravel the nature of the relationships that get established between original and translated films, highlighting the need to analyse films as complex signs and organised wholes, whose various components enter into intricate relations. Along with Toury (1995), he further posits that the translation of films constitutes a typical scenario where norms or patterns of behaviour can be expected to guide the work of audiovisual translators, and suggests ways to study such patterns.

Delabastita (1989) was one of the first scholars to embrace the descriptivist paradigm for the study of AVT, but many academics have subsequently highlighted the benefits of following DTS premises in AVT research. Díaz-Cintas (2004, 31) conceives DTS as "a heuristic tool that opens up new avenues for study, strengthens the theoretical component and allows the researcher to come up with substantial analyses". In a similar vein, Chaume (2012, 161) posits that DTS offer "a powerful interdisciplinary framework for translation analysis" and proposes a two-level, descriptive and semiotic model for the analysis of dubbed texts, which can easily be extrapolated to the study of other AVT modes. The first level is related to the extratextual factors having a bearing on the translation brief, including historical factors (such as year or period of the source and target texts, the translation mode used or the existence of previous versions), professional aspects (deadlines, material available, rates of payment, copyright and royalties, dubbing conventions), communicative factors (client, audience, communicative context, genre, broadcaster) and reception factors (e.g. synchrony requirements, dubbing performance) (2012,161–177). The second level includes both the translational challenges that are shared by other types of translation and those issues that are specific to AVT, articulated through the above-mentioned signifying codes.

Increased awareness of the cultural embeddedness of translation has led to the widening in scope of the topics considered susceptible of being researched. By exploiting case studies centred on a specific audiovisual text or set of texts, AVT scholars have explored the translation of culture-specific references (Pedersen 2011; Ranzato 2016), humour (Zabalbeascoa 1996; Asimakoulas 2004; Martínez Sierra 2005; Chiaro 2006; De Rosa *et al.* 2014), linguistic variation (Ellender 2015), sexual taboo (Yuan 2016), gender stereotypes (De Marco 2012), politeness (Yuan 2012), forms of address (Szarkowska 2013), censorship (Mereu Keating 2016), ideology and manipulation (Díaz-Cintas 2012; Díaz-Cintas, Parini and Ranzato 2016) and multilingualism (Corrius and Zabalbeascoa 2011; De Higes-Andino *et al.* 2013), to name but a few.

Given the inherent limitations of case studies, especially as far as the scope of the research and the generalisation of findings are concerned, scholars have tested other approaches for the study of AVT, taking inspiration from other disciplines such as corpus linguistics. Corpora and corpus-analysis tools have been successfully used in AVT to identify the distinctive features and patterns of translated films systematically, relying on large amounts of data (Freddi and Pavesi 2009; Baños, Bruti and Zanotti 2013). When adopting this approach, scholars have been confronted with many challenges associated with the implementation and compilation of audiovisual corpora. One of the key challenges lies yet again in the complexity and multimodality of audiovisual texts, because any study which analyses audiovisual dialogue on its own, without considering the visual and the acoustic nonverbal components, is necessarily incomplete. This is probably one of the reasons why many corpus-based AVT studies draw on relatively small corpora, since having a more manageable amount of data allows for a qualitative analysis which incorporates not only information transmitted through codes other than the linguistic one, but which also allows the researcher to consider the many other factors that might influence specific linguistic choices (e.g. synchrony, spatio-temporal constraints, semiotic cohesion, etc.). Nonetheless, some academics have devoted substantial energy and resources to compiling fully audiovisual corpora for the study of film translation, such as the Pavia Corpus of Film Dialogue (http://studiumanistici.unipv.it/?pagina=p&titolo=pcfd), a parallel and comparable corpus made up of original Italian films and original English films together with their dubbed Italian translations, or the TRACCE corpus (Jiménez Hurtado and Soler Gallego 2013), containing 300 films audio described in Spanish.

The heuristic potential offered by other conceptual paradigms has also been explored by authors such as Bogucki (2004), who concentrates on relevance theory, and Desilla (2009), who tries to reconcile pragmatics and multimodal analysis in her investigation of subtitled films.

Current debates and future directions

Despite its relative youth, AVT has come of age academically and can be considered a consolidated field of research within the broader area of Translation Studies. The development of AVT as a discipline has been accompanied by an evolution in key topics and debates and, if early studies on the topic can be said to have focused on the distinctiveness and autonomy of AVT, interdisciplinarity and cross-fertilisation are certainly the way forward. The traditional focus of the pioneering scholarly studies conducted in the field of AVT tended to be biased towards the analysis of the role played by language, the challenges encountered when carrying out the linguistic transfer and the translational strategies activated by the translators to overcome them. With the passing of the years, the scope of the research has widened considerably to encompass many other aspects that directly impinge on the transfer that takes place during AVT.

Studies of more traditional practices such as subtitling and dubbing coexist with investigations of media accessibility, and show a shift of focus from the textual idiosyncrasies of the original to the effects that the ensuing translation has on viewers. In this regard, AVT scholars have proved increasingly willing to rely on technology and statistical analysis to interrogate the data under scrutiny, and the study of reception and process has become pivotal in recent academic exchanges, with the viewer becoming the focal point of the investigation. Experimental research based on empirical enquiry has thus become one of the relatively recent developments in AVT as academics are no longer content with describing a given state of affairs or taking for granted certain inherited premises that have been passed on unchallenged in the literature. Rather, contemporary AVT scholars are eager to test the validity of their theories experimentally, to explore the cognitive effort involved in the translational process, or to describe the effects that AVT practices have on the various heterogeneous groups that make up the audience, on translators-to-be and on professionals working in the field and, in these pursuits, they exploit biometric methodologies, new technologies and statistical data analysis tools. Of particular note in this attempt to measure human behaviour is the application of physiological instruments such as eye trackers, frequently used in fields like advertising and social sciences, to the experimental investigation of AVT (Perego 2012). These devices, which offer metrics about visual information by measuring eye positions and eye movement, have helped scholars interested in AVT to move away from speculation to observation of subjects and data-based research. In this new research ecosystem, eye tracking is widely used in experimental research in AVT to gauge the attention paid by viewers to the various parts of the screen, in an attempt to gain a better understanding of their cognitive processes while watching (and reading the subtitles of) the audiovisual programme.

In addition to instruments like eye trackers, and more traditional ones such as questionnaires and interviews, a wide array of other biometric tools are also being used to conduct examinations centred on audience reception, such as galvanic skin response devices to measure participants' levels of arousal, and webcams to record and conduct facial expression analysis to inform researchers about respondents' basic emotions (anger, surprise, joy, etc.), to monitor their engagement and to assess if they are expressing their attitude in observable behaviour. Electroencephalography (EEG) and electrocardiograms (ECG) are also being tested. EEG is a neuroimaging technique that helps to assess brain activity associated with perception, cognitive behaviour and emotional processes by foregrounding the parts of the brain that are active while participants perform a task or are exposed to a certain stimulus material. ECG, on the other hand, monitors heart activity in an attempt to track respondents' physical state, their anxiety and stress levels, which in turn can provide helpful insights into cognitive-affective processes.

All in all, there seems to exist a growing consensus that reception studies are important for the sustainability of the discipline and that it is important to buttress links between the industry and academia. The latter cooperation holds considerable promise for the development and provision of better products for end users. In this collaborative constellation, the media industry is interested in knowing how viewers perceive their subtitled, dubbed, voiced-over, respoken or audio described audiovisual productions; technology companies working on the development of state-of-the-art software and cloud-based systems for AVT can also benefit from the results yielded by experimental research with professionals; trainers of future audiovisual translators can learn about the cognitive load of the translation process and improve their curricula; and language service providers specialising in AVT can profit from the insights gained through reception research, which can help them to adapt their practices to new workflows, to update their style guides to cater for new audiences or to reconsider some of the traditionally accepted spatial and temporal considerations that have influenced the translation and delivery of their audiovisual programmes.

Translation memory tools have had a great impact in other translation specialisations and yet their development has traditionally been curtailed in the case of AVT because of the fictional and literary nature of many audiovisual programmes, which makes them less likely to display the kinds of repetitions of text that translation memory tools generally rely on. However, the fact that increasing numbers of companies and institutions are discovering the virtues of communicating audiovisually, mainly through the internet, is bringing changes to this state of affairs and making it worthwhile for translation companies to employ assisted translation and translation memory tools in the AVT process. The relative ease with which quality subtitled parallel data can be obtained has been the catalyst for the introduction of statistical machine translation (SMT) technology in subtitling (Etchegoyhen *et al.* 2013). Under the auspices of the European Commission, projects like SUMAT, an online service for SUbtitling by MAchine Translation, have focused on building large corpora of aligned subtitles in order to train SMT engines in various language pairs. Its ultimate objective was to benefit from the introduction of SMT in the field of subtitling, followed by human post-editing in order to increase the productivity of subtitle translation procedures, and reduce costs and turnaround times while keeping a watchful eye on the quality of the translation results (Georgakopoulou and Bywood 2014). In an attempt to boost accessibility to audio-visual programmes, primarily for people with hearing impairments, Google and Yahoo announced, in 2009, the launch of machine-generated automatic captions, in the belief that "captions not only help the deaf and hearing impaired, but with machine translation, they also enable people around the world to access video content in any of 51 languages" (Harrenstien 2009, online).

Another area that is experiencing a notable surge in academic interest is the potential of AVT for foreign language teaching and learning. In this respect, subtitling has been the translation mode to attract most interest (Talaván and Rodríguez-Arancón 2014; Gambier, Caimi and Mariotti 2015), though other practices like dubbing and audio description are also being explored. The EU-funded project ClipFlair (http://clipflair.net) is a practical instantiation of an educational platform whose ultimate aim is to foster foreign language learning through interactive revoicing and captioning of clips. Authors have also started to pay closer attention to the didactics of audiovisual translation itself, analysing some of the curricula available (Cerezo Merchán 2012), suggesting potential activities and identifying the challenges of teaching not only dubbing and subtitling, but also of preparing professional translators to be conversant with a wide range of media and AVT modes that often require markedly different skills (Díaz-Cintas 2008).

The affordances of digital technology have nurtured, *inter alia*, the proliferation of closely knit internet communities with shared affinities, and the blossoming of amateur practices like fansubbing and fandubbing. Initially focused on the free translation and distribution of Japanese anime, these netizens' movements have grown in number and their interests have sprawled to cover all sorts of audiovisual texts, from films and TV series to edutainment programmes, documentaries and political broadcasts. This shift towards collaborative practices in social media raises numerous questions that have already attracted the attention of scholars like Pérez-González (2014) and Massidda (2015) and will no doubt continue to dominate the audiovisual landscape in the years to come.

Further reading

Chaume, F. 2012. *Audiovisual Translation: Dubbing*. Manchester: St Jerome.
Chaume provides a detailed overview of dubbing around the world, exploring key historical, professional, technical and methodological aspects of this AVT mode, and delving into general AVT-related issues. This work also contains practical dubbing exercises, outlines the state of the art as far as research in dubbing is concerned and presents an integrated model for the analysis of audiovisual texts.

Díaz-Cintas, J. and Remael, A. 2007. *Audiovisual Translation: Subtitling*. Manchester: St Jerome.
In this key work on subtitling, the authors introduce readers to this AVT mode, providing a detailed account of its semiotics, linguistic aspects and key translation issues, with examples in a wide range of language combinations. Readers will be able to practise the technical considerations, guidelines and conventions described in this work through the practical exercises suggested and the demo version of the professional software WinCAPS, which is also provided.

Pérez-González, L. 2014. *Audiovisual Translation: Theories, Methods and Issues*. Abingdon: Routledge.
Pérez González offers an introduction to fundamental methodological and theoretical aspects of AVT in an attempt to chart and critique influential concepts, models and approaches in audiovisual translation studies. In addition to providing a comprehensive overview of these, this work offers very useful tools for the analysis of audiovisual texts and delves into new developments in this field.

Ranzato, I. 2016. *Translating Culture Specific References on Television: The Case of Dubbing*. London: Routledge.
This book provides a model for investigating the problems posed by the translation of culture-specific references (CSR) in the case of dubbing. Based on a detailed analysis of three TV series dubbed into Italian, and drawing on a corpus of 95 hours, Ranzato proposes a new taxonomy of strategies for the translation of CSRs and explores the sociocultural, pragmatic and ideological implications of dubbing for the small screen.

Related topics

Language and translation on the Web; Translation, interpreting and new technologies; Corpus linguistics, translation and interpreting; Language, interpreting and translation in the news media.

References

Asimakoulas, D. 2004. Towards a model of describing humour translation: a case study of the Greek subtitled versions of *Airplane!* and *Naked Gun. Meta* 49(4), pp. 822–842.
Baños, R. 2014a. Orality markers in Spanish native and dubbed sitcoms: pretended spontaneity and prefabricated orality. *Meta* 59(2), pp. 406–435.
Baños, R. 2014b. "Insights into the False Orality of Dubbed Fictional Dialogue and the Language of Dubbing." In *Media and Translation: An Interdisciplinary Approach*, edited by D. Abend-David, 75–95. London: Bloomsbury.
Baños, R., Bruti, S. and Zanotti, S. 2013. Corpus linguistics and audiovisual translation: in search of an integrated approach. *Perspectives* 21(4), pp. 483–490.
Bogucki, Ł. 2004. *A Relevance Framework for Constraints on Cinema Subtitling*. Lodz: University of Lodz.
Bogucki, Ł. 2013. *Areas and Methods of Audiovisual Translation Research*. Frankfurt am Main: Peter Lang.
Cerezo Merchán, B. 2012. *La didáctica de la traducción audiovisual en España: un estudio de caso empírico-descriptivo*. PhD Thesis. Castellón: Universitat Jaume I.

Chaume, F. 2012. *Audiovisual Translation: Dubbing*. Manchester: St Jerome.

Chaume, F. 2013. The turn of audiovisual translation: new audiences and new technologies. *Translation Spaces* 2, pp. 105–123.

Chiaro, D. 2006. Verbally expressed humour on screen: reflections on translation and reception. *Journal of Specialised Translation* 6, pp. 198–208.

Corrius, M. and Zabalbeascoa, P. 2011. Language variation in source texts and their translations: the case of L3 in film translation. *Target* 23(1), pp. 113–130.

De Higes-Andino, I., Prats-Rodríguez, A. M., Martínez-Sierra, J. J. and Chaume, F. 2013. Subtitling language diversity in Spanish immigration films. *Meta* 58(1), pp. 134–145.

De Marco, M. 2012. *Audiovisual Translation through a Gender Lens*. Amsterdam: Rodopi.

De Rosa, G. L., Bianchi, F., De Laurentiis, A. and Perego, E., eds. 2014. *Translating Humour in Audiovisual Texts*. Bern: Peter Lang.

Delabastita, D. 1989. Translation and mass-communication. *Babel* 35(4), pp. 193–218.

Desilla, L. 2009. *Towards a Methodology for the Study of Implicatures in Subtitled Films: Multimodal Construal and Reception of Pragmatic Meaning across Cultures*. PhD Thesis. Manchester: University of Manchester.

Díaz-Cintas, J. 2004. "In Search of a Theoretical Framework for the Study of Audiovisual Translation." In *Topics in Audiovisual Translation*, edited by P. Orero, 21–34. Amsterdam: John Benjamins.

Díaz-Cintas, J., ed. 2008. *The Didactics of Audiovisual Translation*. Amsterdam: John Benjamins.

Díaz-Cintas, J., ed. 2012. *La Manipulation de la traduction audiovisuelle/The Manipulation of Audiovisual Translation*. Special issue of *Meta* 57(2). Available from: www.erudit.org/revue/meta/2012/v57/n2

Díaz-Cintas, J. and Remael, A. 2007. *Audiovisual Translation: Subtitling*. Manchester: St Jerome.

Díaz-Cintas, J. and Orero, P. 2010. "Voiceover and Dubbing." In *Handbook of Translation Studies*. Vol. 1, edited by Y. Gambier and L. van Doorslaer, 441–445. Amsterdam: John Benjamins.

Díaz-Cintas, J., Parini, I. and Ranzato, I., eds. 2016. *Ideological Manipulation in Audiovisual Translation*. Special issue of *Altre Modernità*. Available from: http://riviste.unimi.it/index.php/AMonline/issue/view/888/showToc.

Ellender, C. 2015. *Dealing with Difference in Audiovisual Translation: Subtitling Linguistic Variation in Films*. Oxford: Peter Lang.

Etchegoyhen, T., Fishel, M., Jie, J. and Sepesy Maučec, M. 2013. "SMT Approaches for Commercial Translation of Subtitles." In *Proceedings of the XIV Machine Translation Summit*, edited by K. Sima'an, M. L. Forcada, D. Grasmick, H. Depraetere and A. Way, 369–370. Available from: www.mtsummit2013.info/files/proceedings/main/mt-summit-2013-etchegoyhen-et-al.pdf.

Fodor, I. 1976. *Film Dubbing: Phonetic Semiotic, Esthetic and Psychological Aspects*. Amsterdam: John Benjamins.

Franco, E., Matamala, A. and Orero, P. 2010. *Voice-over Translation: An Overview*. Bern: Peter Lang.

Freddi, M. and Pavesi, M., eds. 2009. *Analysing Audiovisual Dialogue: Linguistic and Translational Insights*. Bologna: Clueb.

Gambier, Y., Caimi, A. and Mariotti, C., eds. 2015. *Subtitles and Language Learning: Principles, Strategies and Practical Experiences*. Bern: Peter Lang.

Georgakopoulou, P. and Bywood, L. 2014. Machine translation in subtitling and the rising profile of the post-editor. *MultiLingual*, January/February, 24–28.

Harrenstien, K. 2009. *Automatic Captions in YouTube*, 19 November. Available from: http://googleblog.blogspot.com/2009/11/automatic-captions-in-youtube.html.

Hesse-Quack, O. 1969. *Der Übertragunsprozeß bei der Synchronisation von Filmen. Eine interkulturelle Untersuchung*. Munich: Reinhardt.

Ivarsson, J. 1992. *Subtitling for the Media: A Handbook of an Art*. Stockholm: Transedit.

Ivarsson, J. and Carroll, M. 1998. *Subtitling*. Simrishamn: TransEdit.

Jiménez Hurtado, C. and Soler Gallego, S. 2013. Multimodality, translation and accessibility: a corpus-based study of audio description. *Perspectives* 21(4), pp. 577–594.

Laks, S. 1957. *Le sous-titrage de films. Sa technique. Son esthétique.* Paris: Author's property. Available from: http://ataa.fr/revue/wp-content/uploads/2013/06/ET-HS01-complet.pdf.

Luyken, G.-M., Herbst, T., Langham-Brown, J., Reid, H. and Spinhof, H. 1991. *Overcoming Language Barriers in Television: Dubbing and Subtitling for the European Audience.* Manchester: European Institute for the Media.

Martínez Sierra, J. J. 2005. Translating audiovisual humour: a case study. *Perspectives* 13(4), pp. 289–296.

Massidda, S. 2015. *Audiovisual Translation in the Digital Age: The Italian Fansubbing Phenomenon.* Basingstoke: Palgrave Macmillan.

Mayoral, R., Kelly, D. and Gallardo, N. 1988. Concept of constrained translation: non-linguistic perspectives of translation. *Meta* 33(3), pp. 356–367.

Mereu Keating, C. 2016. *The Politics of Dubbing: Film Censorship and State Intervention in the Translation of Foreign Cinema in Fascist Italy.* Oxford: Peter Lang.

Pavesi, M. 2008. "Spoken Language in Film Dubbing: Target Language Norms, Interference and Translational Routines." In *Between Text and Image: Updating Research in Screen Translation,* edited by D. Chiaro, C. Heiss and C. Bucaria, 79–99. Amsterdam: John Benjamins.

Pedersen, J. 2011. *Subtitling Norms for Television: An Exploration Focusing on Extralinguistic Cultural References.* Amsterdam: John Benjamins.

Perego, E., ed. 2012. *Eye Tracking in Audiovisual Translation.* Rome: Aracne.

Pérez-González, L. 2014. *Audiovisual Translation: Theories, Methods and Issues.* London: Routledge.

Pommier, C. 1988. *Doublage et postsynchronisation.* Paris: Editions Dujarric.

Ranzato, I. 2016. *Translating Culture Specific References on Television: The Case of Dubbing.* London: Routledge.

Romero-Fresco, P. 2011. *Subtitling through Speech Recognition: Respeaking.* Manchester: St Jerome.

Szarkowska, A. 2013. *Forms of Address in Polish-English Subtitling.* Frankfurt am Mainz: Peter Lang.

Talaván, N. and Rodríguez-Arancón, P. 2014. The use of reverse subtitling as an online collaborative language learning tool. *The Interpreter and Translator Trainer* 8(1), pp. 84–101.

Titford, C. 1982. Subtitling-constrained translation. *Lebende Sprachen* 27(3), pp. 113–116.

Toury, G. 1995. *Descriptive Translation Studies and Beyond.* Amsterdam: John Benjamins.

Whitman-Linsen, C. 1992. *Through the Dubbing Glass: The Synchronization of American Motion Pictures into German, French and Spanish.* Frankfurt: Peter Lang.

Yuan, L. 2016. *The Subtitling of Sexual Taboo from English into Chinese.* PhD Thesis. London: Imperial College London.

Yuan, X. 2012. *Politeness and Audience Response in Chinese-English Subtitling.* Oxford: Peter Lang.

Zabalbeascoa, P. 1996. Translating jokes for dubbed television situation comedies. *Translator* 2(2), pp. 235–267.

21

Language, interpreting, and translation in the news media

Christina Schäffner

Introduction

Globalisation has resulted in rapid developments in professional practices in multilingual communication and a broadening of the scope of the term "translation", which nowadays also covers activities such as dubbing, subtitling, and localising. Within Translation Studies, these activities have become objects of research and have been widely investigated. Globalisation has also seen a growth of non-professional translation, with fansubbing and fandubbing as cases in point. These developments are closely linked to the globalisation of technology and tools such as Google Translate. Non-professional translators, however, are not only the fan and volunteer translators; other professionals too can resort to translation (and/or interpreting) in performing their usual work. One such group are journalists, for whom information initially provided in another language frequently becomes a source for their own text production. In Translation Studies, this phenomenon of news translation is a relatively new area of interest, as this chapter will illustrate.

Historical perspectives

Although research into the role of translation and interpreting in the news media is relatively recent within Translation Studies, aspects of language use in the media and characteristics of media genres have been addressed in the neighbouring disciplines of Applied Linguistics, Discourse Analysis, Communication Studies, and Media Studies. Among works frequently cited are the monographs by Fowler (1991) and by Bell (1991). Fowler approaches his topic from the perspective of critical linguistics and examines the role of language in mediating reality, illustrated with newspaper representations (and stereotyping) of gender, power, authority, and law and order. Bell's study, which is informed by his own background as both a linguist and a journalist, addresses patterns of media discourse and language styles. Research into media language and discourse conducted from the perspective of Critical Discourse Analysis has dealt with the structure of news (e.g. van Dijk 1985; Bell 1998), ideological aspects (e.g. van Dijk 1998), the functions and conventions of language use in the media (e.g. Conboy 2007; Reah 2002; Richardson 2006), features of journalistic genres (e.g. Straßner

2000), and media discourse in relation to wider social practices (e.g. Fairclough 1995). Such analyses have focused on language use across a range of media, including radio and TV, the internet, and social media.

These studies have identified information selection, deletion, summarisation, and generalisation as major strategies used in dealing with input texts (e.g van Dijk 1988; Bell 1998). Lexical substitutions as well as syntactic and stylistic changes occur, often aimed at standardising the language, maximising the news value, and reflecting the corporate identity of the media institution. In selecting and shaping information, mass media act as filters or gatekeepers. The information selected comes from a variety of sources, including international news agencies and foreign media, often those with which a specific news outlet maintains cooperation agreements. This means that the journalistic text production process also includes dealing with texts in other languages – in short: translation.

Scholars of Linguistics, Critical Discourse Analysis, and Journalism Studies, however, have tended to focus on monolingual texts, and little attention has been paid to the phenomenon of translation in news production. Within the discipline of Translation Studies, the unique role translation plays in the production and dissemination of international news has been addressed more systematically since the mid-2000s, mainly inspired by the project "The politics and economics of translation in global media", funded by the United Kingdom's Arts and Humanities Research Council and conducted at the University of Warwick (see Conway and Bassnett 2006; Bielsa 2007; Bielsa and Bassnett 2009). It investigated the influence of translation on information flows, focusing on the ways in which news agencies employ translation and also studying attitudes to translation prevalent in the world of news reporting. Since then, research into news translation has been enriched by a number of case studies of selected mass media institutions. A search in the Benjamins Translation Studies Bibliography (https://benjamins.com/online/tsb/) showed 59 results for "news translation" in titles, and 169 results each for "news translation" as a keyword and in abstracts (with several overlaps). Of the 59 titles, 55 were published after 2001, and 28 since 2010. One of the first articles with a special focus on news translation is Vuorinen (1997). More recently, several journals have published special issues devoted to news translation, namely *Language & Intercultural Communication* 5(2) (2005), *Across Languages and Cultures* 11(2) (2010), *Meta* 57(4) (2012), and *Perspectives* 23(4) (2015). News in the Arabic context are addressed in a special issue of *Translation Watch Quarterly* 2(1) (2006) and in work by Darwish (2006, 2010).

"News translation" is often used as a cover term for a variety of journalistic genres, such as short news items, news reports, and press releases. Some scholars therefore prefer to speak of "press translation" (e.g. Bani 2006) or "journalistic translation" (Valdeón 2015a). The Warwick project mentioned above focused more narrowly on international news agencies. These produce news for distribution to national or local media and often have their own websites which are accessible to the general public. Some media institutions aim at a wider audience and make their texts available in several languages (e.g. BBC Monitoring Service, Euronews, *Le Monde Diplomatique*). National newspapers and magazines frequently include translations of texts which were initially published by newspapers in other countries. Occasionally, parts of magazines are bilingual; for instance the German news magazine *Der Spiegel* published texts in German and English side by side in its issue devoted to the Brexit referendum (11 June 2016). Some magazines which operate at an international level exist in several languages (e.g. *National Geographic*, *Cosmopolitan*). Journalistic genres, however, are not only produced by mass media. For example, press releases are also produced and translated by governments, companies,

NGOs, etc. (for press releases produced and translated by Amnesty International see Tesseur 2013).

Most research has focused on print media (hard copies and online), with some research on the role of translation and interpreting for TV (e.g. Tsai 2005, 2012) and radio (van Rooyen 2013). There is, however, significantly less research on interpreting in the context of news media. In fact, the Benjamins Translation Studies Bibliography lists only 10 abstracts for "news interpreting", two of which are devoted to sign language interpreting on TV (Wehrmeyer 2015; Xiao, Chen and Palmer 2015). Overviews of the characteristics of various types of media interpreting (for television, radio, Webcasting, etc) are provided by Pöchhacker (2010) and Straniero-Sergio (2012), and a good overview of how research into news translation has developed is Valdeón (2015a). Entries on news translation have also been included in some handbooks on Translation Studies (Palmer 2009; van Doorslaer 2010a; Holland 2012).

Core issues and topics

Research on news translation covers linguistic and textual aspects, translation strategies used and their effects, practices in specific media settings, and agents and their understanding of translation. Conceptual issues are reflected in nearly all of the publications but rarely dealt with as a dedicated topic. Historical aspects of the role of translation in news transmission are addressed by McLaughlin (2015) and Valdeón (2012).

Translation strategies

Investigations into translation strategies, or translation methods, are predominantly text-based, detailed comparisons of the source text(s) and target text(s), often combined with a contextual analysis.

Hursti (2001) focused on textual transformations in transferring international news from the British news agency Reuters to the Finnish News Agency. He identifies reorganisation, deletion, addition, and substitution as major linguistic operations and relates these to situational, organisational, and cultural factors, such as the demands of news journalism (speed of production, readability of the texts) and the cultural desirability of the texts selected. Károly (2012, 2013, 2014) investigates how specific linguistic-textual features, i.e. topical and event structures, rhetorical structure, and referential cohesion, were handled in Hungarian–English news translation and whether functional equivalence was established. She illustrates how translational shifts affected the rhetorical and generic structure of the target texts, the news content, and readers' interpretation. She sees differences between languages, discursive features of the news story genre, and characteristics of news translation as potential motivations for such shifts.

Shifts in translation were also identified by Sidiropoulou (1995), Gumul (2010), Loupaki (2010), Caimotto (2010), Brownlie (2010), and Federici (2010). Gumul investigates the phenomenon of explicitation in Polish translations of English-language press articles, showing that they assume an altered point of view and construct a different conceptualisation of social reality for the target readers. Loupaki investigates how translators deal with ideological conflict evident in news articles, showing that in Greek translations of English news articles the strategies of literal translation, neutralisation, omission, addition, and explicitation result in a shift of the overall position, thus reproducing or erasing ideological conflict, or introducing a new conflict in the target text. Caimotto and Federici show how various Italian newspapers reframe the message of English-language articles, resulting in a different message in the target texts. Brownlie investigates how French texts on the 2007 French Presidential elections were transformed into English for a British audience.

Ideology as a motivation for shifts was identified by Bazzi (2014, 2015) in news production in an English–Arabic translation context and by Floros (2012) in the Cypriot context. Bazzi illustrates ideological motivations behind Arab translators' choices of e.g. metaphors and modal expressions in news reports of political events in the Middle East. Floros (2012) illustrates that Greek Cypriot media use modifiers such as "so-called" when they refer to institutions of the northern part of Cyprus (named the "Turkish Republic of Northern Cyprus" by Turkey, but considered as illegal by the Republic of Cyprus). Since these modifiers also appear in translated texts, he argues that Cypriot newspapers use translation for disseminating national policy and that national ideologies thus violate the desired informativity of news.

Valdeón (e.g. 2005a, 2005b, 2007, 2008) identified differences in the text structure (e.g. use of headlines), syntactic and grammatical structures (e.g. in respect of transitivity), and lexical choices in news articles from the American news corporation *CNN* and the Spanish-language website *CNNenEspañol* and in news web texts of *BBCWorld* and *BBCMundo*, which affect the reporting of a given event. He finds that the English texts were very closely translated, rarely taking audience sensitivity into account, and argues that the image of the world thereby projected to the target audience "accentuates an ethnocentric view of the world whereby Anglophone news is given prominence at the expense of other more international news" (Valdeón 2008, 303).

Other case studies which identify translation strategies based on a comparison of source texts and target texts are Kang (2007) for *Newsweek* and the Korean edition *Newsweek Hankuk Pan*; Hernández-Guerrero (2010a) for the Spanish daily *El Mundo's* translated texts from *The Times*, *The Guardian*, *Libération*, and *Il Corriere della Sera*; Frías and José (2005) on the English edition of *El País*, a supplement to the *International Herald Tribune*; and Schäffner (2005) for *Der Spiegel* and *Spiegel International*. All these studies identify partial translation, omissions, additions, generalisations, specifications, reorganisation, and substitutions as translation strategies. Explicitation and specification often occur in the case of source-culture-specific referents, e.g. politicians and place names. For example, "Otto Schily (SPD)" became "Social Democratic Interior Minister Otto Schily" (Schäffner 2005).

Deletion and rearrangement were also identified by Bielsa and Bassnett (2009) in texts produced by international news agencies. They argue that the overall aim of global news is comprehensibility, which leads to domestication as the overarching approach to news translation. Texts are adapted to suit the target audience, the in-house style, and/or the ideological positions of the newspaper. As Bielsa and Bassnett (2009, 2) say: "Information that passes between cultures through news agencies is not only 'translated' in the interlingual sense, it is reshaped, edited, synthesized and transformed for the consumption of a new set of readers".

The significance of culture in news translation has also been addressed. Bassnett (2005) and Bielsa and Bassnett (2009) illustrate how English versions of Arabic texts in Western media frame a cultural and religious Other. Conway (2006, 2012, 2015), too, investigates news translation as a form of cultural translation, illustrating "the ways in which linguistic re-expression affects and is affected by larger questions of representation of cultural and linguistic otherness" (Conway 2006, 47). However, Davier (2015, 536) argues that the concepts of acculturation and cultural translation "are not fine-grained enough to discriminate between different degrees of cultural mediation in transnational news reporting". Indeed, studies of press translation have revealed that the processes involved in transnational news reporting are complex and include more than making sense of a cultural Other. Factors such as time, ideology, journalistic values, and institutional practices influence the re-perspectivisation (Kang 2007), of news texts. This complexity was already envisaged in the research question formulated by Gambier (2006, 12): "To what extent does news submitted to translation undergo a reframing process, entailing a reconstruction of a constructed reality, already subjected to professional, institutional and contextual influences?"

Practices and agents in specific media settings

Research investigating institutional settings is linked to specific case studies. Palmer (2009) reminds us that translation can occur at different stages in the news production process, i.e. as a part of news gathering, as part of news writing, and in the dissemination process, "when reports are transferred between different news organisations" (Palmer 2009, 187). In news gathering, journalists frequently rely on the help of local interpreters, often called "fixers", who perform various duties for the journalists, including interpreting interviews and translating local media, interpreting usually being a mixture of summary and translation, rather than a word-for-word rendering (for an overview of the use of fixers by Western media personnel in Iraq since the Anglo–US invasion of 2003 see Palmer and Fontan 2007, 10).

Research into institutional practices has revealed a diversity of processes of news production. Bielsa (2007, 2010a) illustrates that news agencies achieve maximum efficiency in the dissemination of news worldwide despite differences in the local practices in their regional centres. Bani (2006) analyses press translations into Italian published in the weekly magazine *Internazionale*. Texts are sent to a translator who works away from the editorial office. When the translations are returned they undergo a complex editing process, with one editor checking the target text against the source text, another proofreading the Italian version, and a copy-editor considering how and where the translation will be placed inside the newspaper. Kang (2007) illustrates the complexity of institutional practices for the Korean edition *Newsweek Hankuk Pan*, which involve translators translating selected texts, checkers revising and proofreading, and top checkers taking the final decision regarding omissions and naturalisation of the text. The published texts result from "the collaborative work of people assuming different roles and engaged in language transfer, cultural adaptation, proofreading, revising, naturalizing, editing and other textual processes that are carried out repeatedly and cyclically" (Kang 2007, 238). Frías and José (2005) found that although professional translators are employed to do some of the translations, journalists in the local office are responsible for post-editing and revising the texts. Schäffner (2010a) compared the practices of *Spiegel International* and the *BBC Monitoring Service*, where some texts are translated by professional translators and others by the journalists in the Berlin office (*Spiegel International*) or by monitors (the label used for translators for the *BBC Monitoring Service*). She argues that the dominant practices are domestication for *Spiegel International*, and foreignisation for the *BBC Monitoring Service*.

Tsai (2005, 2010) and van Rooyen (2013) provide insights into the practices of different media institutions, i.e. television and radio. Based on her own experience as a television news translator in Taiwan, Tsai describes the routine in the newsroom of Taiwan's Formosa Television which determines the production of international news. She shows that news translators use multiple source texts in both print and broadcast format as input for their text production. Van Rooyen analyses news production at the South African Broadcasting Corporation, which caters for several of the national languages. In print media too, journalists regularly use several texts as input for writing their reports, sometimes explicitly indicating their sources, but usually without any reference to the original language. This is because in global news agencies and also in the offices of local media, it is professional journalists with language competence who produce these texts, acting as translators and intercultural mediators in the representation of foreign media, although they have little or no training in translation. However, journalists who work across language frontiers often have "diverse sets of skills, principal of which is recognition of what their target audience expects and can tolerate" (Bassnett 2006, 5ff.). The selection, production, and dissemination of information in global news agencies is governed by the conventions and values of the journalistic profession which aim at reaching global publics with maximum speed and efficiency and leave little space for individual preferences. This is also argued by Chen (2011), who illustrates the translators' constrained subjectivity in the production of news texts with a case study on English–Chinese transediting in the Taiwanese press.

Translation is an integral part of interlingual news writing, and thus is not perceived as a separate activity. As Bielsa (2007, 151) argues, "news translation is doubly invisible, not just because of the need to adopt a domesticating strategy that values fluency and hides its very intervention, but also because of the fact that translation has been successfully integrated within journalism". Moreover, journalists do not consider their work as translation but rather as journalistic writing. Therefore, they do not want to call themselves translators, preferring terms such as "international journalist", or "bilingual journalist". Some scholars in Translation Studies have suggested labels such as "journalators" (van Doorslaer 2012) or "journalist-translators" (Hernández Guerrero 2010b, Matsushita 2015) to account for the fact that translation is involved in journalistic writing.

Conceptual issues related to news translation

Since news texts are often based on several (written and/or oral) sources, one specific source text with one specific author cannot easily be identified. The translated text in its published form too, is rarely the product of one person, which made Kang (2007, 238) speak of news translation as a "collective effort". In news writing, the wording of the input text is much less important than the topic as seen as relevant by the journalists for their respective audience. Or, as Valdeón (2009, 79) says, we have "translation of information, rather than [. . .] translation of texts".

Research has thus revealed a discrepancy between what journalists-qua-translators think translation is and what they themselves actually do. Their own discourse reflects a view of translation as literal translation, as a mechanical process of linguistic transcoding which does not require decision-making beyond linguistic choices. They see their journalistic work as more creative. The journalistic parameters of accuracy and speed of information, readability, and expectations of the target readership result in more or less freely transferred messages. Classical Translation Studies concepts such as equivalence and faithfulness to the original cannot be used for explaining these processes. Davier (2012, 79) thus argues that "[c]lassical translation studies theories are not equipped to ascertain whether or not these different kinds of interlingual transfers can be considered as 'translations'".

It is the amount and the nature of the transformations involved which make researchers reflect on the applicability of the label "translation" to news translation. This unease has made scholars opt for alternative labels, e.g. "adaptation/translation" ("*adaptación/traducción*", Frías and José 2005) or "transformative acts" (Valdeón 2005a, 2005b). The term most often used, however, is "transediting" (e.g. Hursti 2001; van Doorslaer 2009; Chen 2011), which was introduced by Stetting (1989) to account for the fuzzy borderline between translating and editing. Stetting presented five cases where transediting is practised: (i) shortening of text passages for subtitling, (ii) making the text of an interviewed politician idiomatic and well structured, (iii) cleaning up inadequate manuscripts, (iv) journalists drawing on material in other languages for writing their own texts, (v) extracting information from various documents for producing promotional material in another language (Stetting 1989, 373–374). Schäffner (2012) reflects on the power of the term "transediting" to describe the practices in news translation. Bielsa and Bassnett (2009) prefer the simple "news translation" to "point to this particular combination between editing and translating and more specifically to the form that translation takes when it has become integrated in news production within the journalistic field" (Bielsa and Bassnett 2009, 63–64). Schäffner (2012) argues that the processes of translating journalistic texts are "complex and diverse and that replacing 'translation' by another term is not a straightforward solution" (Schäffner 2012, 876). Moreover, using "transediting" instead of "translation" would mean "that 'translation' continues to be understood in a narrower sense of a purely word-for-word transfer process" (Schäffner 2012, 881).

News translation has also been linked to the concept of gatekeeping. Vuorinen considers gatekeeping operations such as deletion, addition, substitution, or reorganisation "part and parcel of the normal text operations performed in any translation, and particularly in news translation" (Vuorinen 1997, 170) for controlling the flow of information. Kang (2007) characterises news translation as an instance of entextualisation in which information is selected, reduced, supplemented, reorganised, and transformed. Orengo (2005, 168) argues that adopting "a theory of 'localisation' rather than conventional translation theories accounts more easily for both the commercial nature and the global scale of news distribution". Similarly, van Doorslaer (2012, 1046) argues that "the borderlines between translation, localization and rewriting have become very blurred in the context of news production". With reference to TV news translation, Tsai (2005, 2006, 2010) suggests studying the theory and nature of interpreting to explore where interpreting and broadcast news translation may converge. Bielsa and Bassnett (2009) too, argue that news translation is close to interpreting, and that therefore methods and insights of Interpreting Studies could be brought to bear on researching news translation.

Main research methods

Studies into the practices and working conditions in media institutions are based on fieldwork, in particular observations and semi-structured interviews. Bielsa (2010a) gathered material through ethnographic observation and interviews with journalists at Agence France-Presse and Inter Press Service, and Davier (2012, 2014) conducted fieldwork in the offices of Agence France Press and Agence télégraphique suisse in Switzerland. Bielsa and Bassnett (2009) combine the results of fieldwork in global news organisations with close readings of different English versions of key Arabic texts. A combination of a textual analysis of translated press releases and ethnographic fieldwork conducted at the local office of Amnesty International Vlaanderen allowed Tesseur (2013) to explain reasons for the choice of particular translation strategies. Tsai (2012) examined authentic news items from a TV news station in Taiwan and interviewed senior TV news translators, concluding that news translators work in a "news ecology that is defined by market values" (Tsai 2012, 1060).

Promising research into news translation processes has recently been conducted by Ehrensberger-Dow and Perrin (2013). They used progression analysis, which was originally developed to study the news-writing processes of journalists at their workplaces, to investigate the translation process. Progression analysis combines ethnographic observation, interviews, keystroke logging, screenshot recordings, eye-tracking, and cue-based retrospective verbalisations. Such a method promises to give new insights into news translation as a situated activity.

Current debates

In addition to a growing body of empirical case studies of news translation practices, the main current debates concern conceptual aspects. Empirical research has gone beyond news in the narrow sense and has included other journalistic genres, e.g. political interviews (Hernández Guerrero 2010b; Schäffner 2008, 2010b). Hernández Guerrero shows that translated interviews in the Spanish newspaper *El Mundo* have undergone journalistic rewriting and a series of mediations, including translation by the journalist if the interview was conducted in a foreign language. Readers of *El Mundo* are given no indication that they are reading a translation, as is generally the case with press translation. Readers receive the mediated voice of the interviewee. Such a mediation of voices can be even more complex if the interview was initially interpreted, and the rendition transcribed and potentially edited further before being translated as a basis for publication in a local newspaper.

Published interviews often undergo omissions, reorganising of information, and changes in genre and style, in order to conform to the newspaper's editorial line or textual conventions, or because of space constraints. Schäffner (2008, 2010b) discusses an interview which the then Russian President Vladimir Putin gave on 1 June 2007 to eight journalists, representing eight newspapers from the G8 countries. Transformations which had occurred in the recontextualisation of the actual interview, which had been interpreted simultaneously, concerned the length of the texts (16,132 words in the Russian interview transcript published by *Kommersant*, 2,291 words in *Der Spiegel*, and 1,461 words in *Le Figaro*), the information selected, the choice of headlines (e.g. "I'm a pure and absolute democrat. It's a tragedy that I'm the only one" in *The Times*, and "Putin threatens to target Europe" in *Globe and Mail*), and differences at the micro level. *The Times* and *Globe and Mail* turned the interview format into a report which included direct quotes. Another example is an interview which the German Chancellor Angela Merkel gave on 25 January 2012 to leading European newspapers, i.e. *El País* (Spain), *Gazeta Wyborcza* (Poland), *The Guardian* (United Kingdom), *La Stampa* (Italy), *Le Monde* (France), and *Süddeutsche Zeitung* (Germany). Only some of the reporters actually interviewed Merkel, apparently in German only, and the interview was then translated by the Translation Service of the German Foreign Office. Ian Traynor, *The Guardian* journalist, confirmed that "unlike the Franco-German papers, we do not usually run straight question and answer interviews, but take the transcript and decide what the news/story/ interest is" (email communication 5 June 2012).

Investigations into potential relationships between certain translation strategies and the types of texts, ideological factors, or institutional policies, including studies of journalistic translations in the Spanish press by Hernández Guerrero (2010b) and Valdeón (2015b), have identified different methods of translation for "stable" sources (e.g. columns authored by experts) and "unstable" sources (i.e. texts not considered final). Stable sources tend to be translated more closely, although Valdeón also uses economic columns authored by Paul Krugman, originally published in the *New York Times* and translated into Spanish by *El País*, to show that certain unstable texts can turn stable.

Current debate concerning conceptual issues addresses questions such as: Is news translation (or journalistic translation) a form of translation, or does it need a separate term (e.g. transediting, adaptation) to capture its specifics? Are such alternative terms best suited to describe what happens in media institutions? May the choice of these labels favour or hinder the development of news translation? What are the theoretical and methodological challenges to researching the phenomena of news translation? Should news translation be researched within Translation Studies at all, or is it rather a matter of journalism studies? Such questions were addressed at panels at congresses of the European Society for Translation Studies (EST) in 2013 (panel theme: "News Translation: Subverting the Discipline?") and in 2016 (panel theme: "News translation challenging Adaptation, Transfer and Translation Studies").

Such conceptual reflections have shown that research into news translation has been pushing the boundaries of the very concept of "translation" and of Translation Studies. Scholars have therefore argued in favour of a broader definition of the term "translation" to include the context of media news production (e.g. van Doorslaer 2010b; Schäffner 2012; Davier 2015). It has also been highlighted that interdisciplinary research can make major contributions to a better understanding of the complex nature of international news production. Some Translation Studies scholars have resorted to methods and theories from related disciplines, such as sociology and globalisation research (e.g. Bielsa 2010b), or imagology (e.g. van Doorslaer 2010b, 2012), in addition to employing methods from Discourse Analysis or ethnography, as illustrated above. These topics of current debates can be expected to dominate future research as well.

Future directions

Despite the increase in research on media translation, journalistic translation is still underrepresented (for example, in an edited volume entitled *Media and Translation: An Interdisciplinary Approach*, only two out of the 14 chapters are devoted to news, compared to seven addressing film (Abend-David 2014). Moreover, research has largely been restricted to a small number of countries (especially Belgium, Canada, South Africa, Spain, Switzerland, Taiwan, and the United Kingdom). However, there is growing research in China (e.g. Pan 2012; Zhang 2013) and Japan (e.g. Matsushita 2015), often related to doctoral studies (see also M'Balla-Ndi 2015 on social values that influence journalistic practices in Vanuatu). Future research is likely to cover a wider range of countries and extend beyond analysis of print media and newswires to include the practices in TV and radio, and more research into media interpreting, voice-over, and re-recording will be useful. Voice-over is frequently encountered on TV when politicians are interviewed. Their original voice is reduced to a low level of audibility, and may only be heard briefly at the beginning and the end, with the voice of an interpreter or an actor superimposed. In this way, journalists "might maintain the illusion that they were able to interview locals in their own language" (Gambier 2006, 15).

More empirical work on practices of news translation will confirm or modify the findings gained so far which reveal that journalistic values (speed, factual accuracy, newsworthiness) and factors such as culture, ideology, and power relations determine the translation process. It would also be interesting to investigate whether media institutions which produce news in several languages follow the same practice for each language. Future research might also investigate the power of languages and media institutions in the circulation of news (e.g. the role of English as a source language or as a lingua franca, e.g. Gambier 2010). Such aspects are linked to credibility, media reception, and media perception (see Samuel-Azran, Lavie-Dinur and Karniel 2014), and we might also ask whether explicit reference to translation or to the source of a quote may encourage readers to interpret a text in a particular way. Research could investigate the effects that journalist-translators' (intratextual and paratextual) interventions may have on receivers' perception if the voice they hear is perceived as that of a friend or a foe.

Bielsa and Bassnett (2009, 67) argue that perspectives change in news translation, and that this is "a perfectly normal operation in journalism if a new angle is justified according to the [. . .] criteria of background knowledge and relevance". But is it actually possible to draw a line between "natural" changes in angle or perspective (perhaps because of differences between languages or speech/writing conventions) and cases of manipulation or deliberate misrepresentation? As we have seen, the voices readers hear are often refracted by translation policies of the respective media institutions. As Holland (2006, 250) asks, can we "distinguish between intercultural communication and 'intercultural spin'"?

Finally, future research can benefit from interdisciplinarity. As mentioned above, Translation Studies scholars make use of concepts and methods of neighbouring disciplines, whereas there is little reference to translation or interpreting in work in Journalism Studies, Media Studies, or Communication Studies. Olausson (2014) analyses reports on climate change in Indian, Swedish, and US newspapers and suggests that we revisit the notion of "domestication" of foreign news in national media (although she does not refer to Venuti 1995). Three discursive modes of domestication are presented: "(1) introverted domestication, which disconnects the domestic from the global; (2) extroverted domestication, which interconnects the domestic and the global; and (3) counter-domestication, a deterritorialized mode of reporting that lacks any domestic epicentre" (Olausson 2014, 711). The deterritorialised nature of news contents as a result of globalisation is also addressed by Kasmani (2014), who compared news production by the BBC World News and Al Jazeera English, focusing on the relationship between the portrayal of Iranian political leaders and the national affiliation of the journalists. He argues that globalisation has redefined the role of foreign journalists, quoting Fürsich (2002) who pointed out that "global journalists in the global media are not 'international journalists who cover foreign news from the perspective of one nation', but global news workers who work for 'transnational media corporations and produce their content for a global market'" (Fürsich 2002, 59, cited in Kasmani 2014, 595). Such a perception of journalistic work can also give new inspiration to researching news translation.

Implications for practice

Translation is a key factor in the chain of journalistic text production, but it is rarely problematised in the media newsrooms, and rarely addressed in academic publications outside Translation Studies. For researchers, problems arise "from the invisible activity of translation rather than the invisibility of the professionals" (Valdeón 2010, 149). Insights gained from interdisciplinary research into news translation, or journalistic translation more widely, can thus have both theoretical and practical implications for both journalists and translators. As illustrated above, some media do use professional translators who, however, usually work outside the immediate context of the media institution and whose translations are revised by journalists to make them fit for publication. In contrast, journalists whose text production process includes translation do not normally have training in translation and are thus guided by their own professional standards and ethics. That is, professionals belonging to different social systems with their own traditions are involved in news production which includes translation. The journalists may be non-professional translators, but as professional journalists they are professionals in their own right. As argued by Antonini and Bucaria (2015, 9–10):

> non-professionals who interpret/translate in the media, in most cases, are unqualified having not received any training in this specific profession, however, this does not necessarily mean that they are incompetent as, over time, they can acquire expertise and competence in a specific area of interpreting/translation in the media.

An exchange between professional journalists and professional translators about their understanding of translation, their practices, and their respective professional codes of conduct should benefit both groups.

Investigating the processes of news translation as well as the factors by which they are influenced can also contribute to raising awareness of the significance of translation not only among journalists, or among Translation Studies and Journalism Studies scholars, but ultimately also among the general public.

Further reading

Bielsa, E. and Bassnett, S. 2009. *Translation in Global News*. London: Routledge.
This book investigates the influence of translation on information flows, focusing on the ways in which news agencies employ translation and what attitudes to translation are prevalent in the world of news reporting.

Language & Intercultural Communication 5 (2) 2005
This special issue of the journal, edited by Kyle Conway and Susan Bassnett, reports on the aims of the Warwick project on "Global News Translation" and presents some initial findings.

Across Languages and Cultures 11 (2) 2010
This special issue of the journal, edited by Roberto Valdeón, addresses translating information in the post-industrial society and includes several articles on news translation.

Meta 57 (4) 2012
This special issue of the journal, edited by Roberto Valdeón, includes articles which deal with topics related to "Journalism and Translation" in a wider sense.

Perspectives 23 (4) 2015
This special issue of the journal, edited by Kyle Conway, is devoted specifically to aspects of "Culture and News Translation".

Related topics

Genre analysis and translation; Narrative analysis and translation; Stylistics and translation; Text linguistics, translating, and interpreting.

References

Abend-David, D., ed. 2014. *Media and Translation: An Interdisciplinary Approach*. London: Bloomsbury Publishing.
Antonini, R. and Bucaria, C. 2015. "NPIT in the Media: An Overview of the Field and Main Issues". In *Non-professional Interpreting and Translation in the Media*, edited by R. Antonini and C. Bucaria, 7–20. Frankfurt am Main: Peter Lang.

Bani, S. 2006. "An Analysis of Press Translation Process". In *Translation in Global News: Proceedings of the Conference Held at the University of Warwick 23 June 2006*, edited by K. Conway and S. Bassnett, 35–45. Coventry: University of Warwick.

Bassnett, S. 2005. Bringing the news back home: strategies of acculturation and foreignisation. *Language and Intercultural Communication* 5(2), pp. 120–130.

Bassnett, S. 2006. "Introduction". In *Translation in Global News: Proceedings of the Conference Held at the University of Warwick 23 June 2006*, edited by K. Conway and S. Bassnett, 5–7. Coventry: University of Warwick.

Bazzi, S. 2014. Foreign metaphors and Arabic translation: an empirical study in journalistic translation practice. *Journal of Language and Politics* 13(1), pp. 120–151.

Bazzi, S. 2015. Ideology and Arabic translations of news texts. *Translation and Translanguaging in Multilingual Contexts* 1(2), pp. 135–161.

Bell, A. 1991. *The Language of News Media*. Oxford: Blackwell.

Bell, A. 1998 "The Discourse Structure of News Stories". In *Approaches to Media Discourse*, edited by A. Bell and P. Garrett, 64–104. Oxford: Wiley.

Benjamins Translation Studies Bibliography. https://benjamins.com/online/tsb/. [Accessed April 2016.]

Bielsa, E. 2007. Translation in global news agencies. *Target* 19(1), pp. 135–155.

Bielsa, E. 2010a. "Translating News: A Comparison of Practices in News Agencies". In *Translating Information*, edited by R. Valdeón, 31–50. Oviedo: Universidad de Oviedo.

Bielsa, E. 2010b. "The Sociology of Translation: Outline of an Emerging Field". In *Applied Sociology in Translation Studies/Sociologia aplicade a la traducció* (Monografias de Traducción e Interpretatción/Monographs in Translation and Interpreting 2), edited by E. Monzó, and O. Diaz Fouces, 153–172. Alicante: University of Alicante.

Bielsa, E. and Bassnett, S. 2009. *Translation in Global News*. London: Routledge.

Brownlie, S. 2010. "Representing News from France". In *Political Discourse, Media and Translation*, edited by C. Schäffner and S. Bassnett. London: Cambridge Scholars Publishing.

Caimotto, M. C. 2010. "Translating Foreign Articles with Local Implications: A Case Study". In *Political Discourse, Media and Translation*, edited by C Schäffner and S. Bassnett, 76–93. London: Cambridge Scholars Publishing.

Chen, Y. 2011. The translator's subjectivity and its constraints in news transediting: a perspective of reception aesthetics. *Meta* 56(1), pp. 119–144.

Conboy, M. 2007. *The Language of the News*. Abingdon: Routledge.

Conway, K. 2006. "A cultural studies approach to translation in the news: the case of Canada and Quebec". In *Translation in Global News: Proceedings of the Conference Held at the University of Warwick 23 June 2006*, edited by K. Conway and S. Bassnett, 47–57. Coventry: University of Warwick.

Conway, K. 2012. Cultural translation, long-form journalism, and readers' responses to the Muslim veil. *Meta* 57(4), pp. 997–1012.

Conway, K. 2015. What is the role of culture in news translation? A materialist approach. *Perspectives* 23(4), pp. 521–535.

Darwish, A. 2006. Translating the news: reframing constructed realities. *Translation Watch Quarterly* 2(1), pp. 52–77.

Darwish, A. 2010. *A Journalist's Guide to Live Direct and Unbiased News Translation*. Melbourne: Writescope.

Davier, L. 2012. Légitimité ou illégitimité de la traduction dans les agences de presse? *Forum* 10(1), pp. 79–114.

Davier, L. 2014. The paradoxical invisibility of translation in the highly multilingual context of news agencies. *Global Media and Communication* 10(1), pp. 53–72.

Davier, L. 2015. Cultural translation in news agencies? A plea to broaden the definition of translation. *Perspectives* 23(4), pp. 536–551.

Ehrensberger-Dow, M. and Perrin, D. 2013. Applying a newswriting research approach to translation. *Target* 25(1), pp. 77–92.

Fairclough, N. 1995. *Media Discourse*. London: Arnold.

Federici, F. M. 2010. "Translations in Italian Media: The Calipari Case and Legitimized Texts". In *Political Discourse, Media and Translation*, edited by C Schäffner and S. Bassnett, 116–141. London: Cambridge Scholars Publishing.

Floros, G. 2012. News translation and translation ethics in the Cypriot context. *Meta* 57(4), pp. 924–942.

Fowler, R. 1991. *Language in the News: Discourse and Ideology in the Press*. London: Routledge.

Frías, A. and José, F. 2005. Traducción y periodismo: *El País English Edition. Puentes* 5, pp. 39–46.

Fürsich, E. 2002. How can global journalists represent the "other"? A critical assessment of the cultural studies concept for media practice. *Journalism* 3, pp. 57–84.

Gambier, Y. 2006. "Transformations in International News". In *Translation in Global News: Proceedings of the Conference Held at the University of Warwick 23 June 2006*, edited by K. Conway and S. Bassnett, 9–21. Coventry: University of Warwick.

Gambier, Y. 2010. "Media, information et traduction á l'ère de la globalisation". In *Translating Information*, edited by R. Valdeón, 13–31. Oviedo: Universidad de Oviedo.

Gumul, E. 2010. "Explicitating Political Discourse". In *Political Discourse, Media and Translation*, edited by C. Schäffner and S. Bassnett, 94–116. Newcastle upon Tyne: Cambridge Scholars Publishing.

Hernández Guerrero, M. J. 2010a. "Las noticias traducidas en el diario *El Mundo*: el trasvase transcultural de la información". In *Translating information*. Edited by R. Valdeón, 51–86. Oviedo: Universidad de Oviedo.

Hernández Guerrero, M. J. 2010b. Translated interviews in printed media: a case study of the Spanish daily. *El Mundo. Across Languages and Cultures* 11(2), pp. 217–232.

Holland, R. 2006. Language(s) in the global news: translation, audience design and discourse (mis)representation. *Target* 18(2), pp. 229–259.

Holland, R. 2012. "News Translation". In *The Routledge Handbook of Translation Studies*, edited by C. Millán and F. Bartrina, 333–346. London: Routledge.

Hursti, K. 2001. An insider's view on transformation and transfer in international news communication: an English-Finnish perspective. *The Electronic Journal of the Department of English at the University of Helsinki* 1, pp. 1–8.

Kang, J.-H. 2007. Recontextualization of news discourse: a case study of translation of news discourse on North Korea. *The Translator* 13(2), pp. 219–242.

Károly, K. 2012. News discourse in translation: topical structure and news content in the analytical news article. *Meta* 57(4), pp. 884–908.

Károly, K. 2013. Translating rhetoric: relational propositional shifts in Hungarian-English translations of news stories. *The Translator* 19(2), pp. 245–273.

Károly, K. 2014. Referential cohesion and news content: a case study of shifts of reference in Hungarian-English news translation. *Target* 26(3), pp. 406–431.

Kasmani, M. F. 2014. The nation-state factor in global news reporting: a study of the BBC World News and Al Jazeera English coverage. *International Communication Gazette* 76(7), pp. 594–614.

Loupaki, E. 2010. "Investigating Translators' Strategies in Rendering Ideological Conflict: The Case of News Translation". In *Political Discourse, Media and Translation*, edited by C. Schäffner and S. Bassnett, 55–75. Newcastle upon Tyne: Cambridge Scholars Publishing.

Matsushita, K. 2015. *Risk Management in the Decision-Making Process of English-Japanese News Translation*. PhD Dissertation, Rikkyo University.

M'Balla-Ndi, M. 2015. On being a contemporary *taasila*: navigating *kastom* and *ol ting blong waet man. Perspectives* 23(4), pp. 599–614.

McLaughlin, M. L. 2015. News translation past and present: silent witness and invisible intruder. *Perspectives* 23(4), pp. 552–569.

Olausson, U. 2014. The diversified nature of "domesticated" news discourse. *Journalism Studies* 15(6), pp. 711–725.

Orengo, A. 2005. Localising news: translation and the "Global-national" dichotomy. *Language and Intercultural Communication* 5(2), pp. 168–187.

Palmer, J. 2009. "News Gathering and Dissemination". In *Routledge Encyclopedia of Translation Studies*, edited by M. Baker and G. Saldanha, 186–189. London: Routledge.

Palmer, J. and Fontan, V. 2007. "Our ears and our eyes": journalists and fixers in Iraq. *Journalism* 8(1), pp. 5–24.

Pan, L. 2012. *Stance Mediation in News Translation: A Case Study of Sensitive Discourse on China 2008*. Doctoral Dissertation, University of Macau.

Pöchhacker, F. 2010. "Media Interpreting". In *Handbook of Translation Studies*. Vol. 1, edited by Y. Gambier and L. van Doorslaer, 224–226. Amsterdam: John Benjamins.

Reah, D. 2002. *The Language of Newspapers*. 2nd ed. Abingdon: Routledge.

Richardson, J. E, 2006. *Analysing Newspapers: An Approach from Critical Discourse Analysis*. Basingstoke: Palgrave Macmillan.

Samuel-Azran, T., Lavie-Dinur, A. and Karniel, Y. 2014. "Accent and Prejudice: Israelis' Blind Assessment of Al-Jazeera English News Items". In *Media and Translation: An Interdisciplinary Approach*, edited by D. Abend-David, 267–290. London: Bloomsbury Publishing.

Schäffner, C. 2005. Bringing a German voice to English-speaking readers: *Spiegel International*. *Language and Intercultural Communication* 5(2), pp. 154–167.

Schäffner, C. 2008. "The Prime Minister said . . .": voices in translated political texts. *Synaps Fag-språk, Kommunikasjon, Kulturkunnskap* 22, pp. 3–25.

Schäffner, C. 2010a. "Crosscultural Translation and Conflicting Ideologies". In *Translation and Cultural Identity. Selected Essays on Translation and Cross-Cultural Communication*, edited by M. Muñoz-Calvo and C. Buesa-Gómez, 107–127. Newcastle: Cambridge Scholars Publishing.

Schäffner, C. 2010b. "Politische Interviews im Blick der Translationswissenschaft". In *Translations-kultur revisited. Festschrift für Erich Prun*, edited by N. Grbic, G. Hebenstreit, G.Vorderobermeier and M. Wolf, 319–339. Tübingen: Stauffenburg.

Schäffner, C. 2012. Rethinking transediting. *Meta* 57(4), pp. 866–883.

Sidiropoulou, M. 1995. Causal shifts in news reporting: English vs Greek press. *Perspectives* 3(1), pp. 83–98.

Stetting, K. 1989. "Transediting: A New Term for Coping with the Grey Area between Editing and Translating". In *Proceedings from the Fourth Nordic Conference for English Studies*, edited by G. Caie, K. Haarstrup, A. L. Jakobson, J. E. Nielsen, J. Sevandsen, H. Specht and A. Zettersten, 371–382. Copenhagen: University of Copenhagen, Department of English.

Straniero-Sergio, F. 2012. "Media Interpreting". In *The Encyclopedia of Applied Linguistics*, edited by C. A. Chapelle, Hoboken: Wiley-Blackwell.

Straßner, E. 2000. *Journalistische Texte*. Tübingen: Niemeyer.

Tesseur, W. 2013. "Amnesty International's Language Strategy Put into Practice: A Case Study of the Translation of Press Releases". In *Emerging Research In Translation Studies*, edited by G. González Núñez, Y. Khaled, and T Voinova. Selected papers of the CETRA Research Summer School 2012. Leuven: KU Leuven. Available from: https://www.arts.kuleuven.be/cetra/papers [Accessed 15 August 2016].

Tsai, C. 2005. Inside the television newsroom: an insider's view of international news translation in Taiwan. *Language and Intercultural Communication* 5(2), pp. 145–153.

Tsai, C. 2006. "Translation through Interpreting: A Television Newsroom Model". In *Translation in Global News. Proceedings of the Conference Held at the University of Warwick 23 June 2006*, edited by K. Conway and S. Bassnett, 59–71. Coventry: University of Warwick.

Tsai, C. 2010. "News Translator as Reporter". In *Political Discourse, Media and Translation*, edited by C. Schäffner and S. Bassnett, 178–197. Newcastle upon Tyne: Cambridge Scholars Publishing.

Tsai, C. 2012. Television news translation in the era of market-driven journalism. *Meta* 57(4), pp. 1060–1080.

Valdeón, R. A. 2005a. The CNNenEspañol News. *Perspectives* 13(4), pp. 255–267.

Valdeón, R. A. 2005b. The translated Spanish service of the BBC. *Across Languages and Cultures* 6(2), pp. 195–220.

Valdeón, R. A. 2007. "Ideological Independence or Negative Mediation: BBC Mundo and CNN en Español's (translated) Reporting of Madrid's Terrorist Attacks". In *Translating and Interpreting Conflict*, edited by M. Salama-Carr, 99–118. Amsterdam: Rodopi.

Valdeón, R. A. 2008, Anomalous news translation: selective appropriation of themes and texts in the internet. *Babel* 54(4), pp. 299–326.

Valdeón, R. A. 2009. Translating informative and persuasive texts. *Perspectives* 17(2), pp. 77–81.

Valdeón, R. A. 2010. Translation in the informational society. *Across Languages and Cultures* 11(2), pp. 149–160.

Valdeón, R. A. 2012. From the Dutch corantos to convergence journalism: the role of translation in news production. *Meta* 57(4), pp. 850–865.

Valdeón, R. A. 2015a. Fifteen years of journalistic translation research and more. *Perspectives* 23(4), pp. 634–662.

Valdeón, R. A. 2015b. (Un)stable sources, translation and news production. *Target* 27(3), pp. 440–453.

van Dijk, T. A. 1985. "The Structures of News in the Press". In *Discourse and Communication: New Approaches to the Analysis of Mass Media Discourse and Communication*, edited by T. A. van Dijk, 69–93. Berlin: de Gruyter.

van Dijk, T. A. 1988. *News Analysis: Case Studies of International and National News in the Press.* Hillsdale, NJ: Lawrence Erlbaum Associates.

van Dijk, T. A. 1998. "Opinions and Ideologies in the Press". In *Approaches to Media Discourse*, edited by A. Bell and P. Garrett, 21–63. Oxford: Wiley.

van Doorslaer, L. 2009. How language and (non-)translation impact on media newsrooms: the case of newspapers in Belgium. *Perspectives* 17(2), pp. 83–92.

van Doorslaer, L. 2010a. "Journalism and Translation". In *Handbook of Translation Studies*, Vol. 1, edited by Y. Gambier and L. van Doorslaer, 180–184. Amsterdam: Rodopi.

van Doorslaer, L. 2010b. The double extension of translation in the journalistic field. *Across Languages and Cultures* 11(2), pp. 175–188.

van Doorslaer, L. 2012. Translating, narrating and constructing images in journalism with a test case on representation in Flemish TV news. *Meta* 57(4), pp. 1046–1059.

van Rooyen, M. 2013. Structure and agency in news translation: an application of Anthony Giddens' structuration theory. *Southern African Linguistics and Applied Language Studies* 31(4), pp. 495–506.

Venuti, L. 1995. *The Translator's Invisibility: A History of Translation.* London: Routledge.

Vuorinen, E. 1997. "News Translation as Gatekeeping". In *Translation as Intercultural Communication: Selected Papers from the EST Congress – Prague 1995*, edited by M. Snell-Hornby, Z. Jettmarova, and K. Kaindl, 161–171. Amsterdam: John Benjamins.

Wehrmeyer, E. 2015. Comprehension of television news signed language interpreters: a South African perspective. *Interpreting* 17(2), pp. 195–225.

Xiao, X., Chen, X. and Levi Palmer, J. 2015. Chinese Deaf viewers' comprehension of sign language interpreting on television. *Interpreting* 17(1), pp. 91–117.

Zhang, M. 2013. Stance and mediation in transediting news headlines as paratexts. *Perspectives* 21(3), pp. 396–411.

22

Corpus linguistics, translation and interpreting

Silvia Bernardini and Mariachiara Russo

Introduction and definitions

During the first decade of the 21st century the corpus methodology established itself as one of the major paradigms in linguistics. Its fundamental assumption is that language should be studied by looking at genuine text samples stored electronically, rather than by relying on introspection and decontextualised, artificial examples. This view of linguistics as the study of language performance (or *E-language* to use Chomsky's (1986) term) rather than language competence (or *I-language*) is compatible with a product-oriented approach to the study of translation and interpreting. In this approach, the focus of attention is on the products delivered by translators and interpreters, rather than on their mental processes. While the latter can be studied through questionnaires, interviews, think-aloud protocols, key-logging, eye-tracking, and so forth, corpus-based translation and interpreting studies (hereinafter CTS and CIS) draw the bulk of their evidence from translated and interpreted texts assembled in *corpora*.

A corpus is a collection of texts, including transcriptions of spoken discourse, selected according to pre-defined criteria to be representative of a language variety, and stored in electronic format for consultation through a corpus query tool. In its simplest form, a corpus can consist of a few dozen text files stored in a local folder and searched through a stand-alone concordancer such as *AntConc* (Anthony 2014) or *Wordsmith Tools* (Scott 2016). However, corpora can also be very large and enriched with contextual metadata (about authors, publication details, intended audience, etc.) and structural and/or linguistic information (about textual subdivisions, graphical emphasis, pauses, hesitations, parts-of-speech, lemmas, etc.). The former, sometimes referred to as "DIY" or "disposable" corpora, are often constructed by single users (students, language professionals, linguists) for a specific task while the latter, requiring both linguistic and computational expertise and substantial efforts, are constructed by teams of corpus linguists and made available to the research community through client/server systems (see Baroni and Bernardini 2013 for further details on corpus preparation and corpus query systems).

Due to the nature of the object of study, positioned at the boundaries of two or more lingua-cultures, corpora for translation and interpreting research tend to be more complex than those used in other corpus linguistics (CL) fields, such as discourse studies or (monolingual) lexicography. Two main corpus typologies are used in CTS/CIS. The first, *monolingual comparable corpora*, include a minimum of two subcorpora, i.e. two collections of texts ("text" here subsumes oral language transcripts) in the same language, similar in all respects but for the existence vs. absence of a constraining source text (henceforth ST). The second, (bilingual) *parallel corpora*, include (transcripts of) STs and corresponding target texts (henceforth TTs) in one or more languages or by one or more translators/interpreters, aligned to each other, usually at the sentence level. Alongside ST–TT alignment in parallel corpora, interpreting corpora and corpora used in audiovisual translation or sign-language research may also include text-to-sound/video alignment, in which case they may be referred to as *multimodal corpora*. These should not be confused with *intermodal corpora*, containing interpreted and translated language and/or samples from different interpreting modalities (see further "Current debates and future directions in CL, CTS and CIS").

Historical perspectives

Originating from the so-called British school of linguistics and heavily influenced by its best-known exponent, J. R. Firth, CL became mainstream in the early 1990s, initially thanks to the work of John Sinclair (starting with the influential 1991 volume *Corpus, Concordance, Collocation*). Firth rejected the idea of an ideal native speaker competence, and believed that "we do not make up our lines as we go along, rather, to a large extent, they are already there for us, stereotyped and narrowly conditioned by our particular type of culture" (Firth 1935, 69). Sinclair further believed that "human intuition about language is highly specific, and not at all a good guide to what actually happens when the same people actually use the language" (Sinclair 1991, 4). The study of large repositories of written and spoken language samples could instead provide new and more revealing data. Corpus-derived insights and analytical methods have since been employed in a large variety of fields, for both descriptive/theoretical and applied purposes. These include, among many others, terminology/lexicography, analysis of register and style, discourse studies, language pedagogy and research on translation/interpreting.

The application of corpora and corpus methodologies to Translation Studies (TS) originates with Mona Baker's (1993) paper in which she famously argued that "the most important task that awaits the application of corpus techniques in translation studies [. . .] is the elucidation of the nature of translated text as a mediated communicative event" (*ibid.* 243). Baker's proposal was successful in establishing a strong connection between a powerful new methodology for the empirical study of language, and contemporary theoretical reflections within TS. Here, attention was shifting from the implicitly prescriptive, source-oriented and equivalence-focused search for translation shifts, to the descriptive, target-oriented and norm-focused account of typical traits of translated language (Toury 1995).

Baker programmatically suggested that the nature of translated text could best be elucidated through the construction and analysis of monolingual comparable corpora. By suggesting that translated language should be compared monolingually against the benchmark of non-translated language, Baker was construing it as any other language variety. The whole expanse of inherently monolingual methods being developed and applied within CL could thus be brought to bear on translated language as an object of study. Corpus-driven observations such as type–token ratio, ratio of lexical to function words, sentence length (Laviosa 1998; Xiao 2010), as well as corpus-based observations of e.g. relative frequencies of specific words, word classes, collocations and lexico-syntactic structures (Dayrell 2007;

Mauranen 2002; Olohan and Baker 2000) could be employed to identify patterning "which is specific to translated texts, irrespective of the source or target languages involved" (Baker 1995, 234); in other words, patterning that is *universal*.

Similar concerns also emerged among interpreting studies (IS) scholars, who advocated a descriptive approach to replace anecdotal observations based on case studies or limited samples, to inform theorisations on interpreters' linguistic output and cognitive processes. The scope of IS could thus be expanded via CL to include the observation of *textual operations* of various kinds – many of them, by multiple interpreters, in multiple settings (conference, institutional assemblies, community, court, media), modes (sign-language, dialogue, simultaneous, consecutive, remote), levels of proficiency (professional, trainee, ad hoc interpreter) and conditions (real-life, simulated, experimental) – and of interpreters behaviour, with insights into their language transfer skills.

The first scholar to highlight the relevance and potential of the corpus-based approach for research into interpreting was Shlesinger (1998, 486), who suggested that the CL methodology could be extended to interpreting, "through (1) the creation of parallel and comparable corpora comprising discourse which is relevant to interpreting; and (2) the use of existing monolingual corpora as sources of materials for testing hypotheses about interpreting". Interpreting corpora would add a new dimension to IS because they would overcome anecdotal observations and also provide information typical of CL, i.e. about word frequencies, grammatical constructions, discourse patterns, co-occurrences, lexical density, type–token ratios, etc. The CL framework would provide for IS what Baker (1993, 248) had envisaged for TS, namely: "a major leap from prescriptive to descriptive statements, from methodologizing to proper theorizing, and from individual and fragmented pieces of research to powerful generalizations".

Core issues, topics and methods

Introduction

As an approach to linguistics that aims to unearth the patterned nature of language performance, and to highlight co-occurrence regularities that escape the traditional categories of lexis and grammar, CL has traditionally focused on phraseological constructs, i.e. those frequently used phrases whose status is intermediate between that of fully lexicalised idioms and that of free word combinations, subject only to the rules of grammar. In particular, the frequency-based notion of *collocation* and the use of lexical association measures to search for collocations in corpora have been central to CL from the start (Sinclair, Jones and Daley 1970). Corpus linguists have also targeted repeated word sequences (for which a variety of terms exist, e.g. clusters, n-grams, lexical bundles), and co-occurrence preferences at the semantic level (semantic preferences), at the pragmatic level (semantic, or discourse, prosodies) and at the lexico-grammatical level (colligations).

At the lexical end of the cline, CL research has developed methods for extracting keywords from general and specialised corpora, i.e. words that are significantly more typical of a given language variety than of the language as a whole. Together with phraseological regularities, these have found application in lexicography (starting with the well-known COBUILD dictionaries) and language learning (e.g. for the development of vocabulary lists (Coxhead 2000) and corpus-informed syllabi (Lewis 2000)).

At the grammatical end of the cline, attempts have been made at developing new approaches to grammar based on patterns found in corpora (Sinclair and Mauranen 2006).

These are consistent with the general shift in theoretical linguistics away from rule-based approaches and towards usage-based accounts of language, in which the idiom principle plays a central role (e.g. frame semantics, construction grammar or cognitive linguistics).

For historical, methodological and practical reasons, and despite the close relationship between corpus-based research into translation and interpreting, their corpus-based investigation has developed separately, with work in TS leading the way, and IS following. For the sake of an orderly account, in the following subsections we follow the chronological order and present the main developments in CTS before those in CIS, pointing out convergences and divergences as appropriate.

Core issues, topics and research methods in CTS

From its early days, CTS research has accompanied the target-oriented turn in TS, focusing on the search for hypothesised typical features, or universals of translation. These include simplification, explicitation, normalisation or conservatism, levelling out or convergence. The search for evidence about such typical features has provided a wealth of new insights about translated language, construing it as a legitimate object of empirical linguistic research, beyond the particularistic perspective of previous theoretical approaches. An early milestone in this sense is the special issue of the journal *Meta*, published in 1998 and edited by Sara Laviosa, which established the corpus-based approach as a new paradigm in TS.

Implicit in the target-oriented turn was the downplaying of source-focused approaches, such as those involving the use of parallel corpora. While some studies based on parallel corpora have been conducted in the past two decades, methodologically these have tended to replicate the text-based comparison of STs and TTs, mainly relying on the direct observation of parallel concordances and focusing on translation shifts, the small changes "that build up cumulatively over a whole text as a result of the choices taken by or imposed on the translator" (Munday 1998, 542). An example of this approach, going beyond single text comparisons, is Shih (2012), who studies the rendering of prepositions in translation from English to Chinese in a composite parallel corpus collection including contemporary fiction, instruction manuals, speeches and advertisements.

A more complex parallel design is used by Øverås (1998), who searches for shifts in cohesion/coherence in the English–Norwegian Parallel Corpus, a bidirectional corpus including STs in English and their Norwegian TTs and (comparable) STs in Norwegian and their English TTs. By carrying out the analysis in both translation directions, Øverås can factor out language-specific effects (the same aim is pursued in monolingual comparable approaches through the inclusion of translations from multiple source languages). She concludes that, in both translation directions, explicitating shifts are more common than implicitating ones, thus providing support for the explicitation hypothesis. A similar corpus (a bidirectional parallel corpus of French and Dutch) is used by Vanderbauwhede, Desmet and Lauwers (2011) in their study of demonstrative determiners, which suggests that around 30% of translation shifts occurring in either direction are due to omissions, additions or reformulations motivated by translator preferences.

Less central to CTS than monolingual comparable corpora, parallel corpora have been used extensively in research carried out at the crossroads of CTS and corpus-based contrastive linguistics (see Johansson 2007; Dom and Declerck 2015). Parallel corpora include "simple" ones, bidirectional ones consisting of STs and TTs in two directions, multi-target ones with one source and many targets, and so forth. Where the contrastive focus predominates, the purpose is to highlight systemic differences between languages. This is the aspect that translation research attempts to factor out in order to highlight translation-inherent shifts occurring regardless of the languages involved. Apart from this fundamental difference, the two fields share a substantial common ground in terms of methods, tools and resources. More importantly, awareness of each other's findings may prove indispensable for the progress of both disciplines, as

> lack of familiarity with [translation studies] findings may lead [contrastive linguistics] researchers to interpret their data in terms of differences between language systems when they result from translation norms or strategies, while [translation studies] researchers may similarly misinterpret their data because of a lack of awareness of a systematic difference between the two language systems established by [contrastive linguistics].
>
> (Granger 2003, 25–26)

The corpus methodology offers a shared framework in which this cross-fertilisation may occur.

The focus on translated language, construed as a mediated variety of the target language, resulted in scholarly attention being drawn not only to universal features shared by all translated texts, but also to radically local patterns, typical of individual translators. Borrowing insights from literary stylistics, studies of translators' style that adopt a mono-lingual comparable corpus approach attempt to identify the stylistic fingerprints of trans-lators, or their "characteristic use of language, [their] individual profile of linguistic habits, compared to other translators" (Baker 2000, 245). Objections have been raised, however, against the total neglect in such studies of the ST, since "many important questions about writer motivation [. . .] may not arise in the case of translated texts unless the texts are seen in the context of their source texts" (Malmkjær 2004, 22). Several ingenious corpus designs have been used to zoom in on such a slippery research object. For instance, Ji (2010) and Marco (2004) adopt a multi-target parallel structure, i.e. a ST and two TTs. More specifi-cally, Ji focuses on phraseology and translators' profiles in two translations of *Don Quixote* into Chinese, while Marco (2004) analyses two translations of Poe's short story, "The Fall of the House of Usher" into Catalan, also factoring in aspects of the style displayed by the two Catalan translators in their own writing. More complex still is the corpus used by Dirdal (2014), namely the fiction component of the English–Norwegian Multiple Translation Corpus (Johansson 2007). Dirdal investigates variation in the use of clause building and clause reduction in 10 different commissioned translations of the same short story (A.S. Byatt's "A Lamia in the Cevennes"), finding that translators differ in their tendency to preserve or modify the syntactic structure of the original, and that this tendency is not to be explained in terms of straightforward "fidelity", since syntactic conservatism is not matched by lexical conservatism. Approaching style in translation between English and Chinese through a series of case studies and multiple perspectives, Huang (2015) concludes that the complexity of the object requires triangulation based on a composite set of corpus resources, both intralingual (or monolingual) and interlingual (or parallel).

Summing up, three main research objectives have attracted the attention of CTS researchers from the beginning: first, the search for textual patterning supporting hypoth-eses about the existence of norms or universals of translation; second, the analysis of translation shifts; and, third, the identification of stylistic fingerprints left by translators in their work. Even though parallel corpora have also been used for these purposes, particu-larly for the search for shifts, there is no denying that the corpus approach has become associated with (various kinds of) monolingual comparable corpora. After initial enthusiasm, however, it is now generally agreed that ST-specific effects should not be ignored by design (Pym 2008).

Core issues, topics and research methods in CIS

Corpora for IS are characterised by a number of specific features requiring the close attention of the researcher. First and foremost, the requirement to transcribe both the source discourse and the interpreters' output is arguably the main cause behind the scarcity of large machine-readable interpreting corpora (one notable exception being the *CIAIR* Simultaneous Interpreting Corpus, with its 182 hours of recordings, amounting to one million words of simulated lectures interpreted by professionals (Tohyama *et al.* 2004)). The lack of user-friendly and shared conventions for transcribing linguistic and paralinguistic features of orality further adds to the problem (Niemants 2015; Cencini 2002; Hu and Tao 2013). All in all, and despite the use of speech recognition software or methods to streamline the transcription procedure (for instance shadowing), transcription remains a major challenge for interpreting corpus projects.

Further challenges to the development of interpreting corpora are multilingualism (source and target texts, language pair and directionality) and situated synchronicity (Setton 2011, 36), as well as the accessibility of interpreting events including both originals and interpreted versions, the need for authorisations and the representativeness of events/speakers/interpreters. In terms of corpus processing, the ST–TT/sound/video alignment is another very demanding feature, due to the laborious manual encoding (alignment software used in CIS includes: CLAN, ELAN, EXMARaLDA, syncWRITER, TRANSCRIBER, TRANSANA, WINPITCH, Niemants 2015). Lastly, at the corpus annotation stage, further work is needed to include metadata concerning the ethnographic dimension of the data (speaker; date, speed and mode of delivery; subject; number of words, timing; location), linguistic features (morpho-syntactic and lexical features), paralinguistic features (disfluencies, prosody, etc.) and, depending on the corpus typology, proxemics, gestural and pragmatic features e.g. for signed language.

In terms of topics and methods, research in CIS before the availability of machine-readable corpora can be divided into several phases. At first, collections of transcripts of moderate size and generally involving only a few interpreters were taken as a basis for theorising on interpreting processes and products. Despite their limits, these studies exerted a great influence on interpreting theories and interpreter education (see e.g. Seleskovitch 1975).

In a second phase, scholars started collecting larger quantities of real-life interpreting data from specific professional settings and carried out qualitative analyses aligning STs and TTs manually. Given their vast amount of field data and the extended recording periods (from months to years), these can be considered as the first genuinely descriptive studies (Toury 1995), providing insights into interpreters' operational norms, styles, strategies, skills and field challenges. For instance, Vuorikoski (2004) evaluated the quality of 30 interpreters' linguistic outputs, in a corpus of 120 original speeches in English, Finnish, German and Swedish and their simultaneous interpretation (SI) into these languages. Her focus was on "accuracy" and "faithfulness". In a subsequent publication (Vuorikoski 2012), she concentrated on speech acts containing modals in English-language European Parliament speeches and concluded that interpreters were not always aware of the functions of speech acts, an issue that she recommended should be incorporated into interpreter training.

The theoretical framework and the methods applied in other studies of this second phase are drawn from sociolinguistics and the ethnography of communication, with interpreting data triangulated with observation notes and interviews with the participants involved (Berk-Seligson 1990/2002; Angelelli 2004), or investigated by means of conversation analysis (Straniero Sergio 2003, 2007). Berk-Seligson investigated how Spanish–English interpreters faced the challenges of legal discourse in 114 hours of interaction in US courtrooms, highlighting the influence on the receivers' perceptions of the way in which people spoke and were interpreted. Angelelli (2004) compiled the *California Hope Corpus*, based on data collected over 22 months, during almost 400 interpreter-mediated hospital encounters including both face-to-face and telephone interpreting. Her objective was to investigate, in particular, the interpreters' perceptions of their role and their actual practice. Straniero Sergio studied quality, interpreters' styles and interpreting norms based on the world's largest multilingual media corpus, his Italian Television Interpreting Corpus (*CorIT*), currently featuring over 2,700 consecutive and simultaneous interpretations broadcast by public and private TV networks. His aim was "to respond to the pressing need for authentic data on SI" (Straniero Sergio 2003, 136), tracing the history of media interpreting and highlighting differences between conference interpreting and other forms of dialogue interpreting. Since 1999, numerous *CorIT*-based studies have appeared (Straniero Sergio and Falbo 2012).

A third phase includes large sets of real-life interpreting data, collected and stored according to criteria inspired by CL, in that they envisage the use of tools to retrieve features of STs and TTs, albeit still manually aligned (Wallmach 2000), or of tools to allow for multiple visualisations of the stored texts (Collados Aís *et al.* 2004). Wallmach recorded 110 hours of SIs by 16 professional interpreters working between English, Afrikaans, Zulu and Sepedi to investigate the effect of speed, complexity and lack of ST–TT equivalents on interpreter strategies and language-specific norms in a South African legislative context. Collados Aís *et al.* (2004) developed the multilingual *ECIS* (Evaluación *de la* Calidad en Interpretación Simultánea) corpus to explore non-verbal, paralinguistic and prosodic features, thus providing a more comprehensive evidence-based evaluative framework for the study of interpreters' performances and their effect on the users.

The turn from collections of computer-stored speeches to the use of CL tools and methodologies has allowed for numerous new perspectives on the investigation of interpreting (hence, fully fledged CIS), thanks to the addition of new features and the speed of information retrieval. What follows is an overview of the most prominent lines of investigation in the interpreting corpora available and their contributions to our understanding of interpreting processes and products.

Between 2004 and 2006, the first free, open, machine-readable, on-line corpus was developed: the European Parliament Interpreting Corpus (*EPIC*), containing English, Spanish and Italian speeches and corresponding simultaneous interpretations. The *EPIC* parallel and comparable design allows for a variety of investigations (Monti *et al.* 2005; Russo *et al.* 2012). Lexical patterns were investigated to ascertain whether the results obtained by Laviosa (1998) for translation held true also for interpreting. Laviosa had found that non-translated texts displayed higher lexical density (content vs. grammatical words) and lexical variety (proportion of high frequency words vs. low frequency words) compared to translated English texts. *EPIC*-based results differed from Laviosa's findings in terms of lexical density, but generally not in terms of lexical variety (Russo, Bendazzoli and Sandrelli 2006). A similar result was obtained by Shlesinger (2009), who applied a different method, calculating the ratio of types to tokens, to identify linguistic richness in her intermodal corpus. Other topics investigated are disfluencies and repairs (Bendazzoli, Sandrelli and Russo 2011), and text-processing strategies (Russo 2011; see also Russo 2010 for an overview of qualitative studies carried out for Master's theses). Building on the expertise gained through *EPIC*,

Bendazzoli (2012) created the Directionality in Simultaneous Interpreting (*DIRSI*) corpus, an English–Italian text-to-sound and ST–TT aligned corpus of medical conferences with a dedicated web interface. A further spin-off of *EPIC* is the European Parliament Interpreting Corpus (at) Ghent (*EPICG*) which is an open, multilingual (French > Dutch and English), partly aligned (time–ST–TT) corpus. Several topics have been explored so far, such as connective markers (Defrancq, Plevoets and Magnifico 2015), and ear–voice span (Defrancq 2015).

Press conference data from a variety of cultural and professional settings are included in three corpora compiled to study communicative interactions and interpreters' strategies and norms: the Football in Europe (*FOOTIE*) corpus, a multimedia, multilingual (French, English, Spanish, Italian) corpus of original speeches and SIs (Sandrelli 2012); the Chinese–English Interpreting Corpus of the Chinese Premier's annual press conferences (*CEIPPC*) recorded over 14 years (Wang 2012); and the Chinese–English Conference Interpreting Corpus (*CECIC*), compiled by Hu and Tao (2013), who found that interpreted texts in the corpus exhibit greater normalisation and explicitation than corresponding translated texts.

Research on interpreter language, or "interpretese", has spurred the creation of small comparable, PoS-tagged, annotated corpora designed to identify lexical and morphosyntactic features. Shlesinger (2009) and Shlesinger and Ordan (2012) developed an English > Hebrew intermodal corpus of ST-interpreted and -translated TTs, and Aston (2018) detected typical lexical patterns in his small corpus of English interpreted speeches at the European Parliament.

An example of a multimodal (audio and video) corpus is the open-source consecutive and simultaneous corpus *CoSi* (House, Meyer and Schmidt 2012), compiled to study the effect of the interpreting mode on the processing of discourse markers, mitigators and proper nouns. Extensive information on the corpus design is provided in this work, to encourage data exchange in CIS.

Finally, studies of dialogue interpreting have gained ground, especially in public service, health and court interpreting. Two large corpora have been developed: the Analysis of Mediated Interaction (*AIM*) multilingual corpus (Baraldi and Gavioli 2012), a sound-to-text and ST–TT aligned corpus of 528 interpreter-mediated medical encounters; and the Community Interpreting Database (*ComInDat*, Angermeyer, Meyer and Schmidt 2012), a corpus of interpreting data from a variety of settings and language dyads, designed to develop common standards for annotating multilingual interpreter-mediated interactions.

Current debates and future directions in CL, CTS and CIS

Consistently with the general trend within CL, the second decade of the 21st century has witnessed three main developments concerning corpus methods in the study of translation, which may continue shaping the field. First, more composite corpus designs counteract the downplaying of the ST, often through a combination of "different components of multilingual corpora as well as of reference corpora not originally created for translation-oriented purposes" (Zanettin 2012, 12). Second, quantitative methods and more sophisticated techniques for data analysis are borrowed from neighbouring research fields, e.g. those employed for authorship attribution and stylometry (Oakes and Ji 2012). Third, new hypotheses and research paradigms are emerging, extending the initial focus on translation universals and combining corpus techniques with other data sources. As concerns CIS, the priorities appear to be the triangulation of qualitative and quantitative approaches, the enrichment of corpus data with information about cognitive and pragmatic constraints and the pooling of resources within and beyond the interpreting community.

Composite corpus designs and sophisticated techniques for data analysis are employed, for instance, by Delaere, De Sutter and Plevoets (2012) in their study of growing standardisation. They rely on a corpus of non-translated Dutch, and Dutch translated from English and French, including six different text types (administrative, journalistic, instructive, fiction, non-fiction and external communication). The novel approach taken in this study consists in splitting the corpus into nine language varieties, six based on the text type and three based on translational status (non-translated, translated from English, translated from French). Using a statistical technique called profile-based correspondence analysis, the authors calculate how different the varieties are in terms of their level of standardisation (measured as the frequency of occurrence of non-standard Belgian Dutch terms for which a standard term exists). Non-translated Belgian Dutch turns out to be (slightly) less standard than Belgian Dutch translated from English and substantially less standard than Belgian Dutch translated from French. The method further reveals that translated fiction, external communication and administrative texts conform to the general trend, while journalistic texts and non-fiction texts do not. Rybicki (2012) adopts an even more complex corpus set-up, carrying out multiple stylometric analyses of translated and non-translated fiction texts from and into several languages, arranged into different groups. He employs the technique known as Burrows's Delta, which is borrowed from the authorship attribution field and known to reliably identify authors on the basis of words that they use frequently, but which proves less apt at identifying translators. If these results somewhat undermine claims about the existence of translators' style, a different picture emerges from a subsequent study by Rybicki and Heydel (2013). Applying the same method to the Polish translation of Virginia Woolf's *Night and Day*, which was carried out partly by one translator and partly by another (who was also responsible for editing the entire text), the authors show that it is possible to identify the point where the second translator took over.

Besides ingenious corpus designs and sophisticated analytical methods, advances in CTS have been pursued through triangulation with other methods and data sources. Alves and Vale (2011) collect and analyse five types of process data (key-logging, screen recording, eye-tracking, recordings/transcriptions of retrospective protocols and questionnaires), as well as the translated texts (both final and interim versions). This composite corpus, which crosses the traditional boundary between process and product approaches, is annotated and searched using specially designed software. The triangulation of product and process is also at the basis of Jiménez-Crespo's (2015) study of explicitation in which he compares translation choices made under experimental conditions with corpus data. This study is innovative in its attempt to isolate the effect of different working methods on the tendency to explicitate (i.e. "traditional" translation vs. selection from a precompiled list). Results suggest that when subjects select their preferred translation from a set of choices – as is becoming increasingly common when post-editing/leveraging machine-translation and translation-memory output – they tend to favour more explicit formulations. Triangulation of methods and data sources is not limited to the process/product dichotomy. Another example is the application of corpus methods to audiovisual translation, for which "an integrated approach is needed to account for the complex semiotic fabric of audiovisual texts, their hybrid nature and multiple codes" (Baños, Bruti and Zanotti 2013, 483). Balirano (2013), combines corpus and multimodal analysis to account for both verbal and non-verbal humour in the TV series *The Big Bang Theory*. On the basis of a parallel corpus containing 87 transcribed episodes in their English and Italian (dubbed) versions, he shows how the Italian dubbed version (which was not as successful as the English one) "lacks both linguistic and semiotic internal coherence" (2013: 573).

In terms of new hypotheses and research paradigms, it is worth mentioning the work pioneered by Shlesinger, at the interface of CTS and CIS. Shlesinger suggested that

> [i]deally, the notion of comparable corpora in interpreting studies should be extended to cover setting up three separate collections of texts in the same language: interpreted texts, original oral discourses delivered in similar settings, *and written translations of such texts*.
>
> (1998, 488, emphasis added).

Bernardini, Ferraresi and Miličević (2016) reproduce Laviosa's (1998) study of simplification using the European Parliament Translation and Interpreting Corpus (*EPTIC*), a bidirectional (English < > Italian) intermodal corpus of interpreted and translated European Parliament proceedings, featuring the parallel outputs of interpreting and translation processes, aligned to each other and to the corresponding source texts. From the monolingual comparable point of view, both interpreted and translated outputs into English and Italian are simpler than the corresponding non-translated/non-interpreted speeches, while at the intermodal level, interpretations are simpler than translations.

Moving on to CIS, there is a widely felt need for commonly shared transcription conventions and information on corpus designs, as well as for the exchange of CIS results, despite concerns about data comparability (Straniero Sergio and Falbo 2012, 37). Several quantitative and qualitative studies have provided evidence of linguistic traits characteristic of interpreted language, thus framing interpreted speech as the result of interpreters' strategic behaviour subject to time, cognitive and situational constraints. This is particularly evident when the outputs of expert and novice interpreters are compared. However, even interpreters with comparable levels of expertise display diverse speech styles and skills. Much remains to be investigated, therefore, through a triangulation of quantitative and qualitative approaches, by zooming in on, among other phenomena, target speeches that are shorter than their sources, fast speech and consequent semantic loss, and mode of delivery (improvised vs. read) in relation to the interpreter's voice quality and comprehensibility.

Further issues in need of exploration within CIS concern cognitive, pragmatic, ethical, socio-cultural and ideological aspects of interpreting (Straniero Sergio 2012). While lexical and morphosyntactic features can be tagged automatically, they need to be transcribed and annotated manually, raising complex methodological questions in terms of objectivity and replicability.

Future directions in CIS also include expanding and aligning existing interpreting corpora and furthering multimodal, intermodal, multiple language/direction/setting corpora, ideally by cooperating and pooling resources within the CIS community. The wide range of research topics expounded in Russo, Bendazzoli and Defrancq (2018) and Bendazzoli, Russo and Defrancq (2017) testifies to the vitality of this research agenda.

Finally, since interpreting corpora are invaluable resources for language learning and Natural Language Processing (development of speech recognition software and synchronous machine speech-to-speech translation), collaboration with these fields could also prove mutually beneficial.

CL, CTS and CIS: Implications for practice

CL has provided a wealth of descriptive data that have found application in a number of fields, from lexicography/terminology to language learning/teaching/testing. Concerning CTS and CIS specifically, translation-driven corpora are employed in applied fields such as machine translation, translation practice and translator education. Statistical machine translation, currently the leading paradigm in machine-translation research, relies on massive parallel corpora for the generation of its translation models (Koehn 2005). In translation practice, some computer-assisted translation (CAT) tools (such as Kilgray's *MemoQ*) now include facilities for performing on-the-fly alignment and search of parallel corpora, alongside better-established resources like translation memories and term bases; more widespread use of corpora as documentation resources is likely to follow, thanks to this inclusion in the standard translation environment and workflow. Lastly it is worth mentioning, in connection with translator education, attempts at building translation learner corpora, i.e. collections of source texts and multiple student translations. These corpora, which can track the development of translation competence over the duration of a degree, typically feature error annotation alongside contextual metadata (Castagnoli *et al.* 2011; Espunya 2014; Kutuzov and Kunilovskaya 2014). They can help learners to develop self- and peer-evaluation skills, provide instructors with innovative teaching resources and offer researchers a vantage point for observing the development of translation competence.

Similar arguments concern practical applications to interpreter education. Access to large interpreting corpora would help trainees hone their analytical and evaluative skills, familiarise themselves with different speech styles, norms and lexical patterns, face real-life interpreting challenges and reflect on ways to meet them. In so doing they would gradually develop the metalinguistic knowledge that favours the shift towards implicit linguistic competence (Paradis 1994) required to perform the complex, time-constrained, multi-componential interpreting task. Professional interpreters too would benefit from exposure to a variety of interpreting styles. Moreover, multiple performances by the same interpreter (sometimes in different language combinations) offer opportunities for self-revision. Interpreters could monitor the pragmatic adequacy and the linguistic quality of their output, and become more aware of their potential.

Further reading

Kruger, A., Wallmach, K. and Munday, J., eds. 2011 *Corpus-Based Translation Studies: Research and Applications*. London: Continuum.
This edited volume is divided into three highly informative sections providing an overview of core concepts and topics in CTS and CIS, methods for the qualitative analysis of contrastive patterns in large translation corpora and studies in specific sub-fields, including an example of simultaneous interpreting.

Laviosa, S., ed. 1998. "L'approche basée sur le corpus/The Corpus-based Approach". *Meta* 43(4) Available from: http://www.erudit.org/revue/meta/1998/v/n4/.
This special issue features 14 contributions addressing a wide range of topics central to CTS from a variety of perspectives, descriptive, theoretical and applied. Most of the studies have been highly influential and are still quoted today. The collection includes Shlesinger's contribution marking the birth of CIS.

McEnery, T. and Hardie, A. 2012. *Corpus Linguistics: Method, Theory and Practice*. Cambridge: Cambridge University Press.
This volume provides an accessible and thorough introduction to CL, surveying its development, methods, findings and applications, and establishing connections with other approaches to empirical linguistics research.

Oakes, M. and Ji, M., eds. 2012. *Quantitative Research Methods in Corpus-based Translation Studies*. Amsterdam: John Benjamins.

This edited volume offers a description of several quantitative research techniques. It is of particular relevance to researchers in TS wanting to move beyond qualitative approaches.

Straniero Sergio, F. and Falbo, C., eds. 2012. *Breaking Ground in Corpus-based Interpreting Studies*. Bern: Peter Lang.

As the title suggests, this is the first volume containing only CIS. The editors' introduction offers a full account of the development of CIS and of key theoretical and methodological issues. It includes the corpus designs of the first large interpreting corpora *CorIT, EPIC, DIRSI, FOOTIE* and accounts of studies based on them.

Related topics

Theories of linguistics and of translation and interpreting.

References

Alves, F. and Vale, D. 2011. On drafting and revision in translation: a corpus linguistics oriented analysis of translation process data. *Translation: Computation, Corpora, Cognition* 1, pp. 105–122.

Angelelli, C. 2004. *Medical Interpreting and Cross-Cultural Communication*. Cambridge: Cambridge University Press.

Angermeyer, P., Meyer, B. and Schmidt, T. 2012. Sharing community interpreting corpora: a pilot study. *Multilingual Corpora and Multilingual Corpus Analysis* 14, pp. 275–294.

Anthony, L. 2014. *AntConc (Version 3.4.3)*. Tokyo: Waseda University.

Aston, G. 2018. "Acquiring the Language of Interpreters". In *Making Way in Corpus-based Interpreting Studies*, edited by M. Russo, C. Bendazzoli and B. Defrancq. Singapore: Springer.

Baker, M. 1993. "Corpus Linguistics and Translation Studies: Implications and Applications". In *Text and Technology: In Honour of John Sinclair*, edited by M. Baker, G. Francis and E. Tognini-Bonelli, 233–250. Amsterdam: John Benjamins.

Baker, M. 1995. Corpora in translation studies: an overview and some suggestions for future research. *Target* 7(2), pp. 223–243.

Baker, M. 2000. Towards a methodology for investigating the style of a literary translator. *Target* 12(2), pp. 241–266.

Balirano, G. 2013. The strange case of *The Big Bang Theory* and its extra-ordinary Italian audiovisual translation: a multimodal corpus-based analysis. *Perspectives* 21(4), pp. 563–576.

Baños, R., Bruti, S. and Zanotti, S. 2013 Corpus linguistics and audiovisual translation: in search of an integrated approach. *Perspectives* 21(4), pp. 483–490.

Baraldi, C. and Gavioli, L., eds. 2012. *Coordinating Participation in Dialogue Interpreting*. Amsterdam: John Benjamins.

Baroni, M. and Bernardini, S. 2013. "Corpus Query Tools for Lexicography". In *Dictionaries: An International Encyclopaedia of Lexicography*, edited by R. Gouws, U. Heid, W. Schweickard and H. Wiegand, 1395–1405. Berlin: Mouton de Gruyter.

Bendazzoli, C. 2012. "From International Conferences to Machine-readable Corpora and Back: An Ethnographic Approach to Simultaneous Interpreter-mediated Communicative Events". In *Breaking Ground in Corpus-based Interpreting Studies*, edited by F. Straniero Sergio, and C. Falbo, 91–117. Bern: Peter Lang.

Bendazzoli, C., Russo, M. and Defrancq, B., eds. 2017. *Corpus-based Interpreting Studies: New Trends in Corpora Development and Exploitation*. Special issue of *InTRAlinea*.

Bendazzoli, C., Sandrelli, A. and Russo, M. 2011. "Disfluencies in Simultaneous Interpreting: A Corpus-based Analysis". In *Corpus-based Translation Studies: Research and Applications*, edited by A. Kruger, K. Wallmach and J. Munday, 282–306. London: Continuum.

Berk-Seligson, S. 1990/2002. *The Bilingual Courtroom: Court Interpreters in the Judicial Process*. Chicago: The University of Chicago Press.

Bernardini, S., Ferraresi, A. and Miličević, M. 2016. From EPIC to EPTIC: exploring simplification in interpreting and translation from an intermodal perspective. *Target* 28(1), pp. 58–83.

Castagnoli, S., Ciobanu, D., Kunz, K., Volanschi, A. and Kübler, N. 2011. "Designing a Learner Translator Corpus for Training Purposes". In *Corpora, Language, Teaching and Resources: From Theory to Practice*, edited by N. Kübler, 221–248. Bern: Peter Lang.

Cencini, M. 2002. On the importance of an encoding standard for corpus-based interpreting studies: extending the TEI scheme. In *CULT2K*. Special issue of *InTRAlinea*. Available from: www.intralinea. org/specials/article/1678 [Accessed 18 March 2016].

Chomsky, N. 1986. *Knowledge of Language: Its Natural Origin and Use*. New York: Praeger.

Collados Aís, Á., Fernández Sánchez, M. M., Iglesias Fernández, E., Pérez-Luzardo, J., Pradas Macías, E. M., Stévaux, E., Blasco Mayor, M. J. and Jiménez Ivars, A. 2004. "Presentación de Proyecto de Investigación sobre Evaluación de la Calidad en Interpretación Simultánea (Bff2002-00579)". In *Actas del IX Seminario Hispano-Ruso de Traducción e Interpretación*, 3–15. Moscú: Universidad Estatal Lingüística de Moscú, MGLU.

Coxhead, A. 2000. A new academic word list. *TESOL Quarterly* 34(2), pp. 213–238.

Dayrell, C. 2007. A quantitative approach to compare collocational patterns in translated and non-translated texts. *International Journal of Corpus Linguistics* 12(3), pp. 375–414.

Defrancq, B. 2015. Corpus-based research into the presumed effects of short EVS. *Interpreting* 17(1), pp. 26–45.

Defrancq, B., Plevoets, K. and Magnifico, C. 2015. Connective markers in interpreting and translation: where do they come from? *Yearbook of Corpus Linguistics and Pragmatics* 3, pp. 195–222.

Delaere, I., De Sutter, G. and Plevoets, K. 2012. Is translated language more standardized than non-translated language? *Target* 24(2), pp. 203–224.

Dirdal, H. 2014. Individual variation between translators in the use of clause building and clause reduction. *Corpus-based Studies in Contrastive Linguistics. Oslo Studies in Language* 6(1), pp. 119–142.

Dom, S. and Declerck, B. 2015. Translating English non-human subjects in agentive contexts: a closer look at Dutch. *Across Languages and Cultures* 16(2), pp. 285–310.

Espunya, A. 2014. The UPF learner translation corpus as a resource for translator training. *Language Resources and Evaluation* 48(1), pp. 33–43.

Firth, J. R. 1935. "On sociological linguistics". Reprinted in *Language in Culture and Society*, edited by D. Hymes, 1964, 66–70. New York: Harper International.

Granger, S. 2003. "The Corpus Approach: A Common Way Forward for Contrastive Linguistics and Translation Studies". In *Corpus-based Approaches to Contrastive Linguistics and Translation Studies*, edited by S. Granger, J. Lerot and S. Petch-Tyson, 17–29. Amsterdam: Rodopi.

House, J., Meyer, B. and Schmidt, T. 2012. "CoSI-A Corpus of Consecutive and Simultaneous Interpreting". In *Multilingual Corpora and Multilingual Corpus Analysis*, edited by T. Schmidt and K. Wörner, 295–304. Amsterdam: John Benjamins.

Hu, K. and Tao, Q. 2013. The Chinese-English conference interpreting corpus: uses and limitations. *Meta* 58(3), pp. 626–642.

Huang, L. 2015. *Style in Translation: A Corpus-based Perspective*. Dordrecht: Springer.

Ji, M. 2010. *Phraseology in Corpus-based Translation Studies*. Bern: Peter Lang.

Jiménez-Crespo, M. A. 2015. Testing explicitation in translation: triangulating corpus and experimental studies. *Across Languages and Cultures* 16(2), pp. 257–283.

Johansson, S. 2007. *Seeing through Multilingual Corpora*. Amsterdam: John Benjamins.

Koehn, P. 2005 "Europarl: A Parallel Corpus for Statistical Machine Translation". http://homepages.inf. ed.ac.uk/pkoehn/publications/europarl-mtsummit05.pdf.

Kutuzov, A. and Kunilovskaya, M. 2014. "Russian Learner Translator Corpus: Design, Research Potential and Applications". In *Text, Speech and Dialogue*, edited by P. Sojka, A. Horák, I. Kopeček and K. Pala, 315–323. Dordrecht: Springer.

Laviosa, S. 1998. Core patterns of lexical use in a comparable corpus of English narrative prose. *Meta* 43(4), pp. 557–570.

Lewis, M. 2000. *Teaching Collocation: Further Developments in the Lexical Approach*. Hove: Language Teaching Publications.

Malmkjær, K. 2004. Translational stylistics: Dulcken's translations of Hans Christian Andersen. *Language and Literature* 13(1), pp. 13–24.

Marco, J. 2004. Translating style and styles of translating: Henry James and Edgar Allan Poe in Catalan. *Language and Literature* 13(1), 73–90.

Mauranen, A. 2002. "Where's cultural adaptation?" *InTRAlinea*, Available from: http://www.intralinea.it/ [Accessed 12 March 2016].

Monti, C., Bendazzoli, C., Sandrelli, A. and Russo, M. 2005. Studying directionality in simultaneous interpreting through an electronic corpus: EPIC (European Parliament Interpreting Corpus). *Meta* 50(4). Available from: http://www.erudit.org/revue/meta/2005/v50/n4/019850ar.pdf [Accessed 18 March 2016].

Munday, J. 1998. A computer-assisted approach to the analysis of translation shifts. *Meta* 43(4), pp. 542–556.

Niemants, N. 2015. "Transcription". In *The Routledge Encyclopedia of Intepreting Studies*, edited by F. Pöchhacker, 421–422, Routledge VitalSource Bookshelf Online.

Oakes, M. and Ji, M., eds. 2012. *Quantitative Research Methods in Corpus-based Translation Studies*. Amsterdam: John Benjamins.

Olohan, M. and Baker, M. 2000. Reporting that in translated English. *Across Languages and Cultures* 1(2), pp. 141–158.

Øverås, L. 1998. In search of the third code: an investigation of norms in literary translation, *Meta* 43(4), pp. 571–588.

Paradis, M. 1994. Towards a neurolinguistic theory of simultaneous translation: the framework. *International Journal of Psycholinguistics* 10(3), pp. 319–335.

Pym, A. 2008. "On Toury's Laws of How Translators Translate". In *Beyond Descriptive Translation Studies*, edited by A. Pym, M. Shlesinger and D. Simeoni, 311–328. Amsterdam: John Benjamins.

Russo, M. 2010. "Reflecting on Interpreting Practice: Graduation Theses based on the European Parliament Interpreting Corpus (EPIC)". In *Translationswissenschaft – Stand und Perspektiven. Innsbrucker Ringvorlesungen zur Translationswissenschaft VI* (ForumTranslationswissenschaft, Vol. 12), edited by L. Zybatow, 35–50. Frankfurt am Main: Peter Lang.

Russo, M. 2011. "Text Processing Patterns in Simultaneous Interpreting (Spanish-Italian): A Corpus-based Study". In *Translation – Sprachvariation – Mehrsprachigkeit: Festschrift in Honour of Prof. Lew Zybatow*, edited by I. Ohnheiser, W. Pöckl and P. Sandrini, 83–103. Frankfurt am Main: Peter Lang.

Russo, M., Bendazzoli, C. and Sandrelli, A. 2006. Looking for lexical patterns in a trilingual corpus of source and interpreted speeches: extended analysis of EPIC (European Parliament Interpreting Corpus). *Forum* 4(1), pp. 221–254.

Russo, M., Bendazzoli, C., Sandrelli, A. and Spinolo, N. 2012. "The European Parliament Interpreting Corpus (EPIC): Implementation and Developments". In *Breaking Ground in Corpus-based Interpreting Studies*, edited by F. Straniero Sergio and C. Falbo, 35–90. Bern: Peter Lang.

Russo, M., Bendazzoli, C. and Defrancq, B., eds. 2018. *Making Way in Corpus-based Interpreting Studies*. Singapore: Springer.

Rybicki, J. 2012. "The Great Mystery of the (almost) Invisible Translator: Stylometry in Translation". In *Quantitative Methods in Corpus-based Translation Studies*, edited by M. Oakes and M. Li, 231–248. Amsterdam: John Benjamins.

Rybicki, J. and Heydel, M. 2013. The stylistics and stylometry of collaborative translation: Woolf's "Night and Day" in Polish. *Literary and Linguistic Computing* 28(4), pp. 708–717.

Sandrelli, A. 2012. "Introducing FOOTIE (Football in Europe): Simultaneous Interpreting in Football Press Conferences". In *Breaking Ground in Corpus-based Interpreting Studies*, edited by F. Straniero Sergio and C. Falbo, 119–153. Bern: Peter Lang.

Scott, M. 2016. *WordSmith Tools Version 7*. Stroud: Lexical Analysis Software.

Seleskovitch, D. 1975. *Langage, Langues et Mémoire. Etude de la Prise de Notes en Interprétation Consecutive*. Paris: Minard.

Setton, R. 2011. "Corpus-based Interpreting Studies (CIS): Overview and Prospects". In *Corpus-based Translation Studies: Research and Applications*, edited by A. Kruger, K. Wallmach and J. Munday, 33–75. London: Continuum.

Shih, C.-l. 2012. A corpus-aided study of shifts in English-to-Chinese translation of prepositions. *International Journal of English Linguistics* 2(6), pp. 50–62.

Shlesinger, M. 1998. Corpus-based interpreting studies as an offshoot of corpus-based translation studies. *Meta* 43(4), pp. 486–493.

Shlesinger, M. 2009. "Towards a Definition of Interpretese: An Intermodal, Corpus-based Study". In *Efforts and Models in Interpreting and Translation Research: A Tribute to Daniel Gile*, edited by G. Hansen, A. Chesterman and H. Gerzymisch-Arbogast, 237–253. Amsterdam: John Benjamins.

Shlesinger, M. and Ordan, N. 2012. More spoken or more translated? Exploring a known unknown of simultaneous interpreting. *Target* 24(1), pp. 43–60.

Sinclair, J. McH. 1991. *Corpus, Concordance, Collocation*. Oxford: Oxford University Press.

Sinclair, J. McH., Jones, S. and Daley, R. 1970. *English Collocation Studies: The Osti Report*. Reprinted 2004. London: Continuum.

Sinclair, J. McH. and Mauranen, A. 2006. *Linear Unit Grammar*. Amsterdam: John Benjamins.

Straniero Sergio, F. 2003. Norms and quality in media interpreting: the case of Formula One press-conferences. *Interpreters' Newsletter* 12, pp. 135–174.

Straniero Sergio, F. 2007. *Talkshow Interpreting: La Mediazione Linguistica nella Conversazione Spettacolo*. Trieste: Edizioni Università di Trieste.

Straniero Sergio, F. and Falbo, C., eds. 2012. *Breaking Ground in Corpus-based Interpreting Studies*. Bern: Peter Lang.

Tohyama, H., Ryu, K., Mastubara, S., Kawaguchi, N. and Inagaki, Y. 2004. "CIAIR Simultaneous Interpreting Corpus". *Proceedings of Oriental COCOSDA 2004*. Available from: http://slp.itc.nagoya-u.ac.jp/web/papers/2004/Oriental-COCOSDA2004_tohyama.pdf [Accessed 18 March 2016].

Toury, G. 1995. *Descriptive Translation Studies and Beyond*. Amsterdam: John Benjamins.

Vanderbauwhede, G., Desmet, P. and Lauwers, P. 2011. The shifting of the demonstrative determiner in French and Dutch in parallel corpora. *Meta* 56(2), pp. 443–464.

Vuorikoski, A. R. 2004. *A Voice of Its Citizens or a Modern Tower of Babel? The Quality of Interpreting as a Function of Political Rhetoric in the European Parliament*. Tampere: Tampere University Press. Available from: http://tampub.uta.fi/handle/10024/67348 [Accessed 18 March 2016].

Vuorikoski, A. R. 2012. "Fine-tuning SI Quality Criteria: Could Speech Act Theory Be of Any Use?" In *Interpreting across Genres: Multiple Research Perspectives*, edited by C. J. Kellett Bidoli, 152–170. Trieste: EUT.

Wallmach, K. 2000. Examining simultaneous interpreting norms and strategies in a South African legislative context: a pilot corpus analysis. *Language Matters* 31(1), pp. 198–221.

Wang, B. 2012. Interpreting strategies in real-life interpreting: corpus-based description of seven professional interpreters' performance. *Translation Journal* 16(2). Available from: http://translationjournal. net/journal/60interpreting.htm [Accessed 18 March 2016].

Xiao, Z. 2010. How different is translated Chinese from native Chinese? *International Journal of Corpus Linguistics* 15(1), pp. 5–35.

Zanettin, F. 2012. *Translation-driven Corpora*. Manchester: St Jerome.

23

Language and translation on the Web

Mark Shuttleworth

Introduction and definitions

The area of "translation and the Web" represents a novel alignment of concepts and subsumes how translation is implemented, enabled, supported, promoted, discussed and made available over the Web. While part of Translation Studies, it also interrelates with the interlocking lines of enquiry referred to as "Web studies", "Web science", "internet studies" or "internet science" (see Consalvo and Ess 2011; O'Hara and Hall 2013).

Two terms need to be defined before we launch into the discussion:

Web 2.0 (or the *"read/write Web"*). Since the early 2000s this term has been used to reflect the collaborativity built into many websites and on-line applications that permits users to interact within virtual communities, creating their own content and contributing to that of other users.
UGC (User-Generated Content). UGC is "any form of content such as blogs, wikis, discussion forums, posts, chats, tweets, podcasting, digital images, video, audio files, advertisements and other forms of media that was created by users of an online system or service" (Moens, Li and Chua 2014, 7).

Historical perspectives

Folaron (2010) approaches translation and the Web from the perspective of Web studies (2010, 449). The present chapter follows Gaspari's (2015) more recent discussion of what he terms "online translation", placing it in the context of language on the Web and adding further topics to his discussion's already extensive repertoire.

Core issues and topic

The language of the English Web

This section describes the English Web; the situation in other languages is believed to be parallel to what is discussed here.

Today's Web contains a proliferation of digital "cybergenres". Some – including advertisements, dictionaries and scholarly papers – are "extant" genres (Shepherd and Watters 1998, 98). "Novel" cybergenres (*ibid.*, 99) include, for example, institutional websites, personal homepages, blogs and FAQs.

A number of factors characterise cybergenres. Some pages are obviously the work of several writers; ongoing updating means that the text associated with a URL may change between visits while dynamic pages are assembled on the basis of the precise information requested by the user (e.g. on-line store or library catalogue pages). Some linguistic heterogeneity and prefabricatedness can therefore be observed.

Another factor that characterises many web pages is their nature as "interrupted linear" (Crystal 2006, 204), where the unidimensional text flow is broken not only by white space and paragraph ends but also by screen ends and, in certain contexts, ellipses to indicate omitted text (e.g. a Google search results list). Alternatively, web pages can be made up of "nonlinear" text fragments (*ibid.*) that can be read in any order, depending on the reader's interest.

In addition, Web documents tend to be hypertext so that moving between different documents is facilitated.

According to Crystal, language usage in cybergenres also tends to be distinctive in vocabulary, orthography, grammar, pragmatics and style (Crystal 2011, 57–77). Lexical innovations include words such as *blogger*, *FAQs*, *netizenship* and *twitterati*. Characteristic orthographic usage includes the use of InterCaps and non-standard spellings. Grammatical innovation is often restricted to certain groups of users, an example being the replacement of plural ending *-s* by *-z* to refer to pirated software (e.g. *tunez*, *gamez*, etc.: see Crystal 2011, 67). As an instance of a pragmatically motivated Web practice, Crystal cites including keywords in a page's title and first paragraph to help ensure a high search-engine ranking (Crystal 2011, 72). Finally, new Web styles include graphic richness, innovative structural elements (e.g. posts, comments, etc.) and the limitation of tweets to 140 characters (Crystal 2011, 77).

Guides on writing for the Web give similar advice. Usability.gov recommends short sentences and paragraphs, the front-loading of important information, and bulleted and numbered lists (Usability.gov 2015). Barr and the Senior Editors of Yahoo! advise shaping text for on-line reading, making it easy to scan, and writing for the world (Barr and the Senior Editors of Yahoo!, 2011, ch. 1). Many cybergenres also display an acceptance of non-native English.

The languages of the Web

With the implementation of successive versions of the Unicode standard (http://www.unicode.org/versions/Unicode8.0.0) on the encoding of characters in different scripts, and following the combined work of the ITU (International Telecommunications Union: http://www.itu.int) and UNESCO (http://en.unesco.org/themes/building-knowledge-societies) on information and communications infrastructure and on access to knowledge as well as that of ICANN (Internet Corporation for Assigned Names and Numbers: https://www.icann.org) on agreeing a set of multilingual and multiscript conventions for the naming of internet entities (Crystal 2011, 84), the infrastructure is in place for the internet to take on a fully multilanguage identity. According to W3Techs, 51.3% "of all the websites whose content language [they] know" use English, Russian accounts for 6.7%, German for 5.6%, Japanese for 5.6%, Spanish for 5.1%, French for 4.1%, Portuguese for 2.6%, Italian for 2.4% and Chinese for 2.0% (W3Techs 2017, figures as of August 2017). In terms of numbers of internet users, English speakers number 952.1 million, Chinese 763.3 million, Spanish 293.8 million, Arabic 173.5 million, Portuguese 155.0 million, Malay 154.7 million,

Japanese 118.5 million, Russian 104.5 million, French 100.6 million and German 83.9 million (Internet World Stats 2017, figures as of August 2017).

Crystal reports identifying 1,000 languages that have "a modicum of presence on the Web" (Crystal 2006, 233). Google searches can be undertaken in 348 languages (Thomas 2015), while as of August 2017 there are 298 Wikipedias, of which 287 are active (List of Wikipedias 2017).

Language learning on the Web

An early mention of Web-Assisted Language Learning (WALL) can be found in Gitsaki and Taylor (1999, 143). WALL can take several forms. The Web can be exploited for authentic materials (Timmis 2015, 133–145), which can be edited and turned into learning activities using software such as Hot Potatoes (https://hotpot.uvic.ca). Language-learning sites, often commercial, offer course materials that can be downloaded or accessed on-line (http://www.rosettastone.co.uk; https://www.linguaphone.co.uk), and software that performs specific language-learning functions – such as testing vocabulary – is also available to download. Sites designed to explain grammar have been in existence for a long time (e.g. http://www.verbix.com).

All of these approaches still play important roles. However, Web 2.0 has enabled a previously unthinkable level of interactivity. Thomas (2009) discusses Skype, virtual learning environments, blogging, podcasts, social networking, video, corpora and courseware management systems. To these may be added wikis (Alm 2006; Shuttleworth 2014) and subtitling (Lertola 2012), for example. Each of these exploits the potential of Web 2.0 for the collaborative development of resources and for making use of UGC. Newer kinds of language-learning application and website have also appeared, including Duolingo (http://www.duolingo.com), Wordreference (http://www.wordreference.com) and Anki (http://ankisrs.net) (Shuttleworth 2014).

On-line machine translation as a utility

Free, on-line translation has been available since the launch of Altavista's Babelfish in 1997, which was based on the rule-based Systran machine translation (MT) system. The original Babelfish service was initially available in 10 language pairs, although that number was gradually increased. Since 1997 websites offering MT have grown in number and diversity: Hutchins (2009) lists 56 free and charging on-line MT services, for example.

In the autumn of 2007, Google Translate (https://translate.google.com), which had been launched the previous year, transferred all its language pairs from SYSTRAN to its own statistical MT system (Chitu 2007), making the addition of further language pairs to the system significantly more straightforward, and free on-line MT more widely available.

The Google Translator Toolkit (https://translate.google.com/toolkit) was launched in 2009 (Garcia and Stevenson 2009, 16). This permits collaboration, interactive use of MT, an enhanced post-editing interface and a limited integration of translation memory and glossaries. In addition, while the direct use of Google Translate remains free, since 2011 (Google Cloud Platform 2015) Google have introduced charges for the use of its API via third-party programs because of "the substantial economic burden caused by extensive abuse" (*ibid.*). Nevertheless, a free Google Translate Website Translator plug-in can be added to any website, and a free mobile app is available.

The second most widely used on-line MT system is Microsoft Translator, launched as Bing Translator (http://www.bing.com/translator) in 2009. This is currently available for

52 languages. An extension of the Translator, the Microsoft Translator Hub (http://www. microsoft.com/en-us/translator/hub.aspx) enables users to build their own MT systems. Other systems include Worldlingo (http://www.worldlingo.co.uk), iTranslate4 (http:// itranslate4.eu/en/) and Systranet (http://www.systranet.com/translate). Baidu (http://fanyi. baidu.com) is the main Chinese system, offering translation between 27 languages within a Chinese-language interface. The original Babelfish service no longer operates, although the similarly named Babel Fish Corporation (https://www.babelfish.com) still maintains a presence.

The output from such systems almost always needs to be post-edited before it can be used for any serious purpose. While much research is being directed towards post-editing (Allen 2003; O'Brien, Simard and Specia 2013) and translation quality (Aiken and Balan 2011; Hampshire and Salvia 2010), the linguistic features of the outputs from different types of MT system have attracted little attention (although see Shen 2010). Likewise, little work exists on the differing characteristics of post-edited MT output and human-translated text.

In the early 2000s the principal uses (all non-specialised) of free on-line MT were to discover information, translate the user's own web page, communicate in another language, provide entertainment and learn a language (Yang and Lange 2003, 201–202). Since then, indiscriminate, uninformed use of on-line MT has led to a number of high-profile gaffs, one of the best known being the decision taken by the Italian government in 2001 to use an on-line MT engine to produce English-language versions of ministers' biographies, which were uploaded to the official government website, apparently without checks (Messina 2001). More recently, unedited output from on-line MT seems to be used to translate Wikipedia content from one of its language versions to another, despite Wikipedia's own deprecation of such a practice (Wikipedia Translation 2015b).

On-line MT may be in the process of bringing about a fundamental change in the way that interlingual communication is being framed and implemented by significant sections of the translation industry. However, views of professional translators on its use vary, with some embracing the new technology while appreciating its limitations and others feeling frustrated when asked to perform post-editing (Stejskal 2010; Kelly 2014a). For reasons of privacy and confidentiality, those who offer services incorporating statistical MT in their workflow are ethically obliged to inform their clients of this as texts that have been translated are generally automatically incorporated in the system's database.

The Web as corpus

The most immediate way to exploit the Web as a corpus is via search engines, an approach described by Bernardini *et al.* as the Web as a "corpus surrogate" (Bernardini, Baroni and Evert 2006, 10–11). This approach can be considerably enhanced through the use of Web concordancers (e.g. http://www.webcorp.org.uk or http://www.kwicfinder.com: see Fletcher 2007), which add some of the features of more standard corpus search tools, such as the KWIC format.

A second approach, designated Web as "corpus shop" by Bernardini, Baroni and Evert (2006, 11–12), involves making a purpose-built corpus by downloading material from the Web. This can involve the use of BootCaT, a set of tools designed to "bootstrap corpora and terms from the Web" (BootCaT 2015) through a series of automated search-engine queries based on "seeds", or "terms that are expected to be typical of the domain of interest" (BootCaT 2015). The idea of "DIY corpora" – defined by Gatto as "corpora created from the web for a specific purpose" such as translation or terminological research (Gatto 2014, 138) – is related but tends to refer to single-use corpora that are *ad hoc* in nature (see Zanettin 2002 and Gatto 2014 among others).

The other two approaches proposed by Bernardini *et al.* are "Web as corpus proper" (Bernardini, Baroni and Evert 2006, 13) and "mega-corpus/mini-Web" (Bernardini, Baroni and Evert 2006, 13–14). The former refers to using the Web as a corpus that can provide representative information on the language of the Web. The latter involves compiling a huge corpus that combines features that are web-like (e.g. size, type of interface, contemporaneity) with those that are corpus-like (e.g. annotation, sophisticated querying language, stability) (see Gatto 2014, 37, 167–171).

Hundt *et al.* point out that "we still know very little about the size of this 'corpus', the text types it contains, the quality of the material included or the amount of repetitive 'junk' that it 'samples'" (Hundt, Nesselhauf and Biewer 2007, 2–3). This, along with the question of representativeness (Gatto 2014, 43–45) and the ephemeral nature of much Web content, which renders replication problematic, has caused some scepticism as to the validity of the "Web as Corpus" concept. Nevertheless, even writers who voice such concerns favour exploiting the Web as a resource for corpus building, and their scepticism only extends to some of the senses described by Bernardini, Baroni and Evert (2006). Gatto argues that while an approach based on the use of commercial search engines does not usually find favour in traditional corpus linguistics, it is "gaining prominence in language teaching, and indeed it is possibly one of the most widespread – albeit unacknowledged – uses of the Web as Corpus even beyond the corpus linguistics community" (Gatto 2014, 3).

On-line translation resources and software

The Web is a repository for terminological and text-based resources, aligned data and specialist software (delivered in the form of SaaS, or "Software as a Service"), all of which can be used to support translators' work.

Enríquez Raído reports that the internet has been the most used source of information for translators for several years, even though the dynamic manner in which sources exist on the Web gives rise to issues of evaluation, selection and use of the information located (Enríquez Raído 2013, 2). There are a wide range of approaches to the task of locating the terminological, textual and information resources that translators need in order to solve problems on an ongoing basis. Ready-made solutions include accessing major on-line databases (e.g. http://untermportal.un.org, http://iate.europa.eu); consulting sites providing links to glossaries and dictionaries (http://www.lexicool.com/dictionary-search.asp, http://lai.com/thc/glmain.html); and searching one of the large translator directories (http://www.proz.com, http://translatorscafe.com; see section on "Translation blogs and translator networking sites" below). More open-ended search strategies include consulting a search engine with a gradually evolving search expression to try to pin down an exact target language terminological usage. A small number of apps either already exist (Terminology by Agile Tortoise: http://agiletortoise.com) or are under development (TermSeeker by UCL: https://termseeker.wordpress.com).

Popular sources for textual assets include Wikipedia and Google Books. Textual resources collected from the internet can be invaluable sources of linguistic and technical information for translators, and, if gathered together and accessed via the appropriate software, can function as DIY corpora. Some corpus linguistics systems boast versions of BootCaT that allow efficient assembly of corpora (http://www.sketchengine.co.uk).

According to Isabelle *et al.*, "existing translations contain more solutions to more translation problems than any other available resource" (Isabelle *et al.* 1993, 1,137), and parallel text (also known as aligned or bilingual text, or bitext) has been described as "the fuel that drives modern machine translation systems", the Web being an excellent source for such data (Smith *et al.* 2013, 1).

However, while large-scale natural language processing projects have exploited resources such as the Internet Archive (http://www.archive.org; Resnik and Smith 2003) and the Common Crawl (https://commoncrawl.org; Smith *et al.* 2013), the options for individual users lacking the necessary expertise are more limited, although resources such as OPUS (http://opus.lingfil.uu.se; Tiedemann 2012) and those of the European Parliament (http://www.statmt.org/europarl) and the United Nations (http://www.uncorpora.org) are available.

Translation memories (TMs), a special type of parallel data, can be downloaded or consulted on-line. One of the first publicly available TMs was the VLTM, or "Very Large Translation Memory" (https://www.wordfast.net/?whichpage=jobs), which started to be offered free for use with the Wordfast translation memory tool in about 2007. Other services include MyMemory (https://mymemory.translated.net) and WeBiText (http://www.webitext.com/bin/webitext.cgi). TAUS (https://www.taus.net/data/taus-data-cloud) offers a large set of aligned data, most of it only available for payment. In all cases, the sharing of translation data has to take place with all due attention to legal considerations (van der Meer and Joscelyne 2013).

Collaborative and crowdsourced translation

Crowdsourcing and crowdsourced translation (Howe 2006; see further "Translation, interpreting and new technologies") has been facilitated by the appearance of Web 2.0. Other terms and concepts such as collaborative, community, volunteer and amateur translation also exist (see O'Hagan 2011a, 13–14).

Fernández Costales argues that the difference between collaborative and crowdsourced translation is one of hierarchy (Fernández Costales 2013, 96): while both use volunteers, the former involves direct networking between equals whereas in the latter the collaborative effort is "managed, directed or sponsored" by an organisation (*ibid.*). The former scenario can be observed in the TED Open Translation Project (DePalma 2009; Olohan 2014; TED Conferences n.d. a), for example, in which over 16,000 translators have collaborated with transcribers to produce some 85,000 translations in 110 languages (*ibid.*) using the Amara on-line subtitling tool (http://www.amara.org). In contrast, before inviting its bilingual users to help translate its interface into the 140 languages in which it is currently available, Facebook put a system in place that ensures that one model of segment translation and quality approval is strictly followed (Ellis 2009; O'Hagan 2009, 112; Facebook n.d.).

Désilets and van der Meer (2011, 30–34) discuss five "common issues" in collaborative translation:

1. *Business goals:* Advantages of the business model used by Facebook include cost saving, community involvement, enhancing brand loyalty, reducing turnaround time, improving coverage of low-density languages and ephemeral UGC, and producing translations that reproduce the linguistic idiosyncrasies of the users of the content (Désilets and van der Meer 2011, 31; see also Ellis 2009). According to Kelly, further attractive features include improvement in quality caused by the involvement of the end-users (Kelly 2009).

2. *Quality control:* In crowdsourcing, this often involves the end-user translators voting for what they consider to be the best translation of each text string, making the translation process self-regulating. Désilets and van der Meer comment that the quality sometimes exceeds that of more traditional processes (Désilets and van der Meer 2011, 32). By contrast, in their "controlled crowdsourcing" (Kelly 2012), the non-profit association Translators without Borders vets volunteers before they start translating because the urgency of many projects allows no time for vetting later (*ibid.*).

3. *Crowd motivation:* Among volunteer translators motivation can be very high because of their emotional investment in the content they are translating (Désilets and van der Meer 2011, 32). In such contexts companies frequently offer intangible benefits, such as Facebook's rewards and leaderboards (Facebook n.d.) and TED crediting (TED Conferences n.d. b).

4. *The role of professionals:* Even though companies such as Facebook have made crowd-sourcing part of their translation strategy, they employ professionals to check quality (Ellis 2009, 236, 238) and to translate legal documentation (Sargent 2008).

5. *Parallelism and de-contextualisation:* Much collaborative translation involves breaking down content for distribution among translators. For example, Asia Online's project of translating the English Wikipedia into Thai (DePalma 2011) involved rapid machine translation of 3.5 million Wikipedia articles followed by large-scale post-editing of the articles in segmented form (Morera-Mesa, Collins and Filip 2013, 11).

Morera-Mesa, Collins and Filip (2013) study workflow patterns used in crowdsourced translation, focusing in particular on questions such as whether alternative translations should be visible to all users and how to assess translations. These and other aspects of crowdsourced work patterns can now be managed by software systems such as Smartling Translation Management System (http://www.smartling.com/platform), Synble Get Localization (http://about.synble.com/?page_id=28), Transifex (http://www.transifex.com) and CrowdFlower (http://www.crowdflower.com) (see also Orr Priebe 2009).

Ethical issues raised by crowdsourced and collaborative translation include the remuneration of participants, the impact on the public perception of translation, the potential positive effect on the visibility of minority languages (McDonough Dolmaya 2011a), the applicability of professional codes to collaborative translation, and the nature of new non-professional codes and the new shared ethos (Drugan 2011).

Wikipedia translation

In August 2017, Wikipedia existed in 298 language versions, of which 287 are active (List of Wikipedias 2017; see also Ayers, Matthews and Yates 2008, 407–418 and Petzold 2012). Articles can be edited by anybody, so that each article becomes a kind of "evolving continuity" (Wikimedia 2014).

Wikipedia's size and scope have led to it being utilised as a corpus in a number of lexical research packages (e.g. http://www.sketchengine.co.uk and http://corp.hum.sdu.dk). In addition, researchers tap into its potential in a range of computational linguistics applications, including entity linking (or "wikification": Milne and Witten 2008), word sense disambiguation (Mihalcea 2007) and measuring semantic relatedness (Explicit Semantic Analysis: Gabrilovich and Markovitch 2006).

Much has been written on the language, style and structure of Wikipedia. For the English version, Ayers, Matthews and Yates (2008, 175) stress the importance of readability and characterise Wikipedia's tone as "direct, crisp, and contemporary" (Ayers, Matthews and Yates 2008, 176). They observe that American English and Commonwealth English coexist (Ayers, Matthews and Yates 2008, 177), a situation that is interestingly mirrored by Simplified and Traditional Chinese on the Chinese version (and sometimes even within the space of a single article). Style recommendations are made in many of the different language versions, with the English articles "Wikipedia Manual of Style" (2016c) and "Wikipedia Writing better articles" (2016e) having 98 and 32 so-called interwiki links respectively. Shuttleworth characterises Wikipedia writing as hybrid in nature as a result of having been authored by multiple writers, and comments on a blurring of the distinction between translation and original writing (Shuttleworth 2015a). Geolinguists Liao and Petzold provide a network graph based on interwiki links and illustrating the encyclopaedia's major language nodes and the routes along which information is disseminated from one Wikipedia to another – which frequently involve the English version (Liao and Petzold 2010, 11).

While it is generally recognised that the encyclopaedia contains material that has been translated from other language versions, it is not certain how much there is or where its greatest concentrations are. The patchwork nature of Wikipedia discourse means that a short translated passage may be present alongside material of a different provenance. Translated material – or material needing to be translated – can, however, be located by referring to the relevant list pages (e.g. Wikipedia "Category Translated pages" 2016b, "Category Articles needing translation from foreign-language Wikipedias" 2016a, "Pages needing translation into English" 2016d). Studying an article's Talk and History tabs can also lead to the identification of specific sections of translated discourse (Shuttleworth 2015b). Human translation appears to be only one of a number of procedures for the cross-language expansion of Wikipedia, others including paraphrase, non-native writing and un-post-edited MT (Shuttleworth 2015a).

Translation blogs and translator networking sites

The practice of blogging has been taken up rapidly, the period of 2006–2014, for example, seeing the number of blogs in existence grow from 35.77m to 260.47m (Meinel *et al.* 2015, 8). As of August 2017, the American Translators Association lists 78 translation-related blogs (American Translators Association 2017), although there may be far more. Translation likewise has a strong presence on the microblogging service, Twitter.

Myers has written an extended study of the discourse of blogs and wikis (Myers 2010). McDonough Dolmaya discusses the "working conditions, emerging technologies, ethical challenges and other aspects of the profession" (McDonough Dolmaya 2011b, 77) and lists the most popular functions within a sample of 50 translation blogs focusing on English, French and Spanish as: offering advice and opinions, sharing news, resources and personal experiences, asking for feedback and sharing material of a personal nature that is not directly linked to translation (McDonough Dolmaya 2011b, 86). In this way McDonough Dolmaya identifies translation blogs as an important means of studying sociological aspects of translation (McDonough Dolmaya 2011b, 91).

There may be up to a couple of dozen English-language translator networking sites. These fulfil the combined functions of directory, portal, discussion forum and marketplace. Possibly the best known is ProZ.com. Founded in 1999 and intended principally for freelance translators, it permits its members to post and/or bid for job offers, provide feedback on clients, collaborate on terminology (via KudoZ, the ProZ.com terminology service) and participate in on-line training (ProZ.com 2016). TranslatorsCafe.com, another highly prominent translator directory, is discussed by McDonough (2007, 804–811; see also Pym *et al.* 2013, 136–138).

The professionally oriented social networking service LinkedIn is also popular among translators. LinkedIn enables users to form networks and increase their professional visibility, to market themselves and conduct more effective job searches, or to advertise for and recruit staff. LinkedIn Groups bring together people with shared purposes or interests, such as networking with clients, sharing advice about translation agencies or discussing specialist areas of translation.

Fansubbing and related practices

Fansubbing is based on a notion of fandom that builds on the concept of the "prosumer" (or person who is simultaneously a "producer" and a "consumer").

In the early 1990s fansubbers worked with VHS copies of Japanese anime series, imprinting the subtitles in the video and distributing tapes by post (Lee 2011, 1,138). Since 2000 the process has gone fully digital, with the "raw" (i.e. unsubtitled) source usually being obtained from DVDs, television broadcasts, peer-to-peer networks or contacts in Japan or elsewhere (Hatcher 2005; Díaz Cintas and Muñoz Sánchez 2006); finished products are likewise typically distributed using the peer-to-peer file-sharing protocol (Lee 2011, 1,137; e.g. via sites such as http://myanimelist.net) or else viewed directly over the Web (e.g. at http://www.crunchyroll.com). The subtitling tool of choice for most fansubbers is Aegisub (http://www.aegisub.org).

Fansubbers are unpaid volunteers, motivated by the desire to share with fellow fans new material from the genres that interest them. Typically they are not trained in subtitling but compensate for this through detailed domain knowledge.

Fansubs can be of a very good quality (Hatcher 2005), although they have been observed to differ from the output of professional subtitlers: for example, they tend to be longer and more oriented towards source text norms, and they contain more features specific to spoken language and also more language errors (Wilcock 2013, 103–6). Furthermore, much modern fansubbing output pursues a relatively foreignising translation approach, with over 90% retaining significant numbers of honorifics (e.g. "san", "sensei") and Japanese words and even displaying explanatory notes on the screen simultaneously with the subtitles (OtaKing77077 2008). However, it has exceeded official translation in terms of the range and variety of material that is subtitled, which has traditionally included titles that would not otherwise have been available, because they either are not well known or are intended for a niche audience (Lee 2011, 1,138; Hatcher 2005).

While technically illegal, fansubbing has been tolerated by the licensed distributors, for a number of reasons: a fansubbed version can help draw a tentative audience towards a new anime series, while the work of fansubbers can help distributors to decide what to license as well as bringing new material – and indeed new translation and subtitling talent – to their attention (Hatcher 2005).

The related phenomenon of scanlation is the process of scanning Japanese manga, Chinese manhua, Korean manhwa and other genres of comic book, translating them and making them available via the Web (Lee 2011, 1,132; see also Lee 2009). Like fansubbing, scanlation is an amateur activity that is almost always carried out without the copyright holder's permission.

O'Hagan argues that the nature of UGTs (user-generated translation) produced by fansubbers and scanlators is likely to have far-reaching consequences for the translation profession, with individual users and consumers becoming empowered as they take their place within a rapidly evolving community of practice (Lee 2009, 115). Fans cease to be seen as "helpless victims of mass culture", taking on instead more positive attributes through their engagement in different forms of resistance (Chu 2013, 260).

Web localisation

One definition of localisation – albeit one that favours the business aspects of the activity – sees it as "the process of modifying products or services to account for differences in distinct markets" (LISA 2007, 11).

The business imperative behind the drive to localise websites and other digital products (such as software, video games and apps) is the geographical distribution of internet users, the preference on their part for an internet experience in their own language and the often excellent return on investment that localisation can yield (Internet World Stats 2015; Globalization and Localization Association 2016). However, other types of material – such as personal homepages or not-for-profit websites – may also require localisation.

Localisation is one of the linked "GILT" processes of globalisation, internationalisation, localisation and translation, which play a role in adapting e-content to different linguistic, cultural and business settings. These processes are frequently referred to by abbreviations – G11N, I18N, L10N and T9N – that are based on each term's letter count.

Globalisation involves the organisational preparations that a company needs to put in place prior to going global (Jiménez-Crespo 2013, 24). Internationalisation, on the other hand, entails "enabling a product at a technical level" (LISA 2007, 17) in order to prevent the need for substantial redesign during the localisation process; this can include allowing space for text expansion and ensuring that the language is as culture-neutral as possible. Once these stages have been completed the website can be localised for use in the target country. This involves replacement of all "user-visible natural-language strings" (Pym 2010, 134) with corresponding TL text strings (translation) and adaptation of date and number formats (part of a website's "locale"), colour scheme, appearance, layout, cultural specificity and conventions for interacting with the interface, making use of all the appropriate technology in the process (localisation). While cultural adaptation often forms a major part of localisation, the internationalisation process can be used to ensure that the presence of features requiring such adjustment is kept to a minimum.

The task of converting the text tends to be outsourced to freelance translator-localisers. Besides being bilingual and bicultural, Jiménez-Crespo describes localisers as translators with "an expandable degree of technological and management competence" (Jiménez-Crespo 2013, 165), including, for example, an understanding of mark-up languages such as HTML and XML, Cascading Style Sheets and scripting languages such as JavaScript and PHP, as well as an ability to conduct quality assurance and other procedures.

Representatives of the localisation industry tend to characterise translation as a mere stage in the complex localisation process (see for example Nichols 2015), and localisation and related processes of adaptation are increasingly distanced from "traditional translation" through the use of terms and concepts such as "glocalisation" (Mazur 2007) and "transcreation" (Bernal Merino 2006, 32; Kelly 2014b; Nichols 2015). In contrast, the translation scholar Gouadec states that "[t]o all intents and purposes, localisers are a particular category of translators who 'translate' material that is embedded in media other than paper or print or audiovisual media" (Gouadec 2007, 114).

Main research methods

The subject of language, translation and the Web is extremely varied, taking in a large number of individual topics. Large amounts of data useful for researching the Web are available on various sites (e.g. http://www.internetlivestats.com, http://www.internetworldstats.com, http://www.alexa.com and https://archive.org) or, for example, for Wikipedia within the encyclopaedia itself (e.g. Wikipedia "Translation" 2015b, "Category Translated pages" 2016b, "List of Wikipedias" 2017 and "List of Lists of Lists" 2015a) so that the principle of using the Web to study the Web, or using Wikipedia to study Wikipedia, seems to apply. Theoretical approaches to the study of language on the Web are drawn from many different branches of linguistics, while when it comes to translation all three of Holmes' original research focuses – i.e. product, process and function (Holmes 2004, 72–3) – are brought into play.

Current debates and future directions

The Web is expected to continue to evolve rapidly and the direction of future research will depend on new developments within its object of study. That said, research paradigms need to be elaborated in greater detail in nearly every area that has been discussed, our current knowledge of most of these being limited.

Implications for practice

The above discussion highlights at least two potential challenges to traditional translation practices, namely MT and crowdsourced translation, both of which have had a significant impact on the translation industry. Furthermore, for certain sectors of the industry, translating "the wiki way" is becoming an increasingly attractive and popular option (Désilets *et al.* 2006). Besides this, there is likely to be an increasing use of corpora among translators although the reliability of data accessed via the Web will probably remain an issue.

Further reading

Ayers, P., Matthews, C. and Yates, B. 2008. *How Wikipedia Works and How You Can Be a Part of It.* San Francisco: No Starch Press, Inc. Available from: http://en.wikibooks.org/wiki/How_Wikipedia_Works [Accessed 29 February 2016].
An excellent all-round introduction to Wikipedia.

Crystal, D. 2011. *Internet Linguistics: A Student Guide.* Abingdon: Routledge.
An introductory overview of the study of internet linguistics.

Gatto, M. 2014. *Web as Corpus: Theory and Practice.* London: Bloomsbury.
A comprehensive and detailed study of how Web content can be exploited and studied using corpus linguistics methodologies.

Jiménez-Crespo, M. A. 2013 *Translation and Web Localization.* Abingdon: Routledge.
A detailed overview of the theory and practice of web localisation.

O'Hagan, M., ed. 2011. *Community Translation 2.0.* Special issue of *Linguistica Antverpiensia New Series: Themes in Translation Studies* 10. Available from: https://lans-tts.uantwerpen.be/index.php/LANS-TTS/issue/view/14 [Accessed 1 March 2016].
A very useful collection of articles on various aspects of collaborative translation.

Related topics

Corpus linguistics, translation and interpreting; Genre analysis and translation; Language and translation in film; Translation, interpreting and new technologies.

References

Aiken, M. and Balan, S. 2011. An analysis of Google Translate accuracy. *Translation Journal* 16(2). Available from: http://translationjournal.net/journal/56google.htm [Accessed 5 October 2015].

Allen, J. 2003. "Post-editing". In *Computers and Translation: A Translator's Guide*, edited by H. Somers, 297–318. Amsterdam: John Benjamins.

Alm, A. 2006. CALL for autonomy, competence and relatedness: motivating language learning environments in Web 2.0. *The JALT CALL Journal* 2(3), pp. 29–38. Available from: http://journal.jaltcall.org/articles/2_3_Alm.pdf [Accessed 24 February 2016].

American Translators Association 2017. *American Translators Association (ATA) Blog Trekker.* Available from: http://www.atanet.org/resources/blog_trekker.php [Accessed 30 August 2017].

Ayers, P., Matthews, C. and Yates, B. 2008. *How Wikipedia Works and How You Can Be a Part of It.* San Francisco: No Starch Press, Inc. Available from: http://en.wikibooks.org/wiki/How_Wikipedia_Works [Accessed 29 February 2016].

Barr, C. and the Senior Editors of Yahoo! 2011. *The Yahoo! Style Guide: The Ultimate Sourcebook for Writing, Editing and Creating Content for the Web.* London: Macmillan (Kindle edition).

Bernardini, S., Baroni, M. and Evert, S. 2006. "A WaCky Introduction". In *WaCky! Working Papers on the Web as Corpus*, edited by M. Baroni and S. Bernardini, 9–40. Bologna: Gedit Edizioni. Available from: http://wackybook.sslmit.unibo.it [Accessed 26 February 2016].

Bernal Merino, M. 2006. On the translation of video games. *Journal of Specialised Translation* 6, pp. 22–36. Available from: http://www.jostrans.org/issue06/art_bernal.php [Accessed 10 December 2015].

BootCaT. 2015. "Simple Utilities to Bootstrap Corpora and Terms from the Web". Available from: http://bootcat.sslmit.unibo.it [Accessed 27 February 2016].

Chitu, A. 2007. "Google Switches to its Own Translation System". Post dated 22 October 2007. In *Google Operating System: Unofficial News and Tips About Google.* Available from: http://googlesystem.blogspot.co.uk/2007/10/google-translate-switches-to-googles.html [Accessed 23 October 2015].

Chu, D. S. C. 2013. "Fanatical Labour and Serious Leisure: A Case of Fansubbing in China". In *Frontiers in New Media Research*, edited by F. L. F. Lee, L. Leung, J. L. Chu and D. S. C. Chu, 259–277. New York: Routledge.

Consalvo, M. and Ess, C., eds. 2011. *The Handbook of Internet Studies.* Hoboken: Wiley-Blackwell.

Crystal, D. 2006. *Language and the Internet.* 2nd ed. Cambridge: Cambridge University Press.

Crystal, D. 2011. *Internet Linguistics: A Student Guide.* Abingdon: Routledge.

DePalma, D. A. 2009. "dotSUB Extends TED's 'Ideas Worth Spreading' to Hundreds of Languages" Post dated 14 May 2009. In *Global Watchtower.* Available from: http://www.commonsenseadvisory.com/Default.aspx?Contenttype=ArticleDetAD&tabID=63&Aid=553&moduleId=391 [Accessed 9 January 2016].

DePalma, D. A. 2011. "The Largest Translation Project … so Far". Post dated 13 January 2011. In *Global Watchtower.* Available from: http://www.commonsenseadvisory.com/Default.aspx?Contenttype=ArticleDetAD&tabID=63&Aid=1180&moduleId=391 [Accessed 24 January 2016].

Désilets, A., Gonzalez, L., Paquet, S. and Stojanovic, M. 2006 "Translation the Wiki Way". In *WikiSym '06: Proceedings of the 2006 Symposium on Wikis.* ACM. Available from: http://citeseerx.ist.psu.edu/viewdoc/download?doi=10.1.1.122.1679&rep=rep1&type=pdf [Accessed 30 August 2017].

Désilets, A. and van der Meer, J. 2011. "Co-creating a Repository of Best-practices for Collaborative Translators". In *Community Translation 2.0*, edited by M. O'Hagan. Special issue of *Linguistica*

Antverpiensia New Series: Themes in Translation Studies 10/2011, pp. 27–45. Available from: https://lans-tts.uantwerpen.be/index.php/LANS-TTS/issue/view/14 [Accessed 1 March 2016].

Díaz Cintas, J. and Muñoz Sánchez, P. 2006. Fansubs: audiovisual translation in an amateur environment. *Journal of Specialised Translation* 6, pp. 37–52. Available from: http://www.jostrans.org/issue06/art_diaz_munoz.pdf [Accessed 12 April 2015].

Drugan, J. 2011. "Translation Ethics Wikified: How Far Do Professional Codes of Ethics and Practice Apply to Non-professionally Produced Translation?" In *Community Translation 2.0*, edited by M. O'Hagan. Special issue of *Linguistica Antverpiensia New Series: Themes in Translation Studies* 10/2011, pp. 111–127. Available from: https://lans-tts.uantwerpen.be/index.php/LANS-TTS/issue/view/14 [Accessed 1 March 2016].

Ellis, D. 2009. "A Case Study in Community-driven Translation of a Fast-changing Website". In *Internationalization, Design and Global Development*, edited by N. Aykin, 236–244. Berlin: Springer Verlag. Available from: http://link.springer.com/chapter/10.1007%2F978-3-642-02767-3_26 [Accessed 10 December 2014].

Enríquez Raído, V. 2013. "Introduction". In *Translation and Web Searching*, edited by V. Enríquez Raído 1–7. New York: Routledge.

Facebook, n.d. "Translation App Guide". Available from: https://www.facebook.com/translations/guide/?cmsid=217893761755049 [Accessed 9 January 2016].

Fernández Costales, A. 2013. "Crowdsourcing and Collaborative Translation: Mass Phenomena or Silent Threat to Translation Studies?" In *Hermēneus. Revista de Traducción e Interpretación*, 15, pp. 85–110. Available from: http://recyt.fecyt.es/index.php/HS/article/viewFile/30295/15892 [Accessed 29 December 2015].

Fletcher, W. H. 2007. "Concordancing the Web: Promise and Problems, Tools and Techniques". In *Corpus Linguistics and the Web*, edited by M. Hundt, N. Nesselhauf and C. Biewer, 25–45. Amsterdam: Rodopi.

Folaron, D. 2010. "Web and Translation". In *Handbook of Translation Studies*, Vol. 1, edited by Y. Gambier and L. van Doorslaer, 446–450. Amsterdam: John Benjamins.

Gabrilovich, E. and Markovitch, S. 2006. "Overcoming the Brittleness Bottleneck Using Wikipedia: Enhancing Text Categorization with Encyclopedic Knowledge". In *Proceedings of the 21st National Conference on Artificial Intelligence (AAAI)*, 1301–1306. Available from: http://www.aaai.org/Papers/AAAI/2006/AAAI06-204.pdf [Accessed 27 January 2016].

Garcia, I. and Stevenson, V. 2009. Google Translator Toolkit: Free web-based translation memory for the masses. *MultiLingual* (September), 16–18.

Gaspari, F. 2015. "Online Translation". In *Routledge Encyclopedia of Translation Technology*, edited by S.-W. Chan, 578–593. Abingdon: Routledge.

Gatto, M. 2014. *Web as Corpus: Theory and Practice*. London: Bloomsbury.

Gitsaki, C. and Taylor, R. P. 1999. "Bringing the WWW into the ESL Classroom". In *CALL and the Learning Community*, edited by K. Cameron, 143–160. Exeter: Elm Bank Publications.

Globalization and Localization Association 2016. "Why Localize?" Available from: https://www.gala-global.org/industry/language-industry-facts-and-data/why-localize [Accessed 18 February 2016].

Google Cloud Platform. 2015. "Translate API FAQ". Available from: https://cloud.google.com/translate/v2/faq [Accessed 26 October 2015].

Gouadec, D. 2007. *Translation as a Profession*. Amsterdam: John Benjamins.

Hampshire, S. and Salvia, P. C. 2010. Translation and the internet: evaluating the quality of free online machine translators. *Quaderns: Revista de traducció* 17, pp. 197–209. Available from: http://www.raco.cat/index.php/QuadernsTraduccio/issue/view/14558/showToc [Accessed 10 December 2014].

Hatcher, J. S. 2005. "Of Otaku and Fansubs: A Critical Look at Anime Online in Light of Current Issues in Copyright Law". Available from: http://www2.law.ed.ac.uk/ahrc/script-ed/vol2-4/hatcher.asp [Accessed 26 November 2015].

Holmes, J. S. 1972/2004. "The Name and Nature of Translation Studies". In *The Translation Studies Reader*. 2nd ed., edited by L. Venuti, 180–192. London: Routledge.

Howe, J. 2006. "Crowdsourcing: A Definition". In *Crowdsourcing Blog*. Available from: http://crowdsourcing.typepad.com/cs/2006/06/crowdsourcing_a.html [Accessed 11 December 2014].

Hundt, M., Nesselhauf, N. and Biewer, C. 2007. "Corpus Linguistics and the Web". In *Corpus Linguistics and the Web*, edited by M. Hundt, N. Nesselhauf and C. Biewer, 1–5. Amsterdam: Rodopi.

Hutchins, J. 2009. *Compendium of Translation Software: Directory of Commercial Machine Translation Systems and Computer-aided Translation Support Tools*. 15th ed. Available from: http://www.hutchinsweb.me.uk/Compendium-15.pdf [Accessed 14 October 2015].

Internet World Stats. 2015. "World Internet Users Statistics and 2015 World Population Stats". Available from: http://www.internetworldstats.com/top20.htm [Accessed 18 February 2016].

Internet World Stats. 2017. "Top Ten Internet Languages: World Internet Statistics". Available from: http://www.internetworldstats.com/stats7.htm [Accessed 22 February 2016].

Isabelle, P., Dymetman, M., Foster, G., Jutras, J.-M., Macklovitch, E., Perrault, F., Ren, X. and Simard, M. 1993. "Translation Analysis and Translation Automation". In *TMI-93: The Fifth International Conference on Theoretical and Methodological Issues in Machine Translation*, Kyoto, Japan, 1133–1147. Available from: http://mt-archive.info/IBM-1993-Isabelle.pdf [Accessed 1 December 2015].

Jiménez-Crespo, M. A. 2013. *Translation and Web Localization*. Abingdon: Routledge.

Kelly, N. 2009. "Freelance Translators Clash with LinkedIn over Crowdsourced Translation". Post dated on 19 June 2009. Available from: http://www.commonsenseadvisory.com/Default.aspx?Contenttype=ArticleDetAD&tabID=63&Aid=591&moduleId=391 [Accessed 29 October 2015].

Kelly, N. 2012. "Translators without Borders Prepares to Bridge the Last Language Mile". *The Huffington Post*, posted 12 March 2011, updated 2 February 2012. Available from: http://www.huffingtonpost.com/nataly-kelly/translators-without-borde_b_1122452.html [Accessed 18 November 2015].

Kelly, N. 2014a. "Why So Many Translators Hate Translation Technology". *The Huffington Post* 19 June. Available from: http://www.huffingtonpost.com/nataly-kelly/why-so-many-translators-h_b_5506533.html [Accessed 9 November 2015].

Kelly, N. 2014b. "Where Transcreation Ends and Localization Begins", 23 July. Available from: https://www.smartling.com/blog/transcreation-ends-localization-begins [Accessed 10 December 2015].

Lee, H.-K. 2009. Between fan culture and copyright infringement: manga scanlation. *Media, Culture and Society* 31(6), pp. 1011–1022. Available from: http://mcs.sagepub.com/content/31/6/1011.full.pdf+html [Accessed 16 February 2016].

Lee, H.-K. 2011. Participatory media fandom: a case study of anime fansubbing. *Media, Culture & Society* 33(8), pp. 1131–1147. Available from: http://mcs.sagepub.com/content/33/8/1131.full.pdf+html [Accessed 12 April 2015].

Lertola, J. 2012. "The Effect of the Subtitling Task on Vocabulary Learning". In *Translation Research Project 4*, edited by A. Pym and D. Orrego-Carmona, 61–70. Tarragona: Intercultural Studies Group, Universitat Rovira i Virgili. Available from: http://isg.urv.es/publicity/isg/publications/trp_4_2012/5-Lertola.pdf [Accessed 24 February 2016].

Liao, H.-T. and Petzold, T. 2010. Analysing geo-linguistic dynamics of the world wide web: the use of cartograms and network analysis to understand linguistic development in Wikipedia. *Journal of Cultural Science* 3(2), pp. 1–18. Available from: http://cultural-science.org/journal/index.php/culturalscience/article/view/47/77 [Accessed 27 January 2016].

LISA. 2007. *LISA Globalization Industry Primer*. Romainmôtier, Switzerland: Localization Industry Standards Association.

Mazur, I. 2007. The metalanguage of localization: theory and practice. *Target* 19(2), pp. 337–57.

McDonough, J. 2007. How do language professionals organize themselves? An overview of translation networks. *Meta: Journal des Traducteurs/Meta: Translators' Journal* 52(4), pp. 793–815.

McDonough Dolmaya, J. 2011a. "The Ethics of Crowdsourcing". In *Community Translation 2.0*, edited by M. O'Hagan. Special issue of *Linguistica Antverpiensia New Series: Themes in Translation Studies* 10/2011, pp. 97–110.

McDonough Dolmaya, J. 2011b. A window into the profession: what translation blogs have to offer translation studies. *The Translator* 17(1), pp. 77–104.

Meinel, C., Broß, J., Berger, P. and Hennig, P. 2015. *Blogosphere and its Exploration*. Berlin: Springer.

Messina, S. 2001. "E Palazzo Chigi creò l'inglese". *La Repubblica*, 8 December. Available from: http://ricerca.repubblica.it/repubblica/archivio/repubblica/2001/12/08/palazzo-chigi-creo-inglese.html?ref=search [Accessed 22 October 2015].

Mihalcea, R. 2007. "Using Wikipedia for AutomaticWord Sense Disambiguation". In Proceedings of HLT-NAACL 2007, Rochester, NY, April 2007, 196–203. Rochester, NY: Association for Computational Linguistics. Available from: http://www.aclweb.org/anthology/N07-1025 [Accessed 27 January 2016].

Milne, D. and Witten, I. H. 2008. "Learning to Link with Wikipedia". In *Proceedings of the 17th ACM Conference on Information and Knowledge Management, Napa Valley, California, USA, October 26–20, 2008*, New York, NY, USA: ACM, 509–518. Available from: http://www.cs.waikato.ac.nz/~ihw/papers/08-DNM-IHW-LearningToLinkWithWikipedia.pdf [Accessed 27 January 2016].

Moens, M.-F., Li, J. and Chua, T.-S. 2014. *Mining User Generated Content*. Boca Raton: Chapman and Hall/CRC.

Morera-Mesa, A., Collins, J. J. and Filip, D. 2013. "Selected crowdsourced translation practices". Paper presented at Translating and the Computer 35, pp. 28–29 November, Paddington, London. Available from: http://www.mt-archive.info/10/Aslib-2013-Morera-Mesa.pdf [Accessed 24 January 2016].

Myers, G. 2010. *The Discourse of Blogs and Wikis*. London: Continuum.

Nichols, B. 2015. "The Difference between Translation and Localization for Multilingual Website Projects [Definitions]". 28 July. Available from: http://content.lionbridge.com/the-difference-between-translation-and-localization-for-multilingual-website-projects-definitions [Accessed 10 December 2015].

O'Brien, S., Simard, M. and Specia, L. 2013. Proceedings of the 2nd Workshop on Post-editing Technology and Practice (WPTP-2), MT Summit XIV Workshop, Nice, France, 2 September 2013. Available from: http://www.mt-archive.info/10/MTS-2013-W2-TOC.htm [Accessed 6 November 2015].

O'Hagan, M. 2009. Evolution of user-generated translation: fansubs, translation hacking and crowd-sourcing. *Journal of Internationalization and Localization* 1(1), pp. 94–121. Available from: https://www.academia.edu/4462788/Evolution_of_User-generated_Translation_Fansubs_Translation_Hacking_and_Crowdsourcing [Accessed 12 April 2015].

O'Hagan, M. 2011. "Community Translation: Translation as a Social Activity and Its Possible Consequences in the Advent of Web 2.0 and Beyond". In *Community Translation 2.0*, edited by M. O'Hagan. Special issue of *Linguistica Antverpiensia New Series: Themes in Translation Studies* 10, pp. 11–23, Available from: https://lans-tts.uantwerpen.be/index.php/LANS-TTS/issue/view/14.

O'Hara, K. and Hall, W. 2013. "Web Science". In *The Oxford Handbook of Internet Studies*, edited by W. H. Dutton, 48–68. Oxford: Oxford University Press.

Olohan, M. 2014. Why do you translate? Motivation to volunteer and TED translation. *Translation Studies* 7(1), pp. 17–33.

Orr Priebe, S. 2009. "Tom Sawyer: A Crowdsourcing Pioneer?". In *tcworld* November. Available from: http://www.tcworld.info/e-magazine/outsourcing/article/tom-sawyer-a-crowdsourcing-pioneer [Accessed 20 January 2016].

OtaKing77077. 2008. "Anime Fansub Documentary PART 2". Available from: https://www.youtube.com/watch?v=yoJ_BWQ9Kow [Accessed 1 March 2016].

Petzold, T. 2012. 36 million language pairs. *Journal of Cultural Science* 5(2), pp. 106–119. Available from: http://cultural-science.org/journal/index.php/culturalscience/article/view/57/87 [Accessed 2 November 2014].

ProZ.com. 2016. *ProZ.com: Company Overview*. Available from: http://www.proz.com/about [Accessed 13 February 2016].

Pym, A. 2010. *Exploring Translation Theories*. Abingdon: Routledge.

Pym, A., Grin, F., Sfreddo, C. and Chan, A. L. J. 2013. *The Status of the Translation Profession in the European Union*. London: Anthem Press.

Resnik, P. and Smith, N. A. 2003. The web as a parallel corpus. *Computational Linguistics* 29(3), pp. 349–380.

Sargent, B. 2008. "Community Translation Lifts Facebook to Top of Social Networking World". Post dated 14 August 2008, in *Global Watchtower*. Available from: http://www.commonsenseadvisory.com/ Default.aspx?Contenttype=ArticleDetAD&tabID=63&Aid=525&moduleId=391 [Accessed 10 January 2016].

Shen, E. 2010. *Comparison of Online Machine Translation Tools*. Available from: http://www.tcworld. info/e-magazine/translation-and-localization/article/comparison-of-online-machine-translation-tools [Accessed 14 October 2015].

Shepherd, M. and Watters, C. 1998. "The Evolution of Cybergenres". In *Proceedings of the XXXI Hawaii International Conference on System Sciences*, edited by R. Sprague, 97–109. Los Alamitos, CA: IEEE-Computer Society.

Shuttleworth, M. 2014. "Approaches to language learning: blending tradition with innovation". *Proceedings of SILK conference, 14–16 February 2014, Hydro Hotel, Penang, Malaysia, CD*. Available from: https://ucl.academia.edu/MarkShuttleworth [Accessed 24 February 2016].

Shuttleworth, M. 2015a. "5th IATIS Conference Wikipedia presentation". IATIS 5th International Conference, Belo Horizonte, Brazil, 7–10 July 2015, slides available from: https://www.academia. edu/13808267/5th_IATIS_Conference_Wikipedia_presentation [Accessed 29 February 2016].

Shuttleworth, M. 2015b. "Wikipedia Translation: Collaborativity, Translation and the Web". *ARTIS@ UCL 2015 Multidimensional methodologies: Collaboration and networking in translation research*, UCL, UK, 15–16 June 2015, slides available from: https://www.academia.edu/12982446/Wikipedia_ translation_Collaborativity_translation_and_the_web [Accessed 1 July 2015].

Smith, J., Saint-Amand, H., Plamada, M., Koehn, P., Callison-Burch, C. and Lopez, A. 2013. "Dirt Cheap Web-scale Parallel Text from the Common Crawl". In *Proceedings of the 51st Annual Meeting of the Association for Computational Linguistics, ACL 2013, 4–9 August 2013, Sofia, Bulgaria*, Vol. 1: *Long Papers*, 1374–1383.

Stejskal, J. 2010. *Freelance Translators Talk about Machine Translation*. Available from: http://www.cetra.com/blog/freelance-translators-talk-about-machine-translation [Accessed 9 November 2015].

TED Conferences n.d. a. *TED Open Translation Project*. Available from: https://www.ted.com/about/ programs-initiatives/ted-open-translation-project [Accessed 9 January 2016].

TED Conferences n.d. b. *Get Started*. Available from: https://www.ted.com/participate/translate/get-started [Accessed 21 January 2016].

Thomas, J. 2015. *The Internet is Killing the World's Languages: Can Google Help?* Available from: http://bigthink.com/connected/language-extinction-google [Accessed 23 February 2016].

Thomas, M., ed. 2009. *Handbook of Research on Web 2.0 and Second Language Learning*. Hershey: Information Science Reference.

Tiedemann, J. 2012. "Parallel Data, Tools and Interfaces in OPUS". *Proceedings of the 8th International Conference on Language Resources and Evaluation (LREC 2012)*, 21–27 May, Istanbul, Turkey, 2214–2218.

Timmis, I. 2015. *Corpus Linguistics for ELT: Research and Practice*. Abingdon: Routledge.

Usability.gov. 2015. *Writing for the Web*. Available from: http://www.usability.gov/how-to-and-tools/ methods/writing-for-the-web.html [Accessed 10 December 2015].

van der Meer, J. and Joscelyne, A. 2013. *Clarifying Copyright on Translation Data*. Available from: https://www.taus.net/think-tank/articles/translate-articles/clarifying-copyright-on-translation-data [Accessed 12 December 2015].

W3Techs. 2017. *Usage Statistics of Content Languages for Websites, February 2016*. Available from: http:// [Accessed 30 August 2017].

Wikimedia. 2014. "Meta: Translate Extension". Available from: http://meta.wikimedia.org/wiki/Meta: Translate_extension, date updated 3 April 2014 [Accessed 27 August 2014].

Wikipedia. 2015a. "List of Lists of Lists". Available from: https://en.wikipedia.org/wiki/List_of_lists_ of_lists [Accessed 21 July 2015].

Wikipedia. 2015b. "Wikipedia: Translation". Available from: http://en.wikipedia.org/wiki/Wikipedia: Translation, date updated 3 November 2015 [Accessed 9 November 2015].

Wikipedia. 2016a. "Category Articles Needing Translation from Foreign-language Wikipedias". Available from: https://en.wikipedia.org/wiki/Category:Articles_needing_translation_from_foreign-language_Wikipedias [Accessed 28 January 2016].

Wikipedia. 2016b. "Category Translated Pages". Available from: https://en.wikipedia.org/wiki/Category:Translated_pages [Accessed 28 January 2016].

Wikipedia. 2016c. "Wikipedia: Manual of Style". Available from: https://en.wikipedia.org/wiki/Wikipedia:Manual_of_Style, date updated 28 February 2016 [Accessed 29 February 2016].

Wikipedia. 2016d. "Wikipedia: Pages Needing Translation into English". Available from: https://en.wikipedia.org/wiki/Wikipedia:Pages_needing_translation_into_English, date updated 28 January 2016 [Accessed 28 January 2016].

Wikipedia 2016e. "Wikipedia: Writing Better Articles". Available from: https://en.wikipedia.org/wiki/Wikipedia:Writing_better_articles, date updated 16 February 2016 [Accessed 29 February 2016].

Wikipedia. 2017. "List of Wikipedias". Available from: http://en.wikipedia.org/wiki/List_of_Wikipedias [Accessed 30 August 2017].

Wilcock, S. 2013. *A Comparative Analysis of Fansubbing and Professional DVD Subtitling*, unpublished MA Thesis, University of Johannesburg. Available from: https://ujdigispace.uj.ac.za/handle/10210/8638 [Accessed 14 February 2016].

Yang, J. and Lange, E. D. 2003. "Going Live on the Internet". In *Computers and Translation: A Translator's Guide*, edited by H. L. Somers, 191–210. Amsterdam: John Benjamins.

Zanettin, F. 2002. "DIY Corpora: The WWW and the Translator". In *Training the Language Services Provider for the New Millennium*, edited by B. Maia, J. Haller and M. Ulrych, 239–248. Porto: Faculdade de Letras da Universidade do Porto.

Translation, interpreting and new technologies

Michael Carl and Sabine Braun

Introductions and definitions

The translation of written language, the translation of spoken language and interpreting have traditionally been separate fields of education and expertise, and the technologies that emulate and/or support those human activities have been developed and researched using different methodologies and by different groups of researchers. Although recent increase in synergy between these well-established fields has begun to blur the boundaries, this section will adhere to the three-fold distinction and begin by giving an overview of key concepts in relation to written-language translation and technology, including computer-assisted translation (CAT) and fully automatic machine translation (MT). This will be followed by an overview of spoken-language translation and technology, which will make a distinction between written translation products (speech-to-text translation, STT) and spoken translation products (speech-to-speech translation, SST). The key concepts of information and communications technology (ICT) supported interpreting, which is currently separate from the technological developments in written- and spoken-language translation, will be outlined in a third section and a fourth will provide an overview of current usages of translation and interpreting technologies.

Written-language translation and technology

There is a great range of MT systems, based on different philosophies and computer algorithms, with different advantages and disadvantages, but a feature they all share is that they are normally used as fully automatic devices, translating a source text into a target language without human intervention. In contrast, human translation, or for short simply translation, is an exclusively human activity without intervention by machines or collaboration between humans and machines, other than interaction with a word processor and perhaps use of electronic dictionaries.

Between these extremes there is a plethora of tools and workbenches available that support human translators in their translation tasks (cf. http://en.wikibooks.org/wiki/CAT-Tools). Depending on the extent to which computers or humans are in the centre of the translation task, a more fine-grained distinction exists between CAT and human-assisted machine translation (HAMT). Using a computer (typically a PC) to draft or format a translation is not normally considered to be a kind of CAT, even though, in a strict sense, this usage of the term would be justified. As the term is commonly used, CAT implies at least the use of electronic mono- or bilingual dictionaries, terminologies, collocation or (bi-)concordance tools, and typically translation memories. In more sophisticated versions of HAMT, an MT system would be at the core of the translation process. As the accuracy and speed of computational devices are increasing, novel forms of human–machine interaction in translation, such as interactive translation assistance, usage of multiple modalities, integration of written and spoken language, gesture and handwriting recognition, optical character recognition (OCR), speech synthesis, etc., are being explored and are likely to become part of professional translation environments in the near future. These tools can – at least in principle – be combined in almost any configuration. In practice a number of workbenches exist to facilitate and support the human translation processes in various different ways.

Translation memory systems (TMs) are often used as a synonym for CAT tools. TMs do not translate by themselves. Rather, they retrieve close matches of a source-language string from a bilingual database (a so-called translation memory) and display the translation(s) associated with the retrieved segments to a translator for him/her to adjust. For this to be possible, a translation memory of aligned translations first has to be created on a segment-by-segment basis. A number of alignment tools are available to carry out this process either interactively or fully automatically. A TM also computes the similarity between the sentence to be translated and similar source-language sentences in the translation memory. The comparison is mostly based on orthographic similarity. The assumption is that similar source sentences have similar translations so that the translator can select and adapt a translation of a similar source segment. Indeed, translators are often paid by the degree of similarity: 100% identical segments are considered to require no work on the part of the translator and are therefore often not paid at all.

Given the increased quality of MT system output, the use of fully automatic translation is constantly growing. Unlike TMs, MT systems generate "proper" translations from source texts, often based on carefully selected and tuned resources. However, depending on the expected quality of the translation product, post-editing of MT output (PEMT) is often necessary to bring the raw MT output in line with the intended purpose of the translation and to erase major translation errors and flaws that would hinder or inhibit the comprehension of the translated text. A number of MT post-editing platforms have emerged recently to facilitate this process. Like TM systems they show each source-text segment together with its MT output for post-editing (O'Brien *et al.* 2014). Post-editors usually receive a translation brief specifying the intended audience and the expected quality of the final translation product. Given the tremendous variety of resources used in an MT system – including bilingual dictionaries, phrase translations and their source-target alignments etc. – integrated MT post-editing platforms are being developed that facilitate interactive human intervention by supporting post-editors in selecting from alternative partial translations, tracing partial translations, visualising confidence scores, etc.

Spoken-language translation and technology

With regard to spoken-language translation, technological developments are still in their infancy. Automatic spoken-language translation systems are a concatenation of automatic speech recognition (ASR) and machine translation (MT) systems with an optional speech synthesis system for spoken target-language output. Transcribed speech (i.e. the output of ASR systems) differs significantly from written text. ASR output therefore requires a number of additional modifications to be suitable input for MT systems. Some of the characteristic features of spoken language, i.e. hesitations (hmm, uh, etc.), discourse markers ("well", "you know"), self-corrections ("it is – it was . . ."), repetitions and incomplete sentences produce ill-formed text that may be difficult to understand even for human readers. In addition, as ASR systems (seek to) generate a faithful transcript of the spoken words, the transcribed output also lacks segmentation and punctuation marks, making it difficult to determine when a sequence ends and is "ready" to be translated. This creates problems for MT systems which normally expect well-formed and sentence-segmented written input text. A number of operations are thus necessary to reformat and map the output of the ASR system to fit the input requirements of MT systems.

Most currently available speech translation systems operate in a consecutive fashion whereby a speaker inputs an utterance, the system processes and translates the spoken signal and outputs the translation either in written form (STT) or spoken form (SST). There are only a few speech translation systems that simultaneously translate unsegmented, continuous speech (Cho *et al.* 2014).

ICT-supported interpreting

Whilst SST is still scarce, the evolution of ICT has created ample opportunities for distance communication in real time and has led to ICT-supported human interpreting as an alternative to delivering human interpreting services onsite. On the one hand, mobile and internet telephony has facilitated conference calls with participants in two or more locations. On the other hand, videoconferencing has established itself as a tool for verbal and visual interaction in real time, including between two or more sites.

Regarding the underlying technology, telephone-based and videoconference-based/video-mediated interpreting are the two established methods of ICT-supported interpreting today. Two main uses can be distinguished on the basis of the physical or geographical distribution of the participants, including the interpreter.

One of these, remote interpreting (RI), is the use of communication technologies to gain access to an interpreter in another room, building, town, city or country. In this setting, a telephone line or videoconference link is used to connect the interpreter to the primary participants, who are together at one site. RI by telephone is often called telephone interpreting or over-the-phone interpreting. RI by videoconference is often simply called remote interpreting in relation to spoken-language interpreting. In sign-language interpreting, the term video remote interpreting has established itself. RI can be used in connection with simultaneous, consecutive and dialogue interpreting.

The second method has emerged from the demand for interpreting in telephone calls or videoconferences between parties at different sites who do not share the same language, i.e. for interpreter-mediated telephone or videoconference communication (e.g. bilingual or multilingual virtual meetings, bail hearings by video link between courts and prisons, doctor–patient phone calls or video links). In this setting, the interpreter is either co-located with one of the parties or at a separate site. The latter configuration leads to a multi-point telephone or videoconference connection. The method of interpreting required in this setting can be termed teleconference interpreting to cover both telephone and videoconference communication. However, the terms, "telephone interpreting" and "videoconference interpreting" have also been used here (Braun and Taylor 2012a; Braun 2015; Mouzourakis 2006).

Remote and teleconference interpreting have different underlying motivations but overlap to a certain extent, most notably in multi-point telephone or videoconferences. In the conference interpreting market, this combination is on the rise due to an increasing number of webinars and other events with distributed participants, and has become known as webcast interpreting. It was included as a new category in the AIIC 2012 conference interpreter survey (AIIC 2014). Webcast interpreting involves conference interpreters working in a team for remote audiences whilst being remote from each other rather than sharing a booth. The connection can be telephone- or videoconference based.

Usage of translation and interpreting technologies

Figure 24.1 summarises the different methods of translation and interpreting. The bottom of the pyramid reflects the market for MT and SST systems, which is known as the "gisting" market. With the emergence of Google's translation service this market segment has grown tremendously and is by now the biggest sector of the translation market. Google started its translation service in 2002 with five languages, and by 2017 served over 100 languages. Google translation services are used by more than 500 million people every month, producing more than 1 billion translations a day. Every day, Google translates more text than all human translators translate together in a whole year. Google translates web pages, tweets, blogs or communications via email or chat systems, using online MT systems as the translation engine. Translation quality is often far from perfect but in most cases users get access to content which would otherwise not be available to them.

Demand for remote and teleconference interpreting varies across fields. In relation to telephone-based interpreting, an analysis of over 1,000 instances by Rosenberg (2007) showed that, at the time of his study, demand for remote interpreting mainly arose from migration and associated language policies, and that it was most widely used in healthcare settings whilst interpreting in three-way telephone conversations was more common in the business world. Variations across fields can also be identified in relation to videoconference-based interpreting. In the commercial conference market, videoconference interpreting in the form of interpreting for remote speakers during a conference is more frequent than remote interpreting but in most regions of the world both categories are outstripped by the emerging method of webcast interpreting (AIIC 2014). However, having conducted initial tests with both videoconference and remote interpreting, the European institutions, which are large users of conference interpreting services, remain mainly interested in remote interpreting (see section on "Core issues and main research methods" below). In healthcare settings, remote interpreting is in high demand, but the growing trend towards tele-healthcare will also require the integration of interpreters into video calls between doctors and patients. In legal settings, both videoconference and remote interpreting have begun to establish themselves.

High-quality translation can be achieved by MT systems for restricted domains and/or controlled languages or when tuning the MT system to the type of texts to be translated. For instance, due to its very particular domain, the Météo system (Chandioux 1988) was a big success story in the history of MT long before the emergence of Google, providing perfect translations for weather forecasts from French into English. Whilst the original Météo implementation was a rule-based system, later statistical implementations on the same domain provided equally good results (Gotti, Langlais and Lapalme 2014). However, the adaptation of the system for another domain (aviation) proved unsuccessful. Fully Automatic High Quality Translation (FAHQT) can thus be achieved for limited domains and by training MT systems to produce a particular type of texts, but for general use with a wide range of text

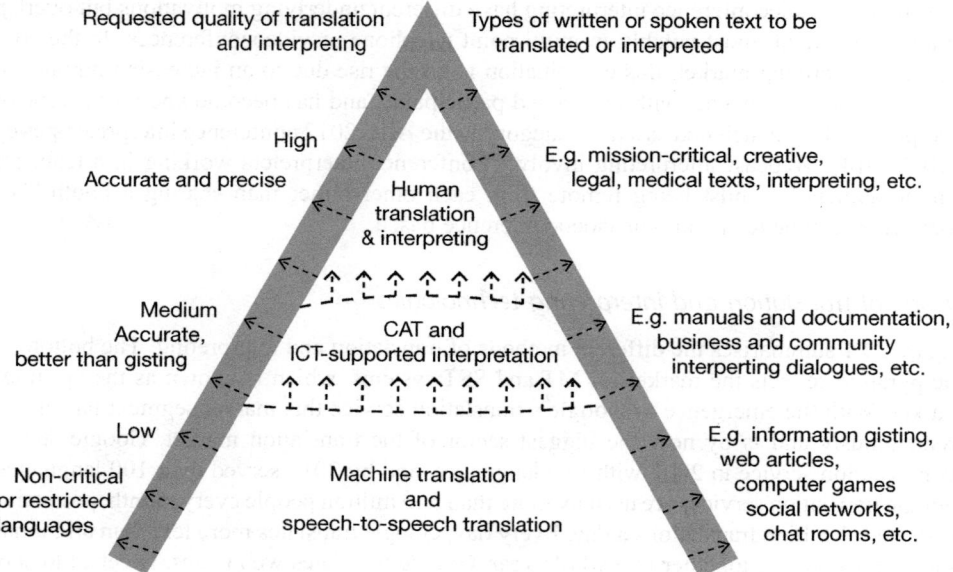

Requested quality of translation and interpreting

Types of written or spoken text to be translated or interpreted

High
Accurate and precise

Human translation & interpreting

E.g. mission-critical, creative, legal, medical texts, interpreting, etc.

Medium
Accurate, better than gisting

CAT and ICT-supported interpretation

E.g. manuals and documentation, business and community interpering dialogues, etc.

Low
Non-critical or restricted languages

Machine translation and speech-to-speech translation

E.g. information gisting, web articles, computer games social networks, chat rooms, etc.

Figure 24.1 Information that users want to have translated

types, it remains "a dream which will not come true in the foreseeable future" (Bar-Hillel 1960), just as in 1960.

The requirement for reliable high-quality translation of less restricted languages can often only be met through from-scratch translation, usage of CAT tools or MT post-editing. However, as discussed above, the market for translation aides and computer-assisted translation is changing and developing at a quick pace, and many new and innovative products are emerging. In contrast to fully automated translation, the post-editor is the integral figure involved in every part during the computer-assisted translation process, to accept or reject translation suggestions, or to insert translation proposals into the target document wherever deemed appropriate.

Professional interpreting is normally required in contexts that are situated at the upper end of the triangle. Some tensions arise from the growing client-side demand for ICT-supported interpreting services, especially remote interpreting, whilst it is currently difficult to be sure whether these methods of interpreting can be associated with the same levels of accuracy and precision as onsite interpreting (Braun 2013; Roziner and Shlesinger 2010).

Historical perspectives

The beginnings of machine translation

In 1949, Warren Weaver became the first person to propose using computers for machine translation. After the successful decoding of German and Japanese military messages during WWII (as generated by the Enigma machine), his idea was that translation of one language into another would be similar to the task of decoding a message. A few years later, in 1954, an MT project at Georgetown University succeeded in correctly translating 60 sentences from Russian into English, resulting in unprecedented euphoria in MT research.

It was then apparent that the process of machine translation would require a formalisation of the syntax of natural language and associated automata for parsing with these grammars; this led to a highly productive period in computer science during which the foundations for programming languages and compilers were laid and pertinent theories of language were postulated in linguistics (Chomsky 1957).

However, 10 years later the Automatic Language Processing Advisory Committee (ALPAC 1966) published a study which expressed doubt that a MT system could ever be produced, based on the assumption that understanding human language relies on information which is not present in the words which make up the message. Instead ALPAC called for investigations of which texts were suitable for automatic translation and which were not, what tools would be helpful to support human translators and how translation aides could be successfully integrated into the human translation workflow. In the 1980s, concrete suggestions for implementing such systems were made (Kay 1998), although the investigation of cognitive processes in CAT received little attention before the early decades of the 21st century (cf. Carl, Bangalore and Schaeffer 2015).

Rule-based machine translation

Interest in MT was revived in the 1980s, following unprecedented development of computer hardware (PCs and cheaper storage capacity), innovative programming languages (LISP and Prolog) and modern linguistic formalisms such as Generalised Phrase Structure Grammar (GPSG; Gazdar *et al.* 1985), Tree-Adjoining Grammar (TAG; Joshi 1985), Lexical-Functional Grammar (LFG; Bresnan and Kaplan 1985), Combinatory Categorial Grammar (CCG; Steedman 1987) and Head-driven Phrase Structure Grammar (HPSG; Pollard and Sag 1994), which were tailored to the new programming languages and suited to formalising the structure of natural languages. A number of theoretical approaches and processing strategies for MT emerged based on these new developments, including direct MT, transfer-based MT and interlingua MT, which, at that time, relied mainly on rule-based formalisms.

The syntactic frameworks were subsequently augmented with formal representations of semantics. The idea was that the semantic expression of a natural-language text would be compositionally derived from the semantic expressions of words in the lexicon and combination rules. The semantic expressions would be devoid of the syntactic variations and vagaries of any particular language and hence two natural-language expressions representing the same "meaning" would result in the same semantic representation. This desideratum is a prerequisite for the Interlingua-based Machine Translation approach (cf. e.g. Eurotra), which, however, has not proved helpful in dealing with general texts at the time of writing.

Statistical machine translation

In the early 1990s, the availability of digitised corpora of real-world texts and translations prompted a technological challenge to process texts using tools from computational linguistics. The plan was to decompose available bilingual texts into large amounts of possible phrase translations, store them in databases and recompose new translations based on combinations of the most likely translation snippets. It soon became apparent that the tools then available for language processing could not deal with the complexities of real-world texts. For example, the tools were designed to provide all possible analyses for a given sentence which could run into thousands of analyses for even simple sentences with no indication of a preferred analysis. Consequently, the computational linguistics community turned to statistical models of language that were prevalent in information theory and speech recognition communities.

A group of researchers from IBM (Brown *et al.* 1988) re-vitalised Weaver's initial idea of translation as a form of language decoding and formalised this approach in terms of a noisy channel model (Brown *et al.* 1993). Given a large amount of data and sufficient computational power, statistical models could be trained on bilingual texts and applied to decode (i.e. translate) unseen sentences. This line of research has been further developed into log-linear modelling (Och and Ney 2002) and into what is known as phrase-based statistical machine translation (PB-SMT). It is now the main MT paradigm that underlies Google translate and a number of research prototypes such as Moses (Koehn et al. 2007) or Thot (Ortiz-Martõnez and Casacuberta 2014). Besides this, tools using rule-based approaches such as Systran and PROMT (see http://www.prompt.com/), developed in the pre-statistical period, have found their niche and continue to survive.

Speech-to-speech translation

Automatic speech recognition (ASR) dates back to the early 1950s, but the principal technological component(s) that are still used in ASR systems (i.e. the Hidden Markov Model, HMM) were introduced in the 1970s in the context of a five-year research project on speech recognition systems funded by the Defense Advanced Research Project Agency (DARPA), an agency of the US Department of Defense responsible for the development of emerging technologies for use by the military (Waibel and Lee 1990).

Automatic *translation* of speech, however, is a more recent development. Research into SST has attracted high levels of funding since the 1990s, including the German VERBMOBIL project (1993–2000), which received approximately €90 million (Wahlster and Karger 2000; http://verbmobil.dfki.de/overview-us.html), the US-led C-Star initiative (1991–2004) and the European PF-Star and TC-Star projects (2002–2004 and 2004–2007). VERBMOBIL aimed at the development of SST in restricted domains (e.g. appointment-making). More recently, after the acquisition of Skype by Microsoft in 2011, Skype Translator was released in 2014. It provides a written translation of a conversation in near-real time (for six languages at the time of writing) and can convert the translated output into speech. It is designed to deal with specific features of spoken language such as incomplete sentences. Whilst these projects have doubtlessly moved the topic of SST forward, at the time of writing they could not be applied to situations in which highly accurate professional interpreting is required. Bilingual and multilingual communication in professional settings often involves complex multi-topic and multi-party interaction and may require simultaneous interpreting (i.e. a rendition whilst a speaker is talking) into, and out of, several languages. At the time of writing, available SST systems struggled to resolve the many pragmatic intricacies of spoken interaction (from e.g. ambiguity, vagueness and differences between what is said and meant to intercultural communication problems and non-native accents/varieties of English) in a reliable manner.

ICT-supported interpreting

The first service for telephone-based interpreting was established by the Australian immigration service in 1973. In the US and in most Western European countries, such services have been offered since the 1980s and 1990s respectively (Mikkelson 2003). Although some telephone interpreting services have been replaced by videoconference-based interpreting services, telephone-based interpreting remains a large market (Commonsense Advisory 2011). With the spread of telephone interpreting, the method has seen improvements in the technology used (e.g. dual-headset phones for clients to listen to a remotely located interpreter).

The development of video-mediated interpreting was originally driven by the interest of supra-national institutions in ICT-supported interpreting as a means of optimising access to interpreters and meeting linguistic demand. The earliest experiment was organised by UNESCO in 1976 to test the use of the Symphonie satellite. It linked the UNESCO headquarters in Paris with a conference centre in Nairobi and involved remote interpreting by telephone, and video link and interpreting in a videoconference between Paris and Nairobi. Similar experiments were organised by the UN later in the 1970s and 1980s (Viaggio 2011; Mouzourakis 1996).

From the 1990s, a series of feasibility studies of video-mediated remote interpreting (in simultaneous mode) was organised by various institutions, including the European Telecommunications Standard Institute (ETSI) in 1993 (Böcker and Anderson 1993), the European Commission in 1995, 1997 and 2000, the United Nations in 1999 and 2001, the International Telecommunications Union (ITU) in collaboration with the École de Traduction et d'Interprétation (ETI) in 1999 (Moser-Mercer 2003), the European Council in 2001, and the European Parliament in 2001 and 2004. The studies revealed a range of physiological and psychological problems which recurred in different technical conditions and which seemed to be caused by the overarching condition of remoteness (Mouzourakis 2006).

Whilst the feasibility studies cited above involved comparisons of real-life or test performances in onsite and remote interpreting, a more recent study conducted by the Fraunhofer Institute for the Interpreting Service of the European Commission (SCIC) in 2010 aimed to define minimum standards for video and audio transmission in the context of remote simultaneous interpreting. This resulted in a comprehensive list of technological recommendations (Causo 2012).

A major driving force of the spread of video-mediated interpreting in legal settings was the increasing use of videoconference technology in the court systems of many Anglo-Saxon countries since the 1990s, e.g. to link courts and prisons for pre-trial hearings (Braun and Taylor 2012; Ellis 2004; Fowler 2013). This entailed a demand for videoconference interpreting rather than remote interpreting whereby the interpreter is co-located with one of the parties. Early videoconference systems, which were ISDN (Integrated Services Digital Network)-based, led to problems with sound and image quality for interpreters. More recent videoconferencing systems that use high-speed internet connections provide better audio and video quality and are more conducive to videoconference-based interpreting (Braun and Taylor 2012). Remote interpreting has been introduced more recently in courts and by the police, mainly as a way of gaining timely access to interpreters and reducing interpreter travel time and cost (e.g. Florida district courts since 2007; the Metropolitan Police in London since 2011).

The spread of videoconferencing has also promoted video-mediated interpreting services in healthcare (Locatis et al. 2010; Price et al. 2012). At the time of writing, healthcare providers mainly need remote interpreting, but developments in tele-healthcare, whereby doctors make video calls to patients who are in their own home, are likely to create more diversified demand for video-mediated healthcare interpreting. At the same time, the availability of web- or cloud-based videoconference services providing varying and unstable sound and image quality, and access to them on tablets and other mobile devices, raises new questions about the feasibility of video-mediated interpreting using such systems.

Core issues and main research methods

Machine translation

One of the main difficulties in MT is the inherent ambiguity in natural languages and the fact that different languages encode information in different ways:

- Analytic languages (such as Vietnamese and Chinese) have little or no inflectional morphology, and individual words tend to consist of single morphemes. In contrast, synthetic languages such as Finnish, Turkish or Japanese make use of inflectional morphology and agglutinate several morphemes into one word. For instance, Turkish "*ev-ler-iniz-den*" (English: "from your houses") can be decomposed as "house-plural-your-from".
- Languages differ widely in the way clause elements are ordered. Most languages have the order, subject-object-verb (SOV), whilst the languages with the greatest speaker numbers, including Chinese and English, use the order, subject-verb-object (SVO). However, each of the possible order permutations is represented in the languages of the world.
- Lexical mismatches occur when translating, for instance, English "brother" into Japanese, where a choice needs to be made between older brother (*anisan*) or younger brother (*otouto*). Similarly, English makes a distinction between "pig" and "pork" according to whether the word refers to an animal or meat, something that may not be specified in all possible source-language contexts.
- Categorial, conflational, structural, thematic and other translation divergences (Dorr, 1994) add to translation difficulties: for instance, Spanish "*tener hambre*" (have hunger; verb (have) + noun) translates into English with a different part of speech as "be hungry" (verb (be) + adjective). Several disconnected words, such as English "make X easier" may translate into a single word, e.g. German "*X erleichtern*". In some cases structural changes are required, as when translating Spanish "*A entrar en B*" into English "A enters B" or a change of the thematic role from Spanish "*John gustar a Klaus*", which is equivalent to English "Klaus likes John".
- Homonyms, words that are written in a similar way but have different meanings can also add to translation difficulties. For instance, English "odd" has two meanings ("uneven" in connection with numbers and "strange") but these meanings are realised differently in other languages. A distinction can be made between homographs and homophones. The latter are words with different spelling but identical or similar pronunciation, whilst homographs have identical spelling but differ in pronunciation (e.g. the present tense and past tense of English "read"). Homophones formed of multiple words or phrases such as "the sky" vs. "this guy" may be difficult for ASR systems to decode correctly.

Unluckily, several of these phenomena may (and often do!) occur at the same time within a single sentence, making translation a difficult endeavour. In addition, these linguistic translation problems are complemented by cultural and contextual adaptations of the translated content.

As pointed out above, the obvious limitations of analytical and rule-based methods led to the use of machine-learning methods in MT in the 1990s, taking advantage of the fact that "existing translations contain more solutions to more translation problems than any other available resource" (Isabelle *et al.* 1993, 205). Accordingly, much translation research in the past two decades has been corpus based and concerned with methods to extract and make accessible from bilingual texts the required knowledge for translation. One bottleneck for data-driven MT methods consists in a lack of a sufficient amount of exploitable bilingual texts (i.e. translations with their source texts). Due to the combinatorial complexity of human languages, millions of parallel source-target sentences are required to extract statistically reliable figures for word and phrase translation relations. In addition, in some cases the necessary translation knowledge cannot even be extracted from the texts alone, but requires "world knowledge" including knowledge about the situation in which the source texts are produced and/or the audience for which the translations are intended to be produced. Machine translation technology therefore increasingly incorporates capabilities for domain adaptation, online learning and incremental learning.

Speech-to-speech translation

In relation to SST, one of the core issues is real-time constraints: SST systems need to be tuned to strike a balance between the size of the acoustic and language models, the search beam (i.e. how many hypotheses are considered in a search graph) and run-time behaviour. Larger search graphs and bigger models allow for more accurate output, but also require more computation time, which, given the complex processing chain ASR–MT–TTS (text to speech), cannot be optimally computed in real time. A balance must be struck to translate the spoken signal within an acceptable timeframe whilst not allowing the quality of the translation to deteriorate to an unacceptable degree.

A different, but related research topic in the development of SST systems centres around removing dysfluencies (hesitations, self-corrections, repetitions, etc.) from the ASR output and tackling ungrammatical or incomplete sentences. A means of inspiration may be human interpreters who often produce condensed target texts, discarding individual words, or substituting longer phrases with shorter target-language versions, particularly in cases of very fast and/or dysfluent speech.

This research topic is also linked to the strategies used to insert punctuation marks into the ASR output, which ensures semantically consistent segments that provide an appropriate basis for generating optimal MT output.

ICT-supported interpreting

Although research topics focusing on ICT-supported interpreting are, on the whole, different from those relating to MT and SST, output quality emerges as a common denominator. Studies comparing the quality of onsite and video-mediated remote (simultaneous) interpreting in conference settings have identified few differences between the two methods, apart from earlier onset of fatigue in remote interpreting (Moser-Mercer 2003; Roziner and Shlesinger 2010). By contrast, research comparing onsite and video-mediated (consecutive) interpreting in legal settings revealed significant quality differences as well as earlier onset of fatigue in remote interpreting (Braun 2013; Braun and Taylor 2012). In the field of healthcare, a comparison of onsite consecutive interpreting and remote simultaneous interpreting via audio connection found higher accuracy levels in the latter (Hornberger *et al.* 1996), although some of the differences may have resulted from the different modes of interpreting.

Many studies have gone beyond researching output quality and also elicited data on ergonomic factors and working conditions. Comprehensive studies on remote conference interpreting, for example, point to a number of psychological and physiological problems including stress, a general sense of discomfort among interpreters when working remotely and interpreters' self-reported fatigue and dissatisfaction with their own performance (Moser-Mercer 2003; Roziner and Shlesinger 2010).

Studies in the field of healthcare and legal interpreting have also elicited user perceptions and preferences. A number of studies conducted from a healthcare management perspective have surveyed medical interpreters, physicians and patients to ascertain the efficiency of ICT-supported interpreting compared with onsite interpreting (Azarmina and Wallace 2005; Locatis *et al.* 2010; Price *et al.* 2012). This work shows that interpreters and physicians generally prefer onsite interpreting and that they prefer video-mediated to telephone-based interpreting. Notably, however, the interpreters surveyed by Price *et al.* (2012) found all three methods satisfactory for conveying information, whilst rating the ICT-supported methods as less satisfactory for interpersonal aspects of communication due to greater difficulties in establishing a rapport with the remote participants. Patients were relatively uncritical in their judgement, possibly because of a perception that any interpretation is better than none. Based on the self-perceptions of the participating interpreters, some of the surveys furthermore suggest that levels of accuracy in onsite and ICT-supported interpreting are similar (Azarmina and Wallace 2005), but research in the legal setting reveals discrepancies between interpreters' self-perception of their performance and objective performance analysis (Braun and Taylor 2012).

Furthermore, qualitative, observation-based research has identified changes in the communicative dynamics in videoconference-based, interpreter-mediated legal communication as well as logistical and communication problems resulting from specific participant distributions (Ellis 2004; Fowler 2007). Experimental research using simulations has explored the cognitive processes and strategies interpreters employ to address the challenges of ICT-supported interpreting (Braun 2004, 2007, 2017). This work has highlighted adaptation processes especially with regard to coordinating the communication, but has also provided evidence for the increased cognitive effort required to resolve communication problems arising, for example, from listening comprehension difficulties and coordination problems in videoconferences as a possible reason for the perception that ICT-based interpreting is more tiring than onsite interpreting.

Current debates and future directions

Machine translation and post-editing

In relation to some language pairs (e.g. English–Spanish) and text types, MT output has reached a degree of quality that makes post-editing (PEMT) effective. In order to facilitate the post-editing process in the best possible way, a number of techniques are being developed and piloted to assist a human post-editor with additional automatised translation aides and real-time techniques.

During Online Learning the MT system incrementally updates its (statistical) models that are involved in the translation process. This enables the system to learn dynamically from corrections during the post-editing process and potentially leads to higher acceptance rates of MT output, since the same translation errors that appear within one text do not need to be corrected over and over again.

During Active Learning the MT re-orders sentences of the source text in a way that enables the best learning results from the modifications produced by a post-editor. The MT system selectively asks a human translator to correct a small portion of the translation so as to optimise the results of the MT system for the remaining sentences.

Interactive machine translation (IMT) assists a human translator by predicting the next piece of text that s/he is likely to input. In the process, the system takes into account all the information it has available both in the source text and in the translation already produced.

A number of browser-based and stand-alone post-editing workbenches are being implemented and piloted for PEMT. The advantages and disadvantages of translation crowdsourcing are subject to ongoing discussion. The term crowdsourcing was coined by Jeff Howe in the *Wired* magazine in 2006 to denote a "process of obtaining needed services, ideas, or content by soliciting contributions from a large group of people, and especially from an online community, rather than from traditional employees or suppliers" (Merriam-Webster).

Translation crowdsourcing is by now well established, and a number of companies have emerged using the web and web portals to realise translation projects. Facebook, for instance, had the entire site translated into French through crowdsourcing in March 2008. The advantages of translation crowdsourcing include shorter delays and lower prices compared to traditional translation. Some companies offer also PEMT for crowdsourcing, which is even more cost-effective. Major issues in translation crowdsourcing are quality control of the translation product and project management.

ICT-supported interpreting

In ICT-supported interpreting one of the points of contention is the quality of ICT-based interpreting performance. Whilst some of the discrepancies highlighted above may be due to different variables, research designs and quality measures, the different findings in relation to conference interpreting (little difference between onsite and remote interpreting) and legal interpreting (significant differences) give rise to questions about the impact of training on the adaptability of interpreters to the challenges of ICT-based interpreting.

A similar issue is the discrepancy between "objective" and "subjective" measures, especially in studies on remote conference interpreting. Whilst these studies found little difference between onsite and remote interpreting in terms of output quality, they revealed a number of differences in the interpreters' perceptions of the two methods (Roziner and Shlesinger 2010). Mouzourakis (2006) contends that this discrepancy ultimately points to a deficit in our current understanding of the notion of remoteness and the challenges associated with it.

A further related point concerns the relative difficulty of remote interpreting (i.e. interpreter completely separated from the main parties) and teleconference interpreting (interpreter co-located with some participants). Remote interpreting is generally perceived to be more challenging, a view that is reflected in the guidance on the use of technologies in conference interpreting issued by the AIIC (2000/2012), which rejects remote interpreting whilst agreeing to teleconference interpreting (under specific circumstances).

Following the increase of videoconference interpreting in the legal sector, one of the questions arising concerns the "best" place for the interpreter. Comparing the options – i.e. interpreter co-located with the judicial authorities vs. interpreter co-located with the minority-language speaker – Ellis (2004) and Miler-Casino and Rybinska (2011) highlight important differences between the two configurations, e.g. concerning the rapport between interpreter and minority-language speaker.

Another point of discussion concerns access to visual information in ICT-supported interpreting and the suitability of telephone interpreting. Kelly (2008) cites a number of advantages, but Ozolins (2011) believes that her description mostly refers to the US, where the size of the market and the dominant role of Spanish have led to a level of sophistication in terms of technology use and logistics that is unlikely to be found in many other countries.

This debate is linked to the interpreters' working conditions. Ko (2006) and Lee (2007), for example, argue that the generally high levels of dissatisfaction associated with telephone interpreting partly stem from the working conditions, including low remuneration, rather than from the use of the technology as such. There is also a debate as to whether ICT-supported interpreting, due to its potential challenges, should command higher fees than onsite interpreting.

One of the most pressing questions for future research into ICT-supported interpreting is to resolve apparent discrepancies in current research findings (see above). Moser-Mercer (2005) and Mouzourakis (2006) suggest that the condition of remoteness or the lack of "presence" may be the most likely common denominator for the problems with remote interpreting. The concept of "presence" and its effects will require a substantial amount of further research.

Furthermore, Moser-Mercer (2005) has raised questions about the ways in which different groups of interpreters adapt to remote interpreting, and the reasons for variations in this process, arguing that experienced interpreters may find it difficult to adapt to the conditions of remote interpreting because they rely on automated processes, whilst novice interpreters, especially when they are subjected to new methods of interpreting during their training, may have a greater potential for adaptation. Braun (2004, 2007) reveals a number of limits to successful adaptation in video-mediated interpreting which lead to a reduction in performance. Roziner and Shlesinger (2010) argue that the maintenance of the performance quality in ICT-supported interpreting comes at a price, i.e. that interpreters put more effort into the interpreting task than they do in other settings and may suffer post-work exhaustion. The issue of adaptation also requires further investigation.

A related consideration is how the physical separation and distribution of all participants and their perception of the situation via technical channels affect aspects such as the processing of information, the communicative behaviour of the primary participants and the communicative dynamic. Moser-Mercer (2005) outlines problems with multi-sensory integration in videoconferences, which she believes prevent interpreters from processing the information and building mental representations of the situation in the usual way. Licoppe and Verdier (2013) suggest that distributed courtrooms change the dynamic of the communication and lead to fragmentation of the communication. The sources and implications of this kind of fragmentation are not very well understood and warrant further study.

Given the speed with which communication technologies develop and spread, the future is likely to bring an increase and diversification of teleconference and remote interpreting. The latest developments which are likely to be relevant for remote interpreting fall into two categories: (i) high-end solutions such as videoconferencing systems (HD and 3D "telepresence" or "immersive" systems) and the merger of videoconferencing with 3D virtual reality technology to create "augmented reality" communication solutions; and (ii) low-end solutions such as web-based videoconferencing services which were originally developed for the home market (e.g. Skype), and video calls using mobile devices and apps. It will be important to investigate how the virtual spaces that these technologies create are able to support the development of "presence" and the dynamic of the communication.

Implications for practice

Translation and interpreting practice has changed tremendously over recent decades. The changes have been brought about by a combination of technological innovation and societal change, especially increased mobility and demand for translation and interpreting in a globalised world.

On the positive side, translators/interpreters have more choices and opportunities to create translations, offer their services, network with colleagues, etc. On the negative side, the introduction of technological tools has often been linked to a deterioration of working conditions and remuneration. Agencies argue, for example, that translators' remuneration can be reduced when translation technology is used to support the production of a translation.

Similarly, the rise of ICT-supported interpreting goes hand in hand with the idea of interpreters being available "at the push of a button" and with an undue simplification of the complexity of interpreting. The introduction of ICT-supported interpreting has thus sparked debate and has raised questions of feasibility and working conditions; but it has also been linked to the efficiency of service provision and the sustainability of the interpreting profession.

Any form of ICT-supported interpreting should be supported by the best possible equipment and connections. Interpreters should be involved in the planning and implementation stages, and an incremental introduction of new technology is recommendable. The room layout, positioning of equipment and seating arrangements for the interpreter and for the other parties need to be considered carefully. Kelly (2008) also highlights the importance of a quiet and undisturbed working environment for the interpreter. She refers to problems that can arise in call centres (or interpreter hubs) where interpreters may disturb each other, and problems caused by background noise when interpreters work from home.

One issue for debate is the length of interpreter-mediated encounters that involve the use of communication technology. Given that research shows a faster onset of fatigue in remote interpreting (Braun 2013; Moser-Mercer 2003), an interpreter's working turn in remote and teleconference interpreting should be shorter than in onsite interpreting.

Given the many challenges of ICT-supported interpreting, interpreters and the users of interpreting services should be trained to work in situations of remote or tele-conference interpreting. The extent of the training required is not yet clear, but recent research in a legal setting suggests that short-term training may not be able to solve all problems (Braun 2017).

Further reading

Braun, S. 2015. "Remote Interpreting". In *Routledge Handbook of Interpreting*, edited by H. Mikkelson and R. Jourdenais, 352–367. New York: Routledge.
This chapter explains the key terms and concepts associated with remote interpreting, gives an overview of the historical development and current trends of remote interpreting in supra-national institutions, legal, healthcare and other settings, referring to practice and to insights from research.

Braun, S. and Taylor, J., eds. 2012a. *Videoconference and Remote Interpreting in Criminal Proceedings*. Antwerp: Intersentia.
This volume covers different configurations of video-mediated interpreting in legal proceedings. The chapters give an overview of practice and research, and presents research findings, suggestions for training and recommendations for best practice.

Roziner, I. and Shlesinger, M. 2010. Much ado about something remote: stress and performance in remote interpreting. *Interpreting* 12(2), pp. 214–247.

Michael Carl and Sabine Braun

This article first gives an overview of research on remote interpreting via telephone and video link with specific regard for conference and medical settings. It compares the findings of two major studies of remote simultaneous interpreting in conference settings.

Schwartz, L. 2017. "The history and promise of machine translation". In *Innovation and Expansion in Translation Process Research*, edited by I. Lacruz, and R. Jääskeläinen. Amsterdam: John Benjamins, ATA series.
An up-to date overview over the history of machine translation.

Related topics

Language and translation on the Web.

References

AIIC. 2000/2012. "Guidelines for the use of new technologies in conference interpreting". *Communicate!* March–April 2000. Available from: http://www.aiic.net/ViewPage.cfm?page_id=120 [Accessed 03 December 2016].
AIIC. 2014. *AIIC statistics: Summary of the 2012 report*. Available from: http://aiic.net/page/6878/aiic-statistics-summary-of-the-2012-report/lang/1 [Accessed 03 December 2016].
ALPAC. 1966. "Language and Machines: Computers in Translation and Linguistics". A report by the Automatic Language Processing Advisory Committee, Division of Behavioral Sciences, National Academy of Sciences, National Research Council. Washington, DC (Publication 1416).
Azarmina, P. and Wallace, P. 2005. Remote interpretation in medical encounters: a systematic review. *Journal of Telemedicine and Telecare* 11, pp. 140–145.
Bar-Hillel, Y. 1960. "A Demonstration of the Nonfeasibility of Fully Automatic High Quality Translation". Appendix III of "The present status of automatic translation of languages". *Advances in Computers* 1, pp. 158–163. Reprinted in Y. Bar-Hillel. 1964. *Language and Information*, 174–179. Reading, MA: Addison-Wesley. Available from: http://www.mt-archive.info/Bar-Hillel-1960-App3.pdf [Accessed 11 January 2016]
Böcker, M. and Anderson, B. 1993. "Remote conference interpreting using ISDN videotelephony: a requirement analysis and feasibility study". In *Proceedings of the Human Factors and Ergonomics Society, 37th Annual Meeting*, 235–239.
Braun, S. 2004. *Kommunikation unter widrigen Umständen? Fallstudien zu einsprachigen und gedolmetschten Videokonferenzen*. Tübingen: Narr.
Braun, S. 2007. Interpreting in small-group bilingual videoconferences: challenges and adaptation. *Interpreting* 9(1), pp. 21–46.
Braun, S. 2013. Keep your distance? Remote interpreting in legal proceedings: a critical assessment of a growing practice. *Interpreting* 15(2), pp. 200–228.
Braun, S. 2017. What a micro-analytical investigation of additions and expansions in remote interpreting can tell us about interpreter's participation in a shared virtual space. *Journal of Pragmatics* 107, pp. 165–177.
Braun, S. and Taylor, J., eds. 2012. *Videoconference and Remote Interpreting in Legal Proceedings*. Cambridge: Intersentia.
Bresnan, J. and Kaplan, R. 1985. *The Mental Representation of Grammatical Relations*. Cambridge, MA: MIT Press.
Brown, P. F., Cocke, J., Della Pietra, S. A., Della Pietra, V. J., Jelinek, F., Mercer, R. L. and Roossin, P. S. 1988. "A Statistical Approach to Language Translation". In *Proceedings of the 12th International Conference on Computational Linguistics, COLING 88*, edited by D. Vargha, 71–76. Budapest: John von Neumann Society for Computing Sciences.

Brown, P. F., Della Pietra, S., Della Pietra, V. and Mercer, R. L. 1993. The mathematics of statistical machine translation: parameter estimation. *Computational Linguistics* 19(2), pp. 263–312.

Carl, M., Bangalore, S. and Schaeffer, M., eds. 2015. *New Directions in Empirical Translation Process Research: Exploring the CRITT TPR-DB*. Berlin: Springer.

Causo, J. E. 2012. "Conference interpreting with information and communication technologies: experiences from the European Commission DG Interpretation". In *Videoconference and Remote Interpreting in Legal Proceedings*, edited by S. Braun and J. Taylor, 227–232. Cambridge: Intersentia.

Chandioux, J. 1988. "METEO: An Operational Translation System". In *Proceeding of the Computer-Assisted Information Retrieval (Recherche d'Information et ses Applications) – RIAO 1988, 2nd International Conference*. Cambridge, MA: Massachusetts Institute of Technology.

Cho, K., van Merrienboer, B., Bahdanau, D. and Bengio, J. 2014. "On the Properties of Neural Machine Translation: Encoder-Decoder Approaches". *arXiv:*1409.1259v2 [cs.CL].

Chomsky, N. 1957. *Syntactic Structures*. The Hague: Mouton.

Commonsense Advisory. 2011. *Trends in Telephone Interpreting*. Available from: https://www.commonsenseadvisory.com/AbstractView.aspx?ArticleID=2102 [Accessed 12 March 2016].

Dorr, B. J. 1994. Machine translation divergences: a formal description and proposed solution. *Computational Linguistics* 20(4), pp. 597–633.

Ellis, R. 2004. *Videoconferencing in Refugee Hearings*. Report to the Immigration and Refugee Board Audit and Evaluation Committee. Available from: http://www.irb-cisr.gc.ca/Eng/transp/ReviewEval/Pages/Video.aspx [Accessed 12 March 2016].

Fowler, Y. 2007. "Interpreting into the Ether: Interpreting for Prison/Court Video Link Hearings". *Paper presented at "The Critical Link 5: Interpreters in the Community"*, Parramatta, Sydney, 11–15 April.

Fowler, Y. 2013. "Business as usual? Prison video link in the multilingual courtroom". In *Interpreting in a Changing Landscape: Selected Papers from Critical Link 6*, edited by C. Schäffner, 225–248. Amsterdam: John Benjamins.

Gazdar, G., Klein, E., Pullum, G. and Sag, I. 1985. *Generalized Phrase Structure Grammar*. Cambridge, MA: Harvard University Press.

Gotti, F., Langlais, P. and Lapalme, G. 2014. Designing a machine translation system for Canadian weather warnings: a case study. *Natural Language Engineering* 20(3), pp. 399–433.

Hornberger, J., Gibson, C., Wood, W., Dequeldre, C., Corso, I., Palla, B. and Bloch, D. 1996. Eliminating language barriers for non-English-speaking patients. *Medical Care* 34(8), pp. 845–856.

Isabelle, P., Dymetman, M., Foster, G., Jutras, J.-M., Macklovitch, E., Perrault, F., Ren, X. and Simard, M. 1993. "Translation Analysis and Translation Automation". In *Proceedings of the Fifth International Conference on Theoretical and Methodological Issues in Machine Translation, TMI '93, Kyoto*, 201–217.

Joshi, A. 1985. "How Much Context-Sensitivity Is Necessary for Characterizing Structural Descriptions/Tree Adjoining Grammars". In *Natural Language Processing: Theoretical, Computational and Psychological Perspectives*, edited by D. Dowty, L. Karttunen, and A. Zwicky, 190–205. New York: Cambridge University Press.

Kay, M. 1998. "Machine Translation: The Disappointing Past and Present". In *Survey of the State of the Art in Human Language Technology*, edited by R. Cole, J. Mariani, H. Uszkoreit, G. Varile, A. Zaenen, and A. Zampolli, 248–251. Cambridge: Cambridge University Press.

Kelly, N., 2008. *Telephone Interpreting: A Comprehensive Guide to the Profession*. Clevedon: Multilingual Matters.

Ko, L. 2006. The need for long-term empirical studies in remote interpreting research: A case study of telephone interpreting. *Linguistica Antverpiensia* 5, pp. 325–338.

Koehn, P., Hoang, H., Birch, A., Callison-Burch, C., Marcello, F., Bertoldi, N., Cowan, B., Shen, W., Moran, C., Zens, R., Dyer, C., Bojar, O., Constantin, A. and Herbst, E. 2007. "Moses: Open Source Toolkit for Statistical Machine Translation". *Annual Meeting of the Association for Computational Linguistics (ACL), Demonstration Session*, Prague, Czech Republic.

Lee, J. 2007. Telephone interpreting – seen from the interpreters' perspective. *Interpreting* 2(2), pp. 231–252.

Licoppe, C. and Verdier, M. 2013. Interpreting, video communication and the sequential reshaping of institutional talk in the bilingual and distributed courtroom. *International Journal of Speech, Language and the Law* 20(2), pp. 247–276.

Locatis, C., Williamson, D., Gould-Kabler, C., Zone-Smith, L., Detzler, I., Roberson, J., Maisiak, R. and Ackerman, M. 2010. Comparing in-person, video, and telephonic medical interpretation. *Journal of General Internal Medicine* 25(4), pp. 345–350.

Mikkelson, H. 2003. "Telephone Interpreting: Boon or Bane?" In *Speaking in Tongues: Language Across Contexts and Users*, edited by L. Pérez González, 251–269. València: Universitat de València.

Miler-Casino, J. and Rybinska, Z. 2011. "AVIDICUS Comparative Studies – part III: Traditional Interpreting and Videoconference Interpreting in Prosecution Interviews". In *Videoconference and Remote Interpreting in Legal Proceedings*, edited by S. Braun and J. Taylor, 117–136. Cambridge: Intersentia.

Moser-Mercer, B. 2003. "Remote interpreting: assessment of human factors and performance parameters". *Communicate!* Summer 2003. Available from: http://aiic.net/ViewPage.cfm?page_id= 1125 [Accessed 12 March 2016].

Moser-Mercer, B. 2005. Remote interpreting: issues of multi-sensory integration in a multilingual task. *Meta* 50(2), pp. 727–738.

Mouzourakis, P. 1996. Videoconferencing: techniques and challenges. *Interpreting* 1(1), pp. 21–38.

Mouzourakis, P. 2006. Remote interpreting: a technical perspective on recent experiments. *Interpreting* 8(1), pp. 45–66.

O'Brien, S., Winther Balling, L., Carl, M., Simard, M. and Specia, L. 2014. *Post-editing of Machine Translation: Processes and Applications*. Newcastle upon Tyne: Cambridge Scholars Press.

Och, F. J. and Ney, H. 2002 "Discriminative Training and Maximum Entropy Models for Statistical Machine Translation". In *Proceedings of the 40th Annual Meeting of the Association for Computational Linguistics (ACL)*, 295–302.

Ortiz-Martõnez, D. and Casacuberta, F. 2014. "The New THOT Toolkit for Fully-Automatic and Interactive Statistical Machine Translation". In *Proceedings of the Demonstrations at the 14th Conference of the European Chapter of the Association for Computational Linguistics, Gothenburg, Sweden, April 26–30*, 45–48. Association for Computational Linguistics.

Ozolins, U. 2011. Telephone interpreting: understanding practice and identifying research needs. *Translation and Interpreting* 3(1), pp. 33–47.

Pollard, C. and Sag, I. 1994. *Head Driven Phrase Structure Grammar*. Chicago: University of Chicago Press.

Price, E., Pérez-Stable, E., Nickleach, D., López, M. and Karliner, L. 2012. Interpreter perspectives of in-person, telephonic, and videoconferencing medical interpretation in clinical encounters. *Patient Education and Counseling* 87(2), pp. 226–232.

Rosenberg, B. A. 2007. "A Data Driven Analysis of Telephone Interpreting". In *The Critical Link 4: Professionalisation of Interpreting in the Community*, edited by C. Wadensjö, B. Englund Dimitrova and A. L. Nilsson, 65–76. Amsterdam: John Benjamins.

Roziner, I. and Shlesinger, M. 2010. Much ado about something remote: stress and performance in remote interpreting. *Interpreting* 12(2), pp. 214–247.

Steedman, M. 1987. Combinatory grammars and parasitic gaps. *Natural Language and Linguistic Theory* 5, pp. 403–439.

Viaggio, S. 2011. *Remote Interpreting Rides Again*. Available from: http://aiic.net/page/3710/remote-interpreting-rides-again/lang/1 [Accessed 24 January 2014].

Wahlster, W. and Karger, R. 2000. "Facts and Figures about the Verbmobil Project". In *Verbmobil: Foundations of Speech-to-Speech Translation* edited by W. Wahlster, 22–30. Berlin: Springer.

Waibel, A. and Lee, K.-F., eds. 1990. *Readings in Speech Recognition*. San Francisco: Morgan Kaufmann Publishers.

Part VI

Applications

Linguistics, translation and interpreting in foreign-language teaching contexts

Anthony Pym and Nune Ayvazyan

The relations between linguistics, translation (including interpreting) and foreign-language teaching can be seen as an interplay of three separate histories that, although once loosely entwined, have been following progressively different paths since the 1970s.

The modern history of foreign-language teaching

When adults sign up to learn a foreign language, they are making a considerable investment in an essentially unknown product: languages are vast, complex and daunting, and it is difficult for any learner to compare the virtues of different teaching methods. Approaches thus demarcate themselves by manipulating a limited set of signals. A course may offer rapid progress, limited effort, proven success, an authoritative source, naturalness and above all, in the age of modernity, newness. On any or all of these points, a new approach must score better than previous approaches. Further, since there are not many more actual values in play, that essential newness requires a clearly visible distinguishing mark with regard to exactly *what* is supposed to be new, habitually selected from the shortlist of things that can be included or not: grammar, pedagogical progress, orality, written correctness, structural repetition, contextualisation and, of course, translation. Not surprisingly, the appeals to "translation" in this discourse have remarkably little to do with what the term might mean for the various linguistic approaches to translation, or indeed with what translators actually do.

The history of language-teaching methods is well rehearsed in the literature (see Kelly 1969/1976; Byram and Hu 2000/2013; Howatt 2004). Kelly (1969/1976, 7) notes that the use of grammar was in vogue in the European Middle Ages and the 18th and 19th centuries, while "during the classical era, the Renaissance, and the early twentieth century it was intuitive command of the target languages that was required". The modern era has seen a movement from the use of the "grammar-translation" method in the 19th century towards a clearer focus on the spoken use of language in situation. The nature of this development, with its implications for translation activities, can best be approached with reference to representative coursebooks, whose introductions and exercises tell a rather more varied story.

Teaching with translation

Since bilingual glossaries date back to 2500 BCE (Kelly 1969/1976, 24), one might assume that some kind of translation has long been associated with some kind of language learning. The clearer association of multilingual dictionaries with translation in the European Renaissance was part of a mode of text-based language learning where Greek and Latin were the essential elements of humanistic education. By the 16th century, classroom learning was closely associated with translating those key texts.

Ascham (1570/1870), Greek and Latin tutor to Elizabeth Tudor, famously recommended teaching a foreign language via a double translation method:

> Let the master read vnto hym the Epistles of *Cicero* [. . .]. First, let him teach the childe, cherefullie and plainlie, the cause, and matter of the letter: then, let him construe it into Englishe [. . .]. After this, the childe must take a paper booke, and sitting in some place, where no man shall prompe him, by him self, let him translate into Englishe his former lesson. Then shewing it to his master, let the master take from him his latin booke, and pausing an houre, at the least, than let the childe translate his owne Englishe into latin againe, in an other paper booke.
>
> (1570, 26)

As expressed, this method actually uses three moments of translation, to which we can add a fourth:

1. *Initial translation*: when the learner confronts the L2 text and construes it mentally into L1, either with or without textual prompts (bilingual glossaries and the like).
2. *Concretising translation*: a spoken or written translation into L1, here used to ground understanding in L1.
3. *Checking translation*: going back into L2 orally or in written form, which in Ascham is an overtly checking process that in effect tests how well the Latin text has been remembered. The union of this activity with translation into L1 can be called, as in Ascham, "double translation".
4. *Communicative translation*: understood as a translation that goes beyond the checking function and is intended primarily as a mode of expression, where the translator can draw on a wide range of resources in order to communicate a message. This kind of translation can be used to illustrate grammatical *differences* between languages, although it is not clear if that was done in Ascham. Ascham's pupil, as Elizabeth I of England, would nevertheless move beyond her language exercises and translate a sizeable body of works to be read by others.

It is not clear how Ascham's use of double translation was to connect with this kind of communicative translation. Indeed, what takes a back seat in this method is close attention to pedagogical *progression*: if the aim is to read and understand Cicero, the beginner is being thrown into the deep end of the pool.

The 17th century saw an influential variant on initial translation for beginners. The Moravian bishop Comenius (Jan Amos Komenský) devised a method for learning Latin that emphasised the importance of direct sensorial knowledge. His *Orbis Pictus* of 1658 had images of everything a child might wish to know about, with a series of short parallel bilingual texts and noun phrases under each image. The prompt was thus initial translation, but the pedagogy did not stop there: where possible, the child should be shown the real thing, then study the picture, speak the names, copy the image and colour it in, in a pedagogy that sought to unite the senses. The first edition of the *Orbis Pictus* was in German and Latin, and then in all major European languages. Tellingly, an edition of Hoole's English translation of the *Orbis Pictus*, published in 1777, adds the sub-title "and the English made to answer word for word to the Latin", with the editors advertising that they have made it easier to pair the English and Latin words by imposing Latin literalism on the English of previous editions (1658/1777, 5). At this initial stage of learning, the pairing of words was clearly more important than any differences in syntax. Such was learning by translation. But it was far from what was to be called "grammar translation".

In both Ascham and Comenius, translation was at work without any close alliance with grammar. This would change with Meidinger's *Praktische französische Grammatik* of 1783, which became the best-selling textbook of its age, spawning many imitations for the learning of European languages. Meidinger (1783/1799, 2) starts from the proposition that "learning from rules is the shortest and safest way to learn French" and then offers comparative grammar lessons, going from simple to complex, with each step checked by having the learner translate short texts, which also go from simple to complex. We thus find pedagogical progression, comparative grammar and translation being used to teach the grammar, not to teach classical texts or sensorial objects. Meidinger explains that the pedagogical work on each text should start from an *oral* question-and-answer routine between student and teacher, in the L2, to ensure the text has been understood. Once the text has been grasped orally, "I read them the story word-for-word in German [L1], and they translate it into French [L2]" (1783/1799, ix). There is thus double translation, as in Ascham. There follows a revision phase based on the checking translation: "Should the learner make a mistake [in the written translation], one does not correct them but underlines the error in red ink and reminds them of the rules, so that they can correct themselves" (1783/1799, viii). A version of Meidinger's method was applied to the learning of English in Fick's (1793/1800) *Praktische englische Sprachlehre*.

These grammar-translation methods were modified in several successful textbooks. Seidenstücker's *Elementarbuch zur Erlernung der französischen Sprache* (1811/1833) begins with the Romantic claim to be following nature: "imitating, as closely as possible, the natural way in which children come to gain knowledge and use their mother tongue" (1811/1833, iii). Although this is ideologically almost the inverse of Meidinger's insistence on grammatical rules as offering a quick and sure path, it does not involve a lesser use of translation, just a change in order. Seidenstücker presents the learner with a bilingual glossary, a text and translation exercises *prior* to working on formal grammar. This inductive approach to the teaching of rules effectively makes translation part of the discovery process. The change alters the nature of the texts to be translated: instead of longish continuous texts, Seidenstücker offers the learner disconnected sentences, designed to indicate the grammatical rule to be discovered. For example:

Vous, ihr, *avez*, habt, *livre*, Buch, *acheté*, gekauft

Vous avez un bon père et une bonne mère. Avez-vous un livre? Le livre est bon. Nous avons acheté un bon livre. Le livre que vous avez acheté, est bon. [. . .]

(1811/1833, 2)

The first lines give the French words with their German equivalents, then the series of French sentences are to be read aloud and translated. The first sentence uses the grammar points previously required; the following sentences use the new words to illustrate new grammatical structures.

Carl Ploetz first published his *Elementarbuch der französischen Sprache* in 1848. His approach is initially inductive, like Seidenstücker's, although he introduces several innovations to help students in their translations. First, in the French sentences, the words pertinent to the grammar point are in italics. Second, syntactic differences between French and German are marked in parentheses in the German sentences. And third, different word orders are also marked by inserted numbers, indicating the order in French. This effectively embedded the grammar lessons within the translation tasks.

The French used a similar method for learning German. Ollendorff's (1836/1838) *Nouvelle méthode pour apprendre à lire, à écrire et à parler une langue en six mois* seeks to present sentences that leaners might actually want to ask about, and bases his method on interaction around those examples: "I was not guided by arbitrary laws, but by the manner in which the child begins to learn his mother tongue" (Ollendorff 1846, vii). But then, these exemplary dialogues begin with: "Have you the bread? – Yes, Sir, I have the bread. – Have you your bread? – Yes, I have my bread" (1846, 10), which would certainly be a strange way for any child to begin learning L1. The learner is also required to render the sentences into L2, which no doubt explains why the L1 English has been made to fit French syntax (avoiding "Do you have the bread?", for example). An American French textbook written by H. G. Sanders to prepare younger students for the Ollendorff method is rather clearer about what "naturalness" actually involves: "Young persons will more readily follow an example than a rule" (Sanders and Hubert 1848, 4) – translation is once again being used inductively, in order to lead to grammar. The originally German-language method had thus reached the United States, where it was initially known (and opposed) as the "Prussian method".

The French pedagogue Marcel (1853, 93) also opposed the "grammar and dictionary" method, which he held to be "in direct opposition to nature". Yet he devised an ingenious argument to make translation akin to what he assumed was the natural acquisition process. Marcel argued that foreign languages should only be taught at *advanced* stages of education, since the young mind first had to learn how to think in L1. Learning an L2 then works, for Marcel, from the written-language forms, the meaning of which is given not by situational context (as in L1 acquisition) but by translation:

> The native expressions addressed to [the child learning L1] are always accompanied by tones, looks, and gestures, which explain them at once. The translation attached to the text [by the advanced learner of L2] interprets the foreign words at once, as the language of action interprets the native [language].
>
> (1853, 93; cf. 1867/1869, 23)

Translation thus somehow parallels "natural" language acquisition. Indeed, Marcel argues that translation is *superior* to L1 learning, since the meaning is given immediately.

Interestingly, Marcel (1867/1869, 11, 14) assumes that L1 acquisition progresses inductively through understanding speech, speaking, understanding writing, then writing. In L2 acquisition, on the other hand, the assumed order is *reading*, hearing, speaking and writing (1867/1869, 22). In this way, Marcel limits the advantages of his initial translations explicitly to reading (the first phase), then includes checking "double translation" exercises in his section on writing.

Marcel was not above envisaging a commercial virtue in his matching pairs: "these reciprocal translations may thus serve both peoples to learn each other's language" (our translation) – the one text might serve two markets. Not surprisingly, the matching equivalents are explicitly contrived, once again, by starting from structures shared by the two languages and bending natural syntax (1880/2013, 14). Marcel (1853, 93) nevertheless sees an advantage in having L2 expressions translated in different ways in different situations, since the differences will lead to greater understanding. Here literal translation has become context-sensitive. Yet translation *into* L2 is not required of the beginner (1867/1869, vi), and all translation is to be phased out at advanced stages. Translation thus operates as scaffolding, to be removed once competence has been constructed.

Line up Meidinger, Fick, Seidenstücker, Ploetz, Ollendorff and Marcel, and you find a series of rather flexible ideas: (1) translation is to be used alongside other methods, especially spoken interaction; (2) it can be adapted to the criteria of pedagogical progression; (3) the relation between translation and grammar can be inductive, deductive or a mixture of both; and (4) L2 acquisition involves a "second nature", quite unlike L1 acquisition. All these writers were working in or for secondary schools; they were concerned with training learners above the age of 12 or so.

Teaching without translation

When Marcel argues that an L2 should not be taught to children younger than about 12, his idea harks back to Rousseau, whose *Émile* (1762) affirms that clear ideas are naturally formed in L1 only, so there is no sense in disturbing them with any L2: "you may give children as many synonyms as you please; you will change the words, not the language; they will never know any but one [language]" (1762/1979, 109).

Rousseau's ideology of the natural subject fed into language education via other routes as well. One of them was in Switzerland, where his influence on the educationalist Johann Heinrich Pestalozzi led to a properly Romantic approach to language teaching. Pestalozzi (1801/1894, 71) insisted on teaching language as an integral part of all other skills, with special attention to "the gradual progress of lessons from sound to word, from word to speech, to attain to the formation of clear ideas". Pestalozzi's main application of psychological progression was in teaching young children to read. Later in his career, he applied his method to the teaching of classical languages to older children. It seems, however, that Pestalozzi's Latin teacher, Stern, also gave grammatical overviews and used back-translations (Roth 1984, 182). Thus, even within a radically naturalistic spoken-language approach, we find methods being drawn from grammar translation and Prussian New Humanism, which similarly sought to engage the student in the inductive discovery of grammar.

Apparently independently of Pestalozzi, the French Latinist François Gouin began working on a method that radically excluded translation. In his *Essai sur une réforme des méthodes d'enseignement* (1880), Gouin gives an account of how he tried to learn German using the available methods, all of which failed miserably – apparently he sought no human teacher, trying instead to do everything from one book after another. Among much else, he found that a week of translating led nowhere: "Translation might be suitable for learning Latin and Greek, but not for living languages" (1880/1894, 16–17; our translation). Then came a communicative epiphany. Gouin by chance witnessed how his three-year-old nephew was learning French by repeating over and over actions he had done. Gouin immediately understood the importance of repeated speech. His method is then based on carefully concocted "series" of sentences, connecting a result with a logical set of actions. Students have to repeat and memorise the sentences. Gouin further claims he can teach "universal grammar", common to the (European) languages involved. He nevertheless remained a strangely marginal figure. Commercial success was to come from elsewhere.

Gottlieb Heness migrated to the United States in 1841 and started teaching German. In explaining his method (1867), Heness interestingly starts from something *between* L1 and L2 acquisition: he explains that children in Germany are brought up speaking local dialects, then go to school and learn High German. They do this through what Heness terms "object-teaching", adapted from Pestalozzi, which involves using a psychologically ordered sequence of activities. Heness (1867/1884, 4–5) argues that the same thing can be done when teaching German to speakers of English.

Heness opened a German-language school in New Haven in 1866. Two years later he employed the Frenchman Lambert Sauveur to teach using the same method, and in 1871 the two were working in their new school in Boston. The course starts from the teacher naming the fingers of their hand (Heness 1867/1884, 23). It then moves from objects or pictures to intensive question and answer routines, with much repetition (Heness 1867/1884, 16–17). Heness (1867/1884, 10) stipulates that his course is for *young* children, for whom the teacher is like a parent. This is because "it is very difficult for the adult to understand and speak without translating", and translation, including mental translation, is precisely the thing to be avoided, along with a dependence on rules.

In contradistinction to the "Prussian" method, Heness and Sauveur designed their courses for students whose first aim was to *speak* the foreign language. This language learning was for four hours a day, five days a week. Heness and Sauveur, as immigrants (along with the critical Marcel, who had learned his English when in Ireland), were speaking from the experience of the displaced person. Their courses were not imitating nature, but immersion abroad.

The American Maximilian Berlitz, an immigrant of German Jewish origins, opened his first language school in Rhode Island in 1878 and expounded his method in a series of publications in the 1880s. As in Heness and Sauveur, use of L1 was excluded, and with it disappeared translation as well. Berlitz initially presented his method as "an imitation of the process followed by nature in teaching a child its mother tongue" (1888, 1). Berlitz (1888/1916, 4) nevertheless also makes an appeal to the "second nature" known by the immigrant: "Instruction by the Berlitz method, is to the student what the sojourn in a foreign land is to a traveller".

The principles of Berlitz's method are: (1) "Teaching of the Concrete by Object Lessons" (as in Pestalozzi, Heness, Sauveur, perhaps Gouin), (2) "Teaching of the Abstract by the Association of Ideas" (as in Gouin), and (3) "Teaching of Grammar by Examples and Ocular Demonstration" (as in almost everyone since Seidenstücker). In practice, Berlitz's system is a clearly ordered sequence of object-based dialogues – as in Pestalozzi, Gouin, Heness and Sauveur – that starts from objects in the classroom, then colours, positions, numbers, and so on, with possible accompaniment by large wall pictures showing the objects mentioned – as in Comenius.

Berlitz's (1888/1916, 3) position with respect to translation was clear: "translation as a means of acquiring a foreign language is entirely abandoned". He gives three reasons for disliking translation:

1. In all translation methods, most of the time is taken up by explanations in the student's mother tongue [. . .].
2. He who studies a foreign language by means of translation, neither gets hold of its spirit nor becomes accustomed to think in it [. . .].
3. A knowledge of a foreign tongue, acquired by means of translation, is necessarily defective and incomplete; for there is by no means for every word of one language, the exact equivalent in the other.

(1888/1916, 3–4)

The translation concept here is clearly one of exact word-for-word matching, of the kind offered in initial prompts in previous methods.

These 19th-century arguments for and against translation did not fundamentally alter in the 20th century. The "against" team did however gain academic respectability.

Enter some linguists

What the Americans called the "Prussian" method came to be known as "grammar translation", although the term seems never to have been used by the writers themselves. It was probably coined in Wilhelm Viëtor's 1882 treatise *Der Sprachunterricht muß umkehren!* (Language teaching must be turned around!). In the early 20th century, the term "grammar translation" was then used loosely to refer to any method that taught grammar and translation, often with the clearly erroneous assumption that this is all that those methods set out to do (Siefert 2013, 1–30).

Viëtor's arguments were picked up by the English phonetician Henry Sweet and then became part of a concerted intervention by university phoneticians: Sweet in England, Otto Jespersen in Denmark and Paul Passy in France. Together with Viëtor, these heavyweights became the Reform Movement (Howatt and Smith 2002).

Even though their insistence on speech chimed in with the L2-only methods of the American-language schools, the phoneticians found translation suitable in the right place and time. Passy (1899/1903, 42–43) actually argued *against* Berlitz's banishment of L1, allowing that translations into L1 and L2 could be useful exercises for advanced students to explore the differences between languages, and that, at beginner levels, checking translations could save time. Passy thus implicitly recognises several kinds of translation: initial word-for-word (which he rejects), explanatory spoken checking into both L1 and L2 (which he accepts) and full (transformational) translation for advanced students.

Sweet (1899), in his *Practical Study*, was even more open to translation. He saw it as enabling a "full understanding" of the L2, to be divided into several stages: the first is "initial translation"; the second is part of contextual "explanation" in L1 and L2, similar to what we have termed "concretising" translation; the third is then the use of translation to highlight *differences* between the languages, and here the reference to "free idiomatic translation" is key: we are approaching a fuller concept of what translation can do, although its function here is ultimately to check on acquisition, with exercises going into both L1 and L2 (1899, 207). In the fourth stage, translation is an *application* of the skills acquired.

Jespersen's (1901/1904) *How to Teach a Foreign Language*, on the other hand, accords a far greater role to inductive work on grammar, and thereby severely limits the role of translation. Jespersen (1901/1904, 70–71) nevertheless admits that "there are many words where an English translation gives the information required more quickly and more clearly than it could be given in a long explanation in the foreign language".

If at this point we look back at the 19th-century discourses, it seems clear that there was never a period where translation was held up as the *only* teaching method: translation was generally to be used alongside spoken activities, visual or situational supports, carefully graded exercises and, from Prussian New Humanism, inductive grammar. Some of the textbooks were remarkably eclectic, suggesting a "pre-method" era, even as their covers promulgated one new method after another. The radical *exclusion* of translation seems to date from the immigrant experience in the United States.

A measure of how complete this break was is found in an anecdote recounted by Heness. A student who speaks only German at school comes home to his mother, who asks what the boy has done at school. The boy "began to stammer, unable to speak intelligibly", then confesses: "'Mother, if you will let me talk in German, I will tell you all;' and he gave a full account of the day's adventures in German" (Heness 1867/1884, 6). This is presented as a hallmark of the method's success: the student is rendered unintelligible in L1.

Developments in the 20th century

The Swiss linguist Charles Bally developed a diachronic stylistics that, privileging spoken interaction, found little place for translation. Bally (1909/1951, 1.2) dismisses the kind of "mechanical translation" performed at the beginning of language acquisition, which he sees as moving from "form to form" rather than passing through the "idea". However, elsewhere he sees his stylistic analyses as preparing the student for quite a different mode of translation, to be used in the final stages of the acquisition process (Bally 1905, 163). He even describes his own linguistics as providing "a veritable method of translation" (1909/1951, 1.138). Bally's *Traité de stylistique française* comprises numerous exercises for learning French stylistics, many of which do indeed involve translation of the more communicative kind. His terms and approach were later picked up by Vinay and Darbelnet (1958/1972), who turned comparative stylistics into one of the foundational pillars of Translation Studies.

A similar double game can be found in Eastern Europe, where the memorisation of spoken L2 dialogues became one of the mainstays of foreign-language learning, in principle excluding the use of L1. Extensive use of translation nevertheless remained. In the classical "Bonk" textbooks (such as Bonk, Kotiy and Lukyanova 1961) translation activities into both L1 and L2 are a part of all lessons, alongside oral practice. In that part of the world, translation never went away.

Audiovisual teaching methods were developed in France from the 1950s. As in the Russian tradition, there were dialogues to be repeated and remembered, but in this case using tape recordings and slides or filmstrips, fleshing out the context in which the L2 utterance was to be understood. The exclusion of L1 was more radical, however. Harvey (1996, 46) reports that ministerial guidelines banned translation from language-teaching methods in the 1950s, although the Association des Professeurs de Langues Vivantes condemned the ban in 1987. Harvey (1996, 46) sees this as a conflict "between teachers faced with the day-to-day reality of the classroom, and official policy makers".

The French ban remains an exception. Elsewhere in the world, the grammar-translation method has remained in force. Adamson and Morris (1997) explain that audiolingual methods and grammar translation were both used from the founding of the People's Republic of China (as indeed they were in the Soviet Union), although grammar translation became dominant after the Cultural Revolution, among other reasons because the audiolingual method was apparently seen as being American.

With the rise of English as a global lingua franca, the teaching methods used around the world have increasingly tended to coincide with those being used to teach English. And in that particular area, the traditional arguments against translation steadily accrued force, albeit through simple repetition rather than conceptual sophistication (see Malmkjær 1995–1996, 58–60; Pym, Malmkjær and Gutiérrez 2013, 12–14). Gatenby (1948/1967, 66) assumed that children learn L1 without translation, so translation is a "departure from the conditions of the natural process of acquiring speech". The argument is backed up by a small cost-benefit analysis: translation is described as "a deceptive process in that, being laborious, it persuades teacher and pupil that a great deal has been accomplished" (1948/1967, 69).

Mackey (1953–1955/1967, 34) added that translation can only produce "mental confusion" due to L1 interference. And Lado (1964, 54) insisted that initial translation was misleading because it relied on word-to-word equivalents. Indeed, the general abstract arguments against translation were so overwhelming that Morris (1957/1967, 61) expressed legitimate surprise that the level of foreign-language skills could be so high in Scandinavia and the Netherlands despite their "excessive resort to translation".

One voice in favour of translation in this period was Dodson's (1967/1972) *Language Teaching and the Bilingual Method*, which combined spoken practice with printed text, picture strips and initial translations as complementary inputs that enabled the learner to act out a given situation in L2. Translation was one input among many, while the goal remained communicative performance. This approach was picked up in Germany by Butzkamm (1980), who argued more explicitly for a "sandwich technique" where the learner is given the L2 expression, the L1 translation and then the L2 expression again:

TEACHER: *Was geht hier eigentlich vor? What's going on here? Was geht hier eigentlich vor?*
STUDENT: *Was geht hier eigentlich vor?*

(from Butzkamm 1980)

The aim is for the student to grasp as quickly as possible what the foreign sentence means, without relying on form-for-form translation (the German word "*eigentlich*", meaning "actually", finds no equivalent here) and assuming that the adult learner would be engaged in mental translation in such cases anyway.

Communicative approaches

The so-called Communicative Approach emerged during the 1970s as a method that advocated real and meaningful communication based on learners' immediate needs (Brumfit and Johnson 1979; Krashen 1982). Once again, that simple idea can be found in various forms throughout 19th-century discourses, albeit mostly with some presumption to restrict or fabricate the learner's "needs" by assuming some natural relation to pictures, immediate objects, simple actions in the world and indeed to the spoken word. Anything could be considered a "need" in the eyes of the pedagogue, except translation, apparently.

The adjective "communicative" owes much to Hymes' (1966) concept of "communicative competence", which stressed that knowing a language system was different from using a language. We thus find Wilkins (1973) shifting attention away from the categories of grammar-based teaching and towards "categories of communicative function".

However, the Communicative Approach was not completely against the use of translation in classrooms. Widdowson, for example, defended the communicative use of translation:

> What we are aiming to do is to make the learner conceive of the foreign language in the same way as a communicative activity. This being so, it would seem reasonable to draw upon the learner's knowledge of how his own language is used to communicate. This is to say, it would seem reasonable to make use of translation.
>
> (Widdowson 1978, 159)

Similarly, Finocchiaro and Brumfit (1983, 92) note that in the Communicative Approach "judicious use of native language is accepted where feasible".

From the late 1980s we find a questioning of communicative approaches. Swan (1985a, 1), for example, points out that the Communicative Approach "fails to take account of the knowledge and skills which language students bring with them from their mother tongue and their experience of the world". He advocates the moderate use of translation activities, even when they "seem to have no immediate 'communicative' value" (Swan 1985b, 83). Alan Maley questioned that supposed lack of communicative value more radically:

> Only recently, as the communicative movement has begun to run short of ideas, has there been a resurgence of interest in traditional practices such as translation. Could it be that it serves some useful purpose after all? Could it be renovated, reinterpreted, humanized, made communicative?

(Maley quoted in Duff 1989, 3)

This question astutely avoids preconceptions of what translation is. The issue is instead how the traditional translation concept can be revamped and put to work, not in opposition to communicative approaches but as part of them.

One of the most significant attempts to reintroduce translation in this way was made in the *Common European Framework of Reference for Languages (CEFR)* (Council of Europe 2001), where "mediation", presented as one of the five basic language skills, includes translation and interpreting, alongside activities such as providing "a paraphrase, summary or record" (*CEFR* 2.1.3). Communicative translation is thus one of the skill sets that the learner is supposed to acquire, in accordance with a vision where the aim of language education is to produce a polyglot who not only knows languages but can move between them. The schoolboy that Heness held up as a model of success because he could not explain himself in L1 would, in terms of the *Common European Framework*, epitomise failure.

In their survey of the use of translation in language learning in 10 countries, Pym, Malmkjær and Gutiérrez (2013) find that the Communicative Approach is the most popular method in virtually all countries, while grammar translation is among the least popular approaches in all countries. That said, translation activities are reported as being used in classrooms in particular ways: the older the students, the more translation is used, and the higher the education system's general foreign-language skills, the more frequent the use of translation. The notable exception to this latter tendency is Germany, where language skills are high yet instructors report not using translation in class: instead they use "mediation", in accordance with the terms established in the *Common European Framework*. That is, translation continues to be used in classrooms, but under a different name and along with a wide range of cross-language communicative activities.

Connections with Translation Studies

The various debates for and against the use of translation have taken place within foreign-language teaching circles; they have not become an issue within Translation Studies or indeed in linguistics as a wider discipline. This is not for want of early contacts between these fields. For example, Bally's stylistics drew on the practical experience of translating with students and provided the basic terms for Vinay and Darbelnet's "method of translation" (1958). Bally, however, did all he could to exclude "mechanical translation" from the classroom, and Vinay and Darbelnet filled their method with examples that are mostly parallel texts, not actual translations. The mistrust of mechanical translation remained.

A more intriguing disconnect can be dated from Holmes' (1972) article "The Name and Nature of Translation Studies", sometimes regarded as the founding document of Western Translation Studies. Holmes' research programme recognised that "priority should be given to extensive and rigorous research to assess the efficacy of translating as a technique and testing method in language learning" (Holmes 1972, 190). Yet the question is mysteriously absent from the graphic representation of Holmes in Toury (1995/2012, 12): the priority was recognised, then quickly forgotten. This was a period when Translation Studies was struggling to establish itself as an independent discipline, in part by insisting that professional translation required skills over and above the learning of a foreign language. Experts in communicative language teaching were free to assume that translation was not communicative, at the same time as translation scholars were quick to presuppose that language learning had nothing to do with translation. Had there been dialogue, of course, exchanges might have dealt with the facile arguments being tossed about both for and against the use of translation, and attention might have been paid to the different *kinds* of translation that can be used in classrooms. As it was, once the translation scholars withdrew from the scene, English-language communicative ideologies were able to rule the roost virtually unchallenged.

The separation of disciplines obscured some positive developments. For example, Alan Duff's excellent 1989 compendium of translation activities for the teaching of English was virtually ignored by translation scholars, while it struggled to find an audience among foreign-language teachers. A decade or so later, though, the translation scholar Malmkjær (1998, 2004) edited two collective volumes on the role of translation in language teaching, the applied linguist Cook (1998) had his arguments in favour of using translation published in the *Routledge Encyclopedia of Translation Studies*, and since then Cook's (2010) *Translation in Language Teaching* has had an impact on both disciplines.

Empirical research

Dodson's (1967/1972) bilingual method was ostensibly backed up by empirical testing: numbers showed that the multiple inputs led to learning faster than just one. This finding is reported as being supported by a series of control-group studies (for example Walatara 1973, with others reviewed in Caldwell 1990). However, none of these studies isolates translation as a variable, since the focus is on the method as a whole.

Other empirical studies have been able to demonstrate the negative effects of translation. Ulanoff and Pucci (1993) tested a situation where the primary-school teacher translates everything as it is said, with the predictable result that the students stopped paying attention to what was said in their weaker language. Much depends, obviously, on the particular *kind* of translation that is used in class, and exactly *when* it is used.

There have been several studies on what students and teachers think of translation as a classroom activity (Altan 2006; Carreres 2006; Liao 2006; Boakye 2007; Fotovatnia 2010; Kelly and Bruen 2014), most of them finding that students generally regard translation as a useful tool. The semi-standardised questionnaires nevertheless include the statement "Learning English is mostly a matter of translating from my mother tongue" (with variants), with which students are requested to agree or disagree. The extreme nature of the statement, which fails to specify what kind of translation is involved or what other kinds of activities might be considered, gives results that seem of little benefit to any seriously balanced discussion of when and where translation can be of real benefit.

Other surveys have focused on instructors' opinions of translation. Pym, Malmkjær and Gutiérrez (2013) found that, except for the special case of Germany, the most negative opinions of translation were in countries were the Communicative Approach and immersion scored highest, which also happened to be the countries where the foreign-language skills scored the lowest (notably France and Spain). This, of course, does not mean that translation itself enhances language skills, since there are numerous other factors involved. But it does suggest that the presence of translation activities in language classrooms in countries like Finland and Croatia, or of mediation activities in Germany, is doing no harm.

Most of the arguments for and against translation have nevertheless tended to remain on the ideological level, without seeking justification in experiments. Indeed, the teaching community has tended to shun empirical testing across the board, since there are always numerous complex factors involved and much depends not just on what is done in the classroom, but what instructors and learners *think* should be done. Rather than comparing methods and seeing what the numbers say, there has been adhesion to a "post-method" condition, where it is accepted that no one method can be demonstrated to be superior to any other, and there should be no need to restrict oneself to the use of just one method (see Stern 1983; Prabhu 1990; Kumaravadivelu 1994). The rejection of rigorous empirical testing has thus led to situations where significant social resources are invested in teaching methodologies whose effectiveness is often no more than a question of beliefs. At the same time, however, acceptance of "post-method" ideology has coincided with a movement away from single teaching methodologies, which has renewed interest in translation.

Further reading

Cook, G. 2010. *Translation in Language Teaching*. Oxford: Oxford University Press.
A timely, balanced and influential restatement of the virtues of translation in language teaching.

Howatt, A. P. R. 2004. *A History of English Language Teaching*. 2nd ed. Oxford: Oxford University Press.
An invaluable reference work, although readers should be aware that it is restricted to the teaching of English.

Malmkjær, K., ed. 1998. *Translation and Language Teaching: Language Teaching and Translation*. Manchester: St Jerome.
One of the seminal texts for the renewed interest in translation.

Pym, A., Malmkjaer, K. and Gutiérrez, M. 2013. *Translation and Language Learning*. Luxembourg: European Commission.
A survey of the institutional and pedagogical relations between translation and language teaching in 10 countries.

Siefert, T. R. 2013. *Translation in Foreign Language Pedagogy: The Rise and Fall of the Grammar Translation Method*. Doctoral dissertation. Harvard University.
Brilliantly documents how the myth of grammar translation was fabricated by its opponents.

References

Adamson, R. and Morris, P. 1997. The English curriculum in the People's Republic of China. *Comparative Education Review* 14(1), pp. 3–25.
Altan, M. X. 2006. Beliefs about language learning of foreign language-major university students. *Australian Journal of Teacher Education* 31(2), pp. 45–52.

Ascham, R. 1570/1870. *The Scholemaster.* 1st ed. 1570, collated with the 2nd ed. of 1571. London: Muir and Patterson.

Bally, C. 1905. *Précis de Stylistique. Esquisse d'une Méthode Fondée sur l'étude du Français Moderne.* Geneva: A. Eggiman.

Bally, C. 1909/1951. *Traité de Stylistique Française.* 2nd ed. Paris: Klincksieck.

Berlitz, M. 1888/1916. *The Berlitz Method for Teaching Modern Languages. English Part.* Revised American ed. New York: Berlitz.

Boakye, N. 2007. Investigating students' beliefs about language learning. *Per Linguam* 23(2), pp. 1–14.

Bonk, N. A., Kotiy, G. A. and Lukyanova, N. A. 1961. *Uchebnik Angliyskogo Yazyka* [Textbook of the English Language]. Moscow: Vneshtorgizdat.

Brumfit, C. J. and Johnson, K., eds. 1979. *The Communicative Approach to Language Teaching.* Oxford: Oxford University Press.

Butzkamm, W. 1980. *Praxis und Theorie der Bilingualen Methode.* Heidelberg: Quelle und Meyer.

Byram, M. and Hu, A., eds. 2000/2013. *Routledge Encyclopedia of Language Teaching and Learning.* London: Routledge.

Caldwell, J. A. W. 1990. Analysis of the theoretical and experiential support for Carl Dodson's bilingual method. *Journal of Multilingual and Multicultural Development* 11(6), pp. 459–479.

Carreres, Á. 2006. "Strange Bedfellows: Translation and Language Teaching. The Teaching of Translation into L2 in Modern Languages Degrees; Uses and Limitations". *Sixth Symposium on Translation, Terminology and Interpretation in Cuba and Canada: December.* Canadian Translators, Terminologists and Interpreters Council. Available from: http://goo.gl/BMs4eK [Accessed March 2016].

Comenius, J. A. 1658. *Orbis Pictus.* Nuremberg.

Comenius, J. A. 1658/1777. *Orbis Sensualium Pictus [. . .] Joh[n] Amos Comenius's Visible World.* 12th ed., translated by Charles Hoole. London: Printed for S. Leacroft, at the Globe, Charing Cross.

Cook, G. 1998. "Use of Translation in Language Teaching". In *Routledge Encyclopedia of Translation Studies*, edited by Mona Baker, 117–120. London: Routledge.

Cook, G. 2010. *Translation in Language Teaching.* Oxford: Oxford University Press.

Council of Europe. 2001. *Common European Framework of Reference for Languages: Learning, Teaching, Assessment.* Strasbourg: Council of Europe, Cambridge University Press.

Dodson, C. J. 1967/1972. *Language Teaching and the Bilingual Method.* London: Pitman.

Duff, A. 1989. *Translation.* Oxford: Oxford University Press.

Fick, J. C. 1793/1800. *Praktische Englische Sprachlehre für Deutsche Beyderley Geschlechts* [Practical English Language Course for Germans of Both Sexes]. 3rd ed. Erlangen: Walther.

Finocchiaro, M. and Brumfit, C. 1983. *Functional-Notional Approach: From Theory to Practice.* Oxford: Oxford University Press.

Fotovatnia, Z. 2010. The effect of individual differences on learners' translation belief in EFL learning. *English Language Teaching* 3(4), pp. 228–236.

Gatenby, E. V. 1948/1967. "Translation in the Classroom". In *ELT Selections 2: Articles from the Journal "English Language Teaching"*, edited by W. R. Lee, 65–70. London: Oxford University Press.

Gouin, F. 1880/1894. *Essai sur une réforme des méthodes d'enseignement. Exposé d'une nouvelle méthode linguistique. L'art d'enseigner et d'étudier les langues*; trans. Howard Swan and Victor Bétis as The Art of Studying and Teaching Languages. 2nd ed. London: George Philip and Son.

Harvey, M. 1996. "A Translation Course for French-speaking Students". In *Teaching Translation in Universities: Present and Future Perspectives*, edited by P. Sewell and I. Higgins, 45–65. London: Association for French Language Studies and Centre for Information on Language Teaching and Research.

Heness, G. 1867/1884. *Der Leitfaden für den Unterricht in der Deutschen Sprache, Ohne Sprachlehre und Wörterbuch, Mit Einer Englischen Einleitung Über Die Lehrmethode der Schule Moderner Sprachen in Boston.* 4th ed. New York: Holt.

Holmes, J. S. 1972. "The Name and Nature of Translation Studies". In *The Translation Studies Reader*, edited by L. Venuti, 180–192. New York: Routledge.

Howatt, A. P. R. 2004. *A History of English Language Teaching*. 2nd ed. Oxford: Oxford University Press.

Howatt, A. P. R. and Smith, R. C., eds. 2002. *Modern Language Teaching: The Reform Movement*. Vol. 5. London: Routledge.

Hymes, D. 1966. "Two Types of Linguistic Relativity". In *Sociolinguistics*, edited by W. Bright, 114–158. The Hague: Mouton.

Jespersen, O. 1901/1904. *Sprogundervisning*, trans. Sophia Yhlen-Olsen Bertelsen as How to Teach a Foreign Language. London: George Allen and Unwin.

Kelly, L. G. 1969/1976. *25 Centuries of Language Teaching*. Rowley MA: Newbury House.

Kelly, N. and Bruen, J. 2014. Translation as a pedagogical tool in the foreign language classroom: a qualitative study of attitudes and behaviours. *Language Teaching Research* 19(2), pp. 150–168.

Krashen, S. D. 1982. *Principles and Practice in Second Language Acquisition*. Oxford: Pergamon.

Kumaravadivelu, B. 1994. The postmethod condition: (e)merging strategies for second/foreign language teaching. *TESOL Quarterly* 28(1), pp. 27–48.

Lado, R. 1964. *Language Teaching: A Scientific Approach*. New York: McGraw-Hill.

Liao, P. 2006. EFL learners' beliefs about and strategy use of translation in English learning. *RELC Journal* 37(2), pp. 191–215. Available from: http://goo.gl/gUksYP [Accessed March 2016].

Mackey, W. F. 1953-55/1967. "The Meaning of Method". In *ELT Selections 2: Articles from the Journal "English Language Teaching"*, edited by W. R. Lee, 9–48. London: Oxford University Press.

Malmkjær, K. 1995–1996. Translation and language learning. *AILA Review* 12, pp. 56–61.

Malmkjær, K., ed. 1998. *Translation and Language Teaching: Language Teaching and Translation*. Manchester: St Jerome.

Malmkjær, K., ed. 2004. *Translation in Undergraduate Degree Programmes*. Amsterdam: John Benjamins.

Marcel, C. 1853. *Language as a Means of Mental Culture and International Communication: Manual of the Teacher and Learner of Languages*. London: Chapman and Hall.

Marcel, C. 1867/1869. *The Study of Languages Brought Back to its True Principles, or, The Art of Thinking in a Foreign Language*. American ed. New York: Appleton.

Marcel, C. 1880/2013. *Rational Method, Following Nature Step By Step, to Learn How to Read, Hear, Speak, and Write French*. London: Forgotten Books.

Meidinger, J. V. 1783/1799. *Praktische Französische Grammatik Wodurch Man Diese Sprache Auf Eine Ganz Neue und Sehr Leichte Art in Kurzer Zeit Gründlich Erlernen Kann*. 15th ed. Frankfurt: Meidinger.

Morris, I. 1957/1967. "The Persistence of the Classical Tradition in Foreign-Language Teaching". Reprinted in *ELT Selections 2: Articles from the Journal "English Language Teaching"*, edited by W. R. Lee, 58–64. London: Oxford University Press.

Ollendorff, H. G. 1836/1838. *Nouvelle Méthode Pour Apprendre à Lire, à Ecrire et à Parler une Langue en Six Mois, Appliquée à L'allemand*. 5th ed. London: Vize Slater.

Ollendorff, H. G. 1846. *New Method of Learning to Read, Write and Speak the French Language*. New York: Appleton.

Passy, P. 1899/1903. *La Méthode Directe Dans L'enseignement des Langues Vivantes*. Brussels: Alfred Castaigne.

Pestalozzi, J. H. 1801/1894. *How Gertrude Teaches her Children: An Account of the Method*. Trans. Lucy E. Holland and Frances C. Turner. Syracuse, NY: Sonnenschein & Co.

Ploetz, C. 1848. *Elementarbuch der Französischen Sprache*. Berlin: Herbig.

Prabhu, N. S. 1990. "There is No Best Method: Why?" *TESOL Quarterly* 24(2), pp. 161–176.

Pym, A., Malmkjær, K. and Gutiérrez, M. 2013. *Translation and Language Learning: The Role of Translation in the Teaching of Languages in the European Union*. Luxembourg: European Commission.

Roth, A. 1984. Die Gestaltung der Altsprachlichen Methode Pestalozzies Durch St. L. Roth. *Pädagogica Historica: International Journal for the History of Education* 24(1), pp. 177–207.

Rousseau, J.-J. 1762/1979. *Emile, or, on Education*. Trans. Alan Bloom. New York: Basic Books.

Sanders, G. and Hubert, J. 1848. *The French Student's First Book: After an Improved and Enlarged Plan Based on Ollendorff's New Method*. Philadelphia: Griffith & Simon.

Seidenstücker, J. H. P. 1811/1833. *Elementarbuch zur Erlernung der Französischen Sprache*. 8th ed. Hamm und Soest: Schulz.

Siefert, T. R. 2013. *Translation in Foreign Language Pedagogy: The Rise and Fall of the Grammar Translation Method*. Doctoral dissertation. Harvard University.

Stern, H. H. 1983. *Fundamental Concepts of Language Teaching*. Oxford: Oxford University Press.

Swan, M. 1985a. A critical look at the communicative approach (1). *ELT Journal* 39(1), pp. 1–12.

Swan, M. 1985b. A critical look at the communicative approach (2). *ELT Journal* 39(2), pp. 76–87.

Sweet, H. 1899. *The Practical Study of Languages: A Guide for Teachers and Learners*. London: J. M. Dent.

Toury, G. 1995/2012. *Descriptive Translation Studies and Beyond*. 2nd ed. Amsterdam: John Benjamins.

Ulanoff, S. and Pucci, S. 1993. "Is Concurrent-Translation or Preview-Review more Effective in Promoting Second Language Vocabulary Acquisition?" Paper presented at the Annual Meeting of the American Educational Research Association. Available from: http://goo.gl/VW9GYz [Accessed March 2016].

Viëtor, W. (Quousque Tandem). 1882. *Der Sprachunterricht muß Umkehren! Ein Beitrag zur Überburdungsfrage*. Heilbron: Henninger. 3rd ed. 1905, Leipzig: Resiland.

Vinay, J.-P. and Darbelnet, J. 1958/1972. *Stylistique Comparée du Français et de L'anglais: Méthode de Traduction*. Nouvelle édition revue et corrigée, Paris: Didier.

Walatara, D. 1973. An experiment with the bilingual method for teaching English as a complementary language. *Journal of the National Science Council of Sri Lanka* 1, pp. 189–205. Available from: http://goo.gl/9CoRGL [Accessed March 2016].

Widdowson, H. G. 1978. *Teaching Languages as Communication*. London: Oxford University Press.

Wilkins, D. A. 1973. "The Linguistic and Situational Content of the Common Core in a Unit/Credit System". In *Systems Development in Adult Language Learning*, 129–145. Strasbourg: Council of Europe.

26

Translation, interpreting and lexicography

Helle V. Dam and Sven Tarp

Introduction

Translation, interpreting and lexicography represent three separate areas of human activity, each with its own theories, models and methods and, hence, with its own disciplinary underpinnings. At the same time, all three disciplines are characterised by a marked inter-disciplinary dimension in the sense that their practice fields are typically "about something else". Translators may, for example, be called upon to translate medical texts, and interpreters may be assigned to work on medical speeches. Similarly, practical lexicography may produce medical dictionaries. In this perspective, the three disciplines frequently come into contact with each other.

This chapter discusses and explores some of the basic aspects of this interrelationship, focusing on the (potential) contribution of lexicography to translation and interpreting and on explaining the basic concepts and methods of the former discipline to the translation and interpreting readership of the present volume.

As we shall show, the relationship between (written) translation and lexicography is strong and well established, whereas the link between interpreting and lexicography is much weaker. With present-day, technology-based lexicographical tools, all three fields, interpreting and lexicography in particular, would have much to gain from closer interaction.

Lexicography and information needs

Lexicography is the discipline that deals with the theory and practice of dictionaries and other reference works. Dictionaries have been designed with many different titles and purposes. They have been produced for more than four thousand years and have been available on clay, papyrus, paper and the digital media. During this long span of time, they have covered almost all languages and areas of human activity and thinking.

The common fundamental characteristic of all these very different works is that they are tools designed to meet a specific category of human needs, namely information needs (Wiegand 1987, 2000). The needs that can be satisfied by lexicographical works may arise in many different social contexts and situations. According to the function theory of lexicography, these needs are always shaped by the specific type of situation where they arise as well as by the characteristics of the person who experiences them in this situation (Tarp 2008, 80–88).

There are various types of situation that are relevant to lexicography. Of these, the two most important, and the ones related to translation and interpreting, are the communicative and the cognitive situations. The former is defined as a situation where a person engaged in the production, reception, translation (and, potentially, interpreting) or revision of texts experiences a problem that disturbs the communication process. A cognitive situation is defined as a situation where a person, for one reason or another, experiences the need to get new or additional knowledge about a specific subject. The corresponding information needs are called "communicative" and "cognitive" needs, respectively (Fuertes-Olivera and Tarp 2014, 48–57).

Nesi (2015, 584) expresses the same idea in the following way: "People typically consult maps, encyclopedias, and dictionaries while they are doing something else". This being the case, users of dictionaries will expect the lexicographical consultation to be finished as quickly and smoothly as possible so that they can return to and continue the "something else" they were doing when their specific information need occurred. As such, the time factor is an important criterion of quality in lexicographical works. If the consultation takes too long, it steals time from the user's main activity. Hence, theoretical lexicography does not only deal with dictionary consultation in the narrow sense of the word, but also with the phases taking place immediately before and after this consultation, as we shall see below.

Transition to the digital media

The decades around the turn of the 21st century saw the rapid transition from printed to digital dictionaries. This development was triggered by the introduction of new disruptive computer and information technologies into lexicography. Today, most dictionaries are published online and can be accessed almost anywhere on earth by means of a variety of devices like laptops, tablets and smartphones. Lexicographical data are now stored in remote databases from which they can be retrieved and presented to dictionary users in real time.

The new technologies and techniques have opened completely new horizons to lexicography. While printed dictionaries provided static articles with static data to their users, the most advanced digital dictionaries now offer dynamic articles with dynamic data, i.e. articles and data that vary from consultation to consultation. This allows for a much more user-adapted and personalised lexicographical product.

Although the concepts of database and dictionary are sometimes mixed up, they are two very different things (Bergenholtz and Nielsen 2013). In fact, one lexicographical database may feed two or more dictionaries and is, as such, exclusively a tool for data storage. Dictionary users do not have direct access to the data stored in the database; they only have indirect access by means of the user interface. The interface is what the users see on the screen. Here, the data addressed to a specific lemma (headword) are structured in the most convenient way. However, not necessarily all data addressed to a given lemma in the database are presented to the user in each consultation. If appropriate information techniques – e.g. data filtering and user identification – are applied, it is possible to visualise only the types and amount of data considered relevant in each case (Bothma 2011).

The data stored in a lexicographical database may be available through various user interfaces which represent either one dictionary with various functions or a number of different dictionaries, each of them with their respective functions. However, even the best-designed user interfaces cannot solve all problems by themselves. Their quality also depends on the design of the underlying database, which should be structured in such a way that each piece of data which may later be displayed separately is given its own number and assigned to its own field with defined relations to other relevant data fields. This makes it possible to retrieve any specific collection of data from the database and present it on the screen in the most user-friendly way (Tarp 2015b). Hence, if both the database and the corresponding user interfaces are well designed, the resulting lexicographical tool will be able to adapt the visualised data to users' specific needs when they experience problems in connection with specific activities such as writing, reading, translating, interpreting or revising texts.

An example of a modern information tool which provides such a differentiated service to its users is the online *Diccionarios de Contabilidad* (Fuertes-Olivera *et al.* 2015), a series of interconnected monolingual and bilingual accounting dictionaries.

This set of dictionaries has various functions; the fundamental one is to provide assistance in connection with the translation of accounting texts. It consists of three main dictionaries (Spanish, Spanish–English and English–Spanish), each with various search options which give access to lexicographical data specifically adapted to different types of information needs. If the user selects the Spanish dictionary, writes a term in the search field and clicks the button *"recepción"* (reception), an article like the one shown in Figure 26.1 will appear on the screen. If one of the other buttons is activated, a completely different article will be displayed. Dictionaries following these basic principles are especially helpful for translators and interpreters with specific information needs related to their profession.

Lexicography and its relation to translation and interpreting

In the mutual relation between translation, interpreting and lexicography, the two former represent the main activity in which translators and interpreters are engaged, whereas the consultation of dictionaries is a secondary activity which is only relevant to the users when they experience information needs during the translation or interpreting process. As such, lexicography is an auxiliary discipline vis-à-vis translation and interpreting.

The task of theoretical lexicography in its relation to translation and interpreting is first of all to study these activities and separate the phases and sub-phases where lexicographically relevant needs may occur, i.e. information needs which can be solved by dictionary consultation. The aim of this endeavour is to determine the lexicographical data that should be selected, prepared and incorporated into the dictionary in order to meet these needs.

Both translation and interpreting studies have developed models that describe the various phases or sub-phases of the respective activities. These models constitute an important source of inspiration for lexicography when studying translation and interpreting, but they cannot be accepted uncritically. Only the phases and sub-phases where information needs that (which can be solved by means of dictionaries) occur are relevant to lexicography. Other phases, sub-phases and needs are lexicographically irrelevant. Translation and interpreting models developed in a lexicographical perspective will therefore to a certain extent differ from those produced within the other two disciplines, as shown in the following sections.

Translation in a lexicographical perspective

There is an extensive academic literature on dictionaries and (written) translation, including a large number of articles and books, among them Snell-Hornby and Pöhl (1989), Piotrowski (1994), Atkins (1998), Sin-wai (2004), Yong and Peng (2007) and Fata (2009). To these

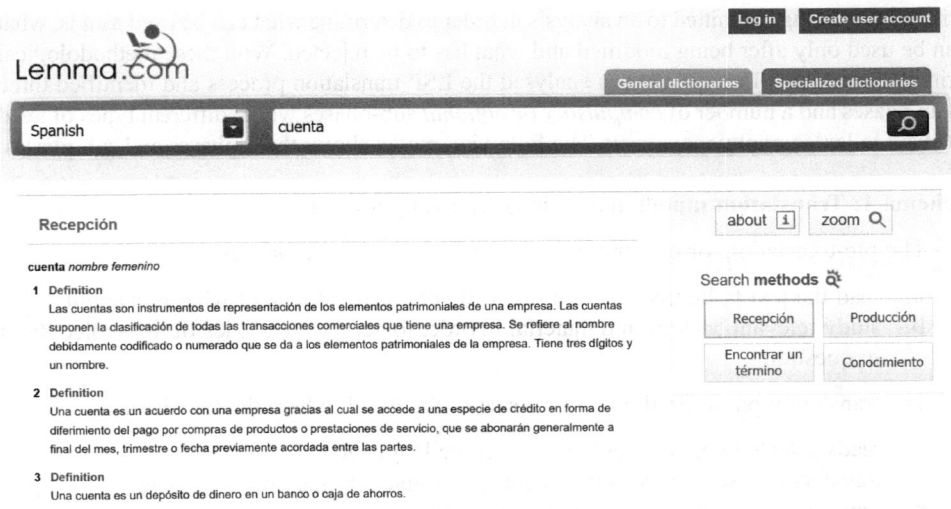

Figure 26.1 Article from *Diccionarios de Contabilidad* – Spanish

can be added thematic issues of specialised journals like *Lexicographica* 29 (2013) and *MonTi* 6 (2014).

Many lexicographers, such as Hartmann and James (2001), Marello (2003) and Adamska-Salaciak (Forthcoming), refer translation problems to bilingual dictionaries without discussing other options. Burkhanov (1998) even defines a translation dictionary as bilingual (or plurilingual). Only a few authors like Tomaszczyk (1989) and Tarp (2013) discuss the relation between lexicography and translation in a more complex manner, discrediting the myth that translation dictionaries are more or less synonymous with bilingual dictionaries.

Most literature deals exclusively with translation for general purposes, and the lexicographical literature on specialised (LSP) translation is relatively scarce. Bergenholtz and Tarp (1995), Fata (2009), Fuertes-Olivera (2013) and Nielsen (2013) are among the relatively few lexicographers who discuss the assistance which dictionaries might provide to LSP translation.

As to the dialogue between lexicography and translation, the state of the art is summed up by Calvo Rigual and Calvi (2014, 42):

> Interest in the sister discipline is evidenced in a number of ways, both from qualitative and quantitative perspectives. Lexicographers have shown concern for meeting translators' needs in the best way possible. Translators have often regretted how inappropriate lexicographical resources are for their needs, but have failed to provide specific suggestions for improvement to lexicographers. A fluent dialogue between the two parties, undoubtedly doomed to understand each other, has been missing. In this sense, it is important to highlight that lexicographers have traditionally been more interested in doing so.

The general picture drawn by the two scholars is very precise. The lack of fluent dialogue between the two "sister disciplines" of lexicography and translation is not particularly surprising, inasmuch as we are dealing with two different disciplines, each with its own superstructure of theories, methods and models that cannot be transferred from one field to the other without first being submitted to an analysis in order to determine what can be used as it is, what can be used only after being modified and what has to be rejected. With these methodological principles in mind, Tarp (2013) has analysed the LSP translation process and identified three main phases and a number of *compulsory or optional* sub-phases where different types of need relevant to lexicography may occur. The following model shows these phases and sub-phases:

Schema 1: Translation model in a lexicographical perspective

1. The pre-translation, or preparation, phase where the translator *may*

    a. read the text to be translated in order to get a general idea of what it is about
    b. study relevant background material in order to get a general idea of the subject field in question

2. The translation phase (in the narrow sense of the word) where the translator

    a. reads selected text segments in the source language
    b. transfers text segments from the source language to the target language
    c. reproduces text segments in the target language

3. The post-translation, or revision, phase where the translator (or another person revising the text) *may*

    a. read the source-language text
    b. read the target-language text
    c. evaluate the text transfer
    d. evaluate the target-language text
    e. correct the target-language text.

The above model has been developed applying the method of deduction and relating it to the usage of dictionaries. Whenever one phase requires different types of lexicographical solution, it has been divided into two or more sub-phases. Furthermore, the model draws on findings from available user research in lexicography, e.g. Tomaszczyk (1989), Mackintosh (1998), Varantola (1998) and Nord (2002). These findings provide empirical evidence to support the sub-phases shown except for those belonging to the revision phase, for which no known user research has been conducted from a lexicographical perspective. The model nevertheless assumes that this post-translation phase consists of a number of compulsory and optional sub-phases as indicated.

It is a matter of course that the phases and sub-phases may vary from translator to translator, and from task to task. Some of the sub-phases may be omitted, repeated or their order may be reversed as the process is not necessarily linear. Contrary to most models developed within Translation Studies, Phase 2 encompasses a distinction between text transfer and text reproduction. The reason is that these two sub-phases require differentiated lexicographical treatment. Frequently, translators do not experience any problems when reading or transferring a text segment, but only when it comes to reproducing it in the target language, especially when this is not their native language.

Lexicographical assistance to translation

In all the phases and sub-phases shown in Schema 1, translators may experience various types of information need which require specific types of lexicographical solutions and data.

The needs may be either cognitive when it is a question of requiring background knowledge, or communicative when it is a question of reading, transferring, reproducing and revising the text. From a theoretical perspective, it is not important how frequent each type of need is, as dictionaries should cater for all relevant types of needs arising during the translation process, including those occurring only rarely. The following model of information needs which may appear in the different translation phases has been developed with this in mind:

Schema 2: Possible information needs during the translation process

1. In the pre-translation phase, translators may need

   a. general background information on the subject field or part of the subject field relevant to the task
   b. definitions of specific source-language terms, words and fixed expressions in order to understand the text to be translated

2. In the translation phase, translators may need

   a. definitions of source-language terms, words and fixed expressions in order to understand the source-language text
   b. equivalents of terms, words, collocations and fixed expressions in order to transfer the text
   c. information about meaning, orthography, gender, inflection, collocations, syntactic properties, word formation and genre conventions in the target language in order to reproduce the text in this language

3. In the post-translation phase, translators or other persons in charge of text revision may need

   a. definitions in both languages in order to understand specific terms, words and fixed expressions or ensure that these are correct
   b. equivalents in order to evaluate the text transfer
   c. information about orthography, gender, inflection, collocations, syntactic properties, word formation, fixed expressions and genre conventions in the target language in order to evaluate and correct the translated text.

One notes that some of the specific information needs, e.g. definitions of source-language terms, are common to two or even three different sub-phases as they were defined in Schema 1. In addition, in all three main phases translators may also need specific background information about specific phenomena, processes and things treated in the text, i.e. information that goes beyond what can be retrieved from traditional definitions. Such background information may be necessary in order to handle specific text passages.

Tarp (2013) has shown how the satisfaction of all these complex needs requires a combination of lexicographical solutions. In fact, a bilingual solution is only compulsory when it is a question of furnishing equivalents, whereas this solution is optional for the remaining data categories. Background information and definitions of source-language terms, etc. could also be furnished in a monolingual solution in this language (best solution when it is the translator's mother tongue). Definitions of target-language terms, etc., as well as data on target-language grammar, collocations, genre conventions, etc. could be provided either in a monolingual solution in the target language (best solution when it is the translator's mother tongue) or in a bilingual one based on this language (best solution when it is not the translator's mother tongue).

If a dictionary is supposed to give real assistance to translators of specialised texts, it should not only incorporate the relevant lexicographical data but also guarantee the easiest possible access to these data as well as their treatment in the most convenient language. In this respect, and based upon the above reflections, *the best overall design* of a dictionary conceived to assist its users in *L1–L2* translation of specialised texts consists of three components:

- a monolingual L1 component
- a bilingual L1–L2 component
- a bilingual L2–L1 component

Similarly, *the best overall design* of a dictionary conceived to assist its users in *L2–L1* translation of specialised texts consists of two components, both of them shared with the dictionary for L1–L2 translation:

- a bilingual L2–L1 component
- a monolingual L1 component

The integration of these three components into one and the same printed dictionary create a number of collateral problems such as the risk of data overload and the need to make additional look-ups in other parts of the dictionary in order to find the required data. These problems may obstruct the consultation process as well as the proper retrieval of the required information. They are inevitable in printed dictionaries but can be avoided in digital dictionaries if appropriate information techniques such as data filtering are used.

An example of a specialised dictionary project which consists of the three components mentioned above and uses relevant information techniques is the online *Diccionarios de Contabilidad* discussed above. The article *cuenta* shown in Figure 26.1 was retrieved from the database using the search method "*recepción*" in the Spanish dictionary. If the user instead chooses the Spanish–English dictionary and clicks the button "*Frases y Expresiones*", a completely different article will be visualised as shown in Figure 26.2.

When fully displayed, the article reproduced in Figure 26.2 contains a total of 50 Spanish phrases and expressions that include the term *cuenta*. A click on any of them will bring the user to the corresponding Spanish–English article where an English translation can be found. The practical experience from a similar Danish–English project (Nielsen, Mourier and Bergenholtz 2015) has shown that professional translators of accounting texts find this particular type of article very useful to their activity.

As to the need for background information indicated above, some specialised dictionaries do in fact offer this kind of information following a long, but relatively unknown tradition going back to the European Enlightenment Era. The French encyclopedist D'Alembert (1754, 958) called them "dictionaries of things". Apart from extensive definitions of terms, they sometimes contain special sections where the reader can get a quick overview of the subject matter treated in them (Bergenholtz and Nielsen 2006).

A recent example of a dictionary of this kind is the English–Spanish *Encyclopedic Dictionary of Gene Technology* (Kaufmann and Bergenholtz 1998), which contains a 43-page systematic introduction to molecular biology structured in 30 thematic paragraphs, each of which can be accessed separately either by means of the index or following cross-references from selected dictionary articles. Apart from offering general information about the subject field, this introduction allows the translator to become acquainted with the basic terminology used within this particular discipline.

Figure 26.2 Article from *Diccionarios de Contabilidad* – Spanish–English

Alternatively, the dictionary can refer the translator to already-existing texts placed on the internet. Various specialised online dictionaries provide external hyperlinks to carefully selected webpages where the translator may obtain relevant and reliable background information. If well prepared, such hyperlinks to reliable sources may facilitate the translator's job and contribute to reducing the total time employed in the information search process.

Unfortunately, the global picture shows that there are still relatively few dictionaries that follow the above principles and pay attention to all relevant information needs which a translator may experience during the whole translation process from the preparation phase to the revision phase. For instance, dictionaries designed to solve communicative needs and those conceived to meet cognitive needs have tended to develop along separate lines with no or little overlap (Tarp 2015a).

If no well-conceived set of dictionaries is available in connection with a specific translation task, the translator typically has to resort to a variety of different lexicographical and non-lexicographical information sources, as has been documented by Nord (2002), among others. Consultation of these sources, which also include human experts, may eventually solve the translator's information needs, but the process tends to be much more time-consuming than if everything could be solved by consulting only one set of dictionaries as described above. In this sense, it is understandable that translators – as claimed by Calvo Rigual and Calvi (2014, 42) – sometimes regret "how inappropriate lexicographical resources are for their needs".

Interpreting in a lexicographical perspective

As we have seen, there is a close and well-established relationship between (written) translation and lexicography, despite certain quibbles between the two disciplines. By contrast, lexicography is largely absent from the literature on interpreting, and vice versa: so far, interpreting has not been explored from the point of view of lexicography. In this and the following sections, and based on an ongoing research project (Dam and Tarp In progress), we shall make a first attempt at bringing the two disciplines together. For this purpose, we shall draw on research carried out in the intersection between written translation and lexicography, as laid out in the previous sections, complemented with insights from interpreting studies. Following the pattern in the previous sections, we shall start by proposing a lexicographical model of interpreting, dividing the interpreting process into phases and sub-phases where lexicographically relevant information needs may occur. After a description of the basic premises, the model itself is presented (Schema 3).

Translation and interpreting share a series of characteristics, but the different conditions under which they are performed have implications for how the two tasks can be modelled lexicographically and, ultimately, for the design of relevant lexicographical tools for each of them. Some of the phases and sub-phases identified for translation in Schema 1 can thus be transferred almost directly to a lexicographically oriented model of interpreting, whereas others need to be adapted or eliminated and new ones must be added.

In widely accepted definitions of interpreting, this activity is conceptualised as an "immediate" form of translation characterised by ephemeral presentation and instant, one-time delivery (e.g. Pöchhacker 2004). This conceptualisation sets interpreting apart from (written) translation on several counts with lexicographical relevance. For one thing, since the target text is not only a first but also a final rendition, there cannot be a separate revision phase in the lexicographical interpreting model, i.e. the post-translation phase described in Schema 1 has no counterpart in Schema 3 below. Interpreters do monitor their own speech output and occasionally correct themselves on the spur, but not in a separate phase. There is also some evidence in the literature that interpreters revise their glossaries after the event (Moser-Mercer 1992a, 1992b; Jiang 2013) or self-evaluate (Kalina 2005). Such post-processes may in principle be interesting from a lexicographical perspective, but they will not be pursued further here.

Secondly, and most importantly, interpreting is a real-time performance conducted under time pressure. Standard information search processes are therefore virtually impossible during the actual task of interpreting, but must to a large extent take place before the event. Consequently, preparation for assignments is a large topic in the interpreting literature (Moser-Mercer 1992a, 1992b; Donovan 2001; Gile 2002, 2009; AIIC 2004; Luccarelli 2006; Jiang 2013; Nicodemus, Swabey and Taylor 2014; Díaz-Galaz, Padilla and Bajo 2015; Kalina 2015).

As source speeches are generally not available to interpreters before the actual task begins (on rare occasions, speech manuscripts are available in advance but speakers tend to deviate from these in any case), interpreters' information search processes are necessarily less targeted towards their actual information needs than those of translators. On the whole, interpreters' preparation is based on anticipated information needs. Thus, rather than preparing for an assignment on the explicit basis of a source text, interpreters tend to rely on meeting documents if and when available (agendas, documents to be discussed, slides, lists of participants, speakers' bios, etc.), complemented with internet searches and the use of "other background information and terminology resources" (AIIC 2004; cf. Donovan 2001;

Gile 2002, 2009; Kalina 2015). From these sources, interpreters extract the information they (believe they) will need to perform their task. The tangible result of interpreters' preparation is normally a so-called glossary of source-language terms and their target-language equivalents to be brought along to the interpreted event, described in more detail below.

The literature contains various classifications of the stages involved in interpreters' preparatory processes (e.g. Gile 2002; Kalina 2005, 2015). A well-known classification proposed by Gile (2009, 144–146) distinguishes between advance, last-minute and in-conference preparation, depending mainly on when meeting documents are made available to the interpreter and, hence, when information acquisition can begin. Interpreters systematically ask organisers and speakers to provide them with meeting documents well ahead of assignments for advance preparation. The standard the International Association of Conference Interpreters (AIIC) contract, for example, stipulates that the documents should be sent at least 15 days before a conference. Meeting documents are, however, often difficult to get hold of. Sometimes they are made available only at the very last minute, if at all. When documents are available only immediately before the interpreted event, on the premises or interpreters are called or assigned at short notice and therefore cannot prepare in advance, they will engage in last-minute preparation. In-conference preparation, on the other hand, is based on documents received after the event has started, speeches and discussions on site and conversations with speakers and colleagues during breaks.

The advance preparation phase has been carried over, without alterations, to the lexico-graphical interpreting model in Schema 3 below. However, the distinction between last-minute and in-conference preparation, though valid for other purposes, is not relevant from a lexicographical perspective as interpreters' information needs, and particularly their pos-sibilities of consulting dictionaries, are very similar in the two conditions: they work under time pressure and are only able to search for relatively simple items such as words, terms and their equivalents. Hence, in the lexicographical model of interpreting, last-minute and in-conference preparation are treated indiscriminately and subsumed under one heading: the so-called on-site preparation phase. This stage, which is conceived as a discontinuous phase surrounding the interpreting phase in the narrow sense (referred to as the online interpreting phase in the model), also encompasses breaks during assignment, i.e. offline periods that are sufficiently long to allow for information acquisition on site.

From a lexicographical perspective, then, the overall interpreting process consists of three main phases and a number of sub-phases where lexicographically relevant information needs may occur:

Schema 3: Interpreting model in a lexicographical perspective

1. The advance preparation phase where the interpreter may

    a. study meeting material (including manuscripts, if available) and other types of background material in the weeks, days or hours prior to the assignment in order to get a general idea of the subject matter, learn about specific topics and become familiar with the relevant terminology

    b. prepare a glossary with terms and equivalents to be used during the task

2. The on-site preparation phase where the interpreter may

    a. use offline periods to solve urgent problems, including to assist a colleague in need of help

    b. read speech manuscripts or other documents to be interpreted, mark the texts and translate problematic terms and words

3. The online interpreting phase where the interpreter interprets in the narrow sense, i.e. listens to source-language utterances and immediately thereafter reformulates them in the target language.

Most sub-phases in the model are optional depending on the interpreter, the context and the task. In fact, the only compulsory phase is the online interpreting phase, Phase 3. In principle, this phase involves the same sub-phases as Phase 2 in the translation model (Schema 1), i.e. reception, transfer and reformulation, but due to the time factor, no "normal" consultation of lexicographical works can take place in this phase. Hence, the three sub-phases in the translation phase in Schema 1 have been merged into one single phase in the interpreting model.

Phase 3 is included in the lexicographical model of interpreting mainly because of interpreters' (potential) use of glossaries – a lexicographical tool *par excellence* – but this phase will probably become even more lexicographically relevant in the future. Handheld mobile devices such as smartphones and, notably, tablets are increasingly making their way into interpreting booths. They are presumably still mainly used for consultation during offline periods (Phase 2), including for assisting a boothmate in need of help, but with increasingly advanced technology, dictionary consultation during online periods (Phase 3) cannot be ruled out as a standard option for the future. In fact, highly experienced interpreters are already able to perform quick searches during online periods using currently available technology.

Information needs in interpreting

In accordance with Donovan (2001), AIIC (2004) and Kalina (2015), among others, the information interpreters seek to acquire during advance or on-site preparation can be divided into three types:

1. information about the communicative context or situation (also referred to as pragmatic information), i.e. information about speakers, their attitudes and affiliations, the composition of the audience, the purpose of the event, the issues at stake, etc.
2. information about the subject matter and topics related to the interpreting task
3. information about the corresponding terminology in source and target languages.

Other classifications of interpreters' information needs have been proposed (Gile 2009; cf. Dam and Engberg 2005), but the one described above is widely used in the field. With respect to type-3 information, it should be noted that, in interpreting, the label, "terminology", is generally used to refer to terms (rather than concepts, cf. Rütten 2015), i.e. lexical items with special meanings and usages in LSP, and usually also includes general lexical items and fixed expressions.

The first type of information needs is beyond the scope of lexicography as dictionaries are unable to provide solutions to such needs, which are always related to concrete and very specific interpreting assignments. The two remaining types, however, bear close resemblance to the needs lexicographers label "cognitive" and "communicative", respectively, and are, as such, highly relevant from a lexicographical point of view, although they have not yet been discussed in this perspective. It is especially interesting to observe how interpreters transform themselves into mini-lexicographers when they compile glossaries during the preparation of an assignment.

Interpreters' glossaries may take many forms, but surveys conducted by Moser-Mercer (1992a, 1992b) and Jiang (2013) show that conference interpreters' preferences are for short and simple lists of source-language terms and their target-language equivalents for easy reference in the booth. Glossaries may in principle contain additional data, but according to the survey by Jiang (2013), interpreters tend to focus on technical terminology in their working languages, along with acronyms and names especially of organisations but also of places and people. Grammatical data, on the other hand, are generally not considered important for glossary purposes, according to the surveys. Grammar is not among AIIC's (2004) recommendations for data to be included in interpreters' glossaries, either. Pronunciation, on the other hand, is recommended for inclusion (AIIC 2004).

The surveys of interpreters' glossary preferences also produced interesting results regarding the preferred medium and format of these information tools. Perhaps surprisingly in the present digital age, the preferred medium for glossaries appears to be loose paper. With respect to format, Moser-Mercer's survey showed that interpreters' preference is for a simple format with "source language terms and target language term(s) parallel on one line" (Moser-Mercer 1992a, 303), a finding that was largely corroborated by Jiang (2013). As pointed out by Jiang, these features suggest that what is important for interpreters at work is instant accessibility. A paper-based glossary provides a broader display than the computer screen, and scrolling is not necessary. All in all, fast and accurate access to information seems vital "to meet the real-time processing needs which are part and parcel of conference interpreting" (Jiang 2013, 91).

However, in a self-observation study where Gile (2002) prepared and used a glossary for interpreting at a technical conference, this tool was found to be a long way from covering the terminological needs that arose during the conference. Based on a crude calculation, the coverage rate was below 20%, perhaps as low as 10%. Despite the fast access to data that glossaries are able to provide, there is thus still room for improvement when it comes to meeting interpreters' actual information needs.

Based on the above considerations, we can now present a model (Schema 4) that links the phases and sub-phases in the overall interpreting process shown in Schema 3 with the various types of information needs interpreters may experience in the course of an assignment, and which can be solved by means of lexicography:

Schema 4: Possible information needs during the interpreting process

1. In the advance preparation phase, the interpreter may need

   a. general and specific background information in order to facilitate comprehension of the overall subject field as well as specific topics related to the task

   b. definitions of terms, words and fixed expressions in order to understand the meeting and other background material

   c. source-language terms, words, fixed expressions, names of organisations and places, acronyms, as well as their target-language equivalents, in order to prepare a glossary and ensure rapid recognition, transfer and reformulation in the online phase

   d. information about pronunciation for rapid recognition of source-speech items and correct reformulation in the online phase

2. In the on-site preparation phase, the interpreter may need

   a. short definitions, equivalents and pronunciation of terms, words, fixed expressions, names of organisations and places, and possible acronyms, in order to solve predicted or observed problems related to the comprehension, transfer and reformulation of the texts (to be) interpreted

b. brief background information in order to facilitate comprehension of specific topics treated at the interpreted event

3. In the online interpreting phase, the interpreter may need

a. equivalents of terms, words, fixed expressions, names of organisations and places, acronyms, as well as information about their pronunciation.

Lexicographical assistance to interpreting

As can be seen in Schema 4, interpreters' needs for information develop progressively from broad and ample information to increasingly narrow categories. On the whole, cognitive needs dominate in the early phase(s), whereas communicative needs increasingly take over as we move from one phase to another. It is, however, more a question of degrees than of types. From a lexicographical point of view, the *types* of information needed are more or less similar in the successive phases (Phase 3 is the only exception, with no cognitive needs listed), but the *amounts* vary. As time becomes increasingly scarce, interpreters increasingly require fast and easy access to increasingly targeted and limited amounts of data.

Except for information about pronunciation, all the needs listed in Schema 4 have already been discussed in connection with the assistance lexicography may give to translation (see Schema 2). On the other hand, in Schema 4 there is no mention of information needs related to gender, inflection, collocations, syntactic properties, word formation and genre conventions. The reason is not that such needs may not occur during the interpreting process, but that interpreters tend to focus their attention on satisfying other types of information need, as explained in the previous section.

There are thus certain differences between translation and interpreting in terms of information needs, but these do not constitute any serious challenge to present-day lexicography. Audio-based data on pronunciation, although relatively expensive to produce, can easily be incorporated into the database discussed in relation to translation above. In addition, it would be fairly straightforward to design an additional set of user interfaces where only the data categories required by the interpreter in each type of situation are displayed. If these interfaces also allow for hidden data on gender, inflection, syntax, etc. to be loaded on the screen, then the interpreter, if needed, could get instant access to these data by means of a simple click or movement over the screen area.

Similarly, an additional interface could be designed to assist the interpreter in the compilation of a special glossary for use in the online phase (Phase 3). This could be done by displaying a dictionary with a reduced and pre-selected number of data fields from which relevant data could be selected (by clicking) and stored in the form of a short and simple glossary to be printed or shown on a handheld device for consultation during the interpreting task.

With respect to the information needs listed in relation to the online interpreting phase in Schema 4, there is little doubt that, objectively, almost all needs described under the translation phase in the previous Schema 2 may also occur during interpreting. However, most of these needs cannot be solved lexicographically, at least at present, due to a combination of time pressure and limitations in available technology. As explained above, information search processes during online interpreting periods cannot be ruled out. Be that as it may, from a lexicographic point of view, it is of no consequence whether interpreters attempt to solve their needs when they are online or they prefer to do so during offline periods. In either case, the task of lexicography is to provide solutions, online or offline, to help interpreters.

Finally, it should be noted that the overview of information needs presented in Schema 4 does not give a complete picture of the needs occurring during the entire interpreting process. Among other reasons, this is due to the fact that, in interpreting in particular, source and target language are dynamic rather than stable categories: what is source language in one moment may become target language the next. This is virtually always the case in dialogue interpreting as performed in, for example, community or business settings. On the other hand, many staff conference interpreters whose first language is a major one, only interpret *into* this language, i.e. it is basically always a target language for them. But then they usually work *from* more than one language, i.e. they normally deal with several source languages, sometimes in one and the same assignment. Language-wise, therefore, interpreters' information needs are often multilingual in nature (rather than bilingual, as is often the case in translation) and in constant flux. This feature needs to be taken into account when designing lexicographical tools for interpreting purposes.

On the whole, if the previously mentioned interfaces are incorporated into the lexicographical tool, the combination of one monolingual and two bilingual solutions in both language directions suggested in relation to translation could also cater for interpreters' information needs in the different phases of the overall interpreting process. Within such a set-up, a common database could feed a set of dictionaries designed to meet information needs occurring during both translation and interpreting. If this set of dictionaries includes more than two languages, it would be even more adapted to the multilingual reality of interpreting. In this perspective, special dictionaries for interpreting, which are bound to have a small audience, could be economically feasible in the digital era.

Future perspectives

The general tendency in current lexicography is the incorporation of sophisticated computer and information technologies with a view to developing still more personalised, web-based information tools. The "stand-alone" dictionary, whether printed or digital, will probably encounter growing competition from dictionaries that are integrated into other types of digital tools and media. The introduction of new techniques is opening new ways of accessing and using lexicographical data.

This development can already be observed in relation to translation dictionaries but will probably also have major consequences for dictionaries designed to assist interpreting. If speech recognition and other techniques are incorporated into devices connected to lexicographical databases, e.g. smartphones and tablets, this may lead to advanced tools capable of meeting other information needs in the interpreting booths than the ones discussed in the previous section.

The introduction of disruptive technologies has created very promising future perspectives for lexicography. We know the point of departure but we still only have a vague idea of where we will eventually arrive. However, in order to overcome all challenges along this road, it is above all necessary to strengthen the dialogue between lexicography, on the one hand, and translation and interpreting, on the other. Such a dialogue between different disciplines, we suggest, holds great potential.

Further reading

Bergenholtz, H. and Tarp, S., eds. 1995. *Manual of Specialised Lexicography.* Amsterdam: John Benjamins.

This classic manual of lexicography provides the student with an easily readable guide including many detailed examples showing how to prepare specialised dictionaries, among them translation dictionaries.

Fuertes-Olivera, P. A. and Bergenholtz, H., eds. 2011. *e-Lexicography: The Internet, Digital Initiatives and Lexicography*. London: Continuum.

In this book, various authors discuss the transition from the printed to the digital media and show how new technologies are transforming lexicography. It contains descriptions of new online information tools as well as visions for the future.

Tarp, S. 2008. *Lexicography in the Borderland between Knowledge and Non-Knowledge*. Tübingen: Niemeyer.

This book provides a comprehensive introduction to the function theory of lexicography with special focus on learners' dictionaries. It includes many detailed examples showing the reader how the theory may guide dictionary making.

Tarp, S. 2013. What should we demand from an online dictionary for specialized translation? *Lexicographica* 29, pp. 146–162.

This article dissects the LSP translation process from a lexicographical point of view. It identifies various phases and sub-phases where information needs may occur and suggests lexicographical solutions to these needs.

Tomaszczyk, J. 1989. "L1–L2 Technical Translation and Dictionaries". In *Translation and Lexicography*, edited by M. Snell-Hornby and E. Pöhl, 177–186. Amsterdam: John Benjamins.

This article describes a case study where the author took note of all look-ups in dictionaries during L1–L2 translation of a specialised book. It shows the variety of lexicographical solutions required to satisfy an LSP translator.

References

Adamska-Sałaciak, A. Forthcoming. "Bilingual Lexicography: Translation Dictionaries". In *International Handbook of Modern Lexis and Lexicography*, edited by P. Hanks and G. M. de Schryver. Berlin: Springer.

AIIC. 2004. *A Practical Guide for Professional Conference Interpreters* [online]. Available from: http://aiic.net/page/628 [Accessed 9 January 2016].

Atkins, B. T. S., ed. 1998. *Using Dictionaries: Studies of Dictionary Use by Language Learners and Translators*. Tübingen: Niemeyer.

Bergenholtz, H. and Nielsen, J. S. 2013. What is a lexicographical database? *Lexikos* 23, pp. 77–87.

Bergenholtz, H. and Nielsen, S. 2006. Subject-field components as integrated parts of LSP dictionaries. *Terminology* 12(2), pp. 281–303.

Bergenholtz, H. and Tarp, S., eds. 1995. *Manual of Specialised Lexicography*. Amsterdam: John Benjamins.

Bothma, T. J. D. 2011. "Filtering and Adapting Data and Information in an Online Environment in Response to User Needs". In *e-Lexicography: The Internet, Digital Initiatives and Lexicography*, edited by P. A. Fuertes-Olivera and H. Bergenholtz, 71–102. London: Continuum.

Burkhanov, I. 1998. *Lexicography. A Dictionary of Basic Terminology*. Rzeszów: Wydawnictwo Wyzszejszkol y Pedagogicznej.

Calvo Rigual, C. and Calvi, M. V. 2014. Translation and lexicography: a necessary dialogue. *MonTi* 6, pp. 37–62.

D'Alembert, J. L. R. 1754. "Dictionnaire". In *Tome IV of Encyclopédie, ou Dictionnaire raisonné des sciences, des arts et des métiers*, edited by D. Diderot and J. L. R. D'Alembert, 958–969. Paris: Briasson.

Dam, H. V. and Engberg, J. 2005. "Introduction". In *Knowledge Systems and Translation*, edited by H. V. Dam, J. Engberg and H. Gerzymisch-Arbogast, 1–13. Berlin: Mouton de Gruyter.

Dam, H. V. and Tarp, S. In progress. *Interpreting and Lexicography: Potential for a Dialogue?*

Díaz-Galaz, S., Padilla, P. and Bajo, M. T. 2015. The role of advance preparation in simultaneous interpreting: a comparison of professional interpreters and interpreting students. *Interpreting* 17(1), pp. 1–25.

Donovan, C. 2001. Interpretation of technical conferences. *Conference Interpretation and Translation* 3, pp. 7–29.

Fata, I. 2009. *Das zweisprachige Translationswörterbuch für Fachsprachen in der wissenschaftlichen Theorie und Praxis.* Budapest: Tinta Könyvkiadó.

Fuertes-Olivera, P. A. 2013. The theory and practice of specialised online dictionaries for translation. *Lexicographica* 29, pp. 69–91.

Fuertes-Olivera, P. A. and Bergenholtz, H., eds. 2011. *e-Lexicography: The Internet, Digital Initiatives and Lexicography.* London: Continuum.

Fuertes-Olivera, P. A., Bergenholtz, H., Nielsen, S., Mourier, L., Gómez, P. G., Amo, M. N., de los Ríos Rodicio, Á., Sastre Ruano, Á., Tarp, S. and Velasco Sacristán, M. S. 2015. *Diccionarios de Contabilidad.* Hamburg: Lemma.com.

Fuertes-Olivera, P. A. and Tarp, S. 2014. *Theory and Practice of Specialised Online Dictionaries: Lexicography Versus Terminography.* Berlin: De Gruyter.

Gile, D. 2002. The interpreter's preparation for technical conferences: methodological questions in investigating the topic. *Conference Interpretation and Translation* 4(2), pp. 7–27.

Gile, D. 2009. *Basic Concepts and Models for Interpreter and Translator Training.* Amsterdam: John Benjamins.

Hartmann, R. R. K. and James, G. 2001. *Dictionary of Lexicography.* London: Routledge.

Jiang, H. 2013. The interpreter's glossary in simultaneous interpreting: a survey. *Interpreting* 15(1), pp. 74–93.

Kalina, S. 2005. Quality assurance for interpreting processes. *Meta* 50(2), 768–784.

Kalina, S. 2015. "Preparation". In *Routledge Encyclopedia of Interpreting Studies*, edited by F. Pöchhacker, 318–320. London: Routledge.

Kaufmann, U. and Bergenholtz, H., eds. 1998. *Encyclopedic Dictionary of Gene Technology: English–Spanish.* Toronto: Lugus.

Luccarelli, L. 2006. Conference preparation: considerations and a course proposal. *Conference Interpretation and Translation* 8(1), pp. 3–26.

Mackintosh, K. 1998. "An Empirical Study of Dictionary Use in L2-L1 Translation". In *Using Dictionaries: Studies of Dictionary Use by Language Learners and Translators*, edited by B. T. S. Atkins, 121–149. Tübingen: Niemeyer.

Marello, C. 2003. "The Bilingual Dictionary". In *Lexicography: Critical Concepts II*, edited by R. R. K. Hartmann, 325–342. London: Routledge.

Moser-Mercer, B. 1992a. Terminology documentation in conference interpretation. *Terminologie et Traduction* 2(3), pp. 285–303.

Moser-Mercer, B. 1992b. Banking on terminology: conference interpreters in the electronic age. *Meta* 37(3), pp. 507–522.

Nesi, H. 2015. "The Demands of Users and the Publishing World: Printed or Online, Free or Paid for?" In *The Oxford Handbook of Lexicography*, edited by P. Durkin, 579–589. Oxford: Oxford University Press.

Nicodemus, B., Swabey, L. and Taylor, M. M. 2014. Preparation strategies used by American Sign Language–English interpreters to render President Barak Obama's inaugural address. *The Interpreter's Newsletter* 19, pp. 27–44.

Nielsen, S. 2013. Domain-specific knowledge in lexicography: how it helps lexicographers and users of accounting dictionaries intended for communicative usage situations. *Hermes* 50, pp. 51–60.

Nielsen, S., Mourier, L. and Bergenholtz, H. 2015. *Accounting Dictionaries.* Odense: Ordbogen.com.

Nord, B. 2002. *Hilfsmittel beim Übersetzen. Eine empirische Studie zum Rechercheverhalten professioneller Übersetzer.* Frankfurt am Main: Peter Lang.

Piotrowski, T. 1994. *Problems in Bilingual Lexicography*. Wroclaw: Wydawnictwo Uniwersytetu Wroclawskiego.

Pöchhacker, F. 2004. *Introducing Interpreting Studies*. London: Routledge.

Rütten, A. 2015. "Terminology". In *Routledge Encyclopedia of Interpreting Studies*, edited by F. Pöchhacker, 416–417. London: Routledge.

Sin-wai, C., ed. 2004. *Translation and Bilingual Dictionaries*. Tübingen: Niemeyer.

Snell-Hornby, M. and Pöhl, E., eds. 1989. *Translation and Lexicography*. Amsterdam: John Benjamins.

Tarp, S. 2008. *Lexicography in the Borderland between Knowledge and Non-Knowledge*. Tübingen: Niemeyer.

Tarp, S. 2013. What should we demand from an online dictionary for specialized translation? *Lexicographica* 29, pp. 146–162.

Tarp, S. 2015a. On the disciplinary and functional status of economic lexicography. *Ibérica* 29, pp. 179–200.

Tarp, S. 2015b. Structures in the communication between lexicographer and programmer: database and interface. *Lexicographica* 31, pp. 219–246.

Tomaszczyk, J. 1989. "L1–L2 Technical Translation and Dictionaries". In *Translation and Lexicography*, edited by M. Snell-Hornby and E. Pöhl, 177–186. Amsterdam: John Benjamins.

Varantola, K. 1998. "Translators and their Use of Dictionaries". In *Using Dictionaries: Studies of Dictionary Use by Language Learners and Translators*, edited by B. T. S. Atkins, 179–192. Tübingen: Niemeyer.

Wiegand, H. E. 1987. Zur handlungstheoretischen Grundlegung der Wörterbenutzungsforschung. *Lexicographica* 3, pp. 178–227.

Wiegand, H. E. 2000. "Wissen, Wissenrepräsentationen und Printwörterbücher". In *Proceedings of the Ninth EURALEX International Congress*, edited by U. Heid, S. Evert, E. Lehmann and C. Rohrer, 15–38. Stuttgart: Institut für Maschinelle Sprachverarbeitung.

Yong, H. and Peng, J. 2007. *Bilingual Lexicography from a Communicative Perspective*. Amsterdam: John Benjamins.

27

Language for Specific Purposes and translation

Stefanos Vlachopoulos

Introduction

This chapter is divided into two parts: the initial part is devoted to the historical background and major trends concerning the interaction of LSP and translation; a second part deals with practical issues.

At the outset of the first part we will start with two tales: the tale of *LSP, Language for Specific Purposes* or *Language for Special Purposes*, and secondly the story of how translation (studies) reacted to LSP. In connection with the tale of LSP, we will argue that the concept of language for specific purposes is no longer viable. Research following Hoffmann's (1993) postulation of a communicative view of domain-specific language use has shown that specialised communication is generated by domain-specific discourse employed to communicate knowledge (Engberg 2010; Eppler 2007). The second tale, of how Translation Studies has reacted to domain-specific communication, will build upon Picht's view (1996) of LSP translation as *intersprachliche Fachkommunikation*, that is, as domain-specific communication across languages. It will demonstrate that translating specialised discourse is actually intercultural knowledge communication (Engberg 2010).

In the second part of the chapter we will examine how translators have handled specialised discourse by analysing samples of translated legal texts, the cultural extreme of domain-specific discourse. The examination of discourse reminds us that we must view a translator's decisions in light of the communicative events both in the source and the target culture and of the knowledge to be communicated. The analysis of the samples will highlight future directions for research in intercultural domain-specific communication.

From Language for Specific Purposes (LSP) to specialised communication

Let us first consider the widespread misconception that the acronym LSP stands for terminology in a given domain, implying that vocabulary alone makes communication happen. After some reflection on communication in general we realise that there is much more to communication than terminology and we come to understand that there are as many LSPs as there are domains and that LSPs change with the domains they serve as instruments of communication. If we take, for example, communication in fields that are all considered as business, we soon realise that there cannot be a single (sub-)language carrying the burden of communication in so versatile a domain. Linguistic structures are used qualitatively and quantitatively differently in accountancy, marketing, banking, etc. as a result of diverging social practices.

In addition to its focus on vocabulary, the LSP school of thought also considered specialised communication to be confined within the borders of each individual domain. The German linguists Möhn and Pelka (1984, 26) defined *Fachsprache* (LSP) as that variety of a language that enables the conceptualisation, the notional designation and the recognition of specialised objects and processes belonging to the domain. However, the communicative reality as we experience it does not know any disciplinary boundaries since intradisciplinary and interdisciplinary communication, as well as communication with laypersons, are routine. The LSP provides common ground for communication by experts with experts from the same or another domain, but it also allows for communication with non-specialists. This means that apart from expert communication within a certain discipline, LSP is used to transfer knowledge across the boundaries of a discipline.

In the late 1970s and 1980s, research contrasted LSP with the common language (Bausch 1976, 128; Henne 1979, 313) focusing on vocabulary and terminology to distinguish the languages of specific purposes from the common language. Research highlighted the interrelation between specialised and non-specialised language and made the mechanisms used visible (Hoffmann 1985, 48; Fluck 1985, 160). Bolten (1992, 153) agrees with Hoffmann and Fluck that the difference between communication using the common language and communication using the LSP is what triggered interest in LSP. At a second stage, research shifted from the study of isolated linguistic issues to communicative aspects of specialised communication (Kalverkämper and Baumann 1996, 355) focusing on the production and the perception of specialised texts (Baumann 2010, 1). Research in domain-specific communication became internationalised and intercultural perspectives on specialised communication developed. Expert communication was studied across cultural borders (Schröder 1993, 517; Baumann 1996, 368).

Buhlmann and Fearns (2000, 12–13) realised that the discourse of certain scientific disciplines results from socialisation and that it reflects structures of thought:

> Therefore, LSP as a means of communication is a result of socialization within a certain scientific discipline. It is characterized as such by reflecting certain thought structures that are determined by the interest in findings and research prevailing in the respective field. LSP is important for the communication of technical contents – objects, operations, processes, procedures, theories, etc. – and, from a linguistic point of view, uses the most concise and precise form.

In other words, LSP is used to communicate patterns of thought within the discipline. These patterns of thought transfer knowledge. The following quotation from Buhlmann and Fearns (2000, 13) reveals a crucial position for LSP research at that time: "LSP is therefore linked to the thought element of the field that the technical terms exist in – the thought structures of the field and the customary communication structures of the discipline". From these words one infers that every domain develops its own, unique, linguistic tools for communication, its own discourse, in Fairclough's (1992) terms, that are linked to the thought patterns of the experts working in the field, and that come into being through socialisation; however, it is a discourse that uses linguistic features of the common language to a great extent: Communication comes into being through fixed stylistic formations (Baumann 1993, 417; Gläser 1978, 463; Grabowski 1992, 17–18; Hoffmann 1984, 47, 231).

The German linguist, Hoffmann, uses the term *Fachsprache* (LSP) in his early work to describe communication within a domain (Hoffmann 1984, 53):

Fachsprache – das ist die Gesamtheit aller sprachlichen Mittel, die in einem fachlich begrenzbaren Kommunikationsbereich verwendet werden, um die Verständigung zwischen den in diesem Bereich tätigen Menschen (und die Popularisierung der fachlichen Inhalte sowie den Kontakt zu bestimmten Nicht-Fachleuten) zu gewährleisten.

(LSP is the sum of all the linguistic resources used in an area of professional communication to enable mutual understanding between professionals in the area (and to communicate the specialist content to the general public and maintain contact with selected lay people).)

About a decade later, Hoffmann abandoned the notion of *Fachsprache* and adopted the term *Fachkommunikation* (specialised communication), which he defined in terms of communication of knowledge (Hoffmann 1993, 614) as follows:

Fachkommunikation ist die von außen oder von innen motivierte bzw. stimulierte, auf fachliche Ereignisse oder Ereignisabfolgen gerichtete Exteriorisierung und Interiorisierung von Kenntnissystemen und kognitiven Prozessen, die zur Veränderung der Kenntnissysteme beim einzelnen Fachmann und in ganzen Gemeinschaften von Fachleuten führen.

(Specialised communication is the externalisation and internalisation, whether motivated or stimulated from the outside or from the inside, of knowledge systems and cognitive processes related to specialised information, which leads to change in individual experts' knowledge systems and in the knowledge systems possessed by entire communities of specialists.)

The definition of specialised communication focuses on the communication as a whole, on the cognitive processes, knowledge systems, the individual interlocutor and the dynamics of meaning, providing an integrated picture of communication in domain-specific settings (Engberg 2010, 53). Moreover, it implies that communication cannot focus solely on isolated linguistic features, such as individual words, syntactic structures, etc. Hoffmann's (1993) definition of specialised communication provides a perspective that considers knowledge and the transformation of knowledge systems to be an integral part of domain-specific communication.

Notwithstanding the definitions by Hoffmann (1984, 1993) and by Buhlmann and Fearns (2000, 13), experts communicate beyond domain borders. The communication of knowledge from expert to non-expert is an endeavour in which language is challenged. Struggling to achieve a communicational goal and transport expert knowledge across disciplinary boundaries – both in writing and in spoken discourse – can stretch the linguistic/communicative competence of the interlocutors.

The pragmatic definition of domain-specific communication as an inherent feature of text and knowledge systems forms a bridge that leads to the scrutiny of communication and the limits of the human mind in acquiring and managing knowledge (Roelcke, 2010, 24). This shifted the examination of domain-specific communication away from linguistic features alone onto communication as such. Moreover, including cognition into the research in domain-specific communication opened up new methods of text classification and provided a new methodo-logical dimension (Baumann 1996, 384). What counts is the degree of domain-specificity of knowledge, knowledge structures, the transfer of knowledge, its linguistic representation and its deployment when communicated within a given domain, etc.

Hoffmann's (1993) definition of specialised communication implies that knowledge and its interiorisation is closely linked to the existing subject knowledge of the receptor. The suc-cessful transfer of knowledge and its reception is subject to a successful assessment of the available subject knowledge: Tsoukas and Vladimirou (2001) identified three important factors concerning knowledge: Firstly, existing knowledge is the basis for the acquisition of new knowledge; secondly, knowledge is created and applied in the mind of the bearer; and, thirdly, knowledge and comprehension are different procedures, where the latter, compre-hension, determines the former. For Risku and Windhager (2009, 4) knowledge is relatively stable in comparison to understanding. They write:

> By "understanding", we mean the process of combining experience-based knowledge with information gathered from the present environment to form a new mental or physical action. Thus, making sense of the environment and understanding are challenges that confront us every single day.

Knowledge can come into being in the mind of the bearer; comprehension needs existing knowledge on the basis of which it can grow. For Eppler, Röpnack and Seifried (1999) the successful communication of knowledge requires the successful transfer and restructuring of that knowledge by the receptor.

Language (for specific communication) as the raw material of domain-specific communication

When it comes to domain-specific communication, what actually occurs is a change in the knowledge system of the individual and the domain; it is the discourse, the fixed, domain-specific, linguistic patterns that experts use when communicating knowledge. As happens with any communication, language is the factor challenged when it comes to the com-munication of knowledge (Welch and Welch 2008). If language is used inappropriately, communication might fail. For Welch and Welch (2008, 354) language is a reconfiguration agent, a mechanism for reconfiguring knowledge.

Given the above, we will isolate LSP from specialised communication in order to shed light on the linguistic mechanisms making up the discourse employed in specialised communi-cation. In order to get a picture of the linguistic raw material in specialised communication, we will examine specialised language as a subsystem of a wider linguistic system. This per-spective provides for a more focused look at the special features of specialised communi-cation, drawing a clearer line between LSP and other varieties of language such as the language of hunters, students, etc. (Fluck 1976, 11). According to Möhn and Pelka (1984, 24), LSPs distinguish themselves as far as choice, use and frequency of particular linguistic features of morphology, vocabulary, syntax and textual properties are concerned. Vocabulary plays a pivotal role in the LSP school of thought. The notion of terminology has – mostly in the past – been treated as a synonym for LSP. Syntactic and textual parameters were con-sidered at a later stage in research. Apart from terminology there is much more to vocabulary in specialised texts. The terms used need complementary lexical material, which allows them to bring about their specific meaning.

Lexically, a specialised text is comprised not solely of terminology but also of other vocabulary. As to terms, in many disciplines they are used for one concept only, while in general language many words have multiple meanings. The term is a special lexical unit that denotes an exactly defined concept within a system that belongs to a domain. Arntz and Picht (1992, 35) provide the following definition of the notion *term*:

> ... *spezifische lexikalische Einheit und einnamige Bezeichnung eines im betreffenden Fach exakt definierten Begriffes oder Gegenstandes, die einen definierten Begriff im System eines Fachgebietes bezeichnet.*
>
> (... a specific lexical unit and the single denotation of an distinctively defined concept or object within the relevant domain, which denotes a concept defined within the system of the specialised domain.)

The very common lack of polysemy within one specialised domain accounts for the context independency of terms. In terminology, the polysemic nature of language is limited; terms are the result of convention, because they are formed on the basis of an agreement between specialists in a given field, and because they are motivated by the intention to facilitate communication in the domain (Sager 1990, 56–57).

Notwithstanding its importance in communication, syntax is neglected when it comes to specialised language. In contrast to the vocabulary where terminology distinguishes the specialised texts from non-specialised, syntax makes use of structures that are known from the common language. Early research in LSP focused on distinct aspects of the specialised language like terminology and – marginally – on syntax. Most work on specialised language limited its involvement with syntax to claiming that the difference between the syntax of common language and specialised language is a qualitative discrepancy in the use of particular syntactic structures (Wüster 1991, 2; Beier 1979, 276; Möhn and Pelka 1984, 19; Buhlmann and Fearns 1987, 50).

Littmann (1983), though, investigated the syntax of German specialised language and identified regularities: Littmann (1983, 98) refers to the relationship between the surface and the deeper logico-semantic structure of language as syntactic structures (*syntaktische Strukturen*), the correlation of the deep structure (*zugrundeliegende Struktur*) and the surface structure (*Oberflächenstruktur*) of a speech act. Littmann bases his approach on the ability of most users of the language to recognise a specialised text from experience and to categorise it as a special text. In his initial approach to a text he identifies the syntactic features of the specialised text on the surface, the *surface structure*. Subsequently, he tries to reconstruct the simplest structure of the verb, the deepest underlying verbal chain (*zugrundeliegende verbale Kette*). By this Littmann (1981, 147, 150) means the verbal phrase, whose environment is fully analysed to its simplest structure. For him the analysis is considered complete when the simplest verbal structure has been produced. In Littmann's words (1981, 150), "*Erst wenn all Leerstellen eines zugrundeliegenden Verbs mit Ausdrücken besetzt sind, die ihrerseits nicht auf zugrundliegende verbale Ketten zurückführbar sind, ist die Analyse abgeschlossen*". (Only if all empty positions of the underlying verb are filled with expressions which cannot be reduced to other underlying verbal chains, is the analysis complete.)

Consider the following sentence from a German contract:

(1) *Wird M die Konzession für diesen Geschäftsbetrieb oder für den Vertrieb einzelner der in § 12 Abs. 1 erwähnten Artikel nach Vertragsbeginn entzogen aus Gründen, ...*

(2) *Wird M die Konzession für diesen Geschäftsbetrieb oder für den Vertrieb einzelner Artikel, die in § 12 Abs. 1 erwähnt werden, nach Vertragsbeginn entzogen aus Gründen,*

(3) *Wenn man M nach Vertragsbeginn die Konzession für diesen Geschäftsbetrieb oder für den Vertrieb einzelner Artikel, die der Verfasser in § 12 Abs. 1 erwähnt, aus Gründen entzieht, . . .*

The first sentence is taken from a German lease. It is semantically very dense due to the use of participles (*erwähnten, entzogen* in version 1). Breaking down the past participles gradually into verbal structures one arrives at the deep structure (*erwähnt, entzieht* in version 3), the simplest verbal chain possible. In the interim phase, version 2, the participle, *erwähnt*, is analysed into a passive voice, a verbal chain.

This is not to imply that the syntax of specialised discourse is necessarily complex in structure. On the contrary: The sentence below taken from the monthly report of the *Deutsche Bundesbank* illustrates exactly the opposite:

> *Mit dem Ölpreisverfall und der Abwertung des Euro, die gegen Mitte des Jahres 2014 einsetzten und sich zum Jahresende markant verstärkten, haben sich einige Eckwerte des globalen Umfelds erheblich verändert.*

(Deutsche Bundesbank 2015, 50)

Nobody would question the high degree of specialisation of the text – simply because of a less complex syntactic structure. It is simply another discourse deploying a different linguistic inventory. The dense occurrence of terms, some of them originating in verbs (*Ölpreisverfall, Abwertung*), signals to the German reader that he has a specialised text at hand.

Apart from lexical and syntactic features, textual patterns are also domain- and culture-specific. Every text is connected to a culture which determines the way the meaning is produced and extracted (Koller 1992, 59). Stolze (1992, 192) connects textuality to domain-specific thought patterns and maintains (Stolze 1992 109, 143) that domain-specific thought patterns differ from culture to culture and are mirrored in a distinct, culture-specific, text structure.

Translating thought patterns

In this section, we will turn to the translation of specialised texts and how translation (studies) deal(s) with it. Picht's coinage (1996) *intersprachliche Fachkommunikation*, (interlinguistic specialised communication), which indicates how specialised translation was viewed at the time, illustrates a tendency to view it rather as a form of specialised communication than as translation. This could explain why, a decade later, Sandrini (2010) concludes that specialised translation is not treated as a field of its own within Translation Studies and that it has not found the place it deserves. Moreover, apart from being largely neglected by Translation Studies proper, it took Translation Studies some time to refocus on pragmatic issues of specialised communication: Stolze (2009, 15) writes that translation theory is too focused on the design of models of the translation process, the discussion of language-specific code transfers, the description of text typologies and text-linguistic structures, the prerequisites for achieving equivalents, the presentation of a model of translation as intercultural communication, the analysis of functional translation problems, and the didactic description of cognitive procedures. In her opinion Translation Studies proper disregards pragmatic aspects of specialised communication.

Much has been written on the translation of domain-specific texts, such as legal texts, engineering texts, business texts, medical texts, etc., but works dealing with specialised translation generally are scarce. The number of books in the field is very limited. Mostly, research in the field is published in journal articles and in collective volumes. Such titles are Hoffmann, Kalverkämper and Wiegand (1998), Kovtyk and Wendt (2002), Rega and Magris (2004), Gotti and Šarčević (2006), Lavault-Olléon (2007), Schmitt and Jüngst (2007), Reinart (2009), Dogoriti and Vyzas (2015) and Vlachopoulos (2015). The books, however, are dedicated to domain-specific translation.

Despite attempts to establish an integrated theory of translation (Snell-Hornby 1986/1994; Hatim and Mason 1990), the work done did not result in a coherent theory of specialised translation. There were, however, attempts to describe the translation of specialised texts generally in the first decade of our millennium. The popular approaches to specialised translation were pragmatic, and culturally and knowledge focused. Stolze (2009) discusses the issues that arise in the course of translating specialised texts against a theoretical backdrop. She urges the translator to compare original texts in the domain with the same text genre cross-culturally and points out that specialised translation can be as diverse as, or even more diverse than, specialised communication. The purpose and the linguistic make-up of the target text genre determine the translator's decisions; specialised intercultural communication is feasible only when we know for what purpose particular norms are used and why specific facts and procedures are denoted in a certain way. Stolze (1999, revised version 2009) is considered a landmark introduction to the field. It discusses the quality of the linguistic, cultural and expert knowledge a translator needs to be able to cope with specialised translations (Stolze 2009, 15) and emphasises the need for an analysis of the aspects of LSP texts on both sides of the cultural rim (Stolze 2009, 13).

The approach of Gerzymisch-Arbogast (2008) is based on a three-step approach based on Nida and Taber (1969) and Dogoriti and Vyzas (2015, 146–148). She proposes the following three steps (Gerzymisch-Arbogast 2008, 13):

- a bottom-up text analysis with text-individual "salient" LSP features in the reception phase (identifiable on an atomistic, hol-atomistic and holistic level), i.e. a phase in which the LSP source text is "understood" and its comprehension is secured and controlled;
- a contrastive analysis phase in which language and cultural LSP features, patterns and/or knowledge systems are compared for translation purposes (transfer phase) and which includes a comparative compatibility analysis of source and potential target text features from all three text perspectives: atomistic, holistic and hol-atomistic;
- a reformulation phase in the target language and culture, in which the individual target text is produced ((re)production phase) against the language and cultural resources identified in the transfer phase. The reformulation process is governed by at least the target text purpose, applicable norms and assumed recipient or text type and interrelates atomistic, hol-atomistic and holistic levels or text perspectives.

She describes a three-step procedure beginning with a bottom-up description of LSP, with the target text purpose and its correlation with the knowledge systems inherent to the domain. The paper acknowledges the importance of the knowledge systems involved in the translation of specialised texts. She points out that not only linguistic features but, most importantly, knowledge systems may be differently structured interculturally, i.e. their "setup" may vary by language and culture (Gerzymisch-Arbogast 2008, 26).

Sandrini (2010) provides, what he calls an attempt to define specialised translation: He proposes the following definition (my translation):

1. skopos-dependent
2. exteriorisation of
3. thematic knowledge-systems and cognitive processes,
4. selected from a pool of available information and weighted (interiorisation),
5. with the intention to disseminate it, in a different linguistic (interlingual) and
6. cultural (cross-cultural) area
7. against the backdrop of the global framework (interculture).

According to Sandrini (2010) each of the above points that make up the framework of specialised translation is a distinct feature of the process. Thus, Sandrini believes that in the widest sense, any communicative act has a skopos, a purpose, and that this has been provided by the initiator who prescribes the translators actions. Features 2 and 3 are taken from Hoffmann's definition of specialised communication and refer to the thematic integration of the translated text into the domain (Hoffmann 1993, 595–617). Feature 4 pays tribute to a basic determinant of Translation Studies, i.e. the choices to be made by the translator when it comes to the purpose-oriented activity of translation. Sandrini points out that the features that differentiate specialised communication from specialised translation are features 5 and 6. These two points account for the fact that translating is about the transfer of knowledge into a different language and culture and the constraints of domain-specific communication in that culture as explained above. Point 7 mirrors the influence of the domain as a global community on the communication processes including translating. The more specialised the translating becomes, the more the general, national culture is pushed into the background and the cultural features of the domain gain importance. Sandrini remarks that this cannot always be attributed entirely to the highly specialised source text; both the envisaged purpose of the target text and the recipient have an impact on the degree of specialisation of the translation.

The texts of a domain are the reflection of the knowledge system and the cognitive structures developed over time to comprehend them. The expert acquires new knowledge on the basis of the existing knowledge. Widdowson's words "no text is an island" (Johns 1997, 35) are confirmed both by linguists such as Hoffmann, Buhlmann and Fearns and by researchers from other domains such as Eppler, and Tsoukas and Vladimirou. Widdowson tells us a general truth: No text stands alone. The understanding of a text relies on the knowledge and experience gained by the individual or the group in the domain. Thus, specialised translation can be seen as an integrated mode of cross-cultural communication – bearing responsibility for a functioning cross-cultural dialogue in a given domain (Sandrini 2010). Indeed, this reconfirms what has been said by Gryzmisch-Arbogast and Sandrini about specialised translation: As an early link in the chain of communication the translator understands a given source text on the basis of existing knowledge. The knowledge s/he comprehends in the course of the translation project is interiorised. The next step is the exteriorisation of this knowledge in a target system in the form of a skopos-appropriate, target knowledge structure.

At this point we will provide a definition of specialised translation based upon the positions put forward so far:

Specialised translation is the communication of intercultural knowledge that takes place when the knowledge from a specialised text inherent to a knowledge system is transferred into a target text embedded in a target culture and aiming at a fulfilling a communicative purpose through transformation of the recipient's knowledge system.

From theory to practice; or how do translators cope with knowledge structures?

In the second part of this chapter we will examine samples of translated specialised communication. We opt for legal texts, the most extreme examples of culturally specific and knowledge-dependent domain-specific communication. The analysis of the samples is conducted against the background of the definition of specialised translation formulated just above.

We will proceed as follows: So far any (specialised) communication has been described as a data-driven process, which cannot disregard the knowledge of language and about language inherent in domain-specific knowledge (communication). Observing the changes in the linguistic inventory is expected to provide feedback on the appreciation of different knowledge structures in different legal cultures by the translators and their awareness of the cross-cultural differences of the appropriate knowledge structures. An examination of the translation process focused on changes in the knowledge systems would direct attention to the translated text as a product of intercultural communication of knowledge and to the interplay between the translator's mindset, the translated text and the management of the available knowledge. The assessment of the (non-)existence of traces of appropriate use of available data to initiate and sustain the communication of knowledge is expected to provide feedback on how translators experience specialised language, if they are aware of the cross-cultural differences and understand why the translators make (no) discourse changes. In particular, scrutiny of the discourse changes (not) made is expected to reveal if the system-inherent particularities on both sides of the cultural rim, and their interplay within the system, have been fully appreciated.

In other words, we will establish whether there are indications of appropriate intercultural communication of structures of knowledge, whether the translator responded correctly to a prompt by an initiator, elaborating on the available data, and whether the target text conforms with the skopos; language will be studied in both systems communicatively – or – the communication will be viewed linguistically. This implies a scrutiny of language in use, language above or beyond the sentence, language as meaning in interaction and language in its situational and cultural context.

Identifying instances in which the translator's decisions are reflected in his or her linguistic choices during the production of a pragmatically sound target text is expected to make systemic discourse properties visible, to highlight cross-cultural differences in the structures of knowledge reflected in the differences between the legal discourses involved, to reveal whether and to what extent linguistic differences between a source system and a target system are being considered and, most importantly for cross-cultural communication in law, to show appreciation of the interplay of system-inherent discourse particularities within the systems of knowledge involved.

The analysis

We will study the translations of two texts. The first text is the 1951 translation of the Greek Civil Code into German, and the second is a German lease translated into Modern Greek for use before a court in Greece. The analysis of the two cases will provide insight into the knowledge systems involved by highlighting the legal background against which the texts were translated. The translations will also be scrutinised for functionality, and the juxtaposition of the discourse properties of the translated text with the source text will allow us to delve into approaches to communicating knowledge appropriately.

The translation of the Greek Civil Code into German

The first case under scrutiny is the translation of a law, the Greek Civil Code, into German. The source text draws heavily on the German Civil Code, which is probably the reason why our examination of the texts does not reveal any problems in the translation of Greek terminology into German. What is interesting, though, is the translation of the sentence structure. In his preface to the translation the translator writes (Gogos 1951, VIII):

> *Bei der Übersetzung des griechischen ZGB wurde versucht, den griechischen Text wörtlich wiederzugeben. Dabei wurde auch an der Reihenfolge der Worte und an der Interpunktion dieses Textes festgehalten, soweit dies stilistisch möglich war. Nur dort habe ich von einer wörtlichen Übersetzung abgesehen, wo durch eine solche der Sinn des griechischen Textes nicht wiedergegeben werden konnte.*

(When translating the Greek Civil Code, I tried to render the Greek text word-for-word, and to retain the word order and punctuation, insofar as this was possible. I have only foregone word-for-word translation in cases where translating in that way could not reflect the sense of the Greek text.)

The translator seeks to stay as close as possible to the source text structure, which is an understandable decision, since the work is published under the auspices of the *Max-Planck-Institut für ausländisches und internationales Privatrecht* for comparativists, who would be interested in gaining insight into the argument structure of Greek law. He commits himself to syntactic fidelity and adds that he will deviate only where any linear reproduction of the source text structure would endanger the comprehension of the original text.

Interestingly, the juxtaposition of the texts shows that he did not act consistently throughout the text. For example, in paragraph 904 the first sentence was restructured as follows:

Source text

Αδικαιολόγητος πλουτισμός

Άρθρον 904

Ο καταστάς πλουσιώτερος άνευ νομίμου αιτίας εκ της περιουσίας άλλου ή επί ζημία τούτου, υποχρεούται εις απόδοσιν της ωφελείας. Η υποχρέωσις αυτή υφίσταται ιδία συνεπεία παροχής αχρεωστήτου ή παροχής δι'αιτίαν μη επακολοθήσασαν ή λήξασαν ή παράνομον ή ανήθικον.

(Enrichment without just cause

Article 904

A person who has become richer without a lawful cause by means or to the detriment of the patrimonium of another shall be bound to restitute the benefit. Such obligation shall particularly arise by reason of a payment made which was not due or of payment for a consideration that did not materialise or that ceased to exist or that was illegal or immoral.)

Translated text

Ungerechtfertigte Bereicherung

904. Wer sich ohne rechtlichen Grund aus dem Vermögen eines anderen oder zu dessen Schaden bereichert hat, ist zur Herausgabe des Vorteils verpflichtet. Diese Verpflichtung besteht insbesondere wegen Bewirkung einer nicht geschuldeten Leistung oder einer Leistung aus einem nicht eingetretenem Grund oder aus einem Grund, der zu bestehen aufgehört hat oder rechtswidrig oder unsittlich ist.

The participle in the first sentence (*Ο καταστάς πλουσιώτερος άνευ νομίμου αιτίας εκ της περιουσίας* ...) was translated in a more transparent way as a relative clause (*Wer sich ohne rechtlichen Grund aus dem Vermögen eines anderen oder zu dessen Schaden bereichert hat* ...). In the following sentence the translator acted in the same way and participles (... *μη επακολοθήσασαν ή λήξασαν ή παράνομον ή ανήθικον*) were transferred into the target system as relative clauses (... *der zu bestehen aufgehört hat oder rechtswidrig oder unsittlich ist*). Complex genitive structures (*Ο ένεκα γενομένων δαπανών υπόχρεως προς αποζημίωσην* ...) were again translated as more transparent relative clauses (*Wer für Aufwendungen zum Schadenersatz verpflichtet ist* ...).

The German language has the same inventory as the Greek language for expressing conditional clauses; however, the translator chose to use an alternative solution instead of being faithful to the original sentence structure. The Greek conditional sentence is introduced by the word *Εάν* while the German language uses either the equivalents *Wenn* or *Falls* or an alternative sentence structure according to which the conditional sentence is introduced by the verb of the conditional clause. The conditional clause *Εάν η εκτέλεσις του τρόπου καθίσταται* .... in paragraph 2016 of the Greek Civil Code could have been translated linearly, but the translator chose a different solution. A linear transfer of the source text structure would have provided a clearer view of the argument structure of the original sentence and served its purpose better. As mentioned in the first part of this chapter, syntax is crucial in the communication of knowledge and syntactic structures may mirror the degree of speciality: The higher the density of the meaning due to a syntactic structure, the more specialised the text.

In this case the translator produced a much too "German" text; despite the fact that the target system provided for solutions closer to the sentence and argument structure of the original Greek text. The comparison of the original and the translation show that the translator did not keep to his initial intention to adhere to the original text structure as much as possible, and therefore he actually deprived the recipient of the chance to gain a better understanding of the source system's argument structure.

As far as translation for the purposes of comparative law is concerned Leckey (2009, 124) writes:

> Although linguistic translation is a key part of comparative law, often it is not texts globally or words individually that comparatists and law makers translate. They translate concepts, in the sense of units of thought combining within themselves the properties and relationships of things. The comparatist objective is to convey the gist of a concept, at a minimum, to readers unfamiliar with its legal system of origin. Respecting legal concepts, they undertake the transference; removal or conveyance from one person, place, or condition to another. The legislative objective is to translate a concept so as to set it to work in the destination legal system: legislatures express a rule or formulate a concept in adapted or modernized terms.

We could not agree more with the above words for comparative purposes. But there are limitations: When it comes to the examination of the argument structure in comparative law, which is reflected in sentence and text structure, and, secondly, in cases where comparability (as in legal disputes) is vital, a translation as linear as possible is more appropriate. In the first case a linear translation of the terminology from one system into another with a differing structure would create confusion about the actual denotations of the concepts. However, in cases where comparability is sought, even linear transfers of terminology can be accepted under certain circumstances.

However, what the examination of this example reveals is that linearity can be the product of a conscious knowledge communication process: The correct use of the information provided might lead to the perception that the translation product cannot be anything else than adherence to the source text structure; this makes the knowledge structure of the source system visible to the target audience. In this case the translator seems to have disregarded the idiosyncrasy of the Greek legal discourse; a linear translation would be a more appropriate solution. Thus he deprived the recipient of a clear view of the existing parallel knowledge structures in the source system.

The translation of a German contract into Greek

The second case concerns the translation of a German contract into Greek; the translation would be used before a court of law and it was translated by a trained and professional translator. The translator of the text researched the terminology and structure and made no mistakes in that respect. For example, the German term Mietvertrag (contract of lease) was translated as *ιδιωτικό συμφωνητικό μισθώσεως* (private lease agreement) despite the lure of a linear translation of the compound noun. The same applies to the translation of the term Glasversicherung (glass insurance), which was translated into the appropriate Greek equivalent, *Ασφάλεια θραύσης κρυστάλλων* (insurance of glass breaking).

As to the sentence structure, the following extract shows that the translator restructured according to Greek legal discourse features:

Source text

Bis Vertragsbeginn kann M durch schriftliche Erklärung gegenüber V von diesem Vertrag zurücktreten, wenn ihm die Konzession für diesen Geschäftsbetrieb oder für den Vertrieb einzelner der in § 12 Abs. 1 erwähnten Artikel nicht erteilt wird, und zwar auch dann, wenn dies aus Gründen geschieht, die in seiner Person liegen. Erfolgt der Rücktritt kürzer als 14 Tage vor Vertragsbeginn, hat M an V den Mietausfall für höchstens 2 Monate zu erstatten.

(Until the contract begins M can withdraw in writing from that contract with V, if he does not receive the licence for the store or for the sale of certain goods as under article 12 paragraph 1, and also if this happens for reasons caused by him. If this withdrawal occurs less than 14 days before the contract starts, M has to imburse a loss of rent for at most 2 months.)

Greek translation

Ο Μ δύναται μέχρι την έναρξη του συμφωνητικού να δηλώσει γραπτώς στον Ε υπαναχώρηση από την παρούσα σύμβαση σε περίπτωση μη χορήγησης άδειας πώλησης μεμονωμένων αγαθών, τα οποία αναφέρονται στην παράγραφο 12, εδάφιο 1, ή ακόμη και σε περίπτωση που η αναφερθείσα κατάσταση οφείλεται στον Μ. Εάν η υπαναχώρηση πραγματοποιηθεί σε λιγότερο από 14 ημέρες πριν από την έναρξη της σύμβασης τότε ο Μ οφείλει να καταβάλει στον Ε αποζημίωση ύψους μέχρι δύο μηνιαίων μισθωμάτων.

The complex German sentence, "*wenn ihm die Konzession für diesen Geschäftsbetrieb oder für den Vertrieb einzelner der in § 12 Abs. 1 erwähnten Artikel nicht erteilt wird*" has been translated as a genitive structure commonly used in Greek legal texts (. . . *σε περίπτωση μη χορήγησης άδειας πώλησης μεμονωμένων αγαθών, τα οποία αναφέρονται στην παράγραφο 12, εδάφιο 1, . . .*). The sentence "*Erfolgt der Rücktritt kürzer als 14 Tage vor Vertragsbeginn, hat M an V den Mietausfall für höchstens 2 Monate zu erstatten*" has been identified correctly as a conditional sentence by the translator. From experience, we know that non-native translators of German often fail to identify a German conditional sentence introduced by the verb and not by a conditional conjunction such as *wenn* or *falls*. In this case, elsewhere in the translation, the translator rendered the conditional sentence with the use of a junction (*εάν - σε περίπτωση που*), since conditional sentences can be formed in Greek only this way. Moreover, the translator recognised the structure *fällig sein* (*Der Mietzins ist monatlich im voraus jeweils am 1. des Monates fällig*) and translated it using a passive structure (*Το μίσθωμα θα καταβάλλεται την πρώτη εκάστου μισθωτικού μήνα*), despite the fact that a linear alternative is available. The translator used the active voice wherever possible (. . . , *wenn die Absicht einen Monat vorher schriftlich angekündigt wurde . . . . – εάν δηλώσουν εγγράφως ένα μήνα προηγουμένως την πρόθεσή τους αυτή*) as is appropriate in Modern Greek legal discourse.

In this case the translator made excellent use of the flexibility the target system inventory provides: There is no doubt that the translator had expert knowledge and provided the recipient with a text showing awareness of the knowledge structures of source and target texts.

What was it all about?

The two cases analysed above demonstrate two points very clearly: In the first case, no knowledge communication process was initiated: There is no trace in the translation of the Greek civil law text into German of any kind of knowledge management: The translator of the Greek Civil Code into German has not taken into consideration the discourse structures of the source and target systems and did not identify these as reflections of domain-specific knowledge structures. This is likely to hamper the process of knowledge communication.

As far as the other case is concerned, our examination shows that the availability and correct assessment of information during translating generated a knowledge communication process as we defined it. The examination suggested that in the course of her/his work, the translator was concerned about the communicative value of the translated text. The translator used an appropriate linguistic inventory to produce a purposeful translation.

Language as a reconfiguration agent in intercultural knowledge communication

Let us return to where we began: We set out to discuss the relationship between LSP and translation. We questioned the use of the term *Language for Specific Purposes* (LSP), argued for the use of the term "domain-specific communication" and defined specialised translation as intercultural knowledge communication, elaborating on the positions of Stolze, Gerzymisch-Arbogast and Sandrini.

But is it indeed knowledge that is being communicated in the course of the translation of specialised texts? First of all, we have shown that in the case in which no use of divergent knowledge structures was in evidence, there seemed to have been little appreciation of either the source or the target language. In particular, in the case of the translation of the Geek Civil Code into German the translator diverged from his or her initial promise to observe discourse properties. On the other hand, the second translator, who translated the German contract, decoded the linguistic system on the basis of his or her knowledge of the source system and the meaning was made available to the knowledge system of the target audience; here the translator resorted to not identical but equivalent linguistic structures to transfer the knowledge structures of the source system communicatively into the target system.

Translating specialised texts is more than replacing source culture terms by target culture terms: It is a complex endeavour of communicating knowledge across cultures. When translating specialised texts, the translator engages in an intercultural knowledge communication procedure. S/he transfers knowledge structures across cultural borders and with the help of language as a reconfiguration agent, this knowledge is embedded in the target knowledge structure, fulfilling a communicative purpose with the transformation of the recipient's knowledge system.

Further reading

Apart from the works cited in the chapter, interested readers should consult the following two online journals. Both publications provide insight into the versatility of (intercultural) specialised communication.

FACHSPRACHE – International Journal of Specialized Communication. Available at http://www. fachsprache.net.
FACHSPRACHE is a refereed international journal that publishes articles on all aspects of specialised communication and provides an interdisciplinary forum for researchers and teachers interested in this field. It is the oldest forum for the exchange of knowledge in the field of LSP.

The Journal of Specialised Translation (JoSTrans). Available at http://www.jostrans.org.
JoSTrans is a multilingual journal specialising in non-literary translation issues. JoSTrans is a free, open-access, electronic, peer-reviewed journal. Going through its archives reveals the breadth and width of issues concerning specialised translation.

References

Arntz, R. and Picht, H. 1992. *Einführung in die Terminologiearbeit*. Hildesheim: Georg Olms Verlag.
Baumann, K.-D. 1993. "Ein komplexes Herangehen an das Phänomen der Fachlichkeit von Texten". In *Fachsprachentheorie 1*, edited by Th. Bungarten, 395–430. Tostedt: Attikon.
Baumann, K.-D. 1996. "Fachtextsorten und Kognition – Erweiterungsangebote an die Fachsprachen-forschung". In *Fachliche Textsorten: Komponenten – Relationen – Strategien*, edited by H. Kalverkämper and K.-D. Baumann, 355–388. Tübingen: Narr.
Baumann, K.-D. 2010. "Specialist Thinking Strategies in LSP Communication of the Natural and Technical Sciences". In *Reconceptualizing LSP: Online Proceedings of the XVII European LSP Symposium 2009, Aarhus*, edited by C Heine and J. Engberg. Available at http://bcom.au.dk/fileadmin/www.asb.dk/isek/baumann.pdf [Accessed November 2015.]
Bausch, K.-H. 1976. "Fach- und Gemeinsprache als kommunikationssoziologisches Problem". In *Fachsprachen. Terminologie, Struktur, Normung*, edited by K.-H. Bausch, W. H. U. Schewe and H.-R. Spiegel, 124–135. Berlin-Köln: Beuth-Verlag.

Beier, R. 1979. "Zur Syntax in Fachtexten". In *Fachsprachen und Gemeinsprache*, edited by W. Mentrup, 276–301. Düsseldorf: Pädagogischer Verlag Schwann

Bolten, J. 1992. "Fachsprache oder Sprachbereich? Empirisch-pragmatische Grundlagen zur Beschreibung der deutschen Wirtschafts-, Medizin- und Rechtssprache". In *Beiträge zur Fachsprachenforschung: Sprache in Wissenschaft und Technik, Wirtschaft und Rechtwesen*, edited by T. Bungarten, 57–72. Tostedt: Attikon.

Buhlmann, R. and Fearns, A. 1987. *Handbuch des Fachsprachenunterrichts. Unter besonderer Berücksichtigung naturwissenschaftlich-technischer Fachsprachen*. Berlin: Langenscheidt.

Buhlmann, R. and Fearns, A. 2000. *Handbuch des Fachsprachenunterrichts*. Berlin: Langenscheidt.

Deutsche Bundesbank. 2015. *Monatsbericht Februar 2015*, 67 Jahrgang, no. 2 . Available at https://www.bundesbank.de/Redaktion/DE/Downloads/Veroeffentlichungen/Monatsberichte/2015/2015_02_monatsbericht.pdf?__blob=publicationFile [Accessed November, 2015].

Dogoriti, E. and Vyzas, T. 2015. *LSP and Specialised Translation*. Athens: Dionicos.

Engberg, J. 2010. Knowledge construction and legal discourse: the interdependence of perspective and visibility of characteristics. *Journal of Pragmatics* 42(1), pp. 48–63.

Eppler, M. 2007. Knowledge communication problems between experts and decision makers: an overview and classification. *Electronic Journal of Knowledge Management* 5(3), pp. 291–300.

Eppler, M., Röpnack A. and Seifried P. 1999. "Improving Knowledge Intensive Processes through an Enterprise Knowledge Medium". In *Proceedings of the 1999 ACM SIGCPR Conference Managing Organisational Knowledge for Strategic Advantage: The Key Role of Information Technology and Personnel*, edited by J. Prasad, 425–436. New York: ACM Press.

Fairclough, N. 1992. *Discourse and Social Change*. Cambridge: Polity Press.

Fluck, H.-R., 1976. *Fachsprachen*. München: Franke.

Fluck, H.-R. 1985. *Fachsprachen*. München: UTB.

Gerzymisch-Arbogast, H. 2008. "Fundamentals of LSP Translation". *LSP Translation Scenarios – MuTra Journal* 2. Available from: http://www.translationconcepts.org/journals.htm [Accessed November 2015].

Gläser, R. 1978. Die funktionalstilistische Komponente in der fachsprachlichen Forschung und Lehre. *Wissenschaftliche Zeitschrift der Humboldt-Universität zu Berlin. Gesellschafts- und sprachwissenschaftliche Reihe* 27(4), pp. 463–465.

Gogos, D. 1951. *Das Zivilgesetzbuch von Griechenland*. Tübingen: Walter de Gruyter.

Gotti, M. and Šarčević, S., eds. 2006. *Insights into Specialized Translation: Linguistic Insights* (Studies in Language and Communication 46). Bern: Lang.

Grabowski, M. 1992. *Fachsprache und Funktionalstil. Ihr Zusammenwirken, demonstriert am Beispiel russischer Fachtexte des Außenhandels (Beiträge zur Slavistik; Bd. 19)*. Frankfurt am Main: Peter Lang.

Hatim, B. and Mason, I. 1990. *Discourse and the Translator*. London: Longman.

Henne, H. 1979. "Fachidiome: Über die eigene Zeit, studiert an der Sprache". In *Fachsprachen und Gemeinsprache*, edited by W. Mentrup, 302–316. Düsseldorf: Pädagogischer Verlag Schwann.

Hoffmann, L. 1984. Seven roads to LSP. *Fachsprache* 6, pp. 28–37.

Hoffmann, L. 1985. *Kommunikationsmittel Fachsprache: eine Einführung. Forum für Fachsprachen-Forschung 1*. Tübingen: UTB.

Hoffmann, L. 1993. "Fachwissen und Fachkommunikation. Zur Dialektik von Systematik und Linearität in den Fachsprachen". In *Fachsprachentheorie*, Vol. 2, edited by T. Bungarten, 595–617. Tostedt: Attikon.

Hoffmann, L., Kalverkämper, H. and Wiegand, H. E., eds. 1998. *Fachsprachen/Languages for Special Purposes: Ein internationales Handbuch zur Fachsprachenforschung und Terminologiewissenschaft/An International Handbook of Special-language and Terminology Research*. Berlin: Walter de Gruyter.

Johns, A. M. 1997. *Text, Role, and Context*. Cambridge: Cambridge University Press.

Kalverkämper, H. and Baumann, K.-D. eds. 1996. *Fachliche Textsorten: Komponente-Relationen-Strategien*. Tübingen: Narr.

Koller, W. 1992. *Einführung in die Übersetzungswissenschaft*. Heidelberg: UTB.

Kovtyk, B. and Wendt, G., eds. 2002. *Aktuelle Probleme der angewandten Übersetzungswissenschaft. Sprachliche und außersprachliche Faktoren der Fachübersetzung*. Frankfurt: Lang.

Lavault-Olléon, E., ed. 2007. *Traduction spécialisée. Pratiques, théories, formations* (Travaux Interdisciplinaires et Plurilingues en Langues Etrangères Appliquées 10). Bern: Lang.

Leckey, R. 2009. "Filiaton and the Translaton of Legal Concepts". In *Legal Engineering and Compartive Law*, edited by E. Cashin-Ritaine, 123–141. Geneva: Schulthess.

Littmann, G. 1981. *Fachsprachliche Syntax: zur Theorie und Praxis syntaxbezogener Sprachvariantenforschung*. Hamburg: Buske Verlag.

Littmann, G. 1983. "Fachsprachliche Syntax". *Jahrbuch Deutsch als Fremdsprache 12*. München: Hueber, 98–109.

Möhn, D. and Pelka, R. 1984. *Fachsprachen*. Tübingen: Max Niemeyer Verlag.

Nida, E. A. and Taber, C. 1969. *The Theory and Practice of Translation*. Leiden: E. J. Brill.

Picht, H. 1996. "Fachkommunikation – Fachsprache". In *Mehrsprachigkeit in der Fachkommunikation*. Vol. 1., edited by G. Budin, 27–45. Vienna: TermNet.

Rega, L. and Magris, M., eds. 2004. *Übersetzen in der Fachkommunikation. Comunicazione specialistica e traduzione* (Forum für Fachsprachen-Forschung 64). Tübingen: Narr.

Reinart, S. 2009. *Kulturspezifik in der Fachübersetzung* (Forum für Fachsprachen-Forschung 88). Berlin: Frank & Timme.

Risku, H. and Windhager, F. 2009. Transcultural communication: managing knowledge and diversity. *Synaps* 23, pp. 3–14.

Roelcke, T. 2010. *Fachsprachen*. Berlin: Erich Schmidt Verlag.

Sager, J. C. 1990. *A Practical Course in Terminology Processing*. Amsterdam: John Benjamins.

Sandrini, P. 2010. "Fachliche Translation". In *Diskurs und Terminologie beim Fachübersetzen und Dolmetschen/Discourse and Terminology in Specialist Translation and Interpreting*, edited by J. Maliszewski, 31–51. Frankfurt am Main: Peter Lang.

Schmitt, P. A. and Jüngst, H. E., eds. 2007. *Translationsqualität* (Leipziger Studien zur angewandten Linguistik und Translatologie 5). Frankfurt: Lang.

Schröder, H. 1993. "Interkulturelle Fachkommunikationsforschung. Aspekte kulturkontrastiver Untersuchungen schriftlicher Wirtschaftskommunikation". In *Fachsprachentheorie*, edited by T. Bungarten, 517–550. Tostedt: Attikon.

Snell-Hornby, M. 1986/1994. *Übersetzungswissenschaft. Eine Neuorientierung*. Tübingen: Francke.

Stolze, R. 1992 *Hermeneutisches Übersetzen: linguistische Kategorien des Verstehens und Formulierens beim Übersetzen*. Tübingen: Narr.

Stolze, R. 1999. *Die Fachübersetzung. Eine Einführung*. Tübingen: Narr.

Stolze, R. 2009. *Fachübersetzen – Ein Lehrbuch für Theorie und Praxis* (Forum für Fachsprachen-Forschung 89). Berlin: Frank und Timme.

Tsoukas, H. and Vladimirou, E. 2001. What is organisational knowledge? *Journal of Management Studies* 38(97), pp. 973–993.

Vlachopoulos, S. 2015. *Intercultural Communication in the Economy: The Translation of Economic Texts from German into Greek*. Athens: ΣΕΑΒ.

Welch, L. and Welch, D. 2008. The importance of language in international knowledge transfer. *Management International Review* 48(3), pp. 339–360.

Wüster, E. 1991. *Einführung in die allgemeine Terminologielehre und terminologische Lexikographie*. Bonn: Romanistischer Verlag.

Index

441